Voice & Vision

Voice & Vision

A CREATIVE APPROACH to
Narrative Film and DV Production

MICK HURBIS-CHERRIER

Illustrations by Gustavo Mercado

AMSTERDAM • BOSTON • HEIDELBERG • LONDON
NEW YORK • OXFORD • PARIS • SAN DIEGO
SAN FRANCISCO • SINGAPORE • SYDNEY • TOKYO

Focal Press is an imprint of Elsevier

Acquisitions Editor: Elinor Actipis
Senior Project Manager: Dawnmarie Simpson
Assistant Editor: Robin Weston
Marketing Manager: Christine Degon Veroulis
Cover Design: Alisa Andreola
Illustrations: Gustavo Mercado

Focal Press is an imprint of Elsevier
30 Corporate Drive, Suite 400, Burlington, MA 01803, USA
Linacre House, Jordan Hill, Oxford OX2 8DP, UK

∞ Recognizing the importance of preserving what has been written, Elsevier prints its books on acid-free
paper whenever possible.

Library of Congress Cataloging-in-Publication Data
Hurbis-Cherrier, Mick.
    Voice & vision : a creative approach to narrative film and DV production / Mick Hurbis-
Cherrier.
        p. cm.
    Includes bibliographical references and index.
    ISBN-13: 978-0-240-80773-7 (pbk. : alk. paper)
    ISBN-10: 0-240-80773-1 (pbk. : alk. paper) 1. Motion pictures--Production and direction.
2. Digital video. I. Title
    PN1995.9.P7H79 2007
    791.4302'3--dc22

                                                        2006034051

British Library Cataloguing-in-Publication Data
A catalogue record for this book is available from the British Library.

ISBN 13: 978-0-240-80773-7
ISBN 10: 0-240-80773-1

For information on all Focal Press publications visit our website at
www.books.elsevier.com

08 09 10   10 9 8 7 6 5 4 3 2

Printed in Canada

This book is dedicated to Frank Beaver, Michelle Citron, and Dana Hodgdon—exceptional professors, mentors, and friends whose teachings have remained with me and whose voices echo throughout the pages of this book.

Contents

Part II ■ **Preparing for Production**

Part IV ■ Tools and Techniques: Postproduction

Acknowledgments

A book of this scope and size could not have been accomplished without the kind help, contributions, and counsel of many reviewers, assistants, and colleagues—friends one and all.

Warmest thanks to the team at Focal Press: Becky Golden-Harrell, Dawnmarie Simpson, and Robin Weston, and to the inimitable Elinor Actipis, whom I cannot possibly thank enough.

I was especially fortunate to have a line-up of excellent reviewers: Jacqueline B. Frost, Michael Kowalski, Andrew Lund, and Catherine Sellars, whose careful, thoughtful, and detailed comments quite simply made this book better. In addition, I was lucky to have Cindy Funkhouser as my copyeditor who contributed with precision and spirit.

I would like to thank my colleagues at Hunter College of the City University of New York, both in the administration and the Department of Film and Media Studies, for their support, advice, encouragement, and patience, especially President Jennifer Raab, Jay Roman, Joel Zuker, Andrew Lund, Ivone Margulies, Joe McElhaney, Kelly Anderson, Michael Gitlin, Renato Tonelli, and Peter A. Jackson. And I thank my dear friend Michael Griffel for his wisdom, kindness, and guidance.

During the writing of this book I was especially touched by the way Hunter film students rallied to my aid. To all of those who gave so willingly of their energy, enthusiasm, and talent, I am grateful: Katherine Allen, Jay Baek, Brian Ferrari, Randi Harris, Yae Mitomi, Alana Kakoyianis, Lucas Pruchnik, Mika Mori, Rosa Navarra, Brian Safuto, Zita Vasilisinova, Rommel Genciana, Michael Gibbs, Miles Adgate, David Pavlosky, Matt Henderson, Jordan Cooke, Jayan Cherian, Ruomi Lee Hampel, Emogene Shadwick, Angel Chicco, and all those who let us onto their film sets to take photographs. But an extra special thank you is in order for the hard, dedicated and superb work put in by: Jessica Webb, Alessandra Kast, Josh Hill, Timothy Trotman, Claudia Didomenico, Gresham Gregory, and George Racz.

I'd also like to thank all the kind people who helped with the technical research and illustrations, including Pete Abel and Anna Feil at Abel CineTech, Will Sweeney at Color Lab Film Corp., Jan Crittenden at Panasonic, Dave Waddell at Fujinon, Lisa Muldowney at Kodak, Charles Darby at DuArt Film & Video, Joe Hannigan at Weston Sound, Frieder Hochheim at Kino Flo, Inc., and John C. Clisham at Mole Richardson Co.

I would be remiss in not acknowledging some of the many other friends whose tangible and inspirational support is woven throughout the pages of this text, especially Abbas Kiarostami, Seifollah Samadian, Madelyn Wils, Peter Scarlet, Sydney Meeks, Raymond Cauchetier, Thelma Schoonmaker, Ellen Kuras, Freida Orange, Edin Velez, Dave Monahan, Pam Katz, Didier Rouget, Kim Doan, Paul Cronin, Timothy Corrigan, Catherine Riggs-Bergesen, Lynne Sachs, Michael Mees, Ramin Bahrani, Alain Thote, Laurent Tirard, Jerry Rudes, Bernard Belair, Kent Jones, and Wes Simpkins. Ken Dancyger deserves credit and special appreciation for prompting me to write a book in the first place and for remaining an encouraging and remarkably perspicacious mentor throughout the process.

But most especially and profoundly, I am grateful and indebted to Katherine Hurbis-Cherrier and Gustavo Mercado, who were in the trenches with me each and every day of the writing and research. This book would not have been not possible without them.

Photograph and Illustration Credits

Figure 1-1 Photo by Seifolla Samadian; **Figure 1-2** Courtesy of Photofest; **Figure 1-8** Photo by Simon Max Hill; **Figure 1-9** Photo by Simon Max Hill; **Figures 2-7** and **2-8** Excerpt from *Ocean's Eleven* granted Courtesy of Warner Brothers Entertainment Inc.; **Figure 2-12** Excerpt from *Sideways* © 2004, Courtesy of Twentieth Century Fox. Written by Alexander Payne and Jim Taylor. All rights reserved.; **Figure 4-1** Photo by Catherine Riggs-Bergesen; **Figure 4-4** Photo by Catherine Riggs-Bergesen; **Figure 4-6** Photo by Catherine Riggs-Bergesen; **Figure 4-8** Photo by Catherine Riggs-Bergesen; **Figure 4-9** Photo by Catherine Riggs-Bergesen; **Figure 5-6** Courtesy of: (L) Photofest (R) George Racz; **Figure 5-10** (L) Photo by Chip Hackler; **Figure 6-9** Courtesy of Abel CineTech; **Figure 7-1 and Cover Image** Photos by Jon Higgins; **Figure 7-4** Photos by Mario Tursi, Courtesy of Pam Katz; **Figure 7-8** Courtesy of George Racz; **Figure 8-33** Courtesy of DuArt Inc.; **Figure 8-42** Courtesy of Kodak Inc.; **Figure 9-12** Courtesy of (L) Sony Corp of America (R) Panasonic; **Figure 9-13** (R) Courtesy of Panasonic; **Figure 9-14** Courtesy of (L) Panasonic (R) Sony Corp of America; **Figure 9-33** Courtesy of Sony Corp of America; **Figure 10-17** Courtesy of Don Fleming at DOFmaster; **Figure 10-19** Courtesy of Dave Eubanks; **Figure 11-2** (L) Photo by David Pavlosky; **Figure 11-4** Courtesy of Sachtler; **Figure 11-6** Courtesy of Sachtler; **Figure 11-11** Courtesy of Didier Rouget; **Figure 11-13** Courtesy of (L) Sachtler, (R) Glidecam; **Figure 11-14** Copyright Raymond Cauchetier-Paris; **Figure 12-3** Photo by Catherine Riggs-Bergesen; **Figure 12-5** Photo by Catherine Riggs-Bergesen; **Figure 12-12** Photo by Catherine Riggs-Bergesen; **Figure 12-13** Courtesy of Ed Rankus; **Figure 13-10** Courtesy of Mole-Richardson; **Figure 13-43** Courtesy of Mole-Richardson; **Figure 13-45** Courtesy of Mole-Richardson; **Figure 13-46** Courtesy of Mole-Richardson; **Figure 13-48** (L) Courtesy of Kino-Flo; **Figure 14-8** Courtesy of Kodak Inc.; **Figure 14-9** Illustration by Wes Simpkins; **Figure 14-16** Courtesy of Kodak Inc.; **Figure 14-30** Photo © The National Gallery, London.; **Figure 15-4** (R) Photo Courtesy PDPhoto.org; **Figure 15-12** Courtesy of D.A. Pennebaker; **Figure 15-13** Photo by Mario Tursi, Courtesy of Pam Katz; **Figure 15-15** (Center) Courtesy of Sound Devices; **Figure 16-1** Courtesy of Sound Devices; **Figure 16-3** Courtesy of (L) Sound Devices (R) Fostex; **Figure 16-4** Courtesy of HHb; **Figure 16-5** Courtesy of (L) Sound Devices (R) Fostex; **Figure 16-9** (L) Courtesy of Sound Devices; **Figure 16-14** Courtesy of Audio Technica; **Figure 16-21** Courtesy of Didier Rouget; **Figure 17-3** Courtesy of: Sound Devices; **Figure 17-9** Photo by Catherine Riggs-Bergesen; **Figure 17-18** Photo by Catherine Riggs-Bergesen; **Figure 18-16** Photo by Catherine Riggs-Bergesen; **Figure 18-17** Photo by Kim Spiegler; **Figure 18-18** Courtesy of Kelly Anderson; **Figure 19-5** Photo by Anthony Young, Courtesy of Sasie Sealy; **Figure 19-13** Courtesy of DuArt Inc.; **Figure 19-15** Courtesy of Color Lab; **Figure 19-16** Courtesy Sam Pollard; **Figure 19-23** Courtesy of DuArt Inc.; **Figure 19-25** Courtesy of DuArt Inc.; **Figure 19-30** Photo by Kerwin Devonish; **Figure 21-1** Illustration by Wes Simpkins; **Figure 21-2** Illustration by Wes Simpkins; **Figure 21-3** Illustration by Wes Simpkins; **Figure 21-4** Illustration by Wes Simpkins; **Figure 21-5** Illustration by Wes Simpkins; **Figure 21-8** (L) Photo by David Leonard ©, Courtesy of Thelma Schoonmaker; **Figure 22-10** (R) Courtesy of Sound One/Ascent Media; **Figure 23-30** (L) Courtesy of Apple; **Figure 24-12** Courtesy of Susan Buice and Arin Crumley

■ ADDITIONAL PHOTOGRAPHY BY:

Gustavo Mercado, Mick Hurbis-Cherrier, Peter A. Jackson, Jessica Webb, Alessandra Kast, and Nicole Pommerehncke

■ ILLUSTRATIONS BY GUSTAVO MERCADO

Introduction

Where does one begin a journey into the world of filmmaking? Film is creative and it is technical. It's a form of personal expression and a universal language. It requires careful logistical planning and inspired spontaneity. It is the product of a single vision and collaborative energy. Film is also the quintessential hybrid art form, finding its expressive power though the unique amalgam of writing, performance, design, photography, music, and editing. And all of it matters. Every choice you make, from the largest creative decisions to the smallest practical solutions, has a profound impact on what appears on the screen and how it moves an audience emotionally.

The central principle behind *Voice & Vision* is the notion that all of the conceptual, technical, and logistical activity on a film project should serve the filmmaker's creative vision. Making a film begins with someone wanting to tell a story, wanting to bring an idea to the screen for the world to see. The next step then involves gathering together the people, equipment, and resources to produce the movie. However, it's quite common these days to hear people who don't want to bother themselves with the technical or conceptual fundamentals of filmmaking say that "it's not about tech, it's not about rules, it's all about the story." That's a little too facile. The fact is, it's not enough to just have a story, no matter how good it is; you have to be able to tell that story well. It's not simply "all about story," it's all about *storytelling,* and in this medium storytelling involves actors, a camera, lights, sound, and editing. To develop your ability to tell a story on film necessarily means understanding the basic visual vocabulary of cinema, the process of production, as well as the function and expressive potential of the tools; like a camera, a light meter, and editing software. In a recent filmmaker's master class the great director Abbas Kiarostami stressed the point that a mediocre idea brilliantly told is preferable to a brilliant idea poorly told. Film is a complex art form and in order to make the right decisions and express oneself successfully you must be clear about what your ideas are and what you want to say, and gain control of the film language, tools, and production process in order to say just that. As James Broughton, one of cinema's great poets, once wrote,

> *Every film is a voyage into the unknown. . . . It is unwise to embark on the high seas without knowing a few of the laws of navigation. To have a shipwreck before you have cleared the port is both messy and embarrassing.*

Voice & Vision elaborates on all of the essential information and skills necessary to ensure that the student filmmaker will acquire the technical, logistical, and conceptual authority needed to "speak in film" with cinematic eloquence and fluency. Think of the book like a map—it may not predict every wondrous sight or challenge you'll encounter on your voyage, but it'll get you sailing into open waters.

Obviously, it is not possible for one book on filmmaking to be a completely comprehensive resource on such a vast and evolving subject. In fact, all of the film books on the bookstore shelves put together don't even manage to say all there is to say—and thank goodness for that. *Voice & Vision* is written for the introductory and intermediate film student or independent filmmaker. This textbook aims to provide a solid foundation in narrative filmmaking, from idea to distribution. This includes essential and detailed technical information on film and digital production tools, a thorough overview of the filmmaking stages and process, and, of course, a discussion of the conceptual and aesthetic dimensions of telling a motion picture story.

FILM AS A COLLABORATIVE ART FORM

The act of making a film, on any scale, is an endeavor that requires enormous effort, concentration, and a broad range of knowledge. It also requires the execution of several tasks simultaneously. For this reason, narrative filmmaking is always a collaborative art form, requiring the collective energy and expertise of a team. A filmmaking team can be anywhere from two to two dozen (or more), but the basic dynamic is the same—a film becomes better when everyone on the team is allowed to make creative contributions and when everyone takes serious responsibility for their practical and technical duties. You will see these ideas of team creativity and responsibility emphasized throughout *Voice & Vision.* This book is also written with the understanding that not every film student will become, or even wants to become, a director. Knowing that students can follow so many creative and fulfilling paths in film (cinematography, sound design, editing, art direction, etc.), I have provided ample technical information, creative context, and discussions of aesthetics to thoroughly engage those many students who are enthusiastic about areas other than directing. Whether they are writing, directing, shooting, or editing, the ultimate goal of *Voice & Vision* is to guide each student of film to develop their own creative voice while acquiring the practical skills and confidence to use it.

FILMMAKING AND TECHNOLOGY IN THE 21ST CENTURY

This book was written in an era when film production is undergoing enormous transformation. Digital media are changing forever the technology and procedures for making movies at every stage of the process. When it comes to the question of film and digital video technology, *Voice & Vision* takes its cues from the professional industry and from students, who have both moved toward an understanding of the application and free integration of these technologies far more quickly than the academy. There is no battle between film and video. There are only movies to be made. The 21st-century filmmaker understands the inherent aesthetic characteristics and creative possibilities of originating on film and originating on digital video, and will use whatever they have at their disposal to make great movies. This ambidexterity is demonstrated in the films of internationally renowned directors like Abbas Kiarostami, Lars von Trier, Rebecca Miller, Steven Soderbergh, Spike Lee, Michael Winterbottom, and many, many others. The modern cinematographer is conversant and expressive across the technologies. This can be seen in the work of trailblazers like Ellen Kuras, Robbie Müller, and Anthony Dod Mantle. The crafts of the editor, sound recordists, art director, and sound designer are not significantly altered if one is working on a film or DV project: just ask any working professional out there. It's all about storytelling! And you can tell stories either way. This book does not favor one technology over the other; instead, I try to provide an understanding not only of the different technologies, but of their inexorable convergence as well. One more note; I often use the word "film" as a synonym for movie or motion picture, which means, in my book, that it can originate on DV, be edited and projected digitally, and still be called a film, and the person who made it is a filmmaker.

TEACHING AND LEARNING FILMMAKING

Film writing and directing cannot be taught, only learned, and each man or woman has to learn it through his or her own system of self education.

Alexander Mackendrick

The great film director Alexander Mackendrick (*The Ladykillers, Sweet Smell of Success*) raises a pertinent issue when he states in his book, *On Filmmaking,* that you cannot teach film, but you can learn it. The interesting twist, however, is that Mr. Mackendrick was also a legendary film *teacher* at the California Institute of the Arts for 25 years, so he must have believed that something about film could be taught, or at least conveyed, and that a teacher plays some role in learning about filmmaking. I believe that you can, in fact, teach a great deal *about* filmmaking. One can teach the essentials of technique, cinematic lan-

PART I DEVELOPING YOUR FILM ON PAPER

from filmmakers ranging in experience from first time feature film directors to legendary masters of cinema.

In the end, however, the best way to learn about filmmaking is simply to make films. Here is some advice from someone who's made a few himself:

The advice I would give today to anyone who wants to become a director is quite simple: make a film. In the sixties, it wasn't so easy because there wasn't even super 8. If you wanted to shoot anything, you had to rent a 16-millimeter camera, and often it would be silent. But today, nothing is as easy as buying or borrowing a small video camera. You have a picture, you have sound, and you can screen your film on any TV set. So when an aspiring director comes to me for advice, my answer is always the same: "Take a camera, shoot something, and show it to someone. Anyone."

Jean-Luc Godard (From *Moviemaker's Master Class,* by Laurent Tirard)

So there you have it. What are you waiting for? It's time to make movies!

guage, the technology, and the expressive capabilities of the instruments of the art form. One can teach an understanding of how the production process itself supports the creation of a movie. One can teach a student a method for recognizing and appreciating exceptional examples of filmmaking from the history of movies. All of this can bring the serious student right to the threshold. The rest of what is necessary, albeit the core of being an artist in any medium, must be learned through example and experience and here a teacher, and a book, can serve as a guide. This core consists of imagination, visual intuition, initiative, an aesthetic sense, and personal style. These qualities can't be taught, but they can certainly be nurtured and developed.

So where do we go to learn those things that cannot be taught? The first thing an aspiring filmmaker must do is watch films, especially the films of the masters, old and new. Writers read great writers, painters look at paintings, and, in fact, often copy the works of masters when developing their craft. It is imperative that young filmmakers look carefully at films for what they express and how the filmmaker actually achieves that particular mood or emotion, or that specific narrative point, or how they develop a theme, or move you to laugh, or cry, or vote, through images, actions, and sound. Movies themselves are our most useful textbooks. Think about it: not one single cinematic storytelling technique in the history of film has become extinct. Every filmmaking technique that has been developed remains part of the lexicon of the art form and it's all there for you to learn from, rework, customize, and apply to your own story. Knowing this, I have included throughout the text numerous illustrations from movies (every one available on DVD). The "In Practice" feature provides brief analyses of scenes or techniques from films that illustrate how a specific technology, process, or technique is used to support a conceptual, narrative, or aesthetic impulse—in essence, the creative application of a principle or a technology. This encourages the student to look at films analytically and to use the wealth of material available for rent as a research tool. You will notice that I reference films from all eras and from all over the world as well as films shot on 35mm, 16mm, Super 16, HD, and standard DV. This book celebrates the vast diversity of voices, approaches, perspectives, and innovations in cinema throughout its history. A smart film student will understand that great movies and creative innovations are as likely to come from Taiwan, Denmark, Brazil, and Iran as Los Angeles. Film is truly a global art form and every continent continues to make vital contributions.

The second way we can learn about filmmaking is to listen to the tales from the trenches of production. Everyone has on-set experience stories: challenges that they faced, puzzles that they solved, issues with that they struggled, ideas that they held on to and those that they had to let go, accounts of their crafty accomplishments, shrewd fixes and innovative work-arounds. It's important to listen to these stories. We learn from the experiences, ideas, ingenuity, solutions, knowledge, advice, strategies, difficulties, disappointments, and successes of other filmmakers, from students struggling with their very first film to seasoned pros struggling with their 30th movie—there are lessons in all of it. Pick up any trade magazine, like *American Cinematographer,* or go to a website like www.filmsound.org, or pick up a book like Laurent Tirard's *Moviemakers' Master Class,* or Walter Murch's *In the Blink of an Eye,* and what you'll find are people with experience in cinematography, sound design, directing, editing, or any other creative aspect of filmmaking, sharing what they've accomplished and what they've learned along the way. You can tuck all of these illuminating stories, all of this first-hand information, into your tool kit and bring it with you to your next project. Then, after you've spent even one day on a film set, you'll have your own stories to share. It's all about storytelling after all.

You will find real world stories sprinkled throughout the book and also in the "In Practice" boxes, which often contain brief anecdotes detailing common and characteristic production challenges from professional film shoots as well as student productions. Many of these on-set stories come directly from the experiences of my students during my 13 years of teaching introductory and intermediate production courses. Some of them come

From Idea to Cinematic Stories

Our first job is to look,
Our second job is to think of a film which can be made.
Abbas Kiarostami (Marrakech, 2005)

There's no doubt about it. Filmmaking is exciting stuff. Working on a set, surrounded by the energy of a great production crew, collaborating with actors, setting up lights, lining up shots, calling out "Roll Camera! Action!" Seeing a film project come to life can be an exhilarating experience. In fact, most aspiring filmmakers simply can't wait to get their hands on a camera and start shooting. Once they get an idea, they're ready to go! But wait. What are you shooting? What is your idea? Are your characters interesting? Does the idea have a shape? Just what are you wanting to say and how will you say it? What does all this activity on the screen add up to? What about the practical side of making this film? Are the subject and visual approach appropriate for your resources? Can you get it done?

Whether your project is a two-minute chase scene with no dialogue or a complex psychological drama, the first step in any narrative film production is coming up with an idea which is stimulating, engaging, and ripe with visual possibilities. The idea is the DNA of the entire filmmaking process—it informs every word written into the script and every shot you take and every choice you make along the way. The better your basic idea is, the better your film will be. But an idea is only the first lightning bolt of inspiration. All ideas have to be developed—fashioned into a story that can be told through the medium of film—this means turning an idea into a story that can be captured and conveyed by that camera you're dying to get your hands on.

■ FINDING AN IDEA

At the beginning of any film, there is an idea. It may come at any time, from any source. It may come from watching people in the street or from thinking alone in your office. . . . What you need is to find that original idea, that spark. And once you have that, it's like fishing: you use that idea as bait, and it attracts everything else. But as a director your main priority is to remain faithful to that original idea.
David Lynch (From *Moviemakers' Master Class,* by Laurent Tirard)

Where do we find ideas? Where does inspiration come from? As Lynch reminds us, ideas can come to us anywhere and at anytime: an act of kindness we witness on the street, an individual we watch on the bus, a piece of music that moves us, an experience a friend relates to us, a memory, or an evocative location that strikes us as a perfect setting for a dramatic story. All are sources of inspiration and ideas. I once attended a reading by the fiction writer Raymond Carver, and someone in the audience asked him if he had any secrets to becoming a writer. He said simply, "You have to be a sponge, you have to constantly absorb the world you live in." If you keep your eyes and ears open, you will discover that material is all around you. Everyday life provides fertile ground for story ideas, visual ideas, and character ideas. Stay alert and connect to the world around you, then you'll be able to connect with your audience.

■ **Figure 1-1** Director Abbas Kiarostami.

In an interview with Houshang Golmakani, the Iranian filmmaker Abbas Kiarostami (Figure 1-1), speaking about inspiration, shared the following thoughts:

Gabriel Garcia Márquez once said: "I don't choose a subject; it's the subject that chooses me." The same goes for me. The subject depends on whatever happens to be keeping me awake at night. . . . I have dozens of stories stored away in my memory. There's a story happening in front of me everyday, but I don't have the time to make a film out of it. In the course of time, certain stories start taking on importance; one of them will end up becoming the subject of a film.

Precisely what strikes us as a good idea, one which could develop into a great movie, is a highly individualistic thing. In fact, where you get your ideas, what strikes you as a good idea for a movie, is *the* thing that makes your films your films and not someone else's. Which is why it is best that ideas come from your own observations and responses to the world around you. The only way that a movie will contain your individual voice is if your core idea comes from you, from your imagination, interests, and perspective. Only Martin Scorsese can make Scorsese films. You may love them, but to try and duplicate them, because they are successful or because you think Mafia violence is the *ne plus ultra* of drama, is to avoid the most important work a filmmaker can do, and that is find out what your unique cinematic voice and contribution might be. Finding your own voice is not easy work, but it's essential, and that process begins with your very first film.

Here is an example from the screenwriter and director Peter Hedges, who is discussing where he got the idea for his 2003 feature film *Pieces of April:*

In the late 1980s . . . I heard about a group of young people who were celebrating their first Thanksgiving in New York City. They went to cook the meal, but the oven didn't work, so they knocked on doors until they found someone with an oven they could use. I remember thinking that this could be a way to have all sorts of people cross paths who normally wouldn't.

(From *Pieces of April: The Shooting Script,* by Peter Hedges)

Hedges jotted the idea down, made a few notes, and then forgot about it. This idea is like many lightning bolts of inspiration—it's interesting and compelling, but not yet fully formed. Hedges would not find the story in the idea until ten years later.

■ FROM AN IDEA TO A STORY

One's initial idea—that first spark of inspiration—more often than not is vague. Sometimes it's no more than an observation or a feeling. In the case of Peter Hedges, the idea was a simple situation that was ripe for interesting interactions, but it wasn't a story yet. The most basic elements of film are images and sound, those things that we can capture with a camera and a microphone. Think about it: when you are in a theater watching a movie, everything you understand about a character, including the story, the mood, and the themes of the film, is delivered exclusively through sound and images. We cannot point our camera and microphone at ideas, desires, intentions, or feelings, but we can record a person who reacts, makes decisions, and takes action as they strive to achieve something, and through those actions we can understand who they are, how they are feeling, what they are after, and what it all means. This is the fundamental principle behind **dramatization**, transforming what is vague and internal into a series of viewable and audible actions and events.

■ NARRATIVE BASICS 1: CONFLICT-ORIENTED DRAMA

The next step in the process is to turn your initial inspiration into a dramatic story. In making this transition, it is important to understand the essential characteristics of a dramatic story. **Narrative films** primarily revolve around **conflict**, and express ideas and concepts through stories in which a character, who needs to accomplish something, encounters obstacles and must struggle to get what they need. The American playwright, screenwriter, and director David Mamet (Figure 1-2) wrote this description of basic dramatic story elements in his book *On Directing Film*:

> *The story is the essential progression of incidents that occurs to our hero in pursuit of his one goal. . . . It consists of the assiduous application of several basic questions: What does the hero want? What hinders him from getting it? What happens if he does not get it?*

This is as good a definition of a dramatic story as I've found anywhere and it describes the three essential elements of drama, namely **character** ("hero"), their **goal**, and **conflict** or **obstacles**. Another word for "hero" is **protagonist**; they are the subject of your story, the central character whom the audience will follow as they attempt to achieve their goal. A character can be a New York City police detective, a lovelorn teenage boy, a clever dog called Lassie, or even an animated lump of clay. It doesn't matter as long as they have an identifiable goal for which they strive. The goal can be obvious (to get the job, to solve the crime) or it can be very subtle (to be left alone, to avoid responsibility, to move into adulthood). It can be an extraordinary goal (to save the world, to steal the diamond) or an ordinary one (to cross the street, to clean the apartment, to get home). Goals can be tasks that our protagonist must accomplish (clean the room before mom gets home or escape from jail) or a personal need (win the girl's love or earn a mentor's respect).

But what about the "progression of incidents" that Mamet mentions? These events are the moments, the actions, reactions, and interactions, all of which make up the plot of your film. The **plot** is the order of events of your film—the unfolding of the story and the scenes. Where do the events come from? The events of your film result from the chemical reaction between three dramatic elements: your *main character* and their *goal* and any complications or obstacles that pose some sort of *conflict*. Conflict is an essential dramatic element because when a goal-oriented character encounters an obstacle, something that "hinders him from getting [his goal]," they are compelled to find a way over, around, or through that obstacle to get what they want. Overcoming the obstacle means that our character must take some sort of *action*, they must do something. The exciting thing about drama is that deciding what they do and how they do it reveals, in a dramatized way, who that character is. So I would add one more to Mamet's list of basic questions—that is, *what is the hero willing to do to achieve*

■ **Figure 1-2** American writer/director David Mamet works extensively in both film and the theater.

■ **Figure 1-3** In Hedges' *Pieces of April* (2003), iconoclastic free spirit April (Katie Holmes) attempts to reconnect with her estranged family by preparing a Thanksgiving meal.

their goal? Now, if we pose a question like this, then it stands to reason that there are things a character is *not* willing to do. Keep in mind that what a character *doesn't* do, what they avoid and how they avoid it can also be revealing of character and create conflicts.

This progression of incidents usually increases in intensity and tension as the film progresses, until the protagonist, in one last-ditch effort to get what they want, brings the film to a **resolution**, which means an end. The resolution answers the question: Did the hero get what they wanted after all? In a happy ending the goal is accomplished; in a sad ending the resolution is not what the hero had hoped. You can have ironic endings, pyrrhic victories, unexpected outcomes, whatever. But the central question— does the main character get what they want?—should be answered or else the film won't have a satisfying resolution.

Peter Hedges transformed his idea into a cinematic story by turning the "group of people" (too vague) looking for a working oven to cook their Thanksgiving turkey into the very specific story of a girl named April, the black sheep of a family (*character*) who decides to cook an all-out, traditional Thanksgiving dinner for her family in her New York City apartment (*goal*). Cooking is the way this highly iconoclastic character tries to reconcile with her mother, who is dying from cancer (*specific and personal motivation*), but April's lovely gesture nearly fails because she has no cooking ability whatsoever and her oven doesn't work (*conflict*). Her dysfunctional family, arriving from out of town, is fully anticipating a disaster. April elicits the aid of her neighbors (*actions*), whom she doesn't know, to help her pull off the meal. In the end April has formed a new family of friends (**Figure 1-3**) *and* has managed to connect with her mom before her mom dies (*resolution*).

The preceding short paragraph describing *Pieces of April* is an example of a film concept. A **concept** is a very brief outline of the basic dramatic elements involved in your story. It describes, in no more than a few sentences, the dramatic engine that will drive the movie: who is in the film, what they want, what gets in their way, and what they do about it. Focusing your idea into a dramatic concept is the first step in the writing process (see Chapter 2).

Hedges did not completely discover the full dimensions of the story for *Pieces of April* until the late 1990s, when he was dealing with his own mother's cancer diagnosis. As he says in his book, "That's when I realized I had a story to tell." He also hung onto that initial spark—"this could be a way to have all sorts of people cross paths who normally wouldn't"—and it emerged as the central theme in the film.

> *A lot of* Pieces of April *to me is about the family you're born into but also the family you find, and it was the family you find that really compelled me to write this particular story.*
>
> **(From an interview with Mark Pfeiffer, *The Film Journal*, Nov. 2003)**

■ SHORT FILM STORIES

Pieces of April is an example of a concept from a feature-length film. The relationship between April and her mother (and the rest of the family) is complicated; add to that the new family April is forging by getting her neighbors involved in her efforts and you have a very rich and complex story. But short films, meaning those films that are thirty minutes or less, are a little different. Shorts can be just as profound as features are, but they must be tight, simple, and efficient. While a short film can tackle just about any subject, the key is to work on a compact scale. Short films usually revolve around a single, simple idea, recognizable characters, and a sharp turning point to make one moment resonate. Short film ideas, of necessity, are narrowly circumscribed because the point must be made in a matter of minutes. You do not have time to complexly develop or slowly transform a character or situation, nor can you examine every angle of a conflict or involve too many extra elements outside of the basic story engine. You don't have room for multiple story layers or for developing a historical context for the actions and characters in the movie. What we look for in a short film is an idea that can be expressed with simple narrative elements and vivid imagery: characters and a situation that we can recognize quickly, a conflict that is streamlined, and actions that are revealing all on their own without a great deal of explication or context.

A good test of a short film concept is to tell it to someone out loud. If you find yourself needing to explain why someone does something, or what happened in that person's past that motivates them, or why it's difficult to achieve the goal, then you know that the basic idea requires more room and context to be expressed and the short form is not the best sized container. Let's look at the plot of a very simple short narrative film (Figure 1-4) that illustrates the use of all of the basic dramatic principles—but on a compact scale.

Abbas Kiarostami's first film, *Bread and Alley* (1970), is a ten-minute-long black-and-white film shot without sound. A young boy, carrying a loaf of bread, is on his way home from school (*goal*). To get home he must travel down a labyrinth of very narrow and deserted alleyways. In one alley his path is blocked by a big dog (*major obstacle/conflict*). Frightened of the dog, the boy freezes. He looks around and sees that there is no alternate route and that the alley is so narrow that he cannot sneak around the dog (*location as source of conflict*). There are no adults around to help him, so he musters his courage and slowly approaches the dog (*1st action*). But the dog growls at him (*obstacle intensifies*), prompting him to stop again. He seems stuck. Just then an old man walks by and the boy decides to follow right behind the man, past the dog (*2nd action, new strategy*). But just as they reach the dog, the old man turns down a side alley into his house, leaving the boy alone and face-to-face with the dog (*conflict intensifies*). Knowing he must do something quickly, the boy breaks off a piece of bread and throws it to the dog (*3rd action*). With the dog now distracted by eating the bread, the boy scampers past. Finished with the morsel of bread, the dog takes off after the frightened boy, which causes the boy to keep feeding the dog more pieces of bread (*4th action*). Soon the dog's tail is wagging happily and the boy reaches home, where he closes the door between him and the dog (*resolution*). The dog lies down in the alleyway until another boy carrying food shows up. The dog growls at him . . . (*coda*).

Pieces of April and *Bread and Alley* show that while the terms "hero," "goal," "conflict," and "action" sound hugely dramatic, they actually work for films of any size and any subject. You don't necessarily need to conceive of a film like *Raiders of the Lost Ark,* in which Indiana Jones (*Hero!*) has to obtain the Arc of the Covenant (*Goal!*), and with the Nazi Army after it, too (*Obstacle!!*). You can use these same dramatic principles on just about any scale project and with any degree of subtlety, such as a young woman who

■ Figure 1-4 *Bread and Alley* (1970), Abbas Kiarostami (writer/director).

wants to connect with her mother by cooking a Thanksgiving turkey, or a little boy who wants to get past a big dog to get home.

■ NARRATIVE BASICS 2: OTHER DRAMATIC QUESTIONS

In the conflict-oriented dramas which we've been examining, the basis for dramatic tension, otherwise known as the "major dramatic question," comes from the question, "Will this person overcome all of the obstacles to get what they want?" But this isn't the only way to engage an audience. Short films in particular can tell stories without direct character conflict if they replace the conflict-oriented dramatic question with something else compelling—another type of mystery, another kind of question, such as "What is this person doing?" or "How is all of this activity related?" This kind of dramatic tension depends on creating a kind of mystery based on ambiguity, which the filmmaker will illuminate in a moment of revelation at the end. Here's a simple example. Jessica Webb, a recent student of mine, made the terrific short film, *Licia,* which follows and inter-cuts the activities of three people: a teenaged boy who pedals his bike, loaded down with dozens of blue irises, to a forest clearing and plants a veritable carpet of flowers in the woods; a middle-aged man who is in his work shed building a large and intricate Kamuro aerial firework; and an elderly woman who travels to a downtown neighborhood to have an iris tattooed on her shoulder. While there is no direct conflict for any of these characters in achieving what they want, there is a compelling dramatic question nonetheless—what do these characters have in common and what do their actions mean? Jessica slyly puts in one clue that binds the three people: a mysterious woman who appears only briefly before any of these people carry out their tasks. The film resolves when the three come together in the end and it is revealed, as they watch the shimmering brilliance of the Kamuro firework (like a blue flower), that they are the son, husband, and mother of a woman who has recently died (the mysterious woman whose fragile presence we saw only fleetingly). The plantings, fireworks, and tattoo were their personal memorials.

The structure here is simple. There is a setup which poses a provocative question, and then a stirring answer to that question emerges from the culmination of what we've seen. Feature films use this storytelling pattern in moments, but it's difficult to sustain tension and engagement like this over the course of an hour and a half—which is why features are almost always conflict-oriented stories. But very short films can work quite well with an approach like this, provided that the question posed is compelling and visual and the answer is satisfying.

There Are No Rules

This discussion of dramatic principles, of course, is only a basic guideline. Cinematic storytelling allows lots of flexibility and room for experimentation. The legendary filmmaker Jean-Luc Godard is commonly paraphrased as saying that films do indeed need a beginning, middle, and end, though not necessarily in that order. Just as the subject matter of drama is virtually unlimited, so, too, are the ways that we can approach these subjects in cinema. The way you tell stories on film can vary depending on what you want to say, how you want a viewer to feel along the way, and what is appropriate for the ultimate point of your movie. As one of my writing professors, the novelist Alan Cheuse, once said of writing in general, "There is only one absolute rule to telling stories, make it work." Nonetheless, an understanding of the basic principles and the conventions that inform most cinematic narrative is an essential starting point. There are countless books on the shelves exploring in great detail the form, structure, and elements of cinematic drama. For the purposes of this book, I've focused the discussion on a few of the most fundamental elements of drama.

■ IDEAS WITHIN LIMITATIONS

The second sentence from the Kiarostami quote, which opens this chapter, "Our second job is to think of a film which can be made," refers to one of the most important skills a filmmaker can develop: identifying ideas that can both be great movies and be accom-

■ FROM IDEA TO CONCEPT

Here's an example from one of my students, George Racz, who was making his second film and his very first film with synchronized sound and color film. George has a four-year-old niece and he was enchanted by her vivid and boundless imagination. He had the idea to somehow capture in a movie her belief in wondrous and magical things. His intention was to charm an audience by allowing us to see the world for a moment through the eyes of this innocent, imaginative four-year old and, as George told me, "Through Panna I want to invite the viewers to rediscover those small magical moments which they once believed in." George's intentions were clear, but it was not yet clear how he would accomplish this on film. *What would he point the camera at? What would the little girl do? What would the audience actually see on screen that would charm them or make them see the world as Panna sees it?* In short, what's the story? George quickly turned his general idea into a specific film concept (Figure 1-5).

■ **Figure 1-5** Frame from *The Miracle* (2006), George Racz (writer/director).

At a huge toy store four year old Kate (main character) is enjoying all the toys when she sees a homeless woman digging through the trash outside the store (conflict). Kate is transfixed. At that moment her parents lead her to a magician in the store, where she assists the magician in a trick. Kate believes she has indeed learned how to perform true magic. Later, at a subway station, she sees a panhandler on crutches unable to walk (conflict re-emerges), and she decides to help the poor man with her new-found magical powers (action). She says the magic words and just as the train pulls away she sees the panhandler count his money and walk away without using the crutches (resolution). The little girl smiles, triumphant.

(See pp. 32–33 for George's finished screenplay.)

Ideas in their raw form are not a film story. Once you have an idea, you need to translate it into a film concept, with specific character, conflict, action. Then, you will be ready to write your screenplay.

plished within the filmmaker's real-world limitations. No matter how good your idea, if it is beyond your resources and experience you will not have a movie to show in the end. Always keep in mind, from the very first stages, that there is a symbiotic relationship between ideas and resources. One must work, from the beginning, with *what one has* rather than what *one wishes one had*. Such resourcefulness will go a long way to ensuring that you will in fact make movies.

Every film project, from a student's first film exercise to huge-budget Hollywood productions, works within limitations. The smart filmmaker will take these limitations into consideration from the very conception of the idea and the earliest development of the screenplay. A filmmaker's job is always to make the best film they can within the realistic limitations of their particular circumstances. You may have a big-budget, epic film waiting to burst out, but if you are taking only your second film class, and your film is due in three weeks, you're using sync sound for the very first time, and you lost one-third of your film funds fixing your car, it may not be the right moment to go for the Oscar. But every project, large or small, is an opportunity to show that you can master the craft of filmmaking, the art of cinematic storytelling, and your specific circumstances to deliver an effective film.

You do not need unlimited resources to be a successful filmmaker; you need to be smart about the resources you have. The following sections describe some real-world circumstances which a filmmaker should consider from a project's earliest conceptual stages.

Length of the Film

Running-time restrictions for a project can be imposed for a variety of reasons, from a professor setting a time limit, to standard television broadcast time limits, which demand accuracy to the fraction of a second. If you are hired by an advertising agency to make a 30-second commercial spot, you will not be allowed to hand in a 32-second spot, no matter how brilliant the extra 2 seconds are.

If you've imagined a terrific idea for a feature film, but only have the resources to make a 15-minute film, it's not a good idea to try to condense your long story into a short form. The story must fit the size and scope of your production. As I mentioned earlier, short films can be about almost anything, but they tell simple stories with a strict economy of means: few characters, one clean plotline, and everything working together to make only one point or one moment resonate. In general, novice filmmakers, still honing their craft, work on short films between 1 and 15 minutes in length.

Production Time

One of the most common mistakes young filmmakers make is underestimating how much time it takes to make a film and overestimating how much they can accomplish in a pre-scribed production period. Your production period can be defined by any number of factors: the limitations of a semester, the availability of an actor, changes in the weather, availability of equipment or crew, delivery deadlines, and, of course, financial resources. Be realistic about the amount of time you have to complete a project and let this inform the idea you choose to develop and the scale of the story you write.

Financial Resources

Being realistic about your financial resources is a vital consideration because it determines many factors that figure into the film concept and, eventually, the screenplay, including the number of characters, the locations, and the props, as well as the time, crew, and equipment necessary to execute certain stories. But working with a limited budget should not stop you from making a great film.

It's obvious to anyone who goes to the movies that bigger budgets alone don't necessarily make better movies, so it also stands to reason that lack of money doesn't necessarily result in a film of inferior quality. Limited funds should never dampen your creativity; in fact, quite the opposite. The fewer financial resources you have, the more creative you have to be, and this often makes for ingenious filmmaking, which is why modest means have often led to enormous innovation. *La Jetée* (1962) by Chris Marker, *Two Men and a Wardrobe* (*Dwaj ludzie z szafa*) (1958) by Roman Polanski, and Maya Deren's *Meshes of the Afternoon* (1943) are all black-and-white shorts, shot with tiny production crews, minimal financial resources, and no synchronized sound, yet they are considered classics of the short form for their incalculable contributions to the art of the cinema (see Figure 1-6). The key with each of these films is that their basic idea was smart, sharp, and elegant and worked intelligently with minimal resources.

Equipment, Location, Props, and Other Resources

You may have a wonderful idea for a short film—say, about a timid oceanographer who wins the heart of his one true love by taking her on a deep sea dive and showing her the wonders of the ocean floor—but if that movie requires real underwater photography and you have no access to an ocean (because you live in South Dakota) nor the equipment you need to shoot underwater, then maybe it's not the best idea to go with, even if it is a winner. Also, keep in mind that there is a direct link between the number of locations and the amount of time and money you will spend. A short film idea conceived with two locations in mind is easier to accomplish than one that involves twelve locations.

Cast and Crew

Small crews can only do so much. There will be many times, especially on low-budget projects, when crew members need to double up on responsibilities, but you need to be

■ **Figure 1-6** Maya Deren's *Meshes of the Afternoon* (1943, left). A landmark American film shot on a minimal budget, with no synchronized sound, and only 18 minutes long. Chris Marker's *La Jetée* (1962, right), one of the great films of the French New Wave, tells its complex and compelling story in 28 minutes, almost exclusively through still images. Despite nominal resources, both short films have an established place in the history of cinema because of their beauty and innovation.

aware, as you write your screenplay, that there is a law of diminishing returns when it comes to overextending your crew. Developing story ideas that require sync sound, moving cameras, careful lighting, crowd management, costumes, makeup, etc. will require crew to address each need. If you are expecting your cinematographer to take care of the camera and the logging and to set up all of the lighting alone and to do the special-effects makeup and arrange the furniture . . . don't be surprised if something goes wrong with the camera work.

Also, keep in mind that the number of characters you write into a film has a direct impact on the financial and logistical burden of the project. The more people you have in front of the camera, the more time and money you can generally expect to spend.

Keep It Manageable

If you're just starting out in filmmaking, it's best to keep your projects manageable. A tight, effective, stylistically exciting five-minute film in which all of your story and technical elements work together to tell a convincing and involving little story is *always* preferable to a sloppy thirty-minute film which loses its way because the filmmaker did not have command of all the cinematic details. Even worse is a film that cannot even be completed because its demands exceed the limits of the filmmaker's resources. Your first opportunity to establish the logistical, financial, and labor parameters of your production happens right in the very beginning, as you develop your idea and begin scripting. It's wonderful and important to be optimistic about your projects, but you must also be realistic.

The short film *Bread and Alley* is a good example of Kiarostami following his own advice. The film involved only elements that were easy for Kiarostami to obtain, especially crucial because this was his first film. The movie is only ten minutes long and required only two crew members and one day to shoot. It used one easy-to-obtain location, one boy, and a couple of extras. Kiarostami needed some bread, some milk, and, the hardest requirement of the movie, a dog. But, of course, the most important thing he had from the outset was a simple yet elegant and touching story idea.

Robert Rodriguez' *El Mariachi* (1992), a feature film produced for $7,000, went on to win major awards and serious Hollywood studio contracts for its director. The first secret to Rodriguez' success is that he came up with an idea that he could make into a film using what he had at his disposal (Figure 1-7).

> *How do you make a cheap movie? Look around you, what do you have around you? Take stock of what you have. Your father owns a liquor store—make a movie about a liquor store. Do you have a dog? Make a movie about your dog. Your mom works in a nursing home, make a movie about a nursing home. When I did* El Mariachi *I had a turtle, I had a guitar case, I had a small town and I said I'll make a movie around that.*
>
> **Robert Rodriguez (From Robert Rodriguez' *10 Minute Film School*)**

By doing the shooting, directing, and editing himself, he required only a small crew of five people; he used few artificial lights, did not shoot with synchronized sound, and used locations that were nearby and easily accessed. The small crew was so lean that Rodriguez could work fast—a method that he calls "frantic filmmaking." The second quality that made his film so successful is that he turned all of these "limitations" into an opportunity to create a flamboyant style that perfectly matched the story and mood of the film. Nowhere is this more apparent than in his energetic camera style, which swoops, pivots, glides, and shoots from a stunning variety of angles. Rodriguez had no lights and no sound,

and therefore no sound crew and a small camera. Realizing that his camera was free of these shackles, he also freed it from the tripod, allowing it to move, handheld, anywhere and everywhere.

> *On* Mariachi *I had two lights, regular light bulbs; they were balanced for indoor film, so [they] look fine. In fact everyone said the lighting looked moody because there was very little light. Your mistakes, your shortcomings suddenly become artistic expression.*
>
> **Robert Rodriguez (From Robert Rodriguez' *10 Minute Film School*)**

When Kelly Reichardt read the short story "Old Joy" by Jonathan Raymond, she knew right away that she not only *wanted* to adapt this story into a film, she *could* actually make the film. The story, which is about two men, old friends who reunite for a weekend camping trip in the Oregon forests, attracted her on many levels. One was the idea of making a film that would involve bringing a very small cast and crew together for a condensed period of time, in a very special, somewhat isolated, place—in this case, the old-growth forests of Oregon. The result was Reichardt's ultra-low-budget and intensely moving feature film *Old Joy* (2006) (Figure 1-8).

All of the requirements were within Reichardt's grasp: a small cast of two principal actors, a car, a dog, and the Pacific Northwest wilderness. She had one more crew person, six, than Rodriguez had, because she was shooting with sync sound and needed another person to mike the scenes and record sound. She also

■ Figure 1-7 A turtle, a guitar case, and a town. Robert Rodriguez crafted the story of his successful *El Mariachi* (1992) around things he knew he had access to or could borrow.

brought to the project Peter Sillen, a cinematographer who had extensive experience on documentaries, so was expert at working with natural light and "working small." True to her original inspiration, Reichardt brought her small cast and crew to Oregon, where they lived together during the production in friend's houses and in a church retreat in the Oregon forests. The film took a mere ten days to shoot. Reichardt had only two lights, which she used in only two scenes. The rest of the time she shot in the magnificent old-growth forests of Oregon under cloudy skies. The location and the quality of natural light made her low-budget film look like a million bucks—the birds, rivers, rain, and foliage all become like another character in the film.

Working small also allowed the cast and crew to be especially agile and made it possible to work in the rugged terrain and around the sudden downpours, which were frequent in Oregon. However, the primary benefit to emerge from the limits of her working conditions involved the intimacy of the group. As Reichardt tells it, "Everyone schlepped equipment up and down the paths, even the actors. And when it rained, all of us would pile into the car and go over lines, do rehearsals and discuss the film until it stopped." The intense and close working conditions created a strong collaborative energy between cast and crew,

which encouraged everyone to contribute to the film. "We knew we were all in this together, we were in a special place having a great experience together, I knew something would come out of it." These sessions generated a deep understanding of the script and some powerful improvisational exchanges, which wound up in the film. In addition, the story itself is as delicate and fragile as the relationship between the two men. So much of what goes on in *Old Joy* remains only barely revealed, and Reichardt's close-knit, small-scale production approach created the perfect environment for nurturing this tone. "I think the intimate approach we took to making the film comes through in the film itself. The limitations all somehow work out for you in the end. Although I sometimes had my doubts, it did work out that way in the end." (See *Figure 1-9*.)

With both *El Mariachi* and *Old Joy*, the aesthetic and conceptual approach to the film necessarily responded to the real-world limitations of the production resources, and yet, each style is so perfectly integrated with the story being told that one doesn't feel pennies being pinched or corners being cut. The stories are right for the resources and the approaches are just right for the stories. We can't imagine these films told any other way.

■ **Figure 1-8** In *Old Joy* (2006), director Kelly Reichardt maintained a minimal crew, isolated in Oregon's Cascade Mountains for the duration of the shoot, creating an atmosphere that perfectly complemented the intimate nature of the story.

■ **Figure 1-9** The bond developed by the close-knit crew and cast of *Old Joy* created an intimacy that was evident on screen. Kelly Reichardt conferring with Daniel London, one of her lead actors.

The Screenplay

A **screenplay** is the literary expression of the story, characters, actions, locations, and tone of your film written in a specialized dramatic script format. Whether you write the script yourself or work with someone else's material, it's important to remember that the screenplay is not the final product. It is an intermediate step in the production of a film and serves many functions in all stages of the project's development. It is often said that the screenplay is the blueprint for the entire process of making a film, in the same way that a rendering of a house serves as the blueprint for the construction of a house. In many ways this is true; however, unlike an architectural blueprint, a screenplay should remain a rather more flexible document throughout the process. It's important to keep in mind that screenplays evolve. They should be revised and rewritten, at every stage of a film's progression, as new ideas or circumstances emerge.

■ STAGES OF SCRIPT DEVELOPMENT

There are a number of stages in the evolution of a screenplay, and each stage usually requires various drafts. Each stage has a specific purpose as you proceed, step-by-step, from a general outline of your story to a script that contains the full dimensions of your film, including locations, actions, dialogue, sounds, movements, etc. This process of working and reworking your film's story material, adding, cutting, or refining details along the way, is called **script development**.

Concept

As mentioned in the previous chapter, the concept is a very brief outline of the basic elements involved in your story. It describes the dramatic engine that will drive the story in no more than a few sentences. Who is in this film (protagonist)? What do they want, what gets in the way, and what do they do (goal + conflict = actions)? And where does it all take place (location)? Once you have determined the basic, but specific, elements of your story, and understand how they work together, you are ready to write a treatment.

Treatment

The **treatment** is a prose description of the plot, written in present tense, as the film will unfold for the audience, scene by scene (Figure 2-1). A treatment is a story draft where the writer can hammer out the basic actions and plot structure of the story before going into the complexities of realizing fully developed scenes with dialogue, precise actions, and setting descriptions. The treatment is the equivalent of a painter's sketch that can be worked and reworked before committing to the actual painting. It's much easier to cut, add, and rearrange scenes in this form, than in a fully detailed screenplay. Generally, a treatment involves writing one paragraph for each major dramatic event, also called a narrative beat. A **narrative beat** is a dramatic event in which the action, decisions, or revelations of that moment move the plot forward either by intensifying it or by sending it in a new direction. In other words, a treatment sketches in the essential events. For a short film, a treatment might be one to three pages long. For very simple short films, you can simply write one sentence describing each scene or each narrative beat. This shorter version is called a **step outline** or a **beat sheet**.

■ **Figure 2-1** A treatment is a simple but comprehensive prose description of a film's plot. George Racz' treatment for *The Miracle*.

THE MIRACLE
Treatment by George Racz

Kate and her parents enter a toy store. The store is huge and filled with every toy imaginable. Kate stands in front of a big stuffed teddy bear and starts to dance with it. As Kate explores other treasures in the store she notices something going on outside. Pressing her nose against the store window, she sees an old homeless woman digging through a garbage can. Kate is soon distracted by a small crowd gathering inside the store; she approaches the crowd to take a closer look. A magician, with a long white beard and a sparkly blue gown is putting on a magic show for the children around him. The magician moves his hands about in preparation for a new trick. Kate mimics his every move. He notices her following his gestures and promptly extends a closed hand in front of her. When he opens his hand she finds it full of gummy bears; she takes one. The magician bends down and whispers magic words in Kate's ear as he hands her his magic wand. Kate repeats the words as waves the magic wand three times. Big magic happens.

Later on, Kate and her parents are waiting for the subway. She is holding the big teddy bear. The subway arrives and they get on. Inside, a homeless man, using crutches, is panhandling. Kate's father gives him a dollar. Kate watches the man struggle with his crutches. The subway arrives at the next station and the homeless man gets off. Kate uses her finger as a magic wand and draws three circles in the air while looking at the homeless man count his change on the platform. She closes her eyes and whispers the magic words the magician told her at the store. When she reopens her eyes, she sees the homeless man suddenly walk normally, dragging his crutches behind him. Kate smiles and hugs her teddy bear as the subway pulls away from the station.

Author's Draft

The **author's draft** is the first complete version of the narrative in proper screenplay format. The emphasis of the author's draft is on the story, the development of characters, and the conflict, actions, settings, and dialogue. The author's draft goes through a number of rewrites and revisions on its way to becoming a **final draft**, which is the last version of the author's draft before being turned into a shooting script. The aim of an author's draft is to remain streamlined, flexible, and "readable." Therefore, technical information (such as detailed camera angles, performance cues, blocking, or detailed set description) is kept to an absolute minimum. It is important not to attempt to direct the entire film, shot-for-shot, in the author's draft. The detailed visualization and interpretation of the screenplay occurs during later preproduction and production stages. We will look closely at some essential principles for script language and for formatting the author's draft in this chapter.

Shooting Script

Once you have completed your rewrites and arrived at a final draft, you will be ready to take that script into production by transforming it into a shooting script. The **shooting script** is the version of the screenplay you take into production, meaning the script from which your creative team (cinematographer, production designer, etc.) will work and from which the film will be shot. A shooting script communicates, in specific terms, the director's visual approach to the film. All the scenes are numbered on a shooting script to facilitate breaking down the script and organizing the production of the film. This version also includes specific technical information about the visualization of the movie, like camera angles, shot sizes, camera moves, etc. Chapter 5 deals with the process of creating the shooting script.

■ FORMATTING THE AUTHOR'S DRAFT SCREENPLAY

The screenplay is a multipurpose document. It is both a literary manuscript, conveying the dramatic story for a reader, and a technical document that anticipates the logistics of the production process and allows everyone involved in your project to see what they need to do. The technical functions of a screenplay are realized in the format of the script, which are standardized to facilitate common film production processes. This is why a screenplay looks unlike any other literary manuscript.

Beyond the technical formatting of a script, the language of the author's draft screenplay, its style and detail, communicates the *spirit* of the visual approach, tone, rhythm, and point of view of the final film. Embedded in the author's draft are your first thoughts on visualizing the story for the screen without the use of camera cues and technical jargon. If written well, an author's draft script should help everyone involved in your project "see" what you are striving for, thematically and visually.

Elements of an Author's Draft Script

There are six formatting elements used in the screenplay form: title, scene headings, stage directions, dialogue, personal directions, and character cues. Let's look at *Kebacle* (2006), a simple screenwriting observation exercise written by my student Alana Kakoyiannis, and label each element. Alana was assigned to observe the people, activities, and interactions in the world around her for two weeks and then render one particularly interesting moment as a scene from a screenplay (Figures 2-2 and 2-3).

General Screenwriting Principles

A screenplay is written as the film will unfold to an audience.

A screenplay is written in the present tense and must follow the progression of the film, moment by moment, scene by scene, as you wish it to appear before an audience. There is no literary commentary in a film script and this necessitates two important practices:

1. *The words on the page present each scene, action, image, character, and series of events to a reader as they would appear to the viewer of the film.* Notice that Alana does not anticipate what is going to happen later by introducing Aamir saying:

   > Aamir is an unlicensed vendor who shouldn't be serving food to people on a public sidewalk.

   We will get to that detail only when it is revealed to the audience. The screenplay builds its story one moment at a time in the same way the film will and in the beginning all we see is a food vendor serving people.

2. *There should be nothing in the script that will not be seen or heard by the film's audience.* In general, nothing goes on the page that cannot be realized on the screen in images and sounds. These are the fundamental tools of a filmmaker and therefore they are the tools of the screenwriter as well. In prose fiction and poetry it is common for an author to explain to the reader what people are feeling, what personal history might be informing an action, what a character is secretly thinking, or even what subconsciously motivates them. In film we must dramatize these internal states. **To dramatize** is to externalize and reveal the internal, through actions, dialogue, and visual context. Notice that Alana does not describe what any character is feeling, their state of mind, or their intentions. She does not write, for example,

The New Yorker is impatient and anxious to get back to work so he calls out his order out of turn.

If you are true to the moment and to the voices of the characters, the intentions behind each line should be apparent. We can already *feel* the impatience, verging on pushiness, in the words and actions of the New Yorker, so there is no need to announce them. It would, in fact, completely ruin the scene if Alana were to write something like

Aamir only pretends to close down by lowering his umbrella because he knows that as soon as the police van drives away, he can get back to business.

While these internal feelings and intentions may be part of what is going on in the scene, expressed this way, they are not cinematic. However, the filmable actions of Aamir folding his umbrella and watching the police drive away, then immediately reopening his umbrella to resume business without missing a beat, all quite vividly *reveal*

■ **Figure 2-2** Screenplay formatting elements.

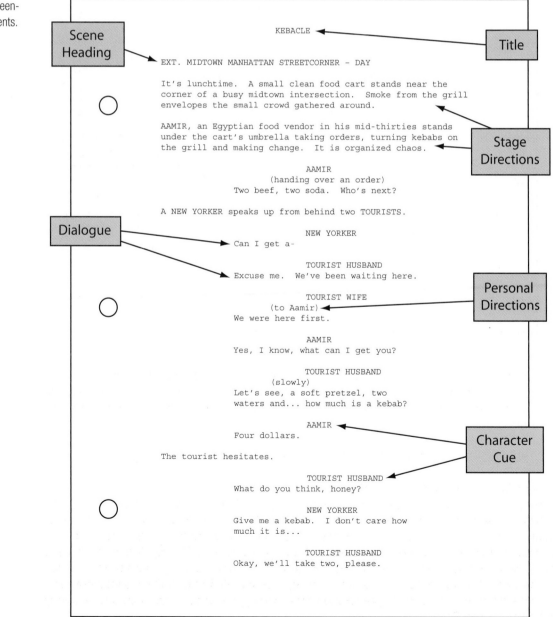

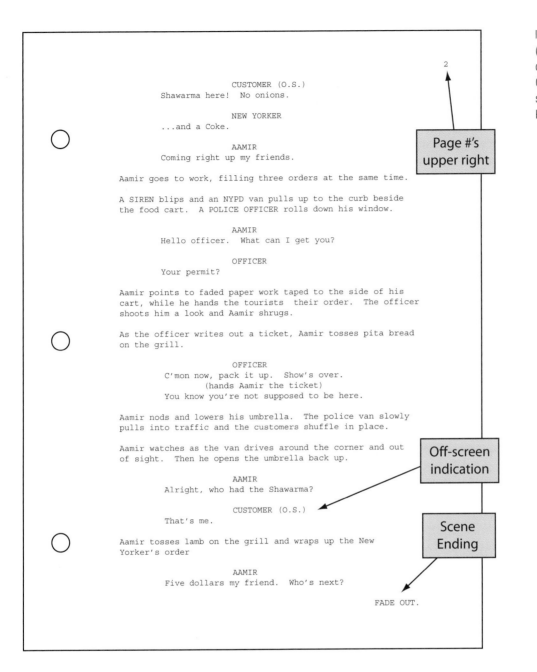

```
                                                            2

                    CUSTOMER (O.S.)
            Shawarma here!  No onions.

                    NEW YORKER
            ...and a Coke.

                    AAMIR
            Coming right up my friends.

    Aamir goes to work, filling three orders at the same time.

    A SIREN blips and an NYPD van pulls up to the curb beside
    the food cart.  A POLICE OFFICER rolls down his window.

                    AAMIR
            Hello officer.  What can I get you?

                    OFFICER
            Your permit?

    Aamir points to faded paper work taped to the side of his
    cart, while he hands the tourists  their order.  The officer
    shoots him a look and Aamir shrugs.

    As the officer writes out a ticket, Aamir tosses pita bread
    on the grill.

                    OFFICER
            C'mon now, pack it up.  Show's over.
                (hands Aamir the ticket)
            You know you're not supposed to be here.

    Aamir nods and lowers his umbrella.  The police van slowly
    pulls into traffic and the customers shuffle in place.

    Aamir watches as the van drives around the corner and out
    of sight.  Then he opens the umbrella back up.

                    AAMIR
            Alright, who had the Shawarma?

                    CUSTOMER (O.S.)
            That's me.

    Aamir tosses lamb on the grill and wraps up the New
    Yorker's order

                    AAMIR
            Five dollars my friend.  Who's next?

                                FADE OUT.
```

Page #'s
upper right

Off-screen
indication

Scene
Ending

what he was thinking and intending to do. Presented this way we also understand that this interaction is routine for him. It is far better to simply show it as it happens and let the audience discover his intentions for themselves—just as Alana did when she witnessed the scene.

Now let's look at each script element used in an author's draft individually.

Scene Headings (or Slug Lines)

The scene heading is our first introduction to each and every scene and establishes the fundamental time and location information in order to set the scene. What is a scene? **A scene** is a dramatic moment that has unity of both time and location. If you make a jump in time, say from day to night, you need to begin a new scene. Change location, and you must begin a new scene—even if that change is only from the living room to the kitchen of the same house. In addition, scene headings play a vital role in the disassembly and reorganization of the script in preparation for creating production shot lists and shooting schedules. (See Chapter 5.)

- *Interior or Exterior Setting:* (EXT.)
  Interior and Exterior are always abbreviated and simply tell us if the scene takes place indoors or outdoors.
- *Location:* (EXT. MIDTOWN MANHATTAN STREET CORNER–)
  The next bit of information is a brief but specific name of the location. We do not describe the location in detail here, but we must be precise. For example, EXT. NEW YORK CITY is brief, but it lacks the specificity to establish the location accurately. Where in New York City does this take place? Brooklyn? Staten Island? Upper East Side? On the street? In a Park? All of these are very different locations with very different associations. EXT. MIDTOWN MANHATTAN STREET CORNER gives the necessary information, as would EXT. TIMES SQUARE or EXT. CENTRAL PARK, for other scenes.

  The location name must always remain constant. If multiple scenes take place on this street corner then the location must be identified the same way each time (for example, don't use MIDTOWN MANHATTAN STREET CORNER for some scenes and AAMIR'S CORNER for others). Also, if you have two similar locations, then you need to make sure you differentiate the two with distinct scene headings. For example, if there were two pushcart vendors on midtown Manhattan corners, then one would need to be, say, AAMIR'S MIDTOWN CORNER and the other JOE'S 32ND STREET SPOT.
- *General Time of Day:* (EXT. MIDTOWN MANHATTAN STREET CORNER—DAY)
  The final bit of information is an indication of whether the scene takes place during the daylight hours, night hours, or in between. You do not need to get too specific with this. THREE AM or TEN-THIRTY PM are too specific. Only DAY, NIGHT, DAWN, or DUSK are generally used. If you want the audience to know the exact hour, then you need to put it elsewhere, like an image (a clock) in stage directions or in dialogue.
- *Other Time Indicators*
  CONTINUOUS, LATER, and SAME are additional time indicators that are commonly used. We use CONTINUOUS in cases when one scene follows the previous one (from one location to another) without any break in time whatsoever. LATER is used when we remain in the same location, but we leap forward a little bit in time (i.e., less than day to night), and SAME is used when two scenes are happening in different locations, but it must be understood that they are happening at precisely the same time.

INT. SCHOOL HALLWAY – DAY

Billy races down the empty hallways, past the sleeping hall monitor and turns into . . .

INT. CLASSROOM – CONTINUOUS

. . . a classroom full of students already working on their exams. Billy heads to his seat and just as he sits down, his teacher places a five page exam on the desk in front of him.

Billy looks it over and swallows hard. He pulls out a pencil and gets to work.

INT. CLASSROOM – LATER

Billy sits in the nearly empty classroom still working on page three of the exam. The only other person in the room is the teacher, who keeps shifting his gaze from the clock to Billy.

INT. SCHOOL PARKING LOT – SAME

Susan sits in her idling car, with her friend Gail, watching as the last few students exit the school.

                              SUSAN
          Where is he?

                              GAIL
          I don't think he's coming. He's totally dis'ing you.
          I told you, Billy was no good.

                              SUSAN
          Maybe you're right.

          Susan sighs, puts the car into gear and drives off.

Stage Directions

Stage directions, also called **scene directions**, are always written in present tense. Stage directions are where most of your creative writing takes place. This is where you describe the actions of the characters, the settings, the images, and all nondialogue sounds of each scene in your script. In short, this is where you write what we see and, other than dialogue, what we hear. We will discuss the role of style and the art of visual writing in more detail later, but as a general rule, you should not elaborate on actions, settings, and movements in extreme detail. Too much extraneous description will bog down your script.

When you write a screenplay, words and space are at a premium, so include only the *essential details* — that is, the essential actions, descriptions, and images — to tell your story. Notice in the *Kebacle* example that Alana describes Aamir's pushcart simply as

          A small clean food cart.

Combined with Aamir's cooking actions, his professionalism, and the food details along the way, there's enough information for a reader (and a set designer and cinematographer) to conjure just the kind of pushcart this man would run and exactly how it would look down to the smallest detail. We don't need to know where the napkins are, or list every item on the posted menu, or if he has a chair next to him, or on which side the pretzels are kept. Later, in the production process, these details and more will be decided, but in the script, they're not essential. The umbrella detail, however, is important to the story, but not, for example, its color.

In terms of essential actions, notice how the author doesn't trace every detail of every action. While we see Aamir give the Tourists their order (to show that he doesn't stop working even as he's getting a ticket) we don't need to write out the entire transaction, including getting money, making change, etc. Also, the author says that he "wraps up the New Yorker's order." But we don't need to know if he uses foil or wax paper, nor do we need to describe him putting the kebab in a bag and then the soda, followed by two napkins and a straw. We don't even see where he puts the ticket after the officer hands it to him. Sure, these details will need to be worked out on the set, but it's not essential to the script.

The *Kebacle* screenplay is exemplary because its script language is lean and yet the scene is vivid. We'll look closely at how this is accomplished in the *Screenplay Language and Style* section.

Other Stage Direction Rules

There are certain instances when words and names need to be written in all capital letters in the stage directions. Again, this is part of the technical function of the screenplay. The following details need to be in all capital letters:

1. *Character introductions.*
   The first time a character actually, physically appears in the film you must use all capital letters for their name when you introduce them in the stage directions. This

■ **Figure 2-4** Text that is meant to be read by the audience, as in this shot from Soderbergh's *Ocean's Eleven* (2001), should be put in quotations in a screenplay. (See **Figure 2-8**.)

allows a producer and casting agent to see at a glance how many characters there are in a given script and it also allows an actor to quickly find their first scene. Once you have introduced a character using all capitals, then you write their name normally for the rest of the screenplay. This rule apples to minor characters as well, but not to extras.

In our Kebacle example, Aamir, the tourists, the New Yorker, and the officer are in all capital letters the first time they appear in the script, but they're never written in all caps again in the stage directions. The other customers are not capitalized because they are **extras**, which means that they are performers who do not have a dramatic role in the film; they simply populate the environment for atmosphere and authenticity.

2. *Sound cues.*

   Any time you have a sound that is not created by a character actually in the scene, like the SIREN BLIP in the example, it needs to be capitalized. This is a reminder that, although the sound is not in the scene as you shoot, the performers will still have to account for it during shooting. If, for example, you are shooting a scene in which a character hears CHURCH BELLS in the distance, the bells will not likely be sounding during actual shooting, yet the characters still need to react as if they were. Also, this is an indication to the sound designer that they will need to find this sound effect to put in later during postproduction.

3. *Readable text.*

   Anything that is intended for the audience to read must be put in quotation marks. This reminds the director and cinematographer that they must compose the shot so that the audience is able to read the text of, say, a banner which reads "Happy Retirement Bob!" or the cover of the book "Being and Nothingness," which a character is reading or a road sign which reads "WELCOME TO KANSAS" (see **Figures 2-4** and **2-8**).

Character Cues

Character cues indicate which character speaks the lines of dialogue, which follow (i.e., AAMIR, OFFICER, or TOURIST WIFE). It's quite simple but there are a few rules to keep in mind.

1. *Keep the name consistent.*

   If my character's name is Aamir Hassan and I decide to give him the character cue AAMIR, then it must remain AAMIR for the entire script. I can't change it to MR. HASSAN later on.

2. *Only one character per name.*

   If I have two characters, Aamir Hassan and Aamir Khan, then they both cannot have AAMIR as a character cue. You should refer to them by their last names.

3. *You may refer to characters by a role.*

   It is common to refer to minor characters by their role, such as OFFICER or TOURIST.

4. *Additional information: Voice-over, off screen, and other delivery indicators.*

   The character cue line sometimes carries other information about the delivery of the dialogue. Occasionally you will have a character speaking off screen or in a voice-over, or the dialogue may come over radio. *Kebacle* has an example of this:

> CUSTOMER (O.S.)
> Shawarma here! No onions.

Off screen implies that the character is present in the time and place of the scene, but they are not visible from the camera's perspective (i.e., they are talking from somewhere in the crowd we can't see or from behind a door). **Voice-over** implies that the person speaking is not speaking from that time or place, like a narrator commenting on the events of a scene from the perspective of memory (Figure 2-5).

Off screen and voice-over indications are always abbreviated—(O.S.) and (V.O.), respectively—and are located after the character cue. You can also indicate (TV) or (RADIO) if the dialogue is being broadcast.

```
INT. ANDREW'S BEDROOM - NIGHT

Andrew rushes into his bedroom, pulls his suitcase out from under the bed
and starts stuffing it with clothes from his dresser. Suddenly, he hears a
NOISE from the bathroom and he freezes.

                        ANDREW
            Who's in there?

                        RUTH (O.S.)
            It's just me Andy. I'll be right out.

Andrew moves to the window and cracks the blinds a fraction of an inch. He
eyes a car that is passing slowly in front of his house.

                        ANDREW (V.O.)
            After that bizarre phone call I started losing my
            mind, I was suspicious of everyone; even Ruth
            seemed to be spying on me.
```

Dialogue

Dialogue is simply what your characters say. Using proper margins and single spacing are pretty much the only formatting rules which apply here. However, dialogue is the other area where your creative writing and stylistic skills come into play. When you consider that dialogue is the "voice" of your character and that everything from the dialogue's content, tone, grammar, rhythm, and accent all serve to define the person speaking those lines and establish their credibility, then you begin to realize that determining "what your characters say" is not so simple. The main principle for stage directions, stick to the essentials, also applies to dialogue. One very common mistake early screenwriters make is to overwrite their dialogue. We will discuss working with dialogue in more detail later in the chapter.

Personal Directions

Personal directions are always very brief, placed in parentheses, and do not have any capital letters unless you use a proper noun. They refer only to the person speaking the lines within which they appear.

Personal directions are one of the most misused elements in a screenplay. Novice writers tend to use personal directions to tell the actors how to perform their lines. This is a mistake in two respects. First, the line itself should evoke the emotional tone of the delivery (sorrowful, joyful, wistful, etc.) without you having to label it as such. If a line is not sarcastic, then labeling it with the personal direction (sarcastically) will not make it sarcastic. Also, generally speaking, actors will try to make

■ **Figure 2-5** *The Thin Red Line* (1998). "Are you righteous? Kind? Does your confidence lie in this?" A Japanese soldier appears to communicate from beyond the grave through voice over narration, a staple of Malick's films.

the best emotional decisions for the lines and the scene. When you use an emotional cue like (sorrowfully) you are closing the door to an interpretation of the line that could, in fact, enrich the moment. The emotional approach should be evident in the situation and dialogue itself, and if there is room for interpretation, then this is worked out between the director and actors in rehearsal and should not be codified in the author's draft. So, when *do* we use personal directions?

1. Important, but very small, actions that must happen on a precise line of dialogue. For example, in *Kebacle:*

> OFFICER
> C'mon now, pack it up. Show's over,
>> (hands Aamir the ticket)
> You know you're not supposed to be here.

It's a nice touch that Alana placed this action right here. The officer's second line is slightly more personal than the others and indicates that they've been through this before. The fact that the ticket is exchanging hands at this moment makes the line seem even more person-to-person.

2. Receiver of dialogue in group scenes. Occasionally it may not be clear to whom your character is speaking, especially in group conversations, so instead of constantly embedding the name of the receiver of the dialogue in the lines, we can simply indicate it in personal directions. For example, in *Kebacle:*

A NEW YORKER speaks up from behind two TOURISTS.

> NEW YORKER
> Can I get a-

> TOURIST HUSBAND
> Excuse me, we've been waiting here.

> TOURIST WIFE
>> (to Aamir)
> We were here first.

> AAMIR
> Yes, I know, what can I get you?

> TOURIST HUSBAND
>> (slowly)
> Let's see, a soft pretzel, two waters and . . . how much is a kebab?

> AAMIR
> Four dollars.

The Tourist hesitates.

> TOURIST HUSBAND
> What do you think, honey?

> NEW YORKER
> Give me a kebab. I don't care how much it is . . .

in practice

Margins, Fonts, and Spacing

Margins, fonts, and spacing are an important part of formatting because they ensure that each script page reflects one minute of screen time, more or less. A fifteen-page screenplay will yield a fifteen-minute film, approximately. There are several computer programs which make this aspect of formatting your script extremely easy (i.e., Final Draft and Movie Magic Screenwriter) or you can very easily create your own screenplay format **template,** using style formatting and macros, in any word processing program, such as Microsoft Word. Simply program in the formatting specification shown in Figure 2-6 for each script element and assign keyboard macros to each set of formatting instructions.

Measurements from the left edge of the page:

Scene Headings:	1.5″
Stage Directions:	1.5″
Character Cues:	4.25″ (names START at center of page)
Dialogues:	2.5″ (cuts off at 6 1/2″)
Personal Directions:	3.75″ (cuts off at 5 1/2″)

Spacing Between Elements

Between Scenes:	3 spaces
Between Scene Headings and Stage Directions:	2 spaces
Between Stage Directions and Character Cues:	2 spaces
Between Character Cue & Dialogue:	1 space
Between Character Cue & Personal Directions:	1 space

Font: Courier 12 point   Page numbers: upper right

■ **Figure 2-6** The industry standard margins and spacing for correct screenplay formatting.

One of the things that makes this moment so sharp is the way the Tourist Husband confronts the New Yorker while the wife appeals to Aamir. They attack on two fronts at once, a strategy that tells us that this is an important matter of principle to them and they *really* feel entitled to order first. If we had left out the personal direction (to Aamir) then the wife's dialogue would appear to be directed to the New Yorker and would have a different effect. Notice also how Alana understood that it was not necessary to write (impatiently) or (exasperated) when the New Yorker places his order. The emotional tone of the line is obvious in the words and context. (Slowly) is not so much an emotion as it is an indication of pace. Alana wants to really draw out this moment, knowing that it adds tension to the situation. Other nonemotional, personal directions you'll see are indications like (whispers), (yells), (with a French accent), and (stuttering).

I have outlined only the basics of screenplay formatting in this chapter. It's definitely worth your time to locate one of the books I mention in the recommended readings section for more detail.

■ SCREENPLAY LANGUAGE AND STYLE

Visual Writing, Character, and Action

"Show Me, Don't Tell Me"

In film, as in life, actions speak louder than words. Someone can say to you, "I love you," and it sounds great, but can you trust it? "I really, really love you": pretty words but perhaps too easy to say. But if that person actually shows their love by leaving a great job, their beloved city, and all their friends to follow you to another state because they can't live without you, then you might think, "Gee, you did that for me? You must really love me."

When you write a script, try to do as much as possible with actions. Converting feelings, intentions, and character traits into actions and behavior is at the heart of screen drama and is essential to establishing an indelible understanding of character. In the *Kebacle* example, just the casual action of Aamir starting business up again after the police van drives away tells us a lot about his essential character: how afraid he is of the law, what he feels he needs to do to run his business, and what his work routine is.

Let's look at some principles for showing character through actions. The focus here will be on the craft of writing visually and on what is revealed through what we see and how

■ **Figure 2-7** Excerpt from *Ocean's Eleven.* Granted courtesy of Warner Brothers Entertainment Inc.

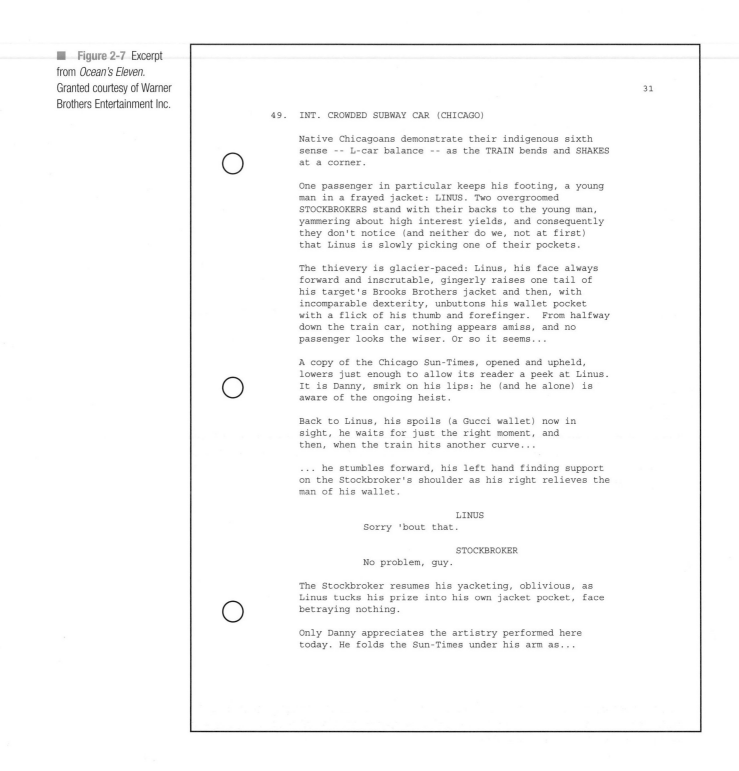

31

```
49.   INT. CROWDED SUBWAY CAR (CHICAGO)

      Native Chicagoans demonstrate their indigenous sixth
      sense -- L-car balance -- as the TRAIN bends and SHAKES
      at a corner.

      One passenger in particular keeps his footing, a young
      man in a frayed jacket: LINUS. Two overgroomed
      STOCKBROKERS stand with their backs to the young man,
      yammering about high interest yields, and consequently
      they don't notice (and neither do we, not at first)
      that Linus is slowly picking one of their pockets.

      The thievery is glacier-paced: Linus, his face always
      forward and inscrutable, gingerly raises one tail of
      his target's Brooks Brothers jacket and then, with
      incomparable dexterity, unbuttons his wallet pocket
      with a flick of his thumb and forefinger.  From halfway
      down the train car, nothing appears amiss, and no
      passenger looks the wiser. Or so it seems...

      A copy of the Chicago Sun-Times, opened and upheld,
      lowers just enough to allow its reader a peek at Linus.
      It is Danny, smirk on his lips: he (and he alone) is
      aware of the ongoing heist.

      Back to Linus, his spoils (a Gucci wallet) now in
      sight, he waits for just the right moment, and
      then, when the train hits another curve...

      ... he stumbles forward, his left hand finding support
      on the Stockbroker's shoulder as his right relieves the
      man of his wallet.

                          LINUS
                Sorry 'bout that.

                          STOCKBROKER
                No problem, guy.

      The Stockbroker resumes his yacketing, oblivious, as
      Linus tucks his prize into his own jacket pocket, face
      betraying nothing.

      Only Danny appreciates the artistry performed here
      today. He folds the Sun-Times under his arm as...
```

```
                                                              32

 50.  INT. UNION STATION / SUBWAY STATION - CONTINUED

         ... The SUBWAY SQUEALS to a stop. Linus jumps out,
         leaving his prey aboard, and a few moments later, Danny
         steps off, too.


 51.  INT. UNION STATION - EVENING

         The hurly-burly of rush hour in Union Station.

         Commuters zig and zag, this way and that, all on
         furious schedules, and Linus slips blithely through
         them, in no hurry, a man who's pulled this job a
         thousand times before.

         He dodges and sidesteps crazed commuters, and except
         for a brief brush with one well-dressed man (the Sun-
         Times tucked under his arm), he escapes the station
         without incident.


 52.  EXT. UNION STATION - EVENING

         Linus exits, casually reaching into his jacket to count
         his winnings. And his face falls.  All he finds where
         the stolen wallet once resided is a calling card. On
         one side, in engraved printing:

         "DANIEL OCEAN." On the flip side, in handwriting: "Nice
         pull. Murphy's Bar, Rush & Division."


 53.  INT.  MURPHY'S BAR -
```

it is presented. We will use a brief sequence from *Ocean's Eleven* (screenplay written by Ted Griffin, 2001) (**Figures 2-7** and **2-8**).

■ *Write with precision.*

The first thing to remember is that when you are writing a screenplay, you are a writer. As a writer, your tools are words, so you need to be precise with your language and find the specific words that will convey not just the action, but also the tone or mood of the situation. The author of the *Ocean's Eleven* script does not say

> Linus lifts up the man's coat, opens his pocket, reaches in and pulls out his wallet.

Yes, that's basically what happens, but put this way, the reader would imagine that Linus is a hapless clod who could not possibly get away with this. So, instead he writes

> Linus, his face always forward and inscrutable, gingerly raises one tail of his target's Brooks Brothers jacket and then, with incomparable dexterity, unbuttons his wallet pocket with a flick of his thumb and forefinger. [and he eventually] . . . relieves the man of his wallet.

The author has written only the actions, but the precision of the passage allows us to really "see" the crime and it also shows us Linus' expert abilities at picking pockets, a skill he will need later on in the film.

Keep in mind that not all actions and details are equally important. In stage directions we stick with only the essentials. The amount of time and words you use to describe something determines its importance in the scene. Lavish special attention and language only on those things that are really critical to the story line.

- *Use images, not camera cues.*

  In an author's draft, we avoid as much as possible the inclusion of camera cues—indications such as CLOSE-UP . . . or ZOOM IN ON . . . or CAMERA PANS TO REVEAL . . ., etc. However, that doesn't mean you can't indicate a close-up or a wide shot if you really feel that it is necessary in the telling of the story. As a screenwriter you need to describe, in prose, an image or action that suggests to the reader or a director a close-up or a long shot or whatever else you intended. This is the essence of visual writing. In the *Ocean's Eleven* example, Ted Griffin writes:

(a) Linus, his face always forward and inscrutable, gingerly raises one tail of his target's Brooks Brothers jacket (b) and then, with incomparable dexterity, unbuttons his wallet pocket with a flick of his thumb and forefinger. (c) From halfway down the train car, nothing appears amiss, and no passenger looks the wiser.

This passage is written to invoke three different shot sizes. In order to show his inscrutable face and lifting up the coattail (a), we'd need something between a long shot (full body) and a medium long shot (from the knees up). Then, for us to really "see" the dexterity in something as small as the flick of a thumb (b), we would need an extreme close-up. Finally, in order to take in the image of other passengers and half the train (c), we'd need a long shot; we cannot visualize this image with the close-up. So the language shows us the shots in prose, rather than labeling them. Again, be careful not to overuse this. Invoke a precise image only when a precise image needs to be invoked to tell the story.

- *Paragraphing stage directions and audience point of view.*

  We use paragraphing in stage directions for three reasons. The first is to distinguish different locations within a single location. Notice how each time the author shows Danny, who is standing at the other end of the train watching, there is a new paragraph. The paragraphing shifts the reader's point of view off Linus and onto Danny, who occupies a different end of the train car. The second reason we use paragraphing is to distinguish dramatic beats and shape the progression of the scene. Paragraphing helps the reader feel when one dramatic moment has ended and a new moment has begun. Yes, this episode on the train is one large dramatic unit; Danny watches Linus pick a businessman's pocket. But tension is created by breaking this task down into smaller dramatic beats and slightly rearranging the details to reveal the situation to the audience in a more suspenseful way.

- (Beat 1, paragraph 1) Average day on a Chicago subway. (Nothing is amiss.)
- (Beat 2, paragraph 2) Introduce Linus and the stockbrokers and Linus is picking this guy's pocket. (Uh, oh . . . a crime and now tension.)
- (Beat 3, paragraph 3) Shows us that Linus is skilled and cool. (Character development.)
- (Beat 4, paragraph 4) He's not alone; Danny is watching the whole thing and likes what he sees. (The plot thickens with this big shift in point of view; now Linus is not just picking a pocket, he's unknowingly being auditioned for a part in a bigger score.)

■ **Figure 2-9** Linus (Matt Damon) and Danny (George Clooney) in the subway car scene in Soderbergh's *Ocean's Eleven* (2001).

■ (Beat 5, paragraphs 5 and 6 w/dialogue and 7) Linus completes the lift and is even polite. (Mr. Smooth the whole way, a real pro.)

■ (Beat 6, paragraph 8) Danny is very impressed (Figure 2-9). (And so are we.)

The third reason to paragraph is to further highlight very important moments or details. *The* dramatic question in this scene, for Danny, Linus, and the reader, is: Will Linus successfully lift the wallet? So *the* climactic moment and action is when he actually picks the pocket. For this reason, the screenwriter has set that moment off in its own paragraph.

Character vs. Voice

In the *Ocean's Eleven* example, the actions we see Linus perform tell us who he is. He's a thief, a skilled thief, who is using his abilities to pull off petty crimes. We believe it because we saw it. **Character** is defined through actions. **Voice**, on the other hand, is the way in which a person presents himself to the world. This could be through their style of dress and the words they speak. Dialogue can be written in harmony with what we understand of that character through actions, or it can provide another layer of complexity, or it can even be contradictory to what we see. With his "frayed jacket" and polite apology, Linus presents himself as an average, nice guy (which the brokers believe), but we know better because we've seen him in action.

Another good example is Hannibal Lecter (Figure 2-10) in Jonathan Demme's *The Silence of the Lambs* (written by Ted Tally). Through his dialogue, Hannibal presents himself as an erudite, cultured, refined, courteous gentleman. At their first meeting he even tells Clarice Starling, "discourtesy is unspeakably ugly to me." This is no one we should fear, right? Until we see him literally rip the face off a police guard! Lecter is a great example of the tension you can create with the dissonance between character and voice. So, if you are able to establish your character's essential nature through their actions, then their dialogue, their voice, can be used to add and refine other facets of their personality. Action = Character, Dialogue = Voice.

■ **Figure 2-10** The two faces of Hannibal Lecter. In Demme's *The Silence of the Lambs* (1991), Dr. Hannibal Lecter presents himself as a sophisticated gentleman when he greets Clarice with the genial "Good morning." Later, we see through his actions, his true murderous nature as he escapes by savagely attacking his guards.

Working with Dialogue: Revealing Emotions, Not Announcing Them

Ideally, dialogue should *reveal* a character to us. It should be illustrative of what that person is thinking, feeling, wanting instead of broadcasting these things directly. In this way, the *show me, don't tell me* principle also applies to dialogue.

This scene from the academy award-winning screenplay for *Sideways* (2004), written by Alexander Payne and Jim Taylor, is a great example of dialogue which is, on the surface, about one topic, in this case wine, but in fact reveals an enormous amount about the internal yearnings and struggles of the lead character Miles (Figure 2-11). Although Miles is clearly lonely, he is finding it impossible to get over his recent divorce and resume his life.

Figure 2-11 Miles (Paul Giamatti) in *Sideways* (2004).

In this scene (Figure 2-12), Miles, who is a wine aficionado, finds himself alone with Maya, an attractive acquaintance, while his buddy Jack is having casual sex in another room with a woman he only met that day. Miles and Maya are sitting on the front porch, drinking wine.

Figure 2-12 Excerpt from *Sideways* © 2004, courtesy of Twentieth Century Fox. Written by Alexander Payne and Jim Taylor. All rights reserved.

38

                         MAYA
            Can I ask you a personal question?

                         MILES
                     (bracing himself)
            Sure.

                         MAYA
            Why are you so into Pinot? It's
            like a thing with you.

            Miles laughs at first, then smiles wistfully at the
            question.

            He searches for the answer in his glass and begins
            slowly.

                         MILES
            I don't know. It's a hard grape to
            grow. As you know. It's thin-
            skinned, temperamental, ripens
            early. It's not a survivor like
            Cabernet that can grow anywhere
            and thrive even when neglected.
            Pinot needs constant care and
            attention and in fact can only
            grow in specific little tucked-
            away corners of the world. And
            only the most patient and
            nurturing growers can do it
            really, can tap into Pinot's most
            fragile, delicate qualities. Only
            when someone has taken the time to
            truly understand its potential can
            Pinot be coaxed into its fullest
            expression. And when that happens,
            its flavors are the most haunting
            and brilliant and subtle and
            thrilling and ancient on the
            planet.

            Maya has found this answer revealing and moving.

Maya, questioning Miles, has found his answer revealing . . . and so have we!

Miles laughs at first because the "personal question" he braced himself for turned out to only be about wine. But in fact, his answer betrays deeply personal things despite its ostensible subject. Through Miles' monologue about pinot noir he reveals his loneliness and acknowledges that he is a difficult, but ultimately worthwhile, person. The implicit question he poses to Maya is . . . are you a "patient and faithful and caring grower?" In revealing himself, he reveals his interest in Maya.

The other interesting nuance in this monologue is the comparison of grape varietals, which serves as a comparison of Miles' personality with that of his friend Jack. His buddy in the other room, who easily picks up women to have sex, is clearly the cabernet grape which can "thrive and grow anywhere," while he is more like the pinot, "thin-skinned, temperamental," and "needs a lot of doting."

Words and Grammar Define Voice
As with stage directions, your choice of language is crucial in dialogue. The words your characters use and the grammar they employ express their unique identity—both who they are and how they wish to be seen. Aamir's ". . . my friend" and the officer's "C'mon now, pack it up. Show's over" are sharp and put flesh on the bones of their characters. Their lines also establish their credibility with the audience.

Throughout *Sideways,* Miles is an exceptionally nervous and awkward character—especially around women. In the scene before our example, he stumbles over himself to describe the novel he is working on to Maya. However, in this scene, Miles is in his element. He is eloquent, even literary, when speaking of wine. This reveals to the audience that not only is he knowledgeable about wine but that, yes, hidden under all the anxiety, Miles also is a passionate, thoughtful and interesting guy—but it's not easy for him at this moment in his life—he must be coaxed into his fullest expression.

▇ REWRITING

The often-repeated axiom for all creative writers is that *writing is rewriting.* It's important to remember that a screenplay is not written in stone. It is not unusual for screenplays (shorts or features) to go through many rewrites. Students in my intermediate production class typically will pen five or six drafts of their ten-minute film before heading into production. Some of these rewrites are simply to improve the script while others are in response to real-world exigencies (like losing an important location), which must be worked into the script in such a way that they *also* improve the script. Screenplays should remain flexible and can be rewritten at every stage in the production process—including the editing process—to respond to new ideas, creative collaboration, production circumstances, practical concerns, and spontaneous inspiration.

▇ CONCLUSION

Whether your project is a two-minute chase scene with no dialogue or a complex, character-driven, emotional drama, narrative filmmakers are storytellers, and the unfolding of events that make up film stories are first hammered out and polished on the page. The first steps in any narrative film production are developing your ideas on paper in concept and treatment forms and then writing a screenplay. The better the script, the better your film will be. So it is essential that one not shortchange these crucial creative steps out of impatience and eagerness to get on a set. It's better to postpone a shoot in order to give yourself the time to get your script in shape.

In writing your script, it is important to follow the rules of formatting closely and yet, within those confines, find a way to be expressive with your language and eloquent with your actions and images, to vividly represent the style, tone, and complexities of your film. It is clearly beyond the scope of this book to fully address all the dimensions of screenwriting. There are many resources for that on the market and I have listed a few useful scriptwriting books in the Bibliography.

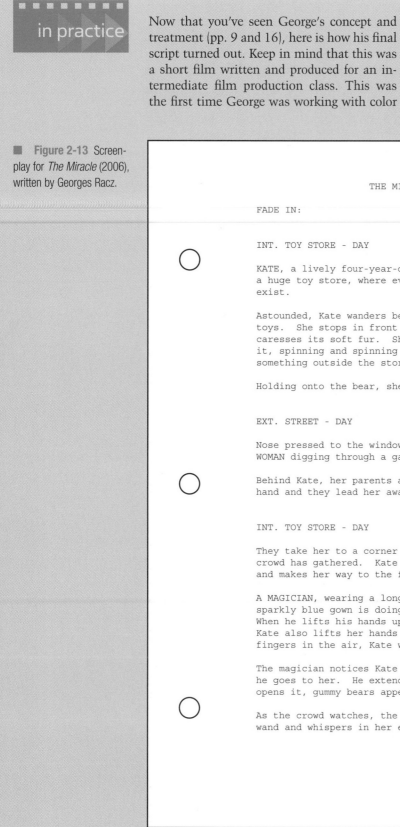

in practice

Now that you've seen George's concept and treatment (pp. 9 and 16), here is how his final script turned out. Keep in mind that this was a short film written and produced for an intermediate film production class. This was the first time George was working with color film and synchronized sound. In addition, he had a crew of four people and only one semester, 13 weeks, to go from a concept to a rough cut of the movie. So, George kept it short and simple.

■ **Figure 2-13** Screenplay for *The Miracle* (2006), written by Georges Racz.

```
                         THE MIRACLE

           FADE IN:


           INT. TOY STORE - DAY

           KATE, a lively four-year-old girl, and her PARENTS, enter
           a huge toy store, where every toy imaginable seems to
           exist.

           Astounded, Kate wanders between the rows and rows of
           toys.  She stops in front of a big teddy bear and
           caresses its soft fur.  She picks it up and dances with
           it, spinning and spinning in circles, until she notices
           something outside the store's window.

           Holding onto the bear, she walks over to the window.


           EXT. STREET - DAY

           Nose pressed to the window, Kate watches an old HOMELESS
           WOMAN digging through a garbage can.

           Behind Kate, her parents approach.  Her mother takes her
           hand and they lead her away from the window.


           INT. TOY STORE - DAY

           They take her to a corner of the store where a small
           crowd has gathered.  Kate squeezes through the crowd
           and makes her way to the front.

           A MAGICIAN, wearing a long white beard, a tall hat and a
           sparkly blue gown is doing a magic show for the kids.
           When he lifts his hands up in preparation for a new trick,
           Kate also lifts her hands up.  When he waggles his
           fingers in the air, Kate waggles her fingers.

           The magician notices Kate mimicking his every move and
           he goes to her.  He extends a closed hand and when he
           opens it, gummy bears appear.  Kate takes one.

           As the crowd watches, the magician gives Kate his magic
           wand and whispers in her ear.
```

in practice

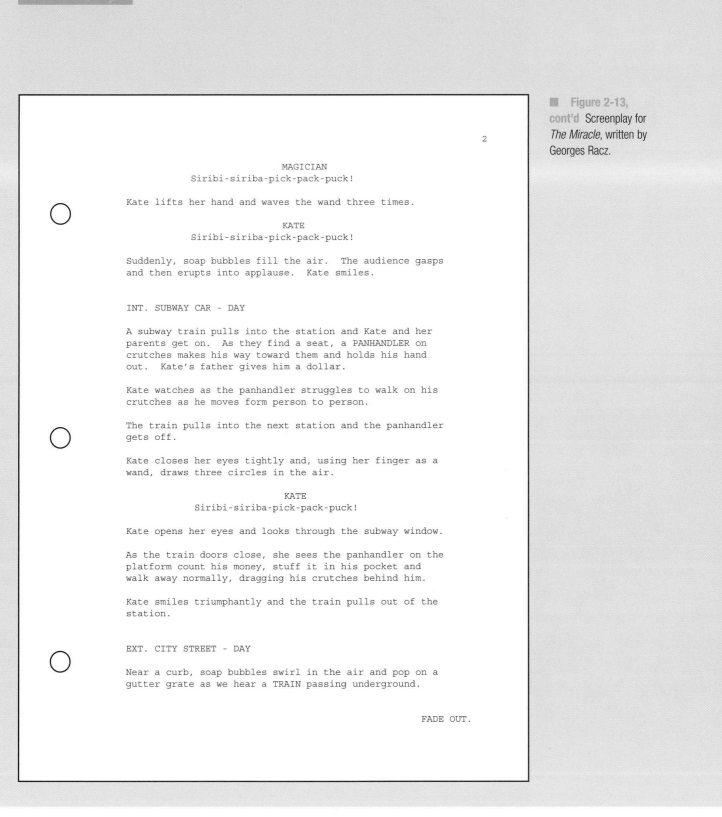

2

                    MAGICIAN
          Siribi-siriba-pick-pack-puck!

Kate lifts her hand and waves the wand three times.

                      KATE
          Siribi-siriba-pick-pack-puck!

Suddenly, soap bubbles fill the air. The audience gasps
and then erupts into applause. Kate smiles.

INT. SUBWAY CAR - DAY

A subway train pulls into the station and Kate and her
parents get on. As they find a seat, a PANHANDLER on
crutches makes his way toward them and holds his hand
out. Kate's father gives him a dollar.

Kate watches as the panhandler struggles to walk on his
crutches as he moves form person to person.

The train pulls into the next station and the panhandler
gets off.

Kate closes her eyes tightly and, using her finger as a
wand, draws three circles in the air.

                      KATE
          Siribi-siriba-pick-pack-puck!

Kate opens her eyes and looks through the subway window.

As the train doors close, she sees the panhandler on the
platform count his money, stuff it in his pocket and
walk away normally, dragging his crutches behind him.

Kate smiles triumphantly and the train pulls out of the
station.

EXT. CITY STREET - DAY

Near a curb, soap bubbles swirl in the air and pop on a
gutter grate as we hear a TRAIN passing underground.

                                        FADE OUT.

■ **Figure 2-13, cont'd** Screenplay for *The Miracle*, written by Georges Racz.

The Visual Language and Aesthetics of Cinema

■ SHOTS, SEQUENCES, AND SCENES

Film scholars and practitioners alike have long referred to the cinema as a language, which means that it is a shared system of terms, symbols, and syntax used to communicate thoughts, feelings, and experiences. In written language we use letters, words, sentences, and paragraphs. In the visual language of cinema we have four basic elements: the shot, the shot sequence, the scene, and the dramatic sequence.

The **shot** is the smallest unit of the film language. A shot is a continuous run of images, unbroken by an edit. Technically speaking, a shot is the footage generated from the moment you turn on the camera to the moment you turn it off—also called a **camera take**. However, these shots are often divided into smaller pieces, which are used individually in the editing stage, and each one of these pieces is also called a shot. Shots can be as short as a few frames or as long as your imaging system will allow before you run out of tape or film. The famous shower sequence in Hitchcock's *Psycho* (1960) lasts about half a minute, but contains over fifty shots, while the film *Russian Ark* (2002), directed by Aleksandr Sokurov and shot on high definition video, is a 96-minute feature film comprising only one continuous shot!

Related to the shot is the broader concept of **mise-en-scène** (a term derived from a French theatrical phrase which means "put on stage"), which in film terms can be defined as everything visible in the frame of a shot: the subject, actions, objects, setting, lighting, and graphic qualities. The mise-en-scène of a shot contains information, a certain meaning, derived from a combination of what we see in the shot and how it is presented (Figure 3-1).

■ **Figure 3-1** In this scene from Gilliam's *The Fisher King* (1991), the close-up (left) apparently shows Anne (Mercedes Ruehl) boldly admonishing her lover Jack for treating her badly, but when the camera alters the mise-en-scène by simply pulling back to a long shot (right), the meaning of the moment changes completely as we can see that he's stood her up again and she's talking to an empty chair.

■ **Figure 3-2** In Malick's *The Thin Red Line* (1998) the long shot of a navy ship is followed by a shot of Private Witt (James Caviezel) in a dark location. Although there are no physical clues to indicate exactly where he is, we assume Private Witt is somewhere inside the ship, because of this juxtaposition.

A **sequence** is an expressive unit made up of editing together multiple shots to define a unified action or event, or passage of time or place. Sequences can be designed to make multiple points. The *Psycho* shower sequence just mentioned not only shows us Marion's murder, but Hitchcock, a master of the macabre, also wants us to feel her terror and wants to establish a new dramatic question—who was that woman who killed Marion?

Each shot in a sequence builds upon the others, so that by arranging shots in a particular order (or sequence), you can contextualize each individual image, to create meaning that is greater than the sum of its parts. Film theorists refer to this concept as **montage** (from the French word "montage," which simply means editing). Broadly defined, **montage** is the film technique in which meaning is derived from the accumulation of information of the various shots in an edited sequence. (For a more detailed discussion of the term montage, see p. 413.)

The term **juxtaposition** is often used when talking about sequences. This means placing two or more shots next to each other so that you highlight a link or contrast between the content in each shot. It's essential for a filmmaker to really understand and put to use the fact that a viewer does not simply interpret each image individually, but almost instinctively creates additional connections between individual shots. If we first show a shot of the United Nations Building, followed by a shot of a group of people seated around a conference table, the audience automatically assumes that this is a conference being held inside the U.N. building. No one needs to announce it, it just becomes a presumed fact. This is a very simple example that, on the surface, seems completely common and obvious, and in fact it is, but on closer analysis you will come to understand the power in the mechanism and the broader creative implications between what's on screen and how an audience assumes connections (**Figure 3-2**).

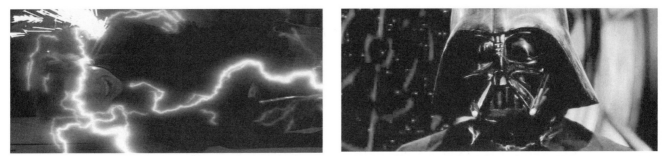

■ **Figure 3-3** The immovable mask of Darth Vader is sufficiently neutral to take on a variety of emotions, depending on the visual context created through juxtaposition. In this scene from *Star Wars: Episode VI—Return of the Jedi* (1983) we detect feelings of sympathy, concern, and alarm that play across the ordinarily intimidating and evil mask of Vader as he watches his son Luke Skywalker get electrocuted.

The most famous examples of this phenomenon are the early film experiments of Lev Kuleshov, who in the early 1920s shot the expressionless face of actor Ivan Mozhukhin and juxtaposed the very same, emotionally neutral shot with various other images. When the face was juxtaposed with a bowl of soup, people saw the face as that of a hungry man; when the same shot was juxtaposed with a child's coffin, people read his expression as sorrowful. Each new juxtaposed image inflected Mr. Mozhukhin's neutral expression with a different emotion. It is important to always remember that images and editing are used in tandem to create meaning and communicate your story, in specific terms, to your audience (Figure 3-3).

Because images and editing function in tandem, they must both be considered as we devise our visual strategy during **pre-visualization**. That's not to say that we try to precisely edit our film, shot for shot, before we go into production (although Alfred Hitchcock very nearly did just that on most of his films), but it does mean that we need to consider not only what we will shoot (mise-en-scène) but also how these shots will fit together (montage). This is what is referred to as **shooting for the edit**.

As stated in Chapter 1, **a scene** is a dramatic unit in which action ostensibly happens in continuous time and within a single location. A scene is usually composed of multiple shots, and there are principles of visual grammar that guide us in putting these shots together to make coherent sense of time, space, and actions; more on this later. Depending on the style of the film, a scene, even those that include multiple camera angles, can also be accomplished in a single shot (Figure 3-4). This approach has been used throughout the history of cinema, from Bresson to Hou Hsiao-Hsien, but is a stylistic deviation from the norm.

■ **Figure 3-4** The "Jack/Zak" scene from Jarmusch's *Down By Law* (1986) is 2 minutes and 45 seconds long and is accomplished in only one shot.

in practice

Alfred Hitchcock is known as a master of montage for the way he was able to conjure complex mysteries through visual means—primarily the precise juxtaposition of simple shots that, with a few edits, accumulate complex meaning. In the second scene of Hitchcock's 1937 film *Young and Innocent* we are presented with a series of shots (Figure 3-5) that, on their own, don't mean so much, but together they mean murder and mystery! A perfect day, a beautiful beach, a lighthouse, and seagulls. These shots resemble kitsch postcards of a summer vacation spot. Wish we were here *(shots 1 and 2)!* Waves break along the shoreline and then an arm flops against the water. The shot tells us that there seems to be a swimmer in the ocean. The swimmer, it turns out, is an unconscious woman who is being tumbled by the waves *(shots 3 and 4)*. Now the viewer starts to ask questions. The swimmer washes onto the shore. Her body is limp and clearly lifeless. Did she drown or was she bitten by a shark? We can't know yet. But a question has been raised, "What happened to this poor woman?" Then . . . a belt washes up on the shore *(shot 5)!*

The shot of the belt all by itself simply means that a belt washes up on a beach—no big deal. Juxtaposed only with the first shot it could mean that the beach is more polluted than we thought, given the beauty of the "postcard" shot, but placed here, next to the shot of the woman's body, it seems to answer our question, "What happened to this poor woman?" The belt immediately and clearly becomes a murder weapon and Hitchcock suggests that the swimmer who washed up on the shore was murdered *with it!* In addition, that idyllic beach becomes an ironic image because, for all its natural beauty, the location has become a sinister crime scene. Suddenly, all those questions, essential to any good mystery movie, flood into the minds of the audience. Who is she? How did she wind up in the ocean? Why was she killed? Whodunnit? All in just a few shots.

■ **Figure 3-5** In this sequence of shots, from Hitchcock's *Young and Innocent,* each image adds a vital piece of information that contextualizes what we've seen and what we are yet to see.

A **dramatic sequence** is made up of a series of scenes that create a larger dramatic unit. The relationship between the scenes can vary, due to cause and effect (the result of one scene triggers the beginning of the next) or parallel action (in which the actions in two or more scenes, happening simultaneously, relate to each other), or the scenes can have other associative connections.

Just as in written language, where we put words together to create sentences, and sentences together to create paragraphs, in film we put shots together to create sequences and scenes, and scenes together to create the larger dramatic events of our story. Theoretically, one could certainly shoot any image at all and place it next to any other image, just as one could configure any string of letters to create sounds that resemble a word—for example, *fluugeproit.* This "word" *fluugeproit* doesn't directly communicate anything, and a sentence like "Bilious for at cake one." makes no sense at all either, even though the meaning of each individual word is perfectly understandable. Neither the "word" nor the "sentence" works within our language's shared system of practices.

Likewise in cinema, there are many commonly understood principles we use for putting the visual pieces together to communicate coherently. This chapter and Chapter 4 explicate some of cinema's "shared systems of practices," including the most pervasive and fundamental visual system, known as *continuity style.* **Continuity style** shooting and editing provides tried and true principles for organizing our images to create a coherent sense of space, time, and movement in a way that is recognized by nearly everyone. Keep in mind that, while continuity style is the fundamental cinematic language, there is always room for innovation and evolution. Only a few years ago "blog," "geek," and "headbanger" meant about as much as *fluugeproit,* but today you'll find them in the dictionary and most of us can actually understand a sentence like "WiFi makes it easy for a geek like me to post my hip headbanger blog." Cinema, too, is a living language with an ever-expanding vocabulary and ever-evolving syntax—the fundamentals in this chapter are just the beginning of how we speak in film. Just as in writing, the cinematic language can be bland or expressive, prosaic or poetic, utilitarian or profound. The development of visual eloquence and your particular style begins with an understanding of the basic vocabulary and the creative possibilities of the film language. And the best place to begin is with the frame.

■ THE FRAME AND COMPOSITION

Cinema is a matter of what is in the frame and what is not.

M. Scorsese

Dimensions of the Frame

Aesthetic considerations concerning the graphic and compositional aspects of your shots begin with the frame. **The frame** has two definitions. The *physical frame* is each, individual, still image captured on film or on video, which, when projected as a series, creates the illusion of motion (see Chapter 8). The *compositional frame* (Figure 3-6) is a two-dimensional space defined by its horizontal (x-axis) and vertical (y-axis) dimensions. Within this space we can perceive a third dimension, depth (z-axis); however, depth and distance are created through graphic illusion.

The frame is your canvas, the rectangular space in which you determine the parameters of the viewer's perspective. We refer to each of the four edges of the frame as **screen left**, **screen right**, **top**, and **bottom**. The frame essentially crops the real-world environment and determines what the audience sees (mise-en-scène) and doesn't see, referred to as **off screen**. Framing your shot, deciding what to show and what *not* to show, is a very important creative decision.

The relationship between the width and the height of the frame is called the **aspect ratio**, and is derived by dividing the width of the frame by the height. There are several different

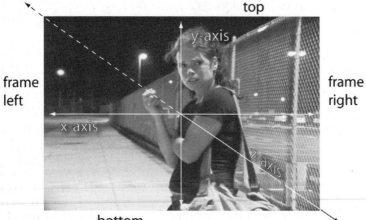

■ **Figure 3-6** The compositional frame. Although we work with only two dimensions (the "x" and "y" axes), it is still possible to create depth in our compositions (by emphasizing the "z" axis). Still from Mercado's *Yield* (2006).

16mm, 35mm full frame and standard video
1.33:1

HDTV video
1.78:1

U.S. Theatrical release
1.85:1

■ **Figure 3-7** The compositional frame: aspect ratios. The ratio of the width to the height of a frame depends both on the shooting and the delivery formats of the film or DV.

aspect ratios used in film and video (**Figure 3-7**). The aspect ratio of a full frame of 35mm film, 16mm film, and broadcast standard video is 1.33:1. In film, this is called **Academy Aperture** (from the technical standards set by the Academy of Motion Picture Arts and Sciences). In video parlance, this ratio is often expressed as 4×3. In any case, the horizontal (width) is one-third longer than the vertical (height).

Movies intended for theatrical release on film or HDTV broadcast are shot with a different aspect ratio which elongates the horizontal dimension. American theatrical release aspect ratio is 1.85:1. European theatrical release aspect ratio is 1.66:1 and HDTV broadcast aspect ratio is 16×9 (or 1.78:1). We will discuss film and video aspect ratios in more detail in Chapters 8 and 9.

Shot Composition and the Graphic Qualities of the Frame

Working within the parameters of a given aspect ratio, a filmmaker has a very broad pallet of aesthetic choices when designing the composition of a shot. There are no absolute rules concerning visual style except that the choices you make should emerge from the dramatic needs of the script and should reflect your own creative ideas. Each compositional principle is expressed in precise terms and it's important that you use the proper terminology when applying them to your script and communicating with your crew.

Closed and Open Frames

A **closed frame** means that all of the essential information in the shot is neatly contained within the parameters of the frame, and an **open frame** means that the composition leads the audience to be aware of the area beyond the edges of the visible shot (**Figure 3-8**). This is not necessarily an either/or choice. A shot can begin as a closed frame and then an unexpected intrusion from beyond the edge of the frame can suddenly disclose the larger off-screen environment. Also, sound or dialogue coming from off screen can serve to open a frame, because it asks the audience to imagine the space beyond the edges of what is visible.

Deep Frames and Flat Frames

We refer to a frame that accentuates the compositional element of depth (z-axis) as a **deep frame** and one that exaggerates the two-dimensionality of the image as a **flat frame**. The graphic factors that are used to create the illusion of depth are the same ones that are minimized to create a flat frame.

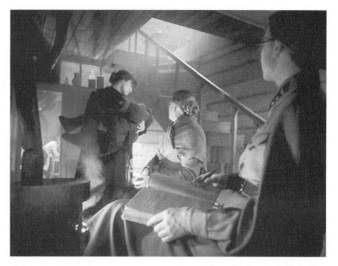

■ Figure 3-8 (Top) A closed frame contains all essential information within the frame, as shown in Jarmusch's *Stranger Than Paradise* (1984). (Bottom) An open frame has a composition that necessarily implies the existence of space beyond what is contained within the shot, like the gunman's hand protruding into this frame from Melville's *Le Samouraï* (1967).

1. *Receding planes*

   We can achieve a feeling of deep space by creating a mise-en-scène in which there are objects placed along the z-axis which define foreground, midground, and background planes (Figure 3-9). By reducing the z-axis space to two or even one plane, we flatten the perspective and the space appears shallow. Related to this is the idea of **object overlapping**, which is the understanding that objects nearer the foreground will cover or overlap objects further in the background. Also, related to the notion of receding planes is **diminishing perspective**, which is the perceptual understanding that objects will appear to be smaller the further they are from the viewer, and conversely, objects will appear larger the closer they are to the viewer. For example, a chicken walking across the foreground of a shot will appear larger than a locomotive far in the background. This phenomenon can be seen with a single object as well. **Foreshortening** is a composition in which one part of an object appears large

■ Figure 3-9 Accentuating depth by using receding planes (top, from Kalatozov's *The Cranes are Flying*) (1957) or by the foreshortening of a subject (middle, from Malmros' *Slim Susie*) (2003) creates deep frames. Reducing the z-axis to a limited number of planes produces a diminished perspective, creating a flat frame (bottom, from Godard's *Masculin/Féminin*) (1966).

because it is very close to the viewer, while another part of the same object appears small because it is further away, creating a dynamic sense of depth within the frame.

2. *Horizontal and diagonal lines*

   Shot head-on, horizontal lines or objects in a horizontal arrangement will obviously look, well, horizontal. But shot from an angle, a horizontal line appears to recede into the distance on a diagonal. For example, if we shoot five people standing against a

■ **Figure 3-10** Shooting horizontal lines head-on creates flat compositions. Changing the shooting angle so that horizontal lines recede into the distance reinforces the depth of the frame, creating a sense of deep space (frames from Singer's *The Usual Suspects*) (1995)

■ **Figure 3-11** Manipulating the amount of focus shown in the frame can direct the attention of the audience to selected areas of the composition. The deep focus in Zvyagintsev's *The Return* (2003) (left) lets the audience see the source of the subject's despair (his friends are leaving him behind), while the shallow focus used in Leigh's *Naked* (1993) (right) hints at the disconnection that exists between the subject and society.

wall for a police line-up head-on, the composition will appear flat; if we move the camera 45 degrees (or more) to the side, so that the line-up now recedes diagonally along the z-axis, then we've created depth in the frame (Figure 3-10). This is a simple yet powerful way to create a sense of deep space. Shooting horizontals head-on minimizes the sense of depth.

3. *Deep and shallow focus*

   The depth of the focus range of a shot can add or eliminate attention to background and foreground information (Figure 3-11). When focus is deep we can see objects along the z-axis, from foreground to background, in crisp detail. Deep focus gives us an awareness of deep space because it is clearly visible. When focus is shallow, meaning that only a single vertical plane is sharply defined and objects in front of or behind that plane are blurry, our attention is limited to a narrow and flat area (see section on the lens, Chapter 4, for information on how to manipulate "depth of field").

4. *Shadows*

   Shadows add depth to just about any image because they accentuate the dimensionality of your subject and their environment (Figure 3-12). Eliminating shadows, therefore, conceals dimensionality and leads to a flatter image (see Chapter 13 for information about controlling light and shadows).

Balanced and Unbalanced Frames

The principle of compositional balance begins with the understanding that objects in your frame carry a certain visual weight (Figure 3-13). Size, shape, brightness, and placement can all affect the relative weight of an object in the frame. How you distribute this visual weight within the frame, equally or unevenly, symmetrically or asymmetrically, gives your composition a sense of stability or instability. There is no value judgment attached to balanced and unbalanced frames; neither is "better" than the other. Like all of the other aesthetic principles in this section, the right choice is the one that is appropriate for the story you're telling and the mood you're creating.

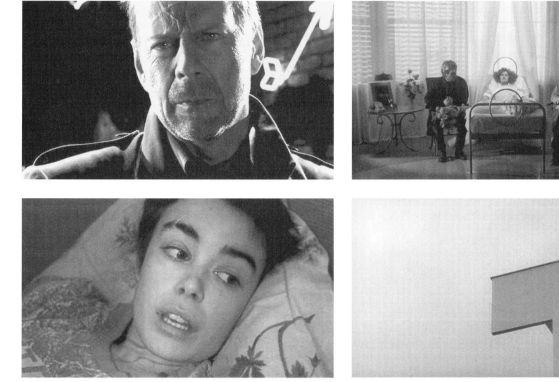

■ **Figure 3-12** Careful positioning of light sources can add shadows and reveal the texture of our subjects, accentuating dimensionality (as shown in Rodriguez' *Sin City,* top). Eliminating shadows conceals texture and dimensionality, creating a flat image (as seen in Zonca's *The Dream-life of Angels,* bottom).

■ **Figure 3-13** The distribution of objects/subjects in the frame can create a sense of stability or instability, according to the needs of the narrative. In Greenaway's *A Zed and Two Noughts* (top), the equal distribution of twins Oliver and Oswald (Eric and Brian Deacon) echoes the film's pre-occupation with the dichotomy of opposites. In Antonioni's *L'Eclisse* (bottom), the placement of the subjects at a corner of the frame hints at an uneasy relationship with their surroundings.

Rule of Thirds (Looking Room, Walking Room)

Cinematic composition, as with any other art form, has certain classic principles that have developed over time. Film, being a two-dimensional representational art form developed after painting and photography, has been influenced by many of their ideas of classical form. One such idea is the **rule of thirds**, which is often used as a guide for framing human subjects and for composition in general.

First, we divide the frame into thirds with imaginary lines (sometimes referred to as "sweet spots") along the horizontal and vertical axes and then place significant objects, focus points, and elements of interest along these lines. For the human form, for example, this would mean placing the eyes along the top ⅓ horizontal line. If your subject is looking or moving toward one side of the screen, then the vertical placement of the figure should be along the left or right vertical ⅓ line *opposite* the direction in which they are looking or moving (Figure 3-14).

This extra vertical space, to one side or the other, is called **looking room**, or **walking room**, for a moving figure. This space provides a sense of balance because the direction of the gaze, or movement, itself carries a sort of compositional weight. This space also keeps the viewer from feeling like the subject is pushing, or about to go beyond, the edge of the frame. Of course, you may *want* to create that uneasy sense. For example, if you want to accentuate the urgency of a character running, you might want that person bumping up against the front edge of the frame, as if the camera itself can't keep up with them! But this is an expressive deviation (Figure 3-15), which is made possible by the common application of the rule of thirds.

■ **Figure 3-14** Typical use of the "Rule of Thirds." Note how the "sweet spots" created by the intersection of the lines located at the thirds of the image are used to position the subject, giving her proper headroom and viewing room. Still from Mercado's *Yield* (2006).

■ **Figure 3-15** Breaking the "Rule of Thirds" for dramatic purposes. In this scene from Meirelles' *The Constant Gardener* (2005), Justin Quayle (Ralph Fiennes) revisits the apartment where he and his recently murdered wife began their relationship. Throughout the sequence he is framed in irregular and unbalanced compositions to emphasize the severe grief he is experiencing as the full emotional impact of his wife's death overcomes him.

Shot Size

Shot size refers to the size of your subject in the frame. The size of your subject is determined by two factors: (1) the proximity of subject to camera (the closer the subject is to the camera, the larger it will appear) and (2) the degree of lens magnification (the more your lens magnifies the subject, the larger the subject will appear). These two approaches are not the same and the differences in their visual perspectives are discussed in detail in Chapter 4.

The frame of reference for any discussion of shot size is traditionally the human form, but the following shot designations work for nonhuman subjects as well.

- *Extreme long shot or wide shot* (ELS) is a shot that shows a large view of the location, setting, or landscape (Figure 3-16). Even if there are people in the shot, the emphasis is on their surroundings or their relationship to their surroundings.
- *Long shot* (LS) is generally a shot which contains the whole human figure. It's a good choice when you need to show larger physical movements and activity (Figure 3-17).
- *Medium long shot* (MLS) frames your subject from approximately the knees up (Figure 3-18). This shot is sometimes called a "cowboy shot" because, as legend has it, of the need to always see a cowboy's gunbelt in the western genre pictures. The French call this shot an "American shot" because of its frequent use in genre movies of the 1930s and 1940s.
- *Medium shot* (MS) frames your subject from approximately the waist up (Figure 3-19). This shot can show smaller physical actions and facial expressions, yet maintain some connection with the setting. However, location is clearly no longer the emphasis of the shot, as the viewer is now drawn closer to the subject.

■ **Figure 3-16** An extreme long shot (Scorsese's *Raging Bull*) (1980).

■ **Figure 3-17** The long shot (Scorsese's *Raging Bull*).

■ **Figure 3-18** The medium long shot (Scorsese's *Raging Bull*).

■ **Figure 3-19** The medium shot (Scorsese's *Raging Bull*).

■ *Medium close-up* (MCU) is generally from the chest or shoulders up (Figure 3-20). The emphasis of this shot is now facial expression, but some connection to the broader physical "attitude" of the body is maintained.

■ *Close-up* (CU) places the primary emphasis on the face or other part of the body (Figure 3-21). Small details in features, movements, and expressions are the subjects of this very intimate shot.

■ *Extreme close-up* (ECU) is a stylistically potent shot which isolates a very small detail or feature of the subject (Figure 3-22).

■ *Two shots, three shots, and group shots:* As these labels clearly state, the two shot includes two subjects, the three shot includes three subjects, and shots that include more than three people are referred to as group shots (Figure 3-23).

■ **Figure 3-20** The medium close-up (Scorsese's *Raging Bull*).

■ **Figure 3-21** The close-up (Scorsese's *Raging Bull*). Close-up of an object (left) and a person (right).

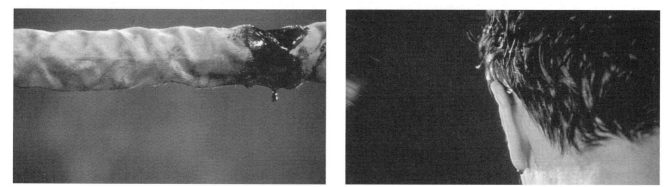

■ **Figure 3-22** The extreme close-up (Scorsese's *Raging Bull*). ECU of an object (left) and a person (right).

■ **Figure 3-23** Two Shots, three shots, group shots. These shots are named according to the number of subjects included within the frame (Scorsese's *Raging Bull*).

■ **Figure 3-24** High-angle, eye-level, and low-angle shots. In an eye-level shot, the camera is positioned at the eye level of the subject, regardless if they standing, sitting, or lying down (middle). Positioning the camera above eye level produces a high-angle shot (top), while putting the camera below eye level produces a low-angle shot (bottom). Extreme low or high angles tend to be emotionally remote, but can produce dynamic frames, as seen in these three examples from Wenders' *Wings of Desire*.

Shot Size and Character Identification

When framing a human subject, the shot size is especially important in establishing the level of intimacy and identification you wish the audience to have with that character. Obviously, an ELS and a LS transmit a feeling of distance and remoteness from the subject. With MEDIUM shots we are close enough to clearly see them, but we're still at an observation distance, which is why this frame is rather neutral in terms of creating an emotional connection with a character. When using a MCU and CU we enter the very intimate, personal space of a character and identification is quite strong. An ECU is so close that it can be either extremely intimate, or in its own way, mysterious and distancing—especially if the ECU obscures a character's eyes. It depends on the subject and composition of the shot. Understanding this, a filmmaker is able to precisely modulate not only the focus of attention within the frame, but also the degree of emotional involvement the audience has with any particular character at any given moment, by carefully selecting shot sizes.

Camera Angles

The orientation of the camera to the subject, the horizontal and vertical angles you are shooting from, has a dramatic effect on your image no matter what size the subject is in the frame. Simply moving the horizontal or vertical position of the camera, relative to your subject, can be a powerfully expressive device that establishes the viewer's relationship to your subject.

High and Low Angles

Let's look first at vertical angles (Figure 3-24). Again, using the human form for our reference, the **eye-level** shot is one in which the lens of the camera is positioned at eye level with your subject, regardless if they are sitting, standing, or lying down. Raising the camera above eye level yields a **high-angle** shot and below eye level gives us a **low-angle** shot. An eye-level shot can encourage a connection with a subject, while extreme high or low angles tend to be more emotionally remote, but they can make for very dynamic frames.

Front to Back Angles

The horizontal position of the camera can be anywhere from directly in front of your subject to directly behind them. A shot in which the subject looks directly at the

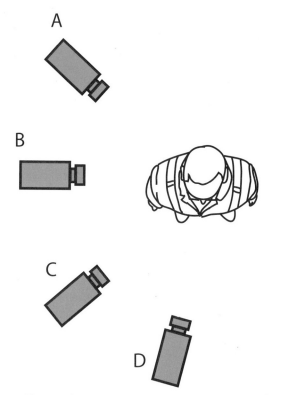

camera is called **direct address** (Figure 3-25). Even though music videos use direct address all the time, eye contact with the audience is rare and is especially powerful in narrative films because it shatters the fictive world by eliminating the separation between the watcher and the watched. Direct camera address is the cinematic version of the theatrical concept of breaking the fourth wall.

■ **Figure 3-26** Front to back camera angle positions: (A) ¾ back, (B) profile shot, (C) ¾ frontal shot and (D) frontal. Unless you want direct camera address, actors should lookl slightly off the side of the lens in a frontal shot.

Much more common are **frontal shots**, in which the camera looks directly at the face of your subject but the subject's sightline glances just off the edge of the frame. Moving the camera along a horizontal arc we progressively move through ¾ **frontal**, **profile shot**, ¾ **back**, and finally to shooting **from behind** (Figure 3-26).

As we move the camera angle from frontal, to profile, to the back of the subject, we lose a degree of intimacy with each step. Looking directly at a subject can elicit strong engage-

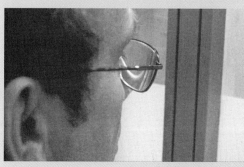

In their film *The Son* (2002), the Dardenne brothers tell the story of Olivier, a carpentry mentor at a rehabilitation center for juvenile delinquents. One day the boy who killed Olivier's son, during a botched robbery, is released from prison and winds up in his carpentry shop as one of his apprentices. On the boy's first day the camera follows Olivier, who is following the boy, as he tries to get a glimpse of the kid who killed his son years ago. For extended sequences the camera remains behind Olivier (Figure 3-27), shooting from a ¾ back angle or completely from behind. This camera angle choice allows the audience to feel like they're peering over Olivier's shoulder, seeing the world from his perspective; however, this angle does not allow us to see how Olivier is reacting to seeing his son's killer. Through this camera angle, the Dardenne brothers build enormous tension by frustrating our need to see what emotions are playing across Olivier's face.

■ **Figure 3-27** Shots taken from behind Olivier (Olivier Gourmet) in the Dardenne brothers' *The Son* (2002) bring the audience into the point of view of the lead character but also serve to obscure his emotional response, since we can't make out his facial expressions.

■ **Figure 3-28** The canted angle shot, also called a "Dutch angle," creates a sense of instability, imbalance, and disorientation, depending on the degree of the lateral tilt used. In *The Crying Game* (1992), director Neil Jordan uses the shot when a desperate Jody (Forest Whitaker) shows Fergus (Stephen Rea) a picture of his "girlfriend" Dil.

ment; a profile shot is a somewhat neutral point of view, and hiding the face by shooting from behind can create a sense of distance, remoteness, or mystery.

One other camera angle that we can consider adjusting is the lateral positioning of the camera. Tilting the camera laterally so that the horizon of your composition is oblique is called a **canted Angle** (or **Dutch angle**) (Figure 3-28). This sort of shot can create a feeling ranging from slight imbalance to extreme spatial disorientation, depending on the extremity of the lateral tilt of your camera.

Creating New Frames and Aspect Ratios

So far, we have been looking at working within the aspect ratio of the film and video frame (1.33:1, 1.85:1, etc.), but you are not entirely restricted to these compositional dimensions. Many filmmakers find interesting ways to alter the aspect ratios of the area that frames their subjects. Because we cannot literally change the aspect ratio of the film or video frame, this technique involves using some element of the physical location and/or lighting to crop the existing frame to new proportions. This is called a **frame within a frame** (Figure 3-29).

■ THE MOVING FRAME

A shot in which the framing remains steady on the subject, without moving or shifting perspective, is called a **static shot** (or **fixed frame**). We can certainly use two static shots edited next to each other to shift the viewer's perspective from, say, a man working at his desk, to the dark window behind him. But there are often important dramatic and stylistic reasons to shift the perspective of the frame and therefore the viewer's attention, horizontally, vertically, or even along the z-axis, during the course of a shot. This is called a **camera move**. Shifting the viewer's perspective, in one continuous motion, from the man at his desk, across the empty room, to the dark window behind him, might provide extra information, or a visual connection, which could be vital to fully grasp that particular

■ **Figure 3-29** Frames within frames. The filmmaker is not restricted to the aspect ratio of the shooting format. Through careful use of composition and/or lighting, it is possible to alter the dimension of the frame to create a dramatically compelling way of presenting a subject (left from Ozu's *Early Summer [Bakushû]* (1951); right from Fassbinder's *Ali: Fear Eats the Soul* (1974)).

scene. For example, by scanning the room between the man and the window, we can see that he is completely alone.

Camera Moves

There are two kinds of moves, stationary camera moves and dynamic camera moves.

Pivot Moves

Pivot camera moves (also called **static camera moves**) are **stationary camera moves**; they involve pivoting the camera, horizontally or vertically, from a stationary spot while the camera is running. This can be done on a tripod or with a handheld camera as long as the location of the camera doesn't change, just its horizontal or vertical angle.

A PAN scans space horizontally by pivoting the camera left or right (PAN LEFT and PAN RIGHT). TILTING refers to shifting the camera perspective vertically, with the lens facing up or facing down (TILT UP and TILT DOWN) (Figure 3-30).

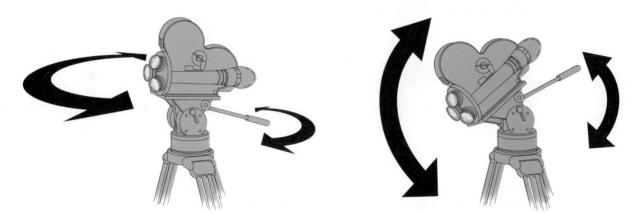

■ **Figure 3-30** Panning and tilting. In a pan, the camera scans space left or right ("pan left" or "pan right") on the tripod's axis. A tilt shifts the camera's perspective vertically on the tripod's axis ("tilt up" or "tilt down").

A pan or a tilt that moves from one subject to another is called **panning from/to** and **tilting from/to**. For example, you pan *from* the man at his desk, *to* the dark window across the room. A pan or a tilt that follows a subject as they move within the space is called a **pan with** or **tilt with** (they are also called **follow pan** or **follow tilt**). For example, the man at his desk thinks he hears a funny noise outside. We can pan *with* him as he walks from his desk to the window to look outside (Figure 3-31).

It is also possible to move in closer or further away from a subject while your camera remains in a stationary spot. **Zooming in** or **zooming out** requires a lens with an adjustable degree of magnification, called a zoom lens or variable focal length lens (see Chapter 4 for details). This lens is common on video cameras, but less common on film cameras. Just as with any other move, one can *zoom from/to* subjects or *zoom with* a moving subject.

Dynamic Moves

Dynamic camera moves involve a mobile camera, which means literally moving the entire camera in space, horizontally (left or right), closer or further (forward or backward), or even vertically (up and down). These moves can be accomplished with special camera mounting equipment or with a handheld camera.

A **tracking shot** is a term used when you move the camera in order to *follow* or *track with* a subject (Figure 3-32). You can *track* left, right, forward, or backward, to follow along with the movement of your subject. Gus Van Sant's film *Elephant* (2003) makes frequent use of long tracking shots, following characters as they walk through the hallways of their high

■ **Figure 3-31** Pan with and pan to. In a scene from Cocteau's *Beauty and the Beast (Belle et la bête)* (1946), the camera pans *with* Beauty (Josette Day) as she explores the Beast's castle. The camera keeps her centered in the frame as she moves from the door to the window (top frames). In a later scene, the camera pans from Beauty, lying on a bed, *to* the Beast (Jean Marais), standing across the room. The camera move follows Beauty's look and *reveals* the Beast, which heightens the surprise and tension of their encounter.

■ **Figure 3-32** When the camera follows a subject as it moves, it is said to be tracking or following it. Tracking shots can be accomplished with dollies, wheelchairs, vehicles, handholding the camera, or, in the case of Van Sant's *Elephant* (2003), with the use of a Steadicam system.

school. Tracking shots can also be from/to shots. **Dolly shots** are generally moving shots in which the camera moves closer or further away from the subject (**Figure 3-33**). To *dolly-in* or *dolly-out* means to move the camera closer to or further away from, respectively. Dolly, however, is a slippery term because it also refers to the wheeled apparatus on which we mount the camera to move it (see Chapter 11). We can certainly move a camera closer or farther away from our subject without using a dolly, for example with a handheld camera. So you'll also hear people say *push-in* or *pull-out* for this camera move, especially when an actual dolly isn't being used.

Lifting the camera up and down is called **booming** (*boom up* or *boom down*). This can be done with a handheld camera or mechanically with a boom or jib arm (**Figure 3-34**).

A **crane shot** is one in which the camera is raised very high in the air, certainly above a human subject's head. This usually requires a special, and expensive, piece of equipment called a crane. The specific equipment and techniques used for camera moves are discussed in more detail in Chapter 11.

All of these moves, pans, tilts, dolly, tracking, booming, and zooming, are very often combined. For example, following the trajectory of a helium balloon, just as a child lets go of

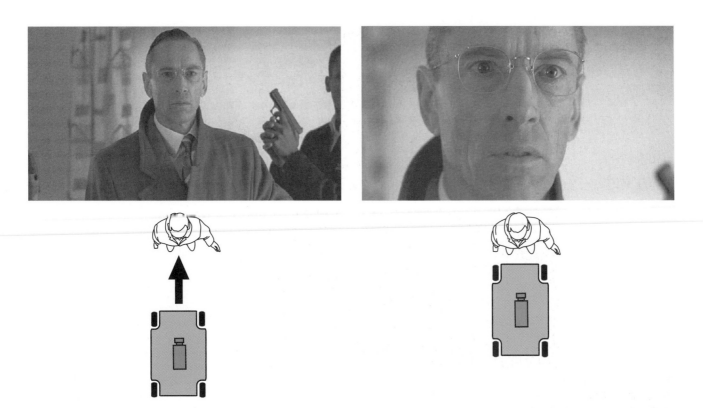

■ **Figure 3-33** In a dolly shot, the camera is moved away or closer to a stationary subject. In this example, from Demme's *The Silence of the Lambs* (1991), a dolly-in move was used to underline the dramatic moment in which Jack (Scott Glen) realizes they've just seized the wrong house, and inadvertently put Clarice (Jodie Foster) in unimaginable danger.

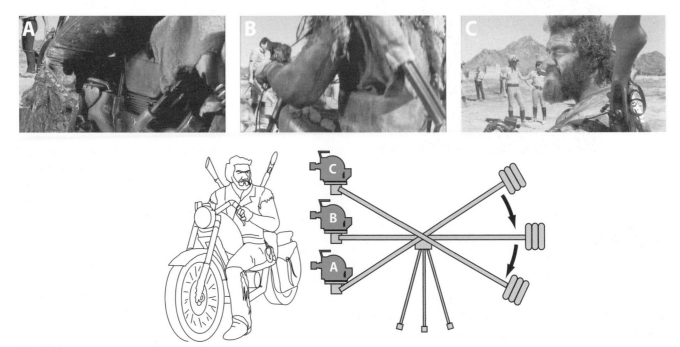

■ **Figure 3-34** This dynamic boom shot, from Joel Coen's *Raising Arizona* (1987), reveals the bounty hunter Leonard Smalls (Randall "Tex" Cobb) from boots to beard, and not only reveals in detail his arsenal of weaponry, but the move also emphasizes his fearsomeness.

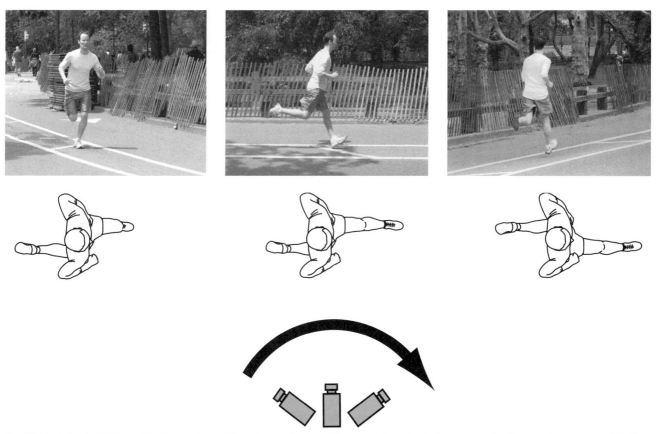

■ Figure 3-35 In a pan, a subject is seen from different angles from a stationary point as the shot progresses. In this example, the runner is facing the camera at the beginning of the shot and is seen from behind at the end of it.

it, would require panning and tilting simultaneously—one might even want additionally to zoom-in. Executing more than one move at a time is referred to as a **combination move** and is very common.

The Moving Frame and Perspective

Although the general directions of the frame shifts are similar (i.e., left to right or up and down), there is a big difference between stationary camera moves (pans and tilts) and dynamic camera moves (dolly, track, and boom). Think of the camera as essentially the seat from which an audience member views the world of your film. With pivoting camera moves this perspective point of reference remains fixed. Panning or tilting the camera is the equivalent of placing the viewer in one spot and then having them turn their head left and right, or up and down. Their seat becomes the pivot point as they scan the world horizontally or vertically. With a mobile camera, you are essentially moving the viewer's seat through the space of the fictive world of the film. This makes for an extremely dynamic feeling of traveling through space.

Here's an example of the difference. Let's say we are filming a runner, jogging down a street. First, let's shoot the run with a follow pan, placing the camera at the halfway mark along his path (Figure 3-35).

The beginning of the shot is quite frontal, looking into the runner's face, as we start our follow pan. When he hits the midpoint mark, directly in front of the camera, he will be seen in profile and, continuing, when he reaches the end of his path, we will be looking at his back. It's the perspective of a stationary spectator—as if we were sitting on a bench watching him run past us.

■ Figure 3-36 Here the camera tracks with the runner, maintaining a consistent profile angle.

Now, let's go back to the beginning of the runner's path and shoot his run with a tracking shot (Figure 3-36). We begin alongside the runner, in profile, and as he moves, our camera tracks along with him. As he reaches the midway point and then the end of the path, the runner remains in profile all the way because we have been following parallel to him. In this shot, the viewer, like the camera, is a runner too, a participant—moving through space just like the runner.

Motivation and the Moving Camera

Camera moves can look very cool, and because they do, they are one of the most over-used techniques in film. Your film, after all, should be about what happens to the characters and not about what's happening with the camera. So, like all film techniques, you need a good reason to employ a moving camera. Camera moves should be **motivated** in two ways. First, conceptually speaking, a camera move must have a narrative function, meaning that it serves as an important storytelling technique. Second, the moment the actual camera move begins needs to be motivated within the scene.

Narrative Motivation (Reveal or Conceal)

A camera move, whether it's a pan, track, or zoom, is a promise—it promises the viewer that they are going to get a new piece of information, or a new understanding, by the end of the camera's little trip. Let's say we're shooting a wide shot of a mountain range and we pan right, the pan promises the viewer that we'll see something in addition to those mountains: maybe the pan reveals a forest fire raging on the south slopes or maybe a cowboy comes into view in the foreground, or perhaps the pan of the mountains goes on and on and on and it is revealed through the move that our character is surrounded by mountains on all sides. But, if you just pan from some mountains to a few more mountains and the move accomplishes nothing more than a static shot would, then the move breaks its promise of showing something else, and it is considered an **unmotivated move**.

Keep in mind that not only can a camera move be used to reveal new information (as in the preceding examples), but it can also be used to conceal information. Horror films use this device all the time. A young woman hears a noise coming from the closet (!) . . . we track with her as she reaches for the doorknob, she turns it, and, just as she opens the closet door, the camera pans away from the closet to show the surprise and terror on her face!! But the move also *conceals* what's in the closet, what she's seeing, and provokes a delicious sense of frustration, mystery, and suspense. Reveal or conceal: two very important considerations when you devise camera moves of any sort.

Short camera moves, like a short **dolly-in** to a character's face (from MED to CU), can be used to punctuate a highly important emotional moment. An example is the very short and slow dolly-in to Miles' face (*Sideways*) as Maya explains why she likes wine (see scene, p. 30). This almost imperceptible move electrifies the moment, as it dawns on Miles that he is attracted to Maya and she to him.

Move Motivation

The moment of the physical movement of the frame also needs motivation within the scene. A move that begins arbitrarily can make the camera apparatus itself very apparent to the viewer, causing them to become aware of the filmmaker manipulating the world of the film. In our previous example of the man at his desk, his look toward the window (off screen) could be the motivation for the pan to begin, because we want to see what he sees. In cases like this we say that we "pan off his look." In the second example, pan with, the action of getting up out of his chair and walking to the window is the motivation for the follow pan as we "stay with our character."

When it comes to the aesthetics of the frame, we have only laid down the groundwork in this chapter. There are many other technical factors that contribute to the graphic qualities of your frame—for example, choice of imaging format, lens selection, lighting design, exposure, frame rate, and the physical location. These tools will be discussed in later chapters and they will also become part of your visual palate as you imagine the film during pre-visualization.

Organizing Cinematic Time and Space

◼ SINGLE CAMERA PRODUCTION AND THE CONTINUITY SYSTEM

Whether you are shooting on film or digital video, fictional narrative movies are generally shot using a single camera. This enables productions to be extremely mobile and to go to any location required by the script, as opposed to multi-camera and control room productions like sit-coms and soap operas, which are produced in a studio. Single camera shooting also allows the energy and expertise of the director and the entire creative team to be focused on each and every shot in the movie. Finally, shooting single camera gives us maximum versatility in editing, because the film has been broken down into its smallest component parts—individual shots—whose intended sequence can be creatively rethought and rearranged throughout the postproduction process to improve the film.[1]

The scenes and shots of a narrative film are rarely shot in the order in which they appear in the script or in the final film. Because of the expense, time, and labor involved in film production, a script is divided and rearranged according to major locations, camera angles, and, finally, shots, and the actual shooting order is organized primarily for efficiency (see Chapter 5). This means that scenes, sequences, and even specific actions are often divided into different pieces and are shot at different times. **Continuity style shooting and editing** is a system that assures us that individual shots, when cut together, will give us the illusion of smooth and continuous time, movement, and space, regardless of the order those shots were taken. The continuity system has been devised in order to present a scene without any confusion about the spatial and temporal relationships of people, objects, and actions. Also, the hallmark of continuity style is to render each edit, the link from one shot to another, as seamlessly as possible. While the principles of the continuity system can, at first, seem a bit like a needlessly complex jigsaw puzzle, they are, in fact, quite simple and can be mastered with relatively little shooting and editing experience.

◼ PRINCIPLES OF CONTINUITY STYLE

Any discussion about the continuity system necessarily concerns both shooting principles and editing principles; there is no way to separate the two and, therefore, the requirements of the editing process must be acknowledged in the shooting process. In other words, a director needs to endeavor to get more than just a collection of great-looking shots; directors need to get shots that will work together in the edit.

Let's start with two shots connected by one single edit. We want to cut shot A with shot B as seamlessly as possible. Invisible edits are the traditional goal of continuity style. Shot A is a long shot of two men at a chess table in the park starting a game of chess. Shot B is a medium close-up of the player with the white pieces making his first move and hitting the clock (**Figure 4-1**).

---

[1]There are some exceptions to this practice. Spike Lee's *Bamboozled,* for example, was shot with as many as ten DV cameras simultaneously, and Lars von Trier's Danish television program "The Kingdom" was shot using two handheld cameras for each take. But these films are exceptions even within the oeuvre of each director. Also, big action sequences that cannot be duplicated, like the spectacular train wreck in Andrew Davis' *The Fugitive,* are often shot with multiple cameras from different angles.

A   B

■ **Figure 4-1** A simple edit. Cutting from a long shot (A) to a medium close-up (B).

Because shooting a movie can take a long time, it's not uncommon that two shots like these might not be shot one right after the other. Perhaps after we shoot the long shot, we decide to break for lunch and shoot the close-up one hour later. Maybe during lunch our actor becomes ill and needs to go home. A week later he's better and we return to the park to get the close-up. To assure that these two shots cut together seamlessly, no matter when they were shot, our first consideration is that the shared visual and aural characteristics in each shot remain consistent.

Continuity of Mise-en-scène

Costume, Props, Sets, and Lights

The clothes our character wears, the things he touches, and his surroundings need to remain the same from one shot to the next. For example, our actor is wearing a necklace in the long shot, but if he removes it during lunch, he might forget to put it back on when shooting commences. Cutting from a long shot with necklace to a MCU without a necklace will break continuity.

Consumable props and set pieces can also cause difficulty. Cigarettes that are short in one shot but longer in the next, or a glass of milk that is drunk down to half empty in the master shot but is suddenly full again in the close-up, or a candle that is tall in the master but just a stub in the close-up—all of these discontinuities are very common problems and avoiding them requires sharp eyes and lots of extra props on hand. In the case of our chess player, the clock needs to be watched carefully. If it starts out showing 5 minutes, but in the one cut it's down to 1 minute, then the illusion of continuous time is broken in a very literal way. For exactly this reason, you must be careful of clocks which appear in the background of shots. You can easily find yourself cutting between 10 am in long shots and 3 pm in close-ups.

The angle and quality of the light in shots A and B must also be consistent if you want to edit these shots together and create the illusion of continuous time. We might be able to shoot one hour later, especially if the chess table is in the shade of a tree, but we wouldn't want to shoot these two shots too far apart in the same day. If the sun is overhead in the master shot, but setting in the close-up (creating long shadows), then continuity will be broken. The angle of the sun is not just a concern for exterior scenes—it's common to shoot your first shot in an interior space with the sun streaming in through the windows, but when you finally get around to the close-up the sun has moved to the other side of the house or clouds have moved in. This is why it's common practice to block windows and then re-create the sunlight streaming in. If your "sun" is a 5,000-watt light on a stand, then that's a sun that'll never set. But even when using all artificial

Not Looking

One of my students was shooting a film and took a break between a long shot and a close-up, to solve an unrelated logistical matter. During the break, the actor decided to go over his lines and put his glasses on to read the script. When shooting recommenced, he got into position for his close-up, and didn't even think about taking his glasses off. He had forgotten, and no one else noticed either, that he wasn't wearing his glasses in the long shot. So, in editing, the student was unable to cut to the close-up without breaking continuity.

Not Thinking

Another story from a student shoot happened on an advanced thesis project. The art department team had done a beautiful job creating just the right look for a kitchen scene, including a lovely bowl of fruit on the dining table. During the crew's lunch beak, however, no one noticed that one of the production assistants, someone with very little filmmaking experience, decided to augment the meal provided by the producer with a few pieces of fruit from the set! Ultimately it wasn't a disaster—it was possible to cut around the missing bananas and grapes—but this does make a good case for using plastic food as set dressing and being careful whom you allow onto your set.

lights, you often tweak and rearrange a few lighting instruments between shots, so you need to remember to be consistent with lighting angles, exposures, and colors from shot to shot.

As much as we all try to maintain continuity as perfectly as possible, many films still have this sort of continuity error. In fact, there are dozens of "blooper" books dedicated to spotting, say, the stick that disappears and reappears in different shots in *My Own Private Idaho* (Figure 4-2). But small continuity gaffes like this are often overlooked if your story is engaging, your performances are good, and the rest of your continuity technique is solid. The truth is, most people don't look for the little stuff if they're engaged in the drama of your film. However, glaring continuity errors can pull the audience completely out of the story. I remember the murmurs and chuckles in the theater during the opening chase scene in *New Jack City* (1991). The chase between Scotty and Pookie starts on a beautifully sunny day, not a cloud in the sky, but in one edit, as Pookie leaps over a fence, everyone on the street is suddenly holding umbrellas to shield themselves from the steady rain. No matter how exciting the chase is, it's hard to overlook a continuity error that big.

On a professional set, the **script supervisor** is responsible for keeping track of these continuity concerns, but small productions and student films rarely have a dedicated script supervisor, so it is important for everyone on the set (especially actors, the director, the cinematographer, and the art director) to be as vigilant and perceptive as possible to

■ **Figure 4-2** Continuity of mise-en-scène. In this shot/reverse-shot sequence from Van Sant's *My Own Private Idaho* (1991), the stick Mike (River Phoenix) uses to stir the campfire (left) disappears when we cut to Scott (Keanu Reeves, right). Small continuity gaffes like this one are common, but mostly go unnoticed by audiences if they are fully engaged in the drama of the film.

maintain the continuity of these mise-en-scène details. Digital still cameras are a great help for continuity of shot content. If you break before completing all of the shots in a continuity sequence, simply take a few pictures of the actors in costume, the props, and the sets to remind you what was in the scene and where it was. Shooting DV does allow you to back up and view the previous take—BUT, a word of caution: I've seen many shots erased because the tape was not properly requeued.

Continuity of Sound

If you are shooting a film with sound, then the shared aural universe between shots A and B also must be consistent. This is especially difficult when it comes to ambient sound. **Ambient sounds** are the sounds that exist naturally in a given location. If you're at the beach the ambient sound world might include breaking waves, seagulls, and footsteps on the boardwalk. However, the human perception of sound has developed such that we unconsciously ignore or "filter out" a lot of ambient sound and "focus" our ears on important sounds. This is a great ability for maintaining one's sanity, but it can be a disaster for the aural continuity of a film.

Let's say that all was quiet in the park when we took shot A, but while we were setting up for shot B the grounds crew decided to trim the grass with a weed-whacker, or maybe a jet airplane is flying overhead at precisely the moment you shoot shot B. These are sounds that we can easily miss at the time, but which will break the illusion of continuous time when you cut the relative silence of one shot right next to the buzz of an off-screen weed-whacker in the next. For this reason, sound recordists are trained to hear absolutely everything in their environment, the same way a D.P. observes everything in the frame. Many shots have been halted by a sound recordist who hears a plane flying overhead. There are ways to "fix" continuity sound problems, but fixes often involve time, money, and compromises. It's best to try to maintain the best possible sound match between the shots—so you should wait for the plane to pass before running the camera, or in the case of the weed-whacker, maybe it would be a good time to break for lunch and shoot the medium close-up when the gardeners are done trimming. Issues concerning continuity and audio recording, editing, and mixing are discussed in detail in Chapters 17 and 23, respectively.

Continuity of Performance, Actions, and Placement

If we are to cut shot A seamlessly with shot B, then the *placement* and *physical actions* of our performer must be consistent. Our character moves the King's pawn with his left hand in the long shot, so he must move the same chess piece with the same hand in the medium close-up, if we are to successfully cut in that spot. This ensures that the visible actions in the two shots match. Also, our character is sitting upright with his right hand in his lap in the LS, so he cannot be leaning forward, resting his chin in his right hand in the medium close-up. Cutting these two shots together would make us feel like there was a chunk of film missing, the chunk in which the character leaned forward in his seat to prop his chin in his hand.

Performance pace is another factor to keep in mind for continuity. If our character in shot A is in a hurry—makes a quick move and hits the clock—BAM!, but is leisurely in the close-up, then it will seem strange that his pace so abruptly switched, making the separateness of the shots very apparent. Also, the *emotional intensity* of a performance must be consistent from shot A to shot B. This can be very difficult to gauge, especially if a lot of time has elapsed between the various takes. Perhaps, in shot A the actor was projecting a sense of chess mastery and confidence when he faces his opponent across the table. But during lunch he decides that his character at this point in the script should be fearful of his opponent and petrified to lose this game in public. Cutting directly from a man exuding confidence to a trembling, fearful wreck will break emotional continuity and confuse the audience. This sort of performance consistency issue is especially difficult when you are recording dialogue. The emotional range of the voice is very wide and it can be tricky to maintain consistency from shot to shot and day to day. Experienced film actors understand all of these issues very well and are trained to keep performance consistent.

Spatial Continuity and the 180° Principle

Spatial continuity is a crucial tenet in the continuity system. In order for the viewer to understand the physical space of the scene and the relationships between characters and objects in that space, we need to maintain coherent and consistent spatial orientation. Spatial orientation begins with the **180° principle**, which, in basic terms, means that we must shoot all of the shots in a continuity sequence from only one side of the action. In other words, when we begin shooting an action from one side, we cannot place our camera on the other side of that action for subsequent shots, or else the orientation of our character and their actions (in fact the perspective of the viewer) will be reversed and the shots will not cut together seamlessly.

Let's say you are watching a chess game and the man playing with the white pieces is to your left. When he looks at his opponent, he faces left to right. The opponent playing the black pieces is to your right—he faces right to left. When white makes the first move it is from left to right, and black's first move is from right to left. This is your spatial orientation from your side of the table. However, for the onlooker who is watching the game from the other side of the table, across from you, everything is reversed. White is to their right, looking and moving from right to left. When we make a film, the camera is the spectator, and to shoot this scene we cannot take some shots from one side of the table and others from the opposite side because that would reverse both the direction of the moves and the direction the players' faces.

In order to understand and utilize the 180° principle, we draw an imaginary line along our action—called the **180° line** (also called the **axis of action**) (Figure 4-3). We draw this line following the directional bearing of our subject, which is the direction a character is looking, called their **sight line**, and/or the direction they travel in the frame, called their **screen direction**. The 180° principle tells us that, to maintain consistent sight lines and screen direction, all shots used in a sequence must remain on one side of the line, giving us a 180° arc where we can place our camera. Crossing the 180° line with the camera reverses both looking and moving directions of our subject and breaks spatial continuity.

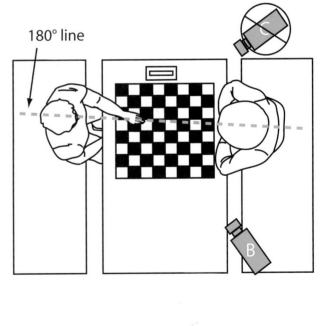

180° line

If we shoot our long shot from the near side of this line, then the viewer's perspective is defined by the man playing white facing screen right (*shot A*). In order to maintain this orientation, we must stay on the same side of the line for the medium close-up (*shot B*). If we place our camera anywhere on the far side of the line to take our close-up, the sight line of the character and the orientation of all actions will be reversed. This is called **jumping the line** (Figure 4-4).

Notice in shot C that our character now suddenly faces screen left and the chess move, which we anticipated going from left to right, is now going from right to left. This shot will not cut with the first shot without causing spatial confusion for the viewer. The viewer might think that the players, for some reason, had suddenly changed places or the edit could be construed, perhaps, as moving us forward in time, hours later, after the two players have switched positions.

Keep in mind that we could have equally chosen to shoot our long shot from the opposite side of the line, meaning that our character would be facing screen left, but then the

■ Figure 4-3 Overhead of shots A, B, and C. Character sightlines establish the 180° line of action and shot A establishes on which side of that line all shots must remain. Shot C, however, crosses the line, effectively reversing all sight lines and movements and potentially causing spatial confusion. (See Figure 4-4.)

■ **Figure 4-4** The images taken from the overhead positions in **Figure 4-3**. Note that while shot B cuts seamlessly with shot A, shot C will not cut smoothly with shot A because character positions, sight lines and movements are abruptly reversed.

close-up would also need to be shot from that side of the line of action. It doesn't matter which side you choose: what matters is that you are consistent with all of the shots that make up a continuity sequence.

20mm/30° Rule

Now let's put a slightly finer point on invisible editing and continuity technique. When we cut from one shot of a subject to another shot *of the same subject,* we need to make sure that each shot is a very distinct composition in terms of frame size and camera angle. If we try to cut together two shots of the same subject when the frames are very similar, then the viewer has the feeling that a single shot has simply lurched forward a little bit—like a battered, old newsreel with missing bits of footage. This is called a **jump cut**, and the awkwardness of the edit calls attention to itself (see later, *Cutting on Action*). In some instances this may be a desirable aesthetic approach (see later, *Style Outside Continuity*), but for the continuity system, it's to be avoided. The 20mm/30° rule ensures that each shot is a distinct composition. Basically, the rule tells us that in order to cut from shot A, the man sitting at the chess table, to shot B, the man making his first move, we must change the shot size of shot B by at least 20mm and the camera angle by at least 30° from its position in shot A (Figure 4-5).

While the 30° rule is easy to understand, the 20mm principle needs a little clarifying. 20mm indicates a shift in the degree of magnification of the lens that alters the size of the subject in the frame, but since we can also change shot size by moving the camera it's better to think about this part of the rule in broad terms. Essentially, the principle is to avoid making the sizes of each shot too similar. Notice how I'm cutting together a long shot with a close-up, very different sizes. If I were to try and cut together, say, a medium long shot with a medium shot, we might get a jump cut (Figure 4-6).

■ **Figure 4-5** 20mm/30° rule. Two shots of obviously different sizes and angles such as shot A (LS profile) and shot B (CU ¾) cut together smoothly, but two shots which are nearly identical, such as shot A (LS profile) and shot C (LS shifted only slightly to the right), will cause a jump cut.

B

A

C

■ **Figure 4-6** Jump cut. The images taken from the overhead positions in Figure 4-5. Shot B will cut seamlessly with shot A, but shot C creates a jump cut.

Cutting on Action

Cutting on action is an effective technique for creating a smooth sense of continuous time and movement from one shot to the next. The **match action edit** means dividing a single movement between two shots in order to bridge the edit. In a match action edit, one part of a movement is in shot A and the continuation of that movement is in the adjoining shot B. Let's say our long shot includes the actions of the player with the white pieces walking into the frame, sitting down at the table, looking up and acknowledging his opponent with a nod, moving the first piece, and hitting the clock. When do we cut to the close-up? Technically there are four strong edit points where we can match the action from the wide shot to a tighter shot:

1. *Match action as he sits down.* The first half of his sitting action in LS, then cut to the MCU for him landing in his seat.
2. *Match action as he looks up at his opponent.* Hold the LS until he tilts his head to make eye contact, then cut to a CU as he nods to his opponent. It could be a very small movement, but it's all we need for a smooth edit.
3. *Match action as he makes his first move.* Stay with the LS until he touches his first chess piece, then cut to a CU as he pushes it forward.
4. *Match action as he hits the clock.* Stay on the LS as he reaches for the clock, then cut to the MCU on the second half of that motion when he actually taps the button.

Duplicating Actions

The ultimate decision for where to cut depends on the dramatic emphasis of the scene, meaning that we need to think about why we are drawing the audience closer to the character at this precise moment, but technically speaking it should be obvious that in order to cut any of these actions we need to overlap or duplicate these action points when we shoot each shot. If we decide to edit on the man moving the chess piece, then we shoot that entire action in the long shot and duplicate the action again in the close-up. Doing this allows us to edit anywhere along that action, from the man reaching for the piece, to

in practice

A strong, tight cut on action creates such a smooth transition that it can effectively hide small continuity errors. In a scene (Figure 4-7) from one of my own films, I shot an extensive MLS master shot of the architect and then later shot the CU of her hand reaching for the telephone. When I framed the CU, I didn't like the composition—there was just a bare white wall in the background and it seemed bland—so I repositioned the colorful pencil can on the drawing table to be behind the phone. Everyone on the set cried "Continuity! Continuity!" but I shot it anyway. I knew that by cutting on the strong action of her grabbing the phone and the relative brevity of the CU, no on would notice the pencil can jump from one side of the desk to the other. After screening this film all over the country, and dozens of times in class, not one person has called me up on it.

That's how smooth and seamless cutting on action is.

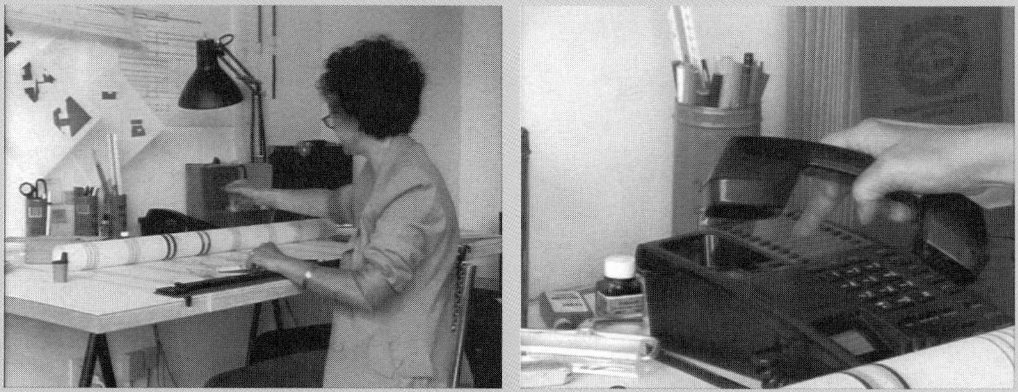

■ **Figure 4-7** When the story is working, small continuity errors, like the moving pencil can in this edit from Hurbis-Cherrier's *Ode to Things* (1998), are generally not noticed.

lifting the piece and placing it down. Going into production, a director should have a sense of where he might want to cut, and shoot ample footage of shared actions so that, in the edit, there is a range of cutting possibilities.

In our chess player example, for instance, the possible cut points are so close that I would probably choose to shoot the entire thing in the long shot (walking in, sitting, acknowledging, moving, tapping clock) and then repeat the actions, from sitting to clock, in the MCU. That would allow me more possibilities in the editing room. If the edit itself is made such that the action is not matched precisely, you can have two problems: accidentally duplicating some part of the movement in both shots, creating double motion and eliminating a part of the motion, even just a few frames, which is not included in either shot. In both cases we get the sense that footage is missing and we have a jump cut.

Cutting on action can also smooth out transitions between shots in which the subject is entirely different. For example, what if your next shot (shot B) is not a match action edit, meaning that there are no shared actions between the two shots? What if we were to cut from the second shot (MCU shot B) to a woman, at a park bench (MED shot), who has noticed that a game has begun? Cutting on an action in the first shot (i.e., moving the pawn) to the woman turning her head and noticing the game makes for a smoother edit than cutting together two perfectly static images.

Six Basic Principles of Continuity

1. Continuity of mise-en-scène (shared shot content)
2. Continuity of sound
3. Continuity of performance
4. Continuity of spatial orientation (axis of action)
5. 20mm/30° rule
6. Cutting on action (match action edits)

■ SCENE STRATEGIES: PUTTING CONTINUITY TO USE

In this section we explore a range of scene and sequence constructions that work with the preceding continuity principles and that make up the fundamental visual approaches to dramatic visualization and scene structure. This is essential information for any filmmaker. One can certainly move beyond or add to these traditional methods, but these approaches are central to the expectations an audience brings to the experience of watching a film, and with these approaches one can find enormous communicative power. In fact, many great films have been made with not much more than the following techniques.

Every concept discussed in the following sections involves the interrelationship between shooting technique (a production process) and editing technique (a post-production process)—it is impossible to detach the two. In addition, because these concepts inform both the creative approach and production plan for your film, they are a vital preproduction concern. Film is an interrelated art form; each stage of the process is intimately connected to the others.

Two-Person and Person/Object Interactions

One of the most fundamental relationships we construct within a scene is between two people, or between a person and an object, in the same space. We have, in fact, already done that with our two-shot sequence of the chess player. But let's make it a little more complicated than just one edit—let's look at a scene in which two people interact over the course of many cuts. The traditional, and still most common way of approaching a two-person (or person and object) interaction is called **the master scene** or **shot/ reverse shot technique. The master scene** consists of three basic shots that are later

■ **Figure 4-8** Cutting from one shot to another should be motivated by the dramatic needs of the scene. Here, we cut from the long shot to a close-up because we want the audience to see that top secret material is passing between the two spies playing chess in the park. We could stay with the LS for this action if we want to remain mysterious about the exchange.

edited together, that is, the master shot and reverse shots of each person (or the person and the object). In addition, there is often a fourth type of shot in a master scene called a **cutaway**.

The **master shot** clearly shows both subjects in the scene and defines the spatial relationship of the two to each other and the space around them, like the long shot (shot A) of our chess players. For this reason, the size of a master shot is usually on the wide side. Often master shots are used to cover the entire scene from beginning to end and can be used as a safety shot, one that you can always stay on or cut back to if the other shots do not edit in smoothly.

Reverse shots (also called **singles**) are closer shots of the subjects in the scene—for example, close-ups of each person. Reverse shots are edited into the master shot at dramatically motivated moments—for example, when you want to draw the audience into a closer identification with one character at a particularly pivotal moment. But where might that pivotal moment, which motivates the cut to a closer shot, be? That depends on your script and how the director interprets the scene. In our previous scene of the chess players, the scene involves a former child grandmaster prodigy who has not played the game in fifteen years; that first pawn move might bring it all back, or might

■ **Figure 4-9** A standard over-the-shoulder shot (OTS).

reveal to him that he's lost his skills completely. So the moment of truth for him is when he reaches for the pawn and recommences his chess playing, and this is where we choose to cut. Or maybe this scene isn't really about chess—maybe he's a spy, sitting across from someone who is supposed to give him an envelope with secret documents; in this case a better place to cut to the first CU would be after a few moves into the game, on the exchange of the top secret material. The first choice emphasizes the game; the second choice emphasizes the covert activity between the two people at the table (Figure 4-8).

Keep in mind that you have many possibilities concerning the size of your frame and the camera angle for the reverse shots and these must be chosen carefully because they are central to the dramatic emphasis and style of your scene. A reverse shot that is from an angle that includes a portion of the other person's shoulder or head is called an **over-the-shoulder shot** (OTS) (Figure 4-9).

We can use the single of only one character in the scene or we can alternate between the reverse shots of both characters. Alternating between the two reverse shot angles is called **shot/reverse shot technique**. Reverse shots are not just about showing a person when they speak their dialogue; there are often times when we wish to see a character who is purely reacting to the moment. This type of reverse shot is called a **reaction shot**. It's also important to note that you can shoot more than one reverse shot of a single character, adjusting the framing and shot size in order to change the tone of the scene or the audience's engagement with that character as the scene evolves.

An example (Figure 4-10) from *Sideways* (read the scene on p. 30) demonstrates the simple master shot, shot/reverse shot technique, but with a variety of reverse shots. The reverse shots for both Miles and Maya progressively move from medium over-the-shoulder shots to tight close-ups as the scene becomes more and more intimate and intense.

Coverage

Practically speaking, typical master scene production technique involves shooting the entire scene in a master shot, then changing the placement of the camera to reshoot sections of the scene for all of the reverse shots of one character, and then changing again to shoot all of the reverse shots of the other character. The side of the 180° line of action from which you choose to shoot the master shot determines on which side you must remain for all of your reverse shots. Each time we move our camera for the reverse shots, we must observe the six basic principles of continuity previously outlined in order for them to cut seamlessly into the master shot. It's very common to shoot the same moment in a scene from two or three different angles and shot sizes (i.e., LS master shot, CU reverse shot of character 1 and CU reverse shot of character 2) or even more. Shooting a scene from various angles is called **coverage**. The amount of coverage you can accomplish for any given scene is determined first by your visual conception of the scene and then, to a large degree, by your time and financial resources. Coverage from multiple angles takes time and continuity coordination, but being able to choose between several angles of the same moment also gives you great flexibility in shaping the dramatic arc and emphasis of the scene later in the editing.

The story and directorial style of some films require extensive coverage while others, like Jim Jarmusch's *Down by Law* (see Figure 3-5), don't use coverage at all, opting instead for one single long take to cover an entire scene. It is also important to understand that not *every* scene within a single film requires the same amount of coverage; some scenes are shot from multiple angles, while others are presented from only one camera angle. For example, the scene from *Sideways* (Figure 4-10) involved numerous camera setups to cover, which requires extra time. But in this case the time was well spent, because this is one of the central moments in the film and each tightening of the reverse shots intensifies the moment. However, in an earlier scene, where Jack warns Miles not to "sabotage" him on their date with Maya and Stephanie, the exchange is presented only in a long, uncut master shot (Figure 4-11).

One additional and important principle that applies to the camera placement for reverse shots is called the sight line match. **Sight line matching** is an important consideration when shooting reverse shots for two characters (or a character and object) who are at different heights. When characters are at different heights and addressing each other, the sight lines established in the master shot are not only traced horizontally (i.e., screen left or right), but the characters' sight lines are also defined diagonally, by one character looking down and the other looking up. So, in addition to observing the 180° line of ac-

■ **Figure 4-10** Shot/reverse shot technique. This scene from Payne's *Sideways* (2004) cuts from medium close-ups (OTS) to increasingly tighter shots as the conversation between Miles (Paul Giamatti) and Maya (Virginia Madsen) becomes more intimate. The framing of these shots effectively reveals the emotions that are embedded in the subtext of their dialogue about wine.

tion, we must also adjust the camera height when shooting the reverse shots, in order to approximate the characters' sight lines, which were established in the master shot. This means shooting the reverse shot of the higher character from a low angle and shooting the reverse shot of the lower character with a high-angle shot. This is especially important if you want your reverse shots to approximate the points of view of the characters in the scene, as is the case in our example. Remember, just as with all other principles in this section, sight line matching also applies to a person and an object (Figure 4-12).

Finally, one further shot commonly found in a simple two-person interaction scene is the **cutaway shot**. The cutaway is a shot of a detail within your scene other than the characters' faces. For example, in our scene of the chess players, one cutaway might be an extreme close-up of the clock counting down the seconds, another could be a shot of a bystander watching their game. Generally, cutaways can have few continuity connections to the main action of your scene. The fewer details a cutaway shares with the other shots in the scene, the easier it is to cut it in. Cutaways are very useful in editing. They can be used for patching together shots where continuity is problematic or as a way to hide post-production alterations (like cutting out blocks of dialogue) or as a way to control pace within a scene.

Shaping the master scene is a central skill in a filmmaker's dramatic vocabulary. The motivation for cutting back and forth between the reverse shots, for deciding where to utilize the master shot and when to use a cutaway, is largely determined by the dramatic rhythms

Figure 4-11 With no dramatic reason to cut to a closer angle, this scene from Payne's *Sideways* plays out in a single, unbroken long shot.

Coverage is often a matter of a director's style: their particular approach to a scene, to the film, and to filmmaking in general. So, in the final analysis, there is no absolute right or wrong way to shoot a scene. As Ethan Coen states in his quote at the beginning of Chapter 3, "That would be too easy." Here are some directors discussing their different approaches (all quotes from *Moviemakers' Master Class*, by Laurent Tirard, 2002):

I don't do any coverage, and I try to shoot every scene in a single shot, or as close to that as I can. I don't cut as long as I don't have to, and I never shoot the same scene from a different angle . . . I never cover anything partly because I'm too lazy, and partly because I don't like the actors to do the same thing over and over.

Woody Allen

I tend to cover each scene a lot, mostly if they're dialogue scenes, because of matching problems. Sometimes I get a

very straightforward scene, where I know there is only one way to shoot it and I stick to that. But that's pretty rare.

Sydney Pollack

As a rule, I don't cover much. It depends on the scene, of course. Very often there is only one way to shoot it. But in some scenes, and especially if the scene is something of a transition, where the story can shift from one point of view to another, then I will do a lot of coverage because it is only in the editing that I will be able to know whether the story should follow this person or that person.

Wong Kar-Wai

When I shoot a scene I cover everything, from wide shots to close-ups, and then I choose in the editing, because that's the moment when I really know how I feel about a scene.

John Woo

■ **Figure 4-12** Sight line angles are usually matched as in this scene from Payne's *Sideways*, in which Miles (Paul Giamatti) is speaking with, and looking down toward, Stephanie (Sandra Oh).

of action and dialogue in the script. We will look at how to give dramatic shape to a master scene in Chapters 5 and 21, on editing.

Multiple Lines of Action

How do we organize space for a slightly more complex scene in which one of our characters moves around, disrupting the original line of action? What happens if a third person comes into the scene, causing our character to shift their sight line? The truth is, we are not once-and-for-all stuck with only one axis of action in every single scene. It's very common for there to be shifts in the line of action, even several times, within a single scene. Each time that there is a shift in sight lines within a scene, we simply need to be clear in showing how and when the axis shifted and then we need to redraw our line of action and shoot any reverse shots accordingly.

It's very common to have a scene in which a moving character crosses the established line of action, causing a complete shift in their looking direction. In this case, it's important to show, in a single shot, the character move and cross the line while the other person follows them with their gaze. Very often this will involve passing in front of the camera. Once they have crossed the axis and settled, they establish a new axis of action from that point onward. Often the movement that establishes the new line of action is shown in a master shot, although it is also possible for us to see a character cross in front of the camera in the reverse shot of the stationary character, where we can also see the sight lines shifting (Figure 4-13).

It's very important to understand that the line of action is not a fixed axis—rather, it shifts when characters and sightlines shift. Very active scenes, like a judo match or a swordfight in which characters circle each other, might involve reestablishing the line of action many times. Finally, moving the camera, from one side of the action to the other, during a single, unbroken shot, also creates a switch in the axis of action.

Creating Point of View

Establishing a character's **point of view** means representing the visual perspective of that character, what they see. By creating a point of view (POV), the audience is not just looking *at* your character, but *with* them. There are two ways to create shots that replicate a character's POV: using a **subjective camera** or constructing a **POV sequence**. Using a subjective camera implies that we are literally looking through the eyes of our character. To produce this effect, the camera often is handled so that its motions are somewhat human (i.e., a handheld camera), and we never get to see the character who is looking, just as we never really see our own faces. Because of the overt artificiality of the device, the subjective camera is not as commonly used (Figure 4-14).

A much more common approach to creating POV involves a three-shot POV sequence, which, visually speaking, only approximates the true perspective of our character, but

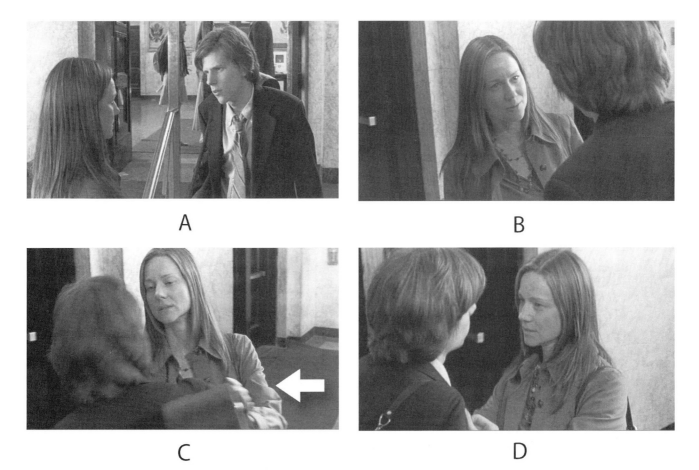

■ **Figure 4-13** This scene from Baumbach's *The Squid and the Whale* (2005) illustrates a very common shift in the line of action. Shots A and B maintain consistent sight lines: screen right for Joan (Laura Linney) and screen left for Walt (Jesse Eisenberg). However, when Walt passes in front of the camera (C) on his way down the steps, the sight lines are reversed and a new line of action is created (D).

which, in many ways, allows us even more intimate access to their perception. The three shots in the POV sequence are: (1) The **looking shot**, which shows your subject turning their gaze toward a person or object. The precise moment their eyes rest on their target, we cut to (2) the **POV shot**, which shows what they are looking at. The POV shot is taken from approximately the looker's perspective, including sight-line matching, but is not a true subjective shot. After the POV shot, we return to the character to see their reaction to what they've just seen, (3) the **reaction shot** (Figure 4-15).

POV sequences follow the same continuity principles as shot/reverse shots, with camera angle positions, to approximate the sight lines of the looker, being especially critical. Practically speaking, while the POV sequence includes three edited shots, we really only shoot *two shots* during production. The looking shot

■ **Figure 4-14** Subjective camera. In this type of shot, we literally "see" the action through the eyes of the character; everyone else interacts with it by looking straight at "us" (frame from Noshir's short film *Fear Eats the Soul*, a brilliant update on how little things have changed since Fassbinder's *Ali: Fear Eats the Soul*).

and reaction shot are in fact just one take that we have divided by cutting-in the POV shot. Inserting a POV sequence during a two-person interaction scene (i.e., one character looks off in another direction) would be another reason that one scene might have multiple 180° lines of action within one scene.

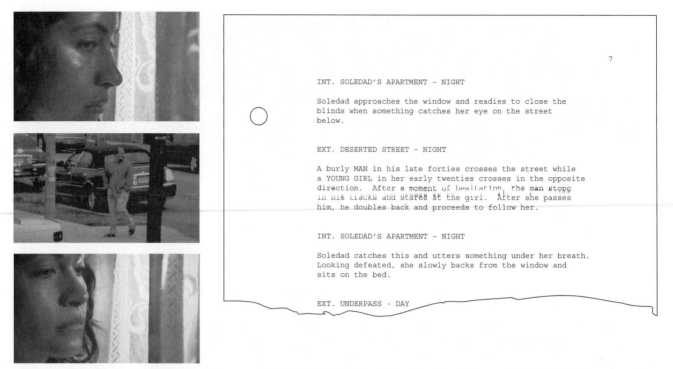

INT. SOLEDAD'S APARTMENT - NIGHT

Soledad approaches the window and readies to close the
blinds when something catches her eye on the street
below.

EXT. DESERTED STREET - NIGHT

A burly MAN in his late forties crosses the street while
a YOUNG GIRL in her early twenties crosses in the opposite
direction. After a moment of hesitation, the man stops
in his tracks and stares at the girl. After she passes
him, he doubles back and proceeds to follow her.

INT. SOLEDAD'S APARTMENT - NIGHT

Soledad catches this and utters something under her breath.
Looking defeated, she slowly backs from the window and
sits on the bed.

EXT. UNDERPASS - DAY

■ **Figure 4-15** By using the three-shot POV sequence (looking shot, point of view shot, and reaction shot) we create the illusion that we are seeing things from the perspective of a given character. In this example from Mercado's *Yield,* the heroine observes as a potentially dangerous situation develops on the street below her bedroom window.

Dramatically speaking, creating a specific point of view is a very strong device. It's powerful to have a character's look send the camera, and the entire audience, to see what they see! This is not an ability to be taken lightly. Establishing point of view signals to the audience who your main character is, from whose perspective the audience is supposed to experience the scene. It can also establish with whom an audience is supposed to identify. Giving the power of POV to one character or another can radically alter the meaning of a scene or even the entire film. Do not squander the intimate connection created through POV on just any character.

Group Interactions

There are many different approaches to shooting groups of people, and each approach is more or less complicated and time consuming. It's advisable for beginning filmmakers, with small crews, to approach these scenes as simply as possible. In general, it's simplest if you can divide your group into two smaller groups (i.e., single vs. group, or ½ and ½) then you can conceptualize the camera placement for the scene exactly like a two-person interaction. For example, take a scene involving a teacher interacting with a class of 20 students. If we conceptualize the teacher as character 1 and all the students as character 2, then we simply draw our axis of action and follow the basic rules of the continuity system. Even if we cut to different close-up reverse shots of various students, they will all follow the same sight line principles (Figure 4-16).

Moving a Person through Space

Movement and the 180° Line of Action

In the continuity system, the 180° line of action also applies to moving a character through space—that is, moving them from one place to another in an edited sequence. The movement of a character (or a car, or animal, etc.) through the frame establishes their screen direction and the axis of action. For us to maintain a sense of strict continuity and progress toward a destination, we must maintain this screen direction from shot to shot by staying on the same side of the 180° line.

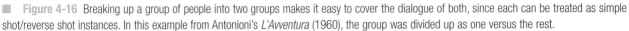

■ **Figure 4-16** Breaking up a group of people into two groups makes it easy to cover the dialogue of both, since each can be treated as simple shot/reverse shot instances. In this example from Antonioni's *L'Avventura* (1960), the group was divided up as one versus the rest.

Let's create a simple, three-shot sequence. Jessica is sitting on a park bench and decides to walk to a food vendor, who is across a field, to get a bottle of water (Figure 4-17). We decide that our three shots will be (A) getting up from the bench and heading toward the vendor, (B) walking across the field, and (C) arriving at the vendor's cart. When Jessica gets up in shot (A) and moves in one direction, say screen right, in order to get to the vendor, it is understood by the audience that the vendor is off in that direction. When we cut to the shot of her walking through the field, we must remain on the side of the action that will maintain her progress, toward screen right, and continue the same screen right progression when she gets to the vendor. Notice that if we were to place the camera on the other side of the 180° line of action (D) it would reverse Jessica's screen direction. This gives the viewer the feeling that she is returning to the bench, or heading in the wrong direction, rather than making her way to the vendor.

Entering and Exiting the Frame

Allowing characters (or a traveling car, running dog, etc.) to enter and exit the frame in each shot is especially useful when it comes time to edit a moving-through-space sequence. Cutting from the moment one exits the frame to the moment one enters the frame is a very smooth edit, although it is not necessarily the one you need make. By allowing a moving character to enter and exit the frame, you give the editor a range of possible places in which to cut into the action.

Movement and Elliptical Edits

Look at the three-shot sequence in Figure 4-17 and take out the middle shot. It still works. We can show this character going from park bench to vendor in two shots, leaving and then arriving. In fact, we could show a person walking from New York City to Dallas, Texas in the same two shots! However, we could show Jessica going from park bench to the vendor in four shots or seven shots or even more! One important question for a director is, how much of a journey, from one place to another, do we want to show? The usual answer is, we show as much of the journey as is necessary to get our dramatic point across. If our character's progress to the vendor is not important, then two or three shots will do. If we need to show that Jessica is in a very rough park, then we might need many shots to show her walking past a snarling pit-bull, two men fistfighting, and a police officer arresting a punk, until she finally reaches the vendor to buy a drink. In this case, the details of the journey and the additional shots have narrative importance.

For the most part, however, getting someone from one place to another usually means cutting out some of the nonessential time and terrain. If our point is simply that Jessica gets up to get some water, then we need not belabor the journey and we can simply show two shots: Jessica getting up from the bench and Jessica arriving at the vendor. This sort

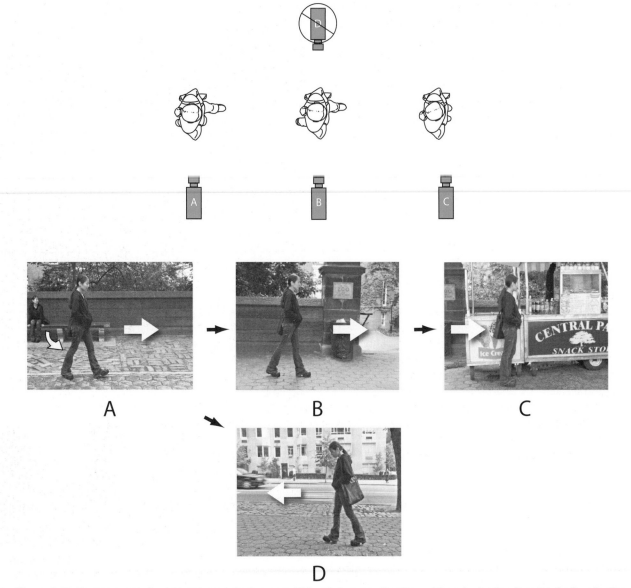

A   B   C   D

■ **Figure 4-17** The movement of a subject through the frame establishes their screen direction and the axis of action. Crossing the line of action (camera position D) reverses the subjects movement through the frame creating the impression that they are suddenly moving away from their original destination.

of time compression is an extremely common cinematic technique. Removing extraneous time and territory in the edit is called **elliptical editing**. Some ellipses are designed to be extreme and obvious (i.e., the guy who walks from New York City to Dallas in two shots), but others, like Jessica walking to the vendor in two or three quick shots, are practically invisible. The remarkable thing about elliptical editing is that you can maintain the feel and seamlessness of strict continuity, even though you have lopped off a good portion of time (Figure 4-18).

Changing Screen Direction
Maintaining only one screen direction over the course of a longer traveling sequence can get somewhat monotonous for a viewer. It's quite possible to change screen direction (i.e., the axis of action) and still maintain the feel of a character's progress toward their destination. Shown in Figure 4-19 are three simple ways we can change screen direction for Jessica, who is walking to the food vendor:

1. *Show the character change direction within a shot.* Given that our character leaves the first shot (Figure 4-19 A) moving screen right, we match screen direction and start the next shot with Jessica following a footpath screen right. But if that path curves around so that she ultimately crosses the front of the camera and exits screen left, she has now reestablished her screen direction. (B) Her journey, from this point on, can progress screen left (F).

2. *Use a neutral shot.* A neutral shot is a shot that has no specific horizontal screen direction, meaning the character is moving either directly toward or away from the viewer. We have not crossed the axis in this shot, rather we are shooting right on the 180° line. (Figure 4-19 C) Since there is no (left/right) screen direction in this shot to match, the following shot can be taken from either side of the axis of action, showing the character moving screen left or right, and it will cut in seamlessly.

3. *Use a POV shot.* Using a POV shot reestablishes the axis of action via a third character and can reverse your character's direction. For example, in shot A Jessica is crossing the field moving screen right. In the background is a mysterious man, sitting under a tree, watching her. We can redraw our line of action between Jessica and the man. (D) Now, if we cut to an over-the-shoulder POV shot of the man (E), Jessica's direction is reversed and her journey can proceed toward screen left (F).

There are, of course, other ways to strategize changing screen direction and to maintain coherent directional orientation. Although these things can be puzzling and even frustrating, at times it's often actually a fun conceptual challenge to devise elegant or even acrobatic approaches to keeping a character's journey as interesting as possible.

Moving People through Space: Following or Converging.

Screen direction is a crucial concern when we create a sequence in which we move multiple people through space, principally in meeting (or converging) scenes and chase (or follow) scenes.

■ **Figure 4-18** A leap in time and space. In this elliptical edit from the Coen Brothers' *Raising Arizona*) (1987) the bounty hunter Leonard Smalls (Randall "Tex" Cobb) is riding his motorcycle in the middle of a vast desert. When he crests a hill his motorcycle takes flight and in one edit lands in the middle of town. The edit maintains perfect spatial continuity while moving us far forward in time and location. The energy contained in this flamboyant edit also adds to the super-human quality of this fierce character.

A **meeting scene** is one in which we intercut between two (or more) people (or other moving subjects) who are in different locations but appear to be moving toward each other. In order to create the impression that two people will meet, we must make sure that their screen direction is oppositional—meaning that one character is moving screen right and the other is moving screen left.

Simply by presenting the movement of two people in oppositional (or converging) directions you can create a very strong anticipation that these people will ultimately meet—long before they do or even if they never do! In shot A (Figure 4-20) we present a young man, moving screen right, and cut to a shot of a young woman (shot B) walking screen left, so the viewer

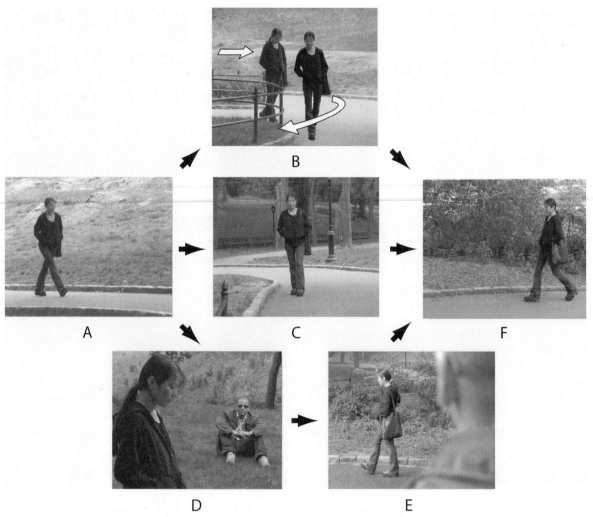

■ **Figure 4-19** Three ways to reverse the screen direction of a subject while maintaining the feeling of forward progress. From shot A (moving screen right); changing direction within a shot (B); cutting to a neutral shot (C); or using another character's POV shot (D and E) will allow us to continue the journey toward screen left (F).

■ **Figure 4-20** Meeting sequence. Maintaining a consistent and oppositional screen direction creates the expectation that two characters might eventually meet.

■ Figure 4-21 To create a sense of one character following (or chasing) another, we shoot them moving in same screen direction. This can be emphasized further by shooting the characters against a shared landmark, in this case a flower bed.

will get the *sense* that these two might bump into each other at some point. With two shots, you have the audience imagining what might happen—in fact they are imagining the story. The more you intercut the characters' converging paths, the stronger this "feeling" becomes, and after a few cross-cuts the audience will *assume* that their meeting is inevitable.

The **chase** (or **follow**) **scene** involves cross-cutting the paths of two (or more) characters who are traveling in the same direction. Simply switch the direction of the young man in the preceding example, so that he is moving screen left, like the young woman, and it will now feel like she is following in his path (Figure 4-21).

This feeling becomes even stronger if there are **shared landmarks** from shot to shot. For example, the young man passes by a park bench and then we cut to a shot of the young woman, walking in the same direction, and she eventually passes the same park bench. Now it's clear she is following along the same path. If you add a POV shot from her perspective, in which she watches the young man and then moves in the same direction, you will have created a sense that she is *intentionally* following him. Further, if you give him a POV shot, looking over his shoulder at her, before he flees screen left, you will create a sense that he *knows* he's being followed and he's trying to elude his pursuer. Now we have a genuine chase scene—someone is fleeing from another person who is in pursuit. The screen direction of pursuer and pursued must be the same in order to preserve the feeling of a chase, while passing common landmarks offers clear points of reference for the proximity of the two. The expectation of a viewer concerning chase scenes is that they are very dynamic sequences. For this reason, chase scenes, especially long ones, often use many neutral shots (and other axis-switching techniques) so that they can change screen direction at any time. Controlling screen direction can allow us to alternate between a close chase (same direction and landmarks) to one in which the pursuer is losing the trail (screen directions become scrambled and landmarks are no longer shared).

Parallel Action Sequence

Parallel action is a narrative technique that involves intercutting between two or more separate areas of action (or scenes) in such a way that the viewer assumes the scenes are occurring simultaneously. Parallel action involves **cross-cutting**, which is an editorial term meaning to alternate between two or more scenes. Parallel action is a powerful technique because it invites the viewer to draw thematic connections or make other kinds of comparisons between the areas of action. Just as we discussed earlier with shots in a

1. *A Classic Meeting Sequence.*

In the magnificent opening to Hitchcock's *Strangers on a Train* (1951), screen direction establishes the eventual meeting between Guy (Farley Granger) and Bruno (Robert Walker) by showing shots of their feet as the men make their way to a train (Figure 4-22). In a display of typical Hitchcockian formalism, a shot of converging train tracks (frame E) foreshadows the course their lives are about to take.

2. *A Classic Chase Sequence.*

The famous "man vs. moped in the subway" (Figure 4-23) chase scene from Jean-Jacques

■ **Figure 4-22** Guy consistently moves toward screen right (frames A, C, F, and H) while Bruno moves toward screen left (frames B, D, and G).

Beineix's *Diva* (1981) uses many of the principles we've discussed above, including:

(A) Maintaining screen direction and shared landmarks between the shots of the chaser, a Parisian cop, and the chasee, Jules (note the poster on the subway wall).

(B) A neutral shot, (B, left) to switch screen direction.

(C) Changing screen direction within a single shot.

(D) Toward the end of the chase the two characters are placed within the same frame to give us the sense that the cop is closing in on Jules and will catch him.

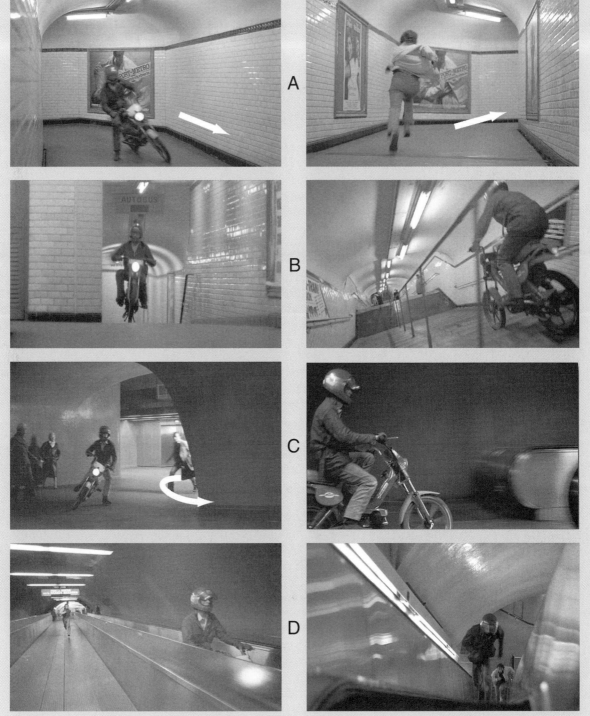

■ **Figure 4-23** These frames represent only one small segment of the extensive "man vs. moped" chase sequence from Jean-Jacques Beineix's *Diva* (1981).

sequence, by juxtaposing the events of two or more scenes a film suggests more than the meaning of each scene individually, because the actions of one area inflect the actions of another area. In order to maximize the substantial potential of parallel action, it must be anticipated *before* shooting, and certainly long before editing, when and where the inter-cutting will occur. An effective parallel action sequence is devised in preproduction, followed through in the shooting stage, and constructed in editing.

The power of parallel action is not realized simply by intercutting areas of action willy-nilly, but by the specific moments, action, and objects, which are linked through the editing. This is what gives an audience the sense that these separate actions are happening simultaneously *and* that encourages intellectual or thematic comparisons as well. Here are five common ways to create provocative links in your parallel action sequences:

1. *Dramatic structure matches:* Intercutting on dramatic narrative beats, meaning that we alternate between the beginnings (intro), middles (development), and ends (result) of each area of action in the sequence.
2. *Content and activity matches:* Cutting on similar activities or details that have different particulars encourages the audience to make direct comparisons between each scene.
3. *Matched action cuts:* We can make very strong associations, along with smooth editing transitions, between the different areas of action by using the matched action cutting technique. As discussed earlier, this would involve a continuity edit that matches the gesture in one area of action to the same action, but performed by a different person, in another location. The second shot is the completion of a gesture from the first shot.
4. *Graphic matches:* We can create strong aesthetic associations from area to area through formal visual links, like matching color, shape, objects, frame compositions, camera or subject movement, etc. Graphic matches also make for smooth editing.
5. *Sound bridges:* Finally, audio can create a bridge between various areas of action. The obvious example would be score music that continues under all of the intercut scenes, but shared sounds within each scene, or dialogue, can also be used as edit points and/or points of comparison and contrast.

Let's look at each juxtaposition technique one-by-one as they are used in two very different films: *Mama, There's a Man in Your Bed,* by Coline Serreau (1989) and *The Godfather,* by Francis Ford Coppola (1972). The French film, *Mama, There's a Man in Your Bed* opens with a parallel action sequence which cross-cuts between the morning routines of two Parisian families: the wealthy white family of executive Romuald Blindet and the struggling, African immigrant family of cleaning-woman Juliette Bonaventure. (**Figure 4-24**). By using both dramatic structure matches and content/activity matches to move back and forth between the same morning activities of each family (i.e., waking, cleaning, eating, leaving), Serreau is able to quickly and vividly reveal the stark contrast in economic status between these two families, raising the issue as a central theme in the movie. In addition, by using parallel action, the filmmaker is able to anticipate the improbable but inevitable entanglement between these two families, who appear to have very little in common.

Dramatic Structure Matches

The narrative events of the sequence in **Figure 4-24** are duplicated within each area of action, Romuald and Juliette's apartments. Each sequence begins with one of the mothers getting out of bed and waking up their children, who then get ready for the day in their respective bathrooms. Next, each of the women prepares breakfast. They then each see their families off to school, and work, and finally they both return to bed. Each of these specific phases is deliberately and carefully paired. This approach not only maintains the sense of linear progression in each of the narrative lines, but also strongly implies the simultaneity of actions. It feels like the activity of each household is happening on the very same morning and at the very same hour.

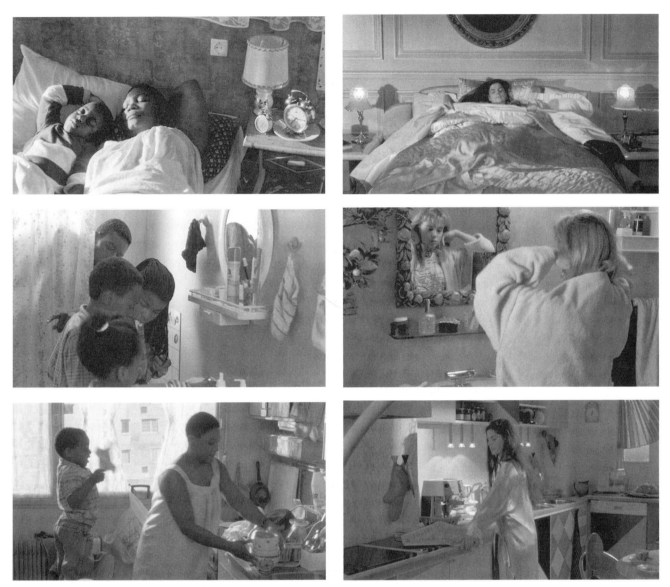

■ **Figure 4-24** Efficiently illustrative and thematic juxtapositions through parallel action open the film *Mama, There's a Man in Your Bed,* by Coline Serreau (1989).

Content and Activity Matches

Because the morning rituals of each family are essentially the same, their juxtaposition encourages us to see the telling differences in their details. At Romuald's apartment, the mother must walk down long corridors in order to get to each of her children's separate rooms. In addition, each child has their own bathroom and brushes their teeth at their own private sink. This is juxtaposed with Juliette's apartment, where she enters her children's one single bedroom, just off her own, and simply claps her hands to wake up all six kids. Teeth brushing time at Juliette's apartment means five children crowded around one tiny sink to brush their teeth while the sixth is showering just behind them in the same bathroom. Simply witnessing the specific conditions of their respective morning routines back-to-back provides all of the evidence necessary to drive home the point that there is enormous economic disparity here. Add to this that Romuald and his children step into a waiting limousine while Juliette's children wait for the bus. By the end of the sequence, when the two mothers return to bed, we understand that Romuald's wife does so because she can afford the luxury (she has a maid who cleans the kitchen), while Juliette does so out of necessity—she is a cleaning woman who works the graveyard shift.

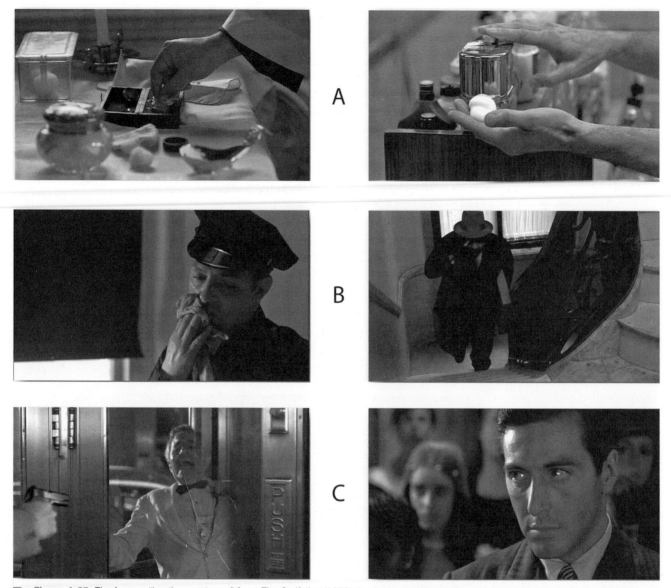

■ **Figure 4-25** The famous "baptism sequence" from *The Godfather* (1972) develops more than six lines of action simultaneously through exemplary parallel action technique.

The justly celebrated "baptism sequence" from *The Godfather* is a masterpiece of parallel action technique. The overall idea behind the parallel action is the harsh juxtaposition of the brutality of cold-blooded murder with the indoctrination of an innocent new life into the spiritual tradition of the church. These are the worlds that the lead character, Michael Corleone, straddles. He is literally both the Godfather to his sister's baby and the Godfather of his "family business." The sequence follows more than six (!) lines of action and utilizes every one of the techniques I have mentioned, both to maintain a sense of coherence and simultaneity and to create a strongly ironic context which reveals the hypocrisy and true brutal identity of the film's lead character, Michael Corleone. One can write an entire chapter on this scene alone, but here I'll just isolate the final three juxtaposition techniques mentioned on p. 78.

Matched Action Cuts and Graphic Matches
Throughout the baptism sequence Coppola sutures together areas of action through matching gestures, shot sizes, movements, and camera moves. Some of these are perfect continuity matched actions, like the cut on two different hit men wiping their sweaty brows (**B, Figure 4-25**). One man starts the gesture in a medium close-up and the other com-

pletes the gesture in a long shot. This creates a seamless edit and provides a strong sense of the simultaneity of action.

Other action juxtapositions have more thematic overtones to them, like the duplication of gestures and camera moves when the barber's hand brings shaving cream to the face of a mafia assassin (the face of evil), juxtaposed directly with the hand of the priest bringing the holy water to the face of the baby (the face of innocence) (A, Figure 4-25). These are not continuity matched action edits, but are formal, graphic matches on camera and subject movement and shot size.

Sound Bridges

Perhaps the most overt thematic bridges in this parallel action sequence occur through Coppola's use of sound to connect the holy baptism to the unholy murders. Michael Corleone's rejection of Satan during the baptism is directly juxtaposed with the savage killings of all his enemies (C, Figure 4-25). Additionally, the somber ecclesiastical organ music from the church is heard throughout the entire sequence, adding an ironic context to the revelation that Michael's allegiance to a life of virtue is, in fact, a lie.

■ STYLE OUTSIDE THE CONTINUITY SYSTEM

At this point in the history of filmmaking, many films do not adhere strictly to the established principles of temporal and spatial continuity from beginning to end. It's common for a filmmaker to deviate from the conventions from time to time to make an especially strong narrative point or to elevate one dramatic moment, like a film's climax, over other moments. In these heightened dramatic scenes the conventional rules go out the window in order to jolt the audience visually to make a more direct and visceral emotional connection. For example, Martin Scorsese's shooting and editing of the fight sequences in *Raging Bull,* especially the "Sugar Ray Robinson: Round 13" sequence, are significant stylistic departures from the rest of the film (see p. 397).

In the case of Fernando Meirelles' *The Constant Gardener* (2005), the moments which *do not* contain essential expository information are shot and edited with a very loose, disjunctive, and noncontinuity style, while the moments that include important verbal information (exposition) calm down considerably and adhere, more or less, to basic continuity principles (Figure 4-26).

It's important not to mistake fast editing or wild, handheld camera work with jump cuts or disjunctive editing. As you have seen, the continuity system is founded on two central precepts. The first is the invisibility of the edit, which is accomplished by maintaining a coherent sense of space, motion, and movement through principles like the 180° line of action, the 20mm/30° rule, and cutting on action. The second is the expectation to elimi-

■ **Figure 4-26** Meirelles' *The Constant Gardener* (2005) freely mixes standard continuity technique with scenes shot in a loose, discontinuous, jump-cut style. The scene in which Justin (Ralph Fiennes) meets Tessa (Rachel Weisz) (left) maintains spatial and temporal continuity, while the scene in which the couple make love for the first time (right) eschews these conventions.

nate extraneous time, action, and terrain through seamless elliptical edits. There are many techniques and aesthetic approaches to shooting and editing that challenge both of these assumptions. Two very common approaches are the intentional use of jump cuts and the long take technique.

The intentional use of jump cuts directly challenges the precept of invisible edits by tossing out concerns like the 180° line of action, the 20mm/30° rule, and/or matching action edits. The legendary French film director, Jean-Luc Godard, has often been credited as the innovator of this technique, and his film *A Bout de Souffle* is generally regarded as the first film to make extensive and aesthetic use of the intentional jump cut. Today the intentional jump (Figures 4-27 and 4-28) is a fairly common formal technique in narrative films used extensively by many filmmakers, including Wong Kar-Wai, Lars von Trier (in his DV movies), and Steven Soderbergh (esp. in *The Limey*). The key to using jump cuts is to utilize them as an *intentional technique,* a stylistic choice around which you plan and organize your shooting and which is fully integrated into the overall aesthetic approach of your project. There's a big difference between the intentional, aesthetic use of jump cuts and the accidental occurrence of jump cuts. One works and the other doesn't.

Another technique that challenges the traditional continuity system is the **long take** (Figure 4-29). The long take technique eschews editing altogether and allows the actions and relationships of an entire scene to develop within a single shot, in real time. These shots are often five, eight, or even ten minutes long! Consider that the average shot length in a conventional motion picture runs around two to six seconds, and you'll have a sense of what a radical aesthetic departure the long

■ **Figure 4-27** Lars von Trier uses jump cuts as an aesthetic device throughout *Dancer in the Dark* (2000) adding a directness, immediacy, and documentary feel to this DV film. The three frames shown here were taken from three consecutive shots.

■ **Figure 4-28** In Wong Kar-Wai's film *Happy Together* (1997) the consistent use of jump cuts throughout the film conveys the feeling of disquiet, displacement, and a pervasive loneliness that denies our protagonist, Lai Yiu-Fai (Tony Leung Ka Fai), any emotional equilibrium.

■ **Figure 4-29** The long take. In the remarkable last scene from Tsai's *Vive L'Amour* (1994) May (Yang Kuei-Mei) first tries to contain her tears, then cries inconsolably. Afterwards, she gathers herself and lights up a cigarette, but after a few moments is once again unable to contain her tears. This unbroken shot lasts a full 6 minutes, and makes the experience of watching May's pain unfold in real time utterly unforgettable.

take is. The irony is that the long take is actually the only technique which gives us true continuity of action, time, and space. Because one essentially never cuts into a master shot, there is no question about matching shot content or actions or spatial orientation. However, for that same reason we are not able to cut out extraneous actions, terrain, or time. This real-time unfolding of events gives the viewer a long time to ponder the image, and *this* is the power of the long take. The viewer is asked to look, think, and then consider again what it is they are seeing, as the film flows on in the real time of everyday life. They are also given the opportunity to choose for themselves what part of the scene to give their attention, rather than have the edit dictate what they should see and when. In the appropriate story, this immersion into a single perspective for a long unbroken period can communicate the feeling of truly being "in the moment" instead of witnessing an abbreviated construction of it, and this can be profound. Many filmmakers make extensive use of this technique, including Tsai Ming-Liang, Jim Jarmusch, and Gus Van Sant (especially in *Elephant*).

In the case of both the intentional jump cut and the long take, the filmmaker understands that the technique will call attention to the artifice of the filmmaking process. Making the process visible, rather than invisible, makes the audience aware that they are watching a movie, a fiction made by people and machines, and this can encourage active viewing, rather than passive reception. Both techniques, among many other alternative approaches to filmmaking, encourage a viewer not only to *feel* but also to *think*.

From Screenplay to Visual Plan

Tell me and I will forget.
Show me and I will remember.
Involve me and I will understand.

Chinese Proverb

Now that you're acquainted with the fundamental aesthetic and conceptual principles of the cinematic language, you're ready to transform a written screenplay into a story, told in images and sound, which plays out across a screen. This transformation is the heart and soul of filmmaking, and the visualization process is where a director does the lion's share of their creative work. However, this is also the beginning of the nitty-gritty logistical work necessary for you to have a successful production period, so a filmmaker needs to wear two hats at this stage: the creative, visual storyteller and the foreman of a production team who has a movie to construct.

Novice filmmakers tend to rush or overlook pre-visualization, but this is precisely the stage which, if done thoroughly and correctly, can ensure a successful production. When it is done right, a filmmaker goes onto the film set knowing what they will shoot, what it should look like, and what everyone must do in order to achieve the unified vision of the film. Knowing your visual approach beforehand allows for two things. First, it makes the production process, the most expensive and stressful stage of making a film, much more efficient and calm. Second, because you are clear about what you are striving for aesthetically, you can more easily respond to the unexpected, adjust visual elements, and improvise on the set.

"[W]e basically make the movie before we even walk on the set. I mean she and I know so well what we want to accomplish and what we want to do that we know what the shots are. We know what we're going to do before we even get there. This kind of collaborative planning, instead of a one-sided approach, is what enables the flexibility on the set, the opportunity to make changes as the need arises," she says. "People who don't plan get themselves so worked up when they actually get to the location that they're so frantic to get something in the can that they're out of their minds . . ."
Ellen Kuras (cinematographer) on preproduction with director Rebecca Miller
(From *Taking the Digital Medium Into Their Own Hands*, by Philippa Bourke)

There are three tools that we use to pre-visualize our film: the shooting script, overheads, and storyboards. We use these tools simultaneously to help us "see" our film and devise the visual and practical strategy that will make the script come alive and the film shoot progress smoothly.

■ THREE TOOLS FOR PRE-VISUALIZATION

The Shooting Script

The ultimate goal of the visualization process is the realization of a shooting script. The **shooting script** expresses the director's visual strategy for every scene in the film. It shows you what shots are used to cover a scene and in how they connect together as an edited scene. Camera angles, shot sizes, and camera moves are marked right on the script itself. Not only does the shooting script clearly communicate the director's aesthetic approach, it also shows, at a glance, many practical and technical details, especially the coverage required for each scene. From the details in the shooting script, you will then devise the logistical strategy for your shoot—the organization of the order in which scenes will be shot. Considerable time, effort, collaboration, and creative attention are required at this stage, because the shooting script functions as both the creative and the technical blueprint for the entire shoot.

Creating the Marked/Shooting Script

1. The first step in creating a shooting script is to number each scene in the script sequentially by placing the scene number in the left margin next to each scene heading.

2. Next, indicate how every action and line of dialogue will be covered by **marking the script** (also called **line-up**), which means drawing a vertical line through the action and/or dialogue covered by a specific shot. The line represents the anticipated duration of the take—where the camera starts rolling and stops (which is always longer than the anticipated edited shot). Each line is labeled with the broad details of the desired shot (i.e., CU or MS PAN WITH or MLS, etc.). When you have finished marking a script, you should be able to see at a glance the anticipated coverage for each scene and if you've inadvertently left any actions or dialogue uncovered by a shot. Keep in mind that some actions may be covered more than one time (drawn through with multiple vertical lines), allowing for options in the editing room. Also, keep in mind that actions on which you anticipate editing should be duplicated in each camera take to allow for a matched action edit. For example, for the two shots in **Figure 4-1** (p. 56) we would duplicate the pawn move in the LS and the MCU (see also p. 62). This concept is known as **action overlapping**.

3. Finally, give every shot a letter identifier. Shots are labeled in alphabetical order beginning with (a) in every scene. Each new scene begins with (a) again. When you are done, every shot in every scene has a unique identification number and a basic shot description. For example, scene #1 will have shots 1a, 1b, 1c, etc., and scene #2 will have 2a, 2b, 2c, etc. This information will become very important when you organize your shot list and shooting schedule (see later, organization of a shoot).

I have devised an example of a **marked shooting script** (**Figure 5-1**) to illustrate how we visualize and indicate some of the cinematic concepts discussed in previous chapters: POV sequences, multiple 180° lines, and moving characters. The three scenes (#13, #14, #15) in the example are from the middle of an imaginary script. Every action and line of dialogue has been marked through and is covered by at least one shot, and every shot is now identified with a scene number and letter. Notice also that for the POV sequence in scene #13 (shots 13b and 13c), we have continued shot 13b right through shot 13c, even though we know there will be an edit from the looking shot to the POV shot. It doesn't make practical sense to separate the looking and reaction shots into two different takes when we can easily shoot the entire action and then cut in the POV shot later.

For short films, the marked shooting script (as in **Figure 5-1**) is certainly all you need to take your film into production. The marked script suffices as your shooting script. Feature films, however, often go through an additional process of rewriting the script to incorporate the shot information into the body of the screenplay itself, in order to create a shooting script. Here is an example:

13. INT. JAKE'S STUDIO APARTMENT – DAY

ANGLE ON DOOR (MLS): Jake rushes in, slams the door behind him, and bolts toward a window in the back of the room.

ANGLE ON WINDOW (CU): He wipes sweat off his forehead as he carefully creates a gap in the blinds to peek outside.

POV LS: Through the gap he sees a black car pulling up to the curb. Two thugs, RALPH and MACKY, emerge from the car and make their way toward Jake's building.

BACK TO CU as Jake's eyes widen with panic and he immediately races toward the door.

ANGLE ON DOOR (MCU): At the door he stops and listens. Convinced that it's safe, he leaves the room, silently closing the door behind him.

On short films, this is an unnecessary, non-creative step. It's best to simply work from your marked screenplay, as it also gives you a more immediate picture of scene coverage.

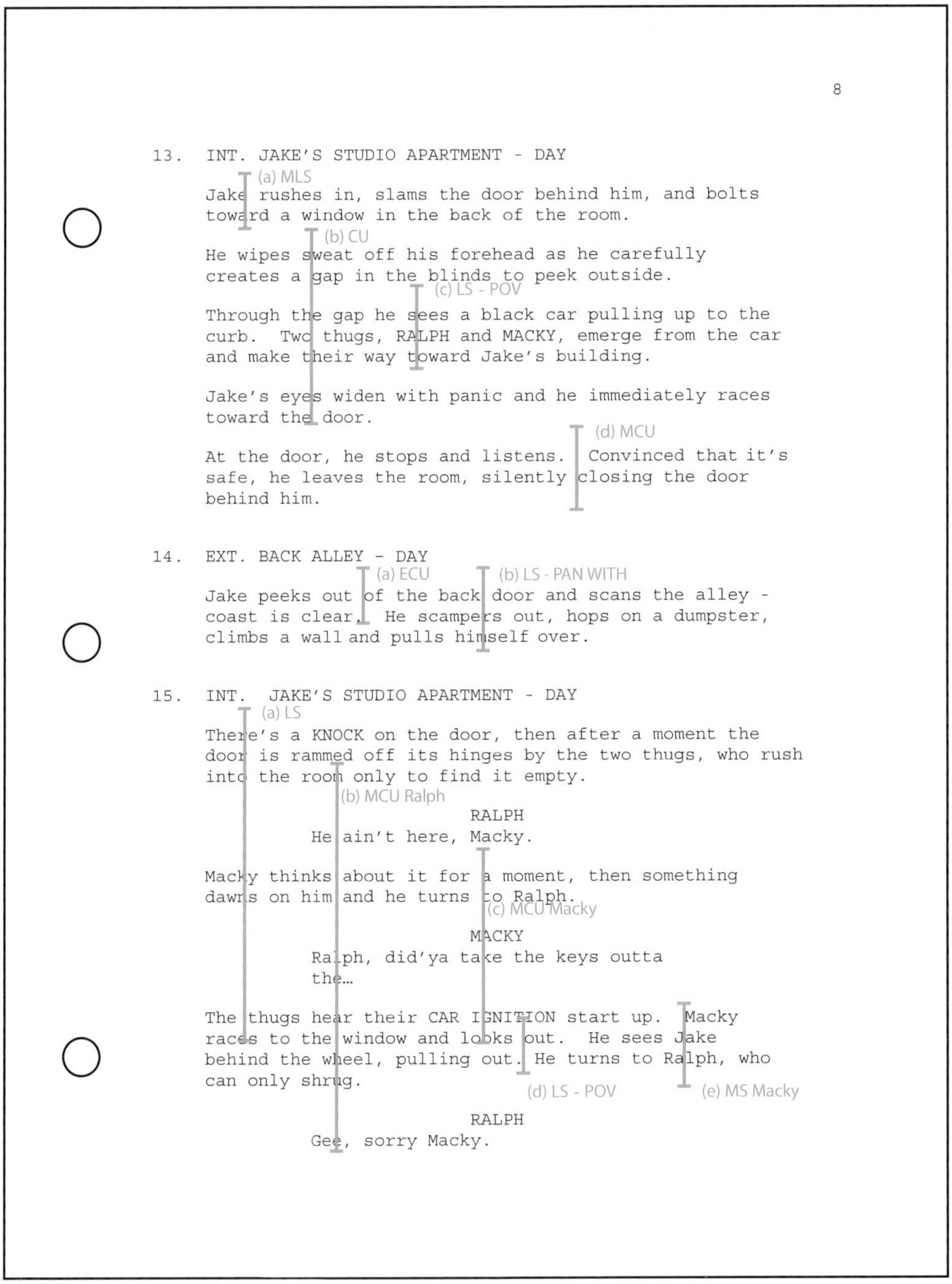

■ **Figure 5-1** Marked shooting script. By drawing vertical lines across dialogue and action on a script to indicate shot coverage, the director can visualize how they will shoot the film. Scenes must be numbered and individual shots identified with letters in descending order per each scene.

Overhead Diagrams

Overhead diagrams (Figure 5-2) are an essential pre-visualization tool worked out and used simultaneously with the development of the shooting script. Overheads are basically drawings of each scene from a bird's eye perspective; they help figure out important details like the axis of action, camera placement, and character **blocking** (the movement of your characters in the space). Overheads are one of the most efficient methods for

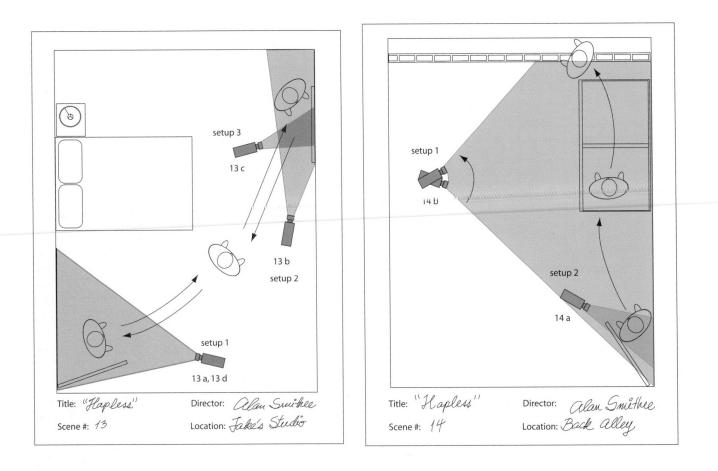

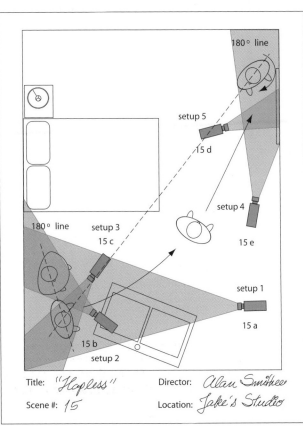

■ Figure 5-2 Overhead diagrams. Drawing simple bird's eye views of locations with camera positions and actor movement sketched in allows for the pre-visualization of scenes. Used in conjunction with a shooting script, this tool makes it possible to shoot footage out of sequence.

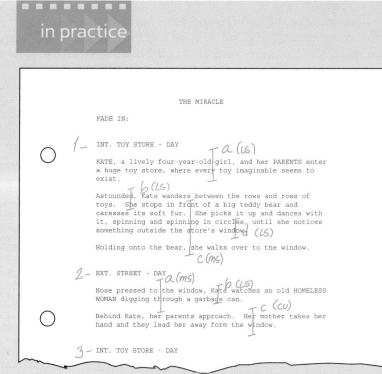

in practice

THE MIRACLE

FADE IN:

1— INT. TOY STORE - DAY

KATE, a lively four-year-old girl, and her PARENTS enter
a huge toy store, where every toy imaginable seems to
exist.

Astounded, Kate wanders between the rows and rows of
toys. She stops in front of a big teddy bear and
caresses its soft fur. She picks it up and dances with
it, spinning and spinning in circles, until she notices
something outside the store's window.

Holding onto the bear, she walks over to the window.

2— EXT. STREET - DAY

Nose pressed to the window, Kate watches an old HOMELESS
WOMAN digging through a garbage can.

Behind Kate, her parents approach. Her mother takes her
hand and they lead her away form the window.

3— INT. TOY STORE - DAY

Handwritten camera annotations: a (LS), b (LS), d (LS), c (MS); a (MS), b (LS), c (CU)

For his film *The Miracle* (also see script on pp. 32–33) George Racz managed to obtain permission to shoot in a famous toy store in New York City (scenes #1 and #2). But he was allowed only one hour (from 11 am to noon) to get all of the shots he needed. To save time, George scouted the location ten times before shooting day! He went alone and with his D.P. He imagined shots, actions, and character movements. He took copious notes and digital photos. He was aware of where all of the toys were and how many shoppers were usually there at that hour. Before production day arrived, he drew overheads of the toy store so that everyone on the set could see where the characters would be, how they would move in the space, and where the camera would be set-up for every shot. George had 12 setups to do in one hour, but he was so well prepared that he got what he needed on the first take, every shot.

One small note: although scene #3 also takes place at the toy store, this scene was in fact shot in a studio, since the real location wasn't necessary, and more time could be taken for lighting and shooting in a more controlled location.

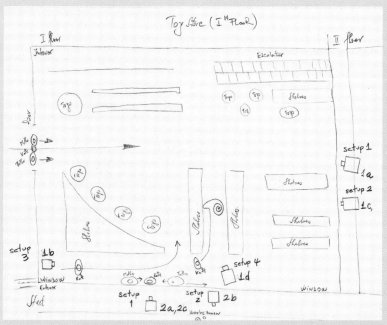
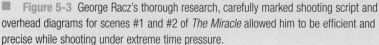

■ **Figure 5-3** George Racz's thorough research, carefully marked shooting script and overhead diagrams for scenes #1 and #2 of *The Miracle* allowed him to be efficient and precise while shooting under extreme time pressure.

figuring out where the camera goes for each shot and for communicating the visual breakdown of a scene to your crew. You may sketch and throw away many preliminary overheads as you work and rework a scene during pre-visualization, but in the end you should always generate polished overheads of your final scene strategy to accompany the shooting script on the set of your film.

Each camera symbol represents a **camera setup**, which is the physical placement of the camera on the set necessary to get each shot in your shooting script. The camera symbol on the overhead represents the approximate location, angle, and move of the camera. Notice the arrows in Figure 5-2 representing the pan in scene #14, shot b. Notice also that in scene #13 we have four shots covering the scene, but we have only three camera symbols. In practice, two shots will be taken from the same camera setup; the one angled on the door is the setup for both shots 13a and 13d. This idea of multiple shots taken from the same camera setup will be an important consideration in organizing your shoot (see later).

You may have also noticed that in order to make accurate overheads, you need to have some sense of the layout of your location, so it's important to do some location scouting ahead of time (see Chapter 6). If it's possible, overheads can also be developed during rehearsals with the actors as you work out the blocking of the scene. Also, if it's available, this can be done in the actual location, but often blocking is done in a mock-up location.

Storyboards

The third pre-visualization tool commonly used is storyboards (Figure 5-4). **Storyboards** are drawings of shots, arranged on paper in the order they appear in a sequence. Storyboards are always drawn in frames with the same aspect ratio as your camera frame. Written under each drawing is a description of the shot and the actions or lines of dialogue it covers (see Appendix 4-4 and 4-5).

Usually, each frame of a storyboard represents one central moment within a single shot; however, long moving shots, which include different framings, might be represented by a number of frames (Figure 5-5). The movement of characters within the shot is indicated with arrows inside the frame, while movement of the camera is indicated by arrows outside the frame.

Storyboards are the most direct way to see what your film will look like before you shoot it. There are several computer programs available to help you create storyboards, including Frame Forge 3D or Storyboard Artist, but hand drawing is still by far the preferred method, especially with short films produced on tight schedules.

It is by no means necessary to storyboard an entire film. In the professional world, storyboard use is quite idiosyncratic. Some people base their storyboards on the shooting script; other people do just the opposite by pre-visualizing with storyboards first and then transcribing the results into the shooting script. Some people create storyboards with detailed and intricate renderings of costumes, sets, facial expressions, and lighting, to establish the style of the film, while others use bare bones sketches to do nothing more than figure out shot size, screen direction, and sequencing. Some people use storyboards for every scene, while others use them only for sequences that involve an intricate interplay of movement, action, and composition in the editing. It is true, that once you get the hang of shot/reverse shot technique, you really don't need to storyboard these scenes; however, sequences that require tricky graphic or movement matches from shot to shot might require drawings.

It's Only on Paper, Not Written in Stone

Once you have completed pre-visualization, resulting in a marked shooting script, overheads, and perhaps storyboards, then you have, in fact, already made your first, fairly complete, visualized version of your film—on paper. You are ready to go into production because you know exactly what shots are needed to tell the story of your film. For some directors the production process is mostly the realization of the creative decisions they've made in preproduction. A look at Alfred Hitchcock's precise storyboards is evidence of his often-stated opinion that production is merely the manual labor of realizing the creative work done before the camera rolls. To be fair, however, this view of Hitchcock has been somewhat overstated. Hitchcock was indeed thorough and exacting with his preproduction, and usually followed his original ideas closely, but he would improvise from time to time on the set.[1] For most filmmakers, however, the pre-visualization pro-

---

[1]For a detailed and fascinating discussion of Alfred Hitchcock and his working method, read *Hitchcock at Work*, by Bill Kohn (Phaidon Press, 2003).

■ **Figure 5-4** Storyboards: scene #13. Storyboards are a useful tool to pre-visualize the composition and editing of a film. They usually depict a central moment of a shot, and include arrows to show actor movement and/or camera movement.

■ **Figure 5-5** Storyboards: scene #14. In the case of complex action or a moving camera, storyboards can include multiple views to make the framing more explicit.

cess is just the next step in the development of the visual strategy of the film. It's not uncommon for a director to rethink choices made in preproduction based on the energy of production: being in the real location, looking through the camera, interacting with the actors, seeing the lighting, negotiating logistical problems, and seeing how the movie is actually coming together. It's very common to hear a director on-set say things like, "Let's combine these three shots into one with a pan left and a tilt up" or "Lose the close-

Professional vs. Simple Storyboards

Although incredibly detailed storyboards can be helpful in illustrating the lighting, art direction, and set design of a film, even simple doodles can work as long as they convey a general idea of the framing of a shot. You don't need to be an expert draftsman to use storyboards. Rough sketches are equally helpful to guide your visualization of a sequence (Figure 5-6). George and his D.P., Tim, devised each shot in these storyboards in preparation for his toy store shoot (see In Practice, p. 89). He was only allowed one hour to shoot in the store, and would not be given a chance to return for reshoots, so he needed to be extra clear about what shots he needed and how these shots would hold together in the final edit.

■ **Figure 5-6** These beautiful storyboards for Alfred Hitchcock's *The Birds* (1963) (left) were created by artist Harold Michelson. But simple storyboards, like George Racz's sketches for scene #1 from *The Miracle* (right), are equally helpful in pre-visualization.

up and let's stay with the two shot; I prefer to keep the tension between the two of them in the same frame when he says that line" or "Look at those trees in the background! Instead of a medium close-up here, let's use a long shot to get them in the frame." This is the importance of having thorough and detailed pre-visualization. When you go onto a set knowing exactly what you need to realize your movie, you actually gain for yourself the freedom and confidence to respond to the moment and improvise with your camera from time to time.

■ THE DIRECTOR AND PRE-VISUALIZING: A METHOD

Framing and editing determine the eye-path of the viewer. It might not be too much to say that what a film director really directs, is his audience's attention.

Alexander Mackendrick (From *On Filmmaking*)

Some people like to do it in the shower, some people like to do it lying in bed, others do it at their desks in the early hours of the morning when everyone else is asleep. Personally, I have always enjoyed doing it while jogging first thing in the morning: imagining how the film will unfold—shot for shot, moment by moment, and scene by scene. The ability to "see," in specific detail, how you want your film to play out in specific images and how sequences hold together to tell a story, is a skill a director must practice and cultivate.

In general, when we first approach a script we begin from the broadest aesthetic concerns and work toward the details. We also want to find an approach that supports the ideas and intentions of the script, rather than imposing a style regardless of the script content. Your job in the pre-visualization process is to find a visual style that will add something to what is on the page, not simply illustrate it and certainly not clash with or undermine it.

The Big Picture

First, consider the overall tone, mood, and pace of the film and determine a general visual strategy. Does the narrative suggest an energetic style involving many quick shots cut together, or is a contemplative pace, with long takes playing out over time, more appropriate? Would a fluid, moving camera feel right, or are highly composed and graphically complex static shots more revealing? What is the overall point of view of the film and how will the camera present this point of view? Will wide objective frames work better than tight, intimate angles, or vice versa? Remember, there is no universally "right" answer and no universally "better" approach. You need to find the style that works best with your specific story material and resources.

The Details

Next, working within your general aesthetic approach, look at each scene individually and determine how every scene and each moment in your film will be visualized, including shot compositions and sequence coverage. As you decide on shots, ask yourself three questions: What is this scene about/what really happens in this scene? Whose scene is this/ from whose point of view should this scene be presented? And finally, are there any important moments, actions, or details that need to stand out above everything else? Answering these questions (and working with overheads and storyboard sketches) will help you to determine specifically what shots and sequences will best convey the content of the scene. Then you'll note them directly on the shooting script, as we saw earlier in the "Creating the Marked/Shooting Script" section (p. 86).

For each shot, sequence, and scene, you are attempting to express a dramatic point through visual choices, so it's important to know what you want to express and then decide how you can best express it. For each moment, there may be several options to consider. Here is a simple example of visualizing a dramatic moment:

A young soldier is saying goodbye to his fiancée moments before he is to leave her to join his platoon on the front lines. We start with a MLS two shot as he says good-bye and they kiss for the last time before he leaves. Then, at the moment he walks out the door, leaving his fiancée alone, we are faced with a choice: which shot is best for this highly emotional moment? Where do we put the camera? Should you cut to a close-up of her face to show her distress and sadness, or do you cut to a wide shot and show her as a small, lonely figure within the emptiness of her surroundings? Again, there is never one "correct" answer, but often there is a "best choice" for what you want to express and for the stylistic unity of your project. This is an example of an emotion that must be conveyed through an image, but you will face similar questions with other details, like visually presenting physical tasks

in practice

Figure 5-7 provides an example of a carefully visualized scene in which the camera is the primary storyteller. In the following interview of Alfred Hitchcock (A.H.) by François Truffaut (from Truffaut's book, *Hitchcock*), Hitchcock discusses his carefully planned and considered shot strategy for a key scene in *Sabotage* (1936) and the role the camera plays in building the tension and revealing the inner thoughts and emotions of the characters. In the scene, where Verloc is "accidentally" killed by his own wife, there isn't one aspect of any shot that is taken for granted. Notice, too, how Hitchcock anticipated editing the sequence as well as the audience's reactions to each shot.

A.H.: We had a problem there. You see, to maintain the public's sympathy for Sylvia Sydney, [the actress playing Verloc's wife] her husband's death had to be accidental. And to bring this off, it was absolutely essential that the audience identify itself with Sylvia Sydney. Here we weren't trying to frighten anyone; we had to make the viewer feel like killing a man, and that's a good deal tougher.

This is the way I handled it. When Sylvia Sydney brings the vegetable platter to the table, the knife acts as a magnet; it's almost as if her hand, against her will, is compelled to grab it. The camera frames her hand, then her eyes, moving back and forth between the two until suddenly her look makes it clear that she's become aware of the potential meaning of that knife. At that moment, the camera moves [cuts] back to Verloc absently chewing his food as on any other day. Then we pan [cuts] back to the hand and the knife.

The wrong way to go about this scene would have been to have the heroine convey her inner feelings to the audience by her facial expressions. I'm against that. In real life, people's faces don't reveal what they think or feel. As a film director I must try to convey this woman's frame of mind to the audience by purely cinematic means.

When the camera is on Verloc, it pans [cuts] to the knife and then back again to his face. And we realize that he, too, has seen the knife and has suddenly become aware of what it may mean to him. Now the suspense between the two protagonists has been established, and the knife lies there between them.

Thanks to the camera, the public is now living the scene, and if that camera should suddenly become distant and

■ **Figure 5-7** The careful blocking of this scene from Hitchcock's *Sabotage* (1936) is designed to instill in the audience the fear that pushes Mrs. Verloc (Sylvia Sidney) to murder her own husband (Oskar Homolka).

objective, the tension that's created would be destroyed. Verloc stands up and walks around the table, moving straight toward the camera, so that the spectator in the theater gets the feeling that he must recoil to make way for him. Instinctively, the viewer should be pushing back slightly in his seat to allow Verloc to pass by. Afterward, the camera glides back to Sylvia Sydney, and then it focuses once more on the central object, that knife. And the scene culminates, as you know, with the killing.

F.T.: *The entire scene is utterly convincing! Someone else might have ruined*

the whole thing merely by changing angles when Verloc rises to his feet, and placing the camera at the back of the room for a full shot before going back to the close shot. The slightest mistake, like the sharp pulling back of the camera, would have dissipated all of that tension.

A.H.: *That would ruin the whole scene. Our primary function is to create an emotion and our second job is to sustain that emotion.*

(From *Hitchcock,* by François Truffaut, Simon & Schuster, 1985)

in shots or sequences, or simply finding the right composition to match the scale and dynamism of an event or action. Thinking in visual terms like this allows the camera to become the storyteller—and that's what cinema is all about.

One conventional way to visualize a scene is to start wide, establishing shots (master shots), and then move in tighter (MCUs and CUs) when tension starts to mount. The tightest shots are reserved for the most climactic moments when seeing the emotional reaction of a character is vital. In the scene from *Sideways* in Chapter 4 (Figure 4-10) Alexander Payne starts with a LS (master shot) and moves in closer and closer as it becomes increasingly clear that Maya is interested in Miles. Toward the end of the scene the tight close-up on Miles shows us that he is both very attracted and very nervous. The subsequent ECU of Maya laying her hand on his is the climactic moment in the scene and puts the question to Miles: "What are you going to do Miles?" The next moment Miles balks and the shots become wider again. He blew it.

Even the Hitchcock sequence in Chapter 3 (Figure 3-5) uses this pattern. We start with ELS establishing shots of the location, then LS of the swimmer in the waves, and then a MLS of her washing ashore, and finally the sequence culminates in the close-up of the belt, which announces to us that there has been a murder.

This conventional pattern, however, is certainly not the only way you can visualize a scene. You could, for example start with tight shots to create a sense of mystery about where we are or who is in the scene and then broaden out to fully contextualize the scene and answer the mystery. For example, we could start our scene of the young man leaving his fiancée with a close-up of the weeping woman. The audience might wonder: Why is she crying? What's going on? Then pulling out to a wide shot and seeing her fiancée next to her in a soldier's uniform might be all an audience needs to see in order to understand her tears. He's been inducted! The choice is yours.

Back to The Big Picture

Just as a painter will step back to see how the small details are working within the broader canvas, you, too, need to step back from time to time to look at the overall picture as you visualize each individual scene. The transitions from scene to scene are especially important to consider. Your scenes may be visualized beautifully, but scenes are not totally distinct dramatic units. You need to look at the larger architecture of the film and determine how each scene will link with those on either side to create the overall shape and rhythm of the film.

For example, I had a student who was making a simple chase film. A tourist in New York City thinks he is being chased by two young hoodlums but discovers in the end that they were only trying to return his wallet, which he had dropped. The chase takes us through several areas of Central Park and mid-town Manhattan. This student carefully considered the larger shape of the film and decided that the pace of the film should speed up toward the end, in order for us to feel that the hoodlums were getting closer and closer. Each successive scene was constructed with increasingly quicker shots, more angles, and more dynamic frames than the previous one, to give us a sense of acceleration. The final sequence was done entirely handheld in order to reflect the main character's anxiety. This film was a success because the student did not think about each scene in isolation; rather, he imagined the film, and composed it, almost as a single, unbroken piece of music.

■ PRE-VISUALIZATION AND COLLABORATION

In the professional world, a director is lucky to be able to make one film every two or three years, but it is not unusual for a cinematographer to shoot two or three films every year. It's important to understand that a director is not alone in the pre-visualization process and that a smart director will draw on the experience and expertise of his crew. The creation of a shooting script, overheads, and storyboards is very often done in collaboration with the cinematographer. Cinematographers are trained to find visual solutions to narrative challenges, and this second set of eyes is invaluable. Cinematographers are also knowledgeable about practical techniques and technical capabilities (from film stocks to lenses), which the director might not know. Even on student shoots, where the director and cinematographer have equal experience, the pooling of knowledge and the additional perspective of the person who is responsible for lighting the scene, choosing the lenses, and using the camera can provide indispensable creative contributions (Figure 5-8).

During pre-visualization, it is also important to include someone from your team, like the producer, who is responsible for the practical and logistical aspects of your production. This person keeps an eye on the feasibility of the director's creative aspirations. They help the director stay within the practical parameters of the project, like how many shooting days there are, how big the crew is, what equipment is available, etc. To imagine dolly shots in every scene when you have a budget to rent a dolly for only one day is counterproductive. To cover a scene with twenty-five shots when you have only two hours at the location is futile. It's very common for an inexperienced director to get overly optimistic during pre-visualization and forget to check their exuberant and expansive creative vision against the realities of production resources. Once, as a student, I was the cinematographer on a project with a four-person crew. The director had many great ideas and some that were not so great. One idea was to send me up on the roof of a six-story building to get a handheld, subjective camera shot for a nightmare sequence. In one swift movement I was supposed to transport the camera from behind a chimney, along the roof tiles and hold it, suspended over the edge of the roof. "It'll be a great shot!" the director insisted. But the producer intervened, "Nope, can't be done." "Why?" the director asked. The producer replied calmly, "One, we don't have access to the roof and I doubt that the University will give it to us. Two, it's dangerous; Mick could fall and die. And three, if the Prof. sees on screen that we were dangling the

■ Figure 5-8 George, going over camera setups during a production meeting with his D.P., Tim, and his A.D., Kanako.

school's camera over the edge of a roof, we'll all lose our equipment privileges for the year." The director said, "Oh, yeah. You're right." and he came up with a different shot. I think it was the idea of losing equipment privileges that ultimately convinced him.

In the professional world there is no shortage of people who perform the role of "reality checker." The production manager, assistant director, and associate producer all function as overseers of the practical, financial, and logistical feasibility and progress of the film. On small crews this could be the producer or associate producer's role. On very small shoots (crew of three or four) a director might ask everyone during pre-visualization to help keep an eye out for the impractical and unachievable and to devise alternative solutions that are equally strong and creative, but more practical.

■ THE SHOT LIST: FROM VISUAL PLAN TO PRODUCTION PLAN

Once you have completed your pre-visualization (marked/shooting script, overheads, and storyboards) you should have a clear and specific idea of every shot you need to bring the script to the screen. Now you need to take the next step and transform your creative visual approach into a practical production plan. As we mentioned earlier, the scenes and shots in a film are rarely shot in the order in which they appear in the script or on the screen. Instead, actual shooting is organized to maximize efficiency of time and resources, which usually means shooting out of sequence. So, how do we know what to shoot first? What setup follows after that? How do we organize the order of our shooting to be most efficient? The answer to these questions lies in understanding how to create a tight shot list. A **shot list** is a list of all of the shots that make up the film *in the order in which they will be shot.* A shot list contains exactly the same shots as in your marked scripted, but they have been rearranged according to the practical and logistical considerations of the production process. With a good shot list the entire crew knows, at a glance, what shot they need to set up for at any time.

Creating a Shot List

The shot list is usually created by the director and the production manager (or associate producer). The shot list is the first step in the larger task of scheduling the production, and the principal factor in organizing the shot list is efficiency. The considerations determining the organization of our shots, in more-or-less descending order of importance, are major location (and time of day), camera setup angle, shot size, on-set logistics, and pick-ups. Additionally, there may be some exceptional considerations that might determine when certain shots must be scheduled.

1. *Location and time of day.*

   The first and broadest organizing principle for order of shots concerns location and time of day. In general, we organize our shooting schedule so that we shoot all scenes occurring in the same location together, regardless of where they appear in the script. For example, if we have a script with four scenes in a restaurant kitchen; one in the beginning, two in the middle of the film, and one at the end, we will, nonetheless, group all of these scenes together and shoot them back-to-back. This way, we minimize the number of times we need to travel to a location and set up lights, camera, sound, etc. Imagine the waste of time if we were to shoot the first kitchen scene, then strike the set to go shoot the next scene somewhere else, and then return to the kitchen location another day and set up all over again.

   In the shooting script example discussed earlier (see also Figure 5-1) we would schedule the alley scene first and then shoot both of the INT. JAKE'S APARTMENT - DAY scenes back-to-back. If it rains on the day of our alley shoot, we will simply move to the apartment scenes and hope that by the time we're finished shooting the weather will have taken a turn for the better.

   For scenes that use natural light, day or night becomes a significant organizing detail. We would cluster all EXT. CENTRAL PARK - DAY scenes together and then shoot all EXT. CENTRAL PARK - NIGHT scenes at another time, regardless of where they occur in the script. Also, in general, we try to shoot all of our exterior scenes first, taking advantage of fair weather when we can, but have an interior scene ready to go as a backup should the weather turn inclement. An interior scene that can be used in case your exterior shoot is cancelled because of bad weather is called a **cover-set**. By scheduling exteriors first, we have our interiors as backups and we waste less time. But if we shoot all of our interiors first, then, when bad weather strikes, all we can do is postpone.

2. *Camera setup angle.*

   As we mentioned earlier, a **camera setup** is the physical placement of the camera for each shot in the marked/shooting script. Once a camera is placed and the shot is framed, a great deal of production time is spent dressing the scene with set pieces and props, lighting that area, and wiring it for sound. Because of this, we cluster all shots with similar setups together on the shot list. This way we move the camera, position the lights and microphones, etc. fewer times. In the shooting script in **Figure 5-1**, scene #13 has two shots taken from the camera angle on the door: shot 13a (Jake entering) and shot 13d (Jake leaving). Even though there are several shots between these two shots, we will take these two shots back-to-back so that we set up the camera, lights, sound, etc. for the angle on the door only once for both shots.

3. *Shot size.*

   Generally speaking, we further organize our shooting to go from wide shots to close-ups. For example, we would shoot master scene two shots, before we shoot the close-up reverse shots in a two-person interaction. We do this for several reasons. First, the master scene generally covers more of the script and requires more set attention, lighting, etc. If we run out of time and have to abandon a shot, it's usually easier to reshoot a close-up later, or even do without it. Keep in mind that many close-ups require fewer cast on camera, so you'd also need to call back fewer people to reshoot a close-up. And, it's much easier to begin with the broadest lighting setup and slightly adjust lights as you move in closer, than it would be to light a close-up and then have to relight the entire scene for a wider shot.

4. *On-set logistics.*

   On-set logistics is where common sense comes into play. It is especially important to avoid keeping your cast and crew waiting needlessly until you get around to their shots. For example, if we have a scene in which a teacher is lecturing to a class of twenty-five students and we plan to cut back and forth between the teacher at the chalkboard and the class taking notes, we would shoot all shots that include the class first (i.e., master shot of class with teacher and the reverse shots of the class). Then we can let the class go home—preferably before lunchtime to save on our food budget!—and shoot the reverse shots of the teacher without the twenty-five people on the set. In the script example (**Figure 5-1**), we don't need to have Jake on the set in order to film shot 13c, the POV shot out the window. We could easily shoot 13c at a different time (or different day) when we have Ralph and Macky on the set for their own scenes.

5. *Pick-up shots.*

   Pick-ups are shots that don't require any actors to be present; pick-ups include shots of landscapes, location-establishing shots, and shots of objects and cutaways (i.e., a looking shot of a clock). Often these shots require only a skeleton crew, so it's not uncommon to have a small crew "pick up" these shots while everyone else goes home. Why keep a sound recordist on the set while you shoot cutaways that require no synchronized sound? Why shoot a close-up of a still life while an actor waits around for her scene to come up?

6. *Exceptional considerations.*

   Every now and then you'll have no choice but to organize your schedule around exceptional considerations. I once made a film in which I needed a police cruiser. The township where I was shooting was willing to let me use a police car for free, but only for forty-five minutes beginning at 5 pm. There was no alternative but to shoot the entire scene (several shots) involving the police car at that exact time—despite the inconvenience. Much of my shot list for that day revolved around this one extenuating circumstance. Actors' schedules, location and prop availability, and equipment availability can all force you to stray from your ideally efficient shot list schedule. In these cases, you just roll with it and do what you need to do—but keep the rest of your scheduling as we have already discussed so that you remain as efficient as possible.

One other special circumstance to consider is directorial and performance approach. There may be times when a director needs to preserve the momentum of the cast's creative and interpretive energy by shooting a scene more or less in order. It may be inefficient, but if you get better performances from sequential shooting, then it is worth the trade-off. This is especially a factor when dealing with nonactors or actors not familiar with single camera style shooting.

Given these six guidelines, the shot list for the three scenes in Figure 5-1 (#13, #14, #15) would look something like the list in Figure 5-9.

```
            SHOT LIST FOR SCENE 14 - EXT. BACK ALLEY -DAY


            SETUP 1: Angle on Dumpster

            1) #14b LS and pan with Jake as he scans the alley and climbs
               on the dumpster, to then jump over the brick wall.

            2) #14a ECU of Jake as he scans the alley through a half-open
               door.


            SHOT LIST FOR SCENE 13 - INT. JAKE'S APARTMENT

            SETUP 1: Angle on Door

            1) #13a MLS when Jake rushes in and slight pan with to father's
               portrait.  Jake exits frame right.

            2) #13d MCU enters frame right and exits out the door.

            SETUP 2: Angle on Window

            3) #13b CU on Jake as he looks, sees, and reacts to car.  Jake
               enters and leaves screen left (if there is time get ECU of
               eyes from the same angle?).

            SETUP 3: Angle on Street through Window (shoot on day we have
               car and thugs)

            4) #13c LS POV.  Show hands opening blinds only.  Car enters
               screen right, parks, and thugs get out.  Close blinds before
               thugs are out of sight.


            SHOT LIST FOR SCENE 15 - INT. JAKE'S APARTMENT

            SETUP 1: Angle on Door

            1) #15a LS two shot of Ralph and Mackie as they break the door
                down, all the way to them hearing their car take off.

            SETUP 2: Angle on Ralph

            2) #15b MCU on Ralph: "They ain't here...".

            SETUP 3: Angle on Mackie

            3) #15c MCU on Mackie as he questions Ralph about the keys.


                                        CONTINUED
```

■ **Figure 5-9** A shot list is a list of all of the shots for each scene listed in the order in which they will be shot.

Scheduling around Extenuating Circumstances

A friend and colleague of mine, Andrew Lund, shot his short film *Finders Keepers* (2006) on the beaches of North Carolina. In the movie there are several scenes that take place under a long pier. Weather during the month of the shooting was wildly variable, so for continuity's sake all of the pier scenes had to be shot on the same day. Additionally, Andrew had to carefully consult the online tide charts and weather reports to determine the exact minutes when he could get the framing he wanted, which included a shot from the ocean to the beach, with the water's edge in the foreground. As they say, "time and tide wait for no man," and you can see in Figure 5-10 that the margin of error was very narrow between getting the shot he wanted and having the shoot washed out.

Scheduling for Special Performance Considerations

Most of Andrew's earlier short film, *Snapshot* (2005), takes place in a much more controlled filming situation—two guys in one room. The drama unfolds around the kidnapping of a celebrated photographer by one of his subjects who is disgruntled about how he is portrayed in a widely reproduced photograph. Although it was not the most efficient use of time, Andrew chose to shoot the scenes in chronological order because he anticipated the real exhaustion of the actor, Henry Darrow, who portrays the photographer and who remains tied to a chair. The fact that his actor would truly be getting more and more fatigued (and anxious) as shooting progressed, Andrew felt, would add something to the scene. The extra shooting time to accommodate this performance strategy paid off. By the time they shot the ending, the lead actor was worn out and at the end of his rope, and the climactic scene contains a truly visceral sense of the frantic anxiety that only a man who has actually spent hours and hours bound to a chair can have.

Figure 5-10 Sometimes it is necessary to accommodate the shooting sequence around location considerations, such as the perfect depth of the tides under the perfect pier in Lund's *Finders Keepers* (2006, left), or around the consistency of a performance, such as the one achieved by Henry Darrow (right) in Lund's *Snapshot* (2005).

■ DAY-TO-DAY PRODUCTION SCHEDULING

As you can see, creating a shot list already anticipates the day-to-day film production scheduling because it divides the script into the smaller production units of location, time of day, angle, and setup. The next step is to schedule your production by dividing up the shot list tasks into specific production days and to generate call sheets. **Call sheets** (Figure 5-11) are simply sheets for each shooting day; they detail what portion of the script is being shot on a specific day, who needs to be on the set, when they need to be there, and how to get to the set (Appendix 4-6). Arrival times include setup times for the crew and makeup and rehearsal times for the cast.

PRODUCTION TITLE: BECOMING

SCENE # : ___17___

INT____ EXT __X__ DAY_____ NIGHT __X__

PAGE COUNT 1 7/8

CREW CALL SHEET SUMMARY

Crew Call

6:30 PM

Shoot Date: 8/18/2006		1		Principal Photography
Dept Title	Name		Phone	Call Time
Camera				
1st Camera Assistant	Tim			6:30 PM
Makeup/Hair				
2nd Makeup Artist	Daphne			7:30 PM
Production				
Producer	Nicole			6:30 PM
Director	Gustavo			6:30 PM
Script Supervisor	Jessica			6:30 PM
Production Designer	Kanako			6:30 PM
Set Ops				
Production Assistant	David			7:00 PM
Production Assistant	Alessandra			6:30 PM
Production Assistant	David			6:30 PM
Production Assistant	Rosa			6:30 PM
Production Assistant	Flonia			6:30 PM
Production Assistant	Megan			6:30 PM
Production Assistant	Taishon			6:30 PM
Sound				
Sound Mixer	Rommel			7:00 PM
Transportation				
Driver	Terry			5:00 PM

Notes: Meeting at the corner of 23rd Avenue and 88th street, Queens. Directions have been e-mailed to everyone. The forecast is: clear overnight, low in the mid 70's.

Producer: _____   Production Manager: _____   1st Asst. Director: _____

This report was created with Gorilla™

■ **Figure 5-11** Call sheets are printed for each shooting day and simply tell cast and crew when they are expected to be on the set.

On very simple shoots involving a crew of three and a cast of two, the "call sheet" might simply be an email to everyone involved. But on more elaborate shoots, it's good to hand the schedule out in hard copy form (and maybe follow up with emails). These days, filmmakers often create blogs or wikis for each project, to keep cast and crew informed of the shooting and rehearsal schedules by posting call sheets online and to discuss other production details. It's the duty of the production manager (and A.D.) to create the call sheets, to see that everyone gets them, and to make sure that the production stays on schedule.

Deciding how much (or how many script pages) you can do on a particular day depends on many factors: the amount of coverage, the style of shooting (e.g., moving cameras take longer to set up than do stationary cameras), the shooting environment (e.g., controlled interior set vs. uncontrolled exterior location), the size of the cast and crew, and the shooting style of the director. The more films you make, the more you will come to understand your own particular production pace and the better you will be able to predict how much you can get done in any given day. One general rule, however, is that it takes some time for a film crew to find its groove and work at maximum efficiency. For this reason, the first day is usually scheduled very lightly. It's a great morale booster for a film production to accomplish everything on the first day's schedule. Conversely, if you try to pack in too much on the first day, and you do not succeed, your crew will feel like they're already falling behind on day one, which can be a drag. But a light, accomplishable first day allows everyone to get to know each other, hit their stride, and fly for the rest of the project.

PART II PREPARING FOR PRODUCTION

Preparing for Production

■ LINE PRODUCING AND THE CREATIVE PROCESS

Making a narrative film, on any scale or in any format, is a multipronged effort. There is, of course, the creative dimension, which involves writing the script, visualizing the shots, working with actors, etc., and then there is the practical dimension of film production, which involves the organization of time and personnel, coordinating the locations, props, and costumes, dealing with film labs and other vendors, and working with budgets. We call these practical considerations the **line producing** or **production management** aspects of a film and we cannot make a movie without them. However, it is essential to remember that these practical tasks are not divorced from the creative element of making movies. Selecting your crew, casting your actors, finding locations, selecting props, scheduling shooting time, and working within a budget are all tasks that will have an impact on what a filmmaker can achieve creatively and what the audience will see on the screen.

How much is enough? For narrative films, our shooting days are the most precious hours of the entire project. A great deal of coordination must happen in order to get everything we need: actors, crew, equipment, and props on location, on time, and ready to go. It can be disastrous if something basic is forgotten or overlooked. Any film professor can list numerous film shoots that had to be scrapped because someone forgot a microphone battery, or no one secured the location, or no one thought to bring the film stock. Countless are the stories of actors getting hopelessly lost because no one gave them directions to the set, or no one checked to see if there was enough electricity for the lights, or there weren't enough crew members on the set to attend to all the technical duties required . . . and on and on. This is production management, and on every film set, someone must see to these details.

However, while many film projects fall apart because not enough attention or care was devoted to production management, the converse can also become a problem. Many films wind up feeling lifeless or mechanical because of an overemphasis on line production, to the exclusion of creative inspiration and exploration. It's not unusual for a producer and director to get so wrapped up in logistics, paperwork, and technical factors that important creative steps like visualization, rewriting, and working with the actors get only cursory attention. One must not let the practical side of filmmaking overwhelm the creative side.

Line producing run amok can also result in a film being "overproduced," which means that the line-producing elements and production technology take precedence over the creative aspects of the film—a good story, or vivid performances, or truly expressive camerawork. In some ways, it's easier to create a technically slick surface than it is to create a film with some depth, poignancy, and originality. In the absence of good ideas and creativity, money, big crews, and technological bells'n'whistles will not make a good film.

The creative side of filmmaking and the practical side of filmmaking remain in close dialogue for the duration of every film project, big or small. Balanced and proper attention as well as a healthy collaboration between the producer and director assure a successful process and satisfying project. Every film shoot, from the smallest to the largest, involves unforeseen challenges, extenuating circumstances, and unanticipated difficulties. In order to deal with these adequately, you must make sure that all of those production elements that you can control, plan, and prepare for are taken care of. The bottom line is that line producing is an essential part of filmmaking and it serves to support the creative efforts of the entire cast and crew.

Art Direction

Art direction is all too often overlooked in low-budget and student films. Many filmmakers just starting out recognize the importance of scriptwriting, directing actors, cinematography, and editing as essential creative elements, but often reduce the process of art direction (and sound, but we'll get to that later) to a purely utilitarian function. The art direction of a film, the look of the environment in which your scenes take place, and the choice and design of the objects and costumes employed in the film have a profound impact on the tone, the characterizations, and the meaning of your movie. I'm constantly amazed at students who take great pains choosing just the right film stock, filters, and lighting scheme to achieve a specific "look" but end up shooting in utterly bland locations, with no thought to the color of the walls, the arrangement of objects in the space, or the background beyond the performers. Recently a student of mine screened a film in which he got great performances in a scene involving two people playing a tense game of cards, but just behind the head of one of the characters was a huge, ugly air conditioner that dominated the shot. I asked the student why he had that thing so prominently in the frame, distracting us from the subtle eye contact during the card game. He answered, "Wow, I didn't even notice that." He hadn't noticed it because he shot in his own apartment where he has become used to everything. All he needed to think about was a little art direction and simply moved the card table a few feet to one side. Remember, the audience responds to everything that is in your frame—yes, obviously the audience sees the performances and camera angles, but they also see the background, the clothes people are wearing, the color of the walls, the kind of lighter a person uses to light their cigarette, and the air conditioner just behind the head of your lead character. Every detail the audience sees is part of the filmic world you are creating and therefore part of your expressive palette (Figure 6-1). We need to think carefully about what we want that location or costume to "say" and how we can use art direction to "say" just that. A "real" or unadorned location may look fine to the human eye, but on camera it might not read the way you intend.

Let's take at a scene shot in a dorm room as an example. A dorm room can look exactly like a prison cell or a cheap motel if the walls are bare cinder block and the room contains nothing more than a bed, a desk, and a garbage can. YOU may know it's a dorm room, but on film it's not so clear. Beyond this, not all dorm rooms are alike. What sort of dorm room does the script require? What sort of student inhabits this dorm room? How would they set up their room? Are they neat or are they slobs? What happens in this dorm room and how is the audience supposed to respond to it? The art director's job is to make sure that this location, in this case a dorm room, has the appropriate look for the film. Just as the cinematographer is responsible for the visual interpretation of the script in terms of lighting and camera work, the art director is responsible for the interpretation of the script in terms of locations, set dressing, costumes, and props. An art director doesn't simply hang a few posters on the wall and throw some dirty laundry on the floor; rather, it is their job to read the script, consult with the director, and imagine what this particular character would have in this specific dorm room—what objects, posters, details, and colors would support the character and the dramatic needs of the script.

■ **Figure 6-1** One glance at the stickers on the door of this neighbor in Hedges' *Pieces of April* (2003) is all we need to know about her convictions, an example of an inspired art direction choice that is both economical and effective.

Let's say our script is about Elise, a classical piano student at an elite music conservatory. The second scene shows Elise walking into her dorm room after expertly ripping through a Chopin polonaise for her professor. She opens her door and we see . . . ? If we were to create a dorm room for her in which there is nothing but a grand piano, piles of sheet music, and a futon wedged under the piano as a bed, we would get one impression of her. If she opens the door and we see a room covered floor to ceiling with rock posters, tie-dyed fabrics, beer bottles, candles, half-smoked cigarettes, and dirty laundry, we would get another impression entirely. A room filled with family photographs, Hello Kitty posters, and stuffed animals will reveal something different about your character than will a room filled with photographs of famous classical pianists and conductors through the ages.

We should also consider what Elise is wearing—her costumes, how she presents herself to the world. Is she in ripped jeans and a leather jacket? Or does she wear modest wool skirts with a coordinated sweater-set? And what about props, like her book bag? Is it a canvas backpack, customized with patches, key chains, and a big sticker? And what does the sticker say? Does it read, "Back Off 200 feet!" or does it say "Save the Planet"? Or maybe Elise carries her sheet music in an expensive designer alligator skin case? What if that designer case were then plastered with a huge "Outkast" bumper sticker? And that's just the second scene! Making these decisions so that your character and the story come alive through their surroundings and details is **art direction**.

Location Scouting

A great deal of art direction is done during preproduction so that everything is available, secured, and in place when the camera starts to roll. One of the first steps is finding your locations. Whether you're making a two-minute exercise or a feature film, you should never arrive at a location on a shooting day without first scouting and surveying that location ahead of time, or you will inevitably get some nasty surprises. Deciding where you want to shoot requires **location scouting**. This means visiting several location possibilities for each setting, to find the one that will work for your film. Here is a simple series of concerns, and questions you should ask as you scout each location to determine if it's right:

- *The Look:* The most important aspect of selecting a location is what it looks like—the physical space, architecture, backgrounds, light, colors, etc.—and what that look can contribute aesthetically to the film. Is the location appropriate for the action of the script? Does the location add to the overall emotional tone of the script and scene? Is this place aesthetically what you are after? If the answer to any of these questions is "NO," then don't waste time; move on and scout another location. If the answers to all of these questions are "YES," then continue on. . . .
- *The Access:* A location that looks perfect doesn't help you if you don't have access to it; this is the next step in determining if a location will work for you. Can you get access to that location? Can you get access to that location on the days and for the hours you need it? If there is rental money involved, can you afford it? If there are strings attached, do you really want to get involved in that way (i.e., you want to use your grandma's house, but she'll ask you to mow her lawn for one solid year in return)? If the answer to any of these questions is "NO," then don't waste time; move on and scout another location. If the answers to all of these questions are "YES," then continue on. . . .
- *The Logistics:* Another factor in determining if a location is workable for you has to do with its functionality as a film set. Is the location safe for people and equipment? Is there adequate natural light, or if you need to use artificial light, is there enough power and access to electricity? Is there enough space to contain your crew, equipment, and cast? Is it possible for everyone to get to the location? Are there bathrooms accessible? If the answer to any of these questions is "NO," then don't waste time; move on and scout a different location. If the answers to all of these questions are "YES," then you might have found your location, if you don't later find an even better one.
- *The Sound:* If your film involves synchronized sound recording, then you'll need to scout for the sound environment as well. Close your eyes and listen to the sounds that exist naturally in the environment (**ambient sound**). Do you hear noisy central air-conditioning motors, a barking dog next door, or kids on a nearby playground? Is

In Jonathan Demme's *Something Wild* (1986), Audrey presents herself as a quirky, offbeat, anything-goes Lower East Side denizen. Her costumes, jewelry, makeup, hair, and accessories, and even her car, are carefully selected to reveal these qualities to the audience (top, Figure 6-2). When her dangerous former boyfriend, Ray, breaks into her New York City apartment, we see that the decor perfectly matches the personality traits associated with her wild New York persona (middle). It is interesting to notice, however, how Audrey's costumes change over the course of the film as her character evolves from reckless and dominant to psychologically vulnerable. This is especially apparent when she is at her mother's house in the suburbs (bottom).

Making her very short first film with no dialogue, Alessandra Kast developed the differences between two characters by emphasizing their personal habits, their clothes, and their environment. One man is a "neat freak" and the other is a "sloppy mess." The art direction of their respective apartments (Figure 6-3) played a major role in defining their characters, which was essential to setting up the story and the lovely narrative twist at the end. As the neat freak walks along the streets, on his way to a job interview, he has several messy accidents, including bumping into a woman who spills coffee on his perfectly cleaned and pressed shirt and stepping in dog nuisance. Yet, in the end, he wins the job from the hiring manager, the messy slob, precisely because he isn't so perfectly neat and tidy, and the messy guy likes that.

◼ **Figure 6-2** Audrey's (Melanie Griffith) internal transformation is externalized through well-thought-out art direction choices in Demme's *Something Wild* (1986).

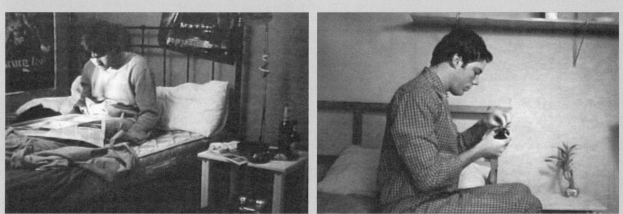

◼ **Figure 6-3** Purposeful art direction establishes the dichotomy between a neat freak and a sloppy mess in Alessandra Kast's short film *Paul and Steve* (2005).

there a highway nearby that creates a constant drone of traffic, or is the location under the flight path of an airport? Is the location quiet enough for you to record sound, or is the ambient noise at least appropriate for the scenes you're shooting? How controllable is the sound environment? How are the acoustics of the location? Does the space have a lot of echo? We will discuss ambient sound and acoustic recording environments in detail in Chapter 15, but if the sound environment is not conducive to location recording, then you should consider finding another location.

■ *Securing the Location:* Securing a location means making sure that you don't lose it between scouting and shooting and that you're not kicked out once you do start shooting. Public spaces often require a **location permit** for you to shoot. Every city has different requirements for obtaining a location permit, so it's best if you go to the City Hall or, if it's a larger city, the film and television office to find out the specific rules. Most places make it fairly simple for students to obtain shooting permits. In some cities there are fees involved; in other cities (like New York) it's free, but you must have production insurance and fill out the appropriate paperwork. I once scouted locations for a film in New Jersey and discovered that each township had completely different regulations for location permits. In one township they required only that you notify the Chief of Police, while the neighboring township required proof of a 2 million dollar liability insurance policy and $250,000 in an escrow account. It was clear that the latter township was discouraging film productions within its borders. To find out more about shooting permits in your area, simply call the local City Hall.

Do you really need a permit to shoot on the street? Think of a permit as a kind of production insurance. No one can stop your shoot or chase you off your location if you have one. In New York, especially in recent years, at least two-thirds of my students' projects got scrutinized by the police. Without a permit, they are often shut down, and this can be disastrous for a project timetable that allows for only three shooting days (Figure 6-4).

Shooting on private property often requires that you obtain either formal permission or a location contract. At the college where I teach, for instance, my students must obtain permission from the Office of Buildings & Grounds before they can shoot on campus. For locations like friend's houses, grocery stores, local restaurants, etc., it's always a good idea to have someone who is truly authorized to do so sign a location contract. (See the sample location contract in Appendix 5-2.) Basically, the location contract protects both parties involved. The filmmaker is protected because their shoot is secure and the owner of the property is protected because the contract releases them from any liability should someone get hurt during the shoot. The contract also usually states that the filmmaker is responsible for any damage to the property.

Whether you are shooting in a public or private space, you must securely establish, well in advance, the availability and reliability of all locations. It's a serious setback for a film when cast, crew, and equipment show up at a location, only to be kicked out.

■ Figure 6-4 Permit hell. Even Al Pacino's celebrity was no match for the NYPD officers asking to see a shooting permit, which he did not have. This real-life event was cleverly integrated into Pacino's innovative narrative/documentary hybrid film *Looking for Richard* (1996).

The Location Technical Survey

Once you have secured your location, you may need to revisit the location to do a thorough survey. A **location technical survey** means closely scrutinizing the location for its technical and aesthetic capabilities. For minor locations the scouting and survey can be done in one visit, but major locations, especially those which require expensive visual planning and lighting, need another visit dedicated to the survey. The director, D.P., and art director often go on location surveys together. If your scene involves extensive and critical sound recording in the field, then your sound recordist might also want to check the location for sound. Also, if your scene involves available light, is important to visit the location at the same time of day that you anticipate shooting.

Try to imagine what shots will work in the space. Think in terms of angles you would like to shoot from, and the size of your shots. Figure out roughly how much of the space will be visible. Is there movement in the shot? From where to where? What will be in the background? How many shots will you need in this location? Takes notes as visual ideas and impressions occur to you. Digital photos are extremely helpful for recalling location details or ideas for shot angles as you later visualize your screenplay or do rough blocking during rehearsals somewhere else.

After you have determined some rough ideas about where and how you'll shoot, the location starts to look more and more like a film set. A **film set** is a location that is being used, customized, and controlled to serve the needs of a film shoot. In order to establish the set you need to consider the following aesthetic and practical elements:

- *Light:* How much of the room will you need to light? Will you be mixing light sources? Research the distribution of the electricity in the location and make sure you know how much power is available.
- *Art Direction:* What does the setting look like in its unaltered state? What are the colors of the walls? What is on the walls? What are the furnishings? What is in the background of all of your imagined shots? And then, what art direction will you need? What will you need to add, remove, or change to make the space look the way you need it to look? Make sure you'll be allowed to do this. Of course, for low-budget films shooting on a tight schedule, it's best to find locations that need as little art direction as possible.
- *Sound:* If you are shooting sync sound at the location, then you'll need to pause a moment, be quiet, and take note of the natural sounds of the location. Are there any sound issues that might pose problems on the shoot? For example, is there a construction site across the street or a German Shepard next door that barks his head off? Get a sense for the aural ambience and acoustic qualities of the location. Is the space acoustically "live" or "dead"? (See Chapter 15.)
- *Other Concerns:* Make sure that there are bathrooms available. And inquire about getting food to the location. Are there food stores nearby? Make sure you know the "house rules," meaning the limits of manipulating the space. Are you allowed to move furniture around? Is there a white carpet that you must cover and protect? Are you allowed to paint a wall?

You will always run into surprises on the set, but the location survey should be thorough enough that those surprises are relatively minor.

Costumes and Props

As we saw with our example of Elise in discussing art direction, the choice of costumes and props is a powerful and efficient element in defining our character. We can't leave the selection to chance. It happens often that a young filmmaker will typecast a friend in a role, thinking that they look perfect for the part, and then assume that they'll arrive on the set dressed as they always are, say in ripped jeans and a baggy sports jersey. But as the day of the shoot approaches, this friend becomes self-conscious about being in front of the camera and arrives dressed the way he wants to be seen, in a suit and tie. When you ask why they're not wearing that sports jersey they've been wearing for the past two months, they'll invariably respond, "It's at my mom's being washed."

Student and independent films often plunder the wardrobes of their actors for suitable clothes. Why not? The clothes fit and the actor is comfortable in them. But you cannot assume that the right thing will be worn when the shooting day arrives. If you're using the actor's real clothes, you should go to their home before the shoot, carefully look over their wardrobe with them, and once you find what you need for the film, mark those items "COSTUMES." Either give the actor instructions to come to the set wearing those clothes or take the clothes away and hold them for the shoot.

Be careful of clothes that have logos on them. It's easy for us to overlook words and graphics on shirts, hats, or jackets, but they will read very strongly in film. If there are words on your costumes, make sure they're appropriate for the character and the scene. I once had a student whose film included a very serious scene of a couple on the verge of breaking up, having an intense argument. It was difficult for the audience to feel the tension of the scene because the actress was wearing a T-shirt which read "C is for Crunk!" I, myself, instead of listening to the argument, was trying to figure out what the heck a crunk is. When I asked the student why he chose that particularly distracting shirt, he replied, "That's all the actress brought with her." That was the very first film this student ever made and the very last time he'll overlook wardrobe considerations.

If you don't find the clothes you're looking for to really bring this character to life, then you'll need to get measurements and either buy, borrow, rent, or make the costume items you need. However, beware of slick costume tricks. I had a friend who needed a wedding dress for a scene. She bought an exquisite wedding dress on her credit card with the clever idea that she'd use it in the film, then return it within two weeks and get her money back. A great idea until the actress dragged the train, and the hem of the dress, through a puddle of Kool-Aid. I think my friend is currently renting that dress out as a costume to help pay off the credit card debt.

Props are those things that our characters actually handle in a scene. The first and most basic rule about props is that they have to be on the set when you need them. This is the sort of detail that can get lost in all of the activity of putting a film together. Someone needs to be assigned the specific responsibility of getting particular props to the set on the days the props need to be there. I recently asked a student why, in his film, he chose to have a burglar tie up the owner of the house with one of the thick orange extension cords from the school's lighting kit. "He was supposed to tie him up with duct tape," came the explanation, "but no one brought any." He glared at the project's production manager, who defended himself by saying "No one *told* me to bring duct tape!"

If your film is about two guys who mix up their identical briefcases, then you need to find identical briefcases and make sure they're on the set when you need them. If your film involves a guitar-playing Don Juan, then you need to get a guitar (with all its strings) on the set and make sure Romeo at least knows how to fake it enough that you can dub in some romantic guitar playing later. And remember, props are not only crucial to the action, as we saw with our example of Elise, the piano player; a prop can also be expressive of character (Figure 6-5).

It is well worth a little extra time to find just the right prop, just the right object that will reflect something about the character using it, or about the time period, or that will carry any other inflection you'd like in your film.

■ **Figure 6-5** Props are not neutral. By carefully selecting hand props you can reveal additional facets of your character. In this scene from Temple's "Rigoletto" segment in the omnibus film *Aria* (1987), film producer Preston (Buck Henry) stands at a urinal with Jake (Garry Kasper), a man who is having an affair with Preston's wife. The length of the men's respective cigars comically reveals other attributes, which are perhaps best left to the audience's imagination.

The Script Breakdown Sheet

The **script breakdown sheet** (Figure 6-6) is the form used in film production to keep track of all the mise-en-scène details that are necessary for each and every scene, including set dressing, hand props, costumes, makeup, and atmosphere (rain, fog, smoke, etc.). Every scene gets its own breakdown sheet so that everyone can see, at a glance, what details are necessary for every scene and so that the responsibility for acquiring it all can be assigned in an organized way.

The script breakdown sheet is usually generated by the A.D. or P.M., but since most of these details fall under the purview of the art department, the art director will usually carefully double-check the list, adding specific details that are part of the art director's interpretation of the scene. For example, an A.D. might not know specifically what posters will hang on the walls of a character's dorm room or what kind of book bag they'll carry, if it's not specifically mentioned in the script (see Appendix 4-3).

Figure 6-6 A script breakdown sheet.

Figure 6-6 A script breakdown sheet:

Scene #: **17**		Date: 8/18/2006
Script Page: 1	**BREAKDOWN SHEET**	Sheet: 1
Page Count: 1 7/8 pgs.	BECOMING	Int/Ext. EXT
		Day/Night: NIGHT

Scene Description: Anna and Sebastian get into car
Setting: DESERTED STREET
Location: FLUSHING PARK PROMENADE
Sequence: _____ Script Day: _____

Cast Members	**Set Dressing**	**Costumes**
1. ANNA	STREET SIGN "ONE WAY"	BLACK SKIRT (ANNA)
11. MAN	WET DOWN STREET AND PARKED CARS	FADED BLACK SHIRT (MAN)
6. OLD MAN		DIRTY SUIT (OLD MAN)
3. SEBASTIAN		VEST AND SUSPENDERS (SEB)

	Special Effects	**Vehicles**
	LITTLE SMOKE	PROP CAR (MIDSIZE)
Props	OCCASIONAL BREEZE	ROWS OF CARS
CRUMPLED PAPER BAG	LIGHT RAIN	
CLIPBOARD		
SMALL PIECE OF PAPER		
PEN		

Makeup	**Greenery**	**Special Equipment**
GLAMOUR MAKE UP		HOSE FOR RAIN
DROPLETS OF BLOOD		LADDER
		HOSE AND SPRINKLER

Mechanical FX	**Extras**	**Stunts**
	YOUNG MAN	

Page 1 — This report was created with Gorilla™

■ BUDGETING YOUR FILM

In many ways, the budget is, as they say, where the rubber meets the road. In a broad sense, **the budget** of a film is basically how much money (and other resources) one has available to make a movie. In a more specific sense, **budgeting** a movie means deciding what specific expenses you will incur and how your available funds will be distributed across the various needs of the project.

There are generally two ways of approaching your budget. One approach is to figure out how much money you have (or can reliably get) and devise the best film you can make with that amount. The other way to go about it is to write the script you want to produce, break it down, and find out how much it will cost to make that film. Then you go out and raise the necessary funds. The latter approach is common practice in the professional industry, but can be risky for a student filmmaker who needs to produce a movie in a few weeks for a grade. There are, of course, many strategies between these poles; for example, you can shoot your film with all of the resources you have, getting it "in the can," and then raise money later for postproduction expenses. In any case, it is essential, before you begin production on your movie, to know just how much it will cost you. Serious sticker shock awaits anyone who makes films on a spend-as-you-go basis. A detailed budget includes a price line for every single item or service that costs money, and will let you know how much your film will cost and where the money will go. It is not a good idea to be blindly optimistic about budgets and about how far a buck will stretch; it's always best to be bluntly realistic. As I mentioned in the very first chapter resources and ideas are inextricably linked so working up a budget often becomes an occasion for rewriting the script.

In student and independent productions many items ordinarily costing money are generally free or can be borrowed. When budgeting a film you must consider *all* of your resources, not just the available cash. For example, in school your production crew, being students themselves, work for free, and basic equipment is generally provided by the school. Facilities like editing rooms and rooms for auditions and rehearsals or screenings are very often provided by a college as well. Introductory and intermediate students also rarely pay actors or have a need for legal work requiring lawyers. But no school covers every expense of a simple film, so working up a budget is still essential (Figure 6-7). In the real world, when you're trying to raise money for a movie, every production company, grant-awarding agency, or investor will invariably ask to see not only the screenplay but also the budget for your movie, so it's a good idea to know what's involved and what it means to translate ideas into financial needs.

The major factors that go into working up an accurate budget are:
- Length of the film and shooting ratio
- Number of shooting days
- Workflow (acquisition and distribution formats and process)
- Equipment
- Supplies
- Facilities
- Personnel (cast and crew)

Obviously not every budget looks the same because not every film project has the same requirements. Figure 6-8 is an example of a budget for a typical short, introductory student movie shot on film.

Film Length and Shooting Ratio

The **shooting ratio** of a film is the amount of footage we shoot compared to the final running time of the movie. If we shoot a total of 20 minutes of film for a

■ **Figure 6-7** The preparation of a realistic budget must include all projected expenses. These students are using a camera and a tripod provided by their school, but the mini-jib necessary for a dramatic shot had to be rented at a cost of $65 per day.

5-minute movie, then we have a 4:1 shooting ratio. How does this happen? Let's say we have a scene in which our actor, sitting at a bar, finishes his beer, puts his coat on, and leaves. In the first take the actor chokes on the beer: "CUT!" In the second take he drinks the beer but then leaves without putting the coat on: "CUT!" In the third take the performance is fine, but the camera operator fails to pan with him as he leaves: "CUT!" The fourth take goes just as planned—beer, coat, pan; perfect: "Keeper!" One good take out of four. We have our shot and we've accumulated a shooting ratio of around 4:1 without much effort at all. Also, the amount of coverage you choose to do on a scene—

■ **Figure 6.8** A sample budget for a 5 minute project shot on film.

SHORT FILM BUDGET

Title: *The Cube and The Calendar*

Director: Jessica W.   D.P.:   Timothy T.   Production Mgr.:   Fannie M.

Length: 5 min	Shooting Ratio: 3:1	Shooting Days: 2

1) PRE - PRODUCTION BREAKDOWN:

Item / Service / Personnel	Unit price / rate	Cost:
Transportation (gasoline)	Allow	$ 25.00
Photocopying	5 copies of 5pp script @ $0.10/sheet	$ 2.50
Miscellaneous	1 @ $6/hr parking	$ 6.00
1) PRE – PRODUCTION SUB-TOTAL		$33.50

2) PRODUCTION BREAKDOWN:

Item / Service / Personnel	Unit price / rate	Cost:
SUPPLIES:		
Film Stock 1	6 100' rolls @ $20 ea. (w/student discount)	$120.00
Gels & Diffusion	6 sheet @ $6.00 ea.	$ 36.00
Misc. Production Supplies	(*e.g.* 2' gaffer tape @ $20.00/roll	$ 37.99
	1' camera tape @ $12.00/roll	
	C-47's @ $0.99/dozen	
	Sharpies @ $5.00/pack	
EQUIPMENT RENTAL:		
(Special Lens i.e., 8 mm)	1 (4x4) @ $50.00/day	$ 50.00
(Polarizing filter)	1 @ $10.00/day	$ 10.00
ART DEPARTMENT:		
Set dressing	1 lace curtain @ $9.99	$ 15.98
	1 "AutoBabes" wall calendar @ $5.99	
Props	1 "Rubix Cube" @ $12.99	$ 12.99
Wardrobe	1 Fez @ $9.99	$ 9.99
LOCATION EXPENSES:		
Transportation/Fuel	4 subway Metrocards @ $8.00/ea.	$ 32.00
Meals	8 lunches @ ~$7.50/each	$ 60.00
2) PRODUCTION SUBTOTAL		$384.95

3) POSTPRODUCTION BREAKDOWN:

Item / Service / Personnel	Unit price / rate	Cost:
LAB WORK		
Film Processing	600' @ $0.19/ft (incl. leader, prep & clean)	$114.00
DV dailies	One-lite 600' @ $0.19/ft	$114.00
Syncing Dailies		N/A
DV tape stock	5 mini DV @ $10 ea.	$ 50.00
FireWire Drive	(Provided)	N/A
DVD stock for copies	1 @ 30.00/ 25 pack	$ 30.00
3) POSTPRODUCTION SUBTOTAL		$308.00
TOTAL		$726.45
Contingency allowance 10%		$ 75.00
GRAND TOTAL:		**$801.45**

for example, shooting a scene from multiple angles to give yourself options in the editing—also increases the shooting ratio. Finally, the more technically complicated your film is (field sound recording, dynamic camera moves, multiple actors, multiple angles, etc.) the more things can go wrong during each take and the higher your shooting ratio is likely to be.

Estimating the shooting ratio is important in budgeting because it helps us calculate how much raw film or tape stock we need to purchase and how many feet of film stock will be processed by the lab and transferred to DV. Keep in mind that many lab services are billed by the foot. This is why movies shot on video enjoy larger shooting ratios; there is no laboratory charging them by the foot for processing!

Shooting Days

The number of shooting days you need for your project is important to calculate in order to arrive at accurate budget figures for things that are paid on a per day basis, including meals, transportation, equipment rentals, location rentals, and personnel who charge by the day. Again, it's best not to be overly optimistic about these figures. If your film will clearly take five days to shoot, then budget for five days. It would be penny-wise and pound foolish to try and cram a five-day shoot into three days.

Workflow and Budgeting

The choices you make concerning your acquisition format (film or digital video) and distribution format (film print, video, DVD, or Internet) have a significant impact on the budget of your project. While it is a mistake to believe that shooting on digital video is, across the board, cheaper than shooting on film (the 2006 Michael Mann film *Miami Vice* was shot on High Definition video at a budget estimated around 150 million bucks!), it is possible to produce very effective movies on digital video, with effects, dissolves, and complex sound tracks for very little money; however, making your movie on film (especially finishing on film) is almost always a costly endeavor because of the unavoidable involvement of a film lab for intermediate prints, transfers, effects, optical track masters, etc. Let's look at just the basic costs of shooting film and shooting digital video to the point of having footage ready to edit. A one-hour professional quality MiniDV tape runs around $8. When we are done shooting we are ready to download the footage into a nonlinear editing system and edit. Shooting one hour of film footage includes processing and transferring to DV tape by a film lab before we can capture our footage. The total cost for one hour of edit-ready film footage comes in around $1,135 per hour of footage. Similar calculations are made for the second

---

in practice ■ ■ ■ ■ ■ ■ ■ ■ ▶ ▶ ▶

The formula for calculating shooting ratios for 16mm film is: $(L \times R)36 = TF$.

"L" is the anticipated final length of your film, "R" is your ratio, 36 is the number of feet of film per minute of screen time at regular sync speed, and "TF" is total footage. So, an 8-minute film, shot on a ratio of 5:1 is calculated like this: $(8 \times 5)36 = 1,404$ feet. We must buy 1,404 feet of film to make our movie.

The cost of one 400-foot roll of Kodak Vision 16mm color negative film (around 11 minutes of footage) is approximately $105 after the 20% student discount.[1] Since we must buy four of these rolls, adding up to 1,600 feet of film (our necessary footage with a little cushion), the cost of our raw film stock will be $420. Then, we need to calculate the cost of processing this film and having the negative transferred to DV tape by a film lab. Both services are charged by the foot, around 21¢ per foot ($1,600' \times 0.21$), totaling roughly $295. So, the cost of film, processing and transferring, for an 8-minute film, shot on a 5:1 ratio, will be around $715. There it is, no surprises later.

[1]If you are a student, always ask for the student discount on anything you buy or rent for the film. You may be surprised at how many places will give you 10% – 20% off the list price.

half of the workflow equation. Do you plan to finished your movie on video or to make a film print? These different processes carry vastly different costs and are covered in detail in Chapter 19.

Facilities, Equipment, and Supplies

Cameras, lenses, lights, digital editing stations, audition rooms, and screening facilities are things that require rental fees, but, happily, schools usually provide students with the basic equipment and facilities necessary to make their films. However, there will be times when something you have planned or something you need for your film can't be accomplished or obtained through the school. Maybe you're shooting a scene through the windshield of a moving car and you need a hood mount for the camera and a polarizing filter to minimize the glare from the windshield. These are not items that schools usually provide, and so the items must be rented. If you need a specialty item, then you must find an equipment rental house near to you and check their catalog for rental prices. Often a catalog listing of resources and rental prices can be found online (Figure 6-9), which is extremely helpful in figuring your budget.

The cost of digital editing software, like Final Cut Pro or Avid DV Express, has come down so drastically in recent years (especially with the educational discounts) that many students, frustrated by the limited access at their school's communal editing facilities, simply put editing software in the budget of their first film, and then they have it for every subsequent project. They find the convenience of editing in their room worth the added expense.

Supplies are those expendable items that everyone needs on the set: gaffer's tape, extra batteries, diffusion paper, color gels, sharpie markers, etc. Take note, these items add up, so make sure you anticipate them in your budget.

Personnel (Cast and Crew)

On a professional film, the fees for cast and crew are significant. Some people on the team are paid a flat rate for the project if they've negotiated their fee in this way, but usually,

Figure 6-9 Some film equipment houses, like AbelCineTech, have their entire rental catalog online, making the preparation of a budget an easy task.

most production personnel are paid a day rate. On small-budget films, any of the principal production team members (e.g., director of photography, art director, sound recordist) can make anywhere between $75 and $1,200 per day. Student productions on the introductory and intermediate level, however, usually use fellow students on their production team, which works out well for both the student filmmaker's pocketbook and the teammates' film experience and education.

Hidden Costs

It's essential that you think very hard about any expense that will likely be part of the project. It's obvious that you have to budget for film stock and processing, but what about transportation costs for a crew who live in totally different areas, or the cost of cleaning up the house you used as a location, or the dry cleaning costs for the tuxedos you borrowed but must return cleaned and pressed? How about the "one-time setup fee" the lab charges you on certain services, or the late fee you had to pay because you returned the equipment late, or the $70 replacement cost for the 2,000-watt bulb that blew during your shoot? What if you're shooting a simple exercise and shoot and budget for only two hundred feet of film, but discover later that the lab has a "minimum service fee" (as many do) that is nearly double what you anticipated? There are a thousand places where hidden costs can sneak up on you. Most hidden costs occur because the filmmaker hasn't done thorough research, especially in the area of lab services, but a lot of budget overruns simply come from not accounting for the little stuff, which can really add up. However, you can never quite predict everything, and it's for this reason that many people figure in a 10% contingency allowance as a line item in the budget. This ensures that the money is at hand to cover any unforeseen expenses.

Professional film production budgets are incredibly long and elaborate documents generated by professional accountants. For the purposes of small, low-budget films we can do with a lot fewer details. The short film budget sheet in Appendix 4-1 and 4-2 should accommodate most introductory or intermediate student films. Keep in mind that you do not need to use every line item on the budget for every film and that you can add line items as you need them.

Figure 6-10 is another sample budget for typical low-budget short film shot on digital video.

Preproduction Paperwork

The key to a creatively successful shoot is organization and planning. Every film production, regardless of the size or budget, encounters extenuating circumstances, unforeseen challenges, and at least one brush with Murphy's Law. Being organized and prepared will ensure that you can meet these challenges without the whole project going under. Here are the preproduction forms we've discussed; these will help you get organized in preproduction and stay organized throughout the production process:

- Marked Shooting Script (pp. 86–87)
- Overhead Diagrams (pp. 87–90)
- Storyboards (pp. 90–92)
- Shot List (pp. 97–99)
- Scene Breakdowns (p. 112)
- Call Sheets (pp. 100–101)
- Budget (pp. 113–118)
- Contact Sheet (pp. 100–101)

■ **Figure 6-10** A sample budget for a 12 minute project shot on DV.

Sample budget for:
TWELVE MINUTE SHORT W /SOUND (shoot MiniDV)

Length: 12 min	Shooting Ratio: 10:1	Shooting Days: 6

1) PREPRODUCTION BREAKDOWN:

Item / Service / Personnel	Unit price / rate	Cost:
Advertising (casting)	1 @ $50.00/ad — 1 @ $25.00/ad	$75.00
Transportation (scouting)	3 roundtrips @ $2.00/subway ride	$12.00
Photocopying	6 copies of 12pp script @ $0.10/sheet	$7.20
Audition facility / equip.	Through College	0
Hospitality	20 refreshments/snacks @ $1.00/each	$20.00
Research	1 ~~prices fabric~~ @ $3.99/bottle	$4.99
Miscellaneous	1 MiniDV@$17.99/4pack (to record audition)*	$17.99.
1) PREPRODUCTION TOTAL		**$137.18**

2) PRODUCTION BREAKDOWN:

Item / Service / Personnel	Unit price / rate	Cost:
SUPPLIES:		
DV Tape Stock	4pack previously bought during pre-pro*	0
Batteries	1 @ $15.00/12pack (AA or AAA-for mics?)	$15.00
Gels & Diffusion	10 @ $6.00/sheet	$60.00
Misc. Production Supplies	(e.g., gaffer tape, replacement tubes, C47's, etc.)	Allow $50.00
EQUIPMENT RENTAL:		
Camera Support (dolly)	1 @ $40.00/day	$40.00
Misc. Camera Dept.	(polarizing filter)	$10.00
Microphones	2 mic. wireless lav. syst. pack. @ $400/week	$400.00
Lighting rental	(2 mini-flow kits) 2 @ $50.00/day (3day week)	$300.00
Misc. Lighting & Grip	(e.g., genny, ladder, dimmer, etc.)	Allow $75.00
ART DEPARTMENT:		
Set dressing	(average seminar type budget)	$200.00
Props	(average seminar type budget)	$250.00
Wardrobe	(seminar type budget) includ. renting tuxedo	$150.00
Miscellaneous	(e.g., make-up, dry cleaning, tailoring, etc.)	Allow $75.00
LOCATION EXPENSES:		
Location Rental	6 @ $50.00/day	$300.00
Van Rental	7 days @ 379.99/wk	$379.99
Transportation/fuel	7 @ $2.21/gal	$15.47
Meals	6 @ $55.00/day	$330.00
Location Stills	10 (36exp) 35mm @ $6.00/roll	$60.00
Miscellaneous	(e.g., trash bags, sunblock, cleaning supplies, etc.)	Allow $20.00
2) PRODUCTION TOTAL		**$2730.46**

3) POSTPRODUCTION BREAKDOWN:

Item / Service / Personnel	Unit price / rate	Cost:
FILM EDIT SUPPLIES & FACILITY:		
FireWire Drives (180 GB)	1 @ ~ $200.00	$200.00
Misc. edit supplies	(e.g., firewire cable, etc.)	$15.00
SOUND:		
Sound Mix Suite	4 @ ~$100/hr	$400.00
Recording Studio Rental	1 @ $300.00/flat rate	$300.00
FINISHING FILM OR VIDEO ORIG. TO VIDEO RELEASE		
Digital Mastering	2 @ $90.00/hr	$180.00
DVD copies	25 @ $2.25/each	$45.00
Packaging	25 cases & inserts @ $1.39/dup	$34.75
Miscellaneous		Allow $50.00
3) POSTPRODUCTION TOTAL		**$1224.75**
	TOTAL:	**$4092.39**

The Cast and Crew

■ THE PRODUCTION CREW

Narrative filmmaking on any scale is a collaborative art form requiring the effort and creative expertise of a team of people. The filmmaking team is the crew and the cast, and choosing the right group of people to pull off the movie you are envisioning is a task of paramount importance. When you build your production crew it is essential to remember that the size of the crew must fit the scale of the project; the size of your team must be adequate to pull off the film, but not so large that it becomes cumbersome. Short narrative films are typically produced with as few as three and as many as fifteen people. The more technical production tasks your project requires, the more people you need. Take the time to build a crew that you can trust and with whom you can collaborate, because your production crew is your creative team. Even in a case where you are assigned a crew in a class, you should take whatever steps are necessary to foster cooperation and a collaborative spirit.

Production Departments

Whether you're shooting on film or video, making a five-minute short or a feature film, or working with a big budget or miniscule resources—the core production tasks for all narrative motion pictures are essentially the same. All film crews are divided up into departments. A **production department** can involve one person or many people who are responsible for a circumscribed set of tasks. In the professional world, where production crews can be large, these tasks have become very narrowly defined and department teams are therefore staffed with many specialists. For example, on a big-budget feature film it's very common for there to be six or more people responsible for the cinematography and functioning of the camera alone (i.e., D.P., camera operator, 1st A.C., 2nd A.C., loader, Steadicam operator, video assist tech, camera P.A.—and then there is the second unit camera crew!). But if we consider the duties of the production departments *broadly* it will give us a good idea for the fundamental tasks on any narrative film of any scope and with any size crew.

- Someone must be responsible for the budgeting and the logistical coordination of the project (time, personnel, production resources). This is the **producing team**.
- Someone must be the definitive creative decision maker of the movie, the person who makes sure that everyone's efforts are working toward a common and expressive end. This is the **director**.
- Someone needs to be in charge of lighting and capturing the image on film or video. This is the **camera department**.
- Someone needs to acquire and manage the costumes and objects used by the actors in the film and to attend to the look of the physical space in which the movie takes place. This is the **art department**.
- Someone must be in charge of recording sound, if it's necessary. This is the **sound department**.
- Someone must appear on camera to perform the dramatic roles in the movie. This is **the talent**.

There is, of course, much more detail involved in the tasks of each department, but considering it in this general way can help you distribute the duties among smaller production teams, where people often need to perform multiple roles.

The Principal Production Crew: Creative Core

The **principal production team** includes those crew members with substantial responsibility and often direct creative input. These people are the heads of the various departments, and in the professional world these key positions are supported by technical teams with highly specific jobs. However, on short films, where budgets, technical demands, and production crews are much smaller, these people often work alone. For our purpose we'll look at the role of each position as it pertains to projects on the introductory and intermediate levels.

The Producing Team

The producer oversees the logistics of the film from preproduction to distribution, including personnel, scheduling, equipment, locations, and other production resources. The producing team makes sure that the project is accomplished on time and on budget. The producer is responsible for providing the director with a realistic assessment of the budget, including what resources are available and how they can be distributed across the various needs of the project. The producer then keeps a close eye on the expenditures of the film for the duration of the project. The producer also helps devise strategies to make maximum creative use of limited budgets. It's considered a high compliment to a producer for someone to say, "The producer made a $5,000 budget look like $50,000!" The producer selects their own support staff, including the production manager, and helps the director choose the rest of the production and postproduction team (Figure 7-1).

The **production manager** (P.M.; sometimes called the associate producer) is the producer's right hand during the production process. While the producer has the bird's-eye view of the project and organizes the big picture, the production manager is responsible for the day-to-day operations of the film set. They manage the master schedule, ensuring that everything and everyone necessary for each and every shooting day will actually be on the set, on time. The P.M.'s job is formidable. They coordinate people, props, equipment, transportation, food, and locations. In many ways the production manager is the linchpin for the entire, logistical effort of film production. The P.M. helps the director break down the script and is therefore acutely aware of the time, material, and personnel needs of the project. The P.M. then creates the shot list, shooting schedule, and breakdown sheets from the shooting script with the assistant director (see p. 112 for a breakdown sheet).

The Director and Assistant Director

The director is the creative driving force of a film project. The director is responsible for bringing the screenplay to the screen and maintaining an appropriate, consistent, and coherent visual approach. Despite the popular impression of the director as some sort of demigod, they are usually more like the captain of a ship. They oversee all creative activity on the film and, working from their own vision as well as the suggestions of the other principle personnel, they make sure that everyone's efforts culminate into an effective and cohesive movie. To this end, the director is responsible for fostering creative input and inspiring enthusiasm and commitment among the cast and crew. More than any other team member the director sets the tone for the production. If the tone is adversarial with the cast and crew,

■ **Figure 7-1** According to Ramin Bahrani (far left) many people assume his film *Man Push Cart* (2006) was made for over 2 million dollars, even though it cost only a fraction of that. He credits his D.P. Michael Simmonds (next to camera) for the film's stunning imagery. Carefully chosen locations also played a big roll in creating the look of the film.

then the experience will be a terrible struggle, which can often find its way onto the screen in the form of unremarkable or sloppy work. If the director has created a collaborative and encouraging environment, then it is remarkable how much great work can be accomplished in a short time with little resources. This is especially important on low-budget shoots when you are not paying people for the hard work of making a movie.

The director is also the ultimate problem solver (Figure 7-2). During the course of any film production, there are countless puzzles to solve and endless questions to answer—for example: Where do we set up the camera and why? What is the actor's motivation? How many setups are required to cover a scene? How long will each take be? From what direction should the light come? What are the color tonalities of the set? When do we move the camera and why? How does an actor move in the location? How do we revise the shot list if we're running out of time? The director's job sometimes can seem like nothing more than answering one long stream of questions and solving one creative puzzle after another. However, the director answers all of these questions, because every one of them determines the expressive style and aesthetic approach of the film. Because of this, a director needs to be broadly knowledgeable in the process, techniques, and creative possibilities of all aspects of film production. Also, a director needs authority, and that authority comes not only from knowing what they are doing, but also from being very clear about everyone else's role in the creation of the film and respecting their contributions. It's equally common for directors to do the question asking. A director might ask a D.P., "I need this scene to feel claustrophobic, tight, suffocating—what lens do you suggest?" or might ask an art director, "This character is a rebellious teenager with a penchant for Goth; what do you think she'd have on the walls of her room?" One final note, the director needs to always keep a level head and should not attempt or demand anything that compromises the safety of anyone on the production team or anything that is in excess of the available resources.

The **assistant director** (A.D.) is to the director what the production manager is to the producer. The A.D. is responsible for the smooth operation of the set. This usually means communicating the director's instructions to the various technical departments (e.g., camera, art, and sound departments) and relating the crew's concerns back to the director. The A.D. makes sure that everyone on the set knows the order of camera setups and what is needed of each department. This leaves the director freer to work with the actors and to make creative decisions on the set. The A.D. works very closely with the P.M. The A.D. helps the director create the shooting script and then, with the P.M., breaks down the script to create a shot list and scene breakdowns (see later). In scenes that involve many extras, the A.D. essentially blocks and directs their actions. On small films, the A.D. is often responsible for keeping track of scene coverage and continuity from shot to shot.

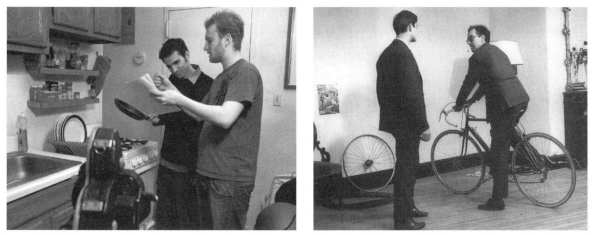

■ **Figure 7-2** Whether you are film student or a cinema legend, the complex job of directing is essentially the same. Director Miles Adgate giving direction to actor Jarret Berenstein on the student film *Discovering* (2006, left) and Director Jean-Luc Godard showing Jean Claude Brialy how he wants him to ride a bicycle in the film *Une Femme est Une Femme* (1961, right) (Godard photograph courtesy of Raymond Cauchetier-Paris).

The Camera Department

The **director of photography** (D.P.; also referred to as "cinematographer") collaborates closely with the director on the visual interpretation of the script and the photographic look of the movie. This involves designing the lighting, choosing film stocks or video format, and devising expressive camera angles, compositions, exposures, and focus. The D.P. knows very well the storytelling capability of the image and is in charge of capturing it all on film or DV. The D.P. collaborates with the director during preproduction, and this collaboration continues into production and postproduction, where the D.P. often oversees final color corrections. While the director has the final say, the D.P. should never hesitate to make creative suggestions if they believe it will enhance the movie. However, a D.P. should never make suggestions simply because they want to play with snazzy camera toys. A good D.P. knows that, in the end, making a movie is not about equipment, it's about visual storytelling (Figure 7-3).

Whether on a professional or a student level, the trust and the creative energy generated between the director and D.P. collaboration are vital to the success of a film. It is important for both people to nurture this relationship. The cinematographer Ellen Kuras described the importance of preproduction meetings with the director in this way:

> *I always, always value the time of the director before photography, because for me the film really gets made during those discussions—in my mind and in our minds. It creates a common language between me and the director to be able to understand the look and what the "third eye" is, in a way. What the vision of the film is.*

Ellen Kuras (From "Where the Girls Are," by Jennifer M. Wood,
***MovieMaker,* Vol. 2, Issue #9)**

Another key position in the camera department is the **assistant camera** person, or A.C. The A.C. is a camera and lens expert. They are responsible for the proper functioning of the camera, which includes setting it up, cleaning the gate, checking and pulling focus, selecting filters and lenses (with the D.P.), etc. They know with precise detail what various cameras and lenses are capable of, both technically and aesthetically. On low-budget shoots, the A.C. is responsible for loading and unloading the film as well as for keeping accurate and orderly camera logs. The acronym F.A.S.T. has become the mantra for working A.C.s. F.A.S.T. stands for the key camera settings that must be checked before each and every shot: Focus, Aperture, Speed (frames per second), and Think meaning that an A.C. should take nothing for granted before the camera rolls.

As movie projects and budgets become larger, the camera department expands to meet the technical demands of the shoot and may include the additional support positions of gaffer and grip(s). The **gaffer** is the hands-on lighting person who implements the lighting designs of the D.P. The gaffer is in charge of the setup and proper functioning of the lights. The gaffer is also responsible for getting the necessary electricity to the set. To ensure the safety of cast and crew, gaffers are almost always certified electricians. Gaffers are in turn supported by camera department grips. **Grips** are the muscle on a film set. They move lights, props, sets, and dollies. They are responsible for the actual physical placement of the lights and props on the set and for the safe use of all lighting equipment. Grips

■ **Figure 7-3** Director George Racz conferring with his D.P. Tim Trotman on the set of his student film *The Miracle* (2006).

in practice ▶

A good friend and colleague of mine was on the crew of Martin Scorsese's *The Last Temptation of Christ* (1988) and told me this story from the shoot in Morocco. *The Last Temptation of Christ* was shot on a remarkably small budget and tight schedule in general, and with a much smaller crew than is usual for a film of that scale. Leading up to the shoot for the crucifixion scene, Scorsese lost the original location, an elevated hilltop in the desert, because it was covered with snow! While the crew continued shooting other scenes, a new location was found, which the art department prepped, day and night, in only two days. As my friend remembers, "That the art department could prep that location in only two days was a miracle."

The location switch only made a tight schedule tighter and the crew had to move fast in order to get everything planned for that location, which included nearly a hundred shots and the crucial crucifixion scene. As my friend tells the story, "Because the sun set early behind the surrounding hills, we had limited hours for each shooting day so we had to work fast. We didn't even have time to break for lunch, we were eating on the run so that we could get all the shots in. This was a key scene in a film that Marty had been dreaming about for years and we were understaffed and had limited time. At one point, when we were moving up the hill to set up a shot, I looked over and saw Marty himself grab two magazine cases weighing about 70 pounds and climb up the hill with them to the next setup. For that moment, Marty Scorsese was doing the job of a P.A. to get the film done. I was impressed."

■ **Figure 7-4** On a film set teamwork is crucial and everyone does what needs to be done to get the film in the can. The famous crucifixion scene from *The Last Temptation of Christ* (1988) required all available hands (right). Time was so tight on this shoot that Scorsese himself schlepped equipment when necessary (pictured in the photo at left with D.P. Michael Ballhaus (middle) and A.C. Florian Ballhaus (left).

are also in charge of the orderly staging and breakdown of the lighting gear. On very small projects with small crews, practically everyone on the set doubles as a grip at one point or another.

The Art Department

The art director is responsible for the look and design of the film as they pertain to locations, sets, costumes, and props. The art director works in close collaboration with the director and makes creative suggestions about the interpretation of story and characters in terms of location choices, the visual design of sets, and specific props and costumes. The art director and cinematographer work very closely, since together they create the total visual environment and style of the film. The art director is also responsible for all safety issues concerning sets, props, and locations.

■ Figure 7-5 Set designer Carol Clements and her art department crew dressing a set before the camera, lighting and sound crews arrive.

■ Figure 7-6 The sound team. In its most common configuration, the sound team consists of a boom person (left) and a sound recordist (right).

The larger the project and budget of a film, the larger the support team for the art director becomes. Often the art director designs the film, but the specific tasks are distributed among a **prop-master**, who locates and coordinates props, the **costume designer**, who finds or makes all costumes and maintains them for the duration of the film, and the **makeup and hair stylist**. On films that require set construction, the art director is also in charge of hiring and coordinating a team of **carpenters and painters** (Figure 7-5).

The Sound Department

The **sound recordist** (also called the location sound mixer) is the head of the sound department and is responsible for recording the best possible quality sound. A perpetual puzzle solver, the sound person chooses the appropriate microphone(s) and microphone placement for each and every scene that requires sound. They also monitor and maintain proper recording levels. Sound recordists are trained to listen to everything in the aural environment of the set and they make technical decisions based on the acoustics of the space and the ambient sounds. They also need to be alert to unwanted sounds intruding on takes, like airplanes flying overhead or a refrigerator suddenly kicking on. The sound recordist often teams up with a **boom operator**, who is responsible for the proper use and actual placement of the microphone(s) for optimum quality (Figure 7-6). Sometimes this means planting a microphone on the talent, or on the set; other times this means holding a boom pole, which suspends the microphone over the action. The boom operator position is extremely important on any film with extensive synchronized sound, since bad audio is as disastrous and irremediable as is bad camera work. On bigger shoots there is also a third person called the **cable wrangler**, who sets up the cables, holds a second boom when necessary, and wrangles the cable when the boom operator follows a moving shot. This position doesn't usually exist on smaller shoots, but I mention it because it is often the entry-level job on a union production sound crew.

Keep in mind that these descriptions are a guide for very small films and student films, which generally do not involve major studios, distributors, lawyers, production office staff, and large crews, with dozens of people and budgets in the millions of dollars. There are many books on the market that define each film crew position in its full professional dimensions (see the Recommended Readings section at the back of this book).

Now that you have a sense for the major production crew positions, remember that fitting the size of the crew to the scale of the project is important. Bear in mind the law of diminishing returns. You want just enough people to get the job done well, but not so many that you waste time and money on unnecessary bodies. As a colleague of mine once remarked about large production crews, more people creates a need for more people because you need extra people to manage and take care of all those people! When you work with small crews, people are required to double or sometimes triple up on duties. It is essential that no matter how you divide up the duties on a project, each person must know precisely what they are responsible for and what is expected of them.

Crew Meetings and Communication

To foster a professional, collaborative, and efficient environment, open and frequent communication is vital. The director/producer should hold regular crew meetings over the course of any project, no matter how small. Crew meetings are essential for convey-

Here are a few examples of what types of projects are appropriate for small film crews and how small teams can be organized.

■ **THREE-PERSON CREW:**

Type of project: Very short films or exercises shot without sound (MOS). Very few locations using only available lighting and relatively little set dressing. Small cast.

Breakdown of duties: (person 1) writer, director, coproducer; (person 2) coproducer, P.M., cinematographer; (person 3) art department, A.D., grip.

■ **FIVE-PERSON CREW:**

Type of project: Short films involving very simple location sound recording. Few locations using limited lighting and set dressing. Small cast.

Breakdown of duties: (person 1) writer, director; (person 2) producer, P.M./A.D.; (person 3) cinematographer, A.C.; (person 4) art department and grip; (person 5) sound mixer, boom operator.

■ **EIGHT-PERSON CREW:**

Type of project: Intermediate to advanced short films involving extensive sync sound, lighting, set design, and multiple locations.

Breakdown of duties: (person 1) writer, director; (person 2) producer; (person 3) P.M./A.D.; (person 4) cinematographer; (person 5) A.C. and grip; (person 6) art department and grip; (person 7) sound mixer; (person 8) boom operator.

ing the creative vision of the project and everyone's specific role in bringing that vision to the screen. Meetings are also indispensable for organizing the general production schedule as well as everyone's individual schedules and duties. No one should show up at the set without knowing exactly what their job is or what the project is about. Finally, crew meetings are where people feel the progress and momentum of a project and where team motivation, connection, and collaboration are fostered. A cinematographer can't make suggestions about the aesthetics of lighting or composition if they never saw a finished script or sat down with the director to discuss the tone, mood, or meaning of the movie. A sound recordist needs to know what the locations and shot selections are like in order to bring the appropriate equipment to the set. An art director needs to be informed of their budget so that they know whether to buy, borrow, or make props

■ **Figure 7-7** A student film production crew meeting in progress. Crew meetings are essential for creative collaboration and logistical coordination.

and set pieces. A grip, like everyone else, needs to know the production schedule so that they can clear their calendar for the necessary shooting days. And so on. . . . One of *the* most common reasons student films fail is that shooting days are scheduled without first meeting with the crew to determine their availability. Then, when the shooting day arrives, principal crew members can't make it because "I have an exam that day and I can't miss it."(Or "I have work that day. If I had two weeks' notice I could have gotten off." The more your teammates know, the more they can do for the project (**Figure 7-7**).

It is always a good idea to include your crew in the initial script reading in order to allow cast and crew get to know each other. After pre-visualization, you should also schedule **technical read throughs** with each department so that you can concentrate on the technical requirements of each area in isolation from the rest. Additionally, you should meet with your crew whenever there are major changes to the visualization, production requirements, locations, or production schedule. Obviously, communication is essential, but can you have too many meetings? Yes. You need to conduct efficient and informative meetings and not hold unnecessary ones just for the sake of meeting. You will respect people's time by not wasting it.

Being a Crew Member

When you are just starting out in filmmaking, it is imperative to crew on as many movies as you possibly can. You always learn an extraordinary amount on well-run productions and on poorly run productions alike. There is no substitute for on-set experience—being part of putting a movie together, watching other people at work and witnessing the travails, struggles, successes, styles, and procedures of filmmaking first hand is by far the quickest and most valuable learning you can do.

As a crew member yourself it is essential that you endeavor to be as informed, skilled, and cooperative as possible. A great deal of time, money, energy, and hope is poured into making a movie, so reliability and resourcefulness from every crew person is essential. Never forget that whatever your role on a film project, no matter how humble, in this business we build our reputation, professional relationships, and careers one film at a time.

in practice

You should be realistic about the scale of your project, your technical needs, and the spirit of the project when building your production team.

- *Too few team members:*
  When I was in film school, another student devised a short film that involved a perpetually moving camera. The scene was a small party and the camera mingled with the crowd and caught provocative snippets of dialogue as it entered into and left people's conversations—not unlike a Robert Altman approach to group scenes. It was a terrific idea but the student filmmaker had only a three-person crew. Practically speaking, he needed a minimum of four people besides himself: one person on camera, one person pushing the dolly, one person holding the boom microphone, and one person on the sound recorder watching the levels carefully. So this director ended up pushing the dolly himself. He also pulled someone from the cast to hold the boom pole. The result was no surprise—unconvincing performances (because the director couldn't pay attention to performances), terrible sound (because the actor knew nothing about positioning a mike), and, even worse, a cast and crew who lost faith in the filmmaker's judgment and abilities.
- *Too many team members:*
  A few years ago, a friend of mine had some significant festival success with a lovely short film she made about traveling out west with her mother. She shot the film all by herself, over the course of the weeklong trip, with a Super-8mm

camera. A professional producer liked her movie and offered to produce her next short film. My friend naturally took her up on the offer and wrote a very delicate and poignant script about two neighbors who get stuck on a city rooftop and almost fall in love. With only one exterior location and only two principal actors, the script was designed to be easy to shoot so that she could really connect with her actors and get some memorable performances. Simple, right? Unfortunately, the very generous producer gave the project the red carpet treatment, and on the day of shooting a twelve-person crew showed up—including two electricians (for a film using no artificial lighting!). My friend called me from the set, almost crying. She said that the overly large crew felt like a huge anchor and kept her from improvising and or even connecting in any intimate way with her cast—yet, she felt obligated to defer to all of these professionals who had made so many films and were there for free. She lost control of her own film. For example, her first idea was to simply hand-hold the camera, but when she saw dolly tracks being off-loaded and laid down, the camera being mounted on the boom arm, and a camera crew of four waiting for instructions, she felt obligated to go that way. The result was a film which looked like a million bucks yet felt stiff, overproduced, and lacked much of the director's individual spirit which was so evident in her first film made with a crew of one.

So, a professional demeanor is essential to develop. The film producer Cirri Nottage (*Girl Six*) once said to my film class that she always keeps her eye out for the person who excels at their job, even if it's a small job like photocopying and stapling script pages. "If that person is the best and most reliable script photocopier I've seen then that person is going to be hired again and promoted, because that's the attitude I want on my film set." Initiative, effort, and energy pay off. If you show these traits, you will find yourself on a lot of film sets. Even if you're in school and taking your very first film production class, the impression you make on your classmates follows you into the intermediate and advanced courses and beyond, into the professional world. This is how any creative community is developed. Very often, the people you call on to help make your first films after graduation are those whom you trusted and collaborated with in school, and if you have proved yourself to be a trustworthy, energetic, and resourceful crew member, you can expect to get a few calls after graduation.

ON-CAMERA TALENT

Casting a film means finding the right people to play each of the various roles in your film and securing their commitment to the project. The formality of this process varies widely depending on the scale of your film, but that doesn't mean you can ever be careless about casting. The success of small films and exercises, all the way up to big-budget features, depends enormously on the quality of the on-camera talent. The on-camera talent can determine the success of a film in two ways—through their performance skill and charisma and through their dedication to the project. Deficiency in either of these can likewise sink an otherwise admirable effort.

Finding an Actor

For very simple projects and film exercises, we often write a script for someone we know or we simply cast a friend (or a friend of a friend) or someone else who seems handy to play a part (**Figure 7-8**).

This practice is fine. You certainly don't need to go through an elaborate audition process for a simple chase scene exercise, but you should be aware of a few pitfalls:

1. Never use one of your crew members as a player in the film. You diminish the size and therefore efficiency of your production team when you pull one of them out. A crew of four people that loses one to become a performer is diminished 25%. Usually this drastic trade-off becomes visible on screen in numerous ways.

2. Try to use someone who has a reason to commit to the film. Filmmaking is arduous and time consuming. Actors and even acting students have a reason to participate in a film until the very end because it's important for them to have "tape," meaning samples of themselves performing. The better the project is, the better their "tape," so they have a strong incentive to perform well. Not only do they get a credit on a film, but the "tape" can also lead to another acting gig. However, a close friend who is an economics major might be willing and even excited about being in your movie, but after the first ten-hour production day, they may start to lose interest. With mid-terms coming up, with an impatient girlfriend to appease and a

■ **Figure 7-8** George with his niece Panna, who was the inspiration for his first three short films, including *The Miracle* (see pp. 32–33). Panna was the obvious choice to play the lead role, Kate, in all three films.

job to maintain, suddenly the thought of sticking around for three more shooting days isn't so appealing. Frequently, really good friends, find the limits of their friendship on film productions.

3. Think twice about casting family members. Family relations are often complex; add to that the stress and arduousness of the filmmaking process, and you're working with a volatile mixture. Besides, do you *really* think you can direct your mom?

4. The super funny guy at parties who does a spot-on perfect imitation of De Niro in *Taxi Driver* can suddenly seem less than convincing once you look at him through a camera lens. The context of a personal relationship is very different from that of a film. What's funny or brilliant between a group of pals kicking back on a Saturday night, a very forgiving circumstance, often doesn't cut it for a broader public.

Casting for type means casting someone because they seem naturally right for the part in some way, whether they look the part, or behave just like your character in real life, or have the same profession your character has. Casting for type can work well, especially if the person happens to also be a fine actor. With nonactors, since they don't necessarily have the skill to perform anything other than themselves, casting for type is the only way to go. But again, one should be careful that the nonactor doesn't suddenly change once the camera is turned on them. I once cast a real-life police officer; mostly because he volunteered to provide two real-life police uniforms for the film, which I needed. The uniforms looked great, but the acting was another question. With the camera rolling, the officer was unable to keep a straight face—to do things he ordinarily does dozens of times a week without cracking a smile. It didn't work so well to have a cop pull up on an emergency call with a silly "Hi Mom" grin on his face. CUT!

With nonactors, you should always do a screen test before you commit them to your movie. Here is what Abbas Kiarostami, who often uses nonactors in his films, says about his casting of nonactors:

> *I sit and talk with them and turn on the camera without them knowing. After seven or eight minutes, once we've found our subject, I pretend to turn on the camera. If you see no difference between the moments before and after this flick of the switch, you know you have a good actor.*
>
> **Abbas Kiarostami (From "Four Golden Rules," interview by Paul Cronin,**
> ***The Guardian,* June 17, 2005)**

That said, it takes a skilled director, and lots of patience, to get a great performance out of a nonactor. For most films, casting skilled actors is important in order to get what you need for your film. Even if your film has no dialogue, a good actor can bring a new interpretive energy, authenticity, and creative resources to the project.

Auditions

An **audition** is an organized process by which you schedule and work with a number of potential performers to determine their suitability to your film. The object of running an audition is to see if a performer is a good fit for the roles you have in the script and to see, to some extent, if you can work with the actors who are auditioning. Always remember that, especially for emerging directors, the actors are auditioning you as much as you are auditioning them. You must represent yourself and your project professionally and always treat actors with respect. The actor is one of your principal creative collaborators. If they feel as though they will not be allowed to be creative or to collaborate, then their interest in your project will certainly diminish.

Running a simple audition is not a terribly difficult task, but it must be well organized in order to convey a sense of your abilities and to provide assurance to the performers. You don't want a chaotic audition to be the actors' first impression of your capabilities, because they are sure to anticipate an equally chaotic shoot and will probably stay away. Here are the steps to running a smooth and productive audition:

1. *Put out an audition call for actors:* An audition call can be as basic as asking filmmakers and actors you know for recommendations (word of mouth) and hanging up fliers in a college acting department, or as broad as paying for advertising in newspapers, trade journals, or online (i.e., *Backstage Magazine,* www.backstage.com, www. NYCastings.com, and even Craigslist). A colleague of mine who needed two actors for his recent short film discovered two wonderful actors performing in a one of his students' films. After getting their contact information, he simply auditioned those two people to make sure they were compatible with the script. When the auditions went well, he cast them. In any case, a public call for actors should have all of the basic information a potential actor needs in order to decide whether they are right for the part and how to contact the filmmaker. **Figure 7-9** is an example of an audition call. When an actor contacts you, a **headshot/bio** is the standard calling card. It usually consists of an 8×10 photograph on one side and a résumé on the other (**Figure 7-10**). Keep in mind, however, that when you open up your search to people with little or no acting experience, you might get a small photograph and a handwritten letter.

2. *Short listing:* Once you have received all of the headshot/bios, and/or personal recommendations, you need to select who you are going to audition by reviewing their credentials and evaluating their photographs. It's tough to judge a person based on one photograph, but for the moment it's all you have. As you review the bios you make "yes," "maybe," and "no" piles. This is actually an illuminating process, because for the first time you are being asked to put a face to your screenplay characters. Occasionally you'll realize that you didn't know as much about your character as you thought. You'll also begin to see a certain flexibility in the character by noticing how they seem to change as you imagine each different face in the role. This is only the beginning of your encounter with the interpretation of your characters through the body and performance of an actor. The "yes" pile of performers, those who both look right for the part and have the performance background you are seeking, is your short list. But be advised— keep it short!

3. *Find an audition space:* To hold the audition, find a space that is large enough for all of the people you need at the audition and for the performers to stand, sit, move, and perform comfortably. The group attending the audition usually includes the director, the producer, and people to read lines with the actors. It is not a good idea to hold auditions in your home. Many potential actors will not go to a private residence to audition for an unknown director. It is also preferable to have a separate, comfortable waiting space to put the next-in-line actor. This is called the **green room**, a place where actors can relax, drink some water, and go over their lines. Incidentally, no one really knows why an actor's reception room is called the "green room," but the term has been part of the theater world since the 18th century.

4. *Decide on audition material:* It is important to be clear about what you want the actors to do in the audition. Obviously, you will need to have them perform a scene or two from your film so that you can see how they fit the role. Reading from script pages that actors are given minutes before the audition is called a **cold reading**. If a cold reading from the script involves dialogue with another person, then you need to have someone of decent ability at the audition to read with all of the actors. Cold readings alone are sometimes not the greatest measure of an actor's abilities, so it's also good to have each actor present a monologue of their own choosing, something they have previously developed, to really give them an opportunity to show what they believe

Female lead (20... be ...rtable around sh...
Send headshots to: Nostromo Productions, 45 Lauriston st. Blixy, NV or e-mail to nostromo@mygama.com

CALL FOR ACTORS FOR FILM "THE HAND-OFF"
City University film student seeking female lead (mid-thirties) male lead (mid-thirties) and boy lead (nine yrs.) for ten minute film exploring the first time a child of divorced parents transfers custody. Non-union, no pay, but meals, transportation and DVD copy provided. Send headshot / bio by November 20 to: Mick Hurbis-Cherrier at City University, City, State, zip. or via e-mail to MHC@cityumail.edu

SHORT FILM "THE MUTE'S CONFESSION"
...ks leads for short film. Liam (45-55) must know

■ **Figure 7-9** A casting call posted in a trade journal or online casting service needs to be brief but must include all pertinent information.

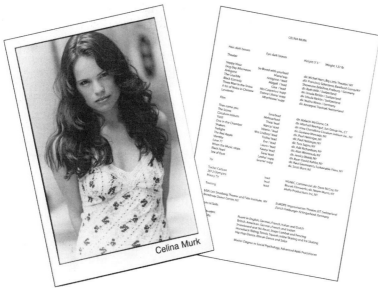

■ **Figure 7-10** A typical headshot. Most serious actors have professional photographs taken for their headshots, and include a résumé listing their acting experience and other skills that may give them an edge in this competitive field.

is their best, most prepared, and most convincing performance. Most trained actors have several monologues prepared and ready for auditions. But you need to know what sort of monologue will allow *you* to see what you need to see from them. A Shakespearean monologue? A modern monologue? Drama? Comedy? If you're doing a silent film with physical humor, maybe you don't want any words at all and need to see a short physical performance. I once made a film based on a series of adaptations of poetry by Pablo Neruda, which required the actors to speak stanzas of a poem to each other as if the lines were dialogue. So I asked the actors auditioning for me to bring in either some modern poetry or a modern monologue that they felt had poetic language. Once you have your short list and your audition space and you've decided on the material you want each performer to present, you're ready to schedule the audition.

5. *Contact and scheduling:* Contact each performer and schedule them with enough time between auditions so that you can reflect and jot notes about what you saw. Do not schedule them in so tightly that their auditions overlap and a waiting crowd starts to accumulate in your green room. When you contact each performer be clear about (a) where the audition is, (b) what you want them to do (i.e., modern monologue and cold read), and (c) how long the audition will last. Also be prepared to answer more detailed questions about the project.

6. *Running the audition:* A typical audition runs something like this: (a) as the actor waits their turn, give them the cold-read script pages to look over. (b) When you are ready for them, bring them into the audition room. Common courtesy is the rule. Greet the actor, introduce everyone in the room, and describe in more detail the project and the specific role. It's important to allow actors to relax and understand just what they're stepping into and who is watching them. (c) Give the actor an idea of your shooting schedule and when they need to be available. If there is an unworkable schedule conflict then there is no need to waste their time, or yours, with an audition. Simply thank them for coming in and call the next person. (d) Have them perform their prepared monologue. If after this you are already sure that they won't work in the role, then there is no need to waste their time, or yours, by keeping them longer. Simply thank them for coming in and call the next person. If you like what they've done, then move on to the cold reading. (e) Give them any necessary context or background for the script pages they are reading and have them do the cold read. Remember, if the scene involves dialogue with another character, you need to have a person at the audition to read with the actor. If after the cold read it's clear that they won't work in the role, then there is no need to waste their time, or yours, by keeping them longer. Simply thank them for coming in and call the next person. If they seem promising then, (f) work with them on the script pages. Try to get a few adjustments and nuances in their performance. Have them try the scene with a different approach or tone. If they seem flexible and respond well to directing, then place them on the callback list (see later). (g) Thank them for coming in and tell them that you'll be in touch. Once they leave, jot a few notes on your audition sheet and call in the next audition.

You should never prolong an audition that you know for certain isn't going well. It's not courteous to keep people working for you after you've already made up your mind, and it's a waste of your time, too. It's always best to politely thank them and let them go. The

shortest audition I ever had ended just after the first handshake. I was casting for the role of Ray, a sweet, overly sensitive and perpetually worried father of a 15-year-old-daughter. One actor strode into the room, shook my hand, and, without allowing me to say one word, proceeded to tell me what he was going to do, in what order, and where he wanted us to sit for his monologue. He also announced that he preferred to do two monologues and skip the cold reading. I simply shook his hand again and thanked him for coming in. I explained that I didn't think he would work out and I didn't want to waste his time. He thanked me, turned on his heel, and left.

Callbacks

Callbacks are second auditions in which you look closely at all of your most promising candidates. Callbacks work primarily with the material of the script, to really establish character/actor compatibility. It's com-

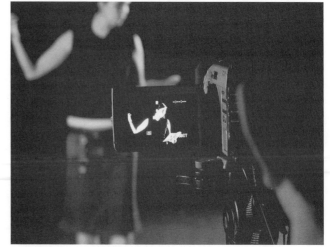

■ **Figure 7-11** Videotaping callbacks is a good strategy to see how a performer responds to the presence of a camera.

mon to send the entire script to your callback choices so that they can be more familiar with the material. Often, if a role involves a close relationship with another character, callbacks can involve pairing up performers to see what kind of chemistry exists between the performers. Although we generally don't videotape the first auditions, it's important to videotape the callbacks as a screen test (**Figure 7-11**). Some actors can perform wonderfully in front of people, but stiffen up when they're on camera. This is especially true of non-actors. You need to know this before you commit to a performer. Also, when taping the callbacks make sure that you take many different angles and shots of the performances. Faces are important, but so is movement and voice. Take time to set up lights and microphones so that you get a high-quality recording. If your shooting is from a single angle, way back in the corner of the room with lousy audio and dim lighting, the tape won't have enough information to help you make your final decisions.

Casting and Commitments

Based on your impression from the callbacks, you should be able to make your decisions and call your chosen actors to tell them you'd like to work with them on the film. Once you have thoroughly explored their availability and secured their commitment, you should inform the other callback actors that they were wonderful, but you decided to go with another performer. Of course, thank them for the time they gave auditioning for you. Actors are extremely valuable for a filmmaker. We need them to turn our literary characters into flesh-and-blood people. You should always be professional and respectful because, as I've mentioned, courtesy is important. Also, you never know when you might need that actor for a future project of yours, or for a colleague's film, and you want them to feel that they'd like to work with you someday.

The Actor as Creative Collaborator

Once you have assembled your cast, you will discover that there is a new energy that actors bring to the filmmaking process. Actors are creative collaborators whose job it is to bring a character off the page and into being. As such, they bring an interpretive energy that a smart director will acknowledge and cultivate. Starting from the callbacks, you are forming both your collaboration method as well as the final form of the characters in your film as you work and rework scenes, gathering from an actor their thoughts, reactions, and insights. This process continues until the last day of shooting. Based on the new insight, expertise, and energy of the performers, don't be afraid to allow your characters to evolve into something you might not have anticipated, as long as it remains appropriate for your story. It's not uncommon during rehearsals, and even during shooting, to rewrite lines and scenes to better fit a new concept of a character.

Rehearsals

Rehearsals are the time you spend in preproduction running through scenes in preparation for shooting. In general, some degree of rehearsing is always necessary. The length and depth of your rehearsal period depend greatly on the needs of the project and the availability of the cast (especially if they are not getting paid). On short student films and low-budget independent films, rehearsals are generally not elaborate or lengthy. Some directors assiduously avoid a lengthy rehearsal period, thinking that it bleeds freshness out of a performance—others engage in long and detailed rehearsals in order to prepare and develop scenes thoroughly in preproduction. Not only do rehearsals allow for the integration of many new ideas, but they also can cut down on production time.

One process that is necessary for any film is a read through. **A read through** is a reading of the script by the actors, with all principal creative people in attendance. The read through allows everyone involved to get to know each other, which is especially important for actors who will be performing together. Also, hearing the script read out loud, in front of people, serves to illuminate any glaring problems with the script, like lines that simply don't work, plausibility problems, or character inconsistencies. It's common for the script to go through a solid rewrite after a read through. A read through is also a place where conceptual ideas—from characterization to visualization—are discussed so that all participants understand what the director is striving for.

Scene work rehearsals are a more detailed examination of specific scenes and aim to refine the interpretation of the drama. Not every scene needs such thorough rehearsals; usually this is reserved for the more dramatically or physically complex scenes. Scene work can include a close script analysis and scene run throughs, in which dialogue, movement, and interactions are examined to develop—for the actors, and often for the director, too—the nuances of characterization, motivation, dramatic context, emotional content, and scene dynamics. Scene work rehearsal also involves rough **blocking**, which is the coordination of the movements of the actors in the scene. More often than not this is done on a mock set, but if it can be done on the actual set, so much the better. I once shot a scene (three setups) on the Coney Island-bound Q train in New York City; the scene involved a woman walking to an available seat in a crowded car, only to have a punky kid jump into the seat just before she gets there (Figure 7-12). The scene was simple, choreographed action, but I knew that the train made only four stops while the train remained aboveground and that I needed to get all three shots within this time or else we'd have to wait to take a Manhattan-bound train back to shoot more shots—and then we'd have to worry about continuity problems on a new train (different posters, etc.). So, using dining chairs, I created a mock-up of the subway car in my living room. We rehearsed the choreography of the

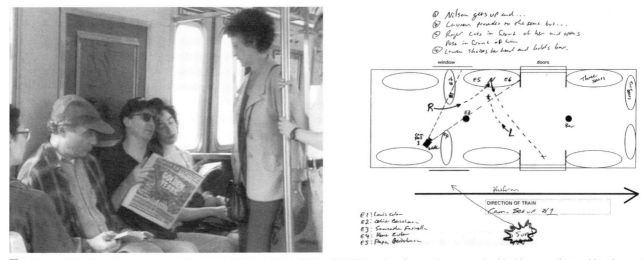

■ **Figure 7-12** To make sure we could get this shot from *Ode to Things* (1998) in only a few station stops, the blocking was thoroughly rehearsed in my living room using chairs configured according to the Q Train overhead diagram (right).

actors and the movement of the extras over and over again until it was automatic. Later that afternoon, we all boarded the Q train and nailed the scene in only three stops! Generally, scene work is done with the director, the actors, and perhaps the A.D. If the rehearsal involves blocking, the cinematographer might be there too.

One final type of rehearsal is actually not part of preproduction, but occurs during the production process. **On-set rehearsals** or **on-set run throughs** are rehearsals during the preparation of the actual shooting on location (see Chapter 18). At this stage, on-set blocking rehearsals are mandatory. They are not only important for familiarizing the actors with the actual location, but they are also essential for the camera and sound departments to know exactly where lights, camera, microphones, and recording levels need to be in any given take. Most of the detailed analysis work should have been done before this point, but actors, directors, and cinematographers will invariably respond to the actual shooting environment and will want to make adjustments to their interpretations along the way.

Working with Extras

If you write a script with a pick-up scene set in a crowded bar, you'll need to find people to play the crowd. If you write a scene in which your hero is the last person in a long line at an ATM cash machine, then you'll need people to make that line. If you need to shoot a scene in which a young professor is lecturing to a class of twenty students, then you'll need to find twenty willing people to sit in a classroom while you shoot. For each of these

---

in practice

Finding Thousands of Extras

In his lovely first film, *Vive le Premier Mai* (1995), the French filmmaker Didier Rouget tells the sweet, simple story of a man who finds his true love but then loses her in the crowd of a huge public demonstration, and finally, through a clever devise, finds her again. Rouget set this film right in the middle of the traditional May 1st worker's demonstration in Paris in which tens of thousands of people march in the streets (Figure 7-13). Cameras are abundant, so no one would notice one more. His film involved a production crew of three and only two principal actors, but a cast of forty-thousand extras!

Figure 7-13 Emmanuel Salinger in Rouget's *Vive le Premier Mai* (1995). Rouget obtained forty-thousand extras for free by setting the story of his short film during the traditional May 1st worker's demonstration in Paris.

Can't Find Ten Extras

Here is a cautionary tale. The producer on a recent student film project managed to acquire, for only a few hours, a very hard-to-get location, Grand Central Station, New York City. The film involved three shoeshine men talking and polishing the shoes of an elite business clientele. Everything was in place for the shoot except one thing, the ten or so extras who would be playing the elite business clientele. The producer and director erroneously assumed that they could simply enlist passers-by and offer them a free shoeshine if they'd be in the movie. But this was Grand Central Station, where everyone is in a hurry. What they discovered was that no one, not one person, was interested in sitting still for ten minutes for a free shoeshine given by an actor playing a role, nor were they particularly interested in being on film.

Rather than scrap the entire shoot (and lose the time and location forever), the crew called up all of their friends and asked them to dress in suits and hurry down to Grand Central Station. A few hours later, about six friends showed up—many with less than convincing suits, several wearing sneakers, and most with haircuts that would not exactly cut it in a corporate boardroom. With time ticking away, the crew shot quickly and eliminated a lot of coverage. In the end they managed to get the basic footage they needed, but the clientele did not look much like they came from an elite business class; rather, they looked like a bunch of dressed-up college undergraduates and the film lost a very important component of its satire and irony.

scenarios, you need extras. **Extras** are those performers who have no lines or important actions in a film, but who populate a scene and give it a sense of realism and authenticity. Extras are one detail that many novice filmmakers take for granted. Inexperienced film-makers are so immersed in the big demands of a film—lead characters, locations, and equipment—that they often think that extras will just be there when needed. Extras have super small roles and no lines, so they must be easy to find, right? The fact is, being an extra requires a lot of time for very little payoff. Extras usually don't even get a credit in the film. It's always difficult to find people willing to stay on a set for hours and hours, do-ing very little, while you shoot your scene. So keep this in mind when you write your script. Small films on tight budgets should try to minimize the need for extras or find a clever alternate solution.

Releases, Minors, and Unions

The shortest, simplest film, if done well, might play in festivals or be picked up for broad-casting. You never know, but you should be prepared for your film's potential success and public exposure. So it's important to obtain a talent release from your actors before shoot-ing begins. A **talent release** (see Appendix 5-1) is a legal document, signed before the cameras roll, simply stating that the performer gives you the right to use his image and voice in your film. Sometimes securing this right involves a fee, and sometimes actors work for free. The talent release protects you should the actor have a change of heart later on. As a student, I remember a classmate's film in which a fairly minor character felt, after the premiere screening, that the director made her "look fat" in the movie. She told the director that she didn't want him showing this film in public and that she'd sue him if he did. The director hadn't obtained a release. Unable to reshoot her scenes, the film ended up in the director's desk drawer.

If you are working with children as talent, it only stands to reason that you need to obtain a release from their legal guardian. Working with minors also requires you to organize your shoots around school schedules and around the parents' or guardians' schedules, since they have a legal right to accompany their child to every film shoot. It is in your best inter-est to have someone to specifically look after the children on the set. Keeping track of a child on a film shoot is a full-time responsibility, and it's best done by the legal guardian. Also, in general, you need to make special assurances for the safety and well being of any child on the set. This means working shorter hours, allowing for regular breaks, and having plenty of healthy food and drinks. You may be able to persuade an adult actor to gut it out and stay an extra couple of hours to get those last shots, but when the going gets tough, kids usually need a nap! Before you proceed with any film involving children, check with your local or state film office: there are usually fairly strict legal requirements that you must know about.

Actors Unions

You'll notice in the call for talent (see Figure 7-9) that the ad clearly states that the call is for a nonunion film. There are two major unions that look after the interest of professional actors who have gained enough credits to become members. The union that most film-makers encounter is the Screen Actors Guild (or SAG). SAG union actors generally work on union films (those that utilize union crews, union directors, etc.). However, exceptions are made for low-budget independent films and student films. SAG has developed a va-riety of contract agreements for student films, shorts, and ultra-low-budget projects. To use a SAG actor in your nonunion student film you must enter into the SAG student film agreement. Generally speaking, this agreement protects the actor by making sure that certain baseline requirements are in place: (1) You must prove you own the copyright on the screenplay that you are shooting. In other words, you have the legal right to make this film. (2) If any money is made from this production (through festivals, broadcast, or other distribution), then the union actor is paid their minimum union wages before anyone else involved in the production is paid. (3) You must adhere to regulation scheduling, meal, and safety procedures and maintain accurate time sheets for each union performer. (4) You must provide proof that the production and the actors are adequately insured. These are just the basics to give you an idea of what it means to use a union actor and to enter into a SAG student contract or independent film contract. (For complete information about these contracts, go to www.SagIndie.org.)

The Contact Sheet

In the intense and creative environment of a movie production, the cast and crew of a film become like a family for the duration of project, and, as I mentioned earlier in the chapter, communication is essential to keep this family involved, engaged, and informed. There is one very simple form that is essential for this necessary communication, the **contact sheet**. A contact sheet is a simple list of who is involved in the project, what their role is, and their contact information (phone and email). It's such an obviously useful list that introductory filmmakers often don't even think of it until the director decides to postpone a shoot or change locations and realizes that they lost that little slip of paper, which was shoved in their pocket, that they wrote so-and-so's number on. So, make a contact sheet and give one to everyone involved in your film. Then, after the film is completed, save that contact sheet! When you make your next film, you may want to get back in touch with some of your extended filmmaking family.

PART III   TOOLS AND TECHNIQUES: PRODUCTION

The Film System

■ THE BASICS OF THE FILM SYSTEM

The essentials of the film system have changed very little since its invention in the 19th century. Film is a mechanical and photochemical motion picture system. It creates the illusion of motion through the rapid presentation of a series of sequential photographic images fixed to a flexible strip of cellulose. At a rate of 24 frames per second, each image is projected onto a screen and held stationary long enough for the viewer to register the image before it is quickly replaced with the subsequent still image, which is again held for a fraction of a second, and so on and so on. The viewer perceives this rapid presentation of still images as motion through the perceptual phenomenon known as **short-range apparent motion**.[1] Simply put, when shown a rapidly changing series of sequential still images in which there is only slight difference from image to image, humans processes this visual stimuli with the same perceptual mechanism used in the visual processing of real motion. This mechanism transforms the series of still images into motion through the psychological and physiological interpolation of information between the still frames (Figure 8-1).

Essential to the perception of motion is that each still image must be held stationary for a fraction of a second and then rapidly replaced with the next stationary image. If we were to simply pull a strip of film smoothly in front of a projector's lamp, the result would be one long vertical blur. A movie projector must have the ability to move one frame into position, hold it steady while the lamp and lens project that image onto the screen, and then repeat this action with the next frame, and so on, at a very precise and regular pace. This regular stop-and-start mechanical action, positioning and holding one frame at a time, is called **intermittent movement**. Both film cameras and film projectors have the same intermittent movement.

Frame Rate

Through a mechanical and photochemical process, the film camera creates 24 photographic exposures per second on a strip of flexible celluloid coated with a light-sensitive emulsion layer. Recording live events through a series of sequential still images at a rate of 24 frames per second (fps) uses 36 feet of film per minute in the 16mm film format (Figure 8-2), and 90 feet per minute in the 35mm format.

Individual photographic images are visible to the eye after the film has been processed by a laboratory. When these images are projected back at the same rate (24 fps) with a film projector, the audience perceives normal motion (Figure 8-3).

It is helpful to think of a film camera and a film projector as essentially the same mechanism, with the transmission of the image reversed. A film camera gathers light from the outside world, through its lens, and focuses that image onto the plane of the film to create the exposures. A film projector pushes

■ **Figure 8-1** The difference between still images in a strip of film is very slight.

[1]"The Myth of Persistence of Vision Revisited," Joseph and Barbara Anderson, *Journal of Film and Video,* Vol. 45, No. 1 (Spring 1993): 3–12.

Tools for Calculating Film Footage

There are also several excellent websites with footage charts and calculators:

http://www.kodak.com/US/en/motion/16mm/resources/

http://www.gregpak.com/filmhelp/tools/footagechart.html#calculator/

TIME	FOOTAGE	FEET	Min:Sec
1 sec.	24 frames	50	1:23
2 sec.	1 ft. 8 fr.		
3 sec.	1 ft. 32 fr.	100	2:46
4 sec.	2 ft. 16 fr.	150	4:10
5 sec.	3 ft.		
10 sec.	6 ft.	200	5:33
25 sec.	15 ft.	300	8:20
30 sec.	18 ft.		
50 sec.	30 ft.	400	11:06
1 min.	36 ft.		
5 min.	180 ft.	500	13:53
10 min.	360 ft.	800	22:13
15 min.	540 ft.		
20 min.	720 ft.	1000	27:46
25 min.	900 ft.	1200	33:20
30 min.	1080 ft.		

16mm Footage & Running Time QUICK REFERENCE
16mm film at 24 fps = 36 feet per minute
1 foot = 40 frames
100 feet = 2 minutes 47 seconds
400 feet = 11 minutes 6 seconds

■ Figure 8-2 Quick reference footage chart for 16mm film running at 24 fps.

24 frames = 1 second

■ Figure 8-3 16mm film strip. Actual size.

light from within the apparatus, through the images and through a lens, to focus and project that image onto the surface plane of a movie screen. The intermittent motion for exposing and projecting the film therefore must be identical.

Twenty-four frames per second is the standard frame rate for all projectors and film cameras running at what is known as **sync speed**. While most projectors do not vary this frame rate, many film cameras are built with **variable-speed motors**, which allows them to alter the frame rate. We can, for example, shoot our film at 8 fps, 12 fps, or 72 fps. When we shoot at a frame rate faster than 24 fps we get **slow motion** when we project at 24fps. The faster our camera's frame rate, the slower the motion will appear when projected. A movement that takes one second in real time, like a glass shattering on the floor, when shot at 72 fps, will take three seconds on screen, and four seconds if you shoot the glass breaking at 96 fps. Conversely, altering the camera's speed to frame rates below 24 fps (i.e., 12 fps or 8 fps) will create motion that appears sped up when projected. This is called **under-cranking**, and the slower the frame rate of the camera, the faster the motion appears when projected (Figure 8-4).

The extreme end of under-cranking is called **time-lapse**, which occurs when one is taking exposures at frame rates as slow as 3 frames per *minute* or 1 frame per *minute*. A camera running at 1 frame per minute will record 24 minutes of movement in only 24 frames. When projected back at 24 fps, those 24 minutes will now happen in one second. With time lapse we can see movements that usually occur gradually over many minutes or hours,

■ **Figure 8-4** In *2001: A Space Odyssey* (1968, left), the use of slow motion adds majesty to an evolutionary leap forward in intelligence, while in *A Clockwork Orange* (1971, right), fast motion makes a caricature of the sexual act (both films by Stanley Kubrick).

■ **Figure 8-5** Time-lapse photography. Shooting at extremely slow frame rates lets you capture events or movements that take several minutes or even hours to complete (as shown in Jonze's *Adaptation*, 2002).

like the sun setting or storm clouds forming, in a matter of seconds (Figure 8-5).

Film and Sound

For all practical intents and purposes, film is a **double system sound** medium, which means that motion pictures shot on film needing synchronous sound recorded with the image must use a second apparatus to record the audio (Figure 8-6). A film camera records the image and a sound recorder (¼″ tape, DAT, or flash memory) records the audio separately. This means that the images and the separate synchronous audio must, at some point later, be brought together. This process, know as **synching dailies**, will be covered later in the postproduction chapter. For now it is just important to note that, unlike DV cameras, which record both image and sound with the same device and on the same material, film cameras do not record sound.

■ THE GENERIC FILM CAMERA

Even though there are many differences between cameras of different manufacturers and from model to model, the very basic components and functions of all film cameras are essentially the same. Film camera technology is not especially mysterious or even terribly complex. Once you understand the basic mechanisms that all film cameras share, you can approach any specific camera with

■ **Figure 8-6** Double system sound. In this student production, a boom person mikes from above to get the best sound possible, while a sound recordist (in the foreground) monitors the levels. Note the use of a softie on the microphone to block wind noise while recording sound outdoors.

a reliable base of knowledge and with the confidence that you can figure out the particularities in no time at all. All film cameras have the following components (Figure 8-7): the body, the gate, the movement, the drive mechanism/film transport, a viewing system, and a lens. Here we'll look at each component in detail except the lens, which has its own section (see Chapter 10).

Body

The body of a film camera is a light-tight chamber in which film can be transported in complete darkness, exposed in a controlled manner, and then taken up in darkness. In many 16mm cameras, small rolls of film can be loaded directly into the body of the camera; other cameras, which use longer rolls, require a **film magazine** (Figure 8-8), which is essentially an extension of the light-tight camera body. (see later, Film Loads).

Gate

The only place where film stock is exposed to light is in the gate. The gate is composed of two plates. The **aperture plate**, located just behind the lens, has a rectangular opening called the **aperture opening**. The dimensions of this opening are the exact full-frame aspect ratio dimensions of the film format. In a standard 16mm camera, the aperture opening is 1.33:1. If you are shooting Super 16mm, the camera will be outfitted with a 1.66:1 aperture plate (Figure 8-9).

The lens focuses all the light gathered from your scene right through this aperture opening, where it exposes (or tags) the film. The film is sandwiched between the aperture plate and the **pressure plate**, which applies constant, gentle pressure to assure that the film lies perfectly flat as it moves vertically through the gate. The light-sensitive emulsion side of the film faces the aperture and the base side of the film is against the pressure plate. The exact position of the film between these two plates is called the **film plane** (or **focal plane**) (Figure 8-10) and it is represented by the symbol ϕ, which is etched into

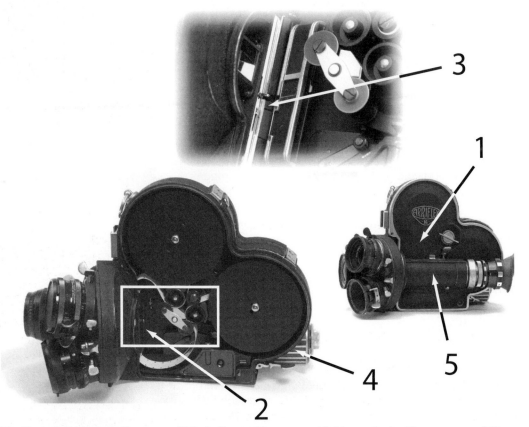

■ **Figure 8-7** The basic film camera: (1) body, (2) gate, (3) movement, (4) drive mechanism/film transport, and (5) viewing system.

■ **Figure 8-8** The magazine. A lightproof extension of the camera body, the magazine permits the rapid reloading of film in a camera. Pictured here is an Arri-BL magazine threaded (left), and mounted and threaded on the camera body (right).

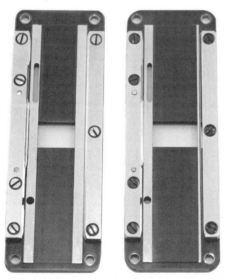

■ **Figure 8-9** A 1.33:1 aperture plate for regular 16mm filming (left) and a 1.66:1 Super16 aperture plate (right).

■ **Figure 8-10** The film plane. All film cameras have a marking on their bodies identifying exactly where the film is exposed to light. Camera-to-subject distance is measured from this precise spot.

the exterior body of the camera. Every frame of your film is exposed right here. The edges of the aperture plate become the edges of each frame. It is therefore essential that you keep your gate clean. An errant hair dancing in the aperture opening blocks light like a shadow puppet (Figure 8-11) and will become part of your image. On a film set, the camera operator should regularly "clean the gate" (see p. 337).

Movement: Claw and Shutter Mechanism

The claw and shutter work in concert with one another to precisely position and expose each and every frame of film (Figure 8-12). A strip of motion picture film is always perforated on one or both sides with **sprocket holes**. These sprocket holes allow the strip of film to

■ **Figure 8-11** Carelessness during the loading of the camera can result in nasty surprises later on, like a hair in the gate becoming a permanent addition to the image; Woody Allen exploited this flaw to comedic effect in his film *What's Up, Tiger Lilly?* (1966).

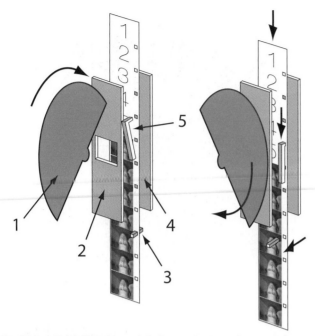

■ **Figure 8-12** The claw and shutter mechanism advances and exposes one frame of film at a time in the gate. Pictured are the shutter (1), aperture plate (2), registration pin (3), pressure plate (4), and claw (5).

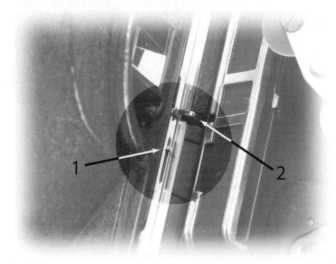

■ **Figure 8-13** The camera movement. A claw (1) advances a film strip one frame at a time while a registration pin (2) holds the frame in place when it is being exposed to light.

be easily, accurately, and gently transported through the camera.

The claw is located on the edge of the aperture plate and is responsible for positioning the film in the gate and holding it steady during the exposure. As the camera runs, the claw moves up and down. On its way up the claw is retracted into the aperture plate, but at the top of its arc, the claw reaches out and hooks a sprocket hole and pulls the film down, or advances the film, placing exactly one new frame into position in front of the aperture opening and holding it in place for exposure. The camera's **shutter** is a rotating half-disk located between the back of the lens and the aperture opening. When the 180° opening of the disk rotates in front of the gate, the film will be exposed; when the solid portion of the shutter spins into place, the film is protected from light.

As the claw advances the film one frame, the shutter rotates closed and blocks the light entering through the lens. Once the claw has positioned the new, unexposed frame of film steady in the gate, the shutter rotates open and allows the light to expose (or tag) the film, creating another frame. This is how the claw and shutter work in tandem: shutter closed, claw advances film; shutter open, claw holds film steady in the gate for exposure. At the standard transport speed this cycle occurs twenty-four times every second. That is to say, the claw and shutter mechanism create 24 frames per second. This cycle—shutter open, film stopped; shutter closed, film moves—is the intermittent movement essential to the film system.

Some cameras have an additional **registration pin** that skewers a sprocket hole to keep the frame steady in the gate. By securing two sprocket holes while a frame is being exposed, the film is held in place with much more stability and therefore a sharper, steadier image is exposed (see Figure 8-13).

Drive Mechanism and Film Transport

The camera's drive mechanism both provides power to run the film through the camera and governs the speed (frame rate) of the film. There are basically two types of motors: spring-wound and DC (direct current) electric (Figure 8-14). Cameras that use DC motors are powered by rechargeable NiCad battery belts or onboard battery packs.

Spring-wound cameras are powered by a large coiled spring much like the spring in a watch; the camera spring requires rewinding after each take. Each type of motor has its own advantages and disadvantages. In the case of spring-wound motors, one never has to worry about running out of batteries or forgetting to charge the battery beforehand. Batteries also lose their charge extremely fast under subfreezing conditions, whereas a spring-wind camera will always provide power, even in extreme weather. The limitation of spring-wound cameras is the relatively short running duration per wind. A single wind from a camera like the Bell & Howell Filmo or the Bolex will give you just under one minute of footage (depending on the age of the spring). While each wind lasts much longer than the average shot in a conventional narrative film, filmmakers who plan to use long takes should

■ **Figure 8-14** There are two types of motors that run film and govern the frame rate in a camera: electric (DC) and spring-wound. The Arri-S uses a DC battery belt (left) to power the camera, while the Filmo uses a spring-wound crank (right).

opt for a battery-powered motor, which will run as much footage per take as you want.

Another distinction of motors is their transport speed capabilities. **Constant-speed motors** run exclusively at 24 fps (sync speed), while **variable-speed motors** have the ability to run at a variety of transport speeds, giving the filmmaker a range of under-cranking or slow motion speeds to choose from (Figure 8-15). Shooting at sync speed (24 fps) is mandatory for scenes in which normal sync sound is needed; however, manipulating your camera's frame rate can be a powerfully expressive technique when used appropriately in shots not requiring sync.

■ **Figure 8-15** Frame rate selector for the Arri-BL. A variable-speed motor adds the capability to record an image at rates other than 24 fps, while a constant-speed motor will only run film at 24 fps.

Most of the other moving parts inside a camera are dedicated to transporting the film to and from the gate (Figure 8-17). They include the **feed and take-up spindles**, which feed the unexposed raw film stock into the gate and then take up the exposed footage. When using larger loads of film, these spindles are located in the magazine. The **drive sprockets** (or drive rollers) are always rimmed with sprocket teeth to transport the film at a steady rate in concert with the intermittent movement of the claw and shutter. The rollers without sprockets are **guide rollers**, which guide the film onto the drive sprockets, ensuring smooth engagement with the film's sprocket holes. Film always travels in between the guide rollers and the drive sprockets.

One additional important element of the drive mechanism, which isn't exactly a physical component but rather an indispensable part of the transport system for both camera and projector, is the **loops** (short for **Latham's Loops**).[2] Loops are small bends of extra film located just above and below the gate. With the drive sprocket feeding film at a steady rate and the claw pulling, holding, and pulling the film, loops act as the shock absorbers of the whole transport system, providing some slack between these two movements, ensuring that the film does not tear in the course of all of this insistent activity. The size of

---

[2]Latham's Loops are named after Major Woodville Latham, who created the loops in order to shoot with and project long, heavy spools of film, rather than limit himself to the 20-second "living pictures" scenes displayed in the enclosed Kinetoscope boxes popular at the time (circa 1894). Latham needed longer lengths and projection because he wanted to cash in on showing boxing prizefights life sized! This proved to be one of the major innovations in the history of cinema.

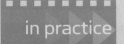 **in practice**

In Wong Kar-Wai's *In the Mood for Love* the tension and drama of repressed desire is protracted and stylized through the use of frequent slow motion sequences. Darren Aronofsky's *Requiem for a Dream* uses fast motion (under-cranked shots) to illustrate the warped state of mind and perspective of characters under the influence of drugs, both legal and illegal.

■ **Figure 8-16** Wong Kar-Wai's *In the Mood for Love* (2000) (top) and Aronofsky's *Requiem for a Dream* (2000) (bottom).

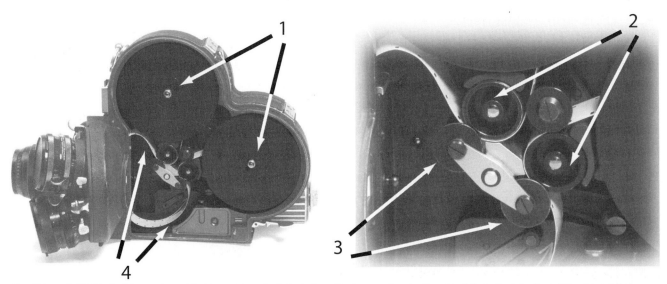

■ **Figure 8-17** Most of the equipment inside a camera body is dedicated to transporting the film to and from the gate. Essential components include: feed and take-up spindles (1), drive sprockets (2), guide rollers (3), and the film loops (4).

the loops needs to be fairly exact. In some cameras loops are created automatically by loop formers, and in others they are created manually, with notches or etchings in the camera to aid the person loading the film to create the proper size loops. While it is indeed maddening, **"loosing your loop"** does not mean that you're ready for the nuthouse; it means that, usually as a result of improper loading, one or both loops shrink until the film is pulled taught between the movement of the claw and the drive sprocket. If you lose your loop the film jumps in the gate and sprocket holes can rip. When this happens all shooting must stop while the camera is reloaded properly (see later, Loading a Film Camera).

Viewing System

All cameras have some sort of viewfinder that allows us to see and evaluate our framing before and during each take (Figure 8-18). Although there are a few different viewfinder systems, most recent cameras utilize a **reflex viewing system**. Reflex viewing means that we see the scene through the same lens

■ **Figure 8-18** A student checking the framing on the orientable viewfinder of an Arri-SRI.

with which we shoot the scene. In other words, the lens for our viewing is the same lens used for exposing the film. This requires that the light coming into the lens must be not only focused on the film plane, but also diverted in some way to a **ground glass** or **fiber-optic viewfinder screen**, for the camera operator to see. There are two different systems commonly used for diverting this light from the lens to the viewing screen: the mirrored shutter and the beam splitter.

The mirrored shutter system (Figure 8-19) utilizes the camera's rotating shutter to divert light to the ground glass viewfinder. The front side of the shutter is a mirror that reflects all of the light coming in from the lens to the viewfinder when the shutter is closed to the film. When the mirrored shutter rotates open to expose the film, all of the light entering from the lens hits the film plane and, for this instant, there is no image in the viewfinder. The mirrored shutter allows 100% of the light to expose your film half of the time and also diverts 100% of the light to your eye, but only half of the time, so there is a "flicker" while you view a scene as the camera is running. Once the camera stops rolling, the viewfinder stops in the closed position and you will have a bright and flickerless image to help you set up your next shot. Because the mirror lining on the shutter adds weight, these shutters are always butterfly shaped, meaning that the 180° opening is divided between two 90° wedges to more evenly distribute the centrifugal force as the shutter rotates.

The beam splitter system works on a different principle. It uses a prism located between the lens and the film plane to divert a small percentage of the light to the viewfinder before it reaches the shutter or gate. The prism diverts around 20% of the light entering from the lens to the ground glass viewfinder screen, leaving 80% to expose the film. This makes for a flickerless viewing image, but one that is not as bright as with the mirrored shutter, especially when the camera is not running. Also, this obviously steals a bit of the incoming light away from the film, which means that some exposure compensation must be made, since not all of the light from a scene is making it to the film emulsion.

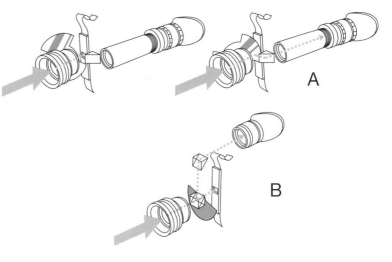

■ **Figure 8-19** The mirrored shutter viewing system (A) and the beam splitter viewing system (B).

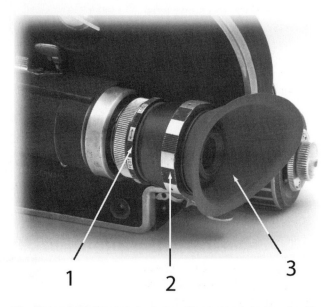

Looking through the viewfinder, you usually see more than just the image on the ground glass viewing screen: you also see **finder markings**, which are etched or painted onto the viewing screen to help you compose your frame. Almost all viewfinders have four sharp corners, slightly smaller than the full area of the viewfinder, which are **camera aperture** markings and **center cross hairs** marking the exact center of the frame (Figure 8-20).

Depending on the specific camera, you may also see **TV safe** markings, which is the same aspect ratio as standard 16mm but is a slightly smaller area to account for the masking used on television sets. TV safe is also referred to as **title safe**, as it is recommended that all your titles and credits fit within these markings to ensure that they are not cut off in any format your film may ultimately be distributed in. If you are shooting on Super 16 film, your camera will have a viewfinder with the corresponding aspect ratio (1.66:1).

One final important component of any viewing system is the **diopter**, found at the end of the viewfinder (Figure 8-21), just behind the eyepiece. The diopter is a simple lens that is focused on the viewfinding screen. Diopters must be adjusted for the specific vision of the person who is looking through the camera. Diopter adjustment allows people who normally wear glasses to go without them and to press their eye right up to the viewfinder to see the entire viewing screen clearly. It is important to remember to adjust the diopter before shooting, because the person before you may have adjusted it to a vision completely different than your own. In this case, every shot will appear soft, even though the lens is focused correctly.

The easiest way to set a diopter is to open up your aperture all the way, aim your camera at an uncluttered area, like a white wall, and de-focus the lens as much as possible. Next, loosen the locking screw on the diopter and rotate it until the finder markings (cross hairs, TV safe, etc.) are sharp. You will also see the grains of the ground glass viewing screen get sharp; then re-tighten the locking screw.

■ **Figure 8-20** The viewfinder of a 16mm camera. Finder markings in the viewfinder commonly include frame-edge brackets, TV-safe markings, and center cross hairs..

■ **Figure 8-21** The Arri viewfinder, with a locking/unlocking ring (1), a focusing ring (2), and the eyecup (3). At the end of the viewfinder is the diopter, a simple lens that focuses the image seen on the viewfinder. This makes it possible for people who wear glasses to look into the viewfinder without them.

■ LOADING A FILM CAMERA

The path that the film takes from the feed reel to the take-up reel is called the **threading pattern** (Figure 8-22). Every film camera model has a unique pattern, but the basic transport elements are common to almost every camera you will encounter, whether you are using a film magazine or loading small 100-foot spools directly in the body of the camera. Even cameras which offer automatic threading are not radically different from those requiring manual loading. Film always travels the same basic route inside the camera:

1. The unexposed raw film stock (on a core or spool) travels from the feed spindle and then . . .
2. passes between the feed sprocket roller and guide, and next . . .

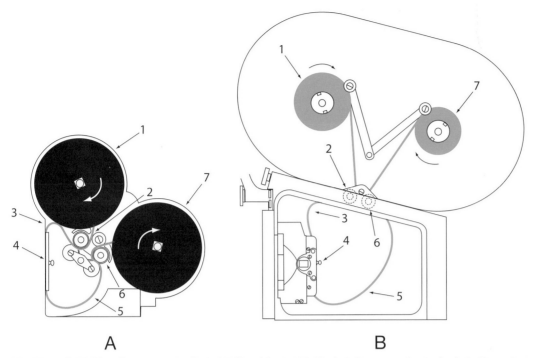

A   B

■ **Figure 8-22** Threading patterns for the Arri-S (A) and the Arri-BL (B). In both cameras the feed spindle (1) sends the film to the feed sprocket and guide (2), forms the first loop (3), passes through the gate (4), and forms the second loop (5), before going through the take-up sprocket and guide (6), and is finally rolled into the take-up spindle (7).

3. forms into the first loop and . . .
4. then passes through the gate (between the pressure plate and aperture plate), emulsion side facing the lens, where it is exposed and then advanced by the claw, and next . . .
5. forms the second loop, before . . .
6. passing between the take-up sprocket roller and guide, after which . . .
7. it is taken up by the take-up spindle (fitted with a core or spool).

Manual load cameras require you to thread the film through each mechanism, which often means separating the guide rollers from the drive sprockets, and the pressure plate from the aperture plate, to thread the film in between. It is essential to secure the film in its path by closing the guide rollers and pressure plate after you thread each mechanism, or the film can jump out of the threading path, rip, lose its loop, or wobble inside the gate. **Automatic threading** cameras simply require you to engage the automatic guide mechanism, trim the head end of the film, and feed it between the first sprocket and guide roller. Even though the threading and even the loop formation are done automatically, you should be familiar with the threading pattern of the camera in case something goes wrong.

Film Loads

Film stocks for 16mm cameras most commonly come in two different configurations for camera loading: **100-foot daylight-loading spools** and **400-foot magazine cores** (Figure 8-23). Be aware that not all cameras use both loads. You must know the film capacity of your camera before you buy your film.

100-foot Daylight-Loading Spools
A 100-foot daylight-loading spool at normal sync speed will give you around two minutes and 45 seconds of footage. The 100-foot spools are very compact and are designed to be loaded inside the body of a camera without the need for complete dark-

ness. You may load a daylight spool in subdued light without ruining the film. The film stock is wound around a solid, black spool that completely and snugly covers the sides so that light cannot enter from the edges and expose the film. The top layer of film is obviously exposed to light during loading, but being opaque, these first layers of film protect the under layers around which they are wrapped, so the bulk of the film load is not exposed to light. When unloading a daylight spool in the open, the tail layers are also exposed. This is important to remember if you have vital footage all the way to the last frames of the film— known as **critical ends.** You will probably not want to sacrifice the ends to light, so you will need to unload your footage in complete darkness (see later for changing bag). Film manufacturers know that a few feet at the head and tail of a 100-foot spool will be exposed, so there is always slightly more than 100 feet of footage on each roll to compensate.

■ **Figure 8-23** Film loads: 16mm film is commonly sold in 400-foot core loads (that require the loading of film inside a lightproof changing bag) and 100-foot daylight-loading spools (that allow the loading of a camera in full daylight without the need of a changing bag).

When loading a 100-foot daylight spool you need to have another, empty 100-foot spool for take-up. Usually, the previous feed spool, now empty after shooting, becomes the take-up spool for the next load of film. To attach film to the take-up spool, fold over and sharply crease three frames into the head end of the film (about an inch) (**Figure 8-24**). Slip the entire doubled end into the cutout slot in the hub of the spool and wind the film around itself a few revolutions so that there is no possibility of the film slipping out of the hub. Then you can put the spool on the take-up post. Never use tape to attach film to a spool.

■ **Figure 8-24** To attach film to a daylight-loading spool, simply bend three frames and then insert them in the slot at the hub of the spool.

400-foot Cores

Longer loads of 16mm film commonly come as 400 feet of film tightly wound around a 2-inch plastic core. The 400-foot cores are always loaded in camera magazines, and since there is no protection from accidental exposure to light, they require loading in complete darkness.

Camera Magazines

A **camera magazine** (**mag** for short) is a light-tight chamber that can be preloaded and easily attaches to and detaches from the body of the camera. There are basically two types of magazines: the **displacement magazine** and the **coaxial magazine** (**Figure 8-25**). The displacement magazine, occasionally called "mouse ears," places the feed and take-up sides next to each other on a single plane and shifts the film from the front (feed side) to the back (take-up side) of the magazine. Also, the feed and take-up are often housed within the same compartment, which requires that the entire film-loading process be completed in total darkness. In coaxial magazines the feed and take-up sides are parallel, side-by-side, and the film shifts from the left to the right side during shooting. Feed and take-up sides are in different compartments, so it's only necessary to load the feed side in darkness. Once the feed side compartment is locked shut, the rest of the threading process can be done in the light, including attaching the film to the take-up core. The other advantage to the coaxial design is its relative compactness compared with displacement mags.

Coaxial mag (left) and displacement mag (right). A coaxial magazine has separate compartments for its feed and take-up rolls, making its threading in the changing bag an easy deal. A displacement magazine has only one chamber for both its feed and take-up rolls,

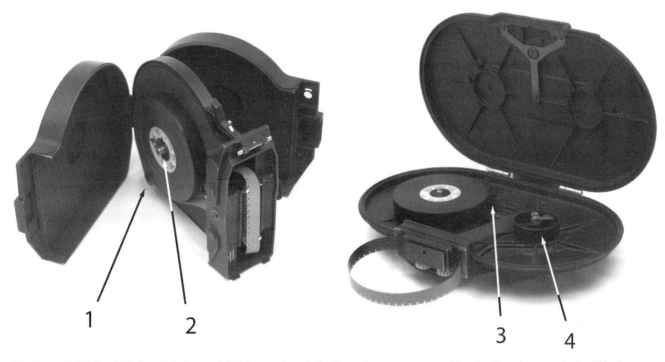

■ **Figure 8-25** Coaxial (left) and displacement (right) magazines. In the illustration we can see a guide roller (1) and a core adaptor (2) in the coaxial mag, and a guide roller (3) and a collapsible core (4) in the displacement mag.

necessitating the use of the changing bag for the whole process of threading the mag. In the illustration we can see a guide roller (1) and a core adaptor (2) in the coaxial mag, and a guide roller (3) and a collapsible core (4) in the displacement mag.

All magazines also have **guide rollers**, which help the film feed smoothly and take up cleanly, and sometimes serve as a footage counter. Without these rollers, the film runs the risk of rubbing the sides of the magazine. Finally, all magazines have posts for the feed and take-up reels, but usually they are simply spindles that do not accommodate the opening of the standard 2-inch core. Many magazines require the use of two **core adaptors**, which lock onto the spindles, before you load the film. Core adaptors must stay inside the magazine for reuse when unloading film, and must not be removed with the core and accidentally sent to the lab. A mag with only one core adaptor is useless.

Not all cameras accommodate the use of magazines (e.g., Bell & Howell Filmo, Canon Scoopic); conversely, not all cameras allow 100-foot spools to be loaded inside the body of the camera (e.g., Arri-BL, Arri-SR). There are, of course, cameras that will accommodate both film loads (Arri-S, Bolex). The mags for cameras that accept only 400-foot core loads have the drive sprockets built right into the magazine, rather than the camera body. In fact, the Arri-SR coaxial magazine (Figure 8-26) contains drive sprockets and the pressure plate. One of the great benefits of using magazines, besides the longer film rolls, is that they allow for the preloading and very quick changing of magazines during the shoot.

■ **Figure 8-26** Arri-SR coaxial magazine. One of the advantages of this mag is its integrated pressure plate (1), which makes loading and reloading a snap.

Not every film camera is suited to every project. Different cameras have different creative capabilities. Here are a few details that you should consider before checking out a camera:

1. *Power:* battery power or spring wind.
2. *Transport speed:* variable speeds or sync sound only (24 fps).
3. *Sync sound shooting:* sync sound camera (quiet) or nonsync camera (smaller).
4. *Film capacity:* 400-foot core (magazines) or 100-foot daylight spools (internal loads) or both.
5. *Lenses:* zoom lens or prime lenses on turret.

■ **Figure 8-27** 400 ft. cores require their loading inside a lightproof changing bag. This is a critical procedure that requires a lot of concentration.

Does all of this have any bearing on the creative aspects of your film? Yes. The film capacity of the camera and even the type of magazine can have some effect on the visual conception of your movie. While allowing for longer loads of film (and very long takes), cameras that use displacement magazines are generally large and cumbersome and limit your mobility and ability to shoot in very confined spaces, like a car. Cameras that use only 100-foot internal loads are often very compact and allow you great flexibility in camera placement and angles, but, of course, they have a very limited film capacity per load. I once had a student who tried to shoot a film in one of New York City's last remaining telephone booths with an Arri-BL (a bulky 16mm camera with a displacement mag). He was simply not able to fit the camera inside the booth and get the focus he needed. So again, you need to be aware of the requirements of your project as you consider the features of available film cameras.

Loading a Mag in a Changing Bag

Because there is nothing protecting the film on a 400-foot core from being accidentally exposed to light, magazines must be loaded in absolute darkness. We could use a darkroom for this, but more often loading is done on the set inside a **changing bag** (also called **dark bag**). A changing bag is simply a large, lightproof bag with a double zipper opening at the base and sleeves on the other end that enable the camera loader access to the inside of the bag without leaking in light (Figure 8-27).

Here is the process for loading a magazine in a changing bag:

1. Make sure the inside of the changing bag is clean. Hair, dust, and bits of film left in the bag by the previous user can easily get inside the magazine and wind up in the camera gate.
2. Put everything you need to load the magazine inside the bag. This includes the magazine (already opened and with core adaptors in place), the take-up core (if you're using a single-chamber magazine), and, of course, the can of film. You should remove the fabric tape from around the can before you put it into the bag, but be careful not to jostle the can open when closing the bag and inserting your arms.
3. Place your arms inside the changing bag, pulling the sleeves up to your elbows to avoid light leaks, open the can of film, and remove the film from its plastic bag. You will notice that the end of the film is taped down with a small strip of paper tape.
4. Remove the tape from the film and stick it to the inside of the film can lid. It is important that you do not let this piece of tape simply float around inside the bag. If it sticks onto your film, it will jam the magazine. You can also reuse this tape to secure your exposed film after you unload it from the magazine later.
5. Feed the film through the feed slot (or through the feed rollers). Now you can put the core onto the feed spindle (with core adaptor), but be careful. You should gently push on the plastic core to get the film onto the post. DO NOT push on the film itself, be-

cause the film could "dish," meaning a portion of film pushes away from the rest of the roll and unspools.

6. Put the feed guide roller into position against the edge of the roll of film.
7. If you're loading a coaxial magazine, you can close and lock the feed side door and remove the magazine to finish loading.
8. If you're using a single-chamber displacement mag, then you'll start to wish for Superman's x-ray vision while you: (a) create the proper loop (by measuring to notches on the magazine by feel), (b) thread the film through the take-up opening in the magazine, (c) attach the film to the 2-inch take-up core, and (d) put the core on the take-up spindle all by feel and within the changing bag.
9. Engage the take-up guide roller and close the door.

You are now free to take the magazine out and secure it to the camera.

To attach the film to the take-up core, fold and crease the tip of the film over itself by half a frame and slip this thicker end into the core slot, with the film wrapping around the core in the same direction as the slot. Then wind the film several revolutions to ensure that the film will not slip out of the core slot (Figure 8-28).

■ **Figure 8-28** Attaching film to a take-up core. Crease half a frame over itself and insert in the core's slit, then roll two or three revolutions to make sure it will stay attached.

After the film is securely attached to the core you may gently push the plastic core onto the take-up spindle (with core adaptor). Never use tape to attach film to the take-up core. Also, while it may seem like a more secure fit, do not wrap the film *against* the direction of the core slot. This will create a slight lump that will only become more pronounced as the core gathers more and more film. This lump can create roller noise and even scrape against the inside of the magazine causing all sorts of trouble.

Miscellaneous Tips for Loading Film

1. Practice, practice, practice. Film is expensive, and properly loading your camera is absolutely crucial. So, before you load real film stock you should always practice loading a camera or magazine with a **dummy roll** (junk film) many times, first in the light and then inside a changing bag, to get familiar with the threading pattern, loop size, and the "feel" of loading that specific camera.
2. Check out your camera. Before you take your camera away from the rental house or check-out facility, run a few feet of dummy film through with the camera door open to make sure it's running smoothly. A maladjusted claw or mistimed drive sprocket can cause you to repeatedly lose your loop.

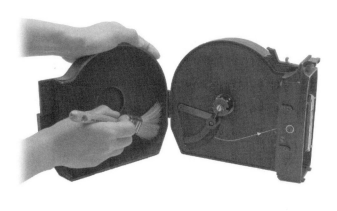

■ **Figure 8-29** It is always a good idea to brush the inside of a magazine to prevent dust, film chips, or fibers to show up on your footage (left). Likewise, taping the door of the magazine (or the camera body) safeguards your footage against possible light leaks.

3. Clean your camera and magazine compartments (Figure 8-29). You may certainly use canned air to clean your magazine of dust, but is not advisable to use compressed air to clean the inside of a camera because this can force dust into the gate and the back of the lens. Cleaning a camera is best done with a white, soft bristle brush. White bristles are used in case the brush loses a hair; you will easily see a white hair in the black interior of the camera body.

4. Tape all of the seams around the door. Not only will this prevent light from leaking into the chamber, but it also is a visual reminder to everyone on the set that there is film inside the camera, so do not open it up!

6. Always have extra take-up cores or spools in case the previous user did not leave one inside the camera. You cannot use the camera without a take-up.

7. Do not hassle the camera loader! Hovering around the person loading the film, trying to get them to move faster, only increases their anxiety and is seriously counterproductive. Let them do their job calmly and carefully.

Removing Exposed Film and Splitting Cores

As you are shooting, when the 400-foot core runs out, the D.P. announces "Roll out," and the magazine on the camera is changed with a fresh pre-loaded one. The exposed film is now completely on the take-up core and must be carefully removed. Keep in mind that your exposed film is the most precious item on the movie set; it contains the results of all of the hard work and long hours of the cast and crew, so take special care when unloading a magazine. The magazine is unloaded in a changing bag (that also contains the plastic film bag and can). When you open the magazine, feel the edges of the film to make sure that it has taken up smoothly. The exposed film will not be wound as tightly as the unexposed stock you loaded, so make sure that you do not pull the film up by the edges or it will dish. Removing an exposed core usually involves first removing the film with the core adaptor and then removing the core adaptor from the core. It's easy to forget this and inadvertently send the core adaptor to the lab—which is a costly mistake. After you've safely done this you can put the film in the bag, the bag in the can, and remove the can. Tape all around the edge to secure the lid shut and label the can (see p. 338 for proper film can labeling).

In cases where you have not used all of your film—say you've only exposed 200 feet out of 400—you can **split the core**. Splitting a core means breaking the film at the loops (which are outside the magazine), and unloading it twice. First unload the exposed footage in the take-up side, tape the can shut and label the can, then unload the feed side, tape up the can, and label that can with the amount of unexposed footage left on the core, the type of film, and the words "**short ends**." This film can be used another day.

■ Film Stocks and Processing

Anatomy of Raw Film Stock

There are two major types of film stocks, **camera film** and **print film**. Print film is used in the laboratory to make the various prints during the postproduction process. Camera film, that is the focus of this section, is the **raw film stock** thar is loaded into a filmmaker's camera.

Motion picture film stock (Figure 8-30) is basically a long strip of strong and flexible material, called the **base**, coated with a photosensitive substance, called the **emulsion**; the film stock is perforated down one

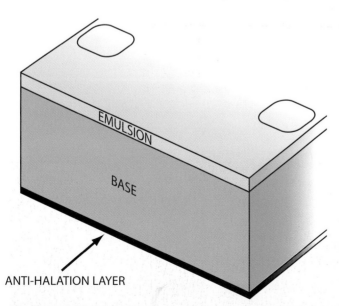

■ **Figure 8-30** A typical black and white negative film stock is composed of a light sensitive emulsion layer containing silver halide crystals, a base, and an anti-halation coating.

edge with **sprockets holes** in order to facilitate transport through the camera. As the vehicle for the photographic image, the film **base** must not only be strong, but must also be optically transparent without any imperfections that might distort the image. Film base for camera films is commonly made from **cellulose triacetate**, which replaced the highly flammable and archivally unsound cellulose nitrate around 1950. The base is between 125 and 130 micrometers thick (around five thousandths of an inch).

The optically clear base is evenly coated with the light-sensitive component of the film stock, the emulsion. Emulsion consists of a layer of microscopic, randomly but evenly distributed, **silver halide crystals** suspended in gelatin and bound to the base with an adhesive layer called the **substratum** or **subbing layer**. The silver halide crystals are highly sensitive to light and are the element that actually creates the photographic image. Black-and-white film, as seen in the Figure 8-30, has only one layer of emulsion, whereas color film has three layers of emulsion (see later). Film which has not been exposed to light is called **raw stock**.

On the other side of the base is a flat black coating called the **anti-halation backing**. This black layer is light absorbent and keeps light, which is passing through the emulsion and then through the base with each exposure, from reflecting back and reexposing the emulsion from behind.

All motion picture film is perforated down one or both edges with **sprocket holes** (also called **perfs**) that allows the camera to gently and accurately advance the film, one frame at a time, through the gate, to create each exposure. Also along the edge of the film are **latent image edge code numbers**, which are imprinted at the time of manufacture. Edge code numbers are a sequential series of numbers along the edge of the film that assign a unique and specific identification number to every frame in the roll. In 16mm film, the edge code numbers are printed every 20 frames (every 6 inches) (Figure 8-31).

To the left of the edge code number is a small black dot indicating the **zero frame**, which means the frame identified by that number—for example, •KM48 1347 3556. Then each frame toward the tail end of the roll is that number plus one frame (. . . 3556 + 1), two frames (. . . 3556 + 2), three frames (. . . 3556 + 3), four frames (. . . 3556 + 4), and so on, until after (. . . 3556 + 19) the next imprinted number switches over one digit (•KM48 1347 3557). The ability to identify and find each and every frame is important throughout the workflow of a project shot on film, especially when we need to identify exact edit point frames, should we wish to go back to our original negative in order to finish our project as a film print (see Chapter 19). These numbers are called *latent image* edge code numbers because they are imprinted onto the film with light and are not visible until after the film is processed.

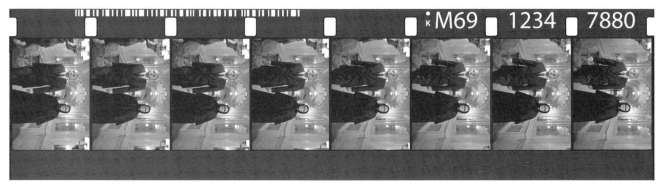

■ **Figure 8-31** Edge code numbers are standard in all film stocks, providing a point of reference to the negative cutter during the conforming process.

Film Processing Basics

When the silver halide crystals are struck by light (actually light photons) there is a chemical reaction to that energy on the atomic level that corresponds to the intensity of the light. The greater the light intensity, the greater the chemical reaction, meaning the more silver halide grains are exposed to light, or "tagged." This is an **exposure**, and when an exposure is taken on one frame of film, essentially what is created is a precise chemical record of the light intensities reflecting off your scene at that moment. A film camera takes twenty-four exposures every second. At this point, the emulsion has what is called a **latent image**, meaning that although the silver halide crystals have become chemically activated, there is not yet any visible change to the crystals (not that you could see it anyway, because exposed film must be kept in absolute darkness). It requires additional chemical processing to produce a visible change. A latent image is an exposure that has not yet been developed, and at this point it is very unstable, which is why you should send your film to the lab as quickly as possible.

At the laboratory, when exposed film goes through the liquid developing agent, those areas that were tagged with light turn into pure **metallic silver particles**, while those grains that were not exposed remain as silver halide. Next the film is run through a **stop bath**, to arrest the developing process at precisely the proper moment, and then through a fixing bath. The **fixer** removes all of the unexposed silver halide particles, leaving behind masses of opaque silver particles in varying degrees of density, which correspond to the various levels of light exposure. A bright area of the image, which exposed many crystals, will be very dense, while a low light area would have exposed only a few crystals and therefore will have a thinner silver particle density. An area that corresponds to a black part of the image will have exposed no crystals and will therefore have no silver particle density at all.

After the development process what we are left with is a **photographic negative**—a perfect record of the scene, in silver particle densities, which is the inverse of the actual light values. Imagine projecting this image, pushing light through this strip of film. The area corresponding to black, with no silver density, would be transparent, with only the clear base between the lamp and the screen, allowing the projector light to pass directly through. The area corresponding to a white detail in the scene would have built up a very dense and opaque mass of silver particles, allowing no light to pass through and would therefore appear black on the screen. Any density in between would be a shade of gray, with the inverse relationship to the actual brightness of the photographed detail (Figures 8-32).

After running through the fixer, the film is washed, the anti-halation backing is removed, and the film is dried (Figures 8-33).

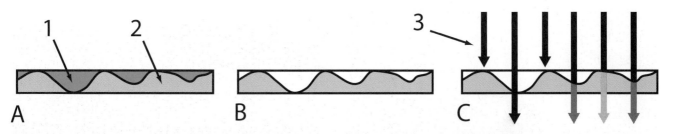

■ **Figure 8-32** When film is exposed to light (A), some of the silver halide crystals change into metallic silver according to the amount of light they received (2), while unaffected crystals remain in their silver halide form (1). During the processing of negative film, the unaffected crystals are removed (B) leaving behind various densities of metallic silver. Areas with heavy silver density block light (3) and areas with little or no silver particles allow light to pass through.

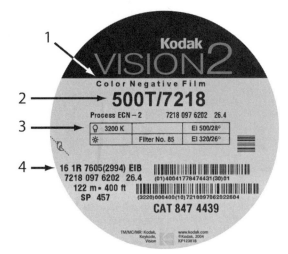

■ **Figure 8-33** During processing and development, film stock is run along rollers that dip it in a chemical soup.

■ **Figure 8-34** A film can will always have the following information: whether it is color or black and white, negative or reversal (1), the Exposure Index (2), a color temperature rating (3), and the gauge (4).

Identifying Film Stocks

We have discussed the basics of all film stocks, but obviously there is more to it than this. All camera film stocks are further identified and ultimately chosen according to five major characteristics:

1. Color or black and white
2. Negative or reversal
3. Film speed (also called the exposure index, or EI)
4. Color temperature balance
5. Gauge/format

Let's take a closer look at each category (Figures 8-34).

Color or Black and White

Obviously, this is a choice between film that renders images as tones of the gray scale (black and white) and films that duplicate the colors of the visible light spectrum as they appear in your scene (color film). As of the writing of this book, Kodak offers twelve different color film stocks but only four different black-and-white stocks for 16mm production. It is clear that black-and-white film is receiving very little research and development attention of late because very few people opt to make black-and-white movies these days—and for those who do, removing the color component is easily done in digital postproduction (Figure 8-35).

■ **Figure 8-35** Woody Allen's *Manhattan* (1979, right) was shot with black-and-white film stock, unlike many contemporary films released in black and white, like Clooney's *Good Night, and Good luck* (2005, left), which are shot on color stock and desaturated in post.

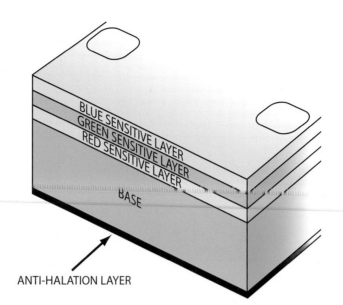

■ **Figure 8-36** The composition of a color film stock includes three emulsion layers, each one sensitive to a primary color. The color dyes that form the image in negative film are the complementary, or opposite, of the emulsion sensitivity. The dye in the blue sensitive layer is yellow, in the green layer is magenta, and in the red layer is cyan.

The basic construction of color film is similar to that shown in Figure 8-30 for black-and-white film stock—emulsion, subbing layer, base, and anti-halation backing—but there is one significant difference. Color film contains three layers of light-sensitive emulsion instead of one. Since every color in the visible spectrum is made up of some combination of the three primary colors of light, red, green, and blue, each of the three layers is sensitive to one of these primary hues.

The first layer is sensitive to blue light, the second layer is sensitive to green light, and the final layer is sensitive to red light. This three-layered emulsion is called **color tripak** (Figure 8-36). Also, since all silver halide emulsions are sensitive to the blue range of the light spectrum, there is an additional yellow filter coating between the first blue layer and the other two emulsion layers. This yellow filter absorbs all blue light before it reaches the green and red emulsions.

Because silver halide photochemistry is exclusively a black-and-white process, color film additionally incorporates **color dye couplers** into the emulsion gelatin along with the silver halide crystals. **Color dye couplers** are grains containing color dye that cluster around the exposed metallic silver sites. During the development process, the couplers release their dye in relation to the density of the exposed silver grains. The greater the density, the more dye couplers bunch up and the more saturated the color will appear. The color dyes that form the image in negative film (as discussed previously) are the complement, or opposite, of the actual color in the scene. Specifically, the dye couplers used in the blue sensitive layers are yellow, the dye couplers used in the green layers are magenta, and the dye couplers used in the red layers are cyan (Figure 8-37).

Negative or Reversal

When **negative film** is developed, the values of light and color are represented in inverse relationship to the actual scene photographed. Light areas are dark and colors are represented by their complement. Camera original negative film is not useful as-is and must be printed onto another strip of film or transferred to DV in order to reverse the image so we can see what we've captured.

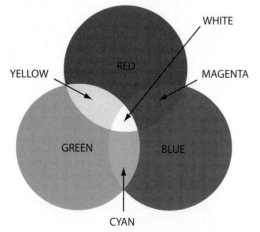

■ **Figure 8-37** The color wheel shows at a glance the three primary colors of light: red, green, and blue and their respective complementary colors directly opposite: cyan, magenta, and yellow. See the color insert in Chapter 13.

In Zhang Yimou's *Hero* (2002), various episodes narrated by Nameless (Jet Li) are clearly demarcated by their use of color and reflect the mythic storytelling style of both the character and the film itself. Details in the costumes, set design, and lighting are carefully controlled to reflect a unified and vividly stylized tone without ascribing a specific psychological state or metaphoric association to the use of a particular color. Zhang and his cinematographer, Christopher Doyle, alternately shot Kodak and Fuji stocks to achieve the specific effect they needed to push color film to the spectacular limits seen in these scenes from *Hero*. Here some thoughts on the use of color written by Christopher Doyle in his journals while making *Hero*:

> *The same story is told in a number of ways, a slightly different version each time that is as much a response to as a compounding of the story that came before. Each elaboration has a color system of its own—white, red, blue, and green are the colors we have settled on. Some will give (and have given) complex explanations for what those colors do or mean, but for me the choices have come as much out of personal taste and convenience as any concept of color or theory of Art.*
>
> *Like the West from Aristotle until Newton, Chinese conceptual systems associate color with elements, objects, parts of the body, and sounds . . .*
>
> *As far as I'm concerned, these colors are nothing more or less than what they are.*

Red
Red is primary in the Chinese world. Red demands. Red takes all in. The red in Hero *can't be* Raise the Red Lantern *red. It has to have a touch more blue so*

it will relate better to the blue part of the film. It also has to be softened but not polluted by our Hu Yang leaves, which are so yellow and light. Our red can't touch the green that is the past (and maybe dreamed) section. It has to be the red of a hero, a red of decisiveness in the face of moral quandary. It has to mean resolve.

Blue
Transparent. Lots of sky. Unreal. Make it beautiful, like a concept. As thin as watercolor. Lots of high-speed. Movement follows story—as little as possible at beginning of the section, then more evident movement.

(From R34G38B25, by Christopher Doyle, Gingko Press, 2004)

■ Figure 8-38 Scenes from Zhang's *Hero*. See the color insert in Chapter 13.

Reversal film creates positive images—images with the same light and color values of the actual scene—right on the camera original film (Figure 8-39).

Reversal films are designed to go directly from camera, to the editing bench, to projection, without the need for additional prints or transfers. In the mid-20th century, 16mm reversal film was the standard format for television news crews. They could shoot a breaking story, like a building fire, on reversal film, get the film to the lab for processing

A   B

■ **Figure 8-39** Reversal film stocks render positive images, just like our subject (A). Negative stocks render a negative image, the exact opposite in terms of brightness and color (B), and need to be printed to create a positive image

and get the footage back to the station, cut it, and put it on the air within a few hours, after which they would probably never use it again. There was no need for additional prints (costing additional money). But in the late 1970s, when video technology completely replaced film for all news gathering, the market for reversal film dwindled to a trickle. Kodak offers only four reversal film stocks in 16mm—two color and two black and white, and they are generally regarded as having the least finesse of all of the films in the catalog. These days, reversal film is considered a specialty item, but enough students still use it to warrant a brief explanation.

The make-up of reversal film emulsion is essentially the same as that of negative film. The difference really comes in the processing. You already understand that the silver halide crystals that have been exposed to light develop into metallic silver of various densities. However, instead of the unexposed silver halide grains being washed away in the fixing process, reversal film undergoes a **bleach process** that washes away the *exposed silver grains* and leaves behind the *unexposed* crystals, which form densities exactly the opposite of negative film—that is to say, densities that correspond positively to the original light values (Figure 8-40).

A white area in the frame, which exposed a lot of silver halide crystals, would have all of those crystals washed away: no crystals means total transparency. A black area, which exposed no grains, would have nothing washed away and therefore would have a deep density of unexposed silver halide, and so on. The unexposed silver halide left behind is then uniformly reexposed under an even and consistent light in a process called **fogging**, and then is developed a second time to transform all of the remaining silver halide crystals into opaque metallic silver. Finally, the film is fixed in a chemical bath. The result is an image that retains the original light values of the scene, forming a positive image.

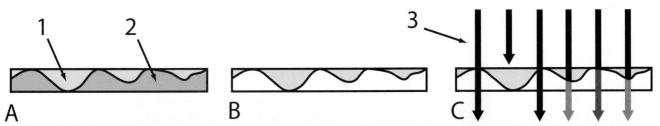

A   B   C

■ **Figure 8-40** Reversal film processing and development works just like negative film, in that exposure to light (A) chemically affects silver halide crystals (1) and turns some of them into metallic silver (2). The difference comes when the exposed metallic silver is removed (B) leaving the unexposed crystals behind; which are then reexposed and processed turning them into metallic silver. This creates a positive image when developed and projected (C). Areas with heavy density block light and areas with little or no silver particles allow light to pass through (3).

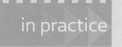

The exposure index scale corresponds exactly to that of the ASA (American Standards Association) scale, which is used for still photography film stocks, and to the ISO (International Standards Association) scale. Although different light meters will label the film sensitivity setting with different indexes, they are all the same scale.

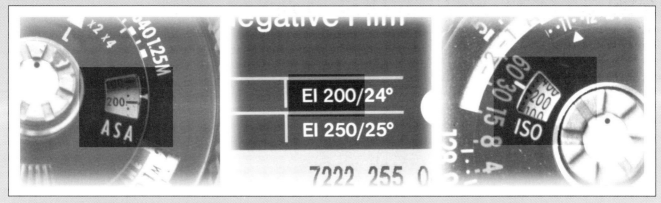

■ **Figure 8-41** EI, ISO, ASA. The Exposure Index (EI), the International Organization for Standardization (ISO), and the American Standards Association scale (ASA) are analogous and can still be found in many film related pieces of equipment. An older incident light meter with an ASA scale (left), a box of film with the EI scale (middle) and a newer incident light meter with an ISO scale (right).

Reversal color film additionally renders the original colors of the scene as a positive image and therefore incorporates primary color dye couplers that match the color sensitivity of each emulsion layer: blue dye coupler for the blue sensitive layer, green dye coupler for the green layer, and red dye coupler for the red layer.

Film Speed (EI)

The sensitivity of a specific film stock to light is referred to generally as the film's speed, and each individual film stock has a specific **exposure index** (or **EI**) that gives us a relative indication of how that stock responds to light. Film stocks that require a lot of light to make an exposure, like EI 50 film, are called **slow films**, while stocks that can create an image in low light situations, like EI 500 films, are called **fast film** stocks. The higher the EI number the faster the film and vice versa.

Some common film speeds for color film stocks, in order of increasing sensitivity to light, are EI 50, EI 64, EI 100, EI 200, EI 400, EI 250, and EI 500. A doubling of the EI number represents a doubling of the emulsion sensitivity, so EI 200 film is twice as fast (twice as sensitive to light) as EI 100, meaning that EI 200 requires only half as much light to make the same exposure.

However, while it is true that using fast film makes production easier in many ways by allowing you to reduce the amount of lighting units you need to light a scene, or even to go without artificial light altogether, there is a trade-off. What makes film more or less sensitive to light is the size of the silver halide crystals in the emulsion. Larger silver halide grains are more sensitive to light, so faster film uses larger grains. However, the grains also become more visible, so fast film appears grainier when projected or transferred to DV.

Fast film also is more contrasty, meaning that it reproduces fewer shades of color and brightness. Fast films tend to lose detail in bright and dark areas and have fewer subtleties in shading overall. Slower film, by contrast, has a much finer grain structure and reproduces an astonishing amount of subtlety in color and gray tones in the image, allowing a cinematographer an enormous amount of control over image details. Slower films also transfer excellently to DV, revealing very little grain.

Until very recently, silver halide grains have always been cubic crystals, but advancements by Kodak have created the **T-grain**, an evenly sized, flat crystal (Figure 8-42). The T-grain

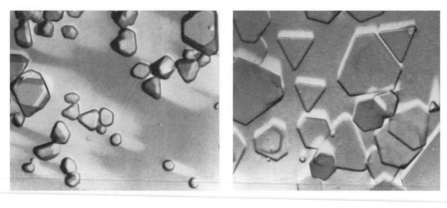

Figure 8-42 Earlier film stocks had cubic-shaped crystals (A), but later developments resulted in the creation of the T-grain crystal (B), providing greater sensitivity while maintaining a fine grain structure.

has transformed motion picture imaging by increasing the sensitivity of each grain, by creating a larger surface area yet maintaining a fine grain structure because the grains lay flat and slightly overlap, kind of like spreading out a deck of playing cards on a table. Fuji film has their own version of this crystal structure, called Σ grain. With T-grain and Σ grain, we are able to purchase relatively fast film stocks, i.e., EI 200 or EI 320, and maintain good contrast and a fine grain look. These film stocks also transfer exceptionally well to DV.

Color Temperature Balance

Different sources of light favor different areas of the light spectrum. For example, the sun is a relatively blue light while the 60-watt incandescent bulb in your desk lamp has a warm, amber hue. The specific hue of a light source is called its **color temperature**. Color temperature is measured by the Kelvin scale, which was devised by Lord William Kelvin in the late 1800s. Lord Kelvin discovered that if he heated a block of black carbon until it was white hot, its glow duplicated all of the colors in the visible light spectrum one-by-one as the heat went up, so he measured the temperature of the carbon at each color stage. The hotter the black body got, the bluer (or cooler) the color turned, and the lower the temperature was, the redder (or warmer) the color of the heated carbon. Color temperature has nothing to do with the actual heat of any light; instead, the color temperatures ascribed to different light sources are simply based on matching the colors between a light's hue and Lord Kelvin's block of heated carbon.

in practice

As with almost every element of film production where you are given a variety of options, there is no film speed that is inherently "better" or "worse"—there is only the "right" film speed for what you need and how you want your film to look and how you need to work. These choices are ideally a matter of aesthetic choice, but very often practical considerations are a major factor.

The Look

In Darren Aronofsky's *Pi* (1998), mathematician Maximillian Cohen searches for a numerical pattern that will allow him to predict fluctuations in the stock market. As he gets closer to uncovering this code, both an investment group interested in using his knowledge for profit and a Hasidim sect whose members believe the code is the se-

Figure 8-43 The paranoid world of mathematician Max (in Aronofsky's *Pi*) is divided between moments of peace (left), shot with lower contrast Plus-X stock, and periods of anxiety (right), shot with higher contrast, grainier Tri-X reversal stock.

■ **Figure 8-44** In George Racz' *The Miracle* (2006) special attention was put into selecting a stock that would render the little girl's environment, toys, and clothing as colorfully as possible. See the color insert in Chapter 13.

cret name of God accost him, throwing his life into turmoil.

The film is told from Max's perspective. His search has turned him into an obsessive-compulsive paranoiac who mistrusts anyone and fears physical contact. Director Aronofsky and director of photography Matthew Libatique chose a highly stylized visual design to represent this character's warped view of the world. This chaotic, paranoid view was accomplished by shooting most of the film in Tri-X reversal film, which renders a grainy, high-contrast image (manipulated further in postproduction to increase this contrast even more). In the scenes in Figure 8-43 the images are made up of only pure blacks and pure whites, with very few grays, as if Max's perception is so warped by his obsessive search for the code that he simply cannot see the world as it really is. There are times, however, when Max is at peace and temporarily out of danger. To mark this change in Max's state of mind, these scenes are shot with Plus-X reversal film, which has a wider latitude and lower contrast than Tri-X. In the scenes of relative calm, Max and his surroundings are rendered in a more realistic way, with softer shades of gray clearly visible. The dichotomy between the look of these two stocks is further emphasized by their content: the organic order of Nature (i.e., the tree branch Max observes when he is at peace) and the inorganic order of numbers (i.e., the computer screens in his apartment).

The Look and Practical Considerations

In George Racz' student shorts—*The Miracle* (see pp. 32–33) and the two other films in his trilogy on childhood *TheFishMiracleSky*—his central idea was to vividly represent the colorful and magical perspective of a little girl. As George himself tells it,

This film is about childhood, where colorful dreamlike images mix with reality. I conferred closely with my D.P. Timothy about the best film stock to use, one which could represent the brilliant colors of the little girl's environment, especially the colors of her red dress, blue leggings, and her room and toys. But we also didn't have very much light for the interior scenes so we needed to go with a high speed film. We shot a few tests and we felt that 7229 (Kodak Vision 2 Expression, 500T Color Neg Film) gave us the most saturated colors for the speed we needed in the interiors, and then we used the medium speed 7205 (Kodak Vision 2, 250D Color Neg Film) for most exteriors. One entire film, Closer to the Sky, was shot outside in the bright sun, so we decided to use 7201 (Kodak Vision 2, 50D Color Neg Film), a slow speed and very fine grained film stock.

The Practical Choice

Practical considerations are another factor in choosing the right EI. Recently, a student group in my class made a short film inside St. Patrick's Cathedral in New York City. The stained glass windows allow very little sunlight into the church and the students were not allowed to bring in any lights. They had no choice but to choose a very fast film stock and take all their shots around the offertory candles and spotlighted statues. The look of that film was dark but this worked wonderfully because, well, it made the audience feel like they were in a dark cathedral.

If we look at a blank sheet of paper it appears white to us, both under the sun or on the desk, because the human eye automatically compensates for the difference in color temperatures, but film stock cannot change its sensitivity to color like this. As a way of compensating, film stocks come balanced for the two most common lighting situations under which we shoot: **daylight (5,600° K)**, which favors a distinctly blue hue, and **tungsten (3,200° K)**, the color temperature of commonly used movie lights, which are quite warm and amber in tint. What it means to balance a film stock to color temperature is to manipulate emulsion sensitivity so that the light source appears to be simply white. Daylight-balanced film emulsion is manufactured such that the blue emulsion layer is slightly less

Color temperatures of common light sources.

COOLER (BLUER)	
sun (overcast sky)	8000°K
daylight (average midday)	5600°K - 6000°K
HMI movie light	5600°K
tungsten movie light	3200°K
halogen light	3000°K
60w household incandescent	2900°K
sunrise / sunset	2500°K
candle flame	1800°K
WARMER (REDDER)	

light sensitive than are the other two layers, and tungsten-balanced film is made with a less sensitive red emulsion layer.

In general, we choose the film stock for our specific shooting situation. If we are shooting outdoors, we choose daylight-balanced film, and if we shoot inside under tungsten movie lights, we choose tungsten film. However, things rarely work out this neatly. What if your film involves some exterior locations and some interior scenes under movie lights? For those times when we are forced to shoot film in situations for which the film is not balanced, we can compensate by using **color conversion filters** (Figure 8-45) in front of the lens to alter the incoming light to match the balance of the film.

If we shoot with tungsten-balanced film under daylight conditions, the image will appear extremely blue, but placing the standard **Wratten #85** amber filter in front of the lens converts the incoming light to 3,200°K. Conversely, if we shoot daylight film under tungsten movie lights, the image will have an overall amber wash to it. By using a **Wratten #80A** blue filter we convert the tungsten light entering the lens to 5,600°K.

When cinematographers have to select one film stock for shooting under different light sources, they will almost always choose tungsten film and convert with an #85 filter for shooting outdoors. This is because color filters work by absorbing certain colors of the light spectrum, which also means that they cut down on the total amount of light entering the lens. In other words, when you place a filter on a lens, you lose light. With an #85 filter we lose ⅔ stop, but with an 80A filter we lose 2 full stops of light. Losing ⅔ stop of exposure when you're going outdoors is not a big deal since the sun is usu-

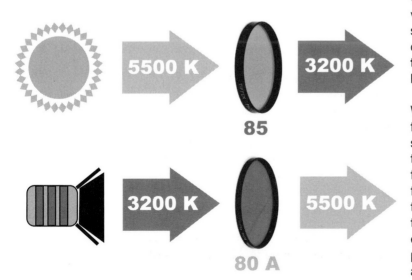

5500 K → 85 → 3200 K

3200 K → 80 A → 5500 K

■ **Figure 8-45** Color conversion filters. Two of the most commonly used filters are the 85 (amber), which turns 5,500°K daylight into 3,200°K tungsten light, and the 80A (bluish), which turns 3,200°K tungsten into 5,500°K daylight. See the color insert in Chapter 13.

ally brighter than most tungsten setups anyway. But losing 2 stops when your source changes from the sun, which is a high-intensity source, to the relatively low intensity of tungsten lights is usually too great a loss. Color conversion filters are so common in film production that color film labels often indicate a specific adjustment to the EI number when these filters are in use, so that you can easily compensate for the loss of light. For example, Kodak Vision2 7217 is a tungsten-balanced film with a normal EI 200, but the label tells us that if we shoot under daylight with an #85 filter, the new EI will be 125. In other words, we compensate for losing $\frac{2}{3}$ stop of light by saying the film is less sensitive and needs more light to achieve a given exposure.

Gauge/Format

A film **gauge** refers to the actual width of the film stock. There are currently only four gauges of film stock manufactured for film production use: 8mm, 16mm, 35mm, and 65mm. The term **format**, however, refers to both the width of the negative film strip and the dimensions of the exposed frame, which are tagged on the film. There can be several formats on the same gauge film. For example, 16mm gauge film is used for both standard 16mm format and Super 16mm film production format, which has a larger image area. Since Super 8mm film is hard to find and harder to get processed, and 65mm film (used for 70mm projection format) is used for large scale, big-budget Hollywood epics and Omnimax productions, I'll restrict my discussion to 16mm and 35mm film formats, which are the most commonly used production formats.

There is no difference in the actual emulsion used for 16mm film and 35mm film of the same type. However, the larger the film format is, the better the quality of the overall recorded image. A regular 16mm film frame measures 0.404″ × 0.295″, super 16 is 0.493″ × 0.295″, and a full frame of 35mm film is 0.864″ × 0.630″. The larger the exposure area of an image, the greater clarity there will be in the rendering of fine details and subtle shades. This is called a format's **resolving power**, and the fact that 35mm has four times the picture area of standard 16mm is the reason it has greater resolving power and higher quality when transferred to DV or HD.

Another reason larger film formats look better than smaller ones is the magnification necessary for projection. Smaller gauge film requires much more magnification when projected, which also includes the magnification of grain and image imperfections. Projecting full frame 35mm film onto a very modest theatrical screen around 20′ × 30′ requires it to be magnified around 158,000 times, but standard 16mm film projected to the same dimensions is magnified 726,000 times. This is one reason why 35mm and 70mm have become the commercial theatrical release standards.

Aspect Ratio

One other major element of a film's format is its aspect ratio (Figure 8-46). We discussed in Chapter 3 aspect ratio as the shape of your compositional canvas, whose dimensions are expressed as a ratio of the width of the frame to its height. But in film there are two aspect ratios that we need to consider, full frame aspect ratio and projection aspect ratio. **Full frame** aspect ratio is the actual dimensions of the frame created by the aperture opening in the gate. The aspect ratios of a full frame of 16mm film and 35mm film are identical, 1.33:1. This is referred to as **academy aperture**. Incidentally, this is the same aspect ratio for a frame of standard National Television Standards Committee (NTSC) video, 4:3, which, in its early development was designed to be compatible with the motion pictures of the time. However, in the 1950s, when color TV entered the market, the film industry felt the need to compete with the TV industry for viewers. After much experimentation with various frame widths the industry eventually settled on 1.85:1 as the standard aspect ratio for theatrical presentation[3] (see p. 40, Language of

---

[3]For a fascinating discussion of the history of projection aspect ratios and the American film industry, see *Widescreen Cinema*, by John Belton, Harvard University Press, Cambridge, MA, 1992.

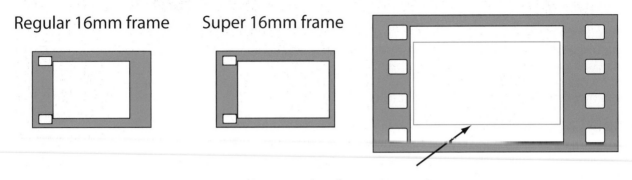

35mm Academy Aperture (1.33:1)

Regular 16mm frame   Super 16mm frame

35mm Theatrical Release (1.85:1)

■ **Figure 8-46** 16mm formats include the standard 1.33:1 aspect ratio (left) and Super 16, with a 1.66:1 aspect ratio (middle). 35mm films (right) are projected at a 1.85:1 theatrical aspect ratio, effectively discarding some of the top and the bottom of the frame in the process.

Cinema). This aspect ratio is much wider and was felt to promise a unique visual experience, one that couldn't be duplicated on TV and therefore would encourage viewers to keep going to theaters. This change in aspect ratio, however, does not alter the actual size of the full 35mm camera frame, only the portion of that frame that is projected. The wider format is accomplished through masking, which involves using a projector gate that cuts off the top and bottom of the full frame to the 1.85:1 proportions. This is common practice in commercial film production, so the final projection aperture (1.33:1 for TV or 1.85:1 for theatrical projection) must be anticipated when shooting. This is accomplished with the finder markings (Figure 8-47) in the viewfinder of a 35mm camera; the markings indicate, through shading, the exact 1.85:1 frame that will be projected and thus aid in framing and composition.

Since we cannot spare any of the area of the smaller frame, 16mm film is usually shot and viewed in its 1.33:1 aspect ratio, however, standard 16mm can be a problem when transferring to any format other than standard NTSC video. Most filmmakers who want to take advantage of the great image quality of film and the lighter, much more affordable 16mm gauge, and who have the intention to later transfer the negative to 35mm (for theatrical release) or DV or HD in the 16:9 aspect ratio, will more often use the Super 16mm format. Super 16 was invented by the Swedish director and cinematographer Rune Ericson in 1961 as a way to use 16mm gauge film to inexpensively produce films for theatrical release. The aspect ratio for Super 16 is 1.66:1, that is the same as standard European 35mm theatrical projection. To create the 1.66:1 dimension, Super 16 uses a gate that is a little bit wider than standard 16mm, which also creates a slightly larger picture area (see Figure 8-46).

This aspect ratio is closer to American theatrical projection (1.85:1), so the transfer, or blow up, from Super 16 to 35mm, is much more compatible than from standard 16mm. The transfer from Super 16 to the 16:9 (or 1.78:1) digital formats is nearly perfect. With television moving more and more toward the wider formats, people are increasingly modifying standard 16mm cameras to shoot Super 16 (not all 16mm cameras do this). In terms of theatrically released films, many low-budget and independent films continue to be shot on Super 16 and are later blown up to

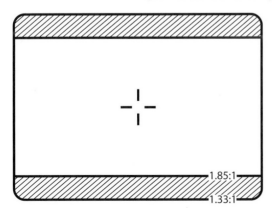

1.85:1
1.33:1

■ **Figure 8-47** The groundglass in a viewfinder usually has some markings to aid in the composition of a frame. Groundglasses come in literally hundreds of aspect ratio combinations (pictured: a 35mm groundglass masking the full frame negative to a 1.85:1 aspect ratio).

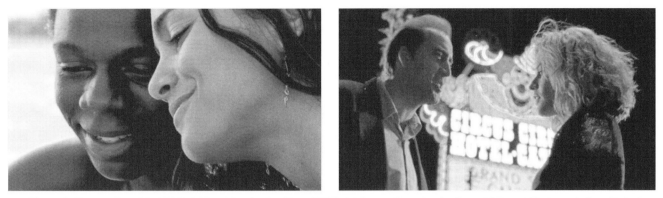

■ **Figure 8-48** Both *City of God* (2002, left) and *Leaving Las Vegas* (1995, right) were shot using the Super 16 format. Figgis wanted a gritty look for *Leaving Las Vegas,* so he purposely blew up the film to 35mm, while preserving much of the grain and flaws of the original stock. Meirelles and Lund's *City of God* used the format mostly for close-ups for its texture, switching to 35mm stock when they needed the extra resolution in longer shots.

35mm for release, not only because it costs less than 35mm costs as a production for-mat, but because the grittier look resulting from the blow-up process contributes a particular edgy aesthetic (Figure 8-48).

It's important to remember that Super 16 is an acquisition format only. There are no Super 16 projectors. All 16mm projectors have the standard 1.33:1 gate. Shooting Super 16 necessarily means that you must transfer to either DV, HD, or 35mm to distribute the movie.

The Digital Video System

While the basic film system has remained virtually unchanged in well over one hundred years, the video system seems to be in a perpetual state of rapid evolution. New video formats are introduced yearly and rapid technological obsolescence is the rule rather than an exception. Lucky for us, with each generation, video's evolutionary trend is toward an electronic image that is sharper and increasingly responsive to the subtleties of light and shadow. Unfortunately, however, the world of video engineers, corporate interests, and government committees has not managed to coordinate their efforts to establish a single national video standard, let alone a worldwide standard. With enormous profits on the line, corporate rivals and nations are all racing to develop their own superior system, in the hope that theirs will become the new standard. Current count reveals 18 different digital video formats, six of them High Definition. Obviously it would be folly to try to cover them all in detail. In addition, one could take the discussion of digital video technology all the way to a highly specialized and arcane scientific discourse on semiconductor theory and the Nyquist-Shannon sampling theorem. The question is, how much information is useful for the creative filmmaker and what can we leave to the engineers and physicists? This chapter tries to demystify the basic technology of video and explain some of the terms, specifications, and processes that are common to digital video formats in general. In the world of digital video, knowing some technical information is imperative for a filmmaker to make informed choices, to understand how their tools can contribute to the aesthetic approach of their movie, and to allow for a smooth and successful creative and technical process from preproduction to distribution. Beyond the information in this chapter, you will find a list of related websites in the Web Resources section at the back of the book, which you can visit to find more details and to stay up-to-date with the most recent changes, facts, and statistics.

■ NTSC BROADCAST STANDARDS

In 1941 a group of television engineers and government policy makers established the standards for creating and broadcasting black-and-white television; these standards are essentially still in effect today. The National Television Standards Committee (NTSC) addressed various technical specifications for image reproduction and reception, ensuring compatibility between every television camera and TV set across the country and with those of any other nation that shared the NTSC system: Japan, Mexico, Canada, and much of South America. In the early 1950s NTSC changed these standards slightly to accommodate the addition of color to the television signal.

NTSC Analog Video Basics
NTSC Frame Rate; Interlaced Scanning
As we mentioned at the beginning of this chapter, film and video share the process of recording a scene as a series of still images and then replaying those images in rapid succession to create the illusion of motion. While film runs at a frame rate of 24 fps, the frame rate for NTSC video is slightly less than 30 frames per second (discussed on p. 172). The major difference, however, is *how* those images are created and then played back. As we've seen, film does this through a mechanical and photochemical process, but NTSC video uses an electronic process known as **interlaced scanning**.

As with film, the creation of the image begins with the lens gathering the light from the scene and focusing it on the image plane. In video, the **imaging plane**, or **target**, is the face of a

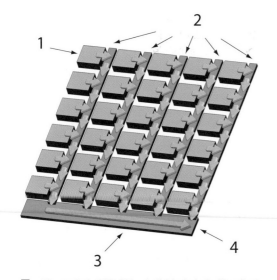

Figure 9-1 CCD Chip. Individual pixels (1) collect brightness information and feed a corresponding charge down vertical registers (2), which carry them to a horizontal register (3). The raw video signal (4) is then fed to an output amplifier. The pixels are read one row at a time at the horizontal charge transfer area; once the information is collected, the row above gets transferred one row down to be collected. The charges in the rows are therefore "coupled" to one another.

CCD chip (for charged coupled device) (Figure 9-1). The CCD chip is a solid state sensor (measuring either ¼″, ⅓″, ½″, or ⅔″ across) composed of hundreds of thousands to millions of light-sensitive photodiodes called **pixels** (short for picture elements), which are linked together (coupled) and aligned in tight horizontal rows.

When these pixels, which are actually tiny capacitors, are struck by the incoming light, they build up an electronic voltage that corresponds to the intensity hitting *that* particular spot. The CCD chip outputs this pixel specific voltage information in two series of stacked horizontal rows, or **scan lines**. First the CCD outputs the odd-numbered horizontal lines (1, 3, 5, 7, etc.), one at a time, from the top to the bottom, creating a half-resolution image that is called a **field** of video. There are exactly 262.5 horizontal scan lines in one field of NTSC video. Then, after hitting the bottom halfway through that last scan line, the scanning pattern returns to the top of the chip (called **vertical retrace**) and outputs the even-numbered rows (2, 4, 6, etc.), from the top to the bottom, to fill in the rest of the information with a second field of video. This second field of video is also composed of 262.5 horizontal lines. These two fields of video are interlaced to comprise one full frame (Figure 9-2).

One full frame of NTSC video, therefore, is made up of 525 horizontal scan lines. The NTSC standard process of reading one field of video and then integrating a second field is called **interlaced scanning**, and the entire process happens at a rate of 30 frames per second, which therefore means that there are 60 fields per second (in fact, slightly slower; see later). This scanning system is often written as 60i (i for interlaced). Interlaced scanning was developed to ensure a "flickerless" image. An additional NTSC standard is the aspect ratio of the video frame—the dimensional relationship between the height and the length of a frame of video. The NTSC standard aspect ratio is 4:3, which is essentially the same dimension as for a frame of 16mm film (1.33:1).

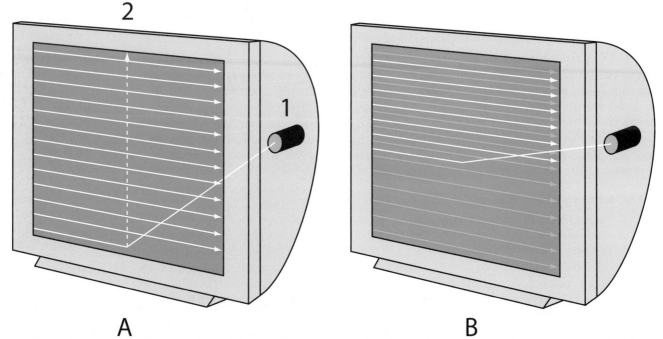

Figure 9-2 Interlaced video is scanned by an electron gun (1) onto a screen coated with phosphors. A single frame is created by scanning two alternate fields; first, only the odd lines are scanned, from top to bottom and from left to right (A). When the electron beam reaches the bottom of the screen, it returns to the top, called "vertical retrace" (2), and scans the second field, this time drawing only the even lines until it reaches the bottom again (B).

Meanwhile, on the inside of a standard video monitor, the whole process is duplicated in reverse and in perfect synchronization. An electron gun at the back of the CRT (cathode ray tube) sprays a stream of electrons with fluctuating electrical voltage against the inside face of the tube (also the **target**), which is lined with hundreds of thousands of voltage-sensitive phosphors (also **pixels**). This stream of electrons excites the phosphors, which glow with analogous intensity to the amount of current with which they are being struck—electricity is turning back into light. As you probably already suspect, the electron gun scans the face of the CRT in exactly the same NTSC standard pattern as we saw with the CCD chip: first one field, top to bottom (262.5 lines), then the second field is interlaced top to bottom (another 262.5), to create one 4:3 frame, with 525 lines of resolution, in 1/30th of a second (Figure 9-3). In fact, the stream of electrons coming out of the CRT gun *exactly* duplicates the electrical current information of the CCD scanning process field by field, scan line by scan line and pixel by pixel.

In a plasma flat screen monitor, the horizontal rows of pixels are made up of hundreds of thousands of tiny colored fluorescent cells that glow when charged by the grid of address electrodes lining the back of the pixel rows. And with LCD (liquid crystal display) flat screens, each pixel is a tiny liquid crystal activated by a transistor. No matter what the display technology, if you are screening an NTSC signal the interlaced lines of information and scanning rate remain exactly the same (Figure 9-4).

NTSC Color Video

In the early 1950s NTSC developed the standards for color television. In an effort to make color television compatible with all preexisting monochrome receivers, NTSC in effect added the color component over the existing black-and-white signal, rather than create a whole new, fully integrated signal. This ensured that even though a program was broadcast in color, viewers who owned black-and-white TV sets could still receive the signal. This decision to ensure compatibility was based as much on economic considerations as on technological concerns. It was certainly not a decision based on the quality of the image, as this "color add-on" policy has numerous shortcomings in terms of image quality.

To achieve a color image the video signal is divided into the three primary colors of light: red, green, and blue (RGB). Achieving a color image involves the additive process of mix-

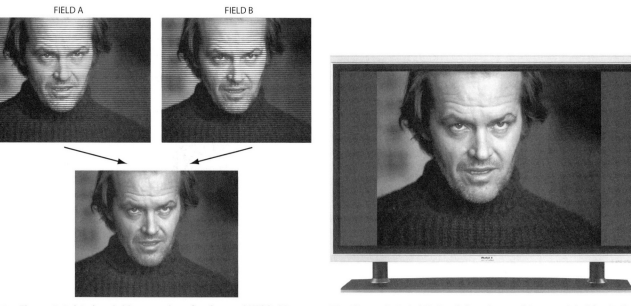

FIELD A   FIELD B

■ **Figure 9-3** Interlaced video scanning. One frame of NTSC video (525 scanlines) is formed by interlacing two video fields; field A is made up of the odd lines (262.5), and field B is made up of even lines (262.5). Interlacing provides flicker free viewing.

■ **Figure 9-4** A 4:3 signal viewed on a widescreen television is displayed with the use of black or gray bars on the sides of the screen, a practice called "pillarboxing."

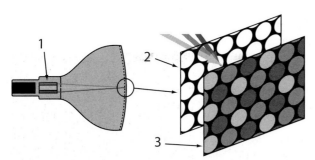

■ **Figure 9-5** Color video uses three electron guns (1) one for each primary color; their output is aimed at clusters of red, green, and blue phosphors on the screen (3). A special masking (2) is used to prevent, for instance, the blue gun from hitting a red phosphor. See the color insert in Chapter 13.

ing these three primary colors to create an accurate color blend, in addition to the brightness information. In a standard CRT monitor there are three electron guns, one for each color, and each pixel comprises three tiny light-sensitive phosphor strips, one red, one green, and one blue. In flat screen displays each and every pixel is made up of three separate cells for each color (Figure 9-5). And correspondingly, in most video cameras there are three CCD chips that are used to record the light intensities of each primary color (see Figure 9-31).

The element of the video image that determines image brightness (shades of black and white) is called the **luminance** signal (also written as Y). The color component of the video signal is referred to as **chrominance** (also written as C, or chroma). Chrominance is made up of hue, which determines the tint of a particular color, and saturation, which determines the intensity of the colors. Rather than fully integrating the color component into the signal, the NTSC system simply superimposes the color signal on top of the existing black-and-white signal along a subcarrier frequency (3.58 MHz). While this has ensured compatibility with all monitors, it has also required a few sacrifices, the most important being literally slowing down the frame rate. The original black-and-white NTSC video signal had a true frame rate of 30 fps, but the addition of color slowed that down to 29.97 fps. So, to be perfectly accurate, the frame rate for NTSC video is 29.97 frames per second and the field rate is 59.94i, although you will usually see this number rounded to 60i.

Summary of NTSC Broadcast Video Standards

■ Frame rate = 29.97 fps interlaced
■ One frame = two interlaced fields (59.94i)

■ Horizontal lines per field = 262.5
■ Horizontal lines per frame = 525
■ Aspect ratio = 4:3

Other Broadcast Standards

As mentioned earlier, NTSC video standards ensure system compatibility in any country that uses it. Unfortunately, there is not a single global broadcast standard. Other television standards that are common around the world are **PAL** (Phase Alternating Line), used by China and most of the countries in the European Union, and **SECAM** (Séquential Couleur Avec Mémoire), used in France, Russia, and many African and Eastern European nations. The primary differences between NTSC and PAL or SECAM are the frame rate and the number of horizontal lines. Both PAL and SECAM contain 625 horizontal lines (producing superior resolution) and they have a frame rate of 25 frames per second (which allows for much easier film-to-tape conversions). If you purchase a video camera in England, it will likely be a PAL system camera. The same model camera in the United States will be NTSC. The various systems are not compatible with each other, so you cannot play video recorded in NTSC on a PAL or SECAM system and vice versa.

Timecode

The system in video by which every frame is assigned a specific and unique number is called **timecode** (T.C.). Recorded right along with the video data for each and every frame is an electronic number with four fields based on the 24-hour clock: hours:minutes:seconds:frames. This numbering system is vital to the workflow of every video project. We use timecode to quickly log, reference, or locate specific frames, to calculate the length of shots, scenes, and entire projects, to maintain audio and video synchronization, to ensure frame-accurate edits, to calculate trims and transitions in editing, etc. In short, timecode is the way we keep track of the frame-by-frame timing of every element, in every stage of a project. All DV cameras have timecode, but some offer a choice of two different flavors: drop-frame timecode and nondrop-frame timecode (Figure 9-6).

Nondrop-frame timecode is simple to understand, but is seldom used. **Nondrop-frame T.C.** simply counts frames according to the original B&W video frame rate, assigning a new number to each video frame at a consistent rate of 30 frames per second. But as we discussed above, the true frame rate of color NTSC video is slightly slower: 29.97 fps. So simply allocating frame numbers to frames 1 to 30 to video that is actually running at 29.97 frames per second means that we are calling 1 second (30 frames) what is in real time 1 second and a fraction—because one second should have turned after 29.97. In essence, nondrop-frame timecode isn't reflecting real time; it is simply counting frames, so we end up accumulating slightly more frame numbers than actual frames per second (30 numbers/second vs. 29.97 actual frames/second) (Figure 9-7).

Because it takes a fraction of a second longer to count off thirty frames, the difference between nondrop-frame T.C. counting time and true video running time is 1.8 frames per minute. That may not seem like much, but when nondrop-frame T.C. counts off 1 hour of time in a program—which looks like this: 01:00:00:00—it would ostensibly have "counted" 108,000 frames. However, in true NTSC running time there are only 107,892 frames of video in an hour-long program.[1] The discrepancy between constant 30 fps counting and true 29.97 video time after 1 hour is 108 frames, or 3 seconds and 18 frames. By using nondrop-frame timecode, when the timecode numbers display 1 hour (01:00:00:00) your video will in fact be shorter by 3 seconds and 18 frames (00:59:26:12). That may not seem like such a big deal, but in broadcast television, where programs and commercials must conform to frame-accurate timing, it is crucial to have a precise frame count.

Nondrop-frame timecode is a bit of an artifact from an era when linear tape editing machines needed perfectly sequential timecode to stay in sync. Today, with DV cameras and nonlinear editing, **drop-frame timecode** is the standard and default method for counting and addressing frames with ID numbers. Drop-frame timecode does not actually drop any video frames, but it does skip over some timecode numbers from time to time in order to adjust the frame count to accurately reflect the true 29.97 fps of NTSC video. To be precise, the drop-frame T.C. system skips over the :00 and :01 frame numbers once every

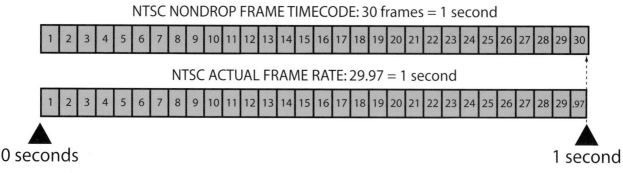

■ Figure 9-6 Timecode assigns a specific number to every video frame according to a format based on hours, minutes, seconds, and frames. Broadcast video uses only "drop frame" timecode, easily identified by its use of semicolons (2), because it is time-accurate. Some applications still provide the option to use "nondrop-frame" timecode, which uses colons as separators (1).

[1] 30 frames/second × 60 seconds × 60 minutes = 108,000 frames, but in reality the counting should reflect 29.97 frames/second × 60 seconds × 60 minutes = 107,892 frames.

NTSC NONDROP FRAME TIMECODE: 30 frames = 1 second

| 1 | 2 | 3 | 4 | 5 | 6 | 7 | 8 | 9 | 10 | 11 | 12 | 13 | 14 | 15 | 16 | 17 | 18 | 19 | 20 | 21 | 22 | 23 | 24 | 25 | 26 | 27 | 28 | 29 | 30 |

NTSC ACTUAL FRAME RATE: 29.97 = 1 second

| 1 | 2 | 3 | 4 | 5 | 6 | 7 | 8 | 9 | 10 | 11 | 12 | 13 | 14 | 15 | 16 | 17 | 18 | 19 | 20 | 21 | 22 | 23 | 24 | 25 | 26 | 27 | 28 | 29 | .97 |

0 seconds   **1 second**

■ Figure 9-7 After exactly one second, nondrop-frame timecode displays that 30 frames have been screened. In fact, NTSC video runs at 29.97 and not 30 frames per second. Drop-frame timecode accommodates for this discrepancy by selectively skipping numbers, not frames, so that the time displayed matches the actual time elapsed.

■ **Figure 9-8** Mike Figgis' *Timecode* (2000), runs four stories on the screen with frame accurate simultaneity. This feat of visual continuity was made possible by matching the time code of each of the four cameras covering the action.

minute, except for the tenth minute. Here is how the T. C. numbers change at each minute of footage (except for every tenth minute): L 00;09;26;28, 00;09;26;29, 00;09;27;02, 00;09;27;03 L This method compensates for the slowed-down video frame rate and, in the end, is completely frame accurate. After an hour of drop-frame timecode counting we will arrive at T.C. 01;00;00;00 for exactly 1 hour of video footage.

■ DIGITAL VIDEO STANDARDS

NTSC broadcast standards were devised in the analog video era. However, film and video production around the turn of the century was manifestly transformed by the digital revolution, and with the revolution came a reappraisal and overhauling of standards. **Analog** video (and audio) means that the creation, recording, playback, and distribution of the video/audio signal are accomplished in videotape via electronic waveforms and magnetic particles, which are, respectively, analogous to the original light values of the image and the acoustic waves of the audio. **Digital video** and audio, on the other hand, create, record, and disseminate video and audio by transforming light values and acoustic energy into binary code, or a series of ones and zeros. There are numerous advantages to digital media: superior resolution, greater flexibility for creative manipulation, the ability to make copies with no generational loss, nonlinear editing, and more stable archiving.

Today, the revolution is complete and we have entered a phase of technological *evolution.* Although NTSC broadcast standards, and analog media in general, are clearly being phased out, both by government mandate and by popular demand, this system still exists side-by-side with a new set of digital video standards established by yet another consortium of engineers and government policy makers, called ATSC (Advanced Television Systems Committee). Emerging from computer technology, digital video standards have introduced changes in a number of areas; most important for us are changes in the aspect ratio and frame rate of video, the number of horizontal lines that make up a frame, and the scanning process itself. It is important to understand the new standards because every time you pick up a DV camera to shoot your movie, you are faced with a menu of possible formats. Should you shoot in high definition (HD) or in standard definition (SD)? Some cameras allow you to shoot at either 60i, 60p, 30p, or even 24p? Should you choose the 4:3 aspect ratio or 16:9? According to the most current count the new ATSC digital television standards allow for eighteen digital video formats, with six of those being for High Definition Television (HDTV).[2] With the standards for digital video somewhat in flux, it's pretty clear that we are still in the middle of this digital evolution. Nonetheless, one thing is for sure: the analog era is over.

In order to fully understand digital video formats it is important to introduce two technical concepts: progressive scanning and vertical lines of resolution.

Progressive Scanning

Progressive scanning (Figure 9-9) is used in computer monitors and some digital video systems. Progressive scanning differs from interlaced scanning in that one frame is not made up of two interlaced fields (odds lines first, then even lines); instead, progressive scanning draws a full frame of video (all horizontal lines) from top to bottom at a rate of 30 frames per second, and in some systems 60 frames per second. These are written as

---

[2]*HDV Filmmaking*, by Chad Fahs, Thomson Course Technology PTR, Boston, MA, 2006, pg. 7.

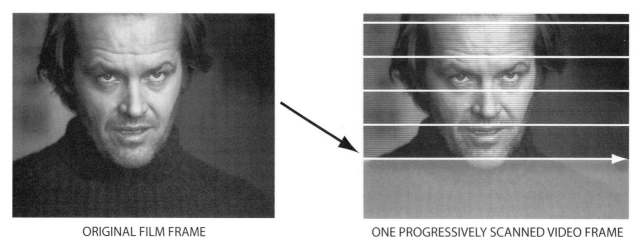

ORIGINAL FILM FRAME ONE PROGRESSIVELY SCANNED VIDEO FRAME

■ **Figure 9-9** Progressive scanning draws a full frame of video with each pass, overcoming the inherent quality drawbacks associated with interlaced video.

30p and 60p. The resolution of progressive scanning is visibly superior to interlaced scanning, and all modern flat screen technologies (like LCD or plasma screens) are compatible with progressive scanning. Progressive scanning is indicated with the letter "p" after the frame rate and interlaced scanning is indicated with the letter "i." For example, the NTSC system scans at 60i (60 interlaced half-resolution fields per second) and one of the high definition systems scans at 60p (60 full resolution frames per second), fully twice as many lines of information.

Resolution

Whenever there is an evaluation of video image resolution quality you will hear the term resolution. **Resolution** generally refers to the ability to reproduce visual detail: sharpness of line, subtlety and degrees of luminance, and accuracy of color. Video resolution is affected by many factors, including lens quality, the scanning system, the number of pixels, data sampling rates, color depth sampling, and data compression (all explained later). All of these variables affect overall resolution, and the general rule of thumb is that the bigger the numbers, the better the resolution. More horizontal scan lines are better than fewer, more pixels are better than fewer, more data sampling is better than less: the more information the compression files retain, the better. Of course, as the resolution statistics for a camera increase, so does another number—the price.

Vertical lines of resolution and horizontal pixels are specific terms: they refer to the number of horizontal lines from top to bottom and the number of pixels that comprise each horizontal line for any given format. Because the vertical dimension of the frame is composed of horizontal lines stacked up on top of each other, the more horizontal scan lines a system has the better the **vertical resolution**. Because it comprises the number of horizontal scan lines, the vertical resolution is fixed by the particular system standard (Figure 9-10).

One detail you should be aware of is that only the **active lines** are counted when describing a system's vertical lines of resolution, meaning only the scan lines that are visible to the viewer. All systems hide some of their scan lines behind a display mask, because the top and bottom edges of the raster are used for video system information (like horizontal blanking pulses and timecode) instead of picture information. As we mentioned above, the NTSC system has a *total* of 525 horizontal scan lines; however, a viewer only sees the 480 lines that make up the image. So, as you will see in Table 9-1, we say that NTSC video has a vertical resolution of 480 active lines. Compare this with the two HD video systems, which have either 720 or 1080 vertical lines of resolution, and you can see why the HD image is clearly superior.

A   B   C

■ **Figure 9-10** The higher the number of horizontal scan lines, the better the vertical resolution of the image. 10 horizontal scan lines make it difficult to see the actual shape of the object (A). 25 horizontal scan lines add significantly more visual information (B). 50 scan lines (C) make it possible to see nuances of shading and volume.

Table 9-1   ATSC Digital Television Standards[a]

	ACTIVE VERTICAL LINES	HORIZONTAL PIXELS	ASPECT RATIO	FRAME RATE
HD	1080	1920	16:9	60i, 30p, 24p
HD	720	1280	16:9	60p, 30p, 24p
SD	480	704	16:9 and 4:3	60i, 60p, 30p, 24p
SD	480	640	4:3	60i, 60p, 30p, 24p

[a]The ATSC digital television standards support 18 different digital video formats. (HD 5 high definition, SD 5 standard definition; i 5 interlaced scanning, p 5 progressive scanning). Source, ATSC.

The ATSC standards also clearly articulate the number of maximum **horizontal pixels** that can make up each scan line. However, the horizontal resolution factor is not fixed. Instead, it is determined by the specific video format you use. Again, the more pixels along the horizontal dimension, the better the resolution of the image. For example, analog VHS tape delivered a resolution of 240 horizontal pixels; consumer DV is capable of around 500 horizontal pixels and professional DV formats, such as DVCPRO, have 720 horizontal pixels (as do commercial DVDs). One can see why VHS vanished so quickly! In fact, the standard analog NTSC broadcast signal can display only 330 horizontal pixels. So the VHS format underutilized the resolution potential of standard broadcast television while the resolution power of DVCPRO is not realized to its fullest. This is precisely why the NTSC analog broadcast system is being replaced with the new digital broadcast standards shown in Table 9-1.

High Definition Video

High definition video (HD, or HiDef) is a term that has generically been used to mean video formats that exceed the visual resolution of a standard definition image. But a more accurate use of the term applies to the six ATSC standards for high definition, meaning video formats with vertical resolution (number of horizontal scan lines) of either 720p, 1080i, or 1080p. All ATSC high definition formats have an aspect ratio of 16:9.

It is important to understand that high definition is a complete system of image creation and display. In order to realize the improved resolution of HD, you not only need to shoot on HD but you also must display that image on an HD-capable display. Shooting HD but displaying the footage on a standard NTSC monitor will only result in the reduction of the quality of your original image to—you guessed it—480 lines of vertical resolution. Shooting HD is recommended if you are ultimately going to display the image on HD or if you plan to transfer your footage to film. In this process, the superior image quality will be fully realized (Figure 9-11).

■ **Figure 9-11** High Definition video transfer to 35mm film. Both Lucas' *Star Wars: Episode II Attack of the Clones* (2002, left) and Medem's *Sex and Lucia* (2001, right) were shot on HD (using Sony's HD24P CineAlta), and then transferred to 35mm film for theatrical exhibition.

What Is 24p?

Of all new video formats, none is as talked about, promising, or as misunderstood as 24p. It should be obvious by now that 24p stands for a video signal with a progressive scan frame rate of 24 frames per second. Sound familiar? The 24p video format was developed specifically to be compatible with and to duplicate the look of motion picture film. At resolutions of 1080 or 720, 24p is considered a high definition format, and when displayed on a system capable of 24p HD, it looks indistinguishable from 35mm film. In fact, feature films are increasingly being shot in this format and then, taking advantage of the simple one-to-one frame correspondence, transferred to film for theatrical distribution (Figure 9-11). While 24p HD has traditionally meant very expensive ($100,000 +) professional cameras, we are beginning to see this HD format making its way into much more affordable price ranges (Figure 9-12).

24p shooting is also available in standard definition DV cameras. While it is clearly visible that standard definition 24p does not have nearly the resolution of 24p HD, 35mm, or even 16mm film, nonetheless, this isn't stopping filmmakers from using this extremely inexpensive, accessible, and mobile format for shooting, and then later transferring and releasing on film (Figure 9-13).

24p differs from standard 60i DV in that the slower frame rate mimics some of the artifacts of film, primarily the way motion is recorded in 24 rather than 30 still images per second, giving it a so called "film look" even

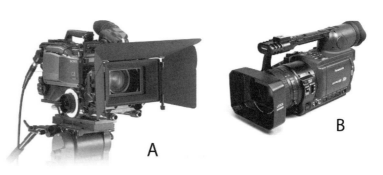

■ **Figure 9-12** While HD previously required the use of very expensive ($100,000+) professional cameras like Sony's Cinealta (A), we are now seeing the HD format make its way into more affordable price ranges with cameras like the Panasonic AG-HVX200 (B).

■ **Figure 9-13** Harrison's *November* (2004, left) was shot in MiniDV with the Panasonic DVX100 (right).

When to Use Which DV Format?

It's not unusual these days to pick up a DV camera that gives you the option to shoot in 24p, 30p, and 60i. Some cameras even give you the additional option of shooting several formats in SD or in HD. So how do you choose? When do you shoot in each format? It all depends on what your finishing format will be and how you plan to distribute your movie.

- **Shoot standard 60i** when you anticipate distributing on standard 60i video (broadcasting NTSC) and don't need or want the so-called "film look" of 24p.

- **Shoot at 24p** when you plan to finish and distribute on film. The one-to-one frame correspondence makes the transfer much easier. Also, shoot 24p if you like the unique visual quality of the format when the film is finished and displayed on standard 60i video (finishing on standard DV).

- **Shoot HD** (720/60p or 1080/60i) if you plan to broadcast with the HD signal or screen on HD-ready equipment. The superior resolution, the ability of HD to handle subtle lighting, and the overall superiority of HD equipment (lenses, encoders, etc.) make this a good format even if you plan to distribute your work in standard definition (even though you will not see full HD resolution with SD finishing).

- **Shoot 24p** HD if you plan to transfer to film and distribute your movie as a film print.

- **Ignore 30p.** To some extent, 30p is a format that is there because the engineers could put it there. There is no advantage to shooting 30p for most applications related to narrative filmmaking.

when played back on standard 60i video monitors. Some people really like the standard DV 24p look, and think it looks like film; others are not as convinced. My recommendation is to do some tests and see if you like the quality. If you think about it, describing an image as "looking like film" admits to a compromise, "Gee I wanted film but all I got was 'looks-like-film.'" If you are shooting DV it's best to simply evaluate 24p as an image with a unique visual quality that is different from, but not necessarily superior, to the unique look of 60i. Ask yourself: Which look is best for the project? Which quality will help you tell the story?

While it is fairly simply to understand how we can transfer 24p video (SD or HD) to film for distribution (frame by frame), one might ask how we can view a video shot at 24 progressive frames per second on a 30 frames per second (60i) NTSC monitor. The answer is, the same way we are able to watch a film shot at 24 fps on television. The transfer process from a 24 fps system to a 30 fps system is called 2:3 pulldown and is explained in detail in Chapter 19.

■ DIGITAL VIDEO CAMCORDERS

Historically, analog video cameras have broken down into neat categories: Professional cameras were big, expensive, and well made and produced high-quality video, while consumer cameras were small and inexpensive and had an inferior image, but above all were easy to use. Then came digital video and everything changed. Now small, affordable cameras are delivering extremely high-quality footage, so much so that the "pros" use them extensively. Today it is possible to get cameras capable of high definition video for well under $8,000! This was unheard of only a few years ago. It seems downright inappropriate to call a camera that is capable of shooting 24p (SD and HD) and 720p at 4:3 and 16:9 a "consumer" camera. Some people use the term "prosumer" for this phenomenon, but I'd rather not do that to the language. The term most used for this range of equipment—which is of high quality yet affordable, but a bit too complex for the average consumer—is "industrial." Industrial video gear is used when a polished and controlled look is important, but a full-blown, high-end, professional outfit would be overkill. Whichever term you use, suffice it to say that the line dividing professional quality gear and nonprofessional access is fading. Price tags on high-quality equipment are so low that virtually anybody can create broadcast and theatrical distribution quality projects on video. Professionals also no longer feel like they need to break their backs or call attention to themselves with a 20-pound, $25,000 camera rig, when a camcorder that fits in your palm will give a perfectly adequate image. Sure, there will always be a line of high-end professional cameras so technologically advanced and tricked-out that buying one requires a second mortgage, just as there will always be a line of super cheap consumer cameras that do everything easily but nothing particularly well, but the range of cameras between those two poles are getting better and more affordable.

The Basic DV Camcorder: Exterior

The standard form of the video camera for location field production is the camcorder, which simply means that the camera and recording device are built into the same unit. Just like film camera, most DV camcorders contain the same basic and essential components. (Figure 9-14).

The Body

Video is a single-system sound format, which means that the body of a video camera contains all of the electronic circuitry to gather and record both audio and video. Generally there are two types of camcorder bodies: shoulder mount cameras and palm camcorders. Shoulder mount camcorders tend to be found on the high-end professional range, where cameras are heavier. A shoulder-mounting camera allows for very stable handheld shots, while the ultralight palm cameras are more difficult to keep steady without a tripod. However, shoulder mount cameras are also more obvious than are the smaller palm-held camcorders. They announce loudly, "Professional camera here! Broadcast!" Many filmmakers find that the unobtrusiveness and mobility of the

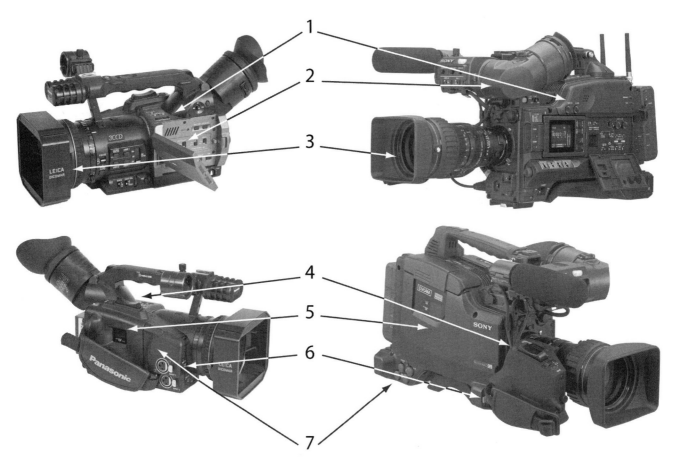

■ **Figure 9-14** Both professional and industrial-grade video cameras have the following features: a body (1), viewfinders and LCD viewscreens (2), a lens (3), a servo zoom control (4), a record media bay (5), external microphone inputs (6), and audio/video inputs and outputs (7).

in practice

After shooting the epilogue to his 1997 film *A Taste of Cherry*, director Abbas Kiarostami was told that the lab had ruined this portion of the film. He could not reshoot because the most beautiful part of the spring season (essential for the story) had already passed and he couldn't wait a full year to get these images again. So, to finish the movie, Kiarostami simply used the footage from a small video camera that had been on the set shooting a "behind the scenes" documentary. The epilogue to *A Taste of Cherry*, as is the case with most Kiarostami films, includes many nonactors. "What dramatically distinguished the performance of the video camera from that of the 35mm camera was the reaction of the simple people who behaved so naturally and spontaneously in front of it. This is something I've always striven to achieve during my 30 year career." In trying to get natural performances from nonactors with large, bulky 35mm film cameras, Kiarostami says that he eliminated as many distractions as possible by paring down his equipment and crew to the bare minimum. "However, when I said 'action,' there was action but it was artificial. . . . There is lighting, tracking, booms, and so on, all of these things keep them from giving a natural performance. . . . [People] know there is nothing natural on the other side off the camera, so why should they be?" But when Kiarostami started to use a small DV camera he discovered something different, "freedom." Nonactors responded with naturalness and spontaneity and Kiarostami was delivered from the large production crews and extra equipment necessary for a 35mm production. "This camera gives the filmmaker an opportunity for experimenting without fear of loosing the essential. It's a liberty for a filmmaker." Kiarostami made his next two films exclusively on DV. "It would have been impossible to shoot a film like *Ten* without a digital [video] camera." (From *10 on Ten*, Abbas Kiarostami, 2004.)

■ **Figure 9-15** Abbas Kiarostami achieved a high level of spontaneity and naturalness from his actors by using small, consumer-grade DV cameras in *A Taste of Cherry* (1997, left) and *Ten* (2002, right).

smaller camera are beneficial in certain situations for a sense of spontaneity, dynamic camera styles, or simply a degree of comfort. One type of camcorder body is not inherently better than the other, but the difference in size and weight does have an impact on what you are able to do with the camera and so should be considered with your visual approach.

Viewfinders and LCD Viewscreens

The viewfinder allows you a close and glare-free look at the video image. The viewfinder is usually a small black-and-white monitor seen through a diopter, but color viewfinders are being used more and more. Just as with a film camera, there is a diopter adjustment that focuses a lens on the tiny viewfinder video screen; the adjustment should be set for the camera operator's eye.

Most palm-held cameras also have a flip-open LCD viewscreen to monitor your video. These screens are not as accurate as the viewfinder is because changes in the viewing angle seriously alter the color and brightness of the image, as does the amount of glare the LCD screen catches from the ambient light. In many situations, especially with wide-angle shots, it is easier to find a precise focus with the viewfinder. It is also important to note that the LCD screen quickly eats up battery power. However, viewscreens are invaluable as a composition aid when you want to shoot from angles or create camera moves that make using the viewfinder difficult (Figure 9-16).

The Lens

The function of the lens is to gather the light reflecting off your scene and focus it onto the CCD chips. In other words, everything visual goes through the lens, so quality is important. A poor-quality lens will give you a poor-quality image. Lens quality is a major de-

■ **Figure 9-16** An LCD allows for shooting angles that would be extremely difficult to frame using only the view-finder.

tail that separates bare bones consumer camcorders from those intended for professional applications. Luckily for us, the dramatic improvement of video resolution and imaging devices has been paralleled by an evolution in optical quality in order to realize the new resolution potential. Higher end cameras have employed many of these advancements by outsourcing the manufacturing of their lenses to highly respected specialists, like Carl Zeiss and Leica (Figure 9-17).

Most DV camcorders come with one zoom lens, which is usually sufficient for most situations, but there are a few camera systems that offer interchangeable lenses (Figure 9-18). Consumer cameras under $1,000 generally come with a single, unchangeable lens that is made with plastic or extremely low-quality glass elements. Plastic lenses are lighter and cheaper, but tend to be less sharp and often result in an image of lower resolution than the camcorder DV format is capable of producing. Virtually all video cameras come with a zoom lens, which means that the lens has a range of focal lengths. The zoom range of any specific lens is expressed in its magnification ability. With a 10× (or 10:1) lens, the degree of magnification increases ten times over its full range, sixteen times with a 16× lens, and twenty times with a 20× lens. The larger the magnification ratio, the greater the magnification power of the lens.

The basic optical functions and compositional attributes of a lens are common to both film and video and are so important to the creative dimension of filmmaking that I have devoted an entire chapter specifically to this topic, where you will find much more detail (see Chapter 10).

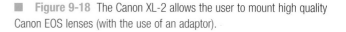

■ **Figure 9-17** Some higher end video cameras outsource their lenses to well-known manufacturers, such as Leica (pictured: a Leica Dicomar lens on a Panasonic DVX100A video camera).

■ **Figure 9-18** The Canon XL-2 allows the user to mount high quality Canon EOS lenses (with the use of an adaptor).

■ **Figure 9-19** The servo zoom rocker-switch allows the cameraperson to glide through the entire range of focal lengths available on the lens. High-end cameras even provide a speed adjustment to this switch, allowing greater control.

Servo Zoom Control

Accompanying the video zoom lens is the ubiquitous **servo zoom control**, which enables you to glide through the zoom range, from wide angle to telephoto, with the touch of a button (**Figure 9-19**). The servo zoom mechanism is usually a "rocker switch," but not all rocker switches are created equal and this is another area that separates the professional cameras from the cheapos. The speed of a good-quality servo zoom is pressure sensitive. The further you depress the mechanism, the faster the zoom, and the lighter you touch the button, the slower the zoom. This enables a camera operator not only to control the rate of a zoom, but also to taper it at the beginning and end. Consumer cameras tend to have only one zoom speed, which lurches on and clunks off when you start and stop.

It's also important to note that there are two types of zooms, optical zooms and digital zooms, and they are not even remotely the same, even though the rocker switch controls them both (**Figure 9-20**). An **optical zoom** adjusts the central lens element to magnify or demagnify the scene being shot. Although the composition and perspective of the image changes, the resolution of the video image remains the same. The optical zoom on most DV cameras falls between 10× magnification range and 20× magnification range. A **digital zoom**, on the other hand is essentially an in-camera digital special effect in which the circuitry in the camera magnifies the captured video signal by selecting the central pixels and blowing them up. The loss of resolution quality is rapid and significant with digital zooms. Cameras that advertise a 100×, 200×, 300×, or more (!) zoom range combine the two types of zooms. Once the rocker switch reaches the telephoto limits of the optical zoom range, the digital zoom (very obviously) kicks in. As the digital zoom enlarges the image, individual pixels become visible and video noise rakes the image. Many of the better quality cameras allow you to turn the digital zoom off, and many professional cameras don't even bother with digital zooms because of the extreme compromises to the image. Most filmmakers would agree that the digital zoom has limited applications; however, I did have a student effectively use the extreme end of a digital zoom to create the sense that an illicit encounter between two people was being observed by a surveillance camera. So think of it as another visual tool in your creative toolbox, albeit seldom used.

■ **Figure 9-20** A digital zoom can greatly augment the size of a subject in the frame, but the resulting image (right) shows severe resolution compromises compared to the far end of the optical zoom range (left).

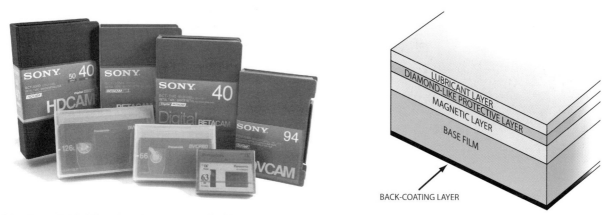

■ Figure 9-21 Although most consumer-grade video cameras use miniDV tape, there are many other formats including DVC-PRO, DVC-PROHD, and DVCAM. Most videotape, however, is usually made up of the same layers.

Media Bay and Recording Formats

The **media bay** is where the video signal is recorded. Historically speaking, this part of the camcorder has been referred to as the video tape recorder (VTR), because magnetic tape was the universal recording format for all video systems since the earliest days of the recorded electronic image. Currently, most consumer and industrial camcorders use MiniDV tape cassettes for recording any standard definition digital video signal, while high-end professional cameras use tape cassettes devised for a specific format (DVCPRO tape, DVCAM cassettes, etc.) to record standard and high definition. The tape stocks in all three formats have a width of ¼ inch but they are not interchangeable. Cassettes for DVCAM and DVCPRO come in larger cassette sizes, run faster tape speeds, and record data on different width data tracks on the tape (Figure 9-21).

The amount of data involved in video recording is enormous compared with that in audio recording. For one hour of DV footage with audio, a MiniDV cassette must record approximately 12 gigabytes of data on magnetic tape that is ¼ inch wide and a little more than 200 feet long. One rule of thumb for recording anything on metal oxide tape stock (e.g., MiniDV tape) is that the faster the tape speed is, the more information you can store on it. However, rather than actually move the tape stock fast, over stationary heads (which would take up an absurd amount of tape), video and audio data is laid down onto the metal oxide surface by two **write heads**, which are mounted on a spinning drum. The movement of the heads greatly increases the "effective" tape speed without using up more tape (Figure 9-22).

Although the actual tape speed of MiniDV is only 18.9 mm per second, the two write heads are spinning at a speed of 9,000 rpm against the direction of the tape, and can therefore lay down all of the data necessary for high-resolution image and audio. In addition, the record heads are mounted on the spinning drum at an angle, so that the data is written along diagonal tracks, called **helical scanning**, giving the heads even more recording space on the tape (Figure 9-23). All video tape formats use this method even though tape speeds from format to format differ. For example, DVCAM tape runs at 28 mm per second and DVCPRO runs at 34 mm per second—these professional formats effectively double the tape speed of standard MiniDV.

All of the video, audio, and auxiliary system data (i.e., timecode) is written in discrete diagonal tracks. In standard DV each track has a width of only 10 microns, while DVCAM and DVCPRO tracks are 15 micron wide. The data for *one frame* of video is written in five revolutions of the two write heads, which lay down ten tracks of data. To appreciate the precision of this system, consider that those ten tracks of audio, video, and auxiliary data measure only 100 microns, or about the width of a human hair!

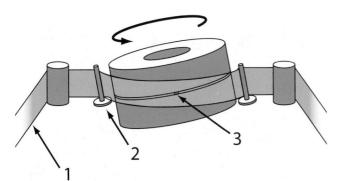

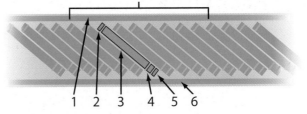

■ **Figure 9-22** When a cassette is inserted into a video camera, the tape (1) is pulled from the casing and it is wrapped around a spinning drum and against the write heads inside (3). Because the drum writes the information using a helical scan, the tape is set at an angle using slant pins (2).

■ **Figure 9-23** A recorded DV tape, in this case the DVCPRO format, has the following information encoded on its surface: cue tracks (1,6), a subcode with data and timecodes (2), a video and auxiliary section (3), an audio and auxiliary section (4), and a reference signal (5).

As remarkable as it is, the DV cassette format has several disadvantages. The first is the "linearity problem," meaning that to move around to different areas of the tape you need to fast forward and rewind through footage, which takes time. Second, a VTR contains numerous moving parts (springs, cogs, wheels, capstans, flying heads, etc.) and moving parts need care and cleaning and eventually break. Finally, the tape stock itself is susceptible to damage from humidity, dust, and heat. With so much data being written on such a small area, even the slightest damage to the magnetic tape surface can result in **drop-outs**, data loss on the tape, which shows as pixel areas in the image with missing video information. So delicate is DV tape, that it is generally recommended that users not mix brands of tape stock. Different brands use different tape lubricants in order to safely glide over the rapidly spinning record heads, and changing brands creates a mixture of different lubricants that can soften the metal oxide, causing particle buildup on the write heads that leads to dropouts.

Although tape continues to be the most prevalent recording media for DV, we are surely witnessing the inexorable transition to solid state recording technology. Currently there are a number of camcorders that record video directly to high-capacity **optical discs** (Sony) or to **P2 flash memory cards** (Panasonic) (Figure 9-24). There are also hard drive recorders that interface with various DV camcorders, allowing you to record direct to hard drive (Firestore).

All of these formats offer the convenience of instantaneous random-access data retrieval and have greatly improved the interface with digital editing systems. In the field you can see thumbnail images of every scene you've recorded, which allows you to see, at a

■ **Figure 9-24** Although recording on videotape has been standard for decades, advances in data storage are prompting the transition to more stable formats, like P2 cards (left) and optical discs (right).

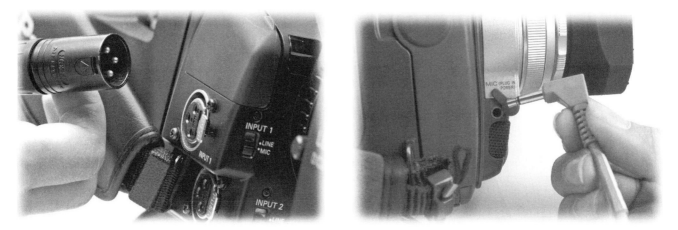

■ **Figure 9-25** While higher-end video cameras come with XLR inputs for professional microphones (left), less expensive consumer-grade cameras only have ⅛" mini-jack connectors (right), which are prone to interference and offer poor quality in the long run.

glance, what script coverage you've recorded at any given time. Footage recorded on any of these formats is immediately available for editing without the need to capture in real time, as is the case with tape. Flash memory cards and hard drives can even be off-loaded to laptop computers in the field, allowing you to reuse them again and again. Another advantage with memory cards is that there are no moving parts.

External Microphone Inputs

External microphone inputs are especially important for narrative film production. The **onboard microphones** that come with many camcorders are generally insufficient for most filmmaking applications where we need to acquire optimum quality audio through very careful microphone placement (see Chapter 17). The microphone input connection is another line demarcating professional/industrial grade equipment, which is suitable for narrative production, from consumer cameras, which are often inadequately equipped for serious productions.

All professional microphones use the three-pronged XLR connector. The advantages of this connector are a secure connection and balanced audio, which means that the cable is grounded and shielded from interference. Many cameras, however, come with a ⅛" mini-plug connector for external microphone input. The primary shortcoming of this connector is its flimsiness. The mini-plug easily breaks or loosens under the rigors of field production, causing a poor connection. This problem is exacerbated when you want to use a professional microphone that requires a mini-to-XLR adaptor. The other shortcoming of the ⅛" mini-jack is that it is not a balanced audio connection and is highly susceptible to interference (Figure 9-25).

It is one of the ironies of the DV world that while image resolution has improved astronomically in recent years, something as simple as audio connectors and circuitry have received practically no attention at all. Because of this, some very fine DV camcorders come with mini-jacks. If this is what you have to work with, don't despair; there are a few solutions that are discussed in Chapters 16 and 17.

Component and Composite Video

Composite video simply means that all of the elements that make up the video signal, luminance (Y) and chrominance (C), are encoded together and transmitted via a single wire, like an RCA or BNC cable. However, on some cameras you will find an **S-video** connector (super-video). S-Video is a four-pin component video connector. **Component video** (or **Y/C video**) keeps the chrominance and luminance components of the signal separate for a superior image. You can only realize this extra quality if both your camera and monitor have S-video connectors and capabilities.

Audio and Video, In and Out

In addition to the external microphone inputs, camcorders usually also have an audio **line signal input and output (I/O)** (Figure 9-26). We use the audio line input when we want to record audio from a line signal device, such as a CD player, or if we are using a portable microphone mixer that sends out a line signal (see Chapter 16). Most cameras also have the standard analog NTSC **composite video and audio** output for viewing footage on a regular NTSC monitor or transferring to an analog format like VHS.

On consumer cameras, audio line signal and composite video connectors are usually the standard RCA plug, but you will occasionally find a mini-jack for audio. Professional gear uses the sturdier and more secure XLR (for audio) and BNC (for video) connectors. Both have lock collars for a very secure connection. However, given the variety of connectors and configurations that can be used for line signals and composite video, you should check your camcorder's specific hardware for getting video and audio in and out.

The only I/O connector on DV camcorders that transmits digital audio and video as data is the **firewire** connector (also called **IEEE 1394**). The firewire cable transfers digital data from the camera to your computer hard drive while capturing footage for editing, or you can connect to a third-party recording device for recording directly to hard drive. The camera end is a small four-pin connector and the computer side is a larger six-pin connector.

■ **Figure 9-26** Consumer-grade video cameras usually come equipped with S-video (1), RCA-type connectors (2), and firewire (3) for audio and video I/O. Professional video cameras additionally have the much sturdier BNC (4) and XLR (5) connectors.

■ Figure 9-27 Common audio and video connectors.

The Audio and Video Connectors for DV Camcorders

1. ⅛″ mini (unshielded, unbalanced line audio and microphone audio with adaptor) male
2. XLR (shielded and grounded microphone audio and line audio if switchable) male
3. BNC plug (composite video) male
4. S-Video (component video) male
5. RCA (line audio and composite video) male
6. Firewire 4 pin (all audio, video, and auxiliary data)
7. Firewire 6 pin (all audio, video, and auxiliary data)

■ Figure 9-28 Video cameras run on batteries available in a variety of sizes and power capacities.

DC Power

Video cameras run on DC power provided by **onboard batteries** or via an adaptor that transforms the unstable AC power coming from the wall outlet into steadier DC current. Despite the unlimited power supply of an AC adaptor, most shooters only use batteries, preferring the freedom of not being tethered by a chord to the wall (Figure 9-28).

Camera Function Menus and Switches

Depending on the make and model of your camera, various camera functions may be embedded inside a menu that can be accessed through buttons and viewed on the LCD viewscreen; some functions may be located as switches and wheels on the outside of the camera body. You need to consult your camera's manual to find out how to access and control all of the functions you require on your shoot (Figure 9-29).

One very important measure of a camera's capability to function as an expressive tool for the visual storyteller is its **manual functions**. Video cameras are designed by engineers and business people, not artists, and the automatic functions on a DV camera—auto focus, auto exposure, auto white balance, and auto sound levels—are designed to give the user easily obtained, generally acceptable sound and image. Point-and-shoot simplicity is what most home video shooters are looking for. The average consumer doesn't have the time or inclination to study their camera; they need to be able to pick it up and simply use it when they need it. This is fine if you are shooting your kid's birthday party, but if you are telling a story with images, something that you want to show to an audience, to move people, to communicate ideas and emotions, you need to be able to control the creative elements as part of your expressive and aesthetic palette. Focus, exposure, color, and sound are central creative elements in filmmaking and each offers a range of expressive possibilities. To leave these creative decisions up to a machine is to give away your voice. All professional video cameras allow for manual control of all of these

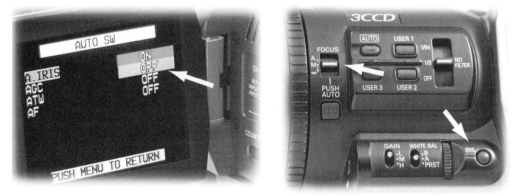

■ Figure 9-29 Some video camera functions are embedded inside menus accessible on the LCD screen (left), while other, more commonly used features (like the manual overrides for focus and iris), are found right on the camera's body (right).

■ **Figure 9-30** A "cheesy" effect. When was the last time you saw a "negative art" effect being used in a film? This hasn't stopped manufacturers from continuing to cram their camcorders with all sorts of dubious special effects.

functions by the camera operator. The better the camera, the more precise and detailed that control can be. Cameras that do not allow us to set our own focus, sound levels, exposure, or white balance, usually the cheapest consumer video cameras, severely limit us in terms of craft and are therefore not so useful for us. Most high-quality DV cameras, even many of the less expensive ones, give us the option of automatic or manual override for these functions, and you should immediately learn how to take control of your own image by turning off the auto functions in favor of manually controlling your shots. We will look closer at how to use manual focus, exposure, white balance, and sound in the sections dedicated to these functions.

The other by-product of cameras created by business people and overly enthusiastic engineers is the inclusion of video functions no one ever asked for or even needs. *Ignore the bells and whistles.* No one asked for three levels of the mosaic special effect, or psychedelic posterizing or a s-t-r-e-t-c-h image function. These functions are there because an engineer could put them there and a marketing executive thought that cramming in more effects would make the camera sell. When you approach a camera, be clear about the functions you need in order to achieve the look you want, and then ignore everything else, especially the "special effects" menus (**Figure 9-30**).

The Basic DV Camcorder: Interior

DV camcorders essentially turn light into data. The best way to understand the interior workings of a basic, three-CCD chip DV camcorder is to follow the progress of an image, which begins as light entering the lens and emerges as a steam of data recorded onto tape (or other record media) (**Figure 9-31**).

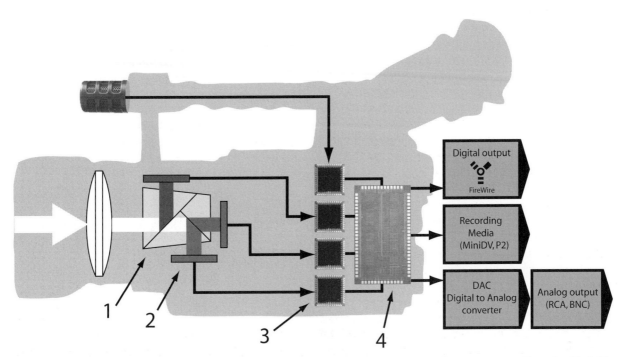

■ **Figure 9-31** A 3 chip video camera produces an image by first dividing the light entering the lens into primary colors with a prism block (1), which are read by 3 CCD chips (2), their signal outputs are converted into digital data by an ADC (3), and are processed by the DSP (4), ultimately outputting the data to the format being used. See the color insert in Chapter 13.

The Prism Block

The light gathered from the lens first passes through the **prism block**, located just behind the lens; this splits the image into the three primary colors of light: red, green, and blue (RGB). These three images, identical except for their color, are reflected onto the face plates of three CCD chips, which register the relative light intensities and create a separate video signal for each color.

Imaging Devices

As we discussed earlier, each CCD chip is made up of tightly packed and linked rows of photosensitive pixels that register the light values of every spot on the image as fluctuations in voltage (explained on p. 170). The electronic information built up in every photosensitive cell is regularly and repeatedly scanned, or "read," according to the system's scanning pattern (NTSC 60i, 24p, 60p, etc.) and then output as an analog signal. We call it an analog signal at this point because the voltage fluctuations are analogous to the various intensities of light in the actual scene.

Most professional and industrial grade camcorders contain three CCD imaging devices for maximum image quality. One-chip cameras exist, but usually on the lower end of consumer equipment. CCD chips come in various sizes depending of the model of your camera. Consumer and industrial level cameras usually have smaller CCD chip sets measuring ⅙″, ¼″, and ⅓″, while high-end industrial and professional cameras have larger chips measuring ½″ and ⅔″. The larger the chip, the greater its resolution capability.

Another factor that has an impact on the resolution capabilities of a chip is the aspect ratio of the chip itself. Most DV cameras can shoot in two aspect ratios: 4:3 and 16:9; however, some cameras use CCDs that are physically a 4:3 chip and use either electronic anamorphic image "squeezing" or selective pixel disabling to crop to the 16:9 format. Both of these processes lead to some compromises in the quality of the image. Recognizing that the 16:9 aspect ratio is quickly becoming very popular with filmmakers and viewers alike, today's higher-end camcorders almost always contain 16:9 CCD chip sets and increasingly consumer cameras have them as well. The slight edge cropping required to then shoot in 4:3 mode for NTSC production has much less impact on image quality (Figure 9-32).

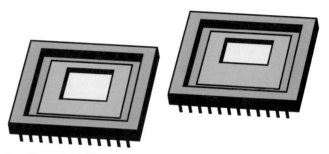

■ **Figure 9-32** Many consumer cameras have 4:3 CCD chips which then crop (disable pixels) along the top and bottom in order to shoot in the 6:9 format. Professional camcorders have 16:9 chip sets providing a higher quality image in "widescreen" mode.

In order for your CCDs to reproduce colors accurately, you must take care to **white balance** your camera each time you change location or lighting conditions. White balancing means adjusting the CCD's color circuitry to match the color temperature of the light source (see p. 162 for color temperature). On nearly every DV camera there are two easily accessible color temperature pre-sets: one for daylight color temperature (5,600°K) and one for tungsten light (3,200°K). In addition, many cameras provide a way to manually set your white balance. This is accomplished by filling your frame with something white (like a white card or sheet of paper) that is lit with representative light, and then engaging the manual white balance button (Figure 9-33). Whether the white card is reflecting the bluish tint of daylight or the amber tint of tungsten bulbs or the greenish hue of fluorescent lights, the camera adjusts the R, G, and B chip sensitivity levels until that card is rendered "white." White balancing must be done every time your lighting source changes.

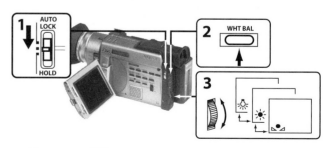

■ Figure 9-33 White balancing. All video cameras have a way to balance the CCD chips to a variety of color temperatures. Common are presets for daylight and tungsten color temperatures and a mode for manual white balancing. (pictured: white balancing instructions for the Sony DCR-TRV900).

Analog-to-Digital Converters

Each CCD then sends its analog electronic signal to separate **analog-to-digital converters** (ADC) where it is transformed into digital data, meaning binary code (a series of 1s and 0s).[3] The process of transforming analog information into digital data is called **quantizing**, and requires the ADC to regularly **sample** the constantly flowing stream of voltage information from each pixel to ascribe discrete digital values. The more times the ADC is able to sample the analog information, the better the resolution and image detail will be (Figure 9-34). ADC sampling rates are referred to as **bit rates**, and camera systems capable of higher bit rates convert more of the original signal information into digital data and therefore deliver superior quality. Most standard definition DV ADCs have an 8 bit or 10 bit sampling rate, and high definition cameras are capable of 12 bit or even 14 bit sampling rates.

The Digital Signal Processor

Once the ADC has crunched the numbers, the raw digital video data from each of the CCD chips and the microphone is then sent to the **digital signal processor** (DSP) to create the final, digital image. The DSP is the most complex part of the entire digital video system and works with algorithms specific to the camera's format (DVCPRO, HDV, HD, etc.). Primarily, the DSP combines the image information from the three CCDs and determines the color value of every pixel in every frame of video to create the full color image, along with incorporating the audio signal. This newly combined image and audio data (now a stream of 0s and 1s) is then sent to the write heads, where it is laid down as tracks of digital information.

Raw DV images contain an enormous amount of data, something on the order of 165 megabytes per second; straight high definition video is five times that size, generating nearly 1 gigabyte per second! This is simply too much data to move around and record, so when processing raw video information, the DSP is forced to reduce the amount of data it sends to the recording media; on the other hand, this reduction of data cannot be accomplished at the expense of too much resolution quality. To this end, the DSP uses highly complex, format-specific, algorithms to reduce data in two ways, **compression** and **color depth sampling**, and both have a significant impact on image quality.

[3]Just as each CCD chip has its own ADC, so, too, does the microphone input signal, which also needs to be converted from an analog electronic signal into binary code.

■ **Figure 9-34** ADC (analog-to-digital converter) sampling rates determine the amount of information and ultimately the resolution of the image being created. An extremely low sample rate, like the one used in the now defunct Fisher Price Pixelvision format (left, from Almereyda's *The Rocking-Horse Winner*, 1997) had an intentionally low quality feel, while the miniDV format (right, from Harrison's *November*, 2004) has an 8-bit rate that produces a polished standard definition image.

Compression and Color Sampling

DV compression is a way of reducing the amount of data flowing from the ADC, by discarding visual detail that is either imperceptible to the human viewer or redundant. The programs that perform this compression are called **codecs** (for compression/decompression). There are several codecs in the world of digital video (i.e., JPEG, MPEG 2, MPEG 4), with new ones being introduced all of the time, but rather than look at them specifically, we'll simply look at the principles of compression, especially as they pertain to the DSP and image quality. Understanding some basics about compression is important because it has a bearing on choosing a DV production format and, ultimately, on what we see on the screen.

Discarding visual information that cannot be perceived by the human eye, like many of those billions of colors and indiscernibly subtle nuances in tonal shades, seems logical enough. Why move it and store it if you can't see it? This is the visual equivalent of tossing out the data for audio frequencies, like those of dog whistles, which the human ear can't hear anyway. This type of compression allows the system to discard nearly half (!) of the data streaming from the ADC; that's a lot of saved space.

Understanding the compression of redundant information is a little more complicated. Redundant information is the data for visual details that are repeated, from pixel to pixel and frame after frame. In video there is a lot of redundant color and brightness information. For example, say we have a shot of an ant crawling across a green wall. The pixels along the path of the ant change from green to black as the ant passes, but the rest of the frame remains exactly the same frame after frame—green. It would take a great deal of space to rerecord all of the common and repeated luminance and chrominance values for every pixel in every frame. In standard NTSC DV resolution (720 × 480) we would need to rerecord the same numeric value for "green" 345,600 times (minus the 30 pixels or so for the ant) for every single frame. The codec, instead, reduces all of this common information to a smaller file size by recording the numeric value for "green" once and then indicating that every other pixel in each subsequent frame (except for the ant pixels) is "just like that first one." The rest of the information is then tossed out. Then later, when we play back that image, the codec **decompresses** that information by reconstructing the data through duplication of that one numeric value for the "green" areas of the frame. It may not be exactly the original data making that image of an ant crossing a green wall, but codecs work so well that it looks just like the original.

Digital video is always compressed for recording and is always displayed decompressed. Discarding imperceptible data and redundant data is called **lossy compression**, because the original data is gone for good. DV codecs reduce video information by 75% to 90%, but there is clearly a limit to the amount of lossy compression we can employ before we see a degeneration of picture quality. In general, the less compression employed, the better the image, but there are many other factors that bear on image quality, so this is not a hard and fast rule. For example, HD video has much greater compression ratios, but with progressive scanning and the increased pixel count, HD more than makes up for the larger compression data loss. Compression ratios for a specific format are expressed as the size of the *compressed* data to the *original* size of the digital information, or **R = C/O**. Most standard definition digital video formats have a compression ratio of 5:1, creating a data rate of 25 mbps. This is why DV, DVCPRO, and DVCAM are often referred to as **DV25**.

High definition video generates five times more data, so it needs a more robust compression system. DVCPRO HD and HDCAM employ a compression ratio of 6.7:1 and the HDV format has a compression of 22.5:1. HDV compression is so high that some people have questioned whether HDV is indeed a true HD format.

There is another type of compression, called **lossless compression**, which warrants mentioning in order to avoid confusion. **Lossless compression** is a kind of compression in which no data is lost at all. This is the sort of compression used for "zip" or "stuffit"

Approximate time to storage ratios for DV25
formats (25 mbps)
- 1 second of footage = 3.5 MB
- 1 minute of footage = 215 MB
- 5 minutes of footage = 1 GB
- 1 hour of footage = 12—13 GB

computer files, in which the original data is compressed into smaller data codes, or "tokens," and then exactly reconstructed upon decompression for a perfect copy of the original. But lossless compression isn't used in digital video codecs . . . yet!

Color sampling (also called color depth) is another way of eliminating unnecessary data in order to save space. Color sampling is the number of times luminance and color information is measured and translated into data by the DSP algorithms. It is expressed as a ratio of luminance sampling to blue sampling to red sampling. The information for green is not sampled because it can be interpolated given the data for luminance of blue and red. Color sampling is done by looking at and averaging out blocks of four pixels rather than every single pixel, which in itself saves space. Because the human eye is capable of perceiving very subtle variations in luminance (brightness) but relatively fewer shifts in color tonalities, all DV formats sample all of the luminance information, but much less blue and red information. A full sample is represented with the integer 4. A color sampling ratio of 4:4:4 would mean that all colors are sampled equally and fully. However, DV25 color sampling comes in at 4:1:1, which means that the color components are sampled only once for every four luminance samples. The resulting image, even after losing three-quarters of the color information, is surprisingly good, as DV has excellent color rendition. Many HD formats have a color sampling rate of 4:2:2. The extra color information takes up much more space, but the quality is clearly superior—which is partly what puts the high definition in HD.

The Lens

CHAPTER 10

■ THE CAMERA LENS

The lens of a camera is often likened to the human eye—in fact, many people have announced that "the lens is the eye of the camera." This is true, in that light enters through and is controlled by the lens and ultimately this light registers an image. However, there are many things that human eyes and human psychology of perception do automatically, which, on a lens, must be accomplished manually. Framing, focusing, and exposure are activities we rarely consciously think about with respect to the function of our eyes, but on a lens, which relies on us to deliberately set each of these functions, we are presented with a range of possibilities. Every lens-related variable offers not just a function, but also an array of creative choices. These choices are, in fact, part of the creative potential of any lens and part of the aesthetic palette of a filmmaker. Often there is no absolute "right" setting; rather, you must find the appropriate setting for what you want to express. In film or video production, registering an image is not done in the blink of an eye. Focus doesn't just happen: we must ask, "Where do we want our focus to be?" There is more to creating a powerful image than simply allowing enough light to see the subject clearly. We get to decide how much light we want and exactly how bright or dark, clear or obscured our subject will appear. On every single shot we must decide, from a wide range of possibilities, the size of the subject and the visual perspective within the frame. Knowing how lenses work will help you choose the right lens and settings to express exactly what you need them to say to your audience. It is helpful to remember that the lens is much more than just the eye of the camera: it becomes the eyes of your audience.

Whether you are shooting on digital video, 16mm film, or 35 mm film, the basic construction and function of the camera lens are the same. All light entering the camera comes in through the lens and this light must be carefully controlled in order to achieve a usable and expressive image.

Broadly speaking, lenses are a series of polished glass sections called **lens elements**. These elements are held parallel to each other in a light-tight housing called the **barrel**, or **lens housing**. The function of these glass elements is to gather the light reflecting off a scene and, through optical refraction, direct that light precisely onto the camera's focal plane. The **focal plane** (also called **film plane**) of a film camera is the emulsion of the film, and every film camera has an external marking which indicates precisely where the film is located. The film plane marking looks like this: ϕ. The focal plane of a video camera is the **face plate** of the CCD chip. In video cameras with three chips, there are three focal planes, all calibrated to exactly the same distance from the last element of the lens (**Figure 10-1**). The lens gathers light reflecting off a three-dimensional scene and projects it as a two-dimensional image onto the focal plane. The image registered on the focal plane is both reversed and flipped. This flipping of the image occurs at the exact optical center of the lens and is later reversed in the projection (film) or scanning process (video).

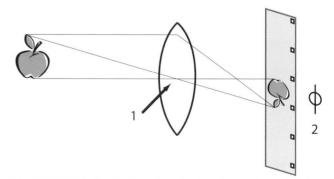

■ **Figure 10-1** Simple image formation by a lens. A lens gathers incoming light and focuses it on the film plane (2). Note that as it passes through the optical center (1), the image is not only flipped, but also reversed.

The type, placement, and number of glass elements in any given lens vary widely depending on the function, quality, and perspective attributes of the lens. There are many lenses to choose from, so understanding lenses in general will help you pick the right one to create the image you need.

Focal Length

The **focal length** of a lens determines the degree of magnification or de-magnification of the scene being shot. Different lenses offer different focal lengths. Focal length is determined by the distance between the **optical center** of the lens (the point at which the image flips) and the focal plane, ϕ. This distance is usually measured in millimeters, although older lenses may be marked in inches. The focal length of a lens affects both the image size within the frame and the **angle of view**, which means how much of the scene the lens takes in horizontally (x-axis) and vertically (y-axis).

■ Figure 10-2 Prime lenses have a fixed focal length, and can be easily identified by reading the engravings on their barrels.

The longer the focal length, the more the subject is magnified and appears closer to the camera. The shorter the focal length, the smaller the image is and the further away it appears. Also, the longer the focal length, the narrower the angle of view becomes and vice versa. There are three broad focal length classifications for lenses: **wide angle** (short lenses), **normal** (medium lenses), and **telephoto** (long lenses) (**Figure 10-2**).

A **normal lens** approximates the same perspective and image size that the human eye would see if one were to stand in the same spot as the camera (not including peripheral vision). While this sounds like a fairly non-scientific description of a normal lens, human visual perspective is indeed the intended reference point. The actual focal length of a normal lens is primarily determined by the size of the imaging format you are using. For the 16mm film format, the focal length for a normal lens is 25mm. For the 35mm film format, a normal lens is 50mm. In video, the normal lens length for a ⅔" CCD is 20mm, for a ½" CCD is 15mm, for a ⅓" CCD is 11mm, and for a ¼" CCD is 8mm. As you can see, the larger the area of the imaging device, the longer the focal length is for a normal lens.

Wide angle lenses are those with focal lengths shorter than normal lenses. Wide angle lenses will reduce the size of the image and broaden the angle of view, compared to the perspective of the human eye. In the 16mm film format, a 15mm lens is considered slightly wide angle, a 10mm lens is wide angle, and an 8mm lens very wide angle. An extreme wide angle lens, with an angle of view greater than 180° (!), is also called a fisheye lens.

Given the small size of most consumer and "prosumer" video imaging devices, which makes for a very short normal lens, it's difficult to find a video camera with an extreme wide angle end to their lens. However, most camera manufacturers offer a wide angle lens attachment as an optional purchase. This is, in effect, another lens that attaches to the camera's existing lens and allows for extreme wide angle shots.

Lenses that have a longer focal length than normal and that enlarge the size of the image and narrow the angle of view are called **telephoto lenses**. In the 16mm film format a 75mm lens is slightly telephoto, 120mm is telephoto, and 250mm is very telephoto. The exact focal length of a lens can be found etched into the front of the lens barrel.

Lens Perspective

Perspective is one of the most important considerations when we think about framing and composition. Perspective is essentially a combination of the angle of view, in terms of both the **horizontal dimension (x-axis)** and the **vertical dimension** of the frame (**y-axis**), and the depth relationship (near vs. far) between objects. This **depth dimension** is the **z-axis**, and since a film image is two dimensional, the sense of depth is an illusion created by the composition of the frame. We have already discussed creating deep frames and flat frames through mise-en-scène in Chapter 3 (*Shot Composition*), but how does lens choice actually affect perspective?

There are two ways to affect the size of an image. The first is to change the camera-to-subject distance—moving the camera itself closer or further from the subject; the other is to alter the magnification of the scene by changing the focal length of the lens you use. There is a significant difference. When you change only the camera-to-subject distance to change the size of the subject in the frame, you are maintaining the same angle of view, and the camera essentially takes in the same horizontal vista. Leaving the camera stationary and changing focal length, longer or shorter, to change the size of the subject in the frame, also alters the angle of view, narrower or wider. This significantly changes the amount of background information contained in the frame (Figures 10-3 and 10-4).

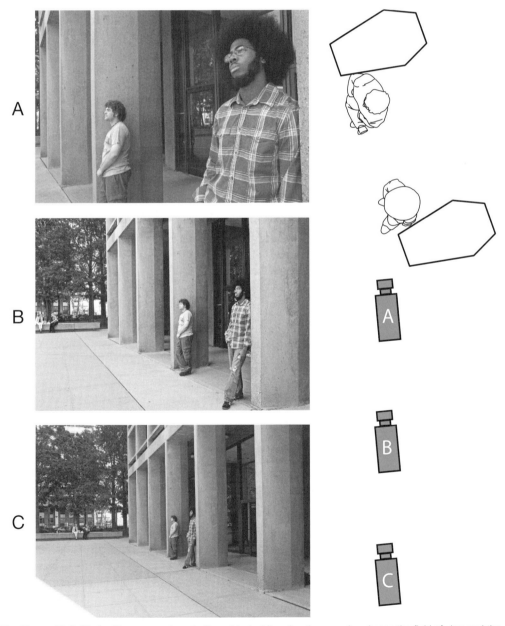

■ Figure 10-3 Moving the camera closer to the subject while using the same lens keeps the field of view and the perspective constant. All positions shot with the same wide angle lens.

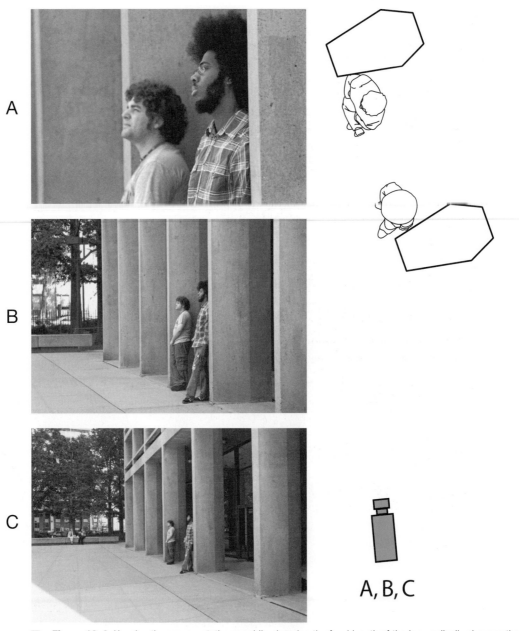

■ **Figure 10-4** Keeping the camera stationary while changing the focal length of the lens radically changes the field of view and the perspective of the image. Telephoto lens (A); normal lens (B) and wide angle lens (C)

The other perspective dimension is that of the perception of depth, or relative distances of objects along the z-axis. A normal lens replicates the sense of depth that our eyes sense. For example, if we frame a subject in a medium shot with another object 5 feet behind, that object will in fact seem like it is 5 feet behind the subject.

Wide angle lenses tend to exaggerate the depth along the z-axis. The space between objects appears to be greater because of the relativity between the camera and objects along the z-axis. For example, if we were to frame the exact same medium shot above with an 8mm lens, we would need to bring the camera in much closer to our subject. Then, the relative distance between the camera and subject will be much shorter than the distance between the subject and background object, causing the object to appear further away than 5 feet. The more wide angle our lens, the more exaggerated the depth of the shot will appear. Wide angle lenses have often been used to exaggerate the space between a person and a destination, in order to stress the sense that they have a long, long way to travel (Figure 10-5).

■ **Figure 10-5** In this single shot from *Goodfellas* (1990) Scorsese used a dolly move and a zoom lens to simultaneously pull back from and zoom in to a conversation between Jimmy (Robert DeNiro) and Henry (Ray Liotta). This technique effectively keeps the subjects the same size in the frame, but creates substantial spatial distortion in the background, which, in this case, vividly reflects Henry's unsettled mental state.

The converse is true for telephoto lenses, which have the effect of compressing space along the z-axis. Again, if we were to frame the same medium shot with a 200mm lens, we would need to pull the camera away from our subject, and the relative distance between the background object and the subject will be much smaller compared to the distance between the camera and the subject. This will cause the object to appear much closer than 5 feet to our subject. The more telephoto the lens, the more compressed the z-axis distance. We have all seen shots of a character walking amongst the crowds on a city sidewalk. It looks as though there is no space at all between all these people and it seems they are practically walking on top of each other. This is accomplished with a very long lens, shooting from a long distance, and the depth compression effect creates the feeling of claustrophobia and extreme congestion.

Prime and Zoom Lenses

Lenses that have one fixed focal length are called **prime lenses**. These lenses are very common in film production. Prime lenses are favored by many cinematographers because their simple design allows them to be made with few glass lens elements, which means that there is less chance for loss of light or lens aberrations to occur (see later, Lens Speed). However, if you are using primes lenses and decide to change the focal length of a lens from one shot to the next (say change from a 25mm lens to a 120mm lens in order to get in closer to the subject without moving he camera), then you need to change your

Understanding how the perception of depth can be manipulated with lenses is certainly vital to creating dynamic compositions, but one must also understand the narrative context of the scene or shot in order to utilize their expressive potential in appropriate ways (Figure 10-6).

Terry Gilliam is known for being a "short lens director" for his frequent use of wide angle lenses, which is an essential part of his unique visual sensibility. In general he is keen on exposing as much of the location and art direction as possible, and wide lenses are the best option for this, given their wide field of view and deep focus capabilities. However, sometimes Gilliam will pull out an extra wide angle lens to infuse a scene with a very particular emotion. In *The Fisher King* (1991) (photographed by Roger Pratt), the protagonist Jack Lucas, in an effort to heal his comatose friend Parry, attempts to steal for him what Parry believes to be the true "holy grail." In fact, the object is merely a worthless trophy cup in a rich person's house. In the scene in which Jack, who is clearly not an experienced thief, must climb a rope to get onto the roof of the rich man's "castle," Gilliam uses an extreme wide angle lens from above and below to exaggerate the sense of height and depth and therefore the sense of mortal danger. These shots convey a strong sense of vertigo, which Jack himself must be feeling—since it looks like it's is a long, long way to the pavement should he fall.

Similarly in Steven Zaillian's *Searching for Bobby Fischer* (1993), in the climactic scene in which the protagonist Josh plays a fearsome opponent in a children's chess tournament, a wide angle lens is used to exaggerate the space that Josh must walk in order to reach the chess table. The wide angle of view also reveals a gauntlet of other players watching his progress to the head table. His apprehension and nervousness in the scene is enhanced by the wide angle lens because it feels (as it must to him) that this is the longest walk of his life.

On the other end of the scale are telephoto lenses which are used to collapse space. Ramin Bahrani's calls *Man Push Cart* (2005) a "long lens" film, meaning that it was shot primarily with telephoto focal lengths. *Man Push Cart* is the story of Ahmad, a Pakistani immigrant in New York City who is trying to start a new life for himself and his son. His primary hope for survival is the tiny food cart that he rents. By shooting primarily with a telephoto lens, Bahrani and cinematographer Michael Simmonds were able to create an overall sense of the packed and claustrophobic environment of New York City. The telephoto lens is used to particularly harrowing advantage in the scenes in which Ahmad pulls his food cart along the roadside to get to his spot early in the morning. The dangers of his morning routine are viscerally communicated in these scenes, which are shot with a telephoto lens from some distance, greatly compressing the space between Ahmad and the huge trucks bearing down on him from all sides.

Figure 10-6 Perspective can be manipulated for dramatic effect by carefully selecting the focal length of your lens. Wide angle lens shots from Gilliam's *The Fisher King* (1991, top left) and Zaillian's *Searching for Bobby Fischer* (1993, top right) and two shots taken with a telephoto lens from Bahrani's *Man Push Cart* (2005, bottom).

lens. With prime lenses, you need to change the lens every time you want a new focal length. For this reason, many 16mm cameras are built with a rotating turret (Figure 10-7). This turret has three lens mounts and will accommodate three prime lenses of various focal lengths. The three lenses mounted on a lens turret usually consist of one normal lens, one telephoto lens, and one wide angle lens. Turrets allow you to switch between lenses by simply rotating and positioning the desired lens in front of the gate.

Zoom lenses, which are also referred to as **variable focal length lenses**, offer precisely that—a continuous range of focal lengths in one lens housing. Zoom lenses are constructed with movable lens elements that slide forward and backward to physically shift the optical center and therefore change the focal length of the lens. **Zooming in** means adjusting the optical center away from the focal plane and therefore increasing the magnification power of the lens (telephoto), and **zooming out** means adjusting the optical center back toward the focal plane, causing the image to become more wide angle. Zooming is accomplished with the adjustable zoom ring, calibrated in millimeters, which allows the filmmaker to manually set the desired focal length. Some zoom lenses, primarily on video cameras, utilize a servo zoom motor, so that you can glide from one focal length to another smoothly during a shot (Figures 10-8 and 10-9).

Different zoom lenses offer a different range of focal lengths, and this range is often stated as a ratio (etched into the lens barrel). A 12:1 zoom lens is one that increases the focal length twelve times over its full range. This can also be stated as a 12× zoom lens. A 10:1 (or 10×) zoom lens might go from 10mm to 100mm or from 12mm to 120mm. The specific millimeter settings are found on the zoom ring itself.

Zoom lenses are wonderfully convenient, as they can offer a wide range of focal lengths in one lens; however, there are trade-offs for this convenience. It requires many more glass elements to make a zoom lens as compared to a prime lens, so zoom lenses are prone to light loss (see later, Lens Speed) and optical aberrations. Video cameras almost always have zoom lenses because, historically speaking, the resolution of the final image would not necessarily benefit from the supe-

■ **Figure 10-7** Switching between prime lenses is a simple task when they are mounted on a rotating turret, like the lenses on the Arri-S.

■ **Figure 10-8** Zoom lenses have variable focal lengths and provide great flexibility during shooting at the cost of some quality; they are widely available for film cameras (top) and standard on video camcorders (bottom).

rior (and more expensive) optics of high-quality prime lenses. However, as the resolution of video increases, especially with the emergence of high definition video, research and development of high-quality zoom lenses is now producing zooms that are being used by cinematographers who shoot 35mm film for theatrical distribution. Conversely, it's not unusual to see HDTV cameras fitted with prime lenses in order to achieve maximum image clarity. In fact, there are currently several "prosumer" digital video cameras on the market designed to take prime lenses. All of these recent improvements in image resolution and lens optics are great news for all moviemakers, whether they work in film or video, because it offers more quality, options, and flexibility.

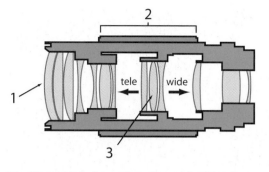

■ **Figure 10-9** A zoom lens changes focal length by shifting the position of a cluster of lens elements internally

■ **Figure 10-10** The focusing ring on a lens has a series of distances engraved in both feet and meters, used to critically focus a subject using a witness mark (arrow) as a reference point.

■ **Figure 10-11** Camera to subject distance is accurately measured from the film plane engraving, found on all film cameras to the subject.

Focus

We all have some sense for what focus is. Images that appear fuzzy and indistinct are "out of focus" and images that are sharply defined and clear are "in focus." But to be more precise about it, **focus** can be generally defined as when a point of light reflecting off the subject is registered as a point of light on the focal plane. The **focus ring** on a lens brings a subject into focus by very precisely moving the front element of the lens forward and backward in relation to the focal plane, which is why the focus ring is always found at the front of the lens.

What you are adjusting when you move the front lens element is called the **focus point**, or **plane of critical focus**—that is, the precise distance in front of the camera, from the focal plane φ, which will be in sharp focus. If you set the focus ring for 5 feet, objects 5 feet from the focal plane will be rendered sharply on the film, and if you set the focus ring to 20 feet, objects 20 feet from the focal plane will be in focus, and so on. Turning the focus ring counter-clockwise moves the plane of critical focus, along the z-axis, away from the camera and vice versa. The range of distances that you find on the focus ring scale will be from the closest to the furthest an object can be and still be brought into focus. This range usually falls somewhere between 3 feet to infinity, which is represented on the focus ring scale with the symbol φ. The focus adjustment scale is etched on the focus ring and is often in both meters and feet. Be careful not to mix up these scales. Setting the focus is done by turning the focus ring until the distance you want is lined up against a **witness mark**, which is a line etched into a nonmovable part of the lens barrel (Figure 10-10).

When shooting video we see the actual image being registered on the CCD chip, either through the viewfinder or through a larger field monitor, so focusing is usually done by eye (see later, Focusing a Zoom Lens). In film, we do not see the image being registered on the film; also, as we discussed, many film viewfinder systems involve either a loss of light, a flicker, or a different viewing lens altogether (nonreflex). For this reason, measuring the distance from the focal plane φ to the subject with a tape measure is common practice on film shoots. Focus has another dimension called depth of field, which will be covered in detail later in this chapter (Figure 10-11).

Pulling Focus

Usually, focus is something you set and leave for the duration of a shot. However, there are times when you may need to change the plane of critical focus during a take, while the camera is running. This is called **pulling focus** and is common practice in film production. The person who does the actual adjustments to the focus ring is called the **focus puller**. There are two kinds of focus pulling. **Rack focus** means shifting the plane of critical focus between two static subjects along the z-axis. For example, let's say we have framed a shot with a flower in the foreground, 10 feet from the focal plane, and a man standing behind that flower in the background, 30 feet from the focal plane. We can shift the plane of critical focus (and the audience's attention as well) from the flower to the man during the shot simply by manually, and smoothly, rotating the focus ring from 10' to 30' (Figure 10-12).

Another type of focus pulling is called **follow focus**. Follow focus is used when your subject is moving along the z-axis either closer to or further away from the camera, and you

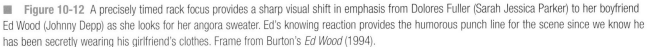

■ **Figure 10-12** A precisely timed rack focus provides a sharp visual shift in emphasis from Dolores Fuller (Sarah Jessica Parker) to her boyfriend Ed Wood (Johnny Depp) as she looks for her angora sweater. Ed's knowing reaction provides the humorous punch line for the scene since we know he has been secretly wearing his girlfriend's clothes. Frame from Burton's *Ed Wood* (1994).

must adjust the plane of critical focus to follow their progress. For example, let's say we have a shot in which a woman begins 30 feet away from the camera, then moves to 20 feet away, and finally comes to a rest 10 feet from the focal plane. In this case we need to set marks for both the actor and the focus puller. **Setting marks** means that we place precise markers on the ground for the actor to hit during the course of their movement. You can use tape if the ground is not seen in the shot, but if it is seen, then you need to use something that will not be too obvious, like leaves or twigs. In any case, these marks are set at precise distances. Then, during the take, the focus puller keeps the subject in focus by smoothly following them with the plane of critical focus—hitting the same feet markings on the focus ring when the subject reaches each mark. Follow focus is usually done in one smooth movement and not in choppy adjustments and can require a few rehearsals to get just right (Figure 10-13).

Aperture

Another adjustable ring found on all lenses used for film production and on all professional video lenses is the **aperture ring** (or **f-stop ring**). The aperture ring controls a slender disk, a diaphragm, inside the lens called **the iris**, which is made up of flat, matte black, metal blades. These blades overlap in such a way that they create an opening that is nearly circular. This opening is called **the aperture** and all light gathered by the lens must pass through the aperture before it is registered on the film plane or imaging device. By adjusting the aperture ring, the iris either opens (creating a larger aperture opening) to allow more light or closes (smaller aperture opening) to allow less light to reach the film or CCD chip. The size of the aperture opening is calibrated to a scale called the **f-stop scale**, which is etched into the aperture ring.

30 ft   15 ft   10 ft

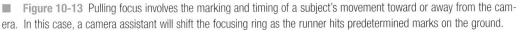

■ **Figure 10-13** Pulling focus involves the marking and timing of a subject's movement toward or away from the camera. In this case, a camera assistant will shift the focusing ring as the runner hits predetermined marks on the ground.

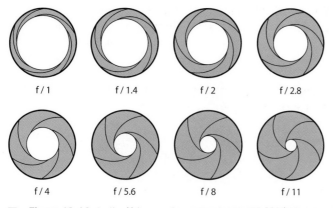

f/1   f/1.4   f/2   f/2.8

f/4   f/5.6   f/8   f/11

■ **Figuro 10 14** Aa the f/stop number grows larger, the aperture opening grows smaller, and vice versa.

The f-stop scale:
f/1.4, f/2, f/2.8, f/4, f/5.6, f/8, f/11, f/16, f/22

At first, f-stops can be a little confusing because the smaller the f-stop number, the larger the aperture opening is and the more light is allowed to reach the imaging device. Conversely, the smaller the f-stop number, the larger the aperture opening is and the more light is allowed through the lens. So, f/2 lets in more light than f/16. This inversion occurs because the f-stop scale is arrived at by dividing the focal length by the diameter of the aperture opening (Figure 10-14). As a filmmaker you don't need to worry too much about *how* this scale was derived as much as you need to understand the relationship between this scale and how it corresponds to the amount of light passing through the lens and exposing your film.

Each number on the scale is called **a stop**. There is one stop between f/4 and f/5.6 and two stops' difference between f/4 and f/2. The difference of one stop has the effect of doubling or halving the amount of light allowed to pass. Expanding the aperture (smaller numbers) is called "**opening up**." Reducing the size of the aperture (bigger numbers) is called "**closing down**" or "**stopping down**." Opening up to f/4 from f/5.6 allows in twice as much light. Closing the aperture to f/2.8 from f/2 cuts the light in half. Each stop, open or closed, doubles or halves the previous number, so that if we open one stop we double the light ($\times2$); if we open another stop it is doubled again 2×2 (four times more light); if we open a third stop we get $2\times2\times2$ (eight times more light), and so on (Figure 10-15).

Iris

The iris is actually a very simple device, but it plays an enormous role in film production. Obviously the simplest application of the iris is to control the amount of light exposing the film, or striking the CCD, in order to give us an "acceptable" image. Allow too much light through the lens and we will have a washed out, overexposed image; block too much light and we will have a dark, underexposed image. This is why it is very easy to believe that there is one "right" exposure for a scene, but nothing could be further from the truth. The interrelationship between the illumination intensities of a given scene and the selection of your f-stop is a central factor in determining the look, tone, mood, and visual content of each and every shot. For any given scene there may be a range of f-stops that will give us an "acceptable" image, but each different setting can inflect the image in various ways. With more than one option, the decision always boils down to the question: What do you want to communicate with this shot? Which f-stop will create the

■ **Figure 10-15** Both film and high-end video lenses have engraved aperture f-stops for precise control over the incoming light.

image that best expresses your idea? In fact, understanding apertures and exposures is so essential to the filmmaker's creative palette, I have dedicated two chapters later in the book to this topic.

Lens Speed

The ability of a lens to gather light is determined by the largest possible f-stop of that particular lens. We refer to this ability as **lens speed**. A **fast lens** can open up to allow more light than a **slow lens**. The larger the maximum aperture can be, the faster the lens is. What limits the ability of a lens to gather light are the optics—the number and quality of the glass elements. For this reason, it is usually the case that wide angle lenses are faster than telephoto lenses (they use fewer elements). A lens with a maximum aperture of f/1.4 is a very fast lens, and can register a readable image with very little light. Zoom lenses tend to be much slower, as their construction requires many more elements. A lens speed of only f/3.5 is not uncommon for a zoom lens. The maximum f-stop number is usually etched into the front of the lens barrel and can sometimes fall between the usual numbers found on an f-stop scale.

T-stops

As we have seen, the f-stop scale is devised through a mathematical formula. This formula, however, assumes a lens with perfect optics; meaning that 100% of the light is transmitted through the lens without any light loss. In effect, f-stops are a theoretical number because no lens has absolutely perfect optics. This can present an inaccuracy in exposure, as many lenses lose quite a bit of light, some as much as one full stop! To remedy this, some lenses show T-stops instead of, or in addition to, f-stops. **T-stops** (short for transmission stops) are f-stops that have been adjusted to take into account the amount of light that is lost, dissipated, or absorbed by that particular lens. T-stops are simply more accurate f-stops. If a lens has T-stops, they will always be found on the aperture ring in red (f-stops are in white). Using T-stops is simple and more accurate. After you determine your exposure (shown as f-stops on your light meter) simply set the T-stop scale instead.

High-quality prime lenses lose so little light that T-stops are not necessary. Zoom lenses, however, utilize many more lens elements and can lose as much as $\frac{1}{3}$ to 1 full stop before the light finally reaches the focal plane.

■ DEPTH OF FIELD

As we discussed earlier, the point at which the lens focus is actually set, and there can be only one setting, is called the plane of critical focus. However, when we look at an actual photographed image, we notice that there is always an area, both in front of and behind this plane of focus, which also appears to be in focus. This range of apparent focus along the z-axis is called the **depth of field** (DOF). The relative depth or shallowness of this area is not fixed. It can be as shallow as a few inches or as deep as infinity (!) depending on a number of variables. Since our eye cannot see the depth of field being registered on the film, it is important to have some way to predict how deep this range will be in order for us to truly know what our final image will look like. Also, what is especially important is that this range can, to a certain extent, be controlled. As with every other controllable variable associated with the lens, depth of field can and should be manipulated in order to serve the content and visual style of your movie (see Figure 3-11 in Chapter 3).

Creating a frame with a shallow depth of field makes your subject stand out from the environment and gain prominence in the frame, because objects both in front of and behind them are out of focus and indistinct. Adopting a deep depth of field increases the amount of information we see along the z-axis and therefore you gain environmental detail that can inflect the mood of the scene and the narrative content. Learning to control depth of field and use it creatively is a big step toward harnessing the aesthetic power of a lens for your needs (Figure 10-16).

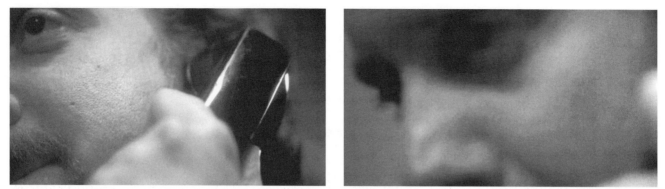

■ **Figure 10-16** The very shallow depth of field in this scene from Payne's *Sideways* (2004) causes Miles (Paul Giamatti) to fall in and out of focus, reflecting his inebriated and confused state when he places an ill-advised call to his ex-wife.

Controlling Depth of Field

The primary factor in determining depth of field is the size of the image format. The smaller the format, the deeper the depth of field tends to be. It is easier to get a deep DOF in 16mm film than it is in 35mm film. And consumer video cameras, with very smaller CCD chips, tend to have very deep depths of field. However, as one of the controllable variables, production format is not especially flexible because it is usually chosen for reasons more pressing than its depth of field potential. There are three other variables that determine the actual range of DOF over which we have some control:

- *The aperture opening.* The larger the aperture opening (smaller f-stop numbers), the shallower the DOF will be, and the smaller the aperture opening (larger f-stop numbers), the deeper the DOF will be. That is why scenes shot in very low light situations have such a shallow depth of field that we sometimes can see an eye in focus, but the ear, just a few inches back, is out of focus. Conversely, scenes shot in brightly lit environments can have a DOF so deep that it appears that everything in the background, as far as we can see, is in focus.
- *The focal length of the lens.* The longer the focal length of the lens, the shallower the DOF will be, and the shorter our lens, the deeper our depth of field will be. Wide angle lenses create deeper depth of field than telephoto lenses.
- *The focus point setting (distance of the critical plane of focus).* The closer to the camera the focus setting, the shallower the depth of field will be, and the further away we place the plane of critical focus, the deeper the DOF will be.

To predict what the DOF for any shot will be, filmmakers consult standard DOF tables like those found in Appendix 6 at the back of this book or in the "American Cinematographer Manual." These tables are very simple to read and will tell you exactly what in your frame will appear to be in focus—so there will be no surprises when you get the film back from the lab. It is then up to you to use this information to creative advantage.

In **Figure 10-17**, you will notice that the four variables for calculating the depth of field are part of the calculation. These two tables are for the 16mm film format. The 35mm film format uses a completely different set of tables. Each table is for a specific focal length lens (located at the top, left of the chart). The two here are for the 25mm and 100mm lenses. The lens focus distance is located on the left vertical column, and f-stops on the top, horizontal column. Let's see how to read these very simple tables.

Look at the DOF table for the 25mm lens (normal lens). If we are focused at 16 feet with an aperture of f/2 we can see that the DOF range is 13′ to 20.9′. All objects between these points will appear to be in sharp focus even though your actual focus point is 16′. The range of apparent focus along the z-axis is therefore 7′ 11″. Now read across and along the f-stop scale for the same focus point (16′) and you will see the DOF get deeper as the aperture gets smaller, and as the aperture opens up the DOF gets shallower. Now, read down the various lens focus distances for f/2 and you will notice that the DOF gets shallower the closer the focus point is, and deeper the further the focus is set.

Now look at the table for the 100mm lens (telephoto) and compare the same settings (focus at 16′ and aperture at f/2), the DOF is 15.8′ to 16.2′ — much shallower. If you go to Appendix 6 and look at the DOF chart for the 10mm lens (wide angle) at the same settings (focus at 16′ and aperture at f/2) you'll see that the range is from 6.5 feet to infinity!

	16mm Camera DOF														
Lens Focal Length: **25mm**														CoC = .015mm (.0006″)	
focus distance (feet)	f/1.4		f/2		f/2.8		f/4		f/5.6		f/8		f/11		f/16	
	Near	Far	Near	Far	Near	Far	Near	Far	Near	Far	Near	Far	Near	Far	Near	Far
2	1.96	2.04	1.95	2.06	1.92	2.08	1.89	2.12	1.85	2.17	1.80	2.25	1.73	2.38	1.63	2.58
4	3.84	4.17	3.78	4.24	3.70	4.35	3.59	4.52	3.44	4.77	3.25	5.19	3.02	5.92	2.74	7.39
6	5.65	6.39	5.52	6.57	5.35	6.84	5.11	7.26	4.82	7.95	4.46	9.18	4.03	11.8	3.54	19.5
8	7.39	8.71	7.17	9.05	6.87	9.57	6.50	10.4	6.03	11.9	5.47	14.9	4.83	23.2	4.15	109
10	9.07	11.1	8.73	11.7	8.30	12.6	7.75	14.1	7.09	17.0	6.33	23.8	5.49	56	4.63	∞
12	10.7	13.7	10.2	14.5	9.63	15.9	8.90	18.4	8.04	23.7	7.07	39.7	6.04	880	5.01	∞
14	12.2	16.4	11.6	17.6	10.9	19.7	9.95	23.6	8.88	33.0	7.72	75	6.51	∞	5.33	∞
16	13.7	19.2	13.0	20.9	12.0	23.9	10.9	29.9	9.65	46.9	8.28	234	6.90	∞	5.59	∞
18	15.2	22.1	14.3	24.4	13.1	28.6	11.8	37.8	10.3	70	8.79	∞	7.25	∞	5.81	∞
20	16.6	25.2	15.5	28.2	14.2	34.0	12.6	47.9	11.0	114	9.24	∞	7.55	∞	6.00	∞
30	22.9	43.4	20.9	53	18.5	79	16.0	241	13.4	∞	10.9	∞	8.63	∞	6.66	∞
40	28.3	68	25.3	96	21.9	230	18.4	∞	15.1	∞	12.0	∞	9.29	∞	7.05	∞
50	33.0	103	28.9	185	24.6	∞	20.3	∞	16.3	∞	12.8	∞	9.74	∞	7.31	∞
∞	97	∞	68	∞	48.4	∞	34.3	∞	24.2	∞	17.2	∞	12.2	∞	8.63	∞

	16mm Camera DOF														
Lens Focal Length: **100mm**														CoC = .015mm (.0006″)	
focus distance (feet)	f/1.4		f/2		f/2.8		f/4		f/5.6		f/8		f/11		f/16	
	Near	Far	Near	Far	Near	Far	Near	Far	Near	Far	Near	Far	Near	Far	Near	Far
5	4.98	5.02	4.98	5.02	4.97	5.03	4.96	5.04	4.94	5.06	4.92	5.09	4.88	5.12	4.83	5.18
6	5.98	6.02	5.97	6.03	5.96	6.04	5.94	6.06	5.91	6.09	5.88	6.13	5.83	6.18	5.76	6.26
7	6.97	7.03	6.96	7.04	6.94	7.06	6.92	7.09	6.88	7.12	6.83	7.18	6.77	7.25	6.67	7.36
8	7.96	8.04	7.94	8.06	7.92	8.08	7.89	8.11	7.84	8.16	7.78	8.23	7.69	8.33	7.57	8.48
9	8.95	9.05	8.93	9.07	8.90	9.10	8.86	9.15	8.80	9.21	8.72	9.29	8.61	9.42	8.46	9.61
10	9.94	10.1	9.91	10.1	9.88	10.1	9.83	10.2	9.76	10.3	9.66	10.4	9.52	10.5	9.34	10.8
12	11.9	12.1	11.9	12.1	11.8	12.2	11.7	12.3	11.6	12.4	11.5	12.5	11.3	12.8	11.1	13.1
14	13.9	14.1	13.8	14.2	13.8	14.3	13.7	14.4	13.5	14.5	13.3	14.7	13.1	15.1	12.7	15.6
16	15.8	16.2	15.8	16.2	15.7	16.3	15.6	16.5	15.4	16.7	15.1	17.0	14.8	17.4	14.4	18.1
18	17.8	18.2	17.7	18.3	17.6	18.4	17.4	18.6	17.2	18.9	16.9	19.2	16.5	19.8	15.9	20.7
20	19.7	20.3	19.6	20.4	19.5	20.5	19.3	20.7	19.0	21.1	18.7	21.6	18.2	22.3	17.5	23.4
30	29.4	30.6	29.2	30.8	28.9	31.2	28.5	31.7	27.9	32.5	27.1	33.7	26.0	35.4	24.6	38.3
40	39.0	41.1	38.6	41.5	38.0	42.2	37.3	43.1	36.3	44.6	34.9	46.8	33.2	50	31.0	56
50	48.4	52	47.8	52	47.0	53	45.8	55	44.3	57	42.3	61	39.8	67	36.7	79
75	72	79	70	80	68	83	66	87	63	93	59	103	54	122	48.5	165
100	94	107	92	110	89	115	85	122	80	135	73	157	66	206	58	369
∞	1547	∞	1094	∞	774	∞	547	∞	387	∞	274	∞	194	∞	137	∞

■ **Figure 10-17** DOF charts for 25mm and 100mm lenses. Depth of field charts are essential on location for determining which areas of the frame are in or out of focus. (16mm film format).

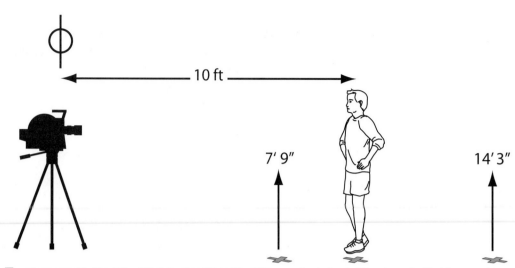

■ **Figure 10-18** The 1/3—2/3 Rule. One third of the DOF range lies in front of the plane of critical focus and two-thirds behind it.

The 1/3 – 2/3 Rule

You may have noticed while you were reading the DOF tables that there seems to be more of the range of apparent focus behind the actual focus setting than in front of it. This is always the case. The **1/3—2/3 rule** for DOF tells us that two-thirds of the depth range along the z-axis is behind the focus point and one-third is in front (Figure 10-18). This is a very important principle to consider when you are trying to move objects into and out of the range of apparent focus (see later, In Practice, *Working with DOF*).

Circle of Confusion

As we have discussed, depth of field is a phenomenon of *apparent* focus along the z-axis range, but lets look a little closer. Focus, as we have defined it, is achieved when a point of light coming off our subject is registered as a point of light on the focal plane and we know that there is only one setting that will be truly in focus (i.e., setting the focus ring to 25′). This means that the light points emanating from the area in front of and behind the plane of critical focus are not registered as a points; rather, they begin to spread larger and larger and get fuzzier the further away their origin is from the focus setting point. However, neither the human eye, nor film stocks, nor CCD chips can distinguish between very small degrees of unsharpness. There is an acceptable size range to which a point of light can spread (be technically out of focus) and still appear to be in focus. For 16mm film, a point of light can spread to a diameter of .015mm or 0.0006″ (that's six ten-thousandths of an inch) on the film, and our eye will see it as in focus. Beyond that, the image starts to appear fuzzy. This measurement of acceptable diameter, which creates the appearance of focus, is called the **circle of confusion (the CoC)**. You will see the CoC for your format at the top, right-hand corner of the DOF table. Each format size has its own acceptable CoC measurement. For 35mm film format, the CoC is 0.001″. In video, the CoC for a 1/4″ CCD is 0.008mm and for a 1/2″ CCD it is 0.016mm. Knowing the CoC allows you to calculate very specific DOF charts of your own by using specialized software or online DOF calculators like those at http://www.dofmaster.com or http://www.panavision.com/tools.php (Figure 10-19).

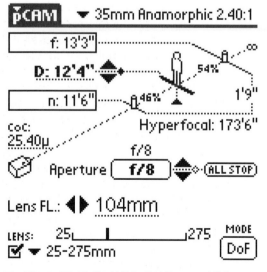

■ **Figure 10-19** David Eubanks' Pcam and Pcine software for the Palm Pilot can calculate depth of field for any conceivable focal length and aperture combination, as well as field of view, filtration compensation, and other calculations.

in practice

Working with DOF

In a final project for an intermediate film production class, Gisela M. ended her film with a shot for which depth of field was a critical element of telling her revenge fantasy story:

> *Joey is a materialistic cad who leaves his sweet girlfriend for a woman who makes very good money. But Joey is quickly dumped when the woman finds out that he has no money himself. In the last scene we see a rejected Joey riding a train, on his way back to reconnect with his girlfriend—but he's out of luck.*

Here is our essential train shot: The train is moderately full; we see Joey in a medium close-up shot, sitting alone and gazing out the window. Passengers in front of him (foreground) and behind him (background) are engrossed in their newspapers. The guy sitting right behind Joey turns the page and we see a photograph of Joey's smiling girlfriend under the headline "Bronx Woman Wins 10 mil. Jackpot" right behind Joey's head. Figure 10-20 is a storyboard of the frame Gisela was after and an overhead diagram of the set-up for this train shot.

Obviously, it is essential for the audience to read the headline. The fact that Joey's girlfriend has struck it rich and that Joey will likely never get her back provides the central irony of the film. Also, this shot allows our audience to know more than the character. We see that his scheming has backfired on him and we can predict the final encounter with the girlfriend, so it's not necessary to show it. This one shot contains both narrative information and the humorous tone of a well-timed punch line.

■ Figure 10-20 Gisela's storyboard shows what must be seen clearly in the frame: Joey's face looking out the train window and the newspaper headline directly behind him.

Here is Gisela's technical information: she was shooting on 16mm film and to get a nice medium close-up on Joey, along with a dynamic composition, including foreground, mid-ground, and background, she was at an 85mm lens with the camera set up 15' away from Joey. The newspaper headline was 3' behind Joey's head, 18' from the film plane. Given the intensity of the light in the train car, Gisela set the f/stop at f.11.

Everything seems fine and a careless filmmaker would simply focus on the face of our subject Joey (set focus to 15') and just take the shot as is. However, when they get the footage back from the lab, they would discover, too late, that the news photo and headline are out of focus and cannot be read. Had they simply consulted a DOF chart they would have seen that, given the variables (85mm lens, f.11, focus at 15'), their DOF range was 13' 7" to 16' 9", not deep enough to include the newspaper.

However, Gisela was a careful filmmaker and she checked the DOF chart and knew she needed to make an adjustment. But which one? Which variable should she choose to get the depth of field we need to see Joey and read the newspaper, to deliver the ironic punch line to resolve the story! Let's look at her options:

- **Changing the Lens**

  If Gisela were to change the lens focal length to 65mm, with all other things remaining the same, her DOF would deepen to a range of 12' 8" to 18' 4". That's great; the newspaper is now in focus—but wait: all things have not remained the same. Changing a lens affects many other aspects of her frame besides DOF. First, with the shorter focal length lens we might not be able to read the newspaper anymore, even if it is in focus, because it appears too far away. Second, Joey is now smaller in the frame and the extras in the foreground take on greater, and maybe excessive, prominence. Also, Gisela's field of view is wider, maybe wide enough to see things she wanted to keep outside the frame, like a light stand or a microphone. Obviously, changing the focal length will require other adjustments: move some lights, shift the extras around, and maybe it's even necessary to move the camera closer to Joey and the newspaper. But wait! We know that a closer camera-to-subject distance will *decrease* DOF and Gisela will lose much of the depth of field she just gained. There's got to be an easier way.

- *Adjusting the Aperture Variable*
  If it's possible to add more light, then Gisela can leave her focal length and camera-to-subject distance as it is and simply close the aperture down. Doubling the intensity of the light means she can shoot at f/16. Consulting the

charts shows that at that f-stop her DOF is 13′ to 17′ 5″. Not quite deep enough. According to the charts, she needs to get to f/22 (even smaller) before the depth of field deepens to 12′ 5″ to 19′. Shooting at f/22 would mean that everything she needs will be in focus and she gets to keep the framing she had in mind. However, adding *four times* the light isn't always that easy; in fact, on a very low-budget shoot, like Gisela's, there was no way to quadruple the amount of light. So what else?

- *Adjusting the Plane of Focus*
  So Gisela couldn't add any light at all and she didn't want to change lenses: what now? Should she rethink the shot completely? Not necessarily. Remember that one-third of the DOF is in front of the plane of focus and two-thirds is behind! Also remember that adjusting the plane of critical focus further from the film plane actually *deepens* the DOF. Obviously, there is no reason to have the plane of critical focus exactly on our subject Joey as long as he falls within the DOF range. So, Gisela simply adjusted her focus ring to 16′ and her DOF shifted back towards the newspaper and deepened slightly to 14′ 3″ to 18′ 1″. The newspaper is now readable and Joey falls within the near end of the DOF range (Figure 10-21).

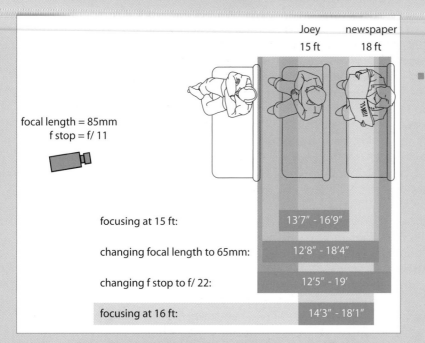

Figure 10-21 After some research, Gisela found the right combination of aperture, camera to subject distance, and focal length to create the shot exactly the way her story needed it.

LENS CONSIDERATIONS ON DV

Although all of the principles of optics apply equally to film and DV lenses, there are a few special details concerning lenses that must be considered when shooting on DV.

DOF and DV

Using DOF tables is standard practice in film production because film camera viewfinders are generally not clear enough to really *see* your range of apparent focus. Since film is projected many times larger than the original frame, absolute accuracy is essential. However, DOF tables are rarely used in video production for two reasons. First, when DOF is absolutely critical to a video project, there is usually a production field monitor on the set for reference (see p. 233). This monitor is many times larger than the viewfinder and allows one to see DOF fairly clearly. Also, it was always assumed that video was a small-screen TV medium, so who could tell DOF to the inch anyway? That, of course, is changing as more and more films originating on DV or HDTV find their way to theatrical release and are projected as big as any 35mm film.

Most consumer and "prosumer" digital video cameras have very small CCD chips; 1/3″ and 1/4″ chips are most common, but there are some that are even smaller! Small imaging devices, as we have discussed, tend toward deeper depth of field. One of the main complaints of D.P.s using video is that the DOF is too deep. There are a number of remedies for this if you want to achieve a shallow depth of field. Most of these strategies involve staying at the widest aperture possible by either keeping the lighting intensity low or, if you cannot control the illumination of the scene (i.e., on a sunny exterior shoot), utilizing the camera's built-in **neutral density** filters to block light and/or using the **electronic shutter control** to reduce the light entering the camera. Either way, reducing the light will force your aperture to open up and your DOF will narrow. Also, you can create your own DOF charts for your specific video camera by going to the DOF calculator websites previously mentioned. Some calculators require you to enter in your chip size to make the calculation and others require you to enter in the CoC.

Focusing a Zoom Lens

Because depth of field becomes narrower as we move toward the telephoto end of a zoom lens, it is possible to have an image perfectly in focus with a wide angle setting, and simply changing the focal length will throw the subject out of focus. The proper way to assure that focus will be maintained throughout the zoom range of a lens is to find your focus at the extreme telephoto end of the range, then pull out to the focal length you want. Going from telephoto to more wide angle will only increase your DOF and the subject will remain in focus. This is especially important to know if you are shooting on the fly—as in many documentary situations. The procedure for focusing a zoom is this: First zoom all the way into the subject you want to have in focus (for example, the eyes of your talent). Adjust your focus until the image is sharp. Now zoom out and find your initial frame. The subject will now remain in focus for the entire zoom range. This is called **presetting focus.**

Video Lenses and Automatic Functions

Unlike film cameras, which oblige us to choose focus and aperture settings manually, most DV cameras provide an automatic setting option for both of these functions. As I mention throughout this book, it is preferable to turn off all automatic functions in your camcorder. Manual settings ensure that the filmmaker is in control of all variables and therefore in control of how their film looks. Remember, choosing your focus is a creative and aesthetic decision: Why would we want to hand that important decision to a machine, with no aesthetic judgment at all? By using automatic focus and exposure, your film cannot help but look like every other film using auto functions.

All professional video cameras employ lenses with focus, f-stop, and zoom rings etched with their respective scales. However, many consumer and industrial DV cameras place some or all of that information within menus. It is important for you to familiarize yourself with these menus and figure out how to access all manual modes for your particular camera before you are on the set and shooting your project (Figure 10-22).

One significant problem with **auto focus** functions is that it favors objects in the center of the frame, which might not be the case for the composition you want, and it tends to shift focus in the middle of a shot when anything moves across the foreground of the frame. Let's say we have a composition in which your subject is tucked over to the right of the frame, with a forest behind her. It's likely that the camera will choose to set focus automatically for that which is in the middle, the forest, leaving the subject fuzzy. Auto focus is also easily confused by images with multiple planes. For example, let's say we wish to shoot a character who is ten feet behind a chain link fence. The auto focus will likely select for the fence in the foreground, especially if your subject is slightly off center. Quite often, auto focus mechanisms will go crazy in a situation like this, shifting

■ Figure 10-22 Most video cameras have a way of switching from automatic to manual focusing, an important feature for maintaining complete control over the way your images are recorded.

■ **Figure 10-23** Video cameras set to auto focus have trouble deciding where to focus in situations where we have multiple planes. Switching to manual focusing solves this problem, letting the users set the focus according to their needs.

arbitrarily from the fence to the character and back to the fence, searching for focus, but never quite settling on it (Figure 10-23).

A common procedure for setting video focus is to zoom in to what you want to be in focus. Allow the auto focus to choose its setting and then flip into **manual mode**. Now when you pull back and readjust your frame, with the subject to one side, the camera will hold your focus point. Also, if a car should pass through in the foreground, your camera will not try to change the focus setting.

Camera Support

It doesn't matter if you are shooting on film or video. Deciding if your camera should move during a shot, and how you want the camera to move, are as important to the tone, style, and meaning of your film as the lighting, locations, or any other creative element. Whether you're panning, tracking, following, or craning, choosing the appropriate camera support is vital. You need to understand the equipment you have available to you and the expressive potential each piece of gear allows so that you can achieve the aesthetic approach you want.

For example, let's say during the pre-visualization process you and the D.P. decided that your film would best be told as a series of meticulously lit and composed, static compositions, where the camera barely moves, as in *Café Lumière* by Hou Hsiao-Hsien, or perhaps you conceived the visual style of your film to be similar to Gus Van Sant's *Elephant,* with extremely long takes that smoothly follow characters down corridors, through doors, and from inside to outside, or perhaps you want that shaky camera look, which restlessly twists, jumps, swirls, and joggles as we see in a film like *24 Hour Party People* by Michael Winterbottom (Figure 11-1).

All three approaches are great, but each requires a different kind of camera support. You need to ask: What will allow me to achieve the particular look I'm after? And, of course: Do I have or can I afford what I need to do that? The way you support your camera is central to achieving any visual style, so choosing your camera support is as important as choosing the right location, lighting approach, or costume. Let's take a look at some options.

■ THE HANDHELD CAMERA

The cheapest and most readily available method of camera support is the human body. "Going handheld" means using your hands and arms for holding small and lightweight cameras (small DV cameras and film cameras like the Arri-S or Bolex), or carrying the camera on your shoulder and bracing it with your arm (large DV cameras and film cameras like the Arri-SR). All video field production cameras are designed for easy handholding (Figure 11-2). Most 16mm film cameras can be handheld, but some, like the Arri-BL, are very heavy and awkward.

Handholding always introduces some human instability in the image, since the camera reflects the human movements of the operator. No matter how steady the camera operator is, a handheld camera is never as stable as one mounted on a tripod; nor should it be. The movement obtained with a handheld camera has an aesthetic quality that recalls the documentary style of Direct Cinema and this quality has been used to great effect to add a sense of immediacy, spontaneity, and direct involvement in numerous narrative films, including *Eternal Sunshine of the Spotless Mind,* by Michel

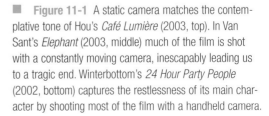

■ **Figure 11-1** A static camera matches the contemplative tone of Hou's *Café Lumière* (2003, top). In Van Sant's *Elephant* (2003, middle) much of the film is shot with a constantly moving camera, inescapably leading us to a tragic end. Winterbottom's *24 Hour Party People* (2002, bottom) captures the restlessness of its main character by shooting most of the film with a handheld camera.

■ **Figure 11-2** Handholding a camera can be an easy task when using a small DV camcorder (left, with the Panasonic DVX-100), but more demanding with a larger film or video cameras (right, with the Arriflex BL).

Gondry, *La Promesse,* by the Dardenne brothers, and *Dancer in the Dark,* by Lars von Trier. All of these films were shot entirely or mostly with a handheld camera.

Using a handheld camera is not as easy as simply slinging a camera on your shoulder and shooting. We've all seen plenty of home movie footage that's so jittery that watching it makes us nauseous. Techniques for handheld shots require practiced skills and a great deal of body control and strength to keep from looking haphazard or sloppy. In many ways, the small, ultra-light DV cameras are more difficult to control because the weight of a camera, especially when mounted on a shoulder, provides some stability. If you decide to go handheld, your movements should be as controlled as possible. Don't worry that it will look like a tripod shot; it won't. It will look handheld. If what you're after are super smooth moves and rock-steady compositions, then don't go handheld in hopes that no one will notice the human movements; they will. Controlled imperfection is the aesthetic point.

Here are a few tips for shooting with a handheld camera:
■ Camera movement comes from the body, not just the hands. Use your entire body—feet, legs, torso, arms, and hands—to perform a camera move.
■ Keep your knees bent and loose, like a skier, for shock absorption.
■ Stay toward the wide angle end of the lens. A telephoto lens only magnifies the jitter and instability of the frame. Use wider angle lenses and move in close for tight shots and out for longer shots.
■ Breathing should be long and steady. Don't hold your breath or you will find the need to gasp for air in the middle of a shot, causing an inevitable jerk of the frame!
■ Don't hold the camera rigid. Rhythm, grace, and controlled movement are key!
■ Take advantage of the pivoting LCD screen and the light weight of palm-held camcorders to go beyond eye-level shots. These cameras allow you to see your compositions even when the camera is dangling low from your arm or held aloft far over your head.
■ Practice, practice, practice. Like any other creative skill, you get better at handholding a camera by doing it over and over again. Great cinematographers who are skilled at handheld technique, like Ellen Kuras, Robbie Müller, Christopher Doyle, and Thomas Mauch, are great because they've handled a camera nearly as often as a great pianist has touched the piano keys, or a tennis pro has swung a racket. No great skill is acquired without effort, learning, and practice.

■ THE TRIPOD

Tripods are perhaps the most common form of camera support. Their design has remained essentially unchanged since the earliest years of cinema (Figure 11-3). Tripods are a three-

■ **Figure 11-3** The tripod has been used since the early history of film-making, as seen in Vertov's seminal film *Man with a Movie Camera* (1929).

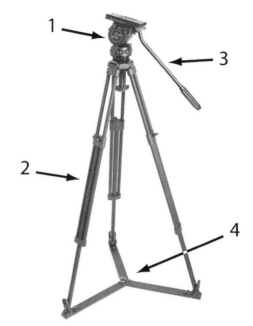

■ **Figure 11-4**
A tripod system will commonly have a head (1), extendable legs (2), a pan handle (3), and a spreader (4).

legged support designed to both hold the camera steady for precise subject framing and also to allow for fluid pans, tilts, and compound moves. Professional tripods are especially adjustable, allowing a filmmaker to frame and maneuver with a precision and fluidity not possible with a handheld camera.

A tripod can be broken down into two major components: The head and the legs (also called sticks). Some less expensive tripods are constructed with the head and legs in one unit, but the most flexible tripods are those that are designed as systems, so that each component is separate and interchangeable to fit a variety of production situations (Figure 11-4).

Tripod Head

In terms of movement precision, the most important component of any tripod is the **head**. The tripod head is where the camera is mounted and is the component that swivels left and right for panning, and up and down for tilting. The quality of the head greatly affects the smoothness of the camera moves. Tripod heads also come in different sizes to accommodate various camera weights. A small head, like the Cartoni C-10 or Action Pro, are designed specifically for small cameras. (Figure 11-5).

■ **Figure 11-5** Picking the right tripod for the job. For smooth, controlled camera moves and even for safety's sake, the tripod should match the weight rating of the camera being used.

Larger heads, like the Cartoni C-20S or the Miller DS60, are built to accommodate the bulk of large video camcorders and heavy film cameras weighing up to 65 pounds.

An important factor determining the quality of the tripod's panning and tilting abilities is the **resistance mechanism**. Smooth moves with a tripod are accomplished by adjusting the resistance of the tripod head against the weight of the camera and the speed of the move. A very slow pan, for example, is smoothest with heavy drag on the pan mechanism. The two types of resistance mechanisms you're likely to come across for DV and 16mm film production are **fluid heads** and **friction heads**. Fluid heads use pressurized hydraulic fluid to provide the adjustable drag necessary for smooth camera moves. Friction heads use the surface friction between internal plates, sometimes lined with cork, to create

Figure 11-6 A professional fluid head has a tilt lock (1), a pan lock (2), tension adjustments for the tilt and pan controls (3, 4), a base plate for the camera (5), and a quick release lock for the base plate (6).

movement resistance. Fluid heads are more expensive but they also give you much more precise and varied adjustments to facilitate your camera move, and they generally have a smoother and more even action throughout the panning and tilting range.

There are several features on a tripod head which are common to all professional tripods, and you should locate these right away (Figure 11-6).

1. **Pan and tilt locks** completely lock down the mechanism keeping the tripod from pivoting at all. The most important lock for you to locate is the tilt lock. If your camera is slightly unbalanced on the tripod (because the magazine load has shifted from the front to the back during the shoot, or from the addition of a heavy battery), this will cause the camera to tilt forward or backward all the way. If unattended, the whole thing can eventually pitch all the way over, sending the camera crashing to the ground. The standard procedure to avoid this catastrophe is to tighten the tilt lock between takes and never leave the tripod and camera unattended.

2. **Pan and tilt dampers** adjust the amount of resistance for their respective movements. Generally speaking, the more slowly you wish to execute a move, the more resistance you want, and vice versa. This assures smoother motion and greater control.

3. **The pan handle** is used to control the movements of the camera. On good tripods, the angle of the pan handle can be adjusted for various tripod heights and personal comfort. Many tripods allow you to mount the pan handle on the left or right, depending on whether you are right- or left-handed. Take the time to adjust the handle for maximum comfort and control. The important cautionary note here is that you should never carry a tripod by the pan handle. Pan handles are usually made of lightweight aluminum and the adjustment threads can easily strip or they could simply break off.

4. The **head mount** is at the base of the tripod head and is where the head mounts to the tripod legs. With modular tripod systems, the head can be used with a variety of sticks offering a broad range of heights. Most quality tripods have claw ball or ball-and-socket mounts, which can be loosened to freely adjust the angle of the tripod head in any direction, to achieve a level base no matter where the tripod is standing. It is much easier to level a tripod by using this adjustment than by varying the lengths of the three legs. Tripods with adjustable heads also usually have a bubble leveler to assist in leveling of the head.

5. Finally, all tripod heads have a **camera mounting plate** where the camera is attached to the tripod head. Cameras are secured to the mounting plate with a threaded mounting screw. Most film cameras and professional DV cameras use a ⅜″ mounting screw, while the small DV cameras use a smaller ¼″ mounting screw. Make sure the mounting screw matches the threads on the underside of the camera.

in practice

You might be wondering why I mention a tiny detail like the size of the camera mounting screw. As I've mentioned before, in film production every little detail is crucial. I have had more than a few students go on location with tripod heads that had the wrong-sized mounting screw. These students often were shooting on MiniDV, but wanted to use a larger tripod or dolly system generally used for 16mm cameras, without stopping to think that they also needed a different mounting screw. These students arrived on location with everything in place: crew, cast, costumes, locations, etc., but had no way to secure the camera on the tripod. In one case they gaffer-taped the camera to the tripod head, which was not only unsteady but also nearly destroyed the delicate camera. Then, they had to untape and retape it every time they needed to change their cassette. In another case the director simply decided to go handheld, and the dolly they had rented sat on the sidelines, unused. Unfortunately, the handheld look was not the aesthetic approach they were after at all. In both cases the look of each project was seriously compromised, all on account of one lil' ol' screw!

It's also important to note that many tripods have adjustable and quick-release mounting plates. An adjustable mounting plate will slide slightly forward and backward on the head. This allows the camera operator to very precisely balance the camera on the tripod. Ideally, you should be able to take your hands off the camera, without the tilt lock engaged or any drag on the mechanism, and the camera will remain level. This way, the operator doesn't fight gravity while executing a camera move. The quick-release function allows you to pop the camera on and off the head of the tripod quickly, which makes moving the tripod and camera from one location to another much faster. You should never carry the tripod around with a camera attached. Quick release also lets you quickly remove the camera from the tripod to go handheld and then pop it back on again for tripod shots.

Tripod Legs

The legs (or sticks) of a tripod are adjustable so that the tripod height, and therefore the camera height, can be easily changed from shot to shot. Also, because the legs are independently adjustable, they provide a firm footing on uneven terrain, like a hillside or on stairs (Figure 11-7). Some tripod systems offer legs in three different heights, on which the same head can be used interchangeably. Typical **standard legs** position the camera between 3 feet and 6 feet. Some standard legs are two-stage legs, which means that they have additional length for extension and offer even higher angles. For shots lower than 3 feet we often use **baby legs**, which have a

Figure 11-7 The individually-extendable legs of a tripod make it possible to use on uneven surfaces, such as a staircase.

height range from 1 foot to about 3 feet (Figure 11-8). Lower than baby legs is a **high-hat**, which is a fixed metal head mount, usually attached to a plywood board. In addition to being the lowest base for a camera, a high-hat can also be attached with clamps in areas where a tripod cannot be used (Figure 11-9).

On many professional tripods, the legs are allowed to open freely out to any width for a stable base of support. To keep the legs from completely sliding out from under the camera, a **spreader** is often used. Some tripods have a built-in spreader, while others require a separate unit. The feet of some tripod sticks have spikes that can be pushed into the ground in exterior locations, but these spikes will obviously slip on hard surfaces, or destroy wooden floors, so you must use a spreader in these situations.

Tripods have remained the single most essential camera support throughout the history of cinema because they are inexpensive, extremely mobile, and give a filmmaker great control and a wide variety of camera angles and fluid camera movements.

Figure 11-8 Yasujiro Ozu's long time collaborator, cinematographer Yuharu Atsuta, demonstrates a quintessential element of the Ozu style: the "tatami" shot, made possible through the use of a baby-legs tripod.

Figure 11-9 A hi-hat allows the camera to be placed closer to the ground than baby legs, or to other surfaces with the use of clamps, as pictured.

■ **Figure 11-10** (Left) A doorway dolly. Inflatable wheels allow for a smooth transit and do not require tracks. (Right) A spider dolly, capable of crab-like lateral moves.

■ **Figure 11-11** Dollies that use tracks can create extremely smooth moving shots, but their setup is a time and labor-intensive endeavor.

■ **Figure 11-12** Innovator Garret Brown operating his Steadicam system in one of the first films to use it, Kubrick's *The Shining* (1980).

THE DOLLY

A dolly is a camera support on wheels that is used when your shot requires a dynamic move (when the camera itself moves through space) and you want it to be smoother and more controlled than what you can achieve with a handheld camera. There are many types of dollies available, from expensive to inexpensive and extremely heavy to relatively portable. Some dollies move on soft, inflated rubber tires and require a smooth, even floor (Figure 11-10). Other dollies run on tracks that are laid out in straight or curved sections along the desired path of the camera movement (Figure 11-11).

Laying dolly track creates extremely smooth camera moves, but it is a time- and labor-intensive task that requires the careful placement of wooden shims to even out the dolly's movement. For this reason, students often think twice about using dollies on tracks. Professional dollies provide a post for you to mount your fluid head so that you can execute smooth pans and tilts while the camera is being moved around; inexpensive dollies require that you mount the entire tripod on the base, which is substantially less stable. There is no doubt: dynamic moves with dollies are wonderful, but you need to be aware that using a dolly can be a very time-consuming addition to your production schedule.

STABILIZING ARM SYSTEMS

Invented by cinematographer Garrett Brown (Figure 11-12) and introduced in the early 1970s, the **Steadicam** stabilizing system completely won over the film world when it was used successfully in films like *Rocky* (1976), *Marathon Man* (1976), and *The Shining* (1980). It has since become a standard tool on large-budget productions.

The Steadicam is basically an articulated arm incorporating a complex system of counterweights and springs to minimize gravitational forces

■ **Figure 11-13** The emergence of DV as a viable filmmaking alternative has prompted the creation of lighter, cheaper stabilizing systems, like the Artemis (left) and the Glidecam (right).

and absorb any shock. On one end of the arm is a camera mount and at the other end is a vest that is worn by the camera operator to carry the weight of the entire apparatus. Combining the mobility and ease of use of a handheld camera with the smooth and controlled movements of a dolly, the Steadicam system allows the operator to move, walk, or run with the camera through space, in any direction, while the articulated arm maintains a steady and easily controlled frame. The downside to Steadicam systems for students and low-budget filmmakers has always been the cost and complexity of the system. However, since the advent of lightweight DV and HD cameras, we are seeing the emergence of a whole range of far less expensive and less cumbersome stabilizing arms (Figure 11-13).

DV stabilizing systems are ultra-lightweight handheld units which use a simple system of counterweights to smooth out the movements of the operator as they move with the camera through space. With a little practice, you can get wonderfully smooth tracks, dollies, and arcs with these systems. The only limitation is that they are designed specifically for lightweight DV camcorders so can't be used for 16mm film productions, where the cameras are heavier.

■ JERRY-RIGGED OR IMPROVISED SUPPORT SYSTEMS

As the saying goes, necessity is the mother of invention, and many people throughout the history of cinema have used their ingenuity to achieve their ends with minimal resources. The cost and complexity of dollies and Steadicam systems have given rise to many wonderful improvised methods for achieving more or less smooth, dynamic camera moves. One of the most common dolly-like devices is a wheelchair (Figure 11-14). The cinematographer simply sits in the wheelchair and is pushed. Obviously this requires relatively smooth surfaces and a stable hand, but this simple solution has been used also by great filmmakers, from Godard to Gondry.

For his *Evil Dead* films, director Sam Raimi invented the "shakey-cam," which was an ultra-inexpensive stabilizing system made by mounting a film camera in the

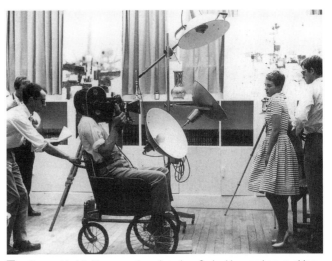

■ **Figure 11-14** New wave icon Jean-Luc Godard is seen here pushing cinematographer Raoul Coutard in a wheelchair for a moving shot during the filming of *Breathless* (1960). (Copyright Raymond Cauchetier—Paris)

■ **Figure 11-15** Raimi's use of a wooden board as a camera support made it possible to execute a dynamic shot in his film *The Evil Dead* (1981).

■ **Figure 11-16** Too dangerous? This image from Vertov's *The Man with a Movie Camera* shows a wonderfully exuberant idea for an improvised moving shot; however, safety should always the first concern of anyone planning an extraordinary shot.

middle of a long wooden board (Figure 11-15). With two grips holding the board on each end, they could run, lift, lower, or tilt the suspended camera, and the board itself absorbed all the shocks. The framing isn't terribly accurate, but the moves, reflecting the POV of a demon as it rushes through the woods, are exceptionally dynamic and sufficiently demonic. So impressed were the Coen brothers with this jerry-rigged system that they used it themselves in *Blood Simple* and *Raising Arizona*.

For one scene in *The Celebration* (*Festen*) (1998), Thomas Vinterberg and D.P. Lars Bo Jensen simply secured an ultra-lightweight DV camera to the end of a long boom pole, and swung it around the room to move the camera in a spiral from ceiling height to eye level. The stories of improvised dynamic camera moves are endless, because, in the final analysis, it doesn't really matter how you arrive at a specific effect (jerry-rigged device or expensive equipment rental), all that matters is what it looks like when the film comes back from the lab (*safely;* see Figure 11-16). The fact that he used a simple wheelchair dolly did not keep Godard's film *Breathless* from being one of the most important films in the history of cinema.

■ AESTHETIC AND PRACTICAL CONSIDERATIONS

The camera support you choose ultimately should help you achieve the look and style you need to tell your story. From the super controlled fluidity of a dolly to the edgy movement of the handheld camera, to the pivot moves of a tripod, different supports offer different "feels." There is no system that is better or worse—there is only what is

■ *Barry Lyndon*
Stanley Kubrick's study of the 18th-century English aristocracy, *Barry Lyndon* (1975), tells the story of Redmond Barry, a relentless and ambitious social climber who attains a name and position among the nobility by marrying the rich widow Lady Lyndon. Much of the film is shot in steady, carefully composed frames, with the camera planted firmly on a tripod, a choice that perfectly reflects the strict and rigid social codes of conduct of aristocratic culture. Even the duels are photographed with poise and containment, which adds to the genteel restraint and cold ritualization of the violence. Late in the film, however, after Barry has spent vast amounts of effort and money to be accepted into the aristocracy, he holds a music recital in his home and invites the elite of the society. In this scene (Figure 11-17),

■ **Figure 11-17** When Barry (Ryan O'Neal) attempts to punish his stepson's (Leon Vitali) transgression in Kubrick's *Barry Lyndon* (1975), the camera's handholding adds a visceral feel to the eruption of instinctive violence (left). Later on, when Barry duels with him, the camera's stability reflects the more civilized nature of ritualized violence in the 18th century (right).

his stepson, incensed that a lowly soldier has married his mother and obtained the family fortune and title, reveals Barry Lyndon's true origins by bringing Barry's real son into the salon. Barry erupts with anger and humiliation and physically attacks his stepson. Suddenly the camera work becomes a raw, unfettered handheld style—reflecting the deep impulsive rage Barry is expressing. These actions are not proscribed by culture anymore, they emerge from an animal instinct, and the camera style telegraphs the uncontrollability of this violence. The contrast with the controlled style of the rest of the film makes this an even more powerful moment, as we are certain that Barry has, in one rash moment, just undone everything he has worked so hard to accomplish.

■ *Nine Lives*

In "Maggie" the final episode of Rodrigo García's film *Nine Lives* (2005), a mother and her 8-year-old daughter visit a grave in a large cemetery. They talk and play; at one point Maggie scolds her daughter for stepping on graves and later keeps a look-out as the little girl takes a pee behind a tree. On a blanket they've laid out in front of a grave, they share some grapes, clearly a favorite fruit of the little girl, and they play patty-cake. It's all very casual and remarkably free from the pathos and gloom usually associated with cemeteries. But, in the middle of the game, Maggie suddenly breaks down in a sudden moment of grief. She tells her daughter "I'm tired," and lays her head on her little girl's lap to sleep (Figure 11-18).

At that moment, the camera begins a long, slow pan, away from the pair by the tombstone and across the beautiful, tree-filled, cemetery. The camera is mounted on a stabilizing arm, so the move feels as if it is gliding, floating across the cemetery. The pan covers a full 360 degrees, and when it returns to the tombstone, Maggie is now alone and folding the blanket to leave. The pan, which lasted only 30 seconds, creates a time ellipsis; clearly an hour or so has passed. After Maggie folds the blanket she lays the grapes on the tombstone. The camera move not only traverses the space of the cemetery but it also initiates a complete perception shift for the audience. What we understood to be true, a mother and daughter's visit to the grave of a long-dead relative, is in fact a grieving mother's visit to the grave of her daughter. Her imagination brought back memories of her little girl so vividly that the daughter took on real flesh and blood beside her. One could say that the camera move serves as a psychological transition, beginning in Maggie's fantasy and ending in reality. This camera move, perfectly placed, serves to completely flip our perspective on the story.

■ *The Balcony*

In her very first film, student Eileen B. chose to explore the beautiful location and views of a 16th-floor wraparound balcony at a public building where she worked. Her film was made up of rock-steady, carefully composed tripod shots displaying beautiful views, comfortable benches where people sit, the modern architecture of the space, lovely planters, etc. Then, at the very end of her film, she used her first and only camera move: a handheld camera racing toward and lurching over the edge of the balcony! The audience at the film screening shrieked when it seemed they were going over the edge. After all of the steady and tranquil compositions, this radical departure shocked us all and effectively expressed the filmmaker's POV. Eileen loves this balcony space but she also suffers from acrophobia (severe fear of heights), and after a few moments on the balcony she is sure she'll fall. That's what she wanted to communicate, what vertigo feels like—and she did just that in 2 minutes and one unexpected camera move.

■ **Figure 11-18** A 360 degree pan takes us from Maggie's (Glenn Close) imagined reality to the sad truth: she's actually mourning the loss of her daughter (Dakota Fanning) (from García's *Nine Lives*, 2005).

■ **Figure 11-19** Small camera reframes are sometimes necessary to maintain a consistent composition of the subject within the frame. In this shot from Meirelles's *The Constant Gardener* (2005), the "rule of thirds" is maintained by a slight camera adjustment when Justin (Ralph Fiennes) leans a little forward and to his right.

appropriate for the conception of your film. Even within a single film, there may be scenes that conceptually work best with a handheld camera while others require the stability of a tripod. But, of course, choosing the right support to move your camera is more than simply a matter of style for style's sake. Whether you handhold a camera, put it on a tripod, or wheel it around on a dolly, both the movement of the camera and the fashion in which it moves must be motivated by the story you're telling. You need to ask yourself: Why move the camera? Why move the camera now? Why move the camera in this fashion?

Always practice moves before you run tape or film. Rehearsals and blocking on the set are not just for the actors; they are also for the camera. The D.P. must know before the camera rolls how to execute a move in relation to the action in the scene. Performing a good camera move, especially combination moves, takes a few rehearsals to get just right.

You should always have a sense for where any camera move begins and ends. Moving the frame means constantly reframing your shot. It is very important to know in advance where your move begins and precisely where it ends and what pace and path you will take to accomplish the move so that you can be accurate with the composition and mise-en-scène from the beginning to the end. It's a common problem with inexperienced filmmakers that they begin a camera move without knowing exactly where they are going, and they wind up fishing around for a place to land, making the move look sloppy.

Camera moves vs. camera adjustments. Whether you're executing a pan, tilt, dolly, or track, a camera move is a clear and substantial alteration of the subject and composition. A **camera adjustment**, on the other hand, is a slight shifting of a frame to maintain your composition on a person or object that is moving only a little. For example, if we frame a character in a medium close-up while they speak to someone off screen, they may shift from one foot to the other or take a step forward or back, or even just shift their gaze from screen right to screen left. Each one of these changes requires a minor adjustment of the frame to maintain a balanced MCU composition. The person operating the camera needs to have a keen sense for the emotional content of the script, the rhythm of the performance, and the body language of the actor to anticipate these little movements and adjust accordingly. For this type of adjustment we say that the camera is "breathing with the subject." Camera adjustments are practically invisible to the audience, but you can spot them by looking, not at the main subject of a shot, but at the edges of the frame. You'll see objects in the background moving in and out of the frame as the camera adjusts to maintain a steady composition on the primary subject (**Figure 11-19**).

Practical considerations need to be measured in deciding on one or another camera support. To begin, moving the camera always adds production time because there are more technical details, like losing focus and camera bobble, which can go wrong, requiring multiple takes. Using a dolly requires more time for camera and subject choreography and for laying down tracks (when necessary), not to mention the addition of dolly grips to your crew. Some camera support systems, like professional dollies and Steadicam systems, are relatively expensive and are a major budget item if you need them everyday. And many professional dollies are so heavy that you need to rent a van to transport them. In the final analysis, you need to be realistic about what practical ramifications there might be with any piece of equipment. You don't want to commit to a major piece of gear only to have it slow you down so much that you don't get your film done.

Basics of Exposure

> *Photography is first and foremost a record of light. You are alone behind the camera, doubling as artist and scientist, hoping that your light—and it is your light—will bring it all to life.*

Tom McDonough (From *Light Years: Confessions of a Cinematographer,* Grove Press, New York, NY, 1987)

This quote by cinematographer and writer Tom McDonough neatly sums up the split personality of the cinematographer's art . . . or is it craft . . . or is it science? The truth is, getting just the right image for the story you are trying to tell, for the mood you want to create, for the connection you're trying to make with the audience, requires the instincts and sensitivity of an artist, the discipline of a craftsman, and the research of a scientist. In other words, when we create the film image we need to know aesthetically what we want and technically how to achieve that. Here and in the next chapter we will look at all of the basic technical factors of exposures and lighting so that you can tell your story with visual impact and eloquence.

■ ELEMENTS OF EXPOSURE

What does it mean to get an exposure? It's all about light: how much of it is bouncing off your scene, into your lens, and tagging your imaging device. But how do we control exposures? How can we assure that the image we imagine in our heads is the one that will make it onto the film or CCD chip? Whether you are shooting film or DV, *every* exposure you make involves an intricate interrelationship between all of the variables that produce, transmit, control, transform, or record light. Here are the primary elements along the path, beginning at the light source and ending at the imaging device:

1. **The light source:** Whether you are shooting under the sun or with artificial lights or a mixture of both, the aesthetic and technical properties or your lighting source have the biggest impact on the look of your image. Of central importance for exposure control specifically is the intensity of light, meaning how much light is falling onto your scene.

2. **The scene:** What are the visual dynamics of your scene? Or more specifically, what are the physical properties of the space, the reflectivity of the objects, the volume of the area, the colors and shadows, and movement? All these need to be considered when lighting and creating an exposure.

3. **Filters:** Lens filters are often employed in film production to alter the quality, color, or intensity of the light entering the camera. We don't always use filters, but when we do, they affect many of the other exposure elements.

4. **The lens and aperture:** As we mentioned, all of the light exposing your imaging device passes through the lens. Lens optics plays a primary role in forming the composition (wide angle, telephoto, etc.), but it is the lens aperture that determines the amount of light that is allowed to pass through to tag the film or CCDs. Aperture control is one of our most flexible variables for creating the best exposure for each image.

■ **Figure 12-1** Legendary Director of Photography Henri Alekan is said to have used almost 40 lights to light this tiny half-trailer from Wender's *Wings of Desire* (1987). Note the incredible range of contrast present in the scene.

5. **Speed and shutter:** The camera's frame rate and the size of our shutter constitute the shutter speed, which determines the duration of each exposure. Shutter isn't a concern only of people shooting film: most DV cameras have an electronic equivalent that equally has an impact on both image quality and exposures.
6. **Imaging device:** Film stocks or CCDs—understanding and factoring in your imaging device's particular and unique sensitivity and response to light is essential in getting the shot down the way you want it.

The ultimate factor is, of course, your creative needs: what you want the audience to see and how you want them to see it. It's easy enough to arrive at a "proper" exposure, but your primary task as a filmmaker is to find the "best" exposure for what you want to express. When determining the exposure for any given scene we are faced with not one solution, but with a range of options, which can involve manipulating any or all of the other exposure factors.

While the *basic* elements for creating exposures are the same for film and digital video, the method by which we determine proper exposure for each is very different. What makes film and DV so different is the simple fact that we can actually see the image being recorded in DV. Shooting on film, we can only predict what we're doing, because the image you see in the viewfinder is not exactly what is on the film, in terms of exposures. The actual image itself is not revealed to us until the film lab has done its work. However, determining the exposure you need follows a very reliable process, because the factors are precisely controllable and measurable and the science is tried and true. The main tool for determining exposures when shooting on film is the light meter.

■ THE LIGHT METER IN FILM

The light meter is like a third eye because it allows us to "see" a scene the way your film stock is "seeing" it. A **light meter** is a small calculator that accurately measures the light intensity values of a scene, and then calculates a "proper" exposure taking into account the exposure variables of the shooting situation. The final exposure suggestion of a light meter is a recommended f-stop. Always keep in mind, however, that the calculations of a light meter are only the starting point for a filmmaker deciding on a "best" exposure (**Figure 12-2**).

Every light meter works with the same set of variables in essentially the same sequence to arrive at an exposure calculation:

1. **Film speed:** The exposure index (EI) for your film stock is the very first variable to set on your light meter. In order for the meter to accurately calculate exposures, it needs to know the sensitivity of your film to light. (For more information on EI, see p. 161.)
2. **Intensity of light:** All light meters utilize a light-sensitive photocell (either selenium or cadmium sulfide cells) that responds to the amount of light entering the meter and generates a light intensity reading via a floating needle or digital

■ **Figure 12-2** Incident light meters, like this the Sekonic L-398, will always have the following features: an Exposure Index indicator (1), a photosphere to sample the light falling on the scene (2), a shutter speed/frames per second scale (3), and an f-stop scale (4).

readout. There are two methods for reading light intensity. The most common for film production is to read the light *falling on* a scene, which is known as **incident light**. The unit of measure for incident light is **footcandles**. One footcandle is equal to the light generated by an "international standard candle" 1 foot away from the center of the flame. If this scale of measure sounds a bit, well, arbitrary, just remember that the inch was derived from the width of *someone's* "average" thumb. The other method is to measure the light *reflecting off* a scene, which is known as **reflected light**. The unit of measure for reflected light is **footlamberts**. Measuring the light that is bouncing off a scene (or an object), otherwise known as the **reflectance value** or just **reflectance**, takes into account the light absorption qualities of objects (see later, Figure 12-5: "What Is Middle Gray?"). So, a footlambert reading therefore measures only the percentage of the incident light being reflected off a surface. Incident and reflected light readings are taken by two different meters called, respectively, an **incident light meter** and a **reflected light meter**. We will look closer at the uses of and distinctions between these two meters later.

3. **Shutter speed:** Once we factor the sensitivity of the film stock, and determine how much light is illuminating the scene, we next need to figure in our **shutter speed,** which is the amount of time a single frame is exposed to light. Shutter speed in film production is far more constant than in still photography, changing only when we attempt a special effect. There are two variables determining the shutter speed of a film camera: the angle of the shutter opening, which rarely changes from the standard 180° (see p. 144), and the film transport speed. Given that the standard frame rate for 16mm sync speed is 24 frames per second, and each frame is only exposed to light by the rotating 180° shutter for half that time, the shutter speed for each exposure is calculated: $1/24^{th} \times \frac{1}{2} = 1/48^{th}$ of a second. *The shutter speed for film running at standard 24 fps is $1/48^{th}$ of a second (often rounded off to $1/50^{th}$ of a second).* Changing transport speed, therefore, changes the shutter speed. For example, if we want to shoot a scene in slow motion we need to speed up the frame rate of the camera to, say, 48 frames per second, which means each frame would stay in the gate half as long ($1/48^{th} \times \frac{1}{2}$), which gives us a shutter speed of $1/96^{th}$ of a second. Because filmmakers alter shutter speed with some frequency, light meters used in film production have a **cine scale**, which shows a range of shutter speeds calculated for different frame rates. Only a few 16mm cameras also allow you to adjust the shutter angle open or closed, which would then require a recalculation of shutter speed, so this is much rarer.

4. **f-stop (aperture opening):** The final step in determining an exposure, and the endpoint for the calculations of the light meter, is the f-stop setting. After all of the other variables are entered into the light meter, the calculations tell us at what f-stop we should set our aperture ring in order to get a "proper" exposure for that reading.

Calculating Exposure

Using a light meter to determine the f-stop setting for a particular spot in the scene is called, **taking a reading**. If your scene is lit evenly throughout, then one reading will do, but very often scenes are made up of areas with different light intensities that would yield different exposure readings. In these cases the "correct" exposure determined through one reading at a single spot might yield an *acceptable* result, but perhaps not the best or most expressive exposure. In order to truly control the visual impact of your images, you should take multiple readings to determine how your film stock sees the variation of exposures in your scene, and then make a creative choice given the range of possibilities. Let's look at a simple example (Figure 12-3).

You are shooting a scene with two subjects in the frame. One subject is standing in the shade and the other is standing in the sun. You get a reading of f/16 in the sun, but when you take a reading in the shade you get f/5.6. So where do you set your f-stop? Which reading is "right?" The truth is, neither reading is right or wrong. If you set your camera f-stop to f/5.6 in order to expose the shade correctly, then the subject in the sun will be three stops overexposed, and if you set your f-stop ring to f/16, then the

f/16   f/5.6   f/8 - f/11

 Figure 12-3 A typical situation shooting outdoors on a sunny day. Exposing for the sunny side, at f/16, underexposes the subject in the shade. Exposing for the shade, at f/5.6, overexposes the subject in the sunny side. A "compromise" exposure, between f/8 and f/11, can be used if both subjects are to be seen with detail.

■ **Figure 12-4** In this scene from Godard's *Masculin Feminin,* (1966) the exposure is set to the outside of the window, resulting in the underexposing of the subject and adding a verité feel to the interview (top). In Nichol's *The Graduate* (1967), this shot of Mrs. Robinson (Anne Bancroft) is overexposed to mimic the glare of sunlight when she speaks to Benjamin who is in the pool (bottom).

man in the shade will be three stops underexposed, but the bright side will be correctly exposed. You could split the difference and set the exposure between f/8 and f/11, in which case one person will be 1.5 stops overexposed and the other will be 1.5 stops underexposed. A little compromise both ways. All three options are technically "correct," so now you need to ask yourself: What do I want this image to express? What is the mood of the scene, the style of the film? What do I want to show the audience, or hide from them? Do I need to show the guy in the shade? Does it matter if the man in the sun is bright? In short, exposures are such an important creative element of your film that they should not be left up to the indifferent calculations of a light meter. Instead, choosing the right exposure is a creative decision determined by the filmmaker, who also considers the other important exposure variables, like the specific visual approach necessary to tell the story. We will revisit this issue of exposure control in detail in the next chapter.

The Incident Light Meter

The **incident light meter** is the most common and versatile meter used in film production (**Figure 12-2**). It measures the intensity of light falling on a scene. This meter is simple to use and gives a consistent reading from shot to shot. All incident meters have a half-globe light diffuser, called a **photosphere** (also called a **lumisphere**), which fits over the photosensitive cell. The photosphere, held near the subject and pointed toward the camera, gathers the light falling on the subject from the front and sides

What Is Middle Gray?

Let's say we have three articles of clothing hanging out on a laundry line to dry: a black towel, a gray T-shirt, and a pair of white jeans. All three are being lit by the same light source, the sun, but each one reflects a different amount of the incident light back to the camera. The black towel reflects very little, about 4% of the light, which is why it looks black on film. The white jeans reflect a lot, about 96%, and so expose the film much more, and the gray T-shirt is somewhere in between, reflect-

ing about 25% of the incident light. Each article of clothing has a different **reflectance value**. Understanding reflectance values is important to understanding how light meters work and in calculating how objects will appear on screen.

The photographer Ansel Adams developed a scale of gray tones, known as the zone system, by dividing up the shades of gray, from black to white, into eleven steps, or zones of luminance (**Figure 12-6**). Each luminance

zone represents a halving or doubling of the brightness (or the reflectance value). For example, zone VI is half as bright as zone VII, and zone IV is twice as bright as zone III. Yes, Adams created the scale so that it would correspond with the way the aperture in a lens halves and doubles light. If we look at the preceding example of the laundry, we can see that the black towel falls closest to zone I, the gray T-shirt falls around zone VI (five zones or stops brighter than the towel), and the white jeans falls in zone IX (three zones or stops brighter than the sweatshirt).

The most important zone for us to consider in order to understand how light meters work is the one right smack in the middle, between pure black and pure white. *Zone V* has a reflectance value of *18%** and is also known simply as *middle gray*. (According to Blain Brown in his book "Cinematography," the true reflectance of middle gray is 17.5%, but it is always rounded off to 18%.) All light meters, incident or reflected, are calibrated to the middle gray tone, although in very different ways. Let's look at how each type of meter works with the middle gray.

Reflectance percentages follow a logarithmic progression, not an arithmetic progression, which is why middle gray is 18% and not 50%.

Figure 12-5 The amount of light a subject reflects is called its "reflectance value." The white jeans reflect 96% of the light they receive, while the black towel reflects only 4%. The gray T-shirt is somewhere in between these two; it reflects about 25%.

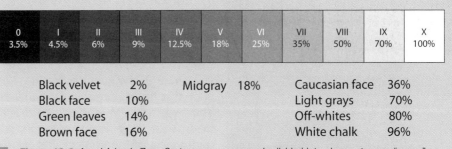

0	I	II	III	IV	V	VI	VII	VIII	IX	X
3.5%	4.5%	6%	9%	12.5%	18%	25%	35%	50%	70%	100%

Black velvet	2%	Midgray 18%	Caucasian face	36%
Black face	10%		Light grays	70%
Green leaves	14%		Off-whites	80%
Brown face	16%		White chalk	96%

Figure 12-6 Ansel Adam's Zone System uses a grayscale divided into eleven steps or "zones". These zones can be used to assign an exposure to a subject according to predetermined reflectance values (percentages from Blain Brown's *Cinematography*, Focal Press 2002).

and averages out these light intensities to arrive at an overall incident light intensity reading (**Figure 12-7**).

The final exposure reading of an incident light meter is derived from the exposure calculation specifically for the middle gray tone. In other words, the f-stop suggestion of an incident meter ensures that, given the intensity of the light falling on that part of the scene, objects with a luminance value of 18% (middle gray) will be exposed correctly (i.e., rendered exactly as middle gray on the film). It then will follow that objects that are lighter and darker (more or less reflective) will appear exactly as they should relative to the middle gray tone, thus duplicating the actual range of brightness values in the scene. In the case of our laundry photo (**Figure 12-5**), because everything was equally lit by the same source, a single incident meter reading assured that the inherent brightness values of each article of clothing would be

Figure 12-7 An incident light meter should always be positioned so that its photosphere is pointing at the lens of the camera.

rendered correctly by following the light meter's f-stop calculation for exposing middle gray correctly. It doesn't matter if the meter reading was f/4, f/5.6, or f/16; by setting the camera

f/16   f/5.6   f/8 - f/11

■ **Figure 12-8** Exposing for middle gray in the sunny areas will underexpose the shaded areas (left frame, f/16), while exposing for middle gray in the shaded areas will overexpose the sunny areas (middle frame, f/5.6). A compromise exposure will slightly overexpose the sunny areas and underexpose the shaded areas (right frame, f/8). Note the effects of exposure change on the middle gray cards (which are all exactly the same shade of gray).

■ **Figure 12-9** A reflected light meter should be pointed at the subject (top), which gives us an average of light values present in the scene. Taking a reflected light reading off a middle gray card (bottom) ensures we will set the aperture for proper tonality, as if we had taken a reading with an incident light meter.

aperture to the f-stop appropriate for the light intensity, which is what the light meter tells us, middle gray and all of the other tones will be rendered correctly. This consistent standard for the exposure calculation assures uniformity from reading to reading. It is often said about incident meters that middle gray is "built-in," which means you don't literally need a middle gray tone in the scene for the meter to make the proper calculation and for the rest of the luminance values in the scene to fall where they would naturally.

But what about a scene in which there is more than one light intensity level? In the scene in Figure 12-8, the young man is standing such that half of him is in the sun and the other half is in the shade. The two readings, sunny side (f/16) and shade side (f/5.6), were taken with an incident meter. If the camera f-stop is set for the bright side of the subject, the middle gray card in the sun is exposed correctly and the luminance of the other objects in the sun (i.e., shirt, jean jacket, background) is rendered appropriately, but the shade side is underexposed. Conversely, when the f-stop is set for the shade side, the middle gray card in the shadow is exposed correctly, along with everything else in the shadows, but the sunny side is now overexposed. Splitting the difference and setting the f-stop in between will cause each side to be slightly overexposed and slightly underexposed, respectively. The choice is yours.

The Reflected Light Meter and Spot Meter

A **reflected light meter** (also called an **averaging meter**) measures the intensity of light reflecting off a scene. A general-purpose reflected light meter has a wide angle of acceptance, which means it measures the reflected light intensity from a fairly wide area, around 45°. A reflected light meter is held near the camera (Figure 12-9) and pointed at the scene and averages out all of the various light intensities bouncing off the objects in the scene, toward the lens. It then assumes that the average reflectance of any scene is middle gray, which may or may not be the case, and gives you an f-stop suggestion for middle gray. However, because these meters always assume a reflectance value of middle gray (18%) for every scene, no matter what, they can be easily fooled. For example, let's say you're shooting a polar bear in the snow. The overall brightness of this scene is close to pure white, but a reflected light meter will suggest an f-stop to render this scene middle gray. This obviously is not the correct exposure. Similarly, if your scene is of a burglar, dressed in black creeping along the shadows, you'll want a scene that is plunged in blackness, but a reflected meter will give you a reading to make the scene middle gray. The same problem exists if we bring the meter in closer, to measure specific objects; for example, if we take a reading off a white car, the f-stop calculation will give us the aperture to render that car as middle gray.

To assure proper tonality in the scene, reflected meter readings are often literally taken off a middle gray card. This way the reading will give the proper f-stop to render that middle gray card, middle gray, and objects lighter or darker will then be rendered in proper relationship to middle gray. In effect, we're back to the way an incident meter functions, but an incident meter is much easier to use. It's not hard to see why incident meters are preferred and standard for general exposure calculations.

Reflected light meters, however, are useful when photographing objects that are themselves a source of illumination—when you need to ascertain the light intensity

■ **Figure 12-10** Use a reflected light meter to get an exposure reading for objects which emit light, as in this shot of a video monitor from *FearFall* (2000).

■ **Figure 12-11** A spot meter is a reflected light meter with an extremely narrow angle of incidence, allowing for very precise readings far from the subject. Shown here are a Pentax spot meter (left), and a Sekonic combination incident/spot meter (right).

of an object that is emitting light, as opposed to the light falling on it—for example, if we are shooting a television set (Figure 12-10), the neon lights of a Las Vegas casino, or the glow of a frosted window pane.

One important variation on a reflected meter is the spot meter, which is commonly used on film sets. A **spot meter** is a reflected light meter with a zoom lens and a very narrow and precise angle of acceptance, usually around 1° (Figure 12-11). A spot meter can pinpoint a small area from a distance. This is useful in measuring a variety of areas to determine the different light reflectance values of various objects in a single scene. It also allows us to take meter readings of areas that are not easily accessible. For example, we can take multiple readings of a city skyline, where some buildings are lit by bright sunlight and others fall into the shadows, from one location. Using a spot meter we can get a very accurate assessment of the relative exposure values of each area from our one setup on the sidewalk (Figure 12-12).

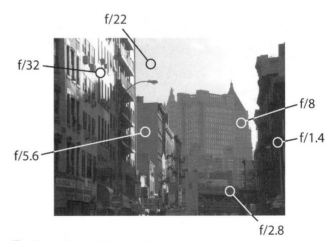

■ **Figure 12-12** Taking readings from subjects far away from the camera is an easy task with a spot meter, but the readings have to be interpreted before setting the f-stop. Setting the aperture for the sky at f/22, for instance, will darken it to middle gray and underexpose everything else. Can you tell what f-stop was chosen to record this image?

The Brightness of Objects On Screen
Keep in mind that the reflectance value of an object does not change. That gray T-shirt in Figure 12-6 always reflects 25% of the incident light. But it can appear more or less bright on screen. The brightness of an object as it appears on screen is determined by three factors with which you are now familiar:

1. Intensity of the incident light (variable).
2. Reflectance of the object (fixed).
3. Lens f-stop setting (variable).

Being a reflected light meter, however, a spot meter reading still needs to be interpreted, because it calculates an exposure to render that area middle gray, whether it's the whiteness of the sun reflecting off a window or a deep, black shadow. However, unlike an averaging reflected meter, the precision of the spot meter allows for easier interpretation. Let's say you meter a precise area in the frame that is clearly white and the spot meter gives you a reading of f/16. You know that the reading tells you where to set your f-stop to expose that white area as middle gray. It's not right, but you also can see from a zone system chart (see p. 227) that the white zone is four zones, or stops, brighter (i. e., the iris should be more open) than middle gray, so you simply open up four stops from f/16, which is f/4, and that will give you not only a correctly exposed white area in the frame, but also, since this f/4 is the correct f-stop, all of the other luminance values will fall correctly into place as well. This is clearly illustrated with the shift in middle gray cards in Figure 12-8.

■ METERING FOR DIGITAL VIDEO

Metering for DV is quite a different matter, for two reasons. The first is that we can see our final image on a monitor and the second is that all DV cameras come with built-in **through the lens** (TTL) **meters**, so handheld light meters are never used. A through the lens meter is a reflected light meter that calculates the aperture setting by averaging out the light from a scene *after* it has entered the lens. That means that it also takes into account any filters you may be using in front of the lens. The fact that the meter is built-in means that it is already calibrated with all of the exposure variables we must enter in manually on a film light meter, like the sensitivity of the CCD chips to light and the frame rate of video.

The range of acceptance on a DV camcorder light meter varies from model to model and it is vital that you understand how your specific camera "reads" the scene. Some models take an average of the entire frame while others take an average reading from a smaller portion of the middle of the frame, assuming that your subject will be framed in the middle of the composition. It is essential to know that, because the meter is located right behind the lens, you can use the zoom capabilities of the lens to turn the TTL meter into a spot meter. Zooming in greatly narrows the angle of acceptance of the meter and allows you to read light values off very circumscribed areas and specific objects.

Exposure Control and DV
Just as we discussed with film exposures, there is not one single "correct" exposure in DV production either. There is a range of possible exposures from which the creative filmmaker must choose in order to achieve the mood, style, and visual meaning they are after. The built-

■ **Figure 12-13** Ed Rankus' short film, *Naked Doom* (1983), is infused with an expressionistic aesthetic seldom seen on analog video; this look required careful control over lighting and exposure.

in meter on all DV cameras can trigger an **auto iris** function (also called **auto exposure**), which will take the average meter reading for your scene and automatically set the camera's aperture. However, exposure control is such a crucial area of aesthetic impact that any serious filmmaker will recognize the folly of relinquishing this important decision to an impassive machine with an automatic function designed to create an *acceptable* image instead of a truly *expressive* one. You should never take the "EZ road" and let the camera select the look of your images for you, especially because the auto exposure mechanism of a DV camera can easily be fooled. Here are three common situations in which auto iris will backfire:

■ **Figure 12-14** The auto iris function gives priority to the center of the frame. As a result, if the subject is placed off-center it will not be read properly by the camera's light meter. In this example, the sunlit traffic in the background (in the center) is exposed properly, but our subject is severely underexposed.

1. *Center averaging:* As we mentioned before, most TTL meters average out the exposure values at the center of the frame, assuming that your subject will always be at the center. But what if your subject isn't in the center? Perhaps the composition you want puts the subject at the edge of the frame. In cases like this, the auto iris can easily choose an unacceptable exposure (Figure 12-14).

2. *Extreme backgrounds:* Auto iris functions are often confused by extreme backlighting or dark backgrounds and will average in portions of the frame that are clearly not average. For example, an actor standing in front of a bright window will cause the auto iris to close down to compensate for the increased exposure value, thus underexposing the subject. Conversely, an actor standing in front of a blackboard will cause the iris to open up and potentially overexpose the subject.

3. *Temporary brightness shifts:* Another common situation that confuses the auto exposure function occurs when a bright object enters the frame during a shot, triggering an adjustment in the exposure during a take. For example, say we're shooting a conversation between two people, and during the shot a passerby in a bright white T-shirt crosses in front of them. The in-camera meter will detect the bright object and trigger the auto iris to quickly close down, to maintain that "average" exposure (Figure 12-15). When the passerby leaves the frame the auto iris will respond to the new average light value and open up again. The same spasmodic iris opening and closing phenomenon also happens if we pan across a scene with various light and dark areas.

■ **Figure 12-15** The sudden appearance of a bright object in the frame will trigger the auto iris function to adjust the exposure in mid-shot to compensate, only to change it again after the object leaves the frame.

■ **Figure 12-16** Many DV cameras allow manual exposure control and can display f-stops on their LCDs, providing a more precise control over the exposure of the subject.

So, the first thing you must do is find out how to turn off the auto iris function (**Figure 12-16**). Look for the **manual aperture override** (also called manual exposure) function on your camera and do it. All professional and industrial grade DV cameras and many (but not all) consumer cameras have manual override capabilities. However, only high-end professional cameras have iris rings that are calibrated in f-stops and actually have the f-stop scale etched on the iris ring. Many cameras, including some very fine industrial DV camcorders, display a quasi-f-stop scale on their LCD screen or viewfinder, while many others have no scale at all, requiring you to use only your eye to judge the exposure.

Manual Exposure Control

Determining your "best" exposure with a DV camcorder requires using a combination of the zoom lens, the in-camera meter, the auto iris, and the manual override functions (**Figure 12-17**). Here are the standard steps for finding your exposure.

1. Decide which part of the frame you would like exposed correctly. This is an aesthetic decision based on the composition, mood, and story.
2. With the camera on auto iris, zoom in tightly to that portion of the composition, preferably so that it fills the frame, and let the auto iris select its "correct" exposure for that small portion of the total scene.
3. Turn off the auto iris by switching to manual override. This will lock in that exposure.
4. Zoom out and compose your shot. It doesn't matter where in the frame you place your subject, or how bright the background is, or what might pass in front of the lens during the take: that exposure is locked in and will not change.
5. Finally, tweak the manual iris to finesse the exposure by looking at the final result in your viewfinder or, preferably, on a high-quality field monitor.

Keep in mind that you can zoom in to any portion of the scene and lock in the exposure there to check out the effect of various apertures. This will give you a clear sense for the range of light values and exposure possibilities within your scene. Metering for film and video are similar in this regard. Multiple readings will give you a better understanding of the range of exposure possibilities that you can choose from.

Using Field Monitors

Unfortunately, it is not uncommon for a filmmaker shooting on DV to be happy with what they're seeing on their LCD screens as they shoot, but when reviewing their footage later, on a professional monitor, to find the exposures are markedly different and to cry out "But

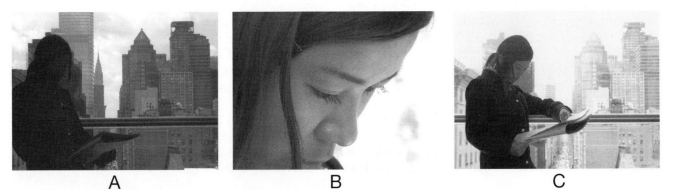

A B C

■ **Figure 12-17** A bright background can throw off the exposure of the subject (A). Zoom in so that the subject fills the frame and the auto iris finds a good exposure. Then switch to manual override locking in that setting (B). Now our subject will remain correctly exposed no matter how we frame the shot (C).

in practice

Determining your "correct" exposure on DV, as with film, is a matter of finding the right aesthetic choice for the narrative content of your scene and the overall look of the film. The frames in Figure 12-18 prove that one need not be timid with digital video. They are great examples of fearless cinematographers pushing DV exposures to their limits.

The first frame (top) is from *Personal Velocity: Three Portraits* (2002), directed by Rebecca Miller and shot by Ellen Kuras. The color palette for the character, Delia, shown standing next to a window, are warm, golden tones, but Delia is a woman whose life is falling apart after she leaves her abusive husband. It's a desperate, messy, and extreme situation, and this "feeling" is wonder-

fully conveyed in Kuras' extreme cinematography, where she often allows Delia's blonde hair to overexpose, looking as if it's practically ignited.

The other frame (bottom), from Thomas Vinterberg's 1998 film *The Celebration*, is at the other extreme. Exploiting DV's sensitivity to light, D.P. Anthony Dod Mantle shot an entire scene exclusively illuminated by the flame of a cigarette lighter. The context for the scene is a young man who encounters the ghost of his dead sister, whom he adored, during a particularly harrowing and revelatory family celebration. Many people will tell you that you can't underexpose DV like this—"there is too much noise in the image, the blacks are murky," they'll tell you. But all of those characteristics of underexposed DV created a devastating moment in *The Celebration*—haunting, surreal, and affectionate all at the same time—because they were "right" for the scene.

Both D.P.s not only capitalized on the unique qualities of the DV image, they also understood the freedom that DV technology provides and they took that freedom to the nth degree.

Figure 12-18 Overriding the automatic iris function allows for expressive uses of exposure, as shown in the DV films (top) *Personal Velocity* (Miller, 2002) and (bottom) *The Celebration* (Vinterberg, 1998).

it didn't look that way when I was shooting it!" The fact that we can see the video image as we shoot can be a great help in evaluating and choosing exposures, but a filmmaker must be confident that what they are viewing in terms of brightness, color, and contrast, while they shoot, is an accurate representation of what is actually being recorded by the camera. The flip-out LCD screens on most DV camcorders cannot be accurately calibrated for critical judgments, which is why they are considered primarily a composition tool, but not a reliable image evaluation instrument. Many DV filmmakers claim that the tiny CRT viewfinder is more accurate for determining exposures and, especially, focus. In many situations, simply white balancing your camera correctly along with careful attention to exposure levels will yield results that are acceptable. Digital video is also flexible enough that minor image adjustments can be made successfully in postproduction. However, when absolute precision is an imperative, most filmmakers will also use a high-quality **portable field monitor** that is attached to the video output of the camera. The color, brightness, and contrast settings for any field monitor, however, must be set to a standard in order to ensure that what we are seeing is indeed what we are getting. All professional and some industrial level DV cameras generate a video test pattern called **NTSC split field color bars**, which are used to calibrate field production monitors (Figure 12-19). NTSC color bars are a standardized set of colored stripes and squares that allow you to easily calibrate your monitor's adjustable settings for brightness (luminance), contrast, hue (tint), and saturation (color level) to ensure faithful display of the images being recorded. Complete instructions for calibrating monitors to color bars are located in Appendix 3.

Unfortunately, not all cameras generate standard colors bars. Many industrial grade DV cameras only generate nonstandard full-field color bars, which are not really that helpful because they rely too much on a subjective understanding of what colors should look like

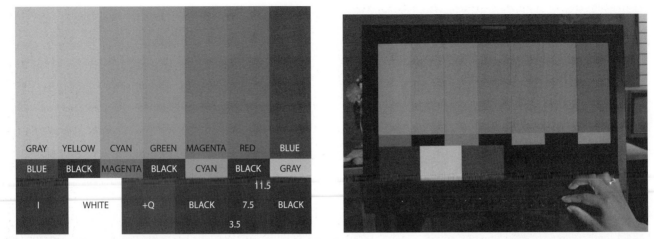

GRAY	YELLOW	CYAN	GREEN	MAGENTA	RED		BLUE
BLUE	BLACK	MAGENTA	BLACK	CYAN	BLACK		GRAY
						11.5	
I	WHITE	+Q		BLACK	7.5		BLACK
			3.5				

■ **Figure 12-19** Monitors can be calibrated with NTSC color bars for luminance, contrast, hue, and saturation, providing an accurate rendition of the video signal from the camera. See the color insert in Chapter 13.

■ **Figure 12-20** The use of a monitor sunshade or hood permits the viewing of an LCD screen even in bright, sunny locations.

and provide no feature for calibrating brightness and contrast. Even more difficult, many DV cameras don't generate color bars at all. In these cases you need to improvise. Some people hook up a small, portable color bar generator to calibrate their monitor, while others record NTSC color bars on a DV tape that they carry with them in the field to play through the camera. It's not the most accurate method, but it's better than nothing.

In addition to calibrating your monitor you also need to take care to protect the monitor screen from the sun or movie lights, which can wash out the image. LCD flip-screen viewfinders are especially vulnerable to being washed out by ambient light; also, viewing LCD screens at a slightly oblique angle can cause dramatic shifts in color, contrast, and brightness. **Monitor sunshades** (also called **hoods**) are often used in the field to avoid these problems (Figure 12-20).

Zebras

Another exposure aid found on many cameras is called **zebra stripes** or simply **zebras**. Zebras are thin, slanted black stripes that show up in the hot spots in your image and can be seen in the viewfinder, but they are not recorded or even visible on an external monitor hooked into the video output. Zebra stripes tell you when a bright area in your image has reached the limits of proper exposure and is in danger of being overexposed. The two most common luminance settings for zebras are **100% white** and **70% white** (sometimes **80% white**). Some cameras allow you to switch between the two.

The **100% white** (or **100 IRE**) setting is considered the absolute upper range of brightness for a video exposure, beyond which your whites "clip" or "burn out," meaning that you've completely lost all detail in that area. When 100% stripes begin to appear in the white areas of the frame, you know you've reached the limits and do not want to open up your aperture any more. For example, lets say we are shooting a man leaning against his white car, and we want that car to gleam nice and bright. The DV camera's auto exposure will see a very bright object dominate the frame and will try to expose the white car closer to a middle gray tone. This won't be acceptable. So we go into manual override and open up the iris to the point when zebra stripes show, and then close down just enough that they begin to disappear. Now that white car is properly white. The benefit of using the zebras is that they give

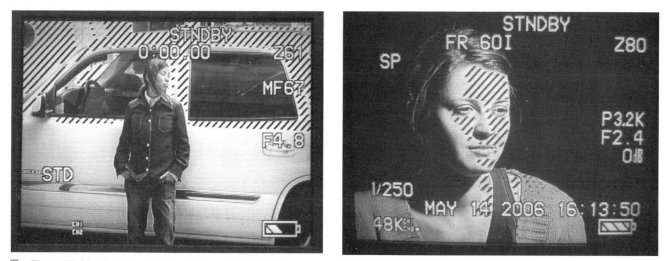

■ **Figure 12-21** The zebra stripe function is useful to control overexposure in our subjects. Zebras are commonly calibrated to display overexposures in white areas (100%) (left), or "correct" exposure for Caucasian facetones (70%) (right).

you the only absolute measure of brightness in your image. Monitors might be slightly off, even after calibration, but zebras will show up at 100% white no matter how you've calibrated the monitor (Figure 12-21).

Some cameras allow you to calibrate zebra stripes to **70%** or **80% white**, which is considered the upper limit of "proper" exposure for Caucasian skin tone. These zebras start to show at 70% white and then disappear around 90%. The logic here is based on the assumption that Caucasian skin is properly exposed around 70% to 80%. When shooting the face of a "Caucasian" subject, you should see zebras in the highlights of the face, like the cheekbones and the forehead. The limitations of 70% zebras should be fairly obvious. Are all Caucasian skin tones alike? Surely not. And what about all of those other skin tones we might want to shoot? In addition, there are many situations where we don't want to use an exposure standard that makes our people look like they're being taped for the evening news. So, 70/80% stripes—if you use them at all—should be considered only as an exposure guide and never as an absolute.

Other DV Exposure Factors

Electronic gain is one way many DV cameras deal with low light situations. **Gain** is an electronic amplification of the video signal coming from the CCD chips, increasing the sensitivity of the imaging system to light. Gain is considered an exposure adjustment of last resort, to be employed when we absolutely need to get the shot, but there simply isn't enough light for a decent exposure. Hit the gain switch and suddenly the image appears much brighter. Gain, however, also involves serious compromises to image resolution and contrast and increases **video noise**, which is unwanted electronic aberrations and artifacts. Most cameras offer three preset gain settings: 0 dB for low gain, 9 dB for medium gain, and 18 db for high gain. Some cameras have the option for even more gain than this. Obviously, though, the noise level increases as the gain level increases. Some cameras also have an automatic gain adjustment which, like most auto functions, should immediately be turned off in favor of the manual settings. Gain requires such serious image compromises that most people stay away from it except under extreme circumstances. That said, gain does have a "look" of sorts that could work well for certain scenes as an aesthetic choice. You never know, so tuck it away into your visual toolbox (Figure 12-22).

■ **Figure 12-22** DV cameras can shoot in extreme low-light situations through the use of the gain function, sacrificing resolution and adding video noise in the process.

■ **Figure 12-23** A slow shutter setting smears the image (left), while a fast shutter captures even fast action without any blurriness (right).

Just because DV cameras don't have a physically rotating 180° shutter light like a film camera doesn't mean they don't have a shutter of sorts. DV cameras have an **electronic shutter** that determines the amount of time each frame of video is exposed. The normal shutter speed for video is 1/60th of a second, but shutters can be manually adjusted over a range. Setting the shutter to slower speeds, like 1/16th of a second, creates longer exposures, allowing more light to fall on the CCD chips and causing movement smears in each frame (Figure 12-23).

Setting the shutter to faster speeds, like 1/4,000th of a second (some cameras have the capability of shooting at 1/15,000th of a second!), creates sharper, crisper images as the speed increases. Fast shutter speeds are great for shots you intend to manipulate, in postproduction, into slow motion because there is no blur in the individual frames. However, when you play back fast shutter speed shots at the normal frame rate, the image can have a staccato or stroboscopic effect, which becomes more noticeable as your shutter speed increases. Just as with the slow shutter speed effect, this, too, can be a desirable aesthetic choice when used appropriately. Keep in mind that the faster your shutter speed, the less light hits your CCD. Ultrafast shutter speeds require a lot of light to create an acceptable exposure.

chapter 13

Basic Lighting for Film and DV

Movie lighting is an art form in which the interplay of light, shadows, color, and movement serve as fundamental expressive elements in the telling of a story. Whether you are shooting on film or video, using only sunlight or using twenty movie lights, with lighting designed for a realistic style or a stylized look, it all comes down to finding a lighting scheme that is appropriate for this scene, at this moment, in this story. Like all art forms, there is really only one absolute rule to dramatic lighting—make it work. If you can justify the lighting design of a scene within the overall intentions of the project, then do it. However, as with all art forms, "making it work" also means having the skill and control to actually pull "it" off. With lighting, the more knowledge you acquire about the history, conventions, and approaches of dramatic lighting, and the more control you develop over the materials, tools, and techniques of the craft, the more successfully you will achieve your vision. In order to gain this sort of control you must start with a solid foundation, which means knowing what tools you have at your disposal and how those tools work. It also means knowing some basic principles of light and lighting. Principles, unlike rules, can be applied creatively, used to improvise, and serve as the foundation for creative exploration and expression.

A thorough understanding of lighting principles is especially important to student and independent filmmakers, who are typically making films on a tight budget and time schedule. Lighting is the most time-consuming and labor-intensive process in making movies. It takes muscle and many hours to get lighting gear onto a set, into position for shooting, broken down afterwards, and loaded back onto the truck. Hollywood films look like Hollywood films because they have all the time, money, and manpower they need for elaborate lighting schemes and setups. But just as with every other element of a filmmaker's

■ **Figure 13-1** Expressive lighting with modest resources. It's beneficial to study the lighting strategies of innovative films like (top, left) Godard's *Masculin, Feminin* (1966), (top, middle) Miller's *Personal Velocity* (2002), (top, right) Wong's *Chungking Express* (1994), (bottom, left) Fassbinder's *Ali: Fear Eats the Soul* (1974) and (bottom, right) Boe's *Reconstruction* (2003).

art, money and size don't necessarily translate into a good or successful film. Ingenuity, imagination, and a practiced eye are your primary resources for using light to tell your story with visual eloquence and impact. If you really want to learn about lighting, stay away from the Hollywood blockbusters, which have an army of grips, gaffers, and electricians and several five-ton grip trucks filled to the brim with state-of-the-art lighting and grip equipment. Not only can these films make you feel that your resources are insufficient, but in fact, this surfeit of resources often proves to be an encumbrance that threatens to supersede the creative impulse with logistics and pure technical procedure for its own sake. Anyone who goes to the movies on a regular basis sees many films that were made with virtually limitless access to lighting gear and labor, but that nonetheless feel lifeless. This feeling comes, in no small measure, from the lighting approach itself, which, for all of its professionalism, often is simply big, blunt, and overproduced rather than uniquely expressive.

Both film students and independent filmmakers should look instead at the filmmakers who have made great movies with very little—whether out of necessity or by choice—and who have conceived of simple, elegant, and expressive lighting designs. For example, look at the brilliantly innovative films from the French New Wave like *Masculin/Féminin* (Godard/Kurant), and the New German Cinema movement like *Ali: Fear Eats the Soul* (Fassbinder/Jürges), and the more recent American Independent and European films like *Personal Velocity* (Miller/Kuras) and *Reconstruction* (Boe/Claro), and, of course, the fearless lighting of recent Asian films like *Chungking Express* (Kar-Wai/Doyle) (**Figure 13-1**). These pictures all had relatively scant lighting resources, but used them with a profound understanding of artistry, sensitivity, and technique, which can teach us far more about lighting, camerawork, and storytelling than can the latest $150,000,000 Hollywood production.

Figure 13-2 An 18,000 watt HMI on location (top) and a flashlight being used as a light source in *The Blair Witch Project* (1999) (bottom). Artificial lights come in any size and can be used according to the narrative needs of your film.

The great cinematographer Néstor Almendros made a critically important point when talking about his work lighting and shooting Eric Rohmer's *La Collectionneuse* (1966). In his interview for the book "Masters of Light" (by Dennis Schaefer and Larry Salvato) Almendros talks about his naturalistic lighting approach, working with Rohmer, and how few lights and crew they discovered they actually needed to make the film: "[We] realized that most technicians had been bull***ing, you know, and inventing uses for enormous amounts of light to justify their importance, to justify their salaries and to make themselves look like someone who knows a secret, when there is technically very little to know."

■ LIGHT SOURCES: A FEW COMMON TERMS

Anything that gives off light, from the blazing midday sun to a candle, can be used as a lighting source in a scene. **Natural light** is a term meaning a light source coming from nature, a source that is not artificial. Usually we mean the sun when we talk about natural light, but the term also applies to light that comes from nonelectric sources, whether or not they are indeed naturally occurring, like campfires, candles, and fireplaces. If your scene included flashes from lightning bolts, that, too, would be a natural light source. **Artificial light** is any light source that generates light though electricity. Artificial lights can be as big as a 50,000-watt movie light or as small as a flashlight (**Figure 13-2**).

The term **available light** refers to using light sources that ordinarily exist in any given location. For example, if we walk into a grocery store with our camera and simply shoot by the light of the

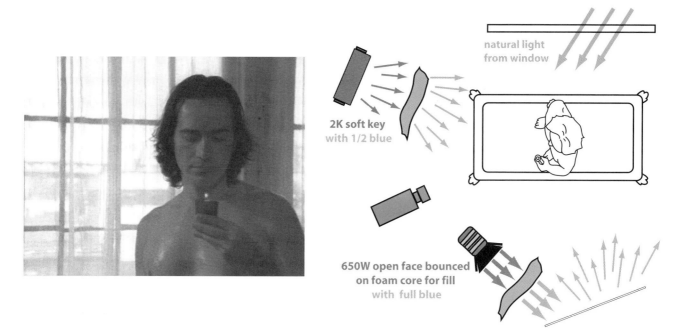

■ **Figure 13-3** In this scene, from Katherine Hurbis-Cherrier's *Ode to a Bar of Soap* (1998) mixed lighting (artificial and sunlight) has been balanced for color temperature and quality. See the color insert in this chapter.

fluorescent fixtures overhead, or if we shoot in a bedroom illuminated only by the sun streaming in from a window, we are shooting with available light. And, as you might suspect, **mixed lighting** means using a combination of available sources and artificial lights to achieve the look we're after. It's very common to use the sun as one light source and artificial lights another (Figure 13-3).

Very often natural and/or available light sources are not powerful enough to create an exposure, but we nonetheless want the audience to feel like that particular source is illuminating the scene. For example, a character is watching TV and we want the audience to believe that the glow from the screen is the only light illuminating her face, but the glow from a TV (or candle, or fireplace, or 25-watt reading lamp, etc.) is almost never strong enough to get a good exposure, especially if your character is some distance away. In this sort of situation we bring in an artificial light to duplicate the color, quality, and direction of the ostensible light source, but at a

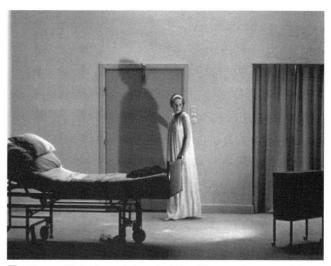

■ **Figure 13-4** The real glow of a TV could not produce enough light for an exposure, so its output was amplified with the use of a movie light in Ingmar Bergman's *Persona* (1966).

higher intensity (Figure 13-4). While this light obviously remains off screen, the ostensible source is often shown in the scene (see later, Specials and Practicals).

This strategy of using movie lights to duplicate where light would logically be emanating from is called **motivated lighting**. Motivated lighting is a central strategy for creating naturalistic lighting designs (see p. 285).

■ THREE ESSENTIAL PROPERTIES OF LIGHT

Light sources don't simply give off generic light: every light source emits a light that has specific characteristics that contribute to the look of your scene. Three of the basic properties of light that give any light source its distinctive character are **intensity**, **hard vs. soft**, and **color temperature**.

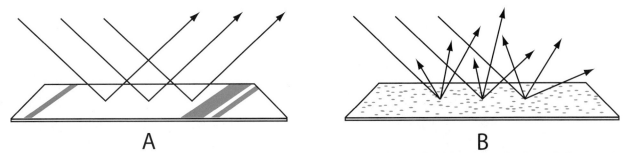

■ **Figure 13-5** A specular surface, like a mirror or a polished reflector (A) maintains the directionality of the light rays it reflects. A diffused surface (B), like foam core or a matte finished reflector, scatters the light rays, changing the quality of the light from hard to soft.

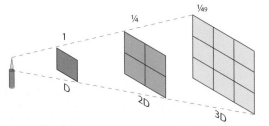

■ **Figure 13-6** The inverse square law. Doubling the distance from the light source to our subject means that the illumination is spread over four times the area and is therefore only one fourth the intensity. Tripling the distance diminishes the intensity to one ninth of the original.

Intensity

Light **intensity** is the strength of the light emitted by a source and, as we mentioned earlier, is measured by a light meter in footcandles. Direct sunlight is obviously a very intense source of light, although the actual intensity changes depending on its angle at various times of day. With artificial light, intensity depends on the **wattage of the lamp** used (500 watts, 1,000 watts, etc.) and on the **reflector system**. When we speak of lamp wattage we use the symbol "K" to stand in for "thousand." So a 1,000-watt light is called a 1K and a 2,000-watt light is called a 2K. (Do not get this K mixed up with the "K" symbol used for degrees Kelvin, when referring to color temperatures.) A very common movie light is a 1K Fresnel with a color temperature of 3,200°K.

Some lighting instruments use a **specular reflector system**. A specular reflector system uses a highly polished, mirror-like surface to reflect the light from the lamp and is very efficient in maintaining the intensity of the lamp wattage. Other instruments use a **diffuse reflector system** to soften the light, and this cuts down the intensity. In addition, some lighting units employ a lens in front of the lamp to help control the directionality of the beam, but this, too, cuts down the intensity of the light (Figure 13-5).

The intensity of incident light on your scene is also greatly affected by the lighting unit-to-subject distance. The further away an instrument is placed from the subject, the weaker the light is falling on the scene. This diminishing intensity as the unit is moved away follows the **inverse square law**, which says that the intensity of light falls off by the square of the distance from the subject (Figure 13-6).

Obviously the converse applies when you bring a light in closer, to increase its intensity on the subject. If the inverse square law seems like a lot of calculation to do on the set, you can simply apply this rule of thumb: if you double the distance between the lighting unit and your subject, say from 10 feet to 20 feet, the strength of the light will fall off four times and will be only one-fourth the intensity compared to the original position. If you halve the distance between the subject and the lighting unit, you will increase the light intensity four times from the original position.

Hard vs. Soft

The lamps for the most commonly used film lights involve a wire filament, enclosed in a glass bulb, surrounded by a vacuum of inert gases, heated to the point where it glows white hot. That glowing filament becomes the **point source** of the lamp's illumination, creating a highly directional beam. Light that travels directly from a lamp to the subject is referred to as a **hard light** or **directional light**, because the light rays, which travel straight and parallel to each other, all fall on the subject from a single angle, causing sharp shadows and bright highlight areas. Lighting instruments with specular reflector systems preserve this hardness because a specular surface, like a mirror, redirects the light rays yet

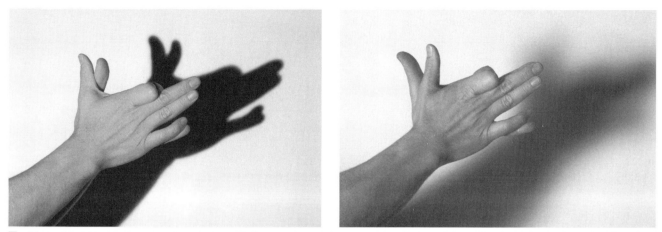

■ **Figure 13-7** Hard light creates sharp shadows (left) because the light beams maintain their parallel direction. Soft light (right), creates diffused shadows because the scattered light beams are reaching our subject from many directions.

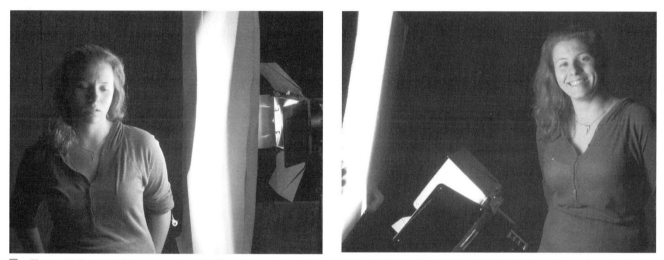

■ **Figure 13-8** Hard light can be softened (diffused) by applying diffusion material in front of it (left) or by bouncing it off a white surface, like foam core (right).

maintains their direct and parallel path. Units that do not illuminate directly from the lamp, but instead reflect the light off an unpolished, white surface, emit a **diffused** or **soft light**. The unpolished surface scatters the light rays in a variety of angles, disturbing their parallel paths (Figure 13-7).

Diffused light rays do not hit the subject from the same angle and therefore create softer shadows and smoother highlights. This sort of lighting instrument is called a soft light. It's important to note that the larger the area of the diffused bounce surface is, the softer the light will be. Understanding this principle, you can see that it is not difficult to soften the light from a hard lighting instrument by simply bouncing it off any diffused surface, like a white wall or a bounce board (Figure 13-8).

You can also soften light from a hard lighting unit by placing **diffusion media** in front of the beam. Diffusion media scatters the light rays in a way similar to that achieved by bouncing light off a diffusing surface (see later, Altering Light with Gels). Be aware, however, that diffusing light either way decreases its intensity. It's also important to understand that the terms "hard" and "soft" describe a characteristic of light and should not be viewed as a value judgment. One is not "better" than the other. As with so many other things, the appropriate choice is based primarily on applying the appropriate aesthetic choice for the content of your story (Figure 13-9).

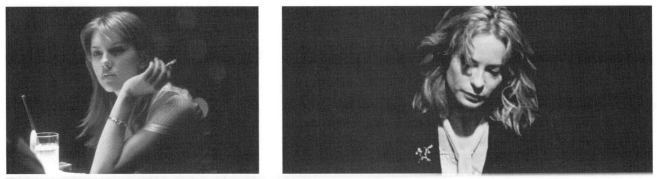

■ **Figure 13-9** The decision to use hard or soft light depends on the aesthetic needs of your film. Although both of these shots use a single source (low-key) lighting approach, S. Coppola's *Lost in Translation* (2003) uses soft light (left) while Boe's *Reconstruction* (2003, right) uses hard light which explains their radically different look and "feel."

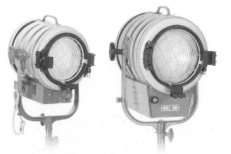

■ **Figure 13-10** Lighting units are designed in either Tungsten (left) or daylight color temperatures, also called HMI's (right) to make the balancing of mixed lighting easier.

Color Temperature

As mentioned in the chapter on film stocks, different sources of light favor different areas of the light spectrum, and the tonality that a light favors is called its **color temperature** (see p. 162 for full description). Color temperature is measured by the Kelvin scale. In discussing film color sensitivity, we already mentioned that average daylight is 6,500°K (quite blue), but the sun can change color temperature quite dramatically over the course of the day. The color temperature of the late afternoon sun can dip to around 4,000°K, and dawn and dusk can be as warm as 2,000°K.

The most common artificial lighting instruments for medium-scale film and DV production are **tungsten lights** (tungsten–halogen) (also called **quartz lights**), which have a color temperature of 3,200°K (quite warm). Tungsten lights are very efficient and powerful for their wattage, but they burn hot and so require ventilation and careful handling. Another kind of light commonly used in bigger budget productions is the HMI (hydrargyrum medium-arc iodide). HMIs are designed to emit a light that matches daylight color temperature, 5,600°K. HMIs are very efficient lights and burn cooler than tungsten lights, but they require a heavy power ballast in addition to the lighting unit itself. This additional encumbrance, along with a higher rental price, make HMIs primarily a professional lighting unit (**Figure 13-10**).

■ CAMERA FILTERS AND LIGHTING GELS

Camera filters and gels are used to change, in some essential way, the quality of light in a scene. The fundamental difference between the two is that **gels** (short for gelatin) are sheets of dyed plastic material that are used in front of a lighting unit (or in a window) in order to alter the quality of that particular light source before it falls on the scene. **Camera filters**, on the other hand, are glass or hard plastic elements mounted in front of the camera lens to change the quality of the light, from all sources, entering the camera.

Altering Light with Filters

Camera filters are mounted in front of a lens in two ways: they either screw directly onto the front of the lens or are held in a matte box. Filters that mount directly onto the lens are usually glass filters inside a mounting ring. These filters come in a wide variety of

■ **Figure 13-11** Matte boxes are useful to block out unwanted light from the lens, and can come equipped with filter holders. They are available for both film and higher-end video cameras.

sizes to match the diameter and mounting threads of various lenses. **Matte boxes** attach to the front of the camera and extend out from the lens to keep unwanted light from glancing off the lens. They usually also have filter holders and slots for holding several rectangular glass or plastic filters (Figure 13-11). It is important to remember that different matte boxes are designed to hold specific filter sizes (i.e., 2×2, 3×3, or 4×4). Make sure that you have the proper size filter for your particular matte box.

There are literally hundreds of different filters on the market, which accomplish a wide range of different effects. Camera filters break down into four broad categories of usage: **color correction**, **exposure control**, **special effects**, and **black-and-white photography**. I have already discussed the two most common color correction filters for film shooting, the Wratten #80A and #85, in the chapter on film stocks (see p. 164). It's not possible to cover every filter available, but the following sections cover a few of the most common and indispensable filters for filmmaking.

■ **Figure 13-12** Neutral density filters are designed to cut the amount of light reaching the lens without changing its color. ND 0.3 (left) reduces light by 1 stop and ND 0.6 (right) cuts the light by 2 stops.

Neutral Density Filters

Neutral density filters (or ND filters) are gray tinted filters that simply cut down the amount of light entering the lens (Figure 13-12). ND filters are exposure control filters and do not affect color at all. An ND 0.3 filter cuts the amount of incoming light in half, or one full stop; an ND 0.6 cuts down two stops and an ND 0.9 cuts down three stops. Obviously, the ND filter is useful if you find yourself shooting with a fast film stock on a brilliantly sunny day; but more frequently, this filter is used when you want to decrease your depth of field without changing your lens, lighting, or composition. By adding ND filters you are forced to compensate for exposure by opening up your aperture, thus decreasing the depth of field.

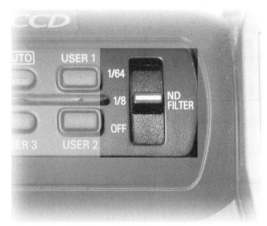

This is especially important when shooting DV where, because of the small size of the imaging device, the depth of field is generally very deep. Many DV cameras have ND filters built-in and accessible either through menus or on a filter wheel (Figure 13-13).

■ **Figure 13-13** Many video cameras come equipped with built-in neutral density filters, accessible through switches or menus; they are especially helpful to decrease depth of field, a common problem with DV cameras.

Diffusion Filters

Diffusion filters are special-effect filters used to soften an image while maintaining sharpness of focus. Exactly how and how much they soften the image is different depending on whether the filter uses a white or black diffusion effect and on the degree of diffusion. **White diffusion** creates a soft haze, from the subtle refracting of white highlights, and **black diffusion** softens the image by delicately flaring the dark, shadow areas of the image. The degree of diffusion is designated by a scale beginning with fractions, ⅛, ¼, and ½ diffusion, and then going from 1 to 5 diffusion. The ⅛, ¼, and ½ diffusion filters show the least amount of diffusion and are not really considered a special effect; the diffusion is barely noticeable except that it slightly smoothes out areas with fine, sharp lines, like skin wrinkles. At 1 and 2 diffusion levels, you will begin to clearly see softer edges on everything and the subtle flaring of white or black areas. By the time you reach a 5 diffusion filter, the soft image becomes a hazy one, creating an overt "dreamy" or "romantic" effect whose use requires some very legitimate narrative motivation (Figure 13-14).

Many shooters feel that the DV image can be excessively harsh and will routinely use a very light, black diffusion (⅛ or ¼) to slightly soften the image's "electronic" edge. For this use, it is important to test various filters (manufacturers and diffusion degrees) to make sure you get the look you are after. Each DV camera responds differently to light diffusion filters.

A   B   C

■ Figure 13-14 Diffusion filters are used to soften the image while maintaining sharp focus. In A, diffusion is minimal. B shows the effects of mild diffusion, while C uses a heavy diffusion filter.

in practice

■ Figure 13-15 Cinematographer Henri Alekan is said to have used a special filter made from his grandmother's silk stockings during the shooting of Wenders' *Wings of Desire* (1987).

It's not uncommon to find cinematographers who make their own diffusion filters by stretching very fine black silk stockings over filter frames, to create a customized diffusion effect. Different cinematographers swear by different brands and grades of hosiery but, anecdotally speaking, it seems that French stockings are preferred. When shooting the black-and-white portions of his film *Wings of Desire* (1987), Wim Wenders had the A.C. try a number of diffusion filters from high-end professional brands, but he was not satisfied with any of their looks. Exasperated, he turned to his D.P., the legendary French cinematographer Henri Alekan, who pulled out of his filter box an old wooden-framed black diffusion filter he made in the 1930s with his grandmother's silk stockings. For Wenders the unique visual quality of this filter, that had been handmade some 50 years earlier, was perfect, and they used it. *Wings of Desire* is acknowledged as being one of the most visually stunning films of all time—thanks to Henri Alekan's grandmother.

Polarizing Filters

When light reflects off shiny surfaces, specifically nonmetallic surfaces like glass or water, it scatters and vibrates in many directions causing glare. A **polarizing filter** (or Pola filter) is used to block light rays that are not parallel when entering the lens. The primary use of a polarizing filter is to reduce or eliminate the obstructing glare and reflections coming off transparent surfaces like glass and water. A polarizing filter is made of two glass elements: one is fixed and one rotates. Each element is manufactured with parallel rows of glass grain, similar to partially opened Venetian blinds. These striated rows block light that is off axis, (Figure 13-16) allowing only light waves that are parallel to one another to pass through the filter. By rotating these layered, parallel grains, a polarizing filter creates an adjustable grid that progressively blocks scattered light (horizontally and vertically) from a selectively wider or narrower axis. Polarizers offer a great amount of creative control because you can easily see, as you rotate the filter, exactly how much glare and reflection you are eliminating (Figure 13-17). Be careful, however, polarizing filters work so well that it is possible to "dial out" all glare and thereby making it seem like there is no glass in a window at all.

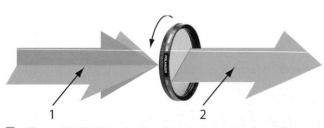

■ Figure 13-16 When shooting shiny, transparent surfaces the reflected and direct light travel together toward the lens (1). To "catch" reflected light, the pola is rotated until it blocks the off axis light rays, so that only direct light (2) passes through.

■ **Figure 13-17** The pola filter at work. Glare on the window makes it difficult to see through it (left). Turning the polarizing filter shows the gradual reduction of the light glancing off the window's surface (middle). At its most effective angle, the pola can almost completely eliminate glare (right).

■ **Figure 13-18** Sometimes reflections can be used as a narrative device, as Wenders did on *Wings of Desire* during the introduction of the angel Cassiel (Otto Sander). The bright neon lights that conceal his presence hint at the ethereal quality of his nature.

Because much of the light that comes from the clear blue part of the sky is reflected light (haze), polarizers are also handy for darkening blue skies to make cloud formations stand out vividly. For this use, the angle of the sun to the filter is important. Darkening blue skies works best with the sun at a 90° angle to the filter, but will not work at all if the sun is along a 180° axis directly in front of or behind the filter.

A polarizer is a neutral filter, so it does not alter the color tonalities of your scene; however, it does take a toll on exposure. Most polarizing filters require a compensation of 1.5 to 2 stops. Also remember that polarizers work through the precise angles between the light and filter elements, so moving the camera by panning or tracking can visually change the polarizing effect.

Graduated Filters

All of the filters discussed so far have an effect on the entire image. **Graduated filters** (also called **grads**), on the other hand, gradually introduce a filter effect into only a portion of the frame, leaving the rest of the frame unaffected. A graduated ND filter, for example, will incorporate a noticeable ND 0.9 at the top of the frame, to darken the sky, but the ND effect will taper off and disappear by the center of the frame, leaving the bottom half of the image completely unchanged. Graduated ND filters are very popular because they reduce the contrast range in an image that might include, say, a bright sky and a shaded area on the ground (Figure 13-19). Graduated color filters are also popular, especially those that affect the color of the sky; examples include the sunset grad filter, which warms up the sky with an amber tint, and the blue grad filter, which deepens blue skies. The

■ **Figure 13-19** Grad filters gradually introduce a filter effect into a portion of the frame, leaving the rest of the frame unaffected. Shown are three graduated ND filters (from left to right) ND 0.9 grad., ND 0.6 grad., and ND 0.3 grad.

■ **Figure 13-20** In Fassbinder's *Veronika Voss* (1982), the dazzling world of celebrated actress Veronika (Rosel Zech) is underlined by the exuberant use of a star filter effect.

transition on all graduated filters, between the effect area and the clear area, comes in two different degrees: **sharp transition**, which means that there is a clearly defined line where the effect tapers off, and **soft transition**, which means that the tapering is much more gradual. Color graduated filters need to be used with some caution, as they are not exactly the most subtle effects you can apply to your image. The effect can be quite noticeable if you fail to conceal the transition area in some compositional element in the scene—for example, placing the transition area in the tree line between the sky and the ground. Camera movement can also reveal the use of the filter.

Black-and-White Photography Filters

Films shot on black and white can benefit from the same ND, polarizing, and diffusion filters mentioned previously, but there are also a few color filters, especially red, green, and yellow, which are commonly used when shooting black-and-white film, to alter contrast and tonality. By employing a color filter, you in effect enhance (or lighten) those colors in the scene that are the same as the filter color and block those that are complementary, darkening those areas in the image. For example, using a green filter will lighten dark green foliage. Using a yellow filter will make a blue sky or blue water darker gray because blue is the complement of yellow and therefore is blocked by the filter. You can control the amount you darken a blue sky by choosing yellow filters that are more or less deeply colored. Amber filters darken blue skies extremely and red filters will turn a blue sky black (which is why red filters are traditionally used when shooting day-for-night special effects). See Appendix 2 for a list of filters often used for black-and-white photography and their effects.

Just as with all craft aspects of film production, when properly used, camera filters can be a powerful tool to refine the look of your film and establish the precise tone or emotional impression you need for your story (Figure 13-20). When unjustified or clumsily employed, however, filters make your footage look downright cheesy. When using camera filters always ask yourself why you've chosen a particular filter, what that filter helps you show or express, and then approach its use with some restraint at first.

Filters and DV Cameras

Not all filters that were made for film cameras work with DV camcorders. The nature of CCD registration, digital resolution, and even DV's inherently deep depth of field can interact poorly with filters made specifically for film camera, causing unexpected results. Fortunately, many companies are now manufacturing filter systems with small-format DV in mind. In any case, always try out your filters, by taking some test footage, before you employ them on the set.

Altering Light with Gels

While filters are mounted in front of the cameras lens and so affect all sources of light, gels, on the other hand, are positioned in front of a specific light source to change the color or quality of that particular light's output before it falls on the scene. There are several different manufacturers of lighting gels offering literally hundreds of different colors, shades, and effects to

■ **Figure 13-21** Gels come in hundreds of colors and intensities, including color correcting, neutral density, and diffusion media. See the color insert in this chapter.

choose from (Figure 13-21). Aside from those designed to create colors, there are also a few utility gels that are absolutely indispensable for the creative filmmaker.

Color Conversion Gels

Color conversion gels are used to change the color temperature of a light source, and they come in two basic flavors: **CTO**, for *color temperature orange,* and **CTB**, for *color temperature blue* (Figure 13-22). Similar to the Wratten #85 camera filter, CTO gels convert daylight (5,600°K) into tungsten color temperature light (3,200°K). CTO gels come in a variety of shades that allow fairly precise control over the change in the color temperature.

■ **Figure 13-22** CTO and CTB gels are used to correct the color temperature of a light source. CTBs are placed on movie lights to make them "daylight," and CTOs are placed on windows to make them "tungsten." See the color insert in this chapter.

Full CTO converts 5,600°K light directly into 3,200°K, but ½ CTO converts 5,600°K daylight to 3,800°K (a little bluer) and ¼ CTO converts 5,600°K daylight to 4,500°K (even bluer). These gels allow the cinematographer a high degree of control in shifting the color tonalities of light sources.

CTB gels convert a tungsten light source to daylight color temperature and are mostly used directly in front of lighting units. **Full blue** converts 3,200°K light into 5,600°K, but CTB also comes in various conversion degrees. For example, ½ CTB converts 3,200°K to 4,100°K (a little warmer) and ¼ CTB converts tungsten to 3,500°K (even warmer).

Color conversion gels and mixed-lighting situations

Whether you are shooting film or digital video, CTO and CTB gels are indispensable for situations in which you have lighting sources with different color temperatures in one location (Figure 13-23). Let's say we have a situation in which we are lighting our subject with tungsten light (3,200°K) but we also have a window with daylight streaming in (5,600°K), visible in the background of the shot. If our camcorder (or film stock) is balanced for daylight, the subject will look as orange as a carrot; conversely, if we are balanced for tungsten, the window light will turn an unnatural blue. What to do? There are two ways we can balance the lighting in this situation.

We can cover the window with CTO gel and white balance the DV camera to tungsten light (or shoot with tungsten-balanced film), since now all lighting sources are tungsten color temperature. The difficulty with this approach is that it's not so easy to cover a window with gel, especially large windows. Lining windows requires that you carefully tape the gel to the window frame, making sure that there are no wrinkles that will refract light and reveal the gel. It can certainly be done, but it takes a little time and prac-

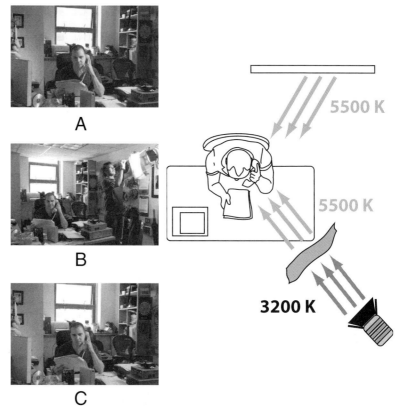

■ **Figure 13-23** Shooting with daylight film (or a DV camera white balanced for daylight) matches the sunlight coming through the window, but records tungsten light as excessively orange (A). Placing a CTB gel over the tungsten unit changes it to daylight (B), matching the color temperature of all sources (C). See the color insert in this chapter.

■ **Figure 13-24** Neutral density gels work just like their glass counterparts, cutting the intensity of light without changing its quality or color. They are usually used on windows to cut down the amount of sunlight coming in. Pictured are ND 0.6 (left) and ND 0.3 (right).

tice. The other option would be to cover your tungsten lights with CTB gel and white balance your DV camera to daylight (or shoot with daylight-balanced film or tungsten film with a Wratten #85 filter), since all lighting sources are now daylight color temperature. While putting a gel in front of a light is easier, there are drawbacks to this approach, too. On a super bright day you might not want to sacrifice any of your tungsten light's intensity, because doing so creates greater contrast between the tungsten areas and the bright sunlight areas. Both solutions work, so choosing one depends on your specific situation. The principle to remember is to use gels to change the color temperature of one source to match the other. Keep in mind that anytime you put a gel in front of a light source you reduce the intensity of that light somewhat. Full CTB reduces intensity around 2 stops and full CTO cuts the light by about ⅔ stop (actual light loss depends on the distance between the unit and the gel).

Also, remember that ½ and ¼ color conversion allows you to truly control the color. Let's say the image you are shooting is a winter scene and you want it to feel like it's cold outside but warm inside the house. You might choose only a ½ blue gel for the interior lights, which would convert them only partially to daylight, maintaining the warmth of your interior sources.

Neutral Density Gels

Just as with ND filters, **neutral density gels** are gray and do not affect the color of a light source: they simply cut down its intensity (Figure 13-24). ND 0.3 cuts intensity by one stop; ND 0.6, by two stops; and ND 0.9, by three stops. Because these gels are very often used in windows to moderate the intensity of light pouring into interior scenes, you will often find ND mixed with CTO in a single gel. A CTO ND 0.6, for example, will change the color temperature of the daylight to 3,200°K and will also reduce the intensity of the window 2⅔ stops (2 stops for the ND and ⅔ stop for the CTO).

Diffusion Media

Diffusion media is used to soften the output of a hard light source (i.e., open face or Fresnel light). Using diffusion instead of bringing along a genuine soft light unit to the location is often more practical, since soft lights tend to be large and bulky (see later). Diffusion can be used as a single layer or doubled or tripled to increasingly soften the light. While softer light is very flattering, especially for lighting faces, the trade-offs are that diffusion can cut light intensity drastically and the spill of diffused light is harder to control with barndoors or flags. Diffusion is not called a gel because there are many different kinds of diffusion, made from a variety of materials that determine the degree and texture of the diffusion. Tough spun (made of spun glass), tough frost, grid cloth and tough opal are some common diffusion materials. The designation "tough" on any gel indicates that it is heat resistant and can be placed on barndoors—with caution (see p. 269) (Figure 13-25).

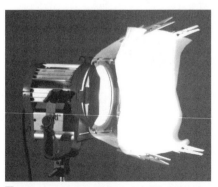

■ **Figure 13-25** While some diffusion and gels can be attached directly to barndoors, it is a good idea to use C-47s (better known as wooden clothespins) to provide an extra level of security against melting and fires.

■ **LIGHT AND DIRECTIONALITY**

When we devise our lighting strategy, among our most fundamental considerations, along with the qualities of light, is the question of directionality. Where is this light coming from? Even if we are simply shooting a film with one actor in a park with no artificial lights, by positioning the actor to face one way or another, in order to have the sun fall in a specific way on our subject, we are in fact controlling the directionality of our light source—we are lighting.

It is crucial to know that the visual emphasis and dramatic potential of lights change significantly given their placement in relation to the illuminated object. The placement of the lighting unit not only determines the

■ **Figure 13-26** The overhead lighting used in Coppola's *The Godfather* (1972) created deep shadows over Vito Corleone's (Marlon Brando) eyes, adding an inscrutable quality to his character. In Welles' *Mr. Arkadin* (1955) a light placed low on the ground throws an ominous shadow as a murderer gets away.

directionality of the light source, but also the direction and length of the shadows. By gaining control of light and shadow you gain control over the motion picture's most powerful elements for creating depth, texture, mood, tone, and even character and narrative meaning in your frame (Figure 13-26).

It is always helpful to remember that the range of light placement options is three dimensional. We can place our lights anywhere in the imaginary globe that surrounds our subject: in front, behind, along the side, high above, below, near, far—any angle, any distance, as long as the lights stay out of the frame of the shot (although this, too, is not an absolute rule). As a point of reference, here are a few basic light angles (see Figure 13-27), which depicts a single, hard light source at the camera's level. Remember, don't just look at the direction of the light, but at the throw of shadows as well.

A. **Frontal light** is illumination that comes essentially from the angle of the camera. Because the light rays duplicate the camera's angle of vision, most of the shadows are not visible to the lens as they fall straight back. Frontal light has a very flat look resulting from the absence of visible shadows.

B. Move the light along an arc, away from the camera, and shadows start to appear and get more prominent as the light moves farther from the camera position. A ¾ **frontal light** is a lighting unit that is positioned 45° from the camera. Notice how the shadows cast by this light are at 45° angles. This light position is often also raised vertically by 45° as well.

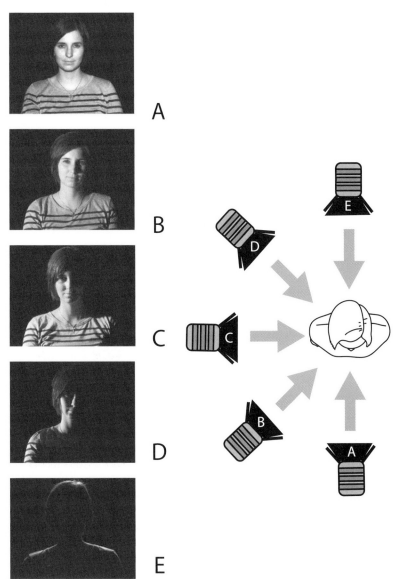

■ **Figure 13-27** The placement of lighting units determines the angle of illumination and the angle at which shadows fall. Placement is a critical factor in creating depth, mood, texture and even a sense of character. Pictured are five standard angles along the same horizontal plane: (A) frontal; (B) 3/4 front; (C) side; (D) 3/4 back and (D) back (rim light).

■ **Figure 13-28** The vertical angle of a lighting unit can dramatically change the look of a subject. Pictured are a high angle frontal (left) and a low angle frontal (right).

C. Move this light another 45° away from the camera so that it is now positioned at a 90° angle from the camera and we have a **side light**. This light comes directly from the side of the subject and has the effect of dividing the illuminated object in half, one side lit and the other in shadows. Side light maximizes shadows and therefore texture as well.

D. Moving this light another 45° away from the camera, we have a ¾ **back light**. The area that this position lights is mostly hidden from the camera, but we do see bright highlights on the top and side edges of the subject. Notice how this angle causes the light to illuminate the shoulder and hair and cuts the light side of the figure out from the background while allowing the other side to blend into the shadows. This placement for a back light is so common that it even has its own nickname, a **kicker**. This light is also commonly raised vertically by 45° as well to catch slightly more of the hair and shoulders.

E. Finally, move this light another 45° from the camera and the light is now 180° across from the camera, illuminating the subject's back. The camera can see only a small sliver of illumination around the top of our subject, as the front falls completely into shadow. This light is commonly called a **rim** light.

In addition to the horizontal angles, you need to also consider the dramatic changes in shadow and mood as you adjust the lighting unit's **height** (or **vertical angle**) from **high angle** to **low angle** (Figure 13-28).

■ FUNDAMENTAL LIGHTING SETUPS AND PRINCIPLES

Like all other art forms, lighting for film requires creativity, craft, experimentation, and experience. When you first start out, movie lighting can seem somewhat mysterious and tremendously time consuming. Simply answering the most basic questions (Where do I physically place the lights with respect to the subject and camera? What quality of light—intensity, hard, soft, etc.—should I use? How does this one light work in combination with the other lights?) can seem intricate and arbitrary. But with a little bit of book research, some hands-on experience, and by listening to the stories of other filmmakers who faced similar lighting challenges, you will quickly develop a repertoire of lighting approaches, styles, and techniques that you can confidently draw upon and build upon from one film to the next. What follows is a discussion of the most commonly used lights in the craft.

Key Light

The key light is the primary source of illumination in your scene. For scenes in which a realistic or naturalistic look is needed, the key light should be a **motivated light source**, which means that when positioning this light we must consider the ostensible and logical source within the scene for that illumination. It might be that we actually use the sun streaming into a window for our key light, or we may use an artificial light to simulate the sun streaming into the window in a naturalistic way. We might place our key light at a high angle to simulate an overhead street lamp on a dark night, or as a side light to simulate a reading lamp on a desk, or at a low angle to simulate the glow from a fireplace. In all of these cases, the placement of the key light is motivated by the ostensible source, visible in the frame or not, and its logical throw. Obviously, the key light can be placed anywhere. In cases where a pool of light creates a silhouette, the key light doesn't even fall on our subject (Figure 13-30). Usually, the key light is a hard and bright light source, but certainly not always. It's not uncommon to see soft keys being used in films.

Always keep in mind that you are not on your own when it comes to devising lighting strategies to tell your story. The works and accomplishments of generations of cinematographers are only a DVD rental away for you to study and learn from. Henri Alekan, Gregg Toland, James Wong Howe, and Karl Freund are four of the early masters of light whose work is more available now than ever before. Their methods and tools were often much simpler than those used in modern films, but their imagination, ingenuity, and understanding of light itself is unparalleled. The images are veritable and valuable textbooks on lighting. Over the years the old li-ons of dramatic film lighting like these (who themselves drew from previous generations of masters of photography, theater, and painting) developed a body of fundamental lighting setups that are used, in some combination, in most film lighting situations today. The basic setups (see Figure 13-31) represent the building blocks of the cinematographer's craft. Knowing these fundamental setups; which combine directionality, quality of light, and function, will help you to understand how to create certain dramatic visual effects, and will also help you determine an answer to the most basic question: Where do I put this light?

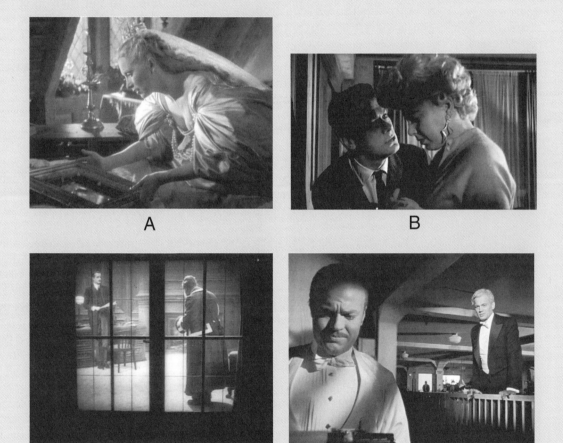

■ **Figure 13-29** Four masters of light and shadow to learn from: (A) Henri Alekan (from Cocteau's *Beauty and the Beast*, 1946), (B) James Wong Howe (from Mackendrick's *Sweet Smell of Success*, 1957), (C) Karl Freund (from Murnau's *The Last Laugh*, 1924), and (D) Greg Toland (from Welles' *Citizen Kane*, 1941).

■ **Figure 13-30** Careful placement of the key light off the subject in Laughton's *The Night of the Hunter* (1955) effectively reverses the conventional association of light with good and darkness with evil by silhouetting righteous Rachel (Lillian Gish) while illuminating evil preacher Harry (Robert Mitchum).

Fill Light

As you can see in the directionality examples (see Figure 13-27), a hard light (like most key lights) casts sharp and dark shadows. When lighting people, this means nose and chin shadows and sunken eyes. A **fill light** is a soft light that is positioned to fill in the shadows created by the key light. Using a fill light is not mandatory, but it is very commonly used in most lighting setups. The reason that fill lights are soft lights is that it would be counterproductive if the light we use for filling in shadows itself created additional shadows.

There are two schools of thought concerning the placement of fill lights. One states that the fill light should be placed opposite the key light, which makes sense, given that it has to fill in the shadows that fall exactly opposite the illuminated area. Other people prefer to place their fill light as close to the lens as possible, creating a soft frontal light. This way, despite it being a soft light, if there are any shadows cast by the fill, they fall straight back and out of view of the camera. Both methods work well, so experiment with this yourself and see which works best in your situation.

The degree to which you decide to fill in those shadows varies depending on the look you are after. You can choose to keep shadows quite dark, but fill in just enough to see some detail in the shadows, or you could almost completely fill the shadows with soft illumination, flattening out the image to create a bright scene in which everything is visible. The critical factor in determining the density of the shadows is the intensity of the fill light. The stronger the fill light, the less prominent the shadows will be (see later, Lighting Ratios).

Fill lights are not generally considered as motivated light sources, although when you're going for a realistic look, you do need to be aware of unnatural fill. For example, if we're shooting a scene in which two characters are talking in front of an idling car in the middle of the night, with the main and only source of illumination ostensibly being the car headlights (key light), you can get away with some very light fill to boost the exposure on the shadow side of the face, because it could be mimicking the way the human eye adjusts in dark conditions. But excessive fill in this situation would look as if the light was coming from an off-camera artificial lighting unit being used by a film crew to light the scene.

Backlight

A **backlight** is a light that separates the subject from the background by positioning a somewhat lower intensity hard to semi-soft light at a high angle and behind the subject. This creates, along the edge of the subject, a rim of light that clearly traces the edges of the figure and helps create depth in the frame. When lighting people, this light is often a ¾ back light (or kicker), positioned opposite the key, which illuminates the hair and shoulders of the subject. Obviously the color of the subject's hair is a factor in determining the intensity of the backlight. Blonde hair tends to thin out and create a halo when intense back lights are used.

Backlights are notoriously easy to overuse. Overly intense backlight coming from seemingly nowhere will give your shot a highly artificial feeling. Automatically employing a ¾ backlight opposite the key can quickly make an image seem generic. For this reason, backlights are often considered a motivated light source needing some logical source; whether it's an existing overhead light, the sun behind the character, a neon sign in the background, or a wall sconce over the subject's shoulder.

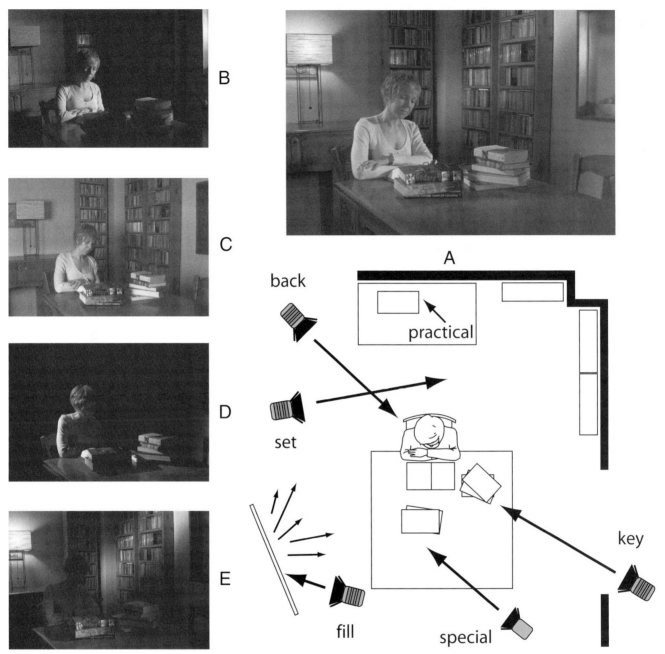

Figure 13-31 The individual elements used in the lighting setup for this typical scene (A) include: The *key light* (B); *fill light* (C); *back light* (D); and a *set light* focused on the shelves (E). There are two other lights as well: a small *special* light on the books and a lamp *practical* (E). Notice that the lamp is not powerful enough to serve as a backlight, but it provides the motivation for the backlight (D).

Backlights are especially helpful when shooting very dark objects that absorb light. An object with low reflectivity, like a black curtain or dark wood bar counter, cannot be adequately lit simply by pouring light onto it, because it simply will not reflect the light back. Instead, a backlight, glancing off the edges of the dark object will create a rim of illumination that will serve to define and highlight its dimensions.

Set Lights

Set lights are used to light the larger area of the set: the architecture, furniture, set dressing, etc. The angle and intensity of set lights are greatly determined by the key light, as the setting often shares the same motivated primary source of light, so this must remain consistent.

Tim Burton's film *Ed Wood* is a good example of the creative use of the basic lighting positions. The lighting design of the film, which was shot by Stefan Czapsky, clearly references the lighting of the B-movie horror genre of the 1950s, but it also manages to appear substantially more polished and expressive. Burton is obviously not making a straight up B-movie; instead, he is telling a poignant, tragic, and at times hilarious story of Ed Wood (Johnny Depp) and Bela Lugosi (Martin Landau), the alienation they experience, and the community of supportive misfits, loners, and outcasts they forge through making movies. Just like the screenplay, the lighting style is at one and the same time humorous, camp, and touching.

Figure 13-32 Three expressive lighting examples from Burton's *Ed Wood* (1994) which make especially dramatic use of: a soft fill light (top); a low angle, hard key light (middle); and hard backlight motivated by visible practicals (bottom).

- **Fill Light:** In the top still in Figure 13-32, Ed takes his new true love Kathy (Patricia Arquette) out on their first date to a carnival and, naturally, they take a turn through Ed's favorite carnival ride, the "Spook House!" In the middle of the ride it breaks down and they're stuck. All of the lights that have been swirling around them stop, and the couple is lit only by soft, low-intensity fill and hard backlights. The lighting creates a calm, flat, and honest tone—no deep murky shadows here. Ed takes this opportunity to tell Kathy that he likes her a lot and that he likes to wear women's clothing, hoping that she'll be okay with all of it. Kathy thinks a moment and then says, "Okay." At that moment the Spook House ride comes alive again, complete with swirling lights.

- **Key Light:** Bela (center still) is lit with a very low-angle, hard key light, making him look especially ghoulish. This is typical of the excessive lighting approach of B-movie horror films; however, the content of the scene is anything but campy. Bela is broke, addicted to drugs, and completely at the end of his tether; he is holding a gun while Ed is trying to keep him from committing suicide. The lighting here creates a profoundly unnerving ironic tension between a genre style that we can't take seriously and desperate human emotions that we must.

- **Backlight:** All of the light (bottom still) in this beautifully designed shot is motivated. The key light comes from the candle (augmented) on the bar counter under Ed, and the backlight is designed to appear to be coming from the chandeliers hanging in the background (also augmented). Notice the important function the backlights serve in illuminating the curves of the bar countertop, Ed's cigarette smoke, and glass ashtrays. Dark objects and transparent material (glass, smoke, water) are difficult to light from the front. Backlighting that glances off the surface creates a gleam that defines the dimensions of the object while keeping the overall look of the scene dark—the way a dimly lit bar should look.

Specials and Practicals

Specials are low-wattage, unobtrusive lights whose function is to kick up the illumination on a specific object or a small area of the frame for special emphasis. Careful control of specials can help create compositional emphasis to guide the viewer's eye by increasing the relative exposure level (by 1 or 1½ stops) on an important area or object in the image.

Lights that are included as part of the mise-en-scène, including wall sconces, household lamps, and overhead fixtures, are called **practicals**. In some cases they can provide some illumination (Figure 13-33), but usually they are not powerful or controllable enough for a good exposure. More often than not, they are set dressing and they also provide the motivation for the movie lighting setup by being the ostensible source, as is the case with the chandeliers in the third *Ed Wood* still in Figure 13-32 and the lamp in Figure 13-31.

■ **Figure 13-33** In this scene from Kelly Lewis' short film *Pretty See, Pretty Do* (2006), practicals were strong enough to provide illumination for the inside of the store, but required additional movie lights for the shots right outside of it.

Three-Point Lighting

Three-point lighting refers to a specific and commonly used lighting strategy that employs a key light (usually a ¾ frontal light, positioned at 45° from the camera and at a 45° vertical angle), a fill light (usually opposite the key), and a back light (usually a ¾ back) (Figure 13-34). You can see three-point lighting used extensively in television dramas and interviews. Three-point lighting is quick and efficient and occasionally a good starting point for a lighting approach. However, it's important not to think of three-point lighting as a rule that must be observed in each and every shot, and it's especially problematic to think that one should *always* light people with the three-point lighting scheme. Automatically following conventional approaches by rote can only lead to bland images.

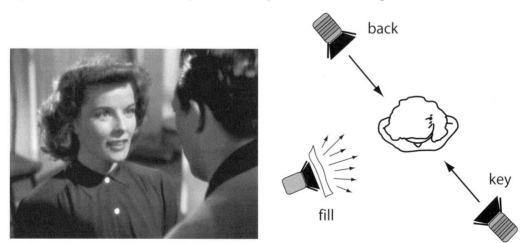

■ **Figure 13-34** A typical three-point lighting setup consists of a key light, a fill light, and a backlight. This setup was considered the standard for decades during the studio system era in Hollywood, as seen in this scene from Hawks' *Bringing up Baby* (1938).

Lighting Ratios

The amount of shadows contained in our scene and their depth relative to the illuminated areas provide our image with a sense of tone, mood, compositional emphasis, and even narrative meaning (Figure 13-35). Through lighting control, we can easily create an image with relatively few shadows or one in which shadows dominate the composition. We can use artificial lights and manipulate the depth of the shadows to create a naturalistic look or an expressionistic tone. The dramatic needs of your story should suggest to you the look you need, but understanding how shadows are measured and controlled is important to getting the look you need.

■ **Figure 13-35** At a key point in Mulligan's *To Kill a Mockingbird* (1962), we are unable to see the face of "Boo" Radley and can't fathom his intentions. When the door is moved and light falls on his face, we realize he was in fact scared. For the dramatic reveal to work, the preceding exposures had to be carefully selected to keep Boo's face underexposed.

Lighting ratios (also called **key-to-fill ratio**) are an indication of the relative intensities of the major light sources illuminating your subject: the key light and the fill light. The key light, as we know, is the primary source of illumination, but the fill light, being a soft source, not only fills the shadows created by the key light, but also spills onto the key side and augments the amount of light falling in the areas lit by the key. For his reason, the ratio between the primary illumination and the fill light is expressed as, **key + fill:fill**. This means that, to find this ratio, you need to first meter your subject with the key and fill lights falling on the scene. Then you meter only the fill light (by blocking the key from the lumisphere or turning it off, if possible) and then divide these two readings. For example, if the key + fill gives a light intensity reading of 640 footcandles and the fill light alone reads 160 footcandles, then the lighting ratio is 640:160, which can be simplified as 4:1. The primary illumination is four times brighter than the fill. This ratio can also be arrived at through a comparison of f-stop meter readings. If the key + fill gives you a meter reading of f/8 and the fill only comes in at f/4, then we have a two-stop difference, for a 4:1 ratio again (each stop doubling the light, 2×2).

Lighting ratios help us specifically determine the relationship between light and shadows, especially when shooting on film where you cannot see your image. A lighting setup with a low ratio, like 2:1 or 3:1, means that the fill light is filling in shadows until they are quite light. A lighting ratio of 1:1 would mean that both key and fill are the same intensity and there are no shadows at all. A lighting setup with a *low* key-to-fill ratio is called (somewhat confusingly) **high-key lighting**. High-key lighting ensures visibility in all parts of your scene with overall bright and even illumination. High-key lighting minimizes shadows, texture, and dimensionality.

Conversely, a high lighting ratio, say 16:1 or 36:1, will yield very dark and prominent shadow areas. This occurs when the intensity of the fill light is considerably lower than the key, allowing areas to be submerged in the shadows created by the key. A lighting setup with a *high* key-to-fill ratio is called, you guessed it, **low-key lighting** (Figure 13-36).

■ **Figure 13-36** Controlling the ratio between the key and the fill produces high-key (left) and low-key (right) images, as done with the lighting of Dorrie (Charlotte Rampling) in Allen's *Stardust Memories* (1980).

in practice

It is difficult, and rather pointless, to ascribe absolute and fixed moods to high-key and low-key lighting approaches (as many film books do). It is true that many comedies, like John Hughes' *Ferris Bueller's Day Off* (1986), employ high-key lighting strategies to create a lighthearted and cheerful mood. One could even say that high-key lighting is closely associated with this sort of comedy movie. But many films use high-key lighting to create a mood of cold, austere alienation. High-key lighting can also be used in situations where flattening out the image might provide a sense of an unforgiving environment, or dramatic irony, or could even infuse a scene with a soft, affectionate tone. Jun Ichikawa's film *Tony Takitani* (2004), for example, is a close examination of a man's profound loneliness and emotional seclusion. The austerity of Tony's surroundings and the flat, high-key lighting accentuate his physical isolation and emotional flatness as well as creating a stark metaphor for the meager resources he has to express his feelings of loss and solitude.

It's the same with low-key lighting, which is commonly used in the darkly lit film noir and

horror genres and psychological dramas. Paul Haggis' 2004 film *Crash*, for example, employs an overall visual look that is decidedly dark and shadowy for its unflinching exploration of the problematic issues of racism and violence in America. But many lighthearted action pictures or horror film parodies have successfully used low-key lighting for laughs. Steven Spielberg's *Raiders of the Lost Ark* (1981) is a good example in which humorous or lighthearted scenes are often lit with heavy shadows and dark tones.

The specific tone that emerges from your image depends on the unique alchemy of your lighting design and your story, characters, settings, and other creative elements. Again, there are no absolutes in the creative process of making a film, from writing the script to conceiving your lighting strategy. Indeed, there are conventions associated with high-key and low-key lighting, but conventions are not rules, and you, as a filmmaker, need to marshal all of your creative instincts and technical prowess into making your movie look and feel the way it should to effectively convey your story and ideas.

Figure 13-37 High-key lighting has been used in such dramatically different films as Hughes' *Ferris Bueller's Day Off* (1986, top left) and Ichikawa's *Tony Takitani* (2004, top right). Low-key lighting can be seen in films with completely different emotional tones like Haggis' *Crash* (2004, bottom left) and Spielberg's *Raiders of the Lost Ark* (1981, bottom right).

The narrative of Woody Allen's semiautobiographical film, *Stardust Memories* (1980) (which is also an homage to Fellini's film, *8½*), follows a famous comic filmmaker who is having a crisis of faith during a weekend retrospective of his films. As he contends with the audience, fans, movie critics, and the stress of finishing his new film, memories of the women in his life, primarily his great love Dorrie, flood back to him. Two specific flashbacks of Dorrie are photographed with starkly different lighting approaches. The first scene is the last time he saw her. Dorrie is in a hospital, suffering from a nervous breakdown, and the relationship is clearly over. The hard source, low-key lighting supports our feeling that this is a woman in total mental distress. Then, toward the end of the film, Allen's character, Sandy, has a flashback to a perfect moment in his life, a brief moment on one beautiful spring Sunday morning, with he and Dorrie simply relaxing and listening to music, when he felt truly happy. In this scene Dorrie is shot in a soft, high-key lighting style that permeates the scene with the affection Sandy has for her and the contentment he feels at this moment (see Figure 13-36).

■ EXTERIOR LIGHTING

Shooting outdoors does not mean simply accepting the light nature has to offer. In fact, the minute you ask your talent to face a specific direction in order to have the sun illuminating them from a particular angle, you are "lighting" the scene. All of the preceding principles about lighting apply to exterior shooting; the only difference is that student and low-budget independent filmmakers usually do not have extensive time, money, or crew to indulge in the sizable lighting equipment (like generators, HMIs, and 20′×20′ silks) needed to artificially enhance the available light of exterior scenes. When lighting exterior scenes we must be crafty concerning the way we control our light sources: the sun during daylight hours and available artificial light during nighttime hours. A few tips are offered in the following sections.

Location Scouting

When lighting is crucial, take the time to scout your location to figure out the period during which the light is just right, and schedule your production around that moment. Remember, the sun is constantly shifting, so when timing is critical make sure to schedule your call early, allowing for setup time and run throughs so you'll be ready to shoot when the

in practice

My colleague Gustavo Mercado recently shot a scene for his feature film *Becoming* (2007) that involved a simple LS two-shot conversation between two people in front of a river.

Mercado wanted to obscure these figures by showing them as silhouettes against the bright sun glistening off the water behind them. The talent would be on the east side of the river, with the camera facing west. Obviously, he needed to shoot somewhat later in the day so that the sun, in the western sky, would be glancing off the water toward the camera. Mercado and his producer took an afternoon to simply sit where the camera would be placed and watched the shifting angle of the sun—occasionally snapping some digital photos. They determined that 5:45 pm was perfect. Two days later they arrived on location at 4:00 pm, set up the gear, ran a few rehearsals, and waited until the moment was perfect. In less than 20 minutes they nailed two good takes and this important scene was in the can.

■ **Figure 13-38** In this scene from Mercado's *Becoming* (2007), careful research into the position of the sun at a specific time of the day was necessary to capture this arresting shot.

light is just right. If your schedule doesn't allow this much flexibility and you are required to shoot whenever you can get the location, you should scout the location at the time you anticipate shooting, to get a good sense for the angle of the sun during your shooting hours.

Check the Weather

To be fully prepared, part of your production task should involve regularly checking the cable or online weather service to determine if it will be sunny, partly cloudy, or overcast, as well as determining exact sunrise and sunset times. The degree of cloud cover drastically changes the tone and mood of your exterior image (Figure 13-39). Overcast days diffuse the sun, creating, in effect, a soft, high-key look. Depending on the thickness of the cloud cover and the angle of the sun, there can be more or less directionality to this soft source. Sunny days produce a hard and bright light, which can create a high contrast situation between the brightly lit portions of your subject

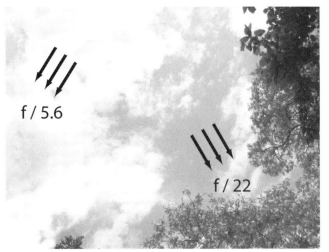

■ **Figure 13-39** A cloudy day can present a difficult exposure challenge, since available light can change in a couple of seconds. The difference between sunny and cloudy areas can be as much as four or five f-stops!

and the accompanying deep, dark shadows. Exposures have to be carefully considered on these days. Partly cloudy conditions, especially on windy days when the sun plays hide-and-seek, are particularly challenging because exposures can shift dramatically from one shot to the next or even within a single take. On these days it's not possible to simply set your exposure and forget it.

Subject and Camera Positions

Just as with shooting indoors using artificial lights, your first lighting consideration when shooting exterior shots is where to place the key light. In this case, you cannot move your key (the sun) to change its directionality, but you *can* move the orientation of your subject and camera to get the angle you desire. Simply by turning your subject you can get a side light, ¾ frontal, ¾ back light, etc.

Sun plus Bounced Light

Perhaps the most useful lighting instrument for exterior shooting is the **reflector board** (also called **bounce board**). A reflector board is a flat, broad, and lightweight board used to bounce light from a source (artificial or sunlight) onto your scene. Whether you make it yourself or buy it, a reflector should have two sides with different reflective qualities. One side has a white, **diffused surface** that simultaneously bounces and diffuses a hard light source, like the sun. The other side is a **specular** (or **hard**) side that reflects and maintains the hard quality of the source, much like a mirror.

If you consider the direct sun as your key light, then you can think of placing a bounce board (diffuse side) opposite the sun, to soften and bounce its light right back to fill in the harsh shadows. One light source (the sun) becomes both a key and fill light (Figure 13-40).

Shade plus Bounced Light

When the direct sun is too intense, you can always simply move your subject into the shade of a tree or a building (if your locations and script allow it). Heavy shade, however, can flatten out the image, and in cases where this is not appropriate, you can always use the specular side of the reflector board to bounce some of that hard sunlight onto your subject in the shade, creating a sharp backlight or side light, to provide a little dimensionality to the image.

Magic Hour

The "*magic hour*" is that time just before sunrise and just after sunset when the Earth's atmosphere bounces the hidden sun's light, creating a diffused and luminous ambient light. People, objects, and landscapes look spectacular during magic hour. While there is certainly enough light to get fine exposures, the problem with shooting during this time is that the window of

■ **Figure 13-40** Direct sun is used as a hard back light and also bounced back onto the talent to provide a soft fill (left). When subjects are in the shade (right), a reflector can bounce sunlight back onto the subject to get a better exposure and a narrower contrast range.

opportunity, before night falls (evening magic hour) or daylight breaks through (morning magic hour), is very short. For most of the continental United States, magic hour lasts around 25 minutes, which makes for very limited shooting time, so it's not terribly convenient in terms of production schedules. The actual duration of magic hour depends on a location's latitude and time of year. One reason you see so many luminous shots of polar bears and penguins is that magic hour can last many hours in the Arctic region (Figure 13-41).

Dusk and Night Shooting

Dusk-for-Night

One very convincing and inexpensive method for shooting scenes that ostensibly take place at night is to shoot dusk-for-night. Just after the sun has set, at the moment when there is still ambient light in the sky but street lights, car headlights, and building lights start to turn on, is the perfect moment to create a full nighttime effect. The dusk-for-night effect is achieved by shooting at dusk and underexposing your film 1½ to 2 stops. Your subject and the surrounding environment will appear dark, but visible, and those streetlamps, head-lights, and building lights will glow like beacons at night. Dusk never lasts long; you usually have a window of about only 25 minutes to get your shots (Figure 13-41).

Shooting at Night

Given the startling developments in CCD sensitivity and film stocks (EIs reaching 500 and even 800!), it is more possible than ever to actually shoot nighttime scenes at night with available light and small portable lighting units to create highlights and emphasis. Obviously, you cannot shoot a scene in a farm field under moonlight and expect to get an exposure, but if you keep your frame tight, shop window lights and bright street lamps can give you more than accept-able exposures. You can also augment these available sources with small, battery-powered lights. Nighttime shooting is tricky, and tests are especially recommended (Figure 13-41).

■ BASIC LIGHTING AND GRIP EQUIPMENT

As I mentioned above, film stocks and CCD chips are increasingly capable of shooting in low light situations. Because of this, the need for huge, bulky, and high-powered lighting units has greatly diminished. For most lighting situations, a student shooting on EI 500, EI 320, or even EI 250 film, or shooting with an industrial grade DV camera, needn't employ any lights that consume more than 2,000 watts of power. Even at that, there is a dizzying array of lights available for low-budget film and DV production, with new ones being devel-oped all of the time. It would be impossible to present them all in this book, but the follow-ing sections present some lighting units that are commonly used by students and low-bud-get independent filmmakers.

- **Magic Hour:** In the 1978 film *Days of Heaven,* directed by Terrence Malick and photographed by Néstor Almendros, many of the scenes were famously shot during magic hour with no artificial lighting. The film is widely considered to be one of the most visually stunning films in the history of cinema. However, shooting extensively during magic hour severely limited the amount of time available per shooting day (according to Almendros, magic "hour" lasted around 25 minutes each day), so the production schedule was drastically extended, so much so that Almendros, contractually obligated to begin another film, had to leave the project before it was finished and the film was completed by another cinematographer, Haskell Wexler.

- **Dusk-for-Night:** Shooting dusk-for-night is a good alternative when lighting is not available for real night shooting. Student filmmaker Jessica Daniels ends her short film *Cycle Unknown* (2006) with a striking shot photographed using the dusk-for-night technique. The lead character, Frank, leaves his laudromat after a long, disappointing day in which he has lost faith in humanity, disillusioned by the object of his desires, the gorgeous Marie, because of her filthy, sloppy laundry. This scene, which takes place at night, was shot at dusk and underexposed a few stops. Notice the im-

portance of the bright point lights in the frame, adding to the illusion of night. Without them, the scene would simply look underexposed and murky.

- **Shooting at Night:** The right-hand still in Figure 13-41 is from Gustavo Mercado's innovative short film *Yield* (2006). The film replays a particularly violent and ambiguous moment that had been witnessed by the lead character—each time she recalls the moment, new clues begin to emerge, but we can't be sure if her memories, and the events of the film, are fact or selective perception. In one very tense scene, the lead character meets up with a girl she perhaps saw brutalized earlier in the day; the scene takes place at a bus station late at night. Mercado was working fast, small, and with minimal equipment resources, so he carefully scouted for a location that, all on its own, had plenty of light to expose the film well, even in the late nighttime hours. He chose a sidewalk next to a rental car dealership that lit its expansive parking lot with very bright sodium street lights. To this he added fill from two cheap, portable, battery-powered flood lights he bought at a hardware store. By using what was available in a resourceful way, Mercado was able, even without a generator, HMI movie lights, and a big crew, to create a stunning nighttime image to match this equally stunning moment in the film.

■ **Figure 13-41** Magic hour cinematography as seen in Malick's *Days of Heaven* (1978, left). A dusk-for-night scene from Daniels' *Cycle Unknown* (2006, middle). A night scene shot at night from Mercado's *Yield* (2006, right).

Like all specialized professions, film production has specific and often colorful terminology for its tools. The jargon isn't just to be cute: using the proper language, names, and common terms is essential to getting things done quickly and precisely. We certainly wouldn't want our heart surgeon to ask the nurse, "Uhh, could you hand me that . . . thing . . . you know it's yea-long and has a hook-like end on it and it holds stuff. . . ." So, too, on the film set you shouldn't be vague by saying things like, "Could you point a light over there?" With a little reading and experience you'll soon be telling your grips, "Grab a stinger and set up that tweenie on a polecat. And let's lose the cookie and go with some spun, so make sure you have enough C-47s."

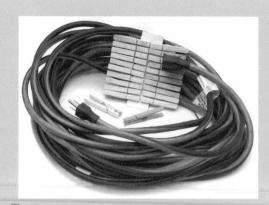

■ **Figure 13-42** Although these may look like wooden clothespins and an extension cord, filmmakers know them as "C-47's" and a "stinger."

Lighting Units

Open-faced Lights

Open-faced lights are units that consist of an open lamp (no lens) and a specular reflector system. Open-faced lights are a hard light source and act primarily as set lights (and occasionally as key lights) and are either used as a direct source or bounced to soften the beam. The **open-faced spot** is a common open-faced unit that has a movable lamp, allowing it to focus its throw somewhat from a broad to a more narrowly defined area. **Broads**, which are open-faced lights with no spotting capability, simply deliver a hard, efficiently bright light. Both lights come in a variety of intensities from 250 watts to 2K (**Figure 13-43**).

Fresnels

Fresnels are one of the most common and versatile lighting units on a film set. What distinguishes a Fresnel is its unique lens and its movable lamp, which allows it to spot its beam with fair precision. Fresnels are named after Augustin Jean Fresnel, the French physicist who designed the shape of the lens. It was already known that plano-convex lenses had the ability to focus light rays and maintain intensity, but they are quite heavy, delicate, and retain a great deal of heat. Monsieur Fresnel simply cut this lens almost in half, but maintained the plano-convex contour by cutting the duplicate curvature into a series of concentric circles. This made the lens lighter and cooler but maintained its ability to focus the beam (**Figure 13-44**). Fresnels are rather hard lights, so the beam is controllable with flags or barndoors, though the textured lens does soften the light somewhat. Fresnels can be either tungsten lights (3,200°K) or HMIs (5,600°K). They also come in various sizes and wattages. The lower wattages (100w–650w) and smaller lens sizes are used as specials and kickers. The medium wattages (650w–2K) are commonly used to light people and can be a key light source. Large Fresnels (2K–10K and large lenses) are used as large area key lights and set lights (**Figure 13-45**).

■ **Figure 13-43** The open faced spot (left) has a movable lamp allowing it to focus its throw somewhat. Broads (right) are open-faced lights with no spotting capability. Both deliver a hard, efficient light and come in a variety of intensities from 250 watts to 2K.

Soft Lights

Soft lights are units that do not throw the light beam directly from the lamp; rather, they emit reflected light. The lamp in a soft light is nestled into a lamp housing and the beam is reflected off the white interior of the **reflector shell** creating a very even and soft source. The larger the reflector shell, the more diffuse the light will be. Very diffuse soft lights are not particularly practical for location shooting because of their girth. The output of a soft light is not particularly efficient and they are used primarily as fill lights and occasionally as soft keys. Soft lights come in a variety of intensities (Figure 13-46); common wattages for small-scale shoots are 650w, 1K, and 2K. Because of the large size of the reflector shell, soft lights can be cumbersome for small crews or tight spaces. When trying to stay light and agile, some filmmakers prefer to create their own soft light source by bouncing light from a hard light unit off a reflector umbrella, a bounce board, or a white wall.

The **Chinese lantern** is a specialized soft light rig that is used exclusively as a fill light. The design of Chinese lanterns is based on the popular collapsible paper lanterns, but the lighting rig that mimics that design is made from flame-resistant material. If you try using a real paper lantern, it will burn! By suspending a low-wattage tungsten lamp, usually 250w, within a globe made of translucent, light-diffusing material, you have a lightweight soft light which can be positioned nearly anywhere, notably much closer to the camera than a stand-alone soft light unit. Chinese lanterns provide a very soft fill that is especially useful for close-ups on faces (Figure 13-47).

Fluorescent Lights

Fluorescent lights are relative newcomers to the shooter's lighting arsenal. Instead of heating a filament to a white-hot point source, florescent lights generate their illumination by passing an electric charge through mercury gas trapped within a hollow tube, causing it to glow. Because of this, fluorescent lamps give off a very soft, flattering light. In addition, they are lightweight and draw very little power. Fluorescent units come is a wide variety of sizes, from large banks holding ten 48-inch fluorescent tubes, to tiny nook fixtures holding one 9-inch fluorescent lamp capable of being tucked under a sun visor for night shots in cars (Figure 13-48). Fluorescent lights have many great advantages: they give off a lovely soft light, they burn cool, they draw very little power, and the units are lightweight and collapsible. Fluorescent lighting units can also be re-bulbed with lamps of various color temperatures, including 3,200°K and 5,600°K. The downside is that they are very delicate.

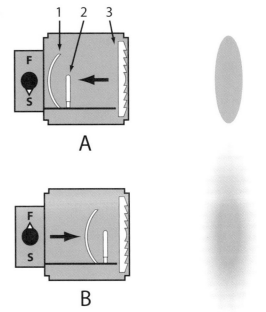

A

B

■ Figure 13-44 Fresnels have a lens (3) that focuses the beam more effectively than open-faced lights. In the spot position (A), the bulb (2) and the reflector (1) are farther from the lens, creating a sharp beam. When flooded (B) the bulb and reflector are brought closer to the lens, creating a wider throw.

■ Figure 13-45 Fresnel lights can come in a variety of sizes and intensities. Shown here are a 220 watt Inkie (left), a 1K Baby (middle), and 2K Junior (right).

Fresnels have specific names depending on the intensity of their lamp and size of their lens. The following Fresnels are some tungsten Fresnel units commonly used by students and independents.

- Inkie: 100w–200w, small lens
- Midget: 500w, small lens
- Tweenie: 650w, small lens
- Baby (also called Ace): 1K, medium lens
- Junior (also called Deuce): 2K, medium or large lens

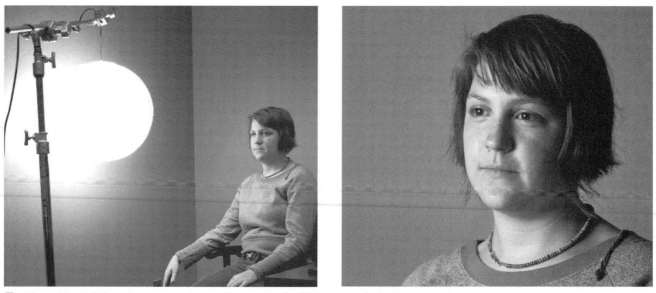

■ **Figure 13-47** Chinese lanterns can also provide a source of soft light, especially for close ups on faces.

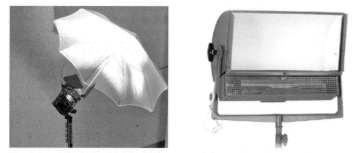

■ **Figure 13-46** Soft lights usually illuminate by bouncing light off some form of reflector. This Lowell ViP light comes with an umbrella for a soft reflector surface (left) and the 2K Baby Zip from Mole-Richardson (right) has a solid reflector shell. Both scatter light beams creating diffused light.

Reflectors

Reflectors (also called bounce boards) are not artificial lighting units per se, but I'm discussing them here because, as an illumination tool, they are as essential to a cinematographer as is any instrument that contains a lamp. As mentioned previously (p. 259), reflectors are lightweight, portable surfaces that bounce light. Reflectors usually have two sides with different reflective qualities: a diffused surface (white) that simultaneously bounces and diffuses a hard light source and a specular side (silver or gold to warm the bounced light) which reflects and maintains the hard quality of the source (Figure 13-49).

■ **Figure 13-48** The Kino-Flo "Vista-Beam" (left) is an extremely soft light source that consumes very little power. It can be used as a fill light or a soft key light. Small, battery powered fluorescent tubes, like these mini-flo lights (right) are often tucked into a car to replicate dashboard lights and provide ample illumination for a good exposure at night.

Basic Grip Gear

Throughout the history of film, grips have been the people who make it all happen. The grips are the muscle behind the movie, and after spending enough time on professional sets you come to realize that phrases like "Sorry, but that can't be done" simply do not exist for a professional grip. If something must be lifted, held, propped up, moved, adjusted, or jerry-rigged, grips do it. Whatever it takes to accomplish the shot the way the director sees it, the grip will pull it off. Over time an entire arsenal of grip equipment has developed, often by inventive grips themselves, in order to make their jobs more efficient and the set safer. There is so much specialized grip equipment that it would be impossible to cover all of it here, but knowing some of the basic gear is important for knowing what your rigging possibilities are on a set.

■ **Figure 13-49** Reflectors are as essential as lighting units to control the quality and quantity of a light. Foam core reflects diffused light (attached to a C-stand on the left), while a foldable reflector can bounce both diffused and hard light.

Stands

Light stands are what we usually position lighting units on, especially when in field production. They are collapsible tripod units that have a telescoping center pole to raise and lower the angle of the light as necessary. **C-stands** are your all-purpose holder, used for hanging, holding, or positioning just about anything (Figure 13-50). They are heavy and stable and their three legs are at different heights, allowing you to place several C-stands, overlapping, side-by-side. Combined with a **gobo head** and **gobo arm** (or multiple gobo arms), C-stands become infinitely adjustable and versatile and can firmly hold virtually anything that is fairly lightweight, at any angle and at a wide range of heights.

Gear for Light Control

It should be apparent by now that, when lighting, we want to be able to carefully control where the light falls and where it does not. Blocking light to keep it from falling where you don't want it is called **trimming** the light, and it's easy to do with hard light units. Soft light, on the other hand, is difficult to trim. With the light rays scattering in all directions, soft light will not create the sharply defined shadow edge necessary for precise trimming. Light that falls where it should not is called **light spill**, and soft light tends to spill.

Barndoors are a standard addition to almost every lighting unit and are designed to help control the coverage of the beam. Barndoors fit onto the front of the lighting unit and consist of two or, usually, four foldable black metal leaves (Figure 13-51). Two leaves control the vertical and horizontal limits of the beam throw.

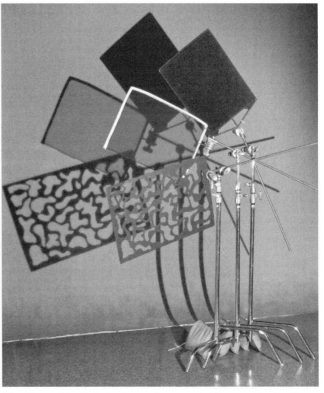

■ **Figure 13-50** C-stands are all-purpose holders used in virtually all film shoots. Pictured: a cookie, a net, and a flag attached to three C-stands with the use of gobo arms and gobo heads.

Right behind barndoors, one can often use **scrims** to reduce the intensity of light. Scrims are wire mesh screens that fit directly in front of the lighting unit. The denser the wire mesh, the more light it cuts. A single scrim cuts the output of the unit by half a stop and a double scrim cuts it by one full stop. You can use multiple scrims to achieve the intensity you need.

When very precise trimming is called for, we often used **flags**, which are free-standing frames covered with black felt, to sharply define where the light falls and where it doesn't. **Nets** are netting material stretched across a frame and, like scrims, are used purely to cut the intensity

■ **Figure 13-51** Foldable barndoors like these are mounted on the front of most movie lights and help control where the unit's light falls.

■ **Figure 13-52** Polecats let you position lights in unusual places where a conventional light stand can not be used.

■ **Figure 13-53** Securing cables with gaffer's tape prevents people from tripping on them.

of light. Nets are designed to cut light by one, two, or three stops. Obviously you can reduce the intensity of light simply by moving it, but by placing the net over *part* of the beam, you can cut intensity on only a part of the scene. **Silks** are like nets, but the material is partly opaque, which not only cuts the light intensity, but diffuses it as well. **Gobo** is the general name given to anything that comes between a light source and the scene, that is, anything that throws a shadow pattern. One specific kind of gobo is a **cookie** (short for **cucoloris**), which is metal or foam core that has had shapes cut into it to create patterns on a wall, floor, or other surface (see Figure 13-50). Once I found myself shooting a scene with a single character against a white wall. The bare white wall appeared severe, overly bright, and flat, so I needed to throw some sort of vague, diffused shadow pattern against it to beak up the glare and give the image some dimension. With time running short I simply grabbed a C-stand, clamped a plastic milk crate (used to carry power cables) to it, and placed this in front of a slightly diffused light. The mesh of the milk-crate bottom cast a very soft criss-cross pattern onto the wall. That's a gobo too, and one that worked well to improve the shot.

Clamps

There are all sorts of clamps used to hold stuff on a film set, but there are two that can be of special use when it comes to placing lights. **Gator clamps** are heavy-duty spring clamps with rubber teeth to ensure a very tight grip on things like doors and tables, and **mafer clamps** are designed to lock onto pipes. Both clamps are built with posts to which you can attach a small light, like an inkie or a tweenie. These clamps allow you to position or hide small lights in uncommon places. **Polecats** are spring-tension, expandable poles, like a shower curtain rod, that are often used with mafer clamps for hanging lights in window frames, doorways, or narrow hallways (Figure 13-52).

A few of the other important items in a grip package would include the **stinger**, which is the on-set name for extension cord, **sandbags**, which are placed over the legs of C-stands and light stands to keep them from toppling over (see safety issues below), and, of course, the indispensable gaffer's tape. **Gaffer's tape** is the all-purpose utility tape on a film set. Gaffer's tape rips easily into any width and length strip you need, it holds well, and it leaves no adhesive residue behind. It is especially useful for taping down cables (called **dressing cables**) to prevent people from tripping (Figure 13-53). Do not substitute common duct tape for gaffer's tape—even though it is much less expensive. Duct tape is designed to be permanent and will leave gum all over your equipment, and anything else it touches.

Electricity and Safety

Film and video production often requires the use of many lights, adding up to thousands of watts of power; using lots of lights means that a filmmaker is harnessing a great deal of electricity. Electricity is dangerous stuff and must be treated properly. A few safety principles and common sense are all it takes to ensure a safe and successful production experience.

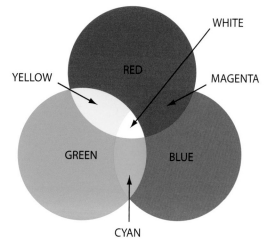

Figure 8-37 The color wheel shows at a glance the three primary colors of light: red, green, and blue and their respective complementary colors directly opposite: cyan, magenta, and yellow.

Figure 8-38 Scenes from Zhang's *Hero.*

Figure 8-44 In George Racz' *The Miracle* (2006) special attention was put into selecting a stock that would render the little girl's environment, toys, and clothing as colorfully as possible.

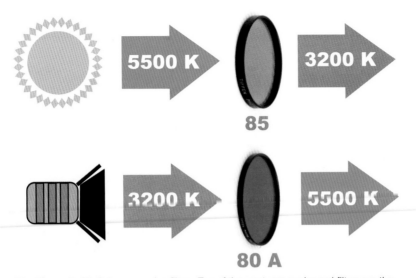

■ **Figure 8-45** Color conversion filters. Two of the most commonly used filters are the 85 (amber), which turns 5,500°K daylight into 3,200°K tungsten light, and the 80A (bluish), which turns 3,200°K tungsten into 5,500°K daylight.

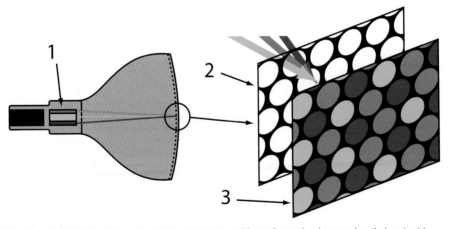

■ **Figure 9-5** Color video uses three electron guns (1) one for each primary color; their output is aimed at clusters of red, green, and blue phosphors on the screen (3). A special masking (2) is used to prevent, for instance, the blue gun from hitting a red phosphor.

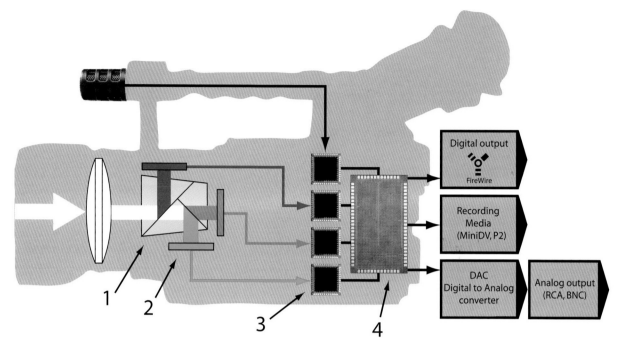

■ **Figure 9-31** A 3 chip video camera produces an image by first dividing the light entering the lens into primary colors with a prism block (1), which are read by 3 CCD chips (2), their signal outputs are converted into digital data by an ADC (3), and are processed by the DSP (4), ultimately outputting the data to the format being used.

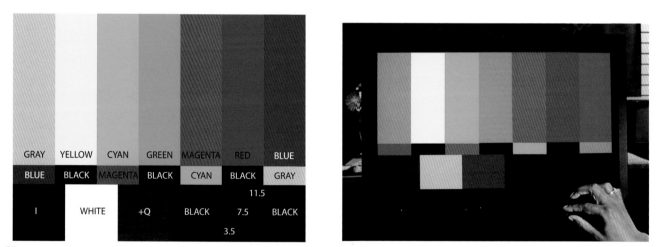

■ **Figure 12-19** Monitors can be calibrated with NTSC color bars for luminance, contrast, hue, and saturation, providing an accurate rendition of the video from the camera.

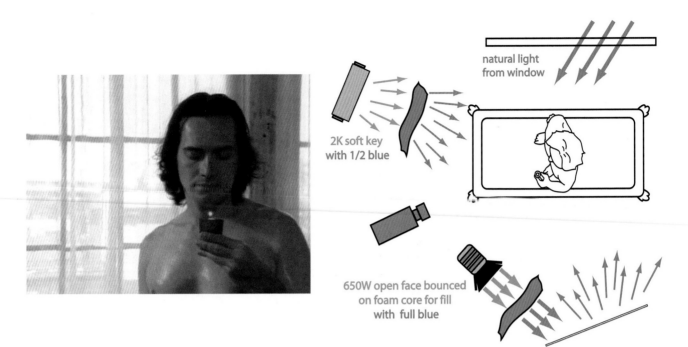

natural light
from window

2K soft key
with 1/2 blue

650W open face bounced
on foam core for fill
with full blue

■ **Figure 13-3** In this scene, from Katherine Hurbis-Cherrier's *Ode to a Bar of Soap* (1998) mixed lighting (artificial and sunlight) has been balanced for color temperature and quality.

■ **Figure 13-21** Gels come in literally hundreds of colors and intensities, including color correcting, neutral density, and diffusion media.

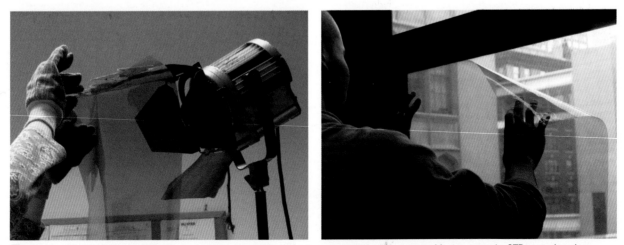

■ **Figure 13-22** CTO and CTB gels are used to correct the color temperature of a light source. Most commonly, CTBs are placed on movie lights to make them "daylight," and CTOs are placed on windows to make them "tungsten."

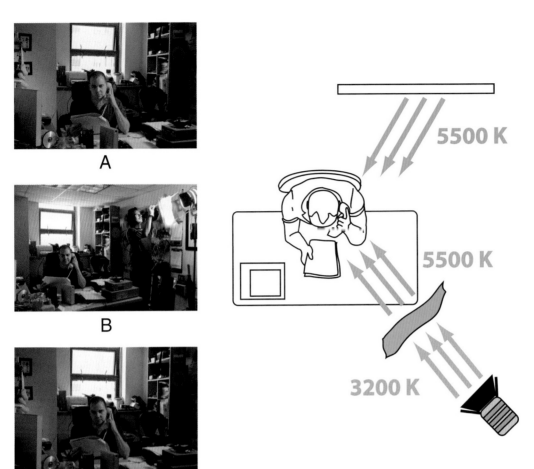

■ Figure 13-23
Shooting with daylight film (or a DV camera white balanced for daylight) matches the sunlight coming through the window, but records tungsten light as excessively orange (A). Placing a CTB gel over the tungsten unit changes it to daylight (B), matching the color temperature of all sources (C).

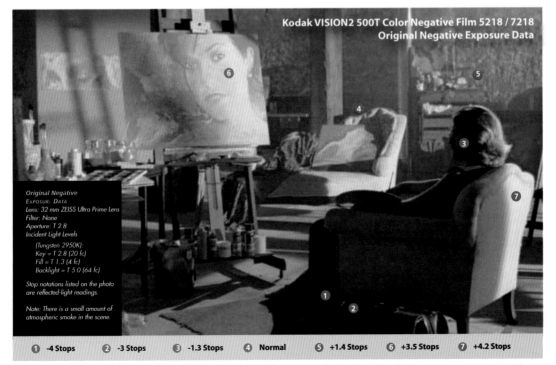

■ Figure 14-16 Kodak provides "original exposure data" examples for their stocks, letting consumers see how they react to an array of exposure values, including normal (N) over (+) and under (−) exposures.

Figure 14-26 Top: Lee's *Do The Right Thing* (1989) has highly stylized lighting that emphasizes the heat of one particularly hot day in Brooklyn (cinematography by Ernest Dickerson). Bottom: In Payne's *Election* (1999), naturalistic lighting provides an ironic subtext (cinematography by James Glennon).

Figure 14-25 The hyper-stylized look created by the masterful interplay of light, shadow, and color in Powell and Pressburger's *Black Narcissus* (1947) serves to visualize the intense emotions felt by a group of Anglican nuns stationed in the Himalayan mountains. (cinematography by Jack Cardiff).

Figure 14-28 Cinematographer Ernest Dickerson lights Bleek (Denzel Washington) using colors that stand for his two main interests, jazz (blue) and women (red), in Lee's *Mo' Better Blues* (1990).

■ **Figure 14-31** Shooting on digital video does not preclude having complex, beautiful cinematography. Ellen Kuras devised 3 completely different visual styles for the 3 characters in Miller's *Personal Velocity* (2002).

■ **Figure 24-1** The Final Cut Pro three way color corrector interface. (1) The luminance slider; (2) the color balance controls (with the balance indicator at center); (3) the color correction control range (blacks, mids or whites). Notice that the shot selected in the timeline is brought up in the viewer for color correction.

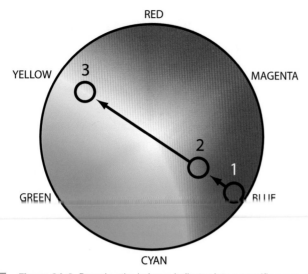

A

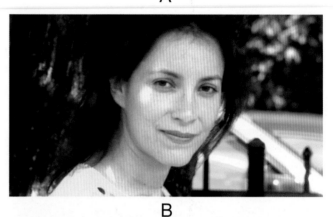

B

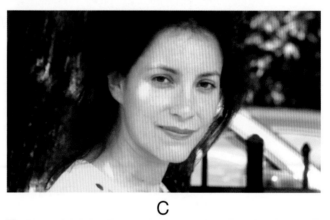

C

■ **Figure 24-3** Dragging the balance indicator into a specific areas of the color wheel balances the image toward that particular color. The closer to the edge you go, the more intense the color becomes. (1) Intense blue; (2) lighter blue; (3) intense yellow.

■ **Figure 24-4** A typical use of color correction. The original image (A) appears somewhat flat and pale. By adjusting luminance values we can create sharper contrast and more depth to the image (B). Adjusting the color further refines the image. In this case adding a slight amber hue provides a sense of the heat of the summer sun (C).

A **ditty bag** is a filmmaker's general utility tool kit and is filled with this, that, and the other thing that you might find useful on the set. Ditty bags are built over time, but here are a few standard items to get you started:

–Lens cleaning fluid/tissues	–AC circuit tester
–Camera tape	–Leatherman tool or Swiss Army knife
–Paper tape	–Jeweler's screwdriver set
–Sharpies	–Screwdrivers: various sizes, regular and Phillips
–Canned air	–Pliers: regular and needle nose
–White-bristled brush	–Allen wrench set
–Orange sticks	–AC plug adaptors (3-prong-to-2 prong with ground loop)
–Tape measure	–Extra take-up cores/spools
–Cable ties	–Extra batteries (AA, 9 v, and whatever mics use)
–Tweezers	–American Cinematographer Manual (or Kodak Cinematographer's Field Guide)
–Magnifying glass	–Pencils and small note pad
–Small scissors	–Leather grip gloves
–Mini-Maglite (penlight)	–Emergency DV tape stock

How Much Electricity?

Before you start plugging lights in, you need to determine how much electricity you have at your location and how it's distributed. This will help you figure out how many lights you can work with and where they can be set up and plugged in. This simple procedure for determining how much power you have and where it is should be done during your location survey. It can save you a lot of time and labor by keeping you from lugging more lights than you could possibly use or by keeping you from having to completely overhaul your lighting scheme when you discover the layout you envisioned at your desk isn't possible, given the facts of electricity distribution on the location.

1. Locate the **breaker box** (or fuse box) for your particular location. A breaker box brings the raw power from the utility company into a building and breaks it out into various circuits distributed throughout the various rooms. Each circuit is rated in **amps** (short for amperes) and has a dedicated breaker switch (or fuse) with the amp rating written right on it. The amp rating tells us how much electricity can safely flow through that circuit. Common circuit ratings found in homes and apartments are 15 amps (most rooms) and 20 amps (rooms that use heavy-draw electrical appliances, like kitchens and bathrooms), but you'll need to check your breaker box to be sure. If you exceed the circuit's rating by plugging in too many lights, the breaker will trip and cut the electricity (with a fuse; a metal filament embedded in the fuse melts and breaks the connection). If the breaker trips, you can simply reset it with the flick of a switch, but you also need to reduce the amount of electricity you are drawing on that circuit or it will trip again (fuses must be replaced). The purpose of breakers is to keep the building from burning down. Excess electricity can heat the internal wiring so much that the insulation melts, leaving super hot and exposed wires to start a fire. If you're using extensive lighting and you do not have access to the breaker box, then it may be too risky to shoot at that location; if you blow a fuse, it's lights out for the rest of the shoot (**Figure 13-54**).

■ Figure 13-54 Electricity on location. This household breaker box has been carefully labeled by a lighting crew after determining where each circuit is located and what the amperage rating is.

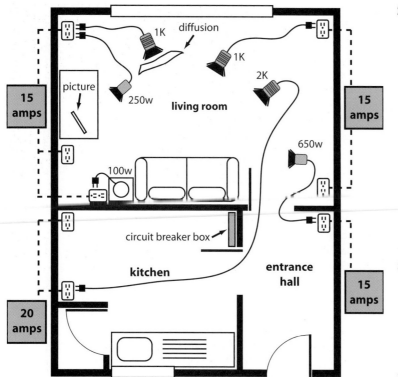

1K diffusion

1K

2K

picture

250w **living room**

650w

100w

circuit breaker box

kitchen

entrance hall

15 amps

15 amps

15 amps

20 amps

■ **Figure 13-55** Overhead diagrams that detail both the distribution of electricity at a location and where each lighting unit will be plugged in are essential in order not to trip breakers during your shoot. Notice that the cumulative wattage plugged in to any given circuit does not exceed its amp rating.

2. The next step is to determine which wall outlets are on which circuits. Usually there are several outlets per circuit, but it's impossible to know exactly how many and how they are clustered without testing them. To determine the distribution, simply turn on one breaker at a time and plug a small lamp or a circuit tester into each outlet. Take note of which breaker controls which outlet throughout your location. Occasionally breakers will be labeled "kitchen," "living room," "master bedroom," etc., but these labels are often flat-out wrong, so it's best to simply figure out for yourself which outlets are connected to which breaker switch.

3. Calculate the amount of electricity you can draw on each circuit. To determine how many watts you can plug into any single circuit, use the following formula:

$$\text{watts} = \text{volts} \times \text{amps}$$

We already know what amps are and their rating can be read straight off the breaker of each circuit. **Volts** (voltage) are the measure of the electromotive force of the electrical current in a system. Volts are standardized by country. In the United States household voltage fluctuates slightly, ranging from 110 to 120 volts. This voltage fluctuation is why our electricity is called AC (for alternating current). Out of respect for electricity, we always use the conservative figure for our calculations:

$$110 \text{ (volts)} \times 15 \text{ (amps)} = 1,650 \text{ (watts)}$$
$$110 \text{ (volts)} \times 20 \text{ (amps)} = 2,200 \text{ (watts)}$$

So, we can plug in up to 1,650 watts of light on each 15-amp circuit and 2,200 watts of electricity on a 20-amp circuit (Figure 13-55). Many gaffers feel that it's not safe to go right up to the limit; if there is a dip in power, you could blow a fuse. Also, be careful to take into account or unplug any appliances that can also draw power. It's easy to forget that the refrigerator is plugged into the kitchen's 20-amp circuit. If lights adding up to 2,100 watts are plugged in while the refrigerator compressor is off, invariably the fridge will kick back on just as your actor is delivering the most moving performance of their career, and BLAM!—the breaker trips and the lights go out. CUT!!

Lighting Safety Tips

1. The first rule of safety is to use common sense at all times. Things can become quite hectic on a film shoot—but you should always take your time and do things correctly. Never cut corners on safety to save time and do not attempt to do things that require the expertise of a trained electrician. I once had a student who was planning an exterior night shoot and he asked about the possibility of tapping into the power of a public street lamp. "It can't be that hard," he said; "I've seen people pop off the covers and rig their own plug-in right on the street." When he saw the incredulous look on my face he added "Yeah, maybe it's not such a good idea." Indeed!

2. Maintain a professional attitude toward your equipment. Abused and manhandled gear will break and, in the case of lighting equipment drawing thousands of watts of electricity, can bite back!

3. Movie lights get very hot and can burn everything from hands to walls. Keep flammable items away from lights. When bouncing lights off walls, keep them back far enough that they will not blister the paint. Always wear leather-palmed grip gloves when handling hot lights. For lighting units of 650 watts and more, never put gaffer's tape or gels in direct contact with the light or even the barndoors; they will melt. When attaching gels to barndoors, clip several C-47s to the barndoor first and then clip the diffusion to the C-47s (Figure 13-56).

Gels designated with the "tough" (tough spun, tough blue, etc.) are flame resistant and can be used near lights, but will melt if not mounted properly. Also, carefully handle the scrims that are used in lights to cut the intensity—they also get super hot. Back when I was a student I was on the set of a classmate who removed a scrim from a 1K baby and dropped it on his mother's carpet. When the shoot was over he went to pick it up off the ground and discovered that it had melted the nap and was fused to the carpet. When his mom came home, he lost the one location he thought he could always count on. Finally, let lights cool down before you pack them away.

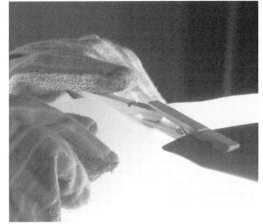

■ **Figure 13-56** Diffusion and gels should be attached to barndoors using a couple of C-47s to avoid melting and fires. Always wear your gloves when handling lights.

4. Related to this, never touch the lamp of a movie light, even if it is cool. Lamps get extremely hot and will obviously burn you. But touching a cool lamp with your bare fingers is also dangerous because your fingers leave oil on the bulb; the oil cooks when the lamp is turned on and eventually causes the bulb to explode. Always use the plastic or paper sheath provided with a new lamp to handle the bulb when you are replacing it.
5. Electricity and water do not mix. Duh! When shooting scenes involving water, like bathtubs and swimming pools, it's best to go with available light. If you must use lighting for interior bathroom scenes, do not set up lights where they could fall into the water. In fact, my students are not allowed to have movie lights in the same room

■ **Figure 13-57** All lights should always be set up so that: the cable is flush against the stand (1), the light is stabilized with one or more sandbags (2), and cables are taped to the floor to prevent accidents (3).

with a full bathtub or running shower. They must bounce light from a unit set up outside the door. In addition, they are required to station a grip at each unit for added safety.

6. When setting up a lighting unit or a C-stand, try to keep the weight as evenly distributed as possible. An unbalanced C-stand can easily topple over; so can a fully extended light stand with a heavy instrument on top. Use a sandbag on any stand that seems even vaguely "tippy" (Figure 13-57). Try not to create unbalanced gobo extensions. In addition, rotate the gobo arm such that the weight of the object pulls the gobo arm in the direction of tightening the gobo head. Do not allow gravity to pull the arm in a direction that would loosen the head.

7. Keep your cables neat. Use stingers to allow cables to fall straight down from the unit to the ground rather than stretching out diagonally to reach an outlot (Figure 13-57). In areas where there is a lot of foot traffic, tape down your cables with gaffer's tape (called **dressing cables**).

8. Put a decent first aid kit in your movie budget and bring it to the set.

Lighting and Exposure: Beyond the Basics

Now that you are familiar with the fundamental concepts and techniques of exposure and lighting, which are applied everyday on every movie set, we can turn our attention to slightly more intricate issues related to image control and interpretation through light. We need to look a little closer at how the film stock, or the CCD chip itself, actually responds to the various light values in a scene, beyond just its general sensitivity (i.e., exposure index). Two additional concepts are essential to a more advanced understanding of lighting and exposure for both film and DV: contrast range and latitude.

■ CONTRAST RANGE AND LATITUDE

Contrast range (also called **luminance range**) is the difference between the brightest and the darkest significant areas of your scene. Remember: "bright" and "dark" consist of a combination of incident light intensity and reflectance values. Contrast range can be expressed either in terms of a ratio or in terms of the f-stops difference between the two luminance extremes. For example, it is not unusual to discover, through multiple light meter readings, that a scene's lightest area is 16 times brighter than its darkest area. We can express this as a contrast ratio of 16:1 or as a contrast range of 4 f-stops. Why? Remember that each stop is a halving or doubling of brightness, so 4 stops from darkest to brightest is: $2 \times 2 \times 2 \times 2 = 16$. It should be noted that 4 stops is a relatively narrow contrast range. In a complexly lit scene, it's not usual to have a contrast range of 256:1, or 8 stops or even more (Figure 14-1)! One central question concerns how much of this contrast range our film stock or CCD chip can faithfully reproduce.

Broadly defined, **latitude** is the range of luminance values your specific imaging device (film stock or CCD chip) can render with detail before falling off into complete overexposure (white) or complete underexposure (black), where no image detail is visible. Latitude is expressed in terms of stops, i.e., the range of stops within which the imaging device will

■ **Figure 14-1** In this scene from Godard's *Masculin/Feminin* we have an example of a wide contrast range (left), where the outside of the café is extremely bright when compared to the darker areas inside. In the kitchen (right) there is very little variation between the tonalities, producing a narrow contrast range for this scene.

see detail. It is often the case that the contrast range of a scene exceeds the latitude range of your imaging device, which means that visual detail will be lost in the brightest or darkest parts of your scene, or both. Different film stocks and different DV formats have different abilities to render detail in bright or dark areas of the image; some fall off into total overexposure (white) and total underexposure (black) sooner than others. So, if we want to truly control our image, it's important to know both the contrast range of the scene and the ability of our imaging device to render it. Once we know this, we can use lighting to selectively bring areas of our scene into or out of the latitude of the imaging device to create visual emphasis and interest.

Although the broader concepts of latitude and exposure are the same for both DV and film, the practical application of these concepts plays out very differently, again, because in video, we are able to actually see the true response of our CCD chip while we are lighting and shooting. In film, however, understanding the latitude of your specific film stock is essential in order to anticipate and control the final image, which you cannot see until after processing.

Latitude, Film Stocks, and Characteristic Curves

There are many different film stocks on the market, each designed for a different shooting situation; there are slow films (EI 50), fast films (EI 500), negative films, reversal films, and color and black-and-white films. Each specific film stock responds to light in a unique way and that response is plotted on a graph called the characteristic curve. The **characteristic curve** is a graphical representation of the way a particular film stock responds to light. In a sense it represents that film stock's "personality." As we discussed in the section on film stocks and processing (p. 156), exposing film is a matter of creating a thicker or thinner silver halide density, depending on the brightness of an object and length of exposure. This is precisely what the characteristic curve measures (Figure 14-2).

The vertical axis of the scale measures the thickness of the silver halide **density**, called "**D**," and the horizontal scale measures the exposure increments in lux-seconds, called

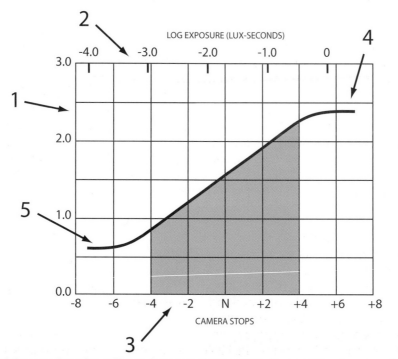

■ **Figure 14-2** A characteristic curve shows how a film stock reacts to light by plotting the correlation along axes of density (1) and exposure (2). The curve is composed of three main sections: a straight-line portion (highlighted), a shoulder (4) and a toe (5). Many curves include a camera stops guide (3) showing the exposure range of the stock (in this case 8 f-stops).

log-e. The log-e scale is commonly translated into a more useful **camera stop** scale on the graph, and that's what we'll use for our discussion. Keep in mind that the graph shown in Figure 14-2 is for a negative film stock, meaning the light values are reversed from the actual values in the scene. So, the range of the "D" scale, moving left to right, goes from D-min (complete under-exposure) to D-max (complete overexposure). D-min means no silver halide crystals were exposed (not enough light and/or exposure time) and the negative image is pure white with no detail. D-max tells us that this area received a great deal of exposure (too much light), which means that the silver halide density is so thick that it registers on the negative as pure black. The straight line between these two luminance extremes (total underexposure and total overexposure) is called, no surprise, the **straight line portion**, and it shows us the proportional response of the film to exposure. The steady and predictable increase of density/luminance values is in response to an increase in exposure (Figure 14-3). Exposures that fall along the straight line portion will show image detail. The straight line portion is of primary importance because it tells us the range of f-stops within which a particular film stock can render image detail before falling off into pure white, total overexposure (D-max), and pure black, total underexposure (D-min). The longer the straight line portion of the curve, the greater latitude the film stock has, which means the greater its capacity to "see" detail in the bright and dark areas. On a characteristic curve that lists camera stops along the horizontal axis, we can easily see how many stops latitude a film stock has. "N" stands for middle gray "normally" exposed. Simply find the exact ends of the perfectly straight portion of the curve, *before* it starts to flatten out, and you can determine how many stops you have where detail will be visible as you move through the various degrees of under- and overexposure.

Negative film stocks typically have a latitude of 8 stops, meaning around 4 to 4½ stops on either side of "N." However, most cinematographers also include those slight curved areas before D-min and D-max, which are called the **toe** and **shoulder**, respectively (Figure 14-4). Indeed, these areas continue to render some visual detail, but they can be tricky. Their curvature tells us that there will still be some image detail just before total underexposure (in dark shadows) and total overexposures (bright highlights), but since the film does not respond to light proportionally here (unlike the straight line portion) it takes some experience to really know what those areas will yield. By including the toe and shoulder in what some D.P.s call the "overall useful range" of a film stock, we can add another 2 stops to our latitude range—or more, depending on the specific stock. So an average color negative film stock's latitude, including straight line, plus toe and shoulder, is around 10 or 11 stops.

Gamma

Closely related to latitude is gamma. **Gamma** (also called **contrast**) represents the capacity of a film stock to differentiate between the various luminance tonalities (shades of gray) in a scene and is represented by the angle of the straight line portion—in other words, the steepness of the slope. The ideal angle for a straight line would be a perfect 45°, meaning a perfectly proportional increase in density to exposure. This would faithfully duplicate all of the subtle shifts in the gray scale (Figure 14-5). Although many color negative film stocks come close, no film has yet reached this ideal. The steeper the

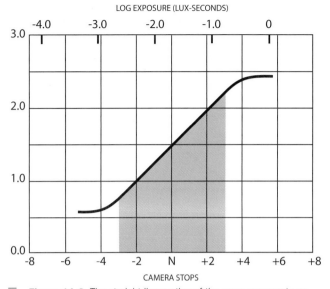

LOG EXPOSURE (LUX-SECONDS)

CAMERA STOPS

■ **Figure 14-3** The straight line portion of the curve represents an equal increase in both density and exposure by the stock. This stock's straight line encompasses 6 f-stops (3 for overexposure and 3 for underexposure).

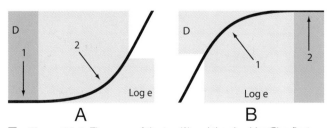

■ **Figure 14-4** The curve of the toe (A) and the shoulder (B) reflect the unequal relationship between density and exposure. When density remains unchanged in the toe, we have complete underexposure, or D-min (1). When density remains unchanged in the shoulder, we have complete overexposure, or D-max (2).

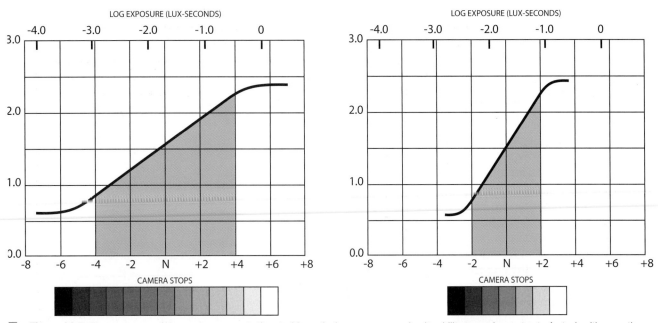

■ **Figure 14-5** The steepness of the curve represents the stock's particular gamma, meaning its ability to render contrast. A stock with a gentle slope has lower contrast (left); it can render more shades of gray. A steep curve (right) indicates a stock with a high contrast; it can only render a few shades of gray.

■ **Figure 14-6** Egoyan's *Felicia's Journey* (1999) abruptly changes from a low-contrast to a high-contrast stock when Hilditch (Bob Hoskins) reminisces about his childhood and his domineering mother.

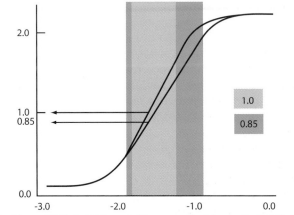

■ **Figure 14-7** A shift in a stock's gamma (in this case by "pushing" the stock during development from .85 to 1.0) can radically alter its contrast. A higher gamma practically shortens the straight line portion of the curve and increases contrast.

angle of the straight line portion, the more contrasty the film is, and the fewer shades of luminance it can differentiate. All films go from absolute black to absolute white, so the steeper the slope is, the fewer stops and tonal ranges will exist between these two extreme poles. Reversal film stock and fast film stocks generally have a steeper gamma slope and have more contrast. Slower stocks and negative film usually reproduce a broader range of subtle luminance values.

More or less contrast is not the basis for a value judgment abut a film stock. Some films can benefit aesthetically from a high-contrast look (Figure 14-6). In fact, given the substantial gamma capabilities of today's negative film stocks, it's quite common for a filmmaker to push film one or two stops (see p. 276) to intentionally shift the inherent gamma angle to create more contrast in the negative (Figure 14-7).

An additional detail of the characteristic curve that is greatly affected by the angle of the curve slope is the toe and shoulder. When the straight line portion of the curve is steep,

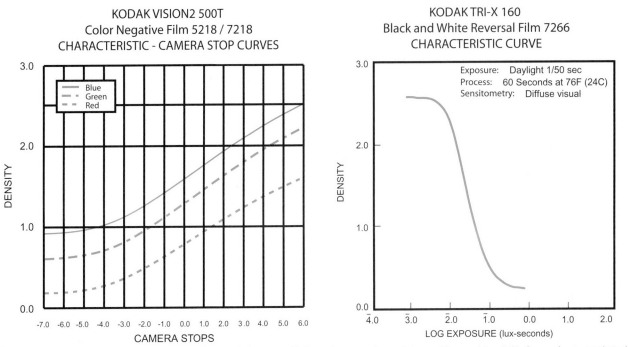

Figure 14-8 A color negative stock has a characteristic curve with three lines, one for each layer of its emulsion (left). Curves for reversal stocks show an inverse relationship between density and exposure, since the image they render is positive, not negative (right).

the angles of the toe and shoulder become more acute, which means that the drop into pure white and pure black (D-max and D-min) is more precipitous than with the gently curving toe and shoulder of a lower contrast stock. With high-contrast film one will see much less into the shadows and highlights of the image, because they plunge more easily into total under- and overexposure.

So far, the characteristic curves we've been looking at have been for black-and-white negative film. Characteristic curves for reversal films, in which the film densities and tonalities are the same as the actual scene, are completely reversed—with D-max representing black areas and D-min representing pure white areas in the image (Figure 14-8). The characteristic curve graph for a color film stock includes three curves, each one representing a different emulsion layer in the color tripack (see p. 158). Each emulsion layer, red, green, and blue, responds to light slightly differently, so each gets it's own curve for analysis.

Quite often, filmmakers select their film stock based on something as simple as exposure index, especially when the lighting situation is somewhat inflexible. For example, when access artificial lighting is limited and shooting is planned for interiors, one might need to simply go with the fastest film stock available. Other times a filmmaker will approach film selection based on the unique color attributes or the grain structure of the stock. Also, it's not unusual to hear cinematographers speak about latitude and gamma as one of the deciding factors for their film stock selection. Then, of course, there are the times when a filmmaker shoots with film that was given to them, or could be purchased inexpensively. When I was a student, my first two movies were made on film stock donated by a production company that had some extra rolls lying around. No matter what criterion (or method) you use in acquiring your film, make sure to study its characteristic curve (sometimes referred to by manufacturers as a **sensitometric curve**); curve data can usually be found on a manufacturer's website.

This basic discussion of the characteristic curve will certainly get you off to a running start, but there is much more to say about how we read a characteristic curve and what it tells us about the way a particular film stock responds to light. I have suggested some additional texts in the Recommended Readings list (at the back of the book) for a deeper study into the technology and techniques of motion picture photography that would be essential for anyone interested in developing their skills as a cinematographer.

What is Pushing Film?

Pushing film (or **push processing**) is a very common exposure tactic when we need a little extra filmspeed to shoot in low light situations or when we want to intentionally add contrast to our image. Say we're using a film stock with a rating of EI 100 but discover there isn't enough light for a good exposure. Pushing the film one stop means pretending that the film in your camera (EI 100) is twice as sensitive (EI 200) and we set our light meter for that doubled sensitivity and proceed with shooting. Obviously, that film is then one stop underexposed. However, when we send this film to the lab for processing we indicate on the film can label to "push one stop." The lab will process that film longer than normal to compensate for the underexposure. This compensation has the additional effect of increasing grain and contrast in the resulting image. We can push film one, two, three, or even four stops. With each increase the processing time gets longer and the image gets more contrasty. Keep in mind that you cannot push only selected shots. You must push entire rolls of film because the entire roll remains in the chemical processing soup longer.

Putting Latitude, Exposures, and Lighting to Work

Great; so now that we know what latitude is, and how we can determine the latitude of our specific film stock, how do we use it? Let's say that we are shooting a simply lit scene with a fast black-and-white negative stock that has a latitude of 6 stops, 3 stops over and 3 stops under (straight line portion only) (see Figure 14-3). Fast films generally have narrower latitude than slow film stocks; also, in reality you will usually get a fraction more latitude in overexposures than in underexposures, but for the sake of simplifying the example, I'll keep everything to full stops.

Knowing the film's latitude, I can set out to light my scene. There are five steps to lighting a scene: (1) rough-in the lights, (2) measure the exposures, (3) visualize and evaluate the options, (4) peg the exposure, and (5) complete the lighting.

1. **Rough-in the lights**.

    The first step to lighting any scene is to **rough-in** the lights. A roughed-in lighting setup is usually little more than setting up the key light and maybe some quick fill. All lights are set up later in relation to the key light and its exposure value. In this case our key is natural light, the sun streaming into the room. It could easily be a 10K Fresnel set up just outside the house, standing in as the sun. The walls of the room are off-white, so provide some natural fill on their own.

2. **Measure the exposures**.

    The next step is to measure the scene thoroughly with a light meter to determine the **exposure range**, which is the range of incident light intensities within your scene. In the scene in Figure 14-9, we are shooting a master shot of two people playing chess in a living room that gets some terrific daylight streaming in from a broad window. There's a lot of light, but it is very directional, yet some of it bounces off the white walls, providing a little ambient fill. There is one other light source (a practical), which is a bright wall sconce that illuminates the portrait on the back wall. We have determined through multiple light meter readings that the brightest part of the scene, the sunlit area outside the window, will be properly exposed at f/22, but the darkest area, the shadows beneath the table where the cat rests, yields an exposure reading of f/1.4. There is a difference of 8 stops between these two meter readings, so we say that the exposure range in this scene is 8 stops. All of the other exposure values fall in between these poles.

3. **Visualize and evaluate the options**.

    Knowing the latitude of our film and the "normal" exposure for each area in the scene, we can now visualize the scene with some accuracy. This means imagining different f-stop choices and how they will affect the other areas of your scene. You certainly don't need to imagine every single possible f-stop, but you do need to know the dramatic context of

■ **Figure 14-9** A typical scene will comprise a number of f-stops. In our scene, the darkest area, f/1.4, and brightest area, f/22, give us a range of 8 f-stops. How this scene will be recorded depends on the range of f-stops our stock can handle.

the scene you are exposing. So ask yourself: Who and what are important in the scene? Where do you want to place visual emphasis? What might you want to expose "normally?" When you hypothetically choose an f-stop setting, you will then be able to imagine how all of the other areas in the scene will be exposed relative to that choice.

The scene in Figure 14-9 is an intense chess match-up between the local grocery boy, Chip (right), and Sandor Micklos (left), the great-grandson of chess Grandmaster and legend Aleksander Micklos, whose portrait hangs Sandor's living room, watching his every move, chess related or otherwise. In this master shot, Chip is playing some cunning moves, while Sandor feels the pressure of an impending loss to a grocery clerk. Sandor is central, as is his great-grandfather's relentless gaze upon him. Seeing the boy's guileless features would also be good for the scene, although secondary. So let's imagine the f-stops for these three visual focal points and see what happens (see table in Figure 14-10).

Film latitude : 6 f-stops (-3 f stops of underexposure from N and +3 f stops of overexposure from N)							
F-stop	**Sandor** f/8	**Chip** f/2.8	**Portrait** f/16	**Chessboard** f/5.6	**Flowers** f/2	**Cat** f/1.4	**Window** f/22
Expose for Sandor f/ 8	N	-3 stops	+2 stops	-1 stop	-4 stops	-5 stops	+ 3 stops
Expose for Chip f/ 2.8	+3 stops	N	+5 stops	+2 stops	-1 stop	-2 stops	+ 6 stops
Expose for Portrait f/ 16	-2 stops	-5 stops	N	-3 stops	-6 stops	-7 stops	+1 stop

■ **Figure 14-10** Taking multiple light meter readings allows you to "see" exposure values the way your fim stock will see them. In this table we provisionally peg our normal exposure at three different f-stops to see where the rest of the exposure values in the scene will fall. Cross reference this table with the characteristic curves in Figures 14-11–14-13.

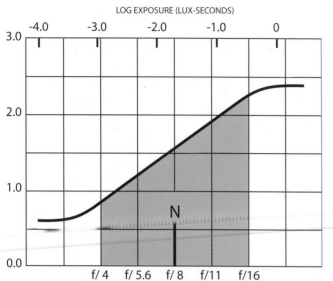

LOG EXPOSURE (LUX-SECONDS)

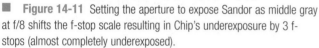

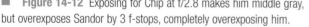

Figure 14-11 Setting the aperture to expose Sandor as middle gray at f/8 shifts the f-stop scale resulting in Chip's underexposure by 3 f-stops (almost completely underexposed).

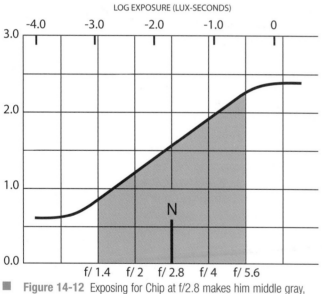

Figure 14-12 Exposing for Chip at f/2.8 makes him middle gray, but overexposes Sandor by 3 f-stops, completely overexposing him.

- *Shooting at f/8: Sandor's Exposure* (Figure 4-11).

Sandor: Sandor is receiving plenty of natural light from the win dow. Shooting at f/8 will expose Sandor's face correctly. Good.

Chip: Chip's face is in shadows created by the sun behind his back. f/8 puts Chip 3 stops underexposed, right at the limit of our film's latitude. He will be very dark and facial detail will be murky. Not so good.

Portrait: The portrait is 2 stops overexposed. That's pretty bright, we can still see some detail in it, but perhaps it's too hot.

Chessboard: The chessboard is only 1 stop underexposed. There is plenty of visible detail so we can see what it is, but it's a bit darker than Sandor, so it won't pull attention away from him. Good.

Flowers: The light from the window falls off fast, plus the flowers are in Sandor's shadow. At f/8, the flowers fall outside the latitude of our film (D-min) and we lose them. Not good.

Cat: Sitting in the darkest area of the scene the cat is 5 stops underexposed and well into the D-min part of the curve. No visible cat. Not good.

Window: The window is 3 stops overexposed. It'll be very bright, but we'll be able to see some detail outside, which is about what we expect from a window where the sun is streaming in. Good.

- *Shooting at f/2.8: Chip's Exposure* (Figure 4-12).

Sandor: Sandor is now 3 stops overexposed, right at the edge of the shoulder. That's way too bright. We'll lose some detail in his face.

Chip: Chip's face is exposed correctly. But he's secondary to Sandor in terms of dramatic emphasis.

Portrait: The portrait is 5 stops overexposed and has fallen beyond our film's latitude into D-max.

Chessboard: The board is 2 stops overexposed, starting to glow too brightly. I'm already not liking this f-stop choice!

Flowers: Now the flowers are only 1 stop underexposed and I can really see them: a bit dark but in detail.

Cat: I can see the cat! At 2 stops under, it's dark, but that's okay for a cat sitting in the shade.

Window: The window is 6 stops overexposed. That's not just bright, that is what we call "blown out." Not only will the window look white with utterly no detail through the glass, but also the brightness will spread around the edges of the window frame, looking like a white blob—dominating the composition with its glare. Definitely not good.

■ *Shooting at f/16: Portrait's Exposure* (Figure 4-13). This is the worst choice. Shooting at f/16 puts Chip's face, the flowers, and the poor cat way out of the latitude range of my film, and I'll lose them all into blackness. The chess board at 3 stops underexposed is simply too dark. All no good. This image will be hard for an audience to make out.

4. **Peg the exposure.**

   Pegging your f-stop simply means deciding on the specific f-stop you're going to use for the shot. That decision in effect pegs N (middle gray, exposed correctly) to a certain spot along the characteristic curve and all other values fall relative to that. So, what f-stop

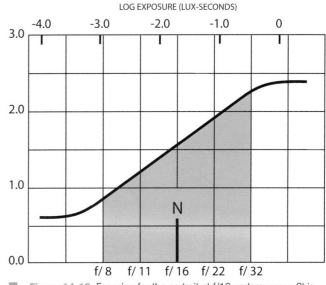

LOG EXPOSURE (LUX-SECONDS)

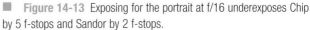

■ **Figure 14-13** Exposing for the portrait at f/16 underexposes Chip by 5 f-stops and Sandor by 2 f-stops.

will I go with for this scene? I choose to shoot at f/8. It's the f-stop that best utilizes my lovely natural key light and brings my overall scene closest to what I'm after. But, as-is, the scene has exposure problems here and there. Since I've thoroughly evaluated all of these areas, I have a good sense for what I need to do to fix them, by adding or subtracting light selectively. Let's take a look.

5. **Complete the lighting.**

   My approach to lighting this scene will be to maintain a naturalistic look, using the motivation of my strong natural key light. So I'll be using artificial lights to augment the natural light to achieve a realistic look. It's the kind of thing we do all the time in film.

The problem areas, according to our evaluation, were: Chip, the flowers, the cat (all too underexposed), and the portrait (too overexposed). To "fix" the scene I would first add a very soft fill on Chip's face to bring his exposure up to 1½ stops to an f/4—5.6 split (1½ stops under). This will give me more facial detail, but keep him on the dark side. Any brighter than that would seem strange, since his back is to the window and we expect his face to be somewhat in shadow. The soft fill would be motivated by the off-white walls and might simply be a bounce board kicking some sunlight back at Chip, or a small lighting unit with diffusion (see p. 241). In either case I must be careful not to cast shadows behind Chip or spill more light onto Sandor, because we don't want to boost his exposure level.

I would do the same with the flowers and cat area, a soft fill to boost that corner of the room so that the exposure drop-off from the window to the table isn't so drastic. Bringing this corner up 2 stops with a soft fill would bring the flowers and cat into the very edge of my latitude. The flowers will be at f/4 (2 stops under) and cat will be at f/2.8 (3 stops under); they will still be dark, which they should be, but we'll see more detail. However, this corner still feels a little dull, not to mention that I went through the trouble of getting a cat, and I'd like to see more of it. So I would try setting up a hard light (like a 1K baby) pushing through a gobo, one that looks like the squares of a window frame (see p. 265). I would position it so that the hard light from a corner of my contrived "window" falls on the floor, cat, and table, just a little bit. The motivation? It would be as if there were, somewhere in the room, another unseen window through which the sun is streaming. This light must be angled so that it appears to be coming from the same angle as the key light. Compositionally speaking, a little slash of light at the lower left of the frame would balance nicely with the bright window in the upper right of the frame, and I would see even more of my cat! Of course, all of my artificial lights will also have CTB to balance these tungsten light

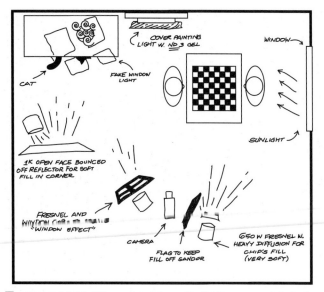

■ **Figure 14-14** This overhead shows the lighting approach that addresses the exposure problems we had. We now can shoot our scene with the knowledge that it will be rendered according to our design.

sources to the daylight color temperature of my key light (see p. 247).

Finally, the portrait is too bright, I like that there is a wall sconce illuminating it, but I need it to be 2 stops lower, to f/8, just like Sandor. To achieve this I can simply cover the sconce bulb carefully with ND gel (see p. 248). That will cut the intensity of the bulb, but since the portrait is lit by both the sconce and the sunlight, I'll need to experiment with one and two layers of ND 0.3 to get it just right. With all lighting problems solved, I'm ready to shoot (Figure 14-14).

I laid this little example out in a very methodical way, but in reality, when you're lighting a scene, it's usually not quite this neat; there is a lot of back and forth, constant remeasuring, and comparisons and reevaluation of exposure values. You might add lights that don't work (like maybe my gobo window effect will seem cheesy once I see it in place) or remove too much light with a flag, or get new ideas as you go along. . . Also, keep in mind that sometimes we peg an f-stop for reasons other than accommodating an exposure range. For example, if the dominant visual approach to the scene is to have a deep DOF, then we start with f/16 as our f-stop and light specifically for that.

Reflectance Values and Latitude

In the preceding example I used an incident meter exclusively. This is the metering instrument of choice on film sets, but we know that contrast range and true luminance values also include the reflectance of objects, not just the incident light intensity. Most of the time, incident readings, which tell you how many stops over or under normal exposure an area is, will give you enough information to imagine how bright or dark that part of the scene will appear on film. The more film you shoot, the more predictable and intuitive exposures will be. But in some cases, where luminance values are critical, you may want a more accurate assessment. This is where a spot meter and the zone system chart are useful (see p. 229).

For example, let's say the preceding gobo idea didn't work, so I simply stayed with the soft fill on the cat, which brought it up to f/2.8, 3 stops underexposed (f-stop pegged at f/8). That's right at the edge of our characteristic curve. We know it'll be very dark, but how dark will the cat truly be? We will probably lose a black cat entirely in the shadows, gone.

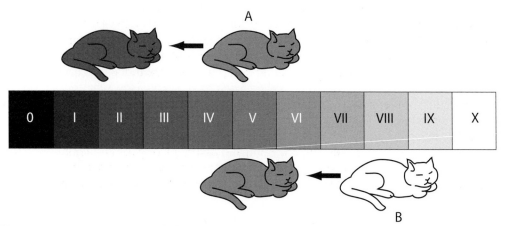

■ **Figure 14-15** A spot meter can give you a more accurate assessment of how a subject will be recorded according to its reflectance. A gray cat (A) underexposed by 3 f-stops will be seen as a dark gray, and a white cat (B) underexposed by the same margin will look grayish, as seen using the zone system scale.

But what about a gray cat or a white cat? Each cat will appear differently on screen even with the same incident meter reading.

So, provided we can get the cat to sit still, we can take a spot meter reading off it (Figure 14-15). If the cat's fur is *exactly* a middle gray tone (Cat A), the spot meter reading will be f/2.8, the same as the incident reading. At 3 stops under we can expect a middle gray cat to look like zone II (three zones darker than middle gray). That's quite dark, but some detail is visible. If that cat's fur is off-white, say at zone XIII (Cat B), then the spot meter reading (giving us the exposure to turn the cat middle gray) will say f/5.6. So now we know the white cat, sitting in the shadows, will be underexposed to the point of looking middle gray. This is why selective spot metering is a regular procedure on film sets when knowing precise luminance values are crucial. Also, a

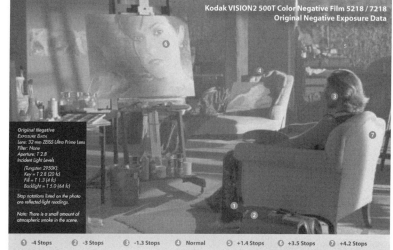

Figure 14-16 Kodak provides "original exposure data" examples for their stocks, letting consumers see how they react to an array of exposure values, including normal (N) over (+) and under (−) exposures. See the color insert in Chapter 13.

black cat, gray cat, and white cat are easy enough to figure out, even without a spot meter, but what if the cat is an orange tabby? What's the reflectance value of orange fur? Spot meters are very valuable in determining the reflectance values of colored objects, like a green apple, a red suitcase, and an orange cat, and placing them onto the zone scale, and it sure is a lot easier than having the art department spray paint your tabby middle gray.

The latitude of a particular film stock (how it reacts to various exposure values) is so critical that most film manufacturers provide original negative exposure samples for each film stock they sell. This allows you to see for yourself the look and response of a particular film stock. The image used in the exposure samples usually includes a wide range of incident light intensities and objects with various reflectance values (see Figure 14-16 on the color insert in Chapter 13).

Latitude and Digital Video

Latitude is one of the central issues that comes up when people compare film and DV images. By now, the reader should know that I'm not a big fan of making value judgments based on film and DV comparisons, because I believe each has its own aesthetic characteristics and a unique and valuable place in filmmaking. Nonetheless, we will build from our understanding of film latitude (read the previous sections if you have not yet done so) to discuss latitude and the video image, so some objective comparison is helpful. It is true that while DV frequently improves its latitude specifications substantially, film manufacturers have answered the challenge with film stocks of unprecedented sensitivity and latitude range. In all likelihood, we will continue to see this game of one-upsmanship continue for some time, while we filmmakers reap the benefits of better and better images in both systems.

At this point it's fair to say that standard NTSC DV video has somewhere around 5 to 6 stops of latitude. Compared with most negative films' 10 to 11 stops latitude, that's significantly narrower. HD video, however, can stand toe-to-toe with any film stock on the market in terms of latitude and ability to see into shadows and detail, as long as it remains an HD signal, of course. However, depending on your camera model, most industrial and high-end standard DV cameras have a few tricks up their sleeves that can electronically extend the latitude.

The three shortcomings most commonly cited with the standard NTSC DV image are slightly high-contrast "crispy" images, the inability to see detail in shadows without video noise, and the abrupt blowing out of whites, called **clipping**, when the image exceeds the

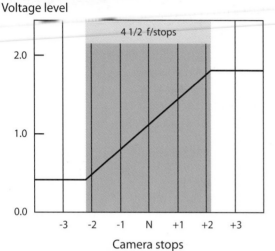

Voltage level

Camera stops

■ **Figure 14-17** The drawback of video formats is their inability to handle extreme over- and underexposure, due to their lack of toe and shoulder. Broadcasted video can only have a range of 4½ f-stops, making it extremely easy to blow out portions of an image (frame from Mercado's *Becoming,* 2007).

factory preset latitude. All of these image details, taken together, have been labeled by some people as "the DV curse." But other people who work with DV extensively use slightly gentler language and refer to these particulars as "artifacts of the digital emulsion" because they understand that much about the performance of the camera's response to light is a function of factory signal presets and that many cameras are now allowing the user the opportunity to tweak these settings. A few of the more common signal adjustments you will find on DV cameras to alter their latitude and contrast range are described in the following sections. Keep in mind that the characteristic curves presented here are purely for illustration purposes. The DV signal is not ordinarily plotted on a film-style characteristic curve.

Black Stretch, Knee, and Cine-Gamma

One of the central causes of "the video curse" is that the factory presets of the video compression circuitry create a signal with no toe and no shoulder, which is responsible for the hard clipping of whites and the abrupt plunge into inky blacks when DV approaches the extremes of under- and overexposure (Figure 14-17). Without a toe and shoulder at the ends of the characteristic curve, the DV image not only loses out on that gradual tapering off of detail toward total black or total white, but it also loses out on a few stops of "useable latitude."

Black stretch is a setting that can extend the CCD's sensitivity range in the darkest parts of the image so that you are able to see somewhat more detail in the shadow areas of the shot. Engaging black stretch is the equivalent of creating a "toe" in the response of the CCD. You will see both a little taper to the extreme underexposures and gain about one stop at the bottom end (Figure 14-18). Black stretch is sort of like a video gain function that selectively boosts only the darkest portion of the image, like intense shadows. However, as with gain, you need to be careful because you

■ **Figure 14-18** The "black stretch" option found on higher-end video cameras can selectively boost darker areas of a scene, practically creating an artificial toe; note how, after the black stretch option is engaged, some detail can be seen inside the arch.

■ **Figure 14-19** The "knee" option found in higher-end video cameras can control the overexposed areas of a frame using compression technology, effectively creating an artificial shoulder. Note how more detail is visible outside the window after the knee option is engaged.

can introduce video noise into an area that was otherwise clean. Some of the work of black stretch can more accurately and more safely be accomplished in two ways: careful lighting of the black areas of the image (when you have lights) or through postproduction color correction (see p. 459).

White clipping commonly shows up in two circumstances; highlights on prominent areas of a subject that reflect the key light, like cheekbones or foreheads, and in situations of extreme contrast ratio, like bright windows visible in a dark interior location. Extreme clipping can be somewhat avoided by careful use of zebras, but even so, bright highlights can cause an extreme and uneven loss of color saturation and detail in the image. **Video knee** (or **pre-knee**) is a signal compression adjustment similar to black stretch, but for the brightest areas in the frame, and is the equivalent of creating a "shoulder" in the signal's response to intense exposures (Figure 14-19). A few cameras allow for the manual setting of the upper signal output levels (near the ultimate white clip level), anywhere between 85% and 95% white allowing more detail to be visible as you approach total overexposure. In my opinion, this is the sort of deep camera signal adjustment better left to experienced engineers. However, many high-end and industrial cameras now have an easily accessible automatic pre-knee setting, called **auto-knee** (also called **auto highlight control**), which is designed to give you maximum detail depending on the highlight values of the particular image in the frame. Auto-knee is one of the few auto settings that you want to actually leave on while you shoot.

Cine-gamma has become one of the most common signal tweaking settings on high-end and industrial level DV cameras. Cine-gamma essentially electronically flattens the straight line portion of the DV signal's characteristic curve (Figure 14-20). This accomplishes

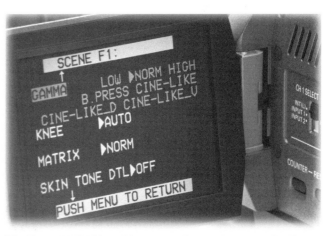

■ **Figure 14-20** Many video cameras have a cine-gamma function that electronically creates a toe and shoulder to more closely resemble the way a film stock responds to light.

two things simultaneously: it slightly extends the latitude of the camera as well as reducing the contrast of the image, thus ameliorating that "crispy" electronic look that some people don't care for. Some manufacturers claim that cine-gamma increases DV's latitude to 7—8 stops (and some claim even more). In effect cine-gamma serves the function of black stretch and pre-knee at the same time because it creates less acute angles at the toe and shoulder of the curve. With cine-gamma, you'll see detail somewhat deeper into the shadows and highlights. The drawback to the cine-gamma setting is that the overall reduced contrast of the image can, in some cases, create washed out midtones and colors. Cine-gamma is a function that will no doubt become more and more sophisticated and convincing with each new camera generation.

Always use caution and moderation when you apply any of these settings. Altering the electronic signal of your camera can have unintended ancillary consequences. If you're interested in using black stretch, pre-knee, or cine-gamma, make sure you shoot tests under similar lighting conditions long before you're on the set and shooting your film. Also remember that adjusting the signal is not a substitute for careful, sensitive, and creative lighting.

■ LIGHTING APPROACHES AND STYLES

As director of photography I am in charge of whatever goes into the making of the image so I am head of the camera, grip, and electric departments. I'm number two to the director so one of the most exciting parts of my job is conceptualizing the visual language that goes into the image. During prep, I sit down with the director and talk about what their visual and narrative influences are. I try to get onto the director's mind's eye in order to be able to enhance and execute that vision. It becomes, for me, a collaborative vision.

**Ellen Kuras, D.P. (From "Cinematography as Poetry,"
interview by Erin Torneo, *indieWIRE*)**

The domain of cinematography is the interpretation of story through images that includes composition, color, lighting, and exposure as the primary tools of expression. By now it should be clear that film lighting isn't just a matter of throwing light onto a scene so that we can simply make out the physical subject. Lighting is communicating visual ideas and inflecting the story with a mood, a tone, a visual context, and a narrative meaning. Lighting can help establish an historical era, a season, or even a time of day. It can provide insight into the psychological state of a character or add an ironic edge to the events in the film. Lighting can evoke any mood from ominous to cheerful. But the name of the game with lighting and exposure is "control." Once you have learned to control your image through lighting and exposure, countless expressive possibilities become available to you, and the more you work, the greater your technical and aesthetic repertoire becomes—so much so that the textbooks become irrelevant. At that point it becomes essential to watch movies, study what cinematographers are actually doing in the field, read the trade magazine interviews, and attend screenings where the director and crew make an appearance. Whenever you watch a movie, try to figure out where the lights are placed and what sources are being used, where the D.P. has pegged the exposure, how they handle the camera, and what lenses they have chosen. Consider the quality of the various sources of light and their relationship to the other lights and to the fictive world. And always think about the story and ask yourself why was this particular lighting and camera approach used in this particular film.

Very broadly speaking, cinematic lighting approaches break down into naturalistic and stylized designs. But you must always keep in mind that these are not strictly delineated approaches or distinct choices—in fact, naturalistic and stylized lighting designs exist along a highly flexible continuum of aesthetic possibilities for your film. These approaches are often also mixed within the same film. That said, for our introduction we'll discuss the unique principles of each lighting philosophy in discrete terms.

Naturalism and Lighting

A **naturalistic** approach strives to appear as plausible and harmonious with the environment as possible. Lighting direction and sources are generally motivated, lighting continuity is usually observed, and the relationship between the various light sources duplicates what we would expect in a real life situation. For this reason, the impact of naturalistic lighting is quite subtle, unobtrusive, and realistic. In fact, the terms naturalistic and **realistic** are often used interchangeably. Obviously, one way to obtain a raw, naturalistic look is to use no artificial lighting—rather, to use only available light. Many films have been shot this way, primarily those that try to evoke a documentary look to draw the audience into the realism of the story. The Dardenne brothers shoot

Figure 14-21 In keeping with the documentary style of their cinematography, the Dardenne brothers shot *The Son* (2002) using mostly available light in real locations (cinematography by Alain Marcoen).

their socially conscious films in a gritty, direct, documentary manner that places very few technical or stylistic layers between the audience and the subjects of their films (Figure 14-21). The Dardennes shoot almost exclusively with natural light in real locations to remain as free from artifice as possible and they consciously use all of the codes of documentary filmmaking. Their visual approach creates the impression that they are not making this stuff up: they are merely reporting on actual human experience from the field.

Naturalistic lighting, however, does not necessarily mean that a filmmaker uses only available light, although many films have been made this way. In fact, naturalistic lighting often requires a lot of artifice, careful light placement, and exposure control in order to "look" natural. The use of strictly available light does not always translate into what the human eye "naturally" sees because no film stock or CCD chip sees light, as-is, quite the way the human eye does. So in an effort to duplicate what an audience expects to see naturally, films employ considerable and careful technique in lighting.

A good example of this can be seen in Erick Zonca's feature film debut, *The Dreamlife of Angels* (1999), which was photographed by Agnès Godard (Figure 14-22). The film takes place in the northern French industrial town of Lille during the wintertime, when the skies are overcast and the light is diffused through a blanket of thick, low clouds. The quality of light during this season is especially thin, gray, and somber, and Godard produced the same quality with the artificial lights to maintain a highly naturalistic feel. For example, the apartment that the two protagonists share in the film had windows that allowed the cold, diffused light to spill in, but Godard nonetheless needed to augment the available light: "Outside it was wintertime, and sometimes we were shooting quite early in the morning—the quantity of light was not high." (Agnès Godard, from "Photographing Angels," by John Calhoun, *Live Design Online*, April 1999.) So she used several HMI lights reflected off bounce boards to bring up the exposures indoors in a way that "duplicated" the natural light of the season. "They were used as a reflecting light, not direct. With the size of the room they were too rude to be used directly." She also used Chinese lanterns for a very soft and subtle source that was more mobile.

Figure 14-22 Zonca's *The Dreamlife of Angels* (1998), shot by Agnès Godard, used bounced HMI lights to maintain the illusion of a typical overcast winter day.

■ **Figure 14-23** The location of the lighting in *Life Lessons,* Scorsese's episode in *New York Stories* (1989), is motivated by where it would be in the real world, a practice favored by the film's cinematographer, Néstor Almendros.

The legendary D.P. Néstor Almendros summed up the naturalistic approach (Figure 14-23) with this statement of his lighting philosophy:

I start from realism. My way of lighting and seeing is realistic; I don't use imagination. I use research. I go to a location and see where the light falls normally and I just try to catch it as it is or reinforce it if it is in sufficient; that's on a natural set. On an artificial set, I suppose that there would be a sun outside the house and then I see how the light would come through the windows and I reconstruct it. The source of light should always be justified.

(From *Masters of Light,* by Dennis Schaefer and Larry Salvato)

Stylized Lighting

Stylized (or **nonnaturalistic**) lighting approaches, on the other hand, are designed to draw attention to the aesthetic by being excessive or exaggerated in ways that make a specific narrative or thematic point—even if that point is simply to highlight the artifice of the narrative. Lighting placement and exposures can be unmotivated or motivated by a logic other than the plausible illumination of the particular physical environment. For example, a stylized lighting scheme might be motivated by the dramatic logic of a scene, by character psychology and point of view, or by the need to create an additional thematic or ironic story layer. Stylized lighting is often associated with nonrealistic film genres, like fantasy films, fables, or films that intentionally invoke an overtly theatrical tone. Film noir is an example of a genre that is associated with an exaggerated lighting scheme whose deep shadows emphasizes the dangers lurking in both the dark criminal underbelly of society and the perils of romantic encounters (Figure 14-24).

■ **Figure 14-24** Stylized lighting, commonly found in film noirs like Curtiz' *Mildred Pierce* (1945), can underline the danger lurking around every corner (cinematography by Ernest Haller).

An extreme example of a theatrical approach to lighting and colors can be seen in Michael Powell and Emeric Pressburger's *Black Narcissus* (1947), which was photographed in Technicolor by Jack Cardiff (Figure 14-25). *Black Narcissus* creates a dream world on an operatic scale. The story revolves around the tale of five Anglican nuns who are trying to establish an order in colonial India's Himalayan mountains. But the surrealistically exotic atmosphere of the remote location causes the nuns to succumb to emotional disorder, sexual desire, and even madness.

■ **Figure 14-25** The hyper-stylized look created by the masterful interplay of light, shadow, and color in Powell and Pressburger's *Black Narcissus* (1947) serves to visualize the intense emotions felt by a group of Anglican nuns stationed in the Himalayan mountains (cinematography by Jack Cardiff). See the color insert in Chapter 13.

Cardiff would freely mix colors in his lighting approach—for example, using green gels over the fill lights and pink gels in his key light (ostensibly the sun) and blue gels over his set lights—in an effort to represent through color the wild mix of emotions that are overwhelming the Sisters of the order. His virtuosic use of various light qualities—soft, hard, and shadows—adds to a world where narrative dramatic mood above all motivates the quality of light. There is no chance that a viewer could take the intense colors and theatrical lighting for anything resembling realism—that encourages us to look beneath the narrative surface for what all this vibrant imagery could mean. The visual style seems to emerge from, and in turn points the audience toward, the surreal internal landscape of human desire, dreams, and fantasy.

It is essential to understand, however, that naturalistic lighting and stylized lighting do not stand as exclusive options for a filmmaker. There is a sliding scale between these two poles, and most filmmakers find themselves working somewhere between strict naturalism and overt stylization. Working with Tim Burton, the master of stylized film technique, the cinematographer Emmanuel Lubezki was free to use a nonrealistic lighting approach for the mythic horror/fantasy film *Sleepy Hollow,* but in the end his approach was somewhere in between, but leaning toward the stylized end of the spectrum.

> *[The screenplay] was a wonderful fantasy with a mixture of horror, romance, drama, and humor . . . What is great is to take something unreal and make it "real"—or, at least, believable—to create a certain reality with material so completely theatrical. [The lighting style] was between naturalism and pictorialism. The aim of pictorialism is to create photographs that are similar to paintings and to establish photography as a valid art form. In this case, [the purpose was] to make images that felt like illustrations from an old book. . . . We were going to enhance the reality and make it more beautiful, but still believable.*

**Emmanuel Lubezki (From *Headless Horror,* by
Pauline Rogers, The International Cinematographers Guild)**

More subtle is the stylized use of color and lighting in Spike Lee's *Do The Right Thing* (1989), which was shot by D.P. Ernest Dickerson. The setting for the film is the Bedford-Stuyvesant section of Brooklyn and the events take place over the course of one summer day—the hottest day of the year. Dickerson used extremely warm colors and hard lighting to evoke the brutal, oppressive heat of an inner-city heat wave in hyperbolic style. The look is both motivated and slightly exaggerated. This visual style makes the audience really feel the intense sun, the heat, the inescapability of it, and it also transforms the literal heat of the weather into a metaphor for the smoldering, inescapable, and explosive racial tensions between the people in the neighborhood (Figure 14-26).

An even more subtle use of lighting that is both naturalistic, but slightly stylized can be found in Alexander Payne's 1999 film *Election.* Shot by James Glennon, the story revolves around the election for student government president at Carver High School, in the American mid-west. Even though the film traces the humiliation and "moral and ethical" debasement of its lead character, the teacher Jim McAllister, the film maintains a consistently bright, cheery high-key look associated with teen comedy movies. The colors are vivid and shadows are all but banished, even though Mr. McAllister is losing his wife, his job, and his good reputation. This lighting scheme,

■ **Figure 14-26** Top: Lee's *Do The Right Thing* (1989) has highly stylized lighting that emphasizes the heat of one particularly hot day in Brooklyn (cinematography by Ernest Dickerson). Bottom: In Payne's *Election* (1999), naturalistic lighting provides an ironic subtext (cinematography by James Glennon). See the color insert in Chapter 13.

■ **Figure 14-27** Stylized lighting can be mixed with naturalistic lighting to effectively emphasize key moments in a film, as Polanski did in *Repulsion* (1965) (cinematography by Gilbert Taylor).

though completely "naturalistic" and motivated by the bright fluorescent lights and industrial white walls of the high school, infuses the events of the film with a sharp ironic tone that encourages us to look beneath the generic surface of this particular, inconsequential high school story and to look also at the film for what it says about human character and America in general.

It is also extremely common for films that are more or less naturalistic in their lighting approach to incorporate scenes and moments with more stylized visual approaches, in order to elevate a particular dramatic moment or bring us into the perspective or psychology of a character. A perfect example can be seen in Roman Polanski's *Repulsion* (1965), the story of Carol, a mentally vulnerable young woman who lives in London with her sister (Figure 14-27). When her sister leaves for a vacation, Carol is left alone and her fears become nightmares, then hallucinations, as she falls inexorably into madness. While the film is presented in a more or less naturalistic mode (albeit quite dark), the lighting approach for the scenes in which we are left alone in the apartment with Carol become highly stylized and low-key. The starkness of the lighting is exaggerated and the high contrast plunges the audience into the dark shadows of Carol's madness. One cannot say the lighting style here is "unmotivated," because Polanski wishes to put us deeply into Carol's point of view, to see the hallucinations as she sees them, so in this case the lighting strategy is motivated by the visions and delusions of a mind in the state of total confusion.

■ FINDING THE APPROPRIATE LIGHTING STRATEGY

So where does one begin to consider the specific approach one should take to lighting a film? In preproduction, of course. The process of devising a lighting strategy is of paramount importance in a movie—even if you're not using any artificial lights at all—and it emerges from the preproduction consultations between the director and cinematographer.

The Overall Look

During the pre-visualization process, the director and cinematographer examine the script to determine how to visualize the story in terms of lighting (and, of course, camerawork as well). Their first task is to determine the overall look of the film. The lighting strategy derives primarily from the story itself. During preproduction meetings, the director and cinematographer ask themselves questions like:

■ What is the film about?

■ What is the director's interpretive angle on the script—the central idea?

■ What mood or tone is suggested by the events and locations in the movie?

■ Does that mood evolve or change over the course of the film?

■ What is the primary element driving this film: Dialogue? Character actions? Juxtaposition of images?

■ From whose point of view are we shooting this film and what is their state of mind?

■ What is the historic era of the film?

■ Does the film reference any existing film genres (screwball comedy, film noir, etc.) that themselves have certain lighting conventions?

■ What are the elements in the script that might suggest a lighting approach (i.e., location, season, time of day, set descriptions, character)?

■ What might be the balance between natural light and artificial light sources?

■ Generally how can lighting support the tone and ideas of the script?

In answering these questions, the director and D.P. will come closer to figuring out not just a lighting strategy, but also the appropriate visual approach for that specific film expressed through lighting, film stocks, exposures, and camera-work that support the story and the director's interpretive idea.

Each script is different. Each tells its own story with characters and emotions. It is that which determines the look of the film. This is why each film should look different.

(Ernest Dickerson, From "Variations on the Mo' Better Blues," by Al Herrell, *American Cinematographer,* September 1990)

For *Mo' Better Blues* (1990), their fourth feature film as a team, Lee and Dickerson derived the look of the film from the two competing elements in the life of the main character, jazz trumpeter Bleek Gilliam: "cool" jazz and "hot" personal relationships, especially with

■ **Figure 14-28** Cinematographer Ernest Dickerson lights Bleek (Denzel Washington) using colors that stand for his two main interests, jazz (blue) and women (red), in Lee's *Mo' Better Blues* (1990). See the color insert in Chapter 13.

women. These are the central narrative elements driving the story. Throughout the film, Dickerson delineates these competing strands of Bleek's life by using cool or warm light sources in various scenes (Figure 14-28). In several scenes he even mixes cool light sources with warm light sources in the same frame to create a stylized, thematic point.

Hot against cool I felt was the best way to exemplify the music—jazz. It also symbolizes the life of the main character, Bleek, and relationships with ladies and his fellow musicians. . . . Whenever you play warm against cool light, these opposite wavelengths seem to vibrate against each other creating a visual tension. They pull against each other, just as Bleek was being emotionally pulled between two ladies.

Given the way Dickerson speaks about light and mixing colors to represent emotions, it comes as no surprise that he has often cited Jack Cardiff, and films like *Black Narcissus,* as a major influence on his work.

Often the process of discovering the appropriate lighting style involves some visual research on the part of both the director and the cinematographer. Obviously, as I mentioned in the previous chapter, the history of motion pictures provides cinematographers and directors a wealth of resources and examples to consider when designing a visual approach to a film. However, beyond looking at movies for inspiration, the other art forms, like painting and photography, are also invaluable for visual research. For *Black Narcissus,* Jack Cardiff studied and used many of the lighting techniques from painters like Vermeer (soft directional lighting), Rembrandt (interplay of bright, golden light and deep shadow), and Van Gogh (expressive mix of colors, in shadows and in light sources).

Cinematographer Darius Khondji often acknowledges the extensive visual research he engages in before each film. When preparing to shoot *Delicatessen* (1991) (Figure 14-29)—directed by Jean-Pierre Jeunet and Marc Caro, who themselves employ a unique visual style—Khondji's research incorporated classic silent films and photography.

Quai des Brumes (Marcel Carné, 1938) and other French Poetic Realist films inspired Jean Pierre and Marc Caro and they showed me those films or selected clips in preparation to Delicatessen. I remember being much more inspired by the pure cinematic style of silent films. I would watch The Wind (1928) by Sjöström, L'Ange Bleu (1930) by Von Sternberg, Vampyr (1932) by Dreyer, Nosferatu (1922) and Sunrise (1927) by Murnau and Von Stroheim's early films. I was also inspired by the paintings of George Bellows and their texture of black, brown, warm red, yellow, and golden colours. I looked at Pictorialists such as Heinrich Kuhn, early Edouard Steichen, Stieglitz, Cameron, and the illustrator, Martin Lewis.

*What I love in Pictorialist photographs is that they were like the "charnier" or "hinge"
between painting and photography, neither painting nor photography, and I found that
very inspiring for my early movies. Before photographing Delicatessen, I didn't go to
the cinema any more. I would only watch black-and-white silent films and avoid being
influenced directly by recent movies.*

**Darius Khondji (From *New Cinematographers*,
by Alexander Ballinger, Laurence King, London, 2004)**

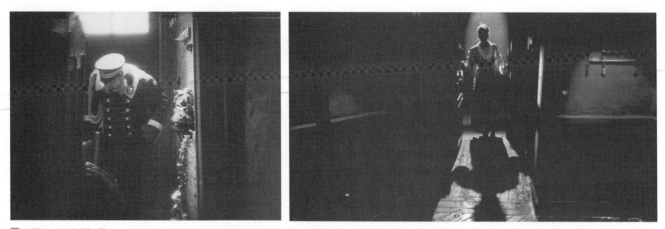

■ **Figure 14-29** Cinematographer Darius Khondji saw nothing but silent film masterpieces like Murnau's *The Last Laugh* (1924, left), in his preparation for shooting Caro and Jeunet's *Delicatessen* (1991, right).

Even small films made on limited budgets can benefit from visual research to find their
lighting style. I was recently the cinematographer on the short DV film *Flesh & Blade,*
which is a dark, 19th-century gothic tale of love and science tragically entangled (**Figure
14-30**). I turned to the wonderful, frightening paintings of Joseph Wright, which depict
both the process of scientific inquiry and the romanticized mysticism that characterized
science in the 18th century, to help determine the overall look of a film that would take
place primarily in a scientist's laboratory.

Other Considerations

As I discussed in the very first chapter of this book, the aesthetic of a film, including the
photographic look of the movie, is also inextricably linked to the practical realities of film
production, especially the resources available to the filmmaker. It doesn't do a project any
good to imagine a style during preproduction if that style cannot be accomplished in the
allotted time or with the resources available. This is a concern, of course, which should
be anticipated and addressed during the very conception and scripting of the film. Again,

■ **Figure 14-30** As part of my visual research for lighting *Flesh & Blade* (2007) (left and right frames), I looked at paintings like *An Experiment on a
Bird in an Airpump* (1768), by Joseph Wright of Derby (center).

when the director and cinematographer explore the screenplay in preproduction, they need to ask themselves practical questions:

- What is the budget of the film?
- What is the shooting format and what is it capable of?
- How much time do we have for lighting (days and hours each day)?
- How large is the crew?
- How many and what sort of lighting units (and grip equipment) are available for the shoot?
- How controllable and accessible are the locations?
- How much power is at each location for artificial lights?
- What are the sources of natural light on the set and how much artificial lighting do we actually need?

However, limited resources never means a lack of style; it means only that the filmmakers need to devise an intelligent, innovative, and resourceful visual approach, which, when perfectly matched with the script, can be as powerful as anything produced with larger budgets. Take the example of the feature film *Personal Velocity* (2002), directed by Rebecca Miller and shot by Ellen Kuras. Kuras recounts the day Miller approached her with the idea of shooting the film:

She wrote a book of short stories and she called me up and said, "Listen, I finally have some money and I can make a short film based on three of my short stories. Would you like to do it?" and I said, "Sure. I'll work with you any time." She said the only thing is "we only have $150,000 and we have to shoot it in mini-DV." I said, "Okay. Well, why don't we shoot it in Super 16?" She said, "We can't, because part of the money is contingent on us shooting mini-DV." Kuras then told Miller, "I'll give you five weeks of my time for free and let's do it—let's make the movie."

(From "Where the Girls Are," by Jennifer M. Wood, *MovieMaker,* Vol. 2, Issue #9)

Even though the shooting format of the film, the most fundamental technical and expressive tool for a cinematographer, was determined by practical considerations, this didn't mean that Kuras was not able to devise an aesthetic and original interpretation of the project. In fact, she turned a limitation into an opportunity.

Kuras first considered the broader concept of working with DV and with literary material and the freedom that allowed her:

I just said, you know what, I'm shooting with this mini-DV medium, I'm going to think of these as short stories and I'm going to make it look and feel like a poem. . . . That means I'm not going to do what everybody says you're supposed to do. I'm just going to do what feels right for the movie.

(From "Taking the Digital Medium into Their Hands," by Philippa Bourke, www.moviesbywomen.com)

Then, in consultation with Miller, Kuras devised a specific lighting and color approach for each woman's story (Figure 14-31).

■ **Figure 14-31** Shooting on digital video does not preclude having complex, beautiful cinematography. Ellen Kuras devised 3 completely different visual styles for the 3 characters in Miller's *Personal Velocity* (2002). See the color insert in Chapter 13.

We had three distinct looks for each of the different narratives. The color palette for Delia's story was warm toned with more yellows and greens and browns. We tried to keep the skin tones neutral . . . Greta's story was cool and austere. The camera moves were on a tripod and were much more mannered. Paula's story was much more frenetic so for the color palette, I wanted to put this kind of blue purple to the shadow areas, and to have some cream colored highlights and then have the flashback sequences be a different color which would be in contrast to what the main color palette was. . . . The contrast is very hard to control using DV unless you have an overcast lighting situation or you're inside. John [Kuras' gaffer John Nadeau] and I basically used the natural light and augmented it, giving it a style unto itself.

(From "Cinematography as Poetry," interview by Erin Torneo, *indieWIRE*)

Kuras has worked extensively on 35mm, Super 16, and DV; she has worked with large budgets and minimal resources and has been supported by fully staffed professional and skeleton crews alike. Her work on *Personal Velocity* is testament to her versatility and artistic virtuosity.

Sound for Production

The digital revolution has not exclusively revolved around the gathering, editing, and presentation of images alone. The past ten years has seen a veritable sea change in the tools and techniques of gathering, mixing, and replaying audio as well. There was a time when distribution on video or through broadcast TV meant that people would be listening to your film on little 3-inch built-in speakers. Today American households are fast equipping their home theater units with super high fidelity, digital surround sound audio. What this means for the filmmaker is that the audience can hear everything! So we are compelled to create the best possible sound tracks possible to accompany our carefully composed and exposed images. The first, and most important, step to this end is to gather the best possible sound in the field during production. Unfortunately, production sound is often the "blind spot" for many filmmakers getting ready to shoot, especially those just starting out. All too often, a lot of time, money, and preparation goes into the production of the images, while inexperienced filmmakers begin to think seriously about sound only after they hear and try to work with the terrible audio they got during production. The production sound team, those people who record sound in the field, are the unsung heroes of the film world—when they do their job perfectly, no one notices them; when the sound is bad, they are cursed. They are sort of like shoelaces: when they do their job properly and keep our shoes on our feet, we don't notice them, but when one breaks, we curse them. Good sound people are invaluable and the smart filmmaker understands that getting good sound in production means a stronger sound design in postproduction, more creative options in editing, and saving time and money. This is why good sound people work a lot and why I've devoted three chapters to the craft of sound recording in the field.

■ WHAT IS PRODUCTION AUDIO?

The final form of a movie's completed sound track consists of layering multiple tracks of sound, anywhere from two to dozens. While many of the sound elements we hear in a final film are gathered during postproduction (i.e., music, sound effects, voice-overs), there are several crucial elements that are recorded in production while we shoot our images: synchronous sound, wild sound, and ambient sound. For many films, short or feature length, the sound elements recorded in the field, like dialogue, constitute the most crucial audio elements on the sound track. These are the elements we will be exploring in this chapter.

■ UNDERSTANDING SOUND

In space, no one can hear you scream.

Tag line for *Alien*

In Stanley Kubrick's *2001: A Space Odyssey,* when HAL 9000 severs Poole's life support cable, sending Poole hurtling through space (**Figure 15-2**), the sound that accompanies his sure demise is—total silence. Why did Kubrick choose utter silence for this highly dramatic moment, even though Poole is struggling and likely screaming his head off? Because sound is produced by some vibrating source creating pressure and displacing air molecules. Much like the ripples in a pool of water when a pebble is thrown in, the displacement of the air molecules create acoustic sound waves, which move through

in practice

Sounds that appear to be emanating from a single location at a single time are actually constructed from many different elements; some are recorded during production and others are collected later, then the different elements are mixed to create a precise aural impression. Here is a simple scene of two friends trying to have a conversation in a noisy coffee shop, just off a busy road, when an off-screen car accident interrupts them. This scene incorporates several distinct sound elements:

Track #1: The friends' dialogue.

Track #2: The ambiance of the coffee shop (i.e., coffee machines, cups clattering, patrons' chatter).

Track #3: The sounds of traffic just outside the coffee shop.

Track #4: The sound of the car crash that interrupts them.

While it is theoretically possible to record all of these sounds in a single take with a single microphone, it would require a prohibitive amount of time and choreography. Instead, we record (or find) each of these elements separately and later, in postproduction, construct a sound design by layering and mixing independent tracks. Each track can be synced to the picture with frame accuracy and also have the ability for independent volume and equalization adjustments. We will explore postproduction sound in detail in Chapters 22 and 23.

■ **Figure 15-1** This seemingly simple conversation in a restaurant has a sound track that combines sync sound, sound effects recorded on location, and prerecorded elements licensed from sound effects collections.

■ **Figure 15-2** Poole's death from Kubrick's *2001: A Space Odyssey* (1968).

the air. If, as in space, there is no air, then there is no sound.

A sound wave is in fact a pressure wave, consisting of an alternating pattern of high pressure (compression) and low pressure (rarefaction), traveling through the air. The vibrating source of this pressure can be a guitar string, a tuning fork, the contact between a baseball and a bat, or human vocal chords. These sound waves are eventually received by some sensitive membrane, like an eardrum or microphone diaphragm, which duplicates the vibration patterns of the original source. And what if there isn't a vibration-sensitive membrane to receive those sound waves? Well, you've probably already pondered the proverbial question of whether or not a tree falling in the woods makes a sound if there is no one there to hear it, right?

There are four basic properties of sound that are essential to understanding audio and the techniques of microphone placement and recording for film production:

- Pitch (frequency)
- Loudness (amplitude)
- Quality (timbre)
- Velocity (speed)

We plot these sound wave characteristics on the graph shown in Figure 15-3. This common sine wave graph measures the compression of the air molecules that are caused by a particular sound. With this graph we are able to see certain properties of a particular sound.

Frequency (Pitch)

Sound waves travel in fairly consistent **wave cycles**. One **wavelength** is the length of one cycle, from peak to peak, which then repeats itself. A wavelength is plotted from one highest pressure point to the very next highest pressure point. The number of these waves that pass a fixed point over the course of one second is the measure of the frequency of the sound wave. This measure of **cycles per second** is referred to as **Hertz (Hz)** and is measured along the graph's x-axis.

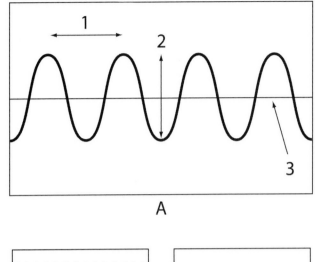

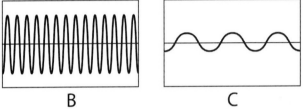

A

B   C

Figure 15-3 A simple sound (A) can be understood in terms of its wavelength (1), and its amplitude (2), or the degree to which it deviates from normal air pressure (3). The higher the number of cycles per second (B) also called Hertz, the higher the frequency the sound will have. Sounds with very low frequencies have fewer cycles per second (C).

A sound that generates 10,000 wave cycles every second has a frequency of 10,000 Hz, also written 10 kHz. This frequency of cycles per second is actually measuring the **pitch** of that particular sound. The fewer cycles per second, the lower the pitch of a sound; the more cycles per second, the higher the pitch (Figure 15-4).

Not all sound frequencies can be perceived by the human ear or a microphone. The range of detectable pitches for a given apparatus is called the **frequency range**. An average, healthy human ear can distinguish pitches from 25 Hz to 20 kHz. Dogs can hear frequen-

5,200 Hz   150 Hz - 2,000 Hz   45 Hz

Figure 15-4 A piccolo (the highest pitched instrument in an orchestra) can reach a frequency of 5,200 Hz, while a tuba (the lowest pitched instrument), can create sounds as low as 45 Hz. The human voice is located in the frequency mid-range, from 150 Hz to 2,000 Hz.

cies beyond 20 kHz; this is why they can hear high-pitched dog whistles that humans cannot. The frequency range that a microphone or a sound recorder can pick up and duplicate is a common measure of equipment quality. The "hearing" range for a particular piece of gear is called its **frequency response**. A professional cassette deck has a frequency response of 30 Hz–15 kHz, which is less than the range of human hearing. A typical professional digital audio recorder has a frequency response of 20 Hz–40 kHz, which is greater than the range of human hearing.

Amplitude (Loudness)

Each peak high and low pressure point along the graph's y-axis has a specific height or **amplitude**, which is a measure of the **loudness** of a sound (see Figure 15-3). The higher the amplitude peak, the greater is the displacement pressure of the sound wave and the louder the sound. Loudness is measured in **decibels** (**dB**). Decibels increase or decrease according to a logarithmic progression. I won't go into the complexities of logarithms; it's sufficient to simply understand that it takes an increase of three decibels (3 dB) to double the loudness and a decrease of three decibels to halve loudness.

The loudness range that the human ear can distinguish falls between the **threshold of hearing** (0 dB) on the lower end, and the **threshold of pain** (120 dB) on the upper end. A normal conversation tone is approximately 55 dB. A whisper is around 25 dB and a scream comes in at around 75 dB. At 150 dB, eardrums will rupture—you'll know when *that* happens.

In most recording situations the loudness of your source fluctuates. For example, many symphonies have quiet passages and loud passages. Listen to the opening of Richard Strauss' "Also Sprach Zarathustra" (which was used in Kubrick's *2001: A Space Odyssey*). The piece begins with the softest, barely audible drone of the double basses and builds to an all-out, full orchestra fortissimo led by crashing cymbals, blaring horns, and pounding tympani, in only a minute and a half! The range of different loudness levels is referred to as the **dynamic range**. "Also Sprach Zarathustra" has an extremely wide dynamic range. A conversation that goes from a whisper to a scream has a wide dynamic range, while a politician delivering a speech in a monotone has a very narrow dynamic range. Wide dynamic ranges can be very challenging for both the sound recordist and the equipment (see Chapter 17, Sound Recording Technique).

Inverse Square Law

The amplitude of a sound wave diminishes according to the **inverse square law** as it travels through space, which means that the intensity of a given sound decreases by the square of its distance from the sound source. This is the same law that governs the drop-off of light intensity as one moves away from the source of illumination (see p. 240), so you can remember it by the same rule of thumb: doubling the distance from the source results in the loudness diminishing four times, and halving the distance from your source will increase the loudness four times. Knowing that sound intensity drops off drastically the further one moves a microphone away from the audio source is essential in determining microphone placement.

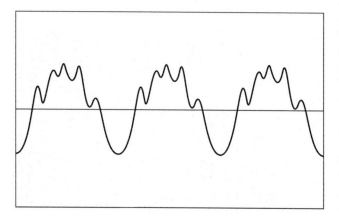

■ **Figure 15-5** Sounds are usually made up of more complex combinations of tiny variations called harmonics and overtones, which mark the difference between, for instance, a piano and a tuba playing the same note.

Quality (Timbre)

The sound waves in Figure 15-3 are representations of pure, electronically generated tones with no character or aberrations. When we encounter the waves of sounds from the real world the curve does not look quite so uniform, with a smooth curve and perfectly symmetrical peaks and dips. Most naturally occurring sound waves include characteristic irregularities in the overall shape

■ **Figure 15-6** Waveforms for a piano playing middle C (A), a violin playing middle C (B), and a human voice singing middle C (C).

and are also accompanied by a series of other waves of lower amplitude and various frequencies, all of which reflect the particular quality of that sound.

The central and dominant shape of the wave is called the **fundamental tone**, but every fundamental tone also resonates with a series of imperfections and coinciding waves that represent **overtones** and **harmonics**. These elements comprise **timbre**, which is the unique tonal composition and characteristics of that sound (i.e., richness, harshness, resonance). Timbre allows us to easily distinguish different instruments playing the very same note. For example, middle C on a piano sounds quite different from the same note played on a trumpet, or on a guitar, or when sung by a human voice (Figure 15-6).

Velocity

Sound is a wave that travels through space, so it has both directionality and speed. The speed of sound is 1,086 feet per second. This is very slow compared to the speed of light (which is 983,571,056 feet per second). This is why, when you're watching the fireworks display on the fourth of July, you see the big flash of light first and hear the boom of the explosion seconds later (Figure 15-7).

■ PRODUCTION SOUND

There are several names for it—**production sound**, **field recording**, and **audio gathering**—but the name of the game is all the same; get the best quality sound possible. Great quality field recordings allow for maximum creative manipulation in postproduction. In some ways it's easier to get away with less than perfect images, than with less than perfect sound. Poor quality audio immediately marks your film as that of an amateur. If you're a stop or two underexposed, well, the audience can at least still see what's going on, but if your recording is too low, they can't hear what people are saying and all meaning is lost. A poor original sound recording can be the utter bane of an entire film. It's often impossible to add what is missing or take away what shouldn't be there, and those times when audio *can* be "cor-

rected in post" it's always difficult and often expensive to do. So the primary responsibility of the sound team during the production phase is to get as clean and strong a sound recording as possible. Getting great production sound means understanding sound, knowing your equipment, and practicing good recording technique.

Location Audio

Location sound is any sound that is recorded in the same environment as the images. Location sound breaks down into roughly two categories: **synchronous sound (sync sound)** and **wild sound** (also called **non-sync sound**).

Sync sound is recorded simultaneously with taking the image, so sound and picture correspond to each other with frame accuracy and are said to be **"in sync"** with

■ **Figure 15-7** In real life, fireworks are usually out of sync with the sound of their blasts, since light travels at a much faster speed than sound. Most films, however, sync them in postproduction, as in Lee's *Brokeback Mountain* (2005).

■ **Figure 15-8** The sound crew, usually made up of a mixer (foreground) and a boom person (standing), is in charge of recording sync sound during the shooting of a film.

one another (Figure 15-8). This could be a character's dialogue, cars zooming past, or the sound of a door closing—anything in which the sound emanating from the scene is recorded in sync with the picture.

In DV production this is not difficult because DV is usually a single-system format, meaning that both audio and video are gathered with the same apparatus (the camcorder) and are recorded in sync on the same media (videotape). However, double-system film production requires additional and specialized equipment for sync sound shooting to ensure that the audio recording machine runs at precisely the same speed as the camera, without fluctuation (see later, Double- and Single-System Recording).

Wild sound is audio that is recorded on location, but not simultaneously with the picture, and so has no corresponding picture to be in sync with. Wild sound functions as a sound design element that either doesn't require synchronization or that can be manually synced to an image later in the editing. Two common types of wild sound recorded in the field are **ambient sound** (also called **room tone**) and **location sound effects** (also called **spot sound effects**). From time to time we might be prohibited from getting a specific sound because of microphone placement or the size of a frame while we are shooting a scene. In these cases a sound recordist will often rerecord specific sounds from the scene as wild sound (without the camera rolling) in order to get a better quality representation that can be inserted in postproduction as a special effect. Ambient sound refers to the entire group of sounds and tonal qualities of a given recording environment. Ambient sound includes both **room acoustics** (also called **presence**) and **background noise** (also called **atmospheric sounds**).

Room acoustics are the general aural qualities of a given space. For example, the acoustics of a small carpeted room filled with old stuffed furniture is quite different from the acoustics of a bathroom with nothing but tiled floors and walls. In the case of the bathroom, any source of audio is surrounded by hard surfaces that will reflect the sound. Sound bouncing off surfaces is called **reverberation (reverb)**. In this situation a microphone will pick up the audio from the source (direct sound) and also pick up the audio reverberating off the walls and floor. The result is a boomy or echo-y sound as the signal duplicates itself over and over again. A recording space like this is called acoustically **live**. The carpets and furniture in the small room, however, are poor reflective surfaces and serve to absorb sounds after they leave the source. This allows only the direct sound source to be recorded. This is known as an acoustically **dead** recording space.

The other factor that affects acoustics is room size. A small tiled bathroom is a very reflective space, but the reverberation intervals will be shorter than in a gothic cathedral, where the sound travels a greater distance to a reflective surface and back to the microphone, increasing the time between the recording of the direct sound and its reflection. The audible difference in the acoustic quality between these two live spaces is the difference in **reverb delay**. Very live acoustics are often difficult to work with. Too much reverberation can create muddy audio.

Background noise or **atmospheric sounds** are all of the sounds that occur naturally in any specific recording location. If we are shooting a scene near a playground, for example, the sound of children playing is part of the environment and therefore is expected to be in the scene. However, we certainly don't want background noises to overwhelm the audio that we are trying to pick up (i.e., the dialogue), so we might want to minimize the sound of children playing while we record our sync sound dialogue as cleanly as possible (through microphone choice and placement), and then record some high-quality "wild sound" of children playing after the camera stops rolling. This way we can place the wild sound under the clean conversation later, and adjust the levels to achieve exactly the volume balance we want under the dialogue. We will discuss specific techniques for recording ambient sound later on in this chapter.

Double- and Single-System Recording

Double- and single-system sound simply refers to the number of machines needed to record your image and sound during a shoot. In general, DV is a single-system sound medium that has the capability to record both audio and video in one camcorder and on the same recording medium—sound and picture are automatically and always in sync. Film, on the other hand is a double-system sound medium, meaning the film camera records the image, and a separate apparatus, a sound recorder, gathers the audio (Figures 15-9 and 15-10).

It's important to know that not all film cameras are capable of shooting sync sound. Nonsync film cameras, like the Arri-S, running at 24 fps, in fact fluctuate between 22 fps and 25 fps. This discrepancy in frame rate isn't noticeable in the image, but can throw the picture out of sync with its cor-

■ **Figure 15-9** Single-system sound uses a single device, like a video camera (2), to record both picture and sound. The addition of a boom person (1) can provide greater flexibility to the way the sound is recorded (see also Figure 16-10).

■ **Figure 15-10** Double-system sound uses two devices: one to record the image, in this case a film camera (3), and another to record the sound, here a digital sound recorder (1) that captures the signal from the boom operator and his microphone (2). Since these two devices work independently, a slate (4) must be used to provide an audiovisual point of reference to sync picture and sound in postproduction.

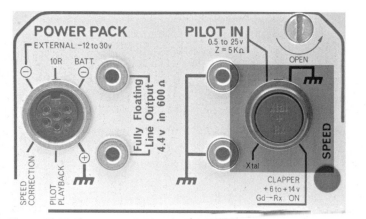

POWER PACK
EXTERNAL −12 to 30v
10R BATT.
Fully Floating
Line Output
4.4 v in 600 Ω
SPEED CORRECTION
PILOT PLAYBACK

PILOT IN
0.5 to 25v
Z = 5KΩ
OPEN
Xtal
Xtal
SPEED
CLAPPER
+ 6 to +14 v
Gd→Rx ON

■ **Figure 15-11** To ensure perfect synchronization in postproduction, film sync sound cameras and sound recorders are outfitted with a crystal sync oscillator that regulates the speed at which they operate (pictured: the crystal oscillator in the Nagra sound recorder).

responding audio. Also, nonsync film cameras tend to have noisy motors, which a microphone would clearly pick up as inappropriate background noise. Sync sound cameras, on the other hand either have a quiet motor or are blimped (encased in metal soundproofing) to keep camera noise from registering on the sound recording. In addition, sync sound cameras are outfitted with a **crystal sync oscillator** to ensure a constant and compatible speed. The crystal oscillator emits a steady 60-cycle-per-second pulse that precisely governs the transport speed of the camera. A crystal sync camera running at sound speed (24 fps) remains accurate to plus or minus half a frame over 400 feet of film (16,000 frames), a standard magazine load. The recording "speed" of digital recorders, on the other hand, is precisely regulated by their constant sampling rate, which is also based on 60-cycle oscillations (see later, Sampling). So one second of steady 24-fps film transport will perfectly match one second of steadily sampled digital audio. In the case of analog tape recorders, like the Nagra, they too must be outfitted with a crystal oscillator to govern their speed and remain in sync with the film camera (**Figure 15-11**).

In some situations DV production, too, can be approached as double-system sound. People usually choose to shoot double-system DV under two circumstances: if the camera they are

Crystal sync film production was developed long before the digital era by documentary filmmakers D. A. Pennebaker and Richard Leacock. Pennebaker and Leacock wanted to

■ **Figure 15-12** Documentary filmmakers D. A. Pennebaker and Richard Leacock pioneered the creation of crystal sync sound cameras. From Pennebaker's *Don't Look Back* (1966).

do away with the sync cable, which had previously regulated the speeds of both the camera and the analog recorder but that necessarily tethered the sound recordist to the camera. These filmmakers wanted the camera operator and the recordist to move about independently, yet maintain sync between sound and picture, so they attached the crystal oscillators found in the newly introduced Bulova Accutron watches to both a Nagra tape recorder and a heavily modified Auricon camera. These highly accurate 60-MHz oscillators precisely regulated the speeds of both camera and tape deck, and crystal sync was born. Their innovation was used in documentary films, such as *Don't Look Back* (1966) and *Monterey Pop* (1967).[1]

[1]*Film Style and Technology*, 2nd edn., by Barry Salt, Starword, London, 2003.

Figure 15-13 Double-system sound always requires a way to sync the picture and sound in postproduction, with the use of a slate being by far the most common method. Still from Scorsese's *The Last Temptation of Christ* (1988). (Photo courtesy of Pam Katz.)

Figure 15-14 A properly shot and recorded slate is the perfect audiovisual point of reference in postproduction. The frame where the slate is clapped is marked in the video file (1), and then the sound file is positioned so that the sound of the slate clapping (2) is aligned with the marker. Video and audio are now in sync.

using offers substandard audio quality (i.e., 32 kHz, 12-bit audio only) and those dreadful, unshielded mini-plug audio inputs, or if being tethered to the camera with a microphone cable is not flexible enough for a particular recording situation (which is precisely what Pennebaker and Leacock overcame back in the early 1960s!).

Whether you're shooting on film or on DV, double-system sound always requires the additional step of syncing audio to the picture in postproduction. This is where the slate comes in (Figure 15-13). The **slate** (also called **clap sticks** or **sticks**) is used for two reasons: one is to place a positive visual identification at the head of every take (including, scene, shot, take, and sound number) and the other is to create a one-frame, easily identifiable reference "moment" with which to line up the picture and sound later in post-production. That "moment" is the sharp closing of the slate sticks, which is recorded by the camera and the audio record deck at the beginning of every take (see Chapter 20 for full procedure). Later, when syncing up the image with the sound, it is easy to find the exact frame in which the slate sticks make contact. Next, you find the "clap" of the two sticks meeting on the audio track; which can be heard and *seen* using the visual waveform function on your editing software. Then you simply line up the clap image with clap audio and everything after that point, for that take, should be in sync (Figure 15-14).

Another method of syncing double-system audio is by using a **timecode slate**. If your recording deck generates timecode (like the Nagra IV-S or Sound Devices 702T), then you can use a timecode (T.C.) slate, which receives the same timecode numbers (via wireless or cable link) that are being laid down on the sound track (Figure 15-15). When the clapper sticks snap together during slating, the timecode number freezes at that moment and then returns to 00:00:00:00. With a timecode slate, syncing is done by reading the last timecode number off the slate picture and then simply typing in the same timecode number to locate the exact sync point on the sound track. We will discuss syncing footage in more detail later in the postproduction chapter.

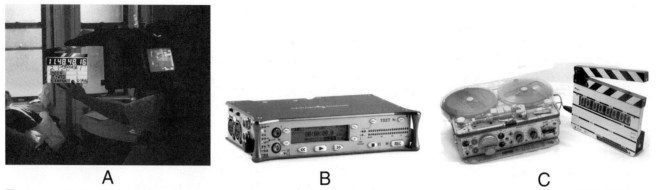

■ **Figure 15-15** A timecode slate (A) makes synchronizing even easier, since it displays the timecode being recorded with the audio. The Sound Devices 702T (B) and the Nagra IV S (C) have T.C. capability.

■ DIGITAL SOUND RECORDING

The Basic Signal Path

Let's look at the basic signal path of a digital recording situation to see how sound starts out as an acoustic source, which is transformed into an electronic signal, then is turned into data, only to be transformed back into acoustic sound again in the end (Figure 15-16).

1. Sound recording begins with the **source** of sound, which emits acoustic energy (sound waves).
2. These sound waves enter the microphone, where a diaphragm, magnets, and coil (see Figure 16-11) convert the acoustic energy into fluctuations of electrical voltage that is analogous to the original sound waves. This fluctuating voltage created by a microphone is called a **microphone** (or **mic**) **signal**, which is sent to the digital audio recorder (or a DV camcorder) via a microphone cable.
3. The relatively low-voltage mic signal first passes through a **pre-amp**, where the signal is boosted, and then goes to an **analog-to-digital converter** (**ADC**), which samples the analog audio information and translates it into binary code (a series of 1s and 0s). The sequencing of binary data ultimately represents the aural characteristics of the source sound. The digital information is stored on some form of recording media; this could be a hard drive, flash drive, or digital audio tape (DAT), depending on the recorder you use. In the case of DV camcorders, the audio is recorded onto the DV tape.
4. When playing the audio back, the data is sent to a digital-to-analog converter (DAC), which changes it back into electronic energy and outputs a **line signal**, which is the

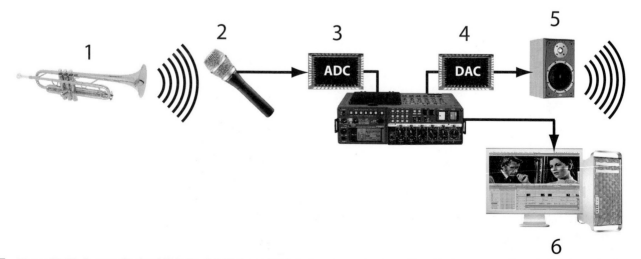

■ **Figure 15-16** An acoustic signal (1) is translated into an electrical charge by a microphone (2) and is then converted into digital information via an analog-to-digital converter chip (3). This data is stored in the record format (hard drive, DAT, flash memory) and can also be sent via firewire to a computer for editing (6). A DAC (4) reverses the process when we play the recorded sound (5).

audio signal between audio components. Be careful not to mix up line and mic signals—a line signal is much stronger.

5. The audio line signal can then travel to speakers or headphones, where magnets, sound coils, and cones convert the electronic energy back into acoustic sound waves that travel through the air and are received by our ears.

6. The audio data can also be sent digitally via firewire or USB connection to the hard drive of a digital editing system.

Digital Audio—Quality Matters

The number one factor in determining the quality of any digital recording has nothing to do with the cost of your equipment, quantizing, sample bit rates, or signal-to-noise (S/N) ratios—any professional sound mixer will tell you that microphone choice/placement and recording technique can make lower end recording gear sound great, or a state-of-the-art recording system sound terrible. We will discuss recording and microphone technique in depth in the following section.

The other, more objective parameters that determine recording quality are found primarily in the analog-to-digital conversion process, basically in relationship to how thoroughly and accurately the analog information is measured before it is assigned its representative data.

Sampling

Similar to digital video, **audio sample rates** determine how many times a sound (the sine wave of that sound) is measured per second. One **sample** is a single measurement of amplitude, sort of like a snapshot of a piece of that sound, and primarily determines the frequency response of the recording. The more samples (the higher the sample rate), the more accurate the reproduction will be because more frequencies will be measured. Higher sample rates produce better quality sound, but take up more storage space on your tape or drive. The most common sample rate for recording on either a DV camcorder or a digital audio field recorder is 48 kHz (that is, 48,000 sample measurements per second). The standard sample rate for audio CDs is 44.1 kHz, and you'll find this sample rate on a few recorders and camcorders as well. Occasionally you'll see sample rates on DV camcorders as low as 32 kHz. This substandard rate is used to save space on DV tape and allows for four channels of audio instead of the standard two channels. It's a devil's bargain, however, because having four channels of poor audio does no one any good. In general it's best to stick with two channels recording at 48 kHz (Figure 15-17).

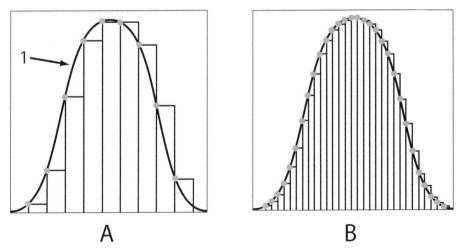

A   B

■ Figure 15-17 The process of converting analog sound (1) to a digital format involves sampling the signal at regular intervals. The lower the sampling rate (A), the less accurate the digital version will be; a higher sampling rate (B) creates a more faithful reproduction of the original sound.

The second, and perhaps more easily perceptible measure of audio quality is **bit depth**. **Bit depth** (also called **word length**) is a measure of the accuracy and detail of each audio sample, determined by the number of binary digits (bits) assigned to each sample. The greater the bit depth, the better your audio quality will be because the sine wave, in all of its complexity, is more accurately defined. Imagine having a ruler that is divided into ¼-inch units. If any measurement falls between the ¼-inch marks it will be rounded up or down. This ruler doesn't give you particularly accurate measurements. Now imagine a rule that is divided into ¹⁄₄₈ths and another that is divided into ¹⁄₉₆ths. These rulers will measure far more accurately because measurements that fall between markings need to be rounded only slightly. Bit depth works the same way, with a sound being measured, more or less accurately, through the number of sampling "levels." A 4-bit sample will measure 16 levels, an 8-bit sample will measure 256 levels, and a 16-bit sample will measure 65,536 levels. With each bit you add, you double the number of values defining that sound, so with 24-bit audio, there are 16,777,216 levels! With greater depth a more accurate picture of the original sine wave can be rendered and consequently the more space the data needs for storage. The process of rounding up or down areas of the sine wave that are not measured is called **quantizing**. With more bits, you reduce the quantizing error of the recording. In the field you will often encounter 12-bit audio (substandard), 16-bit audio (great quality, the standard bit depth for CDs and DV), 20-bit audio (usually only on HD camcorders), and 24-bit audio (superior quality on professional sound recorders).

The mechanism described here, for digitally converting an analog signal by taking a sequence of discrete individual samplings and then storing that data in a sequential binary format, is called **PCM audio (pulse code modulation)**. PCM audio it is by far the most pervasive digital recording method for professional audio field recorders and DV camcorders. The standard PCM sample rates and bit depth for high-quality audio for use in film production are 48 kHz and 16 bit.

Production Sound Tools

■ SOUND RECORDERS

The Generic Digital Sound Recorder

All portable digital sound recorders used for film production record PCM audio and are essentially the same in their basic features and operation (Figure 16-1). These features include microphone inputs, record level controls and meters, recording controls, and audio outputs. However, the difference between digital recorders centers on how the audio data is stored. We will look at that later in this chapter.

Microphone Inputs and Preamps

True XLR microphone ("mike") inputs are essential for film production. XLR connectors are the professional standard connector for microphones and mike cables (see p. 312). Not only do they lock into position for a secure connection, but they are also grounded and shielded, which means that they are protected from audio interference like radio waves and AC hum. Stay away from any recorder with mini-plug inputs, which you often find on consumer audio equipment. Portable field recording decks typically have between two and four separate microphone inputs, also called **channels**, which allows multiple microphone setups. Each channel can be monitored, controlled, recorded, and transferred as a distinct audio track. Decks with more than four inputs are indeed available, but start to become cumbersome for small-scale film production.

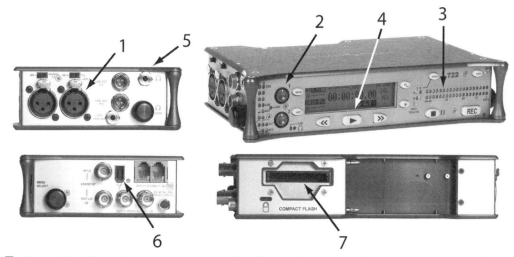

■ Figure 16-1 Most professional sound recorders have the same features: mike inputs and preamps (1), level control potentiometers (2), a peak meter (3), controls for playback and searching (4), headphone jack(s) (5), audio outputs (6), and the format to which they record (in this case compact flash memory) (7).

Preamps in the recorder boost the mike signal input. However, the quality of your audio not only depends on the sampling rate and bit depth, but on the quality of the components inside the recorder. Cheap preamps can be a major source of unwanted system noise and will "dirty up" your 48-kHz, 16-bit audio so much that it sounds terrible. **System noise** is electronic junk that contaminates the audio signal we want to record. The specifications for the system noise of any particular recorder are measured by its **signal-to-noise** (S/N) ratio, which is the ratio between the audio that we want to record (signal) and unwanted

interference (noise) that contaminates that signal. Signal-to-noise ratio is measured in decibels and the higher this ratio is, the "cleaner" your audio signal will be when it's recorded. For example, an audio deck that has a signal-to-noise ratio of 55 dB (55:1) means that 1 dB of noise will be detectable when a signal of 55 dB is played back after recording. A signal-to-noise ratio of 95 dB (95:1), however, means that the playback signal can be as high as 95 dB before we detect any noise at all. Professional digital field recording decks should come in at 80 dB or higher—which is extremely clean audio. Again, the first indicators of cheap audio circuitry are mini-plug audio inputs (Figure 16-2).

■ **Figure 16-2** Lower end audio recording equipment commonly uses a mini plug for connecting microphones. This connection is flimsy and prone to interference and should be avoided if possible.

Level Controls and Meters

Adjusting and monitoring the strength of your audio signal is at the heart of the sound recordist's craft. The term **levels** refers to the strength of your audio as it enters the recorder and the degree to which we boost or lower that audio with manual **level controls**, sometimes called **gain controls** or **pots** (short for **potentiometers**). This adjustment determines the strength of the audio signal recorded and is called **setting levels**. On professional recorders you will have one level control for every microphone channel, allowing you to adjust the levels of each microphone independently. Setting levels is aided by a **peak reading meter** (Figure 16-3). The peak meter is a highly sensitive instrument that has a one-to-one level correspondence with all sounds entering the recorder. In other words, it reacts to and measures every sound. This allows the recordist an accurate indication of absolute peak levels in any recording situation. Each mike input will have its own corresponding peak meter. Meter displays can be quite different from machine to machine, including pivoting needles, colored LED lights, or backlit LCD displays, but they are all calibrated in decibels that run from $-\infty$ dB on the extreme low end, through -40, -30, and -20 dB, and so on, to 0 dB on the high end. At $-\infty$ dB there is no signal at all and you will record no sound. If your signal strength exceeds 0 dB your audio is too strong and will become distorted. We will discuss recording techniques and using gain controls and meters in detail in Chapter 17.

Controls and Outputs

Play/Record/Stop control buttons obviously control the starting and stopping of audio recording and playback (to check sound quality and details after recording). A **headphone jack** is standard, since fully isolated headphones are essential for monitoring audio during recording. Headphone outputs often have their own volume control. Beware, however, that you do not mistake the headphone volume level for the record volume level. Headphones are used primarily to monitor the content of your audio, NOT the audio levels as

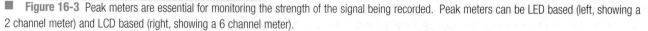

■ **Figure 16-3** Peak meters are essential for monitoring the strength of the signal being recorded. Peak meters can be LED based (left, showing a 2 channel meter) and LCD based (right, showing a 6 channel meter).

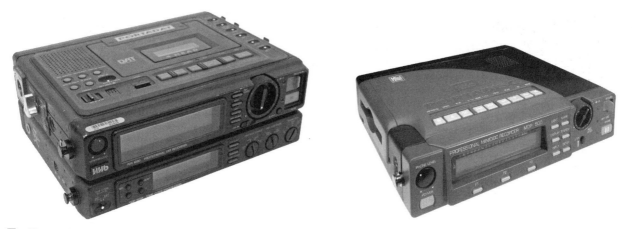

■ **Figure 16-4** Digital Audio Tape recorders (DAT's) record to a proprietary audio cassette (left), while mini-disc recorders (right) record to tiny discs using magneto-optical technology.

they are being recorded—the peak meter is the device by which we determine record levels (see Chapter 17). When I was a student shooting my very first sound film, my mixer had the headphone volume turned all the way up, but the record levels, which he never looked at, were way below standard. The result was audio that he could hear okay in the headphones, but that was recorded "in the mud." In the end I couldn't fix that audio and I was forced to reshoot those scenes. **Audio outputs** send the recorded signal out, either to your computer for capturing with editing software, or to whichever format you are transferring your image (i.e., MiniDV) for the direct syncing of video dailies. It's important that your recorder has digital audio outputs—some consumer formats, like mini-disc, are manufactured without digital outputs for fear of music pirating.

Digital Recording Formats

Beyond the common features of any digital field production recorder, the primary difference between field decks is their recording **format**—meaning how they store the audio data. Digital recording formats come and go as the technology evolves, but there are a few standard formats that one is likely to come across.

Digital Audio Tape and Mini-disc

Digital audio tape (**DAT** for short, or **R-DAT** for rotary head digital audio tape) is an audio-only cassette format that uses a magnetic tape 3.81mm wide and that writes its data in a helical scan pattern with a flying record head—much like a DV video camera. Professional DAT recorders have a frequency response around 20 Hz – 22 kHz and the signal-to-noise ratio is outstanding at around 90 + dB. The drawback to DAT machines is their fragility in the field. They seem especially vulnerable to dust and humidity and can jam up in extreme conditions. The other drawback is their linearity—meaning that one needs to fast-forward or rewind to find sound takes, rather than access them through the instantaneous random access of hard drives and other recording formats. The DAT format is clearly phasing out in favor of digital recorders with no moving parts. Industry reports indicate that there are no new DAT recorder models in the pipeline, but since many production companies and film schools are heavily invested in these machines, their ubiquity and their superb audio quality ensure that they will likely be with us for some time (Figure 16-4).

There are still many **mini-disc** recorders in use, but this is a recording format that will soon disappear. Based on the Sony consumer mini-disc music format (that is quickly vanishing), the main attraction of this format was its relative compactness, but the quality of these recorders is highly variable. Consumer models offer only mini-plug mike inputs, questionable circuitry, and often no ability to control record levels. Professional models, however, have all of the necessary features and excellent audio specs. As the format fades away, the mini-disks themselves are becoming more difficult to find.

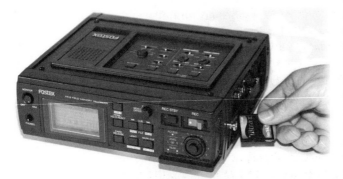

Figure 16-5 Some high-end digital sound recorders store data directly to an internal hard disc, like the Sound Devices 722 (top), or to DVD-RAM media like the Fostex PD6 (bottom) Both formats make random access possible.

Hard Drive Recorders

Hard drive recorders write their data directly to a hard drive—what could be simpler? Depending on the size of the hard drive, these recorders can store many hours of audio without changing media. Hard drive recorders also interface with computer editing software seamlessly and have a reputation for being quite robust; temperature, humidity, and motion have little effect on the functions and recording. The convenience and robustness of hard drive recorders come at a price, however, as they are among the most expensive machines available. **DVD-RAM** recorders function similarly to hard disk recorders. DVD-RAMs write the audio data in concentric tracks (like hard drives) instead of one long spiral track (like DVD+R and −R, which are entirely different formats). DVD-RAM does not need DVD burning software and, using a DVD-RAM reader, they can be loaded and read instantly on any PC or Mac computer system. This is one of the newest formats, but also one of the most promising (Figure 16-5).

Flash Memory Recorders

Almost every major brand making portable sound recording equipment is developing **compact flash memory** recorders. Compact flash (CF) records audio directly to **data cards**, which can be transferred into computer hard drives for storage and then reused again and again. Compact flash also contains no moving parts, which means there is less to break down, they are reliable in extreme conditions, and they use very little battery power. Although the storage capacity of compact flash cards was limited at first, we are currently seeing exponential leaps in storage space even as the price per gigabyte becomes cheaper. If there is one drawback it is that not all compact flash cards are compatible with type 1 and type 2 cards, being different thicknesses (Figure 16-6).

The Nagra Analog Recorder

The last holdout from the era of analog sound recording is the trusty **Nagra** ¼" tape reel-to-reel tape recorder. It's extremely common, even on big-budget film productions, to see a Nagra sitting under an entire rack of state-of-the-art digital audio gear, running as a backup. This machine has an established place in the history of film because it was the first high-quality, portable audio recorder, and it remained the gold standard until only a few years ago. There is a great deal of lore surrounding the Nagra and its creator Stefan Kudelski, who has achieved deity status among sound professionals. When I was trained to use a Nagra, I was told, "The Nagra is the perfect sound machine. It takes two hours to learn it, and two years to understand it." This Zen audio koan aside, the Nagra is indeed an exceptional sound recording machine. Not only is it reliable (handmade in Switzerland) and rugged (the body is bored out of a solid piece of titanium), but the Nagra also offers exceptional frequency response, dynamic range capabilities, and signal-to-noise ratios. There are many different makes and models of the Nagra but the two most commonly in use today are the **Nagra 4.2** and the **Nagra IV-S** (with stereo and timecode); both are crystal synced for sync sound film production. Nagras record audio on standard or low-noise ¼" reel-to-reel audio tape and run on AC power or twelve D cell batteries for 8 hours of field use (Figure 16-7).

Figure 16-6 The falling price of compact flash memory cards makes digital recorders that use this format enticing; with no moving parts and consuming very little power, they are particularly sturdy.

As with all longitudinal analog tape recorders, tape speed is a major determiner of audio quality, with faster

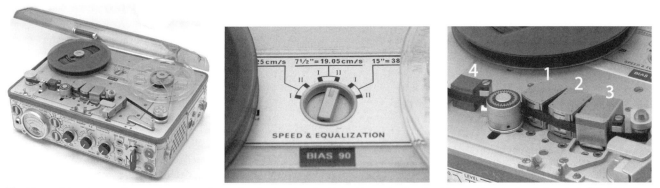

■ **Figure 16-7** The workhorse of sync sound recording for decades. the Nagra is a professional-quality analog recorder. It records to ¼″ magnetic tape and offers three record speeds (center). The recording mechanism is simple, it consists of: erase (4), record (1), pilot tone (2), and playback (3) heads. The pilot tone head records the 60-cycle sync pulse.

speeds providing better quality (but using up more tape). Between the feed reel and take-up reel is a switch for tape speeds and tape equalization (standard and low-noise tape stock). The Nagra 4.2 offers three tape speeds from which to choose: 15 ips (inches per second), 71/2 ips, and 33/4 ips. While 15 ips offers the best quality audio, 71/2 ips is the standard record speed for sync sound film production and has a frequency response of 30 Hz −16 kHz (very near the sensitivity range limits of the human ear) and a S/N around 75 dB. The slowest speed, 33/4 ips, is substandard audio quality, but can be used when high-quality audio is not as important as getting a lot of material on a single roll of tape (as with interviews for transcribing).

Threading the Nagra is extremely simple. With the pinch-wheel level opened the tape is lined up around the two outside tension rollers and across the heads. The tape is then securely wound around the take-up reel. When the pinch-wheel control lever is closed, a stabilizer roller and the pinch wheel push the tape across the three heads—erase, record, and playback. Another head, the pilot tone head, records the 60-cycle pulse generated by the crystal sync right onto the tape itself, so that subsequent playback on any other Nagra will be governed by the pulse on the tape. One of the most attractive features of Nagras is not only the ease of use, but also that the entire transport mechanism is extremely gentle on the tape. There is little chance, given proper use, that this machine will ever tangle, mangle, wrinkle, or stretch your precious master audio tapes.

Finally, the Nagra's level meter (called the **modulometer**) is a highly sensitive and accurate peak meter. While the modulometer is also calibrated in decibels, the scale is slightly different than peak meters on digital recorders, because analog recording is more forgiving with audio peaks and overmodulation (see Chapter 17).

Sound Recording on DV Camcorders

When you are recording signal system sound on DV, the camcorder is your sound recorder as well as your video recorder. As we mentioned in the previous chapter on DV technology, DV camcorders that use tape as their record medium write PCM digital audio along a helical scan with a flying head (see p. 184). Most camcorders of any quality have high recording specifications: 48 kHz and 16 bit. In theory, these are great audio specifications, however, as we've discussed before, there are other factors that contribute to audio quality.

Mini-plug audio inputs are especially a problem with low-end DV camcorders. The connections are fragile and prone to poor contacts, and mini-plugs are unshielded and unbalanced. Many people use an XLR-to-mini adaptor (called a pigtail) so that they can use professional external microphones. This, of course, is better than nothing, but the problem with this solution is that it converts your lovely balanced, shielded audio into an unbalanced signal, vulnerable to interference and noise. A few years ago I was shooting a short film on DV and using a professional microphone connected to the camera

with an XLR-to-mini adaptor. After a few takes into our shooting, the sound recordist noticed that we were picking up a Top-40 radio station. When we played back the tape we could hear it. It was very faint, but sure enough, there was Britney Spears leaking onto my audio track!

Camera-mountable adaptors with pre-amps and XLR connections are available for DV camcorders that have only mini-plug audio inputs (Figure 16-8). These adaptors allow you to use XLR cables and some even provide a shielded mini-cable to the camera, two big advantages. However, where you find mini-plugs you may also find cheap preamps and audio circuitry adding system noise to your signal. Many consumer DV camcorders have terrible signal-to-noise ratios (between 40 dB and 50 dB).

Figure 16-8 Although it is possible to get an XLR-to-mini cable (top) to use professional microphones with ⅛" mike inputs, a mountable adaptor like the Beachtek (bottom) provides a sturdier solution for long term use.

Most industrial and professional camcorders that provide true XLR connectors usually have two microphone inputs with independent level controls. The preset for many cameras is **automatic gain control**, meaning the camera will set your levels for you. Just as with auto focus and auto exposure, you should turn off this blunt tool and set your levels manually. The problem with auto gain is that it doesn't just allow soft noises be soft and loud noises be loud, it tries to bring every sound to a middle volume, so it is constantly responding to peaks and pauses in audio, adjusting levels up when there is quiet and down when a loud noise occurs, however briefly. The background sounds, too, rise and fall very noticeably with each auto adjustment. In Chapter 17 we explore in detail the proper method for setting levels manually.

Portable Field Mixers

Portable field mixers (also **microphone mixers**) are small audio consoles that allow for independent level control of multiple microphone inputs (usually from one to four) and that output this audio as either a microphone or line signal to your camcorder (Figure 16-9). Many sound recordists working with DV single-system setups find portable mixers an indispensable tool, because camcorder level controls are located right on the camera itself and it can be very awkward to have the sound recordist hovering around the camera setting levels. Using a field mixer enables the sound recordist to precisely monitor and control levels (and use multiple microphones) at a distance. The output of a field mixer can connect with the camera via a standard XLR cable, or via a wireless connection for true independence of movement (Figure 16-10). It is vital, however, to calibrate the gain levels of each device (mixer and camcorder or mixer and sound recorder) in order to maintain audio level consistency from mixer to recorder. This process is discussed in detail in the section on setting levels in Chapter 17.

Figure 16-9 Field mixers allow precise control over the recording levels of several inputs without having to access the audio controls on the video camera.

Located in the signal chain between the microphones and the camcorder audio input, field mixers are small enough to be worn in a carrying case over the shoulder, if there is only one sound person who is also holding the boom. Field mixers are also handy when shooting double-system sound because of their capacity for multiple microphone inputs.

■ MICROPHONES

Simply put, a microphone is a device that converts acoustic energy (sound waves) into electrical energy (electrical signal). All microphones are constructed with a **diaphragm**, a thin membrane that is extremely sensitive to the vibration of air particles. The vibra-

■ Figure 16-10 A typical single system sound configuration. Boom operator (1) sound recordist adjusting levels with field mixer (2), audio recorded on camcorder (3).

tions of the diaphragm, which correspond to the sound waves buffeting it, are translated into fluctuating voltage. One of the ways we identify different microphones is by the method they employ to make this conversion.

Dynamic, Condenser, and Electret Condenser

A very common type of microphone for film and video field production is the **dynamic microphone**, which generates a signal through electromagnetic principles. This microphone is sometimes called a **moving coil microphone**, after the element that converts the acoustic energy into an electrical signal. Basically, a dynamic microphone element consists of a highly acoustically sensitive diaphragm to which a wire coil, with a permanent magnetic charge, is attached. This coil is called the **voice coil**, and is suspended around a permanently fixed magnet. As the diaphragm responds to a particular sound source, the coil moves up and down with the vibrations of the diaphragm. The movement of the magnetized coil through the electromagnetic current of the permanent magnet produces an electrical output that is analogous to the original acoustic vibrations.

Dynamic microphones are renown for their rugged construction, which makes this kind of microphone a favorite on location shooting. They are also less expensive than other types of microphones. Naturally, many of the technical factors, such as sensitivity and frequency range, depend on the manufacturer of the mike, but as a general rule dynamic mikes are fairly sensitive and also have a fairly good frequency response. In close mike situations they are more than adequate, which is why news reporters who report from the field usually use these mikes. When greater sensitivity and frequency response are necessary, then we usually turn to the condenser microphone (Figure 16-11).

Condenser and **electret condenser** microphones work on a similar principle; however, instead of using an electromagnetic current (like the dynamic mike), condenser and electret condenser mikes work on voltage fluctuations within an electric **capacitor** (another name for condenser). The capacitor is made of two round plates oriented parallel to each other, with a very narrow space between them called the **dielectric**. One plate is the microphone's diaphragm, a movable acoustically sensitive membrane; the other is a

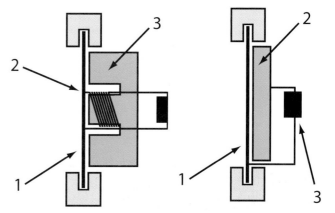

■ Figure 16-11 A moving coil (left) microphone works by converting the movement of a diaphragm (1) into an electrical charge when the coil (2) attached to it moves up and down while suspended around magnets (3). A condenser microphone (right) uses a positively charged diaphragm (1) and the negatively charged backplate (2) to form a capacitor; the movement between these two electrically charged plates creates voltage fluctuations that are sent to a preamp (3).

fixed plate called the **backplate**. Both of these plates are charged with polarized voltage. When sound waves buffet the diaphragm the voltage relationship between these plates changes correspondingly, which results in the audio signal. The output signal of this capacitor is very low and so condenser microphones have a **preamplifier** built into the microphone (**Figure 6-11**).

In order for the capacitor to work, both plates require some source of power to provide the necessary polarizing voltage; the preamp also requires some power. Condenser mikes can be powered through the use of **phantom power**, which is power provided by the record deck or a mixer, delivered to the microphone via one of the three XLR cable prongs, or through the use of a **battery power source**, which is usually located in an intermediary capsule connected to the microphone (**Figure 16-12**).

The **electret condenser** microphone works on exactly the same capacitor principle as does the condenser microphone, but one of the two plates in an electret condenser is manufactured with a permanent charge, so there is no external power source necessary. The preamp, however, still requires power, but much less than is required by a standard condenser. This is usually accomplished by a small battery located in the microphone itself (sometimes AA, or the smaller N battery, or the even smaller LR44 1.5 volt). The low power requirements allow for a more compact design, which is always welcome in field production. Condenser microphones are generally more sensitive than dynamic mikes, both in terms of pick-up distance and frequency response. They are especially good with high-frequency audio. However, they cost more than dynamic mikes and are considerably more fragile.

■ **Figure 16-12** Condenser microphones, like the Sennheiser shotgun pictured, need a battery to provide the power necessary to charge the capacitor.

Most professional-quality microphones send a **balanced output** utilizing the standard XLR professional microphone connector (**Figure 16-13**). A balanced output means that the signal is running in opposite directions along two wires within the microphone cable. This effectively cancels out any noise. A balanced line also incorporates a shield, a wire mesh that covers the two hot wires and is connected to ground. This shield greatly protects the signal from interference caused by AC or fluorescent hum and radio frequencies. This is precisely the shortcoming of the ⅛" mini microphone inputs on some consumer-level recorders and DV camcorders. In general, mini-plugs are neither balanced nor shielded. The other advantage to the XLR connectors and cables

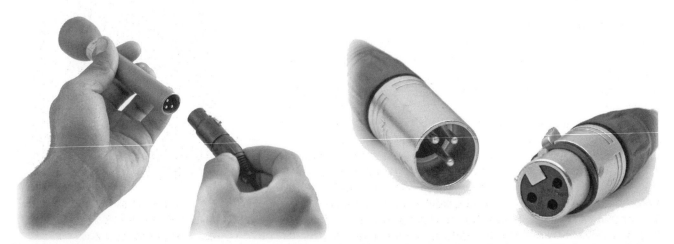

■ **Figure 16-13** The standard professional audio cable is the XLR, a tough and inexpensive solution for sending balanced, distortion-free audio between microphones and recorders.

is that the actual connectors are rugged and the male end of the connector fits with the female end through a tongue-and-groove fit and a spring lock, providing for a strong and stable connection that cannot be inadvertently pulled loose. This is especially useful when linking a number of cables together to lengthen the reach of the microphone.

Microphone Frequency Response

Frequency response refers to the sensitivity of a given microphone to frequencies in the sound spectrum. This measurement is represented on a frequency response graph (Figure 16-14). The x-axis on this graph measures the microphone's response in dB and y-axis measures the frequency. A perfect microphone would have an equal response throughout all frequencies of the sound spectrum. If we were to plot this perfect response on a graph, the line would appear perfectly flat. This would be the theoretical, perfect **flat response**. Flat response in the real microphone world means that, given a large frequency range, a microphone can respond fairly equally throughout. For most microphones, when the extremes of their capabilities are reached, the response dips. All professional microphones come with a spec sheet that will indicate the instrument's frequency range.

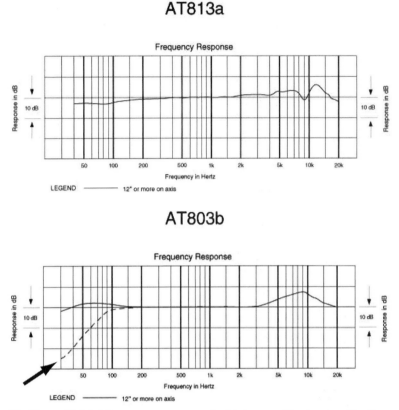

■ **Figure 16-14** A frequency response graph plots how sensitive (measured in dB, on the "x" axis) a microphone is to a range of frequencies (measured in Hz on the "y" axis). A perfect response would be represented by a flat graph. Note that the AT803b, an omnidirectional lavalier condenser microphone, has a "roll off" option that affects its sensitivity to low frequencies (arrow).

Some microphones come with two **low-end roll-off** settings so that one can choose to make the microphone less sensitive to low frequencies, which are often caused by wind or machine noise in the field. A roll-off switch usually has two symbols. It is generally agreed that it's always best, if given a choice, to leave the microphone on flat response, gather as much of the frequency range as possible, and then tweak your audio in postproduction, where graphic equalizers can be much more precise in removing unwanted frequencies (Figure 16-15).

Microphone Directionality

In addition to the method of generating the electronic signal (dynamic vs. condenser), we also identify mikes by their **directionality** (also called **pick-up pattern**), which distinguishes the area and range within which the microphone will respond optimally. This is a critical factor in choosing the right microphone for any given recording situation, as different microphones are constructed to have specialized directionality characteristics. In simple terms, directionality is sometimes described by a microphone's basic **angle of acceptance**, which is the area from which a microphone will gather sound. Mikes are often broadly categorized as **nondirectional** (wide angle of acceptance), **directional** (limited to a medium angle of acceptance), and **ultra-directional** (very narrow angle of acceptance). However, the **polarity pattern**, represented in **polarity graphs**, is a more accurate three-dimensional conceptualization of a microphone's pick-up pattern.

■ **Figure 16-15** Some microphones have a "low end roll-off" setting (2) that makes them less sensitive to low end frequencies, usually caused by wind or machine noise. The flat response setting (1) is preferable for most situations.

Omnidirectional

A omnidirectional microphone (Figure 16-16) picks up audio from all directions equally (called a broad or wide pick-up pattern). This microphone is a good choice for recording general ambient sounds, like crowd noises, or for miking a scene where sound emanates from a number of different directions, or for groups of people (i.e., four friends gathered around a table for dinner). This is a good choice for interviews in which you want both the interviewer and the interviewee to be miked and recorded equally. A **lavaliere** microphone (**lav** for short) usually has an omnidirectional pattern, but also has a highly specialized function. Lavalieres are tiny, clip-on mikes that can be attached to a lapel or tie, or easily hidden under a collar, and are used for close miking talent (Figure 16-17). However, as tiny omnidirectional mikes, they are handy for hiding in the middle of a scene, say behind a candle during a dinner table sequence. One must be aware, though, that these mikes are intended to be placed near the chest of a speaker, where a great deal of bass is generated, so many lavs employ some degree of low-frequency roll-off (see Figure 16-14). Using them as an omnidirectional mike in a crowd situation can result in somewhat thin sound.

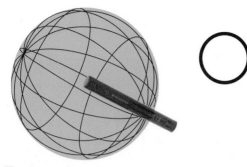

■ Figure 16-16 The pick-up pattern of an omnidirectional microphone allows it to capture sound equally from all directions.

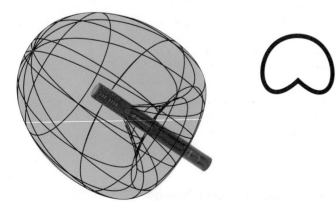

■ Figure 16-17 Lavaliere microphones must be carefully hidden on talent (right) and are perfect for situations where a boom microphone cannot be used or when close miking is needed. When lavaliere is wireless, the transmitter (left) must be concealed as well.

Cardioids

The pick-up pattern of a **cardioid** microphone (Figure 16-18) is just as its name suggests (cardioid/cardiac): heart shaped. The pick-up pattern is somewhat directional, so the mike can be aimed specifically at the source of the audio, which minimizes extraneous noise yet still provides a natural ambient feel. Its sensitivity is primarily in front, with some sensitivity to the sides, but the mike picks up very little from behind, which is usually where the equipment and crew are. This is the most common microphone used in film production because it offers both control and extremely high quality. When miking a single person speaking, this is the microphone of choice.

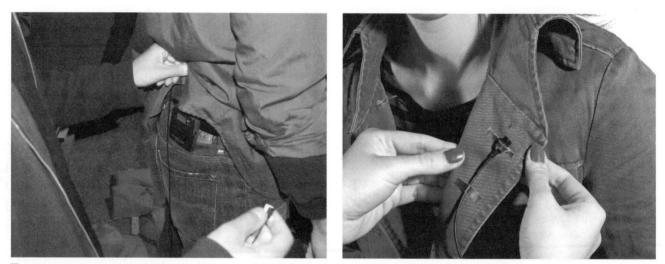

■ Figure 16-18 A cardiod microphone has a pickup pattern that favors sound coming from the front and sides, but not from behind.

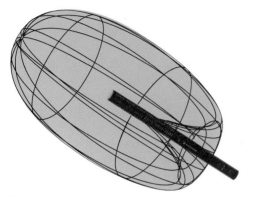

■ **Figure 16-19** A hypercardiod microphone pickup pattern has a narrow range of acceptance and increased sensitivity. It greatly favors sound coming from the front and not from the sides or back.

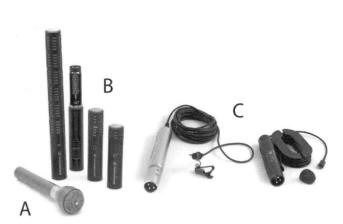

■ **Fig. 16-20** Picking the right microphone for the job. A dynamic cardioid microphone (A) is an ultra sturdy and reliable sound tool. A modular system, like the Sennheiser K-6 condenser mike kit (B) provides great flexibility with 3 interchangeable heads: omni, cardioid, and super-cardioid. Lavalieres and wireless microphones (C) complete the sound person's microphone arsenal.

Hypercardioids and Shotguns

Hypercardioids and **shotgun mikes** (also called **super-cardioid** or **line mikes**) (Figure 16-19) both generally duplicate the heart-shaped pick-up pattern, but these mikes are considerably more sensitive than the cardioid and are used when close miking isn't possible (i.e., because of wider camera framings). Their pick-up patterns are highly directional, meaning that they are considerably narrower than a cardioid and that they can be held at a greater distance. The shotgun mike is the more sensitive and directional of the two. There are drawbacks, however, to using both of these microphones. Because these mikes are so sensitive, one must be careful when using them indoors. Not only will they pick up the sound directly from the source, but also they will easily pick up the reflections of that sound, resulting in a boomy quality to the audio. These mikes are quite successful outdoors, but here, too, one must be careful about sounds reflecting off surfaces within the mikes' direct pick-up pattern. For example, a couple is seated at a small table in a garden restaurant. There is a wall behind them and a small fountain in the garden. A shotgun microphone can pick up and exaggerate the sound of the fountain reflecting off the wall behind the subjects, even if the fountain is behind the microphone.

Wireless and On-Board Microphones

Wireless Microphones

Wireless microphones (also called **radio mikes**) consist of a small pocket-size transmitter to which a microphone (very often a lavaliere) is attached, which transmits the electrical audio signal via VHF high-band or FM frequencies to a receiver; the receiver itself is connected to the input of the record deck. Using wireless lavalieres allows close miking while maintaining the talent's freedom of movement, since they carry both the concealed microphone and the transmitter on their person (see Figure 16-17). In addition to wireless lavalieres, there are many radio mike systems on the market that allow you to adapt virtually any professional microphone into a wireless mike with a plug-on transmitter, which means that even the boom operator need not be tethered to the sound recorder by an XLR cable. In both cases, wireless mikes allow a sound mixer to get great audio no matter how wide the framing! If there is a downside to wireless microphones, it is that they are vulnerable to interference, especially the further the transmitter is from the receiver. Some systems use a "diversity" system that is constantly searching for the clearest transmission channel. Nonetheless, you should always have XLR cables handy.

On-Board Microphones

Another specialty microphone that should be mentioned is the **on-board microphone** (also called **camera microphone**) found on a DV camcorder. These are often factory-provided microphones that are fixed to a mount above the lens. Professional cameras allow you to mount your own microphone. Generally these microphones are for news

in practice

A filmmaker friend of mine, Didier Rouget, shot his short film *Urban/Suburban* (2006) in the Sahara Desert. He conceived of very wide, landscape shots as we followed two yuppies who, even though they are hopelessly lost in the desert, cannot stop talking about real estate investments. Clearly, wireless lavaliere mikes were the best choice, so this is what the sound recordist brought to the desert location. As the crew was setting up for a champion shot that included the actors in the foreground with a dazzling setting sun behind them, they discovered that they could not find a clean VHF channel to transmit the audio. Even though they were in a remote corner of the Sahara Desert, they discovered that this area was North Africa's "Grand Central Station" for innumerable radio signals, and using their wireless system was impossible. As Didier himself wrote to me, "We actually postponed the shoot until we finally found other wireless mikes with different VHF channels that work in this area. But I never found time enough to take this shot with the sun. Eventually, I was able to take only one shot, under a very cloudy sky. We all called this shot 'the damned shot.'" In the end, only Didier and his crew know that they missed a perfect shot, because the film works beautifully nonetheless, but what's most important is how Didier concluded his letter to me: "It would have been better to shoot the first day as scheduled without sound, and postsynchronize it. Once more, I learned a lot with this experience. . . ." Indeed, in film we learn every single time we're on a set, as much from hardships as from successes.

■ **Figure 16-21** "Waiting on sound!" Director Didier Rouget's film set, in the Sahara, sits and waits until a wireless microphone problem is corrected. Production still from *Urban/Suburban* (2006).

■ **Figure 16-22** Camera mounted microphones are commonly found on even the cheapest video cameras, but the inability to control their position in relation to talent makes them of very limited use for narrative filmmaking purposes.

gathering or down-and-dirty documentary shooting where the camera operator is alone. The controllability of on-board mikes is too limited for most narrative filmmaking needs (**Figure 16-22**).

The pick-up patterns of these microphones are different from camera to camera. Lower end camcorders often use an omnidirectional microphone, and broadcast electronic news gathering (ENG) cameras will use the more directional supercardioids. Some on-board mikes are switchable from omnidirectional to directional. Obviously, the more directional the on-board microphone is, the more the audio pick-up is restricted to the direction the camera is facing. Conversely, omnidirectional camera microphones often pick up noises from the camera operator and from the camera mechanisms, such as the servo zoom or tape transport. In any case, the on-board microphone's positioning is obviously restricted by the camera angle and camera-to-subject distance. For this reason, in narrative film production, these microphones are either not used or they are used to pick up general ambient sound when specific audio, like dialogue, is not necessary to the scene.

Location Sound Techniques

■ THE SOUND TEAM

The basic production sound team on a small-scale film project usually consists of two people, the **sound mixer** (also called the **sound recordist**) and the **boom operator**. Occasionally, on shoots with very simple location audio requirements, you'll see one person performing both roles, but when gathering sync sound, like dialogue, is part of the production, two people are recommended. The mixer and boom operator are a tight team and must communicate well. The sound mixer is the head of the sound department and is responsible for getting the best quality audio onto the recording format. This not only means setting the record levels on the sound recorder but also includes understanding the acoustics and ambient qualities of a given location and choosing the most appropriate microphones for the situation. The sound mixer works very closely with the boom operator in strategizing optimal microphone placement. The boom operator is responsible for placing the microphone where it needs to be, whether that means holding it aloft over a scene or hiding it inside an actor's collar, or both.

As I have mentioned before, getting good location sound is as important to a film as getting great images, but all too often people think about audio only at the last minute and choose the sound team either from people on the set who don't look busy or from people with utterly no experience but who are "willing to do anything" to be on a film set. To ensure the success of your shoot and your editing, it is important to choose a competent and knowledgeable sound crew who will dedicate themselves exclusively to the task of getting great sound (Figure 17-1).

Good recording technique and postproduction mixing are more important now than ever. The digital revolution has made great quality sound recording and reproduction technology within everyone's reach—even to the point where many homes are equipped with super high-fidelity surround sound home movie systems. So a filmmaker no longer can

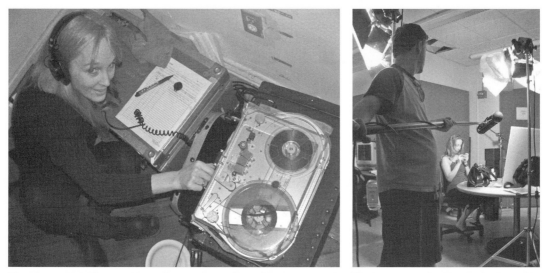

■ **Figure 17-1** The sound team: the sound recordist and the boom operator. The importance of getting the best possible sound quality for your film rests on their shoulders.

While taking a break from writing this book, I was strolling through Washington Square Park and found myself watching a group of students from a nearby university shooting a sync sound film exercise. They, of course, had no idea I was a film professor taking notes for a textbook. The director very seriously selected his shot and blocked the actors' movement through the scene, all the while communicating brilliantly with the cinematographer. Off to the side, lying on the ground unattended, was the sound recording gear. After the actors and camera operator rehearsed the scene two or three times, the director turned to the others in his small production group and asked, "Who's gonna hold the boom this time?" The group shuffled their feet and cast glances at one another, but no one volunteered. "C'mon, we need someone on the boom," pleaded the director. Finally, another actor, who was not in this particular shot, stepped forward and said "Alright, I'll do it." He grabbed the boom, planted its base in his stomach, near his belly button, and dangled the mike in the general vicinity of the camera. The director ran around to the sound recorder, slipped on the headphones and called, "Roll Camera!" He then rolled sound and yelled "Action!" As the take played out he closely watched the movements of the actors, never once looking at the sound levels. "CUT!" he yelled. And then, tossing the headphones aside, said, "That *looked* great! Next shot." He probably had a take that did look good, but he also had one that would undoubtedly give him massive audio headaches in postproduction. And me? I got a nice cautionary tale for my book.

expect that their final product will be heard through a built-in 3-inch, mono speaker on the family TV set. Nor can a low-budget filmmaker expect to show their work only as a 16mm film print with its accompanying poor quality optical track. These days you really need great sound, because in almost every screening venue—it shows! Three factors play a major role in getting the best audio in the field: recording technique, microphone technique, and simply using your ears.

■ RECORDING TECHNIQUE

The **sound mixer** is the head of the sound department and his job is to get the best possible recording of all field production audio, including dialogue, location sound effects, and wild ambient sound. Good recording in the field allows for more creative flexibility in postproduction. On a narrative film set, the mixer usually works in collaboration with the **boom operator** (see later) in strategizing the best approach for each recording situation. Recording the "best quality audio possible" means several things: cleanly picking up and isolating the sounds you want from the unwanted background noise, recording a strong signal, and ensuring the greatest frequency range. It also means being fast, reliable, and consistent, fitting yourself around the lighting, camera, and art department setups and constantly and creatively adjusting to shifting audio conditions. Solving audio issues on the set is a constant challenge and it takes resourcefulness, ingenuity, and knowledge. Good sound recordists are not easy to come by, but by the same token, good sound people are in high demand and work—a lot.

Setting Levels

The term **levels** refers to the **loudness** of a signal as it enters the audio recorder, which in turn determines the strength of the recorded audio signal. As mentioned earlier, all professional recorders offer manual level controls, allowing the sound recordist to control the strength of the signal; this is called **setting levels**. Getting strong audio levels depends on a combination of microphone placement and manual audio level adjustment. The craft of the sound mixer centers on the ability to find proper levels, which generally means setting the loudest possible record level without overmodulating. This provides for the best sound signal for playback and postproduction. For the sound mixer, the most important tool for monitoring and setting audio levels on a digital recorder or DV camcorder is the **peak meter** (Figure 17-2).

Setting Levels on a Peak Meter

Peak meters are found on DV camcorders and stand-alone digital audio recorders and measure the strength of the incoming signal. Peak meters are calibrated in decibels, from −50 dB on the low side to 0 dB on the high side. If your audio level exceeds the maximum, 0 dB, then your audio will become **overmodulated** or **overloaded**, which means the signal is too strong to be sampled accurately and the result is distorted sound. Sudden and loud transient sounds, like a car door slamming shut, which **spike** above 0 dB are especially a problem, because even these brief noises can cause crackling on the sound track. You cannot fix overmodulated sound in postproduction. On the other hand, if we record a level that is too low then we will be required to turn up the volume in postproduction to transfer or even hear this weak signal. By turning up the volume of the recorded signal, we also turn up the volume of the unwanted audio noise and the result is greater background and system noise. Recording too low is called recording "**in the mud**," the mud being system noise. Be careful, however; recording too low is different than recording soft sounds, which sometimes, appropriately, barely register on the peak meter.

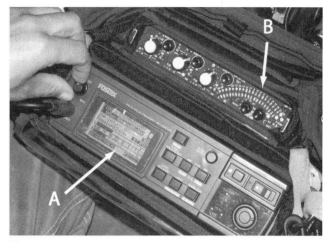

■ **Figure 17-2** The peak meter on a sound recorder (or field mixer) lets the recordist monitor and adjust the loudness of the signal being recorded. Peak meters can have LCD displays (A), or LED displays (B).

To make sure you obtain a good, strong signal, but protect yourself from overmodulation, you should set your levels so that the loudest audio in the scene peaks around −12 dB on the peak meter. For example, if you have a scene in which a man is arguing with a store clerk and his last line ". . . and I'm never coming back to this dump!" is the loudest the actor projects in the scene, then, during rehearsals, you will set your levels so this line of dialogue registers around −12 dB on the peak meter. The rest of the actor's dialogue will register lower on the meter, as it should. The range between −12 dB and 0 db is called **headroom** and it gives us a buffer for any unforeseen and sudden audio spikes—like the man slamming the door on his way out. The record level for normal dialogue should generally fall between −20 dB and −18 dB (Figure 17-3).

When we initially set levels for dialogue, this "normal" dialogue level is often our first reference. It is the job of the sound mixer and boom operator to find approximate mike placement and levels as quickly as possible and then make adjustments to improve the audio with each rehearsal and with each take. This initial **sound check** is usually done with the actors as the crew makes final adjustments to the lights and camera. You should try to find a moment with the actors, before the director runs through the take, to have them speak into the microphone. Sometimes they'll run through a few lines, or you can ask them a question that they need to answer at length. Remember, this is only a starting point. Actors often speak louder or softer than their normal speaking voice once the camera rolls and they're performing. The first run through or first take will usually help you to tweak your levels (and microphone placement) to get a better signal on subsequent takes.

When setting record levels, it is best to avoid extremes on the level control knobs. We never want to have our gain control set all the way to its loudest point or too close to its lowest setting. These extremes usually mean there is either something wrong with your microphone placement or you have some technical problem along the signal path. Not all sounds need to be recorded between −20 dB and −10 dB, especially when recording soft sounds. Very low sounds, like papers rustling as someone studies in the library, are fine to record at a low level like −40 dB or −30 dB. Trying to get this soft sound to peak at −20 dB will

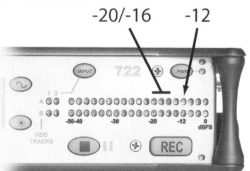

■ **Figure 17-3** Normal dialogue should be recorded around −20 to −16 dB on the peak meter. Loud sounds should peak at −12 dB or else they risk overmodulating.

force you to turn the levels up to their maximum, which will increase the extraneous room noise (ambient sound) to an unnaturally high level. This will also exaggerate unwanted system noise. If a fairly strong source, say a person speaking, is registering very low on the meter, then it's preferable to move the microphone in closer instead of boosting the recording levels all the way. And vice versa, if a very loud, consistent noise, like an un-muffled motorcycle engine, is spiking the levels, it's advisable to move the microphone away rather than turning the record levels nearly all the way down. In short, through careful microphone placement (of course, respecting the pick-up range of the mike), you should keep your pots within the middle three-fourths of its range.

As already mentioned, the difference between the loudest and softest sounds in any single recording situation is called the dynamic range, and setting levels for a sound situation with a wide dynamic range is a mixer's greatest challenge. It's a temptation to raise and lower the recording levels during recording as the sounds increase and decrease; this practice is called **riding levels** (also called **riding gain**). But riding levels causes unnatural fluctuations in the background noise and it can also be a problem with sudden loud or soft passages that were not anticipated and therefore spike above 0 dB or fall into the mud. The main problem with riding levels is that a range of loud and soft sounds is simply natural. If you constantly raise and lower the levels so that every sound records at the same level, the effect is terribly unnatural. Occasionally riding levels may be necessary, especially in uncontrolled situations. But for most controlled environments, we anticipate (or rehearse through) the loudest possible sound for a given situation, set that level at −12 dB, and leave the sound levels alone.

Setting Levels on a VU Meter

Occasionally, you may come across a **VU meter** (short for **volume unit meter**), especially if you use a field mixer for setting levels. As we mentioned previously, peak meters respond to all sounds directly entering the recorder. The VU meter, on the other hand, indicates an average sound level. It is, therefore, not highly sensitive to short, sharp, percussive sounds (transient sounds). For example, a slamming door the middle of a moderately quiet scene will cause the needle to jump a bit, but not to the true decibel level of that slam, because the noise is too brief for the needle to respond directly. In addition, although the VU level range is calibrated in decibels it has a slightly different scale and runs from −20 on the low end to +3 on the high end, with 0 dB as the audio peak level. The point on the scale from 0 dB to +3 is highlighted by a thicker, red bar on a needle scale, or red lights on an LED scale (**Figure 17-4**).

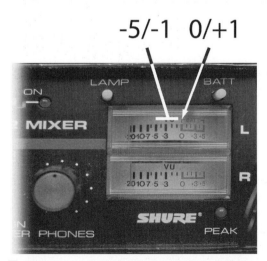

As a general rule, the loudest sounds in a given recording situation should peak at 0 dB. Occasionally, the reading can fall into the red zone but should not spend too much time there, and in no situation should the VU meter needle "pin" against the +3 side of the scale. A +3 on the VU scale means overmodulation and distorted sound. Normally spoken dialogue voice is usually set to average around −3 dB so that any sudden, loudly expressive moments might peak between −1 dB and 0 dB. Very low sounds, like our previous paper rustling in the library, can be set to register around −10 dB.

Setting Levels on the Nagra Modulometer

The modulometer on a Nagra is a peak meter with a highly sensitive needle, but with a scale that approaches that of a VU meter. All of the same principles for setting levels apply on a modulometer, but the scale is slightly different (**Figure 17-5**). Setting peak levels with the modulometer is similar to setting the VU meter levels; one doesn't want the needle to go above 0 dB with any regularity and never should the needle pin against the extreme high end of the decibel range. However, the difference is that, since the Nagra uses a highly responsive peak meter, you'll notice yourself hitting the danger zone

■ **Figure 17-4** The scale of a VU meter is slightly different from that of a peak meter. In this type of meter, the loudest signal should peak between 0 dB to +1 dB, with normal dialogue registering between −5 dB to −1 dB.

more often. Normally spoken dialogue should register around −6 dB to −4 dB; this gives you ample head room for louder sounds.

Reference Tone and Calibration

Reference tone (also called **line-up tone**) is a 1-kHz pure tone that is used as a reference for calibrating a chain of audio devices in the field. For example, let's say we are plugging our microphone into a field mixer (with VU meters) that we will use to set levels during the shoot. The mike signal then goes from the mixer into the DV camcorder (with peak meters), where it is recorded. But how do we know where to set our gain control on the camcorder so that we get the same audio levels we are setting on the mixer? All field mixers have a button that, when depressed, will generate the 1-kHz reference tone, which allows us to set the camcorder levels so that the camcorder will record exactly the audio signal levels the mixer is sending. The 1-kHz tone registers exactly as 0 dB on all VU meters; the equivalent level on digital peak meters (according to NTSC) is −20 dB.[1] So, when you send the reference tone from the field mixer

■ **Figure 17-5** The peak meter on a Nagra is called a modulometer. In this scale the loudest signal should peak at 0 dB, with normal dialogue being recorded at a level between −6 dB to −4 dB.

to the camcorder, simply set your camcorder levels to −20 dB and then forget them; the camcorder input level is now calibrated to record the same audio levels you are setting on your mixer (Figure 17-6). The Nagra also has its own reference tone button, but on the Nagra modulometer scale the 1-kHz tone registers at −8.

One final note about reference tone. It is standard practice to record 30 seconds of reference tone at the head of every tape so that audio transfers in postproduction can also be calibrated with the original audio source tape (in other words, if you need to transfer from, say, Nagra ¼″ tape to MiniDV for digital editing). This is called **headtone**. The record level of the DV deck that is recording the Nagra audio can then be calibrated to the tone you laid down at the beginning of each tape. What you hear is what you get!

■ Figure 17-6 Because of the different scale systems, a 1 kHz reference tone falls on different numbers depending on the machine being used. A digital device (left) registers the reference tone at −20 dB, an analog device with a VU meter (middle) at 0 dB, and the analog modulometer at −8 dB (right).

Manual vs. Automatic Functions

Manual vs. Automatic Level Control

Most consumer and industrial camcorders have a setting for **automatic level control**, sometimes called **auto gain**. Auto gain gives away the control for setting audio levels to the recorder, which assumes that there is a single proper level for all sounds. In low-volume situations the record level automatically increases, and in loud environments the signal is depressed—like a robot relentlessly riding the gain. Auto gain is easily fooled by sudden, sharp sounds (called **transient sounds**) or drastic dips in volume. If we are shooting a scene where two people are talking in a normal tone of voice around a dining

---

[1]Many professional sound mixers I've spoken with believe that the −20 dB reference standard is slightly too low and prefer to set their camcorder or digital recorder peak meter at −18 dB against the reference tone.

room table and suddenly a plate is dropped and smashes on the floor, the auto gain will compensate for this sudden, loud noise by immediately lowering the volume. If a character then speaks directly after this, their initial dialogue will be recorded way too low until the gain readjusts itself back to the dialogue level—which always takes some time. Conversely, if two people are speaking in expressive tone of voice and suddenly stop talking, the auto gain will respond to this quiet moment by adjusting the volume up, resulting in a conspicuous boost in room noise. If your camera has the option for **manual override**, use it. A sound recordist is better off maintaining full control of the audio signal being laid down on the tape (Figure 17-7).

■ **Figure 17-7** The auto gain control, found in many video cameras, should be turned off to have precise control over the recording level of the audio signal.

Limiters and Frequency Filters

Other automatic audio controls that you will encounter on record decks and field mixers are limiters and frequency filters. **Limiters** are volume controls that only come into effect when an audio signal reaches overload. At this point the limiter suppresses the loudness by **clipping** off the sounds before they can peak. The danger with employing a limiter is that it can be difficult for an operator to tell if the levels are properly set, since volume extremes never peak. In controlled audio situations, try not to use the limiter at all, though they can be useful when a single person is both booming and setting levels and you anticipate some erratic loud noises in the scene. In these cases, set the levels for the most common audio first, then employ the limiter.

Frequency filters automatically remove unwanted portions of the frequency range (a feature often built into microphones). The most common filters are designed to cut off low frequencies and are variously called **bass**, **bass roll-off**, **low-pass**, or **low-frequency attenuation filters**. Bass roll-off is common because we very often encounter wind noise (wind hitting the microphone diaphragm) and low machinery hum (like rumbling HVAC systems) in the field. For example, perhaps we are filming in a factory where there is a constant, low-frequency machinery hum that is making the dialogue between two actors difficult to record. A low-frequency filter will automatically suppress frequencies, say, below 50 Hz (the specific frequencies rolled off are variable depending on the system). In general, it is not a good idea to use any sort of frequency filters in the field. The equalizing capabilities in postproduction are far more sophisticated and precise than those on field recording equipment and should be used instead. The sound recordist should gather the widest possible frequency range and then be more selective (and creative) about equalizing frequencies out of the audio later in the sound mixing stage.

Headphone Monitoring

In the field, sound monitoring is always done through headphones during actual sound recording. Headphones with isolation pads are essential so that the sound person can be certain that what they are hearing is only the audio being picked up by the microphone. It is important to remember that we use the meters when setting and monitoring audio levels and NOT judge levels by what we hear through the headphones. Most professional audio recorders and camcorders offer a separate headphone level adjustment, so it is quite possible to have the headphone level set so high that audio sounds fine to your ear but is being recorded at an unacceptably low level. First set your audio to the proper levels with your meters, and then set the headphone to a comfortable volume. You shouldn't need to change the headphone volume again (Figure 17-8).

■ **Figure 17-8** Large headphones that completely cover the ears should be used to monitor audio, since they block out noise.

Headphones are used to monitor the types of sounds being recorded, and to listen for sound problems (loose connections, signal interference, unwanted background noise, etc.). Headphones are also used to evaluate other aural qualities of the recording situation, like the acoustics of the recording location. Once the gain levels are set, the sound mixer and the boom operator (who should be wearing headphones as well) can also monitor the accuracy of the microphone placement, being sure to keep it on axis and the subject-to-mike distance consistent (see later).

Just as a cinematographer is trained to see every light source on the scene, a sound mixer is trained to hear every sound on the location that might wind up on the recording. However, humans have developed highly selective hearing. It is very easy for us to ignore or "filter out" inessential sounds and focus only on the sounds we need to hear in a particular situation. It's easy to go through an entire day and never really "hear" the air conditioning droning in the background, or the constant buzz of crickets out your window, or the hum of the cooling fan in your computer. Background noises just like these can be anything from distracting to disastrous on an audio recording, so a sound mixer needs to develop an "objective ear" and must communicate to the director when unwanted sounds are infiltrating the scene, especially when they are intermittent sounds, like a plane flying overhead, or a news radio coming through the wall from next door, or the refrigerator in the kitchen kicking on. Chances are, no one else on the set has heard any of these noises.

■ MICROPHONE TECHNIQUE

Balance, Consistency, and Being On-Axis

A typical field recording situation includes dialogue (between one, two, or three characters) and background sounds. The keys to getting good audio in the field are **balance** and **consistency**; balance is finding the right relationship between the audio we want (dialogue) and the background sounds, and consistency is maintaining this balance, as well as audio levels, from setup to setup. Recording in the field always means picking up some background sounds, but too much background noise can obscure the audio. Background sound in recording is like salt in cooking: you can always add a little more later, but you cannot take it out if you've put in too much.

Balance is controlled by two important factors: microphone choice (directionality) and distance. The distance between the microphone and the audio source, say an actor speaking dialogue, is as crucial as proper record levels. Getting the microphone in as close as possible is essential because the stronger the signal from our desired sound source, the lower we can set our record levels and therefore the lower the extraneous noise will be. The further the microphone is from the source of audio, the more background sounds will infiltrate the recording. This is why we always try to get the microphone as close as possible to our actors. It is also important to understand the pick-up pattern of your microphone and to place the projection of the audio source (i.e., the mouth of an actor speaking lines) **on-axis**, which means directly within the microphone's optimal sensitivity range (Figure 17-9). As a rule, first get your microphone in its optimal position (as close as possible and on-axis) before you adjust gain levels on the recorder. Boosting input gain to compensate for a badly positioned microphone will yield poor results.

■ **Figure 17-9** Microphones should be positioned "on axis" according to their specific pickup pattern. Note how the microphone is pointing directly at the actor's mouth from above and slightly in front.

The microphone of choice most often for recording voices is the cardioid. It usually offers the flattest frequency response and a certain degree of directionality, so we have control over the source/background balance. Some cardioid microphones are manufactured with a **speech bump**, which means the microphone is especially sensitive to frequencies where the average human voice falls (mid-range) and is less sensitive to high and low fre-

Good sound mixers hear everything. Not only are their ears attuned to the ambient noise, acoustic qualities, and problematic transient sounds of a given location, but they remain aware of aural opportunities as well, including wild sounds that might be useful later in postproduction. This is creative listening! On a recent film of mine, we had to postpone an exterior scene because a flock of crows flew in and squawked obnoxiously over all that nice dialogue I had written. So, I decided to break for an early lunch, and later, when the crows had flown off to bother some other neighborhood, we continued the scene in peace. I discovered later that while we were at lunch, Michael (my sound mixer) had remained behind and recorded a few minutes of crows squawking. "Just in case you need it later," he said to me, adding that "it sounded really cool." My short film *Fear-Fall* is about Ray, a middle-class man from the suburbs who descends into paranoia over his new next-door neighbors, whom he never sees. Sure enough, Michael was absolutely right. That little piece of ambient sound, recorded impromptu, was pure gold in postproduction. I inserted those squawking, nagging crows as ambient sound in certain scenes later in the film, as Ray's paranoia gets the better of him. Those birds, which seemed to me a nuisance at the time, provided me with the perfect sound to subtly represent Ray's growing anxiety and fearful state of mind.

quencies. If your framing allows you to position your microphone within 4 feet of the talent, then a regular cardioid will do; if the framing of your shot is wider than this, causing you to position a microphone from 4 to 10 feet, then a hypercardioid is a good choice. Beyond 10 feet, you could use a shotgun microphone, but remember: while this is a fine solution for exterior shots, in interior locations a shotgun will sound "boomy."

One indispensable tool for microphone placement, and a common sight on any film production, is the **boom pole** (also called **fishpole boom**), which allows us to position a mike as close as possible to the source but still remain outside the boundaries of the shot (Figure 17-10). A boom pole is a long, lightweight pole that telescopes out to various lengths. At one end is a **shock mount** that holds the microphone in place. Shock mounts come in many different styles but the principle for all is the same. The microphone is suspended securely in place by a series of rubber bands that absorb any vibrations or handling noise from the boom pole (Figure 17-11).

The boom allows the operator to suspend the microphone on-axis precisely over and in front of the speaker (pointing directly at the source of audio), just out of the edge of the

■ **Figure 17-10** A boom pole is essential to keep microphones as close to the actors as possible while keeping the mike and boom person off frame.

■ **Figure 17-11** A shock mount keeps the microphone secured and prevents it from picking-up vibrations caused by moving the boom pole.

frame. Occasionally, it is advantageous to hold a boom below the talent and angle the microphone upward, but this can be tricky, as you may pick up background noises from above, like airplanes flying overhead if you are outdoors.

Boom Technique

Using a boom requires careful technique. Below are a few tips:

1. Consistency is essential. A boom operator must maintain both a consistent distance between the speaker and microphone and the proper on-axis mike angle during a take. Pulling the boom away from a speaker, even a few inches, or slightly positioning the microphone off-axis, will drastically shift the balance between the audio you want (i.e., dialogue) and the background noise.

2. Booms should be handled with fingertips to reduce vibration on the pole, which can be transmitted up to the microphone (Figure 17-12). You can change the angle of the microphone to keep an actor on-axis by rolling the pole in your fingers. You can even pivot a single cardioid microphone (shift the axis 180°) between two speakers by simply rolling the pole on your fingertips.

3. A boom operator should monitor the audio with their own headphones to hear exactly what they are picking up.

4. The boom operator must communicate with the camera operator to determine the limits of the frame. During rehearsals and just before each take the boom operator tests the framing by slowly lowering the mike into the scene. When the camera operator sees the mike at the edge of the frame, the boom operator should back off a few inches, to obtain some buffer.

5. Care must taken not to cast a boom shadow over the set or on the talent. Usually, the boom operator sets up after everything is ready to go and fits in around the existing camera and lighting situation.

■ **Figure 17-12** Handling the boom pole with the fingertips allows for silent repositioning of the microphone

■ **Figure 17-13** Talent in motion can be especially difficult to keep "on axis" while recording sound; rehearsals and knowledge of the script are necessary for good results.

6. Often boom operators are called upon to follow moving talent. Sometimes this means pivoting the body; other times, as with dolly shots, it may mean walking alongside the talent. Care must be taken to move quietly and maintain consistent subject-to-mike distance and pick-up axis. Boom operators should practice these moves, know where they are going, and be especially aware of casting boom shadows when moving through a set (Figure 17-13).

7. A boom operator should be familiar with the script in order to anticipate movements and dialogue.

8. Remember, rehearsals are not just for the actors—they are for the crew as well. The sound team should perform their duties on every run through as if it were a real take and adjust their strategy along the way.

9. Some boom poles are made so that the mike cable runs inside, but in cases where the mike cable swings free, the cable should be loosely wrapped a few times around the pole to avoid having it slapping against the sides and transmitting noise to the mike.

10. In situations that are too tight for a boom pole, it is also possible to mount a microphone on a small handheld device called a **pistol grip** (with a shock mount) (Figure 17-14).

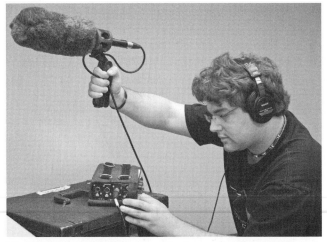

Figure 17-14 Recording sound in close quarters can make handling a boom cumbersome; for these situations a pistol grip is more convenient.

Using Lavaliere Mikes

There are certain situations for which booming is not a viable option. For example, long shots might not allow you to position a mike close enough to get decent audio, or perhaps character movement is so elaborate that a boom operator could not possibly follow the action. In these cases you may consider using a lavaliere microphone planted on your talent. Hiding lavaliere mikes requires a little bit of ingenuity, tact, and gaffer's tape (see **Figure 16-17**).

Lavalieres are also a good choice in very noisy environments or when you are working within wide shots. The extremely close miking of a lavaliere allows the sound mixer to lower the input volume, thereby reducing the background noise; additionally, you can position the actor so that their body acts as an absorbing sound buffer and blocks unwanted sounds.

While lavalieres indeed give you great sound, there are a number of factors to be considered:

1. *Perspective problems.* The very close, intimate audio presence of a lavaliere will seem odd in long shot situations. The sound is close but the image is distant. Perspective problems can be fixed in postproduction if you have access to the proper equipment, so before you use this strategy, know what is available to you in postproduction.

2. *Pick-up axis.* Lavs need to be placed carefully with regard to vocal projection and possible direction shifts. For example, let's say we've hidden a lavaliere microphone under the left side of a performer's collar, but during the course of the take the performer turns and speaks over the opposite shoulder. The drop-off in the performer's audio level can be extreme (**Figure 17-15**).

3. *Noise.* Hiding a lavaliere microphone on the talent can pose an unwanted noise problem, as this type of mike is particularly vulnerable to "rustle" noises from clothes or fabric. Take care to tape down lavaliere microphones to clothes or to the body, such that there is no possibility of other fabric rubbing against the mike as the actor performs—for example, at the sternum in the little depression between the pectoral muscles. Every working sound person has their own home remedy for rustle-free lavaliere mounting. On of the most common methods is to wrap a Band-Aid around the body of the mike to keep clothes from direct contact. One guy showed me an elaborate, bent-paperclip cage he made, a sort of teeny-tiny shock mount. It worked well, but unfortunately, I never could duplicate his sculptural creation on my own.

4. *Mobility.* Using a standard lavaliere microphone still means that the talent is tethered to a microphone cable that extends from their body (usually out of their pant leg) all the way to the recording deck. This can restrict movement. In instances where long shots are required and an actor's mobility is essential, a wireless microphone set can be used (see p. 315).

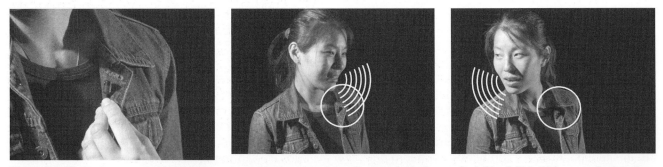

Figure 17-15 Because of their tiny size, lavaliere microphones can be easily concealed in the actor's clothing (left), but it becomes the talent's responsibility to stay "on axis" (middle). A turn of the head can make the signal difficult to record (right).

5. *Feelings.* Hiding a microphone on talent usually means working under a person's clothing, so you need to be tactful when approaching an actor to wire them. Less experienced actors will tell you "Give me the mike and I'll put it on myself." But this isn't a great idea for obvious reasons. It's best to wire your performer in a discreet place (don't, for example, ask them to take their shirt off in the middle of a busy set). Also, let them know why all this is necessary; if you tell them that you're trying to record their lovely voice and their brilliant lines as cleanly as possible, then they're more likely to allow you to gaffer tape a microphone to their bra or to run an XLR cable down their pants.

Miking and Perspective

Obviously, the closer we can put the microphone to the speaker the stronger our signal will be. But when we record for film we also need to consider the **perspective** of a person's voice and how the audio recording will relate to our expectations, given the frame size and the proximity of the camera to the subject. It will feel odd to have an extreme close-up on a character and to hear their dialogue as if it's coming from a great distance, and vice versa. Fortunately, in narrative production much of this problem is solved on its own, because even though we try to get the microphone in as tight as possible, the dimensions of the visual frame determine how close we can actually go before the mike shows up in the frame. A tight close-up allows us to place a microphone close to the subject, which will give us a better frequency response, warmer, more intimate sound, and less ambient noise intrusion. A wide shot will require us to keep the microphone a distance away, and this change in **perspective** is usually appropriate for the camera-to-subject proximity.

Using Multiple Microphones

Occasionally you may have a situation in which one microphone simply doesn't cover all the bases. This is especially the case with shots that involve a dialogue between two people who are far apart, or with long shots that involve substantial character movement. The former often require a combination of booming and planting microphones on the set where characters will stand to deliver lines, while the latter case can simply mean hiding wireless lavalieres on your talent (**Figures 17-16** and **17-17**). Each location and each miking situation is unique and poses a variety of challenges. To a large extent, that's the fun of this job! As a sound mixer and boom operator you need to understand the capabilities and limitations of your equipment and be resourceful and creative in devising strategies to obtain the best possible audio under any circumstances.

■ **Figure 17-16** In this scene from Lund's *Snapshot* (2006), the framing made it necessary to use multiple mikes. A boom mike slightly off frame left was used for Nathan (David Andrews, foreground) while Marcello (Henry Darrow, background) was miked with a wireless lavaliere.

Audio Continuity: Ambient Sound

Concerning ambient sounds, we also need to consider **audio continuity.** Continuity is usually discussed in visual terms, relating to making sure the actors are wearing the same clothes from shot to shot, or holding their glass with the same hand, but continuity is essential for audio also, and continuity problems usually come from radical shifts in ambiance from shot to shot. For example, in a simple dialogue scene we would never mike character "A" with a lavaliere for their close-up reverse shots and then mike character "B" with a cardioid for their close-up reverse shots. We would obviously get a drastic shift in presence and environmental noises. But this ambient shift also happens when we shoot a wide master shot with a hypercardioid and then switch to

■ **Figure 17-17** In this scene from Robert Altman's *Nashville* (1975), a six-way overlapping dialogue situation is recorded live thanks to the use of wireless lavaliere microphones on all of the talent. The same situation would be impossible to accomplish if shotgun microphones were used instead.

regular cardioids for close-ups, something that would not be uncommon. Ambient shift can also occur if we use the same microphone but change the distance from sound source to microphone from shot to shot; because the recordist is required to change levels in this situation, we'll get a shift in ambient sound and therefore a discrepancy in audio continuity. If the background noises shift from shot to shot, it creates a tough situation for an editor who is trying to invisibly cut two shots together to create the illusion of continuous time and space. For this reason we always record one minute of **ambient sound** (or **room tone**) at each and every location. After the last "Cut" is called by the director, before anyone starts striking the set, the mixer needs to ask everyone to be quiet for one minute of room tone.[2] The mike is then opened at the normal, speech level and the boom operator announces the sound take by stating the location and announcing "one minute of room tone." Then everyone stands stock still while they record one minute of general ambient sound. After one minute, the mixer calls "End Ambience" and the set can be struck. It is important to do this while the crew and equipment are still on the set. Remember, they, too, were part of the ambient atmosphere during each take (the bodies absorb echoes, etc.). This is a practice that people usually have very little patience for on a hectic film set, but it pays off big dividends in the editing room, because the editor can use this baseline ambience as a separate track to smoothly suture together shots with differing ambience (see Chapter 23).

Miscellaneous Recording Challenges

When a director scouts a location, they are usually evaluating the visual qualities of the set, rather than its aural qualities. It happens frequently that a sound person will find themselves on a set that looks terrific to the camera, but that has serious problems for sound recording. **Reverberant spaces** are one such problem. Earlier in the book we spoke about "live" recording spaces with hard surfaces that bounce sound back and forth, creating sound reverberations. Too much reverberation, however, can create indistinct audio with muddy highs and boomy low frequencies. **Sound blankets** (often just mover's blankets) are used very often when reverberation threatens to compromise sound quality. By hanging blankets just off screen and laying them on tiled floors, between the sound source and the reflective surfaces, you in effect absorb the sound before it can be reflected. The more blankets, the more sound is absorbed (Figure 17-18).

■ **Figure 17-18** Careful positioning of sound blankets off screen will absorb sound before it bounces off hard surfaces.

Another very common sound challenge—this one for exterior location recording—is **wind noise**. Microphones are particularly vulnerable to wind noise because the wind acts like sound waves and buffet the highly sensitive microphone diaphragm. High winds can sound like a freight train, but soft winds, too, can contaminate sound by generating a low-frequency rumble. To this end, many microphones are manufactured with built-in **windscreens** that are foam wind buffers surrounding the head of the microphone. Windscreens dampen the effects of the wind on the diaphragm without altering the incoming sound waves. Built-in windscreens, however, are rarely enough protection from even the slightest breeze. Thankfully, there are many windscreens on the market that fit the head of almost any microphone, and you should always bring one to your exterior locations (Figure 17-19).

■ **Figure 17-19** Windscreens are necessary to cut wind noise when shooting outdoors. There are models available for most microphones, even for tiny lavalieres (lower right).

[2]Do this even before you turn off any movie lights, because they will make little pinging noises as the metal cools.

On Set!

CHAPTER 18

There are many ways to shoot a narrative film. The complexity of the project, the size of the crew, the nature of the location, and the style of the director all have an impact on what actually occurs on the film set. Director Kelly Reichardt shot her third feature film, *Old Joy,* with a crew of six, a principal cast of two, predominantly exterior locations and available light, and with everyone bunking together on location for the duration of the shoot (see p. 12). Filmmaker Didier Rouget shot his first short film, *Vive le Premier Mai,* in one afternoon, on the streets of Paris, with two other crew members, two actors, no lights, and no sound (see p. 133). The shooting processes for these productions are bound to be different than those for your standard industry blockbuster film, with crew members numbering into the dozens and a veritable convoy of equipment trucks and trailers. There are many books on the market that explain in complex detail all of the tasks and procedures on a standard commercial feature film, but be careful: a production must adjust its personnel size and on-set procedures to the scale of the project, especially on short films, in order to keep the creative process from being weighed down by excessively elaborate logistics. This chapter will look at the basic on-set process for an average short narrative film with sync sound. While certain tasks and procedures can be scaled to fit larger or smaller projects and crews, there's nothing in the following discussion that you can cut entirely.

■ WALKING ONTO THE SET

So you've thoroughly completed your preproduction. You've talked to everyone, rehearsed and discussed the script with the cast, and figured out the aesthetic and technical approach to each scene with the crew. Everything and everyone necessary to accomplish the day's shooting is here, the location is secured, and you are armed with your marked shooting script, overheads, and shot list. Now what? Now you get down to the work of building your film one setup at a time, take after take, with the knowledge that being well prepared allows you to respond creatively to what is happening on the set. When you walk onto a film set for the first time, whether you're a director, D.P., actor, art director, or sound recordist, you will feel something remarkable—the energy of a group of people who have come together to make a movie. You will also, probably for the first time, be in the actual shooting space and watching those actors in their costumes moving in that location. As you collaborate with the cast and crew, new ideas will start to emerge. If you know clearly the shots you need to make the film, then you are freer to improvise, cut, alter, or adjust, to accommodate new ideas or unexpected obstacles. Use the chemistry of all of those creative people gathered in one place and the inevitable surprises that occur on the set to improve the project at every turn. So, get down to work, but remember that production is rarely just the mechanical realization of the film that had been developed in preproduction; rather, it is another creative stage in the evolution of your idea (Figure 18-1).

■ **Figure 18-1** On the set. The creative intensity and collaboration that are generated by a focused and involved cast and crew are among the great experiences of the filmmaking process.

■ WHO DOES WHAT, WHEN

Whatever the scale of your production, the basic stages for a shooting day are the same: (a) arrive at the location and dress the set (also called prepping the set), (b) run through the scene in the actual space, then set up your camera and, if necessary, lights and sound based on that rehearsal, (c) run the scene a few more times until all cast and crew feel ready, and then (d) take the shot. Repeat these steps until your film is done. After a while, this routine becomes completely automatic for everyone on the project and, at last, you're making a movie. But let's look a little closer at each step for an average short film project, using lights and sound, and fill in some essential details.

Dressing the Set

The first team to arrive on a set, in addition to the director and producing staff, is the art department. The art department **preps the location**, **dresses the set**, and prepares wardrobe and props in advance of the rest of the crew. Often, the art department will be prepping the next day's location while everyone else is shooting the current day's scenes. On small films, however, it's not always possible to have access to a location a day ahead of time, nor is it necessary if the set needs are minimal, which is often the case for exterior shoots, for example (Figure 18-2).

Loading In

When the rest of the crew arrives on the set, they begin the process of **loading in**, which simply means getting all of the necessary equipment onto the location. A very simple shoot might only involve enough equipment to fit in the trunk of one car, while larger projects, especially those with extensive lighting needs, might require trucks full of gear. No matter how much equipment you're using, it is critical that you establish a designated area, near the actual set, where all of it will be held. This is called the **staging area** (Figure 18-3). When you need something, you'll know where to find it; when you're done using something, you'll know where to return it. Orderliness is essential! When equipment gets lost, nine out of ten times it's because there is no established staging area and equipment gets sprayed all over the location in the course of a shooting day. In this scenario, almost without exception, something gets lost. It may be something small, like a zoom handle or a filter, but it could be something expensive or essential, like a battery cable, a microphone, or a roll of exposed film from the day's shoot!

■ **Figure 18-2** Before lights, camera, action! (or sound), the art department arrives and does their job prepping the set. Production still from Sharone Vendriger's *Baloon Girl* (2007).

Tech Rehearsal

With all the equipment now loaded in at the location, the question everyone is asking is, how and where do we set up? Each department should have their own copies of the marked shooting script, overheads, and shot lists, so they should already have an idea of the basic setups, but the director and actors will also stage a **tech rehearsal** in the dressed set (Figure 18-4). This is a basic run through of the scene to be shot, including dialogue and blocking, so that the various departments get a more accurate sense for where to set up the camera, lights, and sound. The tech rehearsal is also the director's first time running the scene in the actual location and viewing the framings from the camera. Changes to the visual conception of the scene at this point are common. Slight (or major) adjustments to the framing, merging shots, rethinking the blocking of the actors: all are part of the tech rehearsal. Also, during the tech rehearsal the camera crew might lay **focus marks** on the floor. These are small pieces of tape that follow the path of a character's movement in the space. They are measured to the camera so that focus can be accurately pulled as the character hits their marks, meaning as they move from mark to mark during the scene (see p. 201). Once the scene has been staged, the departments get to work.

Setup

After the tech rehearsal the actors leave the set to get into costume and makeup and, if there is time and it is necessary, the director will run lines or quick rehearsals with them off the set. This is an important time between an actor and director. The director's task at this point is to get the actor **into character**, meaning get them into the emotional and psychological space necessary to pull off the scene, and to remind the actors of the performance decisions that were made during preproduction rehearsals and read throughs (see later, "The Director and Actors on the Set").

Meanwhile, the camera department preps and sets up the camera, meaning cleaning the camera, selecting the right lens, setting camera speed, mounting the camera on the camera support, and loading the film magazines. If you are shooting on DV, this is where you will white balance the camera, and set all other necessary video adjustments. As the lighting crews set up the lights, the D.P. takes countless light meter readings and consults the depth-of-field charts to makes sure that lighting setup, exposures, and focus are in line with the visual strategy established in preproduction.

From time to time the director will check on the progress of the lighting, camera placement, and look of the set. Also, the D.P. may ask an actor to stand here or there, or walk through their blocking again so that lights, camera, and focus can be more accurately established. If an actor is not available (e.g., they're rehearsing or in hair and makeup), then a **stand-in** is used (Figure 18-5). Ideally a stand-in and the actor have approximately the same height and coloring, and on major film productions there are specific people who are hired as stand-ins for particular stars. But on small shoots a stand-in can be any available crew member. During the lighting setup the art department is also on set and ready to adjust set pieces or furniture in order to create a better composition.

■ Figure 18-3 Designating a staging area for equipment is necessary to keep tabs on where everything is and where everything should be once shooting is finished.

■ Figure 18-4 A tech rehearsal, where actors do a basic run through of a scene, is essential to establish the lighting, blocking, and camera placement.

■ **Figure 18-5** The use of stand-ins instead of actors to focus lighting instruments can save a lot of time during production, especially when the actors are in rehearsal or makeup.

■ **Figure 18-6** While the crew sets up, the sound department devises a recording strategy and tests equipment.

While all of this is happening the sound department sets up their equipment (Figure 18-6). Their first task is to strategize how to mike the scene given the environment, the blocking, and the framing. Should the recordist decide to boom the scene, they will wait until the lighting crew has finished their work before establishing the position for the boom operator, in order to fit themselves around the lights so boom shadows do not fall onto the set. If lavaliere microphones are used, then the recordist must find the talent and wire them for sound. Also, the sound crew will set up and test their recording gear to be certain they are getting a clean audio signal. In a single-system sound situation that means making sure the audio chain (mike → field mixer → camera) is hooked up, calibrated to the 1 kHz reference tone, and transmitting clean audio (see p. 321). The same goes for double-system sound (mike → field mixer → recorder), except that the sound recordist will additionally record a **verbal slate** at the head of each new DAT or ¾" tape which includes: (a) the name of the project and director, (b) the roll number, (c) the date, (d) the recording sample rate (or ips record speed for Nagras), and, if your recorder has a tone generator, (e) the headtone level (i.e., −18 dB digital or −8 dB Nagra). Then the recordist will record 30 seconds of reference tone, which is used to calibrate the postproduction sound transfers. After this, the tape is ready for the first take.

Final Run Throughs

When all of the technical setup has been completed and everyone is ready to go—camera in place, lighting set up, sound in position—the director will call for a **run through** (also called **dress rehearsal**). During the run through everyone proceeds as if you're actually filming. Without running any film or tape, this allows everyone to make final adjustments: actors make final adjustments to movements and performance; the camera operator gets to refine the focus, camera moves, and the overall visual composition; the lighting team tweaks the lights to get them just right; the art department addresses whatever set piece, prop, costume, or makeup issue needs addressing; and the sound team establishes boom position and final record levels. And all of this activity is happening under the watchful eye and instructions of the director, whose job it is to make sure that everyone's creative and technical energies are working toward a single, unified cinematic goal (Figure 18-9).

Sometimes a crew will go through several run throughs before everyone feels they're ready to roll; however, you need to be careful. You can tweak, adjust, fix, and rehearse endlessly. If too much time is being wasted splitting hairs or fixing things that no one would ever notice, the producer or P.M. must step in and push things along by reminding everyone how little time there is and how many setups they must accomplish before the day is over, and that they generally need to "move it." This efficiency nudge hopefully prompts the director to say, "Okay everyone, let's try a take."

in practice

The Slate and Production Logs
First Level of Information

The **slate**, the **camera report**, and the **sound log** are all used to keep a running record of each and every **camera take**. A **take** is defined as the moment the camera is turned on at the beginning of a shot to the moment it is turned off after the director has called "Cut!" Slate and production logs contain two levels of information; the first is general information:

- *Title of the project*
- *Name of the director*
- *Name of the camera operator (or sound recordist on sound logs)*
- *Date*

This information doesn't change much, but the second level of information, which identifies which scene is being shot and how many times it has been attempted, changes with each and every take on both the logs and the slate (Figure 18-7).

■ **Figure 18-7** Roll, scene and take numbers. The information on a slate is vital in postproduction, so care should be taken to keep the slate updated, accurate, and readable.

Second Level of Information

- *Roll number.* The roll number refers to the DV tape cassette or roll of film (or other media, like P2 cards). When you change your DV tape, say after an hour of footage, or put a new roll of film in the camera (or fill up a P2 card), you will change the roll number. Roll numbers run sequentially, the first being roll #1, then roll #2, roll #3, etc.
- *The scene/shot number.* The scene and shot you are currently shooting (e.g., scene 13 b) is taken from the shot list (which itself corresponds to the marked shooting script). The scene/shot number changes to the next on the list after the director believes that a good take, called a **keeper take**, has been achieved.
- *The take number.* This is the number of times you've attempted a scene/shot. This number changes each time you make another attempt at the same shot (e.g., scene 13 b, take 1; scene 13 b, take 2; scene 13 b, take 3, etc., until you achieve a keeper take).
- *Sound number.* The sound number always runs sequentially (e.g., snd 1, snd 2, snd 3, . . .) even across different rolls (Figure 18-8).
- Additionally, sound and camera logs include *footage* or *timecode information* for each take; this information is also filled in after each take. This not only helps find and cue specific takes on a tape later, but it gives you an accurate time count of how long each individual take is and it helps you keep track of how much film or tape you've used and how much you have left before you need to change rolls.

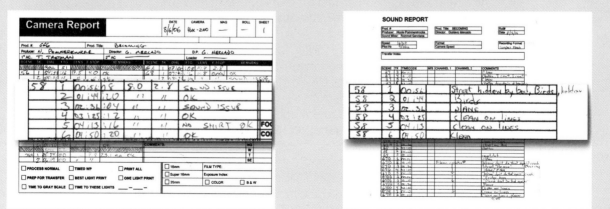

■ **Figure 18-8** The information on the camera report (left) and sound logs (right) should remain perfectly coordinated with the slate throughout the shoot. Spot checks are recommended.

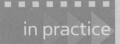

In narrative production, slates and logs are used to label every take, whether you're shooting on DV or film. On small-scale films, like student shorts, the A.C. generally keeps the camera reports and updates the slate, while the sound recordist keeps the sound logs. But if the A.C. is busy with other tasks, like pulling focus, or elaborate dolly moves, the A.D. can also load the slate. In either case, establish a routine and stick to it; it is essential for a smooth and efficient postproduction process that the production logs and the slate are kept in perfect coordination.

■ **Figure 18-9** Run throughs are essential to getting your actual takes just right, especially on tricky shots like this moving escalator set-up from Mercado's film *Yield* (2006).

■ **Figure 18-10** It is up to the camera people to make sure the slate is in framed properly, in focus and readable. Here the A.C. uses a flashlight in a dark location to ensure that the slate is visible.

■ SHOOTING A TAKE

This is the moment of truth. All of the preproduction preparation, all of the setup and rehearsals, boil down to what happens in front of the camera while film (or tape) is rolling. A take begins with the director (or A.D. on larger shoots) asking for "quiet on the set" and for everyone to get into their positions. Actors, camera crew, and sound crew all position themselves where they need to be. Then the A.C. (or whoever was assigned to load the slate) steps into the scene holding the updated slate (clapper arm already opened) for the camera to see. The camera operator must be able to clearly read the slate in the viewfinder. A slate that is halfway out of the frame, out of focus, or too dark to read is useless (Figure 18-10).

After everyone is in position and it's quiet on the set, the director (or A.D. on larger shoots) then calls the shot. **Calling the shot** is a standardized routine for every sync sound take on a double-system film production. The order and commands are designed to make syncing dailies in postproduction routine. Here's how the director calls a shot:

(a) DIRECTOR: "Is anyone not ready?" If no one says anything, then . . .

(b) DIRECTOR: "Roll sound."

(c) SOUND REC.: Starts recorder, and when it is up to speed, calls out, "Speed" (speed is achieved after a 5-second preroll for digital recorders or when the "sync flag" shows on the Nagra).

(d) DIRECTOR: "Roll camera."

(e) CAMERA OP.: Starts camera and calls, "Rolling."

(f) A.C. (or other slate person): When the slate person hears "Rolling," they call out the scene and take numbers, "Scene 13 b, take 1," clap the slate closed, and move quickly out of the scene and settle down quietly!

(g) DIRECTOR (after a pause): "Action!"

(h) The take plays out and the director will wait a beat after the scene has ended before calling out . . .

(i) DIRECTOR: "Cut!" No one can call cut except the director and no one stops their jobs until the director calls "cut." There may be a great reaction or tableau at the end of a scene that the director wants to linger on, and if the camera operator simply turns off the camera because they thought the scene was over, they've lost a great moment. Also, a director should not call "cut" exactly at the end of the shot; it's wise to wait a beat or two to give yourself handles for the editing process. However, the director can certainly call "cut" before the scene is done if something egregious has occurred; like a piece of the set falling over, or the actor speaking the wrong lines, or a police car driving past with the siren wailing.

(j)   When "cut" is called, the take is over and the camera is turned off. The sound recordist, however, will record two short beeps with the recorder's tone generator before stopping. This helps you to quickly cue sound takes in postproduction. Finally the camera report, sound logs, and slate are updated.

Evaluating the Take

Technical: Performance and Continuity

After the take, the director first checks with camera and sound for confirmation. If there was a technical problem, it must be communicated to the director at this point so that he or she can determine if a **retake** is needed.

- *Camera:* If the camera lost focus, or bobbled in the middle of the shot, or if a pan didn't follow the actor or got the edge of a light stand in the frame, then a retake might be necessary.

- *Sound:* If the microphone drifted off-axis too much, or the actor delivered their lines so loudly that the levels clipped, or if the mike picked up extraneous noise (like a dog barking or a lawnmower starting up next door), or any other problem like this, you'll probably require another take.

- *Performance, New Ideas:* The director also evaluates the performances. Did the actor drop some lines? Was the performance not as good as it could be? Were the actions awkward or incorrect? Maybe everything was fine, but the director got some new ideas while watching the scene unfold. All of these things could also lead to a re-take.

- *Continuity:* Continuity issues also must be considered. Did the actor have a cigarette in the long shot, but not in this close-up take? Was the actor wearing a coat in the long shot, but is now wearing only a shirt for the close-up? Is there a problem with matching screen direction or performance intensity from shot to shot? These issues also can require a retake. On projects that require a lot of continuity shooting, it is a good idea to have a dedicated **script supervisor**, whose job it is to pay attention to continuity details and to mark off shots that have been completed (see later, The Lined Script). Script supervisors also can do spot checks with the logs and slates to make sure that they're corresponding properly.

If the director decides that another take is needed, then the problem with that take is noted in the camera and sound logs "comments" area and, after making the necessary corrections (technical or performance), then the whole process is repeated for "take 2." Keep in mind, the "comments" notes are important because not all "bad takes" are a complete loss. Sometimes a technical or performance problem isn't a problem throughout the take, and there are some good moments that can be used in the editing. These should be noted as well (Figure 18-11).

If the director is happy with the take, then it is marked as a "**keeper**" in the logs and everyone moves on to the next scene/shot on the shot list. After all of the shots from a particular camera angle are completed, the camera and lighting move to the next angle and setup begins again. This system is repeated, take after take, setup after setup, scene after scene, day after day, until you've got your movie "**in the can**."

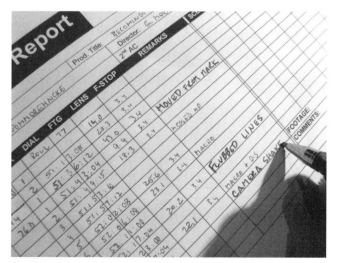

■   **Figure 18-11** A camera report contains comments and technical information about every shot taken.

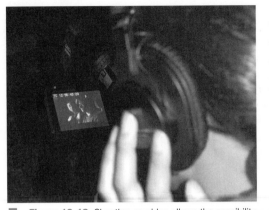

Figure 18-12 Shooting on video allows the possibility of reviewing material that has been shot. In film, this is only possible if a video assist system is used during production.

Other Retake Factors

There will be times when everything on a take went relatively well, but the actor or D.P. feel that they could have done better or want to try something new, or feel that with one more take they can really do something extraordinary. In these cases they should ask the director for another take. If you can afford the time and the footage, it's usually a good idea to listen to these requests.

Sometimes, when cast and crew nail the scene on the very first take, a bizarre superstition takes hold of everyone and they think, "It can't have been *that* easy." Or "What if something happens to that take? It's the only one we've got." In these cases the director may call for another take, "just for safety's sake." This is called a **safety take**. The funny thing is, there is often some problem with the safety take (technical or performance) and then people will inevitably want to do retakes of the safety take. . . . Still, safety takes are a good idea, if only to give you some options in the editing room.

There will also be times when you are running out of time or film or both and simply not getting the entire shot you're after in a single take. This situation calls for the director to be crafty. Perhaps you have everything you need, but it is distributed in good moments among several "imperfect" takes. Maybe all you need to do is shoot a cut-away, or a simple reaction shot of someone else, which will then allow you to piece together the best parts of various takes seamlessly. It's important that a director keep in mind during the shooting process the flexibility that editing affords.

Checking Video

If you are shooting on DV, and you are undecided about the quality of a take, you can always rewind the tape, or cue the P2 card, and watch the shot. People shooting on film can also do this if they have video assist (**Figure 18-12**). **Video assist** (or a **video tap**) is a small video pick-up device, attached to the camera viewing system, which records low-quality video of each take. Video assist is standard issue on big- to moderate-budget films, but it requires three things that put it out of reach of many introductory film students. First, it requires additional funds for the rental of the video tap; second, it requires an additional crew person to operate the video assist gear; and, finally, it requires a camera that will accommodate video assist. Video assist is usually overkill for small film projects, which can do just as well relying on the observations of the director, D.P., and sound recordist.

In either case, evaluating shots by checking the video can be helpful, but it can also be extremely time consuming if you have to rewind videotape to check each and every potential keeper take. P2 cards and DVD-RAM recording have the advantage of instantaneous random access, but still you need to watch the take in real time. Watching video also can drive you a little crazy in the quest for absolute perfection. You may find yourself doing retakes for things that no one would ever notice, but that you see as a flaw. Directors who do get into the habit of rewatching everything they've shot on the set can expect, and should schedule, a longer shooting period.

Additional Shooting Procedures and Tips

MOS and Single-System Sound

If you are shooting without sound, called shooting **MOS**, or shooting single-system sound, all takes are still slated but the commands for the sound recorder are obviously omitted and there is no need to clap the slate, since there is no microphone, or in the case of single system, no postproduction syncing to be done. With both single-system and MOS shooting, slating is purely for visual reference, so the slate (with the proper scene information) is simply held in front of the camera for a few seconds after "roll camera." Then the slate person steps away and settles so that action can be called. It is very common to have a mix of sync takes and MOS takes in a single shooting day.

Tail Slates

Sometimes you need to get a shot off right away, or you'll lose a special moment (like a boat cruising unexpectedly in the background or a perfect wind blowing through the trees), or you may simply want to roll camera without breaking the emotional focus of an actor with the whole slating procedure. In these cases we use a **tail slate** to mark the take. A tail slate simply means that the verbal marker and slate clap are done at the end of the shot, but before the camera is turned off. To avoid confusion with the next shot, tail slates are held upside down.

Checking the Gate

When shooting film the D.P. (or A.C.) should check the gate after each "keeper" take. **Checking the gate** means taking a close look at the aperture plate in the camera's gate to make sure there are no hairs or debris that would show up permanently on the image. Finding a hair in the gate can also be a reason to do a retake. Checking the gate involves using the inching knob to swing the shutter away from the gate, removing the lens and with a small flashlight and magnifying glass, looking at all four edges of the aperture plate opening (especially the bottom edge) to make sure it is free of hair and dust. If it is clean, then shooting can continue. If the gate is dirty, then the offending hair should be removed with a soft wooden **orangewood stick**. Outside the film world, "orange sticks" are used for pushing back fingernail cuticles and can be bought at any drugstore. On a film shoot, orange sticks are a standard item in a shooter's ditty bag because they are soft and will not damage the gate and do not leave debris behind (Figure 18-13).

With zoom lenses, you can check the gate without removing the lens. Simply swing the shutter away from the gate, set the lens aperture to wide open, and bring the zoom lens all the way in. The lens acts like a magnifying glass, so the D.P. need only shine the flashlight through the front of the lens and scan the edges of the gate. If the D.P. finds a hair, then the lens, of course, will need to be removed to clean the gate.

The Lined Script

After each keeper take that particular scene/shot is then "lined off" with a red squiggly line on a lined script. A **lined script** is a copy of the screenplay that contains a record of what parts of the script have been successfully shot and from what angle. The lined script looks like a marked shooting script (see p. 87), but the difference is that it reflects the actual shots taken rather than the shots as they were anticipated in preproduction. Most of the time you will be drawing squiggly lines across the shots you've drawn-in during preproduction, but during the production process the coverage might change in some scenes; perhaps some camera angles were added or omitted or merged. Maybe the director decided that the master shot was all that was necessary and that close-ups were not needed. Or maybe the director realized on the set that adding a new close-up angle would be a powerful shot to cut to. All of these types of decisions are reflected in the lined script. The lined script also allows everyone to see at a glance if everything has been covered. Any part of the lined script without a red squiggly line was not covered and still needs to be shot (Figure 18-14).

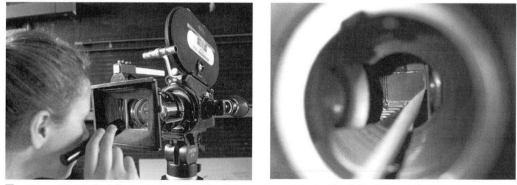

■ Figure 18-13 An A.C. checks the gate using the zoom lens as a magnifier (left). Soft orangewood sticks are the standard tool for safely cleaning a gate of debris (right).

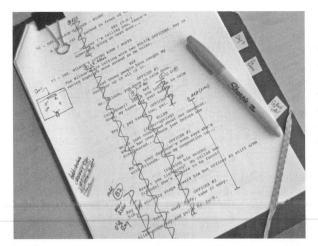

■ **Figure 18-14** A lined script is regularly updated during the shoot to reflect what shots have already been taken; it is also a record of last-minute changes done by the director.

There must only be one lined script on the set, and updating it is the job of a **script supervisor**, but on smaller shoots it can be done by the A.D. or even the director. Any notes about each take or reminders about how a particular scene was covered (especially for scenes that changed during production) should also be noted in the margins or on the back of the corresponding page, making this particular document a very important record of the director's ideas during production, which can be highly useful in the editing process.

Roll-Out

When a camera roll reaches its end (the end of a DV tape or the end of a camera load) the D.P. will tell the director, "roll-out," and the production will halt while the film spool or magazine, or DV tape or P2 card, is changed. If you've kept careful camera logs, roll-out should be anticipated so that it doesn't happen right in the middle of a long and elaborate shot. If you know you have a minute or so left on a roll, you should inform the director. After removing your DV tape or your film (in a changing bag if you're using a 400´ magazine load), you should immediately put it back in its case or can and label it. Film cans should also be securely retaped closed. This footage is the most valuable thing on the set and you don't want an unmarked, unidentified can or tape kicking around the film set.

■ MISCELLANEOUS (BUT IMPORTANT) PRODUCTION DETAILS

A film set is an exciting, intense, and often pressure-filled environment filled with energetic people who are focused, driven, and usually working with limited time and resources. In this environment there is often a temptation to cut corners to get the job done. But cutting certain corners often proves to be counterproductive—or worse, downright foolish and dangerous. The following sections cover the essential set procedures, protocol, and etiquette that should always be observed.

Labeling Film Cans and Tape Cases

It's important to take a little time out to properly and neatly label your film cans or tape cases right after roll-out and put them in

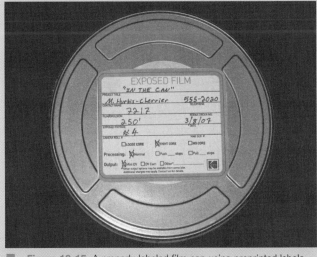

■ **Figure 18-15** A properly labeled film can using preprinted labels available online from Kodak.

a secure location. Film cans, DV tapes, and sound rolls must be neatly labeled with the following information:

- Project title
- Roll number
- Director's name and contact information
- Shooting date
- Film cans should additionally contain *processing instructions* (e.g., process normal or pushed one stop), *type of film* (e.g., 7297), and *footage* (e.g., 400´).
- Sound rolls should additionally contain *record sample rate* (e.g., 44.1 kHz) or 3/4″ *tape speed* (e.g., 7½ ips), and *headtone level* (e.g., −18 dB).
- If you are splitting a film core (see p. 154) then the can containing the unexposed film should be labeled with the *type of film* (e.g., 7297), *footage* (e.g., 220´), and *date*.

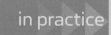
in practice

Takes, Retakes, and Mistakes

1. The camera and sound crew must be alert, aware, and honest about evaluating the technical qualities of a take. Everyone makes mistakes; this is what retakes are for. One time, while my class and I were shooting a brief scene on 16mm for an in-class production exercise, we shot a take of two guys playing "rock-paper-scissors" as if their lives depended on winning. The close-up shot involved a slow pan from one player's face, to their hands, then to the other player's face. The actors really nailed the performance and after calling "cut," I turned to the camera operator and asked, "Was that good for camera?" The response was a less than confident "Uh, yeah, s'pose so." "Was it good, or not?" I pressed. "Yeah, yeah, it was good." When we got the dailies back from the lab, we all saw that the pan wasn't great; it mostly missed the hands playing the game and the end of the move didn't really find its final composition on the second player's face, landing instead somewhere around his shoulder. The student knew the pan wasn't good, but he didn't want to admit to his teacher that he messed up the shot so he was less than honest with his evaluation. Unfortunately, and predictably, the photographic evidence was right there and undeniable. Obviously, it's so much better to simply say "the pan was off" and do another take, than to discover in postproduction that there's only one poor take to edit with. Shooting on DV, I could have checked it in the field myself, but shooting on 16mm film (without video assist), the crew needs to be especially exacting and forthcoming.

2. In one of my own films, I had a scene in which a business executive delivers distressing news about imminent lay-offs to his management team. The problem was, I couldn't get the executive to deliver his speech in one clean take. Not only did he flub his lines, but also the multiple takes were making him feel increasingly on the spot, and we discovered that when he got nervous, he'd start to stutter. After about five takes I became concerned about the amount of film I was burning on this relatively small moment. Since I planned to intercut the executive's speech with the reactions from one particular worried manager, I came up with a work-around. I figured I had the first three sentences of the speech covered in one of the live takes. Then I imagined exactly where I could cut into the scene and we simply had him deliver two other, tiny chunks of the speech (no more than two sentences each) for the camera. After these two short shots, which he achieved in one take each, I sat with him on location and recorded the entire speech as a sound take only. This way, he could read the speech, sitting down, without the lights and camera on him. He was terrific, and I had both my images for intercutting and the rest of the speech to insert as audio under the anxious face of the manager.

3. A colleague of mine recounted a time when, on her film set, she had an actress who was great during run throughs but who got "big" when the camera was actually recording. "It was totally unconscious, but she couldn't help it. She would turn up the intensity a few notches whenever she knew we were doing a real take." In addition, retakes only made her performance even bigger. So the director told camera and sound that they'd secretly roll tape during the "run though" and then they'd also take some scenes after the run through, so that the actress wouldn't catch on. Since they were shooting on DV, they put a little strip of black tape over the red light, which indicates when the camera is rolling. The plan worked and the actress' performance in the film was convincing, ". . . but we had no slates for her good takes otherwise; if we had slated, she'd know we were rolling."

Set Protocol and Etiquette

Courtesy and Respect

Everyone on a film set should be treated with courtesy and respect. This is not just a top-down issue (i.e., producers respecting the grips), but goes for all crew members toward each other. As they say in the business, when you come onto a film set, leave your ego at the door. Courtesy and respect also include being on time. When you are late, you waste other peoples' valuable time. The film industry places a very high premium on promptness and if you have a reputation for being late (even on the level of film school) you will not be asked to work much.

Safety and Common Sense

We have covered safety issues with respect to the director's role (p. 121) and electricity (p. 266). But it's important enough to be mentioned again. No one on a film set should request anything of anyone that would even remotely jeopardize their safety. Also, there are many things on a film set, like electricity, which can do grave harm if not handled with care and respect. By far, the preponderance of accidents that happen on the set occur because people forget to use common sense. In a rush to get a setup done, someone will try to single-handedly carry the camera, the tripod, and a 1K baby up a steep flight of stairs, or plug a light in with the cable strung across a heavily trafficked corridor, or get a panoramic shot from the peak of a steep rooftop. Equipment too must be treated with respect and with an eye toward keeping it safe. Here is an example of dangerous carelessness: A group of students in one of my classes (I'm sorry to say) were making a film outside an all-night bodega. The scene they were shooting involved a big American car pulling up to the bodega and the lead character strutting out. They thought it would be cool to set the camera up in the parking spot so that when the car came to a halt at the curb, the front grill would be framed in a tight wide angle (ECU!). Already we can see that common sense was not in play here. A wide-angle ECU meant that the car would need to stop about a foot in front of the camera. But they, and I mean a crew of five with no objections from anyone, decided to go with it and put the tripod and D.P. off the curb, where the car would pull in. The driver of the car, another member of the crew, all on his own decided that it would be even cooler to come to a *hard stop,* with the tires screeching a bit and the front grill bouncing in front of the lens. Well, you can guess what happened. The car hit the camera, smashing the lens, and the D.P. ended up with a broken finger. The entire crew was banned from using school equipment after that and, needless to say, the movie never got made. It's a sad story, but hopefully it'll encourage everyone reading this book to use common sense and keep their wits about them at all times.

Food and Breaks

Twelve-hour work days are not unusual on a film production. When a crew finds its groove and they're knocking down setups and keeper takes with the smooth efficiency of a well-oiled machine, everyone on the set enters an altered state, and time becomes relative. Four hours can pass and will seem like moments. However, the body knows that it's been working hard for hours. In order to maintain the morale and physical stamina of the crew, well-timed breaks for food are essential. You cannot expect people to work long hours for you if you do not feed them. And giving people meal breaks will only make them a happier, healthier, and more productive crew. You also need to make sure that the food is somewhat interesting. When I was a student I once worked as a grip (for free) on a low-budget seven-day (12 hours/day) film shoot. To save money, the producer decided to serve the crew pizza for lunch and pizza for dinner. He also decided not to spring for coffee in the morning. The thought of seven days of pizza was more than any of us could bear. After four days he had a very disgruntled crew who organized a meeting with the producer to demand some variety for our meals. The next day we had sandwiches, but from that point on, the crew referred to him as the "pizza producer" and we all vowed never to work for him again.

Protect the Location

Making movies often involves renting or borrowing locations that are ordinarily not film sets. The unwritten rule of film production is that you should leave a location in exactly the

same condition *or better,* when the filming is over. It's important to observe this rule if we are to maintain the good faith of those kind people who open their homes, shops, restaurants, and property for the sake of our movies. This requires that you instruct everyone on the team to be careful to protect and respect the location. Additionally, a few extra precautions are standard:

1. Lay down clean tarps on carpets, before you load-in your equipment.
2. Carefully assess the electricity distribution so you don't overload internal wiring.
3. Designate a single place for the production team to dispose of garbage.
4. Place delicate objects well out of harm's way.
5. Be aware of the placement of hot movie lights: they can blister paint, burn drapes, etc.
0. Assign someone the job of monitoring the condition of the location. If necessary, this person can suggest that the crew take some time out to clean the space.

Protecting the location also requires a little common sense, like not taping cables to painted walls, or you'll peel the paint right off when you remove the tape. It is also a good idea to take photographs of the space before you start to move furniture around, so that you remember exactly where everything belongs when it comes time to returning the space back to normal. From time to time an accident may occur and the location might sustain some damage. For example, while moving a C-stand, the gobo arm gouges the wall. Don't try to hide the damage and get away with it; tell the owner of the property and offer to fix it. Also make sure you have some contingency money in the budget to professionally clean and/or repair the location if it is necessary.

Production Insurance

The boom operator is holding the microphone aloft over the scene, then the actor walks a bit further than in the previous take, so the boom operator steps back but trips over a sand bag and breaks a leg. It can happen to anyone. When the boom operator gets back from the emergency room, he's got a cast and a medical bill for $6,000. If you've arranged for production insurance, you're covered; if not, well then your low-budget movie isn't so low budget anymore. Production insurance is necessary for all film shoots, regardless of the size, scale, and budget. Insurance protects the project from catastrophe should there be any injury to cast, crew, or equipment. In fact, if you want to use a SAG actor you must show proof of insurance before they can enter into a student agreement contract with you. Additionally, many rental houses and locations require proof of insurance. If you're a student, your department should have information about where and how to acquire production insurance. If you're an independent filmmaker, then there are several insurance companies that provide production insurance for low-budget films. The Independent Feature Project (IFP) website is a good place to start your search (http://www.ifp.org).

After the Shoot

Striking the Set

After the last "cut" has been called and the day's final keeper take has been logged, the work is not over. The last task of a film crew's day is to **strike the set**. Because this happens at the very end of a long day, you can be sure that *everyone* on the set is exhausted and wants to get home—and for this reason *everyone* must contribute to striking the set. It is a serious breach of film production ethics to participate in a shoot, but then skip out when it comes time to strike. No one leaves until everything is packed up and squared away. When a crew member commits to a film, they must commit to the bitter end, which means that they need to clear their schedule and be there when it's time to put all the toys away (**Figure 18-16**).

■ **Figure 18-16** Everyone helps strike the set. Putting gear away should be done carefully and methodically.

Striking the set must be done neatly, carefully, and thoroughly. If you simply toss the equipment aside to get it out of the way, you will only make the load-in and setup for the next day's shoot all the more difficult and time consuming. Even worse, carelessly striking a set can damage equipment. Each department is responsible for striking their own gear, but everyone pitches in until it's all packed neatly away and the set is put to rights, meaning it's clean and orderly. If you're striking a set to which you will not return, make sure you return that location to its original condition or better, as was discussed in a previous section (see Protect the Location).

When the director announces to "strike the set," all lights are immediately powered down first, but they are one of the last things to get packed away. This allows them to cool before you fit them back into their cases. Also, the sound recordist and D.P. should take some time to organize and label all of the day's camera and sound rolls. If you're shooting film, the D.P. (or A.C.) needs to go some place quiet to unload the last film magazine, which often means splitting the core (see p. 154). Remember, exposed film needs to get to the lab for processing and transfer ASAP after a shoot.

That's a Wrap!

After the last "cut" has been called on the very last day of the shoot, and all of the coverage for the movie has been accomplished, the director will gleefully exclaim, "That's a Wrap!" This means that the production phase is officially over. The last set strike is called the **wrap out** and includes returning the last location to its former state, and all equipment to the rental house, school checkout facility, or wherever it came from, and getting the last of the exposed film to the lab. After the last set strike is completed there is nothing left for the film crew to do but attend the wrap party.

The Wrap Party!

The **wrap party** is exactly what it sounds like. It's a party that is thrown soon after the final shooting day and which brings together the entire production team, cast, and crew, one last time (Figure 18-17). But this time it's not to work on the film, it's to have a good time, eat some good food, dance, share stories, and generally get to know each other outside of the intense and harried environment of a film set. The feeling of camaraderie at a wrap party bonds the team as they communalize the production experience that they have all recently been through. It's also a way the producer and director can express their gratitude for all of the team's efforts and for a job well done. Take note: I don't mention the wrap party to be cute, but I mention it because it's an important part of this process. If your experience with the cast and crew was positive, you very well might call on them again in the future. In fact, they may call each other for their own projects in the future. One director friend of mine always hands out cast and crew contact sheets to everyone involved in the film. A good wrap party leaves everyone with a better final experience than a set strike, and it's quite simply an essential part of creating and maintaining your film community. It should also be a line item in your budget!

■ **Figure 18-17** A group of American and Moroccan filmmakers participating in the Marrakech/Tribeca Filmmaker's Exchange (2005) celebrate the conclusion of an intense but successful production period with a well earned party.

■ THE DIRECTOR AND ACTORS ON THE SET

I have already detailed the roles of the director, producer, and other crew in Chapter 7: *The Cast and Crew.* That chapter also addressed actors and rehearsals, but a little more should be mentioned about the unique connection an actor and director have on the film set. In a significant way, an audience can overlook many small problems in a film if the performances are compelling and convincing. By the same token, a film that is technically flaw-

less, or even spectacular, can fall flat if the performances are not persuasive. This is not just an issue on highly dramatic films with complex emotional situations and dialogue. A very simple film, with simple actions, can also be dragged down if the performances go awry. Here is a good example: In an introductory film class, one production group made a very simple silent film about someone doing their laundry. This was, in fact, their very first film. The laundromat was beautifully picturesque and the shots were perfectly focused, exposed, and wonderfully composed. The lighting was simple but effective and the scene coverage and editing was sharp. In every way it was a successful film, except that the actor, who was not an actor but rather a buddy of the filmmaker, had this ever-so-slight goofy grin on his face. The grin said "Yo, I'm on camera!" and it shattered the fictional illusion that the director had so carefully created. The film ended up not being about a guy doing his laundry, but about a guy who was aware of being filmed while doing his laundry. It was the director's job to not only organize the sequence of events, compose the shots, and determine the coverage, but also the director should have noticed that revealing grin and find a way to get the talent to drop it and to do this routine cleaning chore as he had done a hundred times before. Fundamental to the art of film directing is getting performances that are truthful and that emerge from the dramatic moment.

To this end, it's important that a director not allow technical considerations to pull them away from the actors. This is why the producers, the A.D., and/or the P.M. are important; they transmit the director's wishes to the crew and keep them going, allowing the director to work with the actors. This is also why a reliable and resourceful crew is important; they can take their direction and run with it.

The process of working with actors is dependent on many factors, including acting styles and training, directing styles, and the actor/director relationship. This is a topic that is clearly beyond the scope of this book, but I have recommended some texts in the Recommended Readings list in the back of the book, to introduce you to the essential aspects of working with actors in dramatic filmmaking. However, there are three basic directorial responsibilities that are crucial for any narrative film made on any level, from a simple short film made in an introductory film class, to a dramatically complex feature film heading to the Cannes Film Festival.

The first is that you, as the director, must help the actor understand the script, which means not only understand the story, but also understand what you want to do with that story and how you intend to present and inflect the characters, actions, and dialogue in the script. For example, do you want to make a simple film about a guy who is doing his laundry as a routine, bi-weekly, chore? Or do you want him to do it like a guy whose mom has always cleaned his clothes and this is the first time he's doing his own laundry? Maybe he's supposed to be an expert at cleaning and folding laundry, or maybe he's ridiculously obsessive about getting details exactly right. The possibilities are great, even with the smallest action. But you, as the director, have to know what you're after first, and then find a ways to communicate that to the actors so that they can achieve the performance energy, mood, and nuance the movie needs.

Second, it is important to remember that we do not shoot a film in sequential order; rather, scenes are rearranged in the shot list to create the most efficient order from a production perspective. It's not unusual, for example, to shoot the end of a film in the first few days of a shoot. It's not easy for a performer to jump around to the various scenes of what is supposed to be an organically unfolding linear story. This means that the director must serve as the guide for the actors, reminding them, with each camera setup, where they are in the story, what their character has been through up to that point, and where they need to be emotionally in the current moment when the camera rolls. For example, if you're shooting the clothes-folding scene first (which would be near the end), you need to remind the actor of all of the difficulties he had washing and drying the clothes before he got to the folding stage, so that he can bring into the scene the accumulated frustration he needs to be truthful in the moment.

And third, as I mention in Chapter 7, the actor/director relationship is a collaborative one. Don't forget to listen carefully when an actor brings an idea to you. It might be something you haven't thought of before and it might just improve the movie. Allow for this collaboration. If the suggestion is off the mark, then you need not incorporate it. But having been listened to and consulted in earnest, the actors will feel like they are respected participants, which they are, as everyone else on the set should be.

in practice

The director Kelly Anderson told me this story of using a very simple and ingenious device for getting actors in the right emotional space while she was directing *Shift*, her first narrative film. *Shift* (1999) tells the story of Melanie, an unhappily married waitress who develops an intimate phone relationship with a telemarketer who, it turns out, is also a prison inmate. The scene Anderson was shooting was a wide two-shot of Melanie and Diane, another waitress, behind the counter of the diner, speculating about what Melanie's telephone/inmate boyfriend might look like, since she's never even seen a photograph. They kid around as they refer to various male customers off screen ("I'll bet he looks like him over there. . ."), some cute and some less than attractive. Because they're looking and pointing to guys off screen, Anderson had her first A.D. stand off camera to give the waitresses a point of focus for sightlines. The tone of the scene was supposed to be lighthearted and full of fun, saucy girl talk about guys. But during the run throughs, Anderson says, "It was flat.

Flat, dull, staged and not fun." She gave her actors some direction but nothing seemed to infuse the performances with the lively spirit she was after (Figure 18-18). She did a few takes and it didn't improve. Then she remembered that, while the actresses were in makeup prepping for the scene, she overheard them talking about how "hot" the intern production assistant was. On the next take she switched the A.D. for the intern just as the camera rolled, so that the waitresses would be looking at someone they truly had a little crush on. "Immediately the tone switched. When they saw this really cute intern standing there they were both surprised and started to giggle and blush. Now they had something to work with and I got that fun, girlish spontaneity I was looking for" (Figure 18-19).

What made this little directorial ploy possible was that Anderson could spend time with her actors while the crew set up, listening and responding to them even while they were in makeup.

■ Figure 18-18 On a set, one of the primary duties of the director is to help the actors find the emotional tone necessary for each scene. The director confers with actors before each take to make necessary performance adjustments [as director Kelly Anderson did during the shooting of her film *Shift* (1999)].

■ Figure 18-19 Anderson got the performance she was after as Diane (Marla Sucharetza) cannot help but giggle as she talks about guys with Melanie (Alethea Allen).

PART IV TOOLS AND TECHNIQUES: POSTPRODUCTION

Postproduction Overview and Workflow

After the director has gleefully announced, "that's a wrap," after all of the equipment has been packed up and returned, after you shake the last hand at the wrap party, and after the last video daily comes back from the lab, there's still quite a way to go before you've truly finished making your movie. The next step is postproduction. **Postproduction** encompasses all of those creative and technical processes that go on after the shooting stops:

1. Reviewing and evaluating footage.
2. Editing the picture.
3. Editing the sound.
4. Creating and mixing the sound design, which can include music.
5. Adding visual transitions and effects and fine-tuning color.

Every one of these steps offers tremendous creative potential for the continuing evolution of your motion picture. The possibilities can include large structural changes in content, like cutting out entire characters or rearranging the events of the plot, or subtle alterations in mood through adjustments in the image color, or insightful thematic additions like the inclusion of a sound track that creates a new tone or subtext or associations with the image; in other words, the possibilities are endless.

Naturally, the director follows the project into postproduction. Often, you will find directors actually editing their own film; this is especially true on short projects, but less so on feature-length films. Just as there are creative specialists in the other areas of filmmaking (cinematographers, art directors, writers, etc.), there are also specialists in postproduction who can bring a fresh perspective, imaginative energy, and technical expertise to the movie. Editors, sound designers, composers, and colorists are the postproduction contingent to the filmmaking team. Again, if you are shooting a five-minute film for an introductory film class you will probably do all, or most, of the postproduction tasks yourself. In fact, when you are starting out, it's a good idea to do as much of the postproduction as possible yourself. The more postproduction you encounter first hand, the more you will understand the expressive possibilities of this phase. This is especially true of editing. Film is an integrated art form, and editing is a storytelling tool of equal power and importance to cinematography, directing, and screenwriting.

■ THE GOLDEN RULE OF POSTPRODUCTION

The one piece of advice that I would impart to anybody who is looking to be an editor or any other aspect of this business is always remember that making movies is about investigating all possibilities. You should always be open to different options. If you get focused into making something one way, you may not make the best film.

The thing that you learn when you're writing a film is that it's the template; it's the foundation. It gives you the opportunity to have a template in front of you. Then when you go into the editing room, that process is the next level of the template. First you have it on paper, now you have it visually and then you have to make it a film.

Sam Pollard (From "Things I've Learned as a Filmmaker,"
***MovieMaker,* Vol. 3, Issue #4)**

■ **Figure 19-1** Producer and editor Sam Pollard works extensively in both narrative and documentary forms.

Professionals who work in postproduction, primarily directors, editors, and sound designers, understand this one fundamental principle: *make the film from what you have, not solely from what is written in the script.* Some time ago I was discussing the process of editing with Sam Pollard (**Figure 19-1**), an accomplished editor (*Mo' Better Blues, Juice, Bamboozled*), producer (*Eyes on the Prize II, The Blues: "Feel Like Going Home"*), and educator, who told me that he tries not to read the script more than once or twice before he starts to edit—and after that he rarely refers to the script again. Why would this be? There are two reasons.

Figure 19-1 Producer and editor Sam Pollard works extensively in both narrative and documentary forms.

First, if the director, cinematographer, and art director have done their jobs correctly, they will have improvised here and there and altered details to improve the film from its incarnation as a screenplay. So the actual results—the scenes, performances, footage—coming from production may be quite different from the script. Hopefully the footage reflects a beneficial transformation of the material and one that has taken the editing process into account. Second, as anyone who has been on film sets will tell you, "stuff happens." Just as you may find shots and scenes that weren't in the script that improve the project, you might equally have run out of time and left a few things out, or even forgotten a detail or two; the sound from one day can be junk, or an actor had an off day, or the camera was running at 30 fps and no one noticed—it happens to everyone. This certainly doesn't mean you don't have a film, it just means you have a slightly different film, one that you will find in the editing process. Whether the footage contains everything called for in the shot list and then some, or is missing pieces here and there, the bottom line is that when you bring your footage into postproduction, stay loose and work from what you have. Don't stubbornly hang on to preproduction ideas that are not in the footage, or even if they are—let the idea evolve. Look for new possibilities that will emerge during the cutting and sound design process—they will present themselves to you.

One of the primary reasons that the filmmaking process breaks a film-in-process down into little pieces—every shot separate from the others and every type of audio distinct from the others and from the picture—is to allow for maximum creative flexibility in postproduction. We can put any shot next to any other shot as we see fit, or we can lay down any audio track under any sequence, or we can layer tracks and tracks of audio in any configuration that our heart desires. Whatever works best for the film. So remember: postproduction isn't just the mechanical construction of the original idea, but postproduction also constitutes the further creative development of your story. It is often said that editing is your second chance at directing. Something happens when you start connecting one shot with another—a whole new chemistry occurs and new storytelling options emerge. And when you put a piece of music behind your sequences, or a slightly different ambient background, the film takes on new life and new energy again. That's the power of postproduction.

The director Sidney Lumet, in his book "Making Movies," wrote this about editing: "Like everything else in movies, editing is a technical job which has aesthetic ramifications." There it is again, that inevitable mix of artistry and technology. In movies we express our ideas through the tools and processes of film and digital technologies. In order for us to harness their power, we need to understand something of the science and procedures that are an inherent part of the medium. For this chapter we'll begin with the big picture: workflow.

"Fixing it in Post"

We've all heard the old adage that we can learn as much, or more, from our mistakes as from our successes; but just like Alexander Fleming's accidental discovery of penicillin, mistakes can be more than hard-knock lessons: they can also be blessings in disguise—if you stay open to the creative possibilities available in postproduction.

Figure 19-2 Cinematographer Christopher Doyle and director Wong Kar-Wai turned a mistake into stylistic innovation by artfully integrating footage shot on bad film stock at key points in *Fallen Angels* (1995).

Bad Color, Good Concept

Wong Kar-Wai's 1995 movie *Fallen Angels* is widely considered to be the most visually bold, original, and groundbreaking of his early films. The deliriously hedonistic, over-the-top visual style of *Fallen Angels,* which was shot by cinematographer Christopher Doyle, was celebrated by critics and audiences alike (Figure 19-2).

"We f***** up with the film stock. It was old," said Doyle in an interview with Vicente Rodriguez-Ortega ("Zen Palette," *reverse shot online,* summer 2004). "We couldn't reshoot . . . so of course it was foggy in color. We said: 'maybe this can represent something so let's pick some other pieces,' and that's what we did. Because of a mistake, a certain structure came out of the film . . . What happened was that we gave it a system, so we made the most important parts of each scene in black-and-white. But that was a solution to the problem, not an original concept. We just appropriated the mistake and made it work." It not only worked but also firmly established the Kar-Wai/Doyle team as a force of cinematic innovation in international cinema. Turning your mistakes into cinematic innovation in the edit . . . *that* really is innovative.

Sound Design Saves the Picture

In the bold documentary/narrative hybrid film *Close Up* (1990), Abbas Kiarostami follows the real trial of Hossain Sabzian, a man who posed as the famous Iranian film director Mohsen Makhmalbaf, and ingeniously intercuts this documentary footage with a recreation of the events of the crime—showing how the man gradually insinuated himself into the good graces and home of the unsuspecting Ahankhah family. Sabzian and the family portray themselves in these reenactments. Kiarostami planned all along to have the film culminate with a surprise meeting between Sabzian (the imposter) and the real Makhmalbaf on the day he is released from jail. Like the rest of the film, this scene was shot in a documentary style, but with a telephoto lens, from a long distance so that the men wouldn't feel under a microscope. Each man was wired with a wireless lavaliere to pick up his dialog from a distance as Kiarostami's film and sound crew follow them, in a trailing van, as they drive from the jailhouse to the home of the Ahankhah family on a small motorcycle (Figure 19-3).

Figure 19-3 A faux microphone malfunction, created in postproduction, allowed Kiarostami to salvage the emotional climax at the end of his film, *Close Up* (1990).

The first moment is shattering. When Sabzian encounters Makhmalbaf outside the jail, he breaks down in tears and embraces his idol, whom he impersonated. But then, as Kiarostami tells it, Makhmalbaf dominated the conversation and it veered into territory that dissipated the intensity and honesty of Sabzian's moment. Kiarostami felt that his climactic scene was ruined and with it his entire film. This was not a scene that could possibly be reshot, and he felt that he had lost the only possible ending for his movie. Kiarostami says that he went four sleepless nights wondering how he could salvage his film. Then the solution came to him: creative postproduction sound mixing. Kiarostami created a static-y sound effect as if there was a bad microphone connection, which allowed him to simply cut the sound intermittently, whenever he chose. He then inserted the off-screen voices of the ostensible "director" and the "sound man," from the trailing van, complaining about the bad connection and about the sound coming in an out. The contrived sound equipment malfunction allowed Kiarostami to preserve what was best about the scene and eliminate what might have destroyed it. It was also a device completely in keeping with the vérité style of the movie. In the end the climax remains Sabzian's moment—utterly moving. *Close Up* went on to establish Kiarostami as one of the foremost directors in the world. The filmmaker himself has said that this is one of his favorite moments in all of his films.

Trash or Treasure?

In my introductory film production class, Jonathan and his crew of two, shooting their very first film, decided to do a portrait of a New York City neighborhood called the "meatpacking district." Their angle was to show the incongruities of a neighborhood in the middle of a rapid transition from a decrepit wholesale meat warehouse district into an ultra chic, super fashionable, hotspot. They contrasted the decayed and dilapidated exteriors with the interior of a stylishly designed, exclusive, and trendy nightclub. They only had several shots involving people, and those were meatpack-

ers, smeared in blood, loading a truck with sides of beef. When they viewed their raw footage, they discovered that everything they shot came out perfectly except the shots of the meatpackers, which were inexplicably in slow motion. Somehow, the camera malfunctioned and for half a roll was running somewhere around 48 frames per second—not at all what they wanted (Figure 19-4).

With the screening deadline fast approaching they could not reshoot. Jonathan decided to use the shots anyway, but in a slightly different way than he originally conceived. He used them as a transition from the bleak exterior to chic interior and cut them into the film in such a way that the slow motion made the movements seem like something from a bygone era, too slow to keep pace and therefore fading fast. When Jonathan screened his film in class, everyone agreed that the slow motion effect was brilliant—the best part of the whole film. At first, Jonathan took full credit for his creative decision to shoot slow motion, "Yeah, I had a feeling it would be pretty great that way." But then later on, fearing that a classmate might get stuck with a malfunctioning camera for the next assignment, he disclosed the truth. In fact, I told him, I was even more impressed that he saw the potential in footage that others might have thought ruined.

Naturally you want to enter postproduction with the best possible footage you can get, meaning everything you need to tell your story. Most footage problems, like carelessly shot scenes or missing material, simply cause headaches and compromises that ultimately weaken your movie; nonetheless, what these stories bring into high relief is the power of an open mind and the transformative potential of the various areas of postproduction.

■ **Figure 19-4** Film student Jonathon Gibson encountered a camera malfunction while shooting his very first movie. He saw potential where others might have seen a mistake and used the footage to the benefit of the final film.

■ WORKFLOW AND FORMAT INTERFACE

One essential factor that a filmmaker must consider from the very beginning of a project is workflow. **Workflow** is the format path your project will take from origination to exhibition, including acquisition/shooting format, editorial format, finishing (mastering) format, and distribution format. At this point in the evolution of the medium, there are a wide variety of paths one can take, and each course has a significant impact on the budget of the film, the technical process, and the range of exhibition possibilities. More than any other technical area, filmmakers can lose their way in the workflow stream, with unexpected and often expensive results. A little bit of research, at the very beginning, into the technical stages of your project and the way various formats interface with each other, will go a long way toward minimizing nasty surprises. The primary questions you must ask yourself right up front in preproduction are:

1. What am I shooting on, film or DV?
2. How am I editing?
3. How do I want to finish and screen the project once it's done: as a film print or on some DV format?

With the advent of inexpensive and user-friendly editing software, digital nonlinear editing (NLE) has all but superseded film editing, so for all practical intents and purposes, the answer to the question #2 is "digitally." However, the interface between the digital NLE and the shooting and finishing variables (film or DV) determines an enormous amount concerning the technical postproduction pathway and, consequently, your budget.

Overview: Four Common Workflow Paths

Most low-budget projects, especially on the introductory and intermediate levels, finish on one of the digital videotape formats and are ultimately screened on a television monitor or with video projection:

1. Shoot: DV / Edit: Digital / Finish: DV tape / Release: DVD
2. Shoot: Film / Edit: Digital / Finish: DV tape / Release: DVD

Both of these workflows are not only very common for students and independent filmmakers, but are also standard for any project on any level that will ultimately find its audience through television broadcast (**Figure 19-5**). The preponderance of primetime television dramas and comedies shot on location (i.e., single-camera style, not three-camera studio method) follow the second workflow, with comedies shot primarily on 16mm or super 16mm and one-hour dramas (and made-for-TV movies) originating on 35mm film. However, the current trend is away from film origination as many television programs switch to high definition DV with the audience not even noticing. The world of film festivals, too, has realized that projecting submissions on DV is essential if they are to remain current and represent the full spectrum of films out there—documentary or narrative—regardless of their acquisition format. For example, in 2006 the Tribeca Film Festival in New York City, one of the world's premier festivals, screened over half their programs on HDCAM, and the Avignon International Film Festival (that showcases emerging filmmakers) is 100% HD projection.

There are, of course, times when you may want to finish your movie as a film, on cellulose acetate, with sprocket holes, to be projected by a movie projector. This could be because the festivals you want to enter screen film prints or simply because you want to see your film as a "film." Thus we have the third and fourth workflows:

3. Shoot: Film / Edit: Digital / Finish: Film / Release: Film and DVD
4. Shoot: DV (SD or HD) / Edit: Digital / Finish: DV Tape / Release: Film and DVD

The third workflow, shooting film, editing digitally, and then finishing on film is currently the standard procedure for theatrically released feature films. I say "currently" because of the significant inroads high definition digital projection has made in the commercial market in recent years, and the future promises even more HD projection in commercial theaters. Why ship a 35mm film print weighing over 75 lbs to 1,000 theaters across the country when you can send a hard drive weighing only a few pounds, or, even better, simply transmit your movie via satellite hookup to 1,000 theaters at the scheduled projection time. But for the moment, this is still the stuff of the future (albeit, near future). While many advanced film production students and independent filmmakers who can foot the bill continue to shoot and finish on film, for projects on the introductory and intermediate levels, this is a rare workflow option.

■ **Figure 19-5** Sasie Sealy's award winning student film *Dance Mania Fantastic* (2005) followed a common workflow. It was shot on 16mm film, cut digitally and mastered on HD. She has sent the film to festivals on both HD and BetaSP formats.

in practice

The video origination-to-film distribution barrier was first broken down by documentary films that were so compelling that they found an audience in the commercial theatrical market, despite the obvious image compromises inherent in transferring and projecting a low-resolution format like standard NTSC video. Once it was clear that commercial theater audiences didn't resist the look of films shot on standard definition video, pioneering narrative filmmakers quickly developed stories that incorporated and benefited from the "video aesthetic" (Figure 19-6).

Figure 19-6 *Hoop Dreams* (1994), directed by Steve James, was one of the first documentaries shot on video to achieve a wide theatrical release.

contrivance, production philosophy. Thomas Vinterberg's landmark Dogma film *The Celebration* (1998) even won the Jury Award at 1998 Cannes Film Festival. You can go to http://www.dogme95.dk/ to read the "Dogme 95" manifesto and their "vow of chastity."

Following the success of the Dogma films, there was a virtual wave of films by upstarts and major filmmakers alike produced on standard DV, including *Bamboozled* (2000), *Timecode* (2000), *Chuck & Buck* (2000), *Personal Velocity* (2002), *24 Hour Party People* (2002), *Pieces of April* (2003), and *Open Water* (2003), to mention just a few (Figure 19-8). Many people, it seems, are keen on adopting this highly versatile and spontaneous production method. The list of films shot on standard definition DV and distributed theatrically as

Figure 19-7 Sánchez and Myrick's *The Blair Witch Project* (1999, left) was shot on both 16mm film and Hi8 video and Vinterberg's *The Celebration* (1998, right) was shot on standard DV. Both films enjoyed wide theatrical release and inspired many filmmakers to turn to video as a production format.

Eduardo Sánchez and Daniel Myrick's *The Blair Witch Project* (1999) was an early example of a film, shot on 16mm and the now obsolete Hi8 consumer video format, which was transferred to film for national release (Figure 19-7). Lars von Trier and the Danish Dogme ("Dogma") filmmakers made the consumer DV format the liberating centerpiece of their look and their minimal intervention, minimal

film prints has grown steadily, and it is likely that the tape-to-film process will become even more common as the price of high definition video drops to an affordable level for independent, low-budget filmmakers—that is, until the day that the standard for "commercial theatrical release" is itself an HD format—then no one will need to go to film. Stay tuned!

Figure 19-8 Peter Hedges' 2003 film *Pieces of April* (left) was shot on standard definition video while *You, Me and Everyone We Know* (2005, right), by Miranda July was produced on HD video. Both films were distributed theatrically on 35mm film.

The fourth workflow scenario, shooting and editing on video but releasing on film, is becoming more and more common on two fronts. More features films, even large-budget Hollywood productions, are being shot on high definition DV, then transferred and released on film for commercial theatrical projection—since digital projectors are still rare in commercial theaters. And interestingly, many films that originate on standard definition DV are also being transferred to film for widespread commercial theatrical distribution.

■ THE TECHNICAL PROCESS OF WORKFLOW

Each of the four workflow options has their own advantages and challenges. It's important to keep in mind that the picture and audio often follow different technical paths, especially in double-system sound production. Let's look closer at the specific technical process for each workflow scenario.

Shoot: DV / Edit: Digital / Finish: DV Tape / Release: DVD

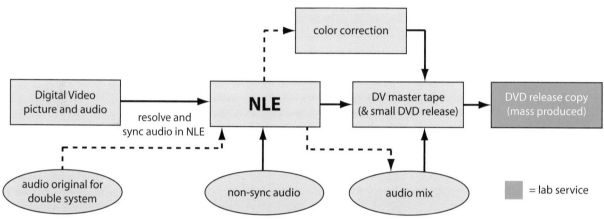

■ Fig. 19-9 Picture and audio paths for workflow 1: Shoot: DV / Edit: Digital / Finish: DV tape / Release: DVD.

The Picture Path

Staying entirely in the digital domain—shooting on DV, capturing the footage directly from your camera original tapes into the computer nonlinear editing (NLE) system, and outputting back onto digital videotape—is by far the most straightforward and cost effective workflow process because nowhere does it rely on the services of a laboratory. **Capturing** is the term used for transferring your DV footage from a tape format into a computer editing system. This can be done directly from the camera via a firewire cable, but is best accomplished with a separate DV deck to avoid wear and tear on your camcorder (Figure 19-10). Tapeless formats, like P2 memory cards, require a simple data transfer that is faster than the real time required for capturing from tape.

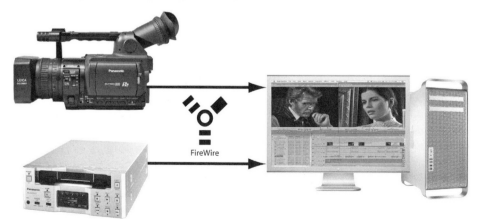

■ Fig. 19-10 You can use either your camcorder or a DV deck to capture footage, but be aware that using your camera causes extra wear and tear on an vital production tool.

After you have edited your film, the output of your final program, or "print to video" function, is just as straightforward. This tape of your final edit becomes your film master. For the most part, people will master on the most robust format they have access to. DVCAM, DVCPRO, and DigiBeta formats are better than standard MiniDV for mastering because the tape is thicker and dropouts are less likely. Because there is always some data compression involved, DVDs are not a mastering format.

The Audio Path

If you have shot single-system sound, then the audio path is the same as the picture path. The sync audio and the picture are captured at the same time and should remain in sync. However, if you shoot DV in a double-system sound setup, then your audio is captured separately and each scene must be synced in the NLE timeline, either by lining up the image and audio reference timecode, or lining up the image and audio of the slate closing (see p. 386). All nonsync audio sources, music, sound effects, etc. must also be captured from their original format, into the NLE for editing and mixing.

With standard DV resolution continually increasing in quality and high definition video consistently coming down in price, DV as an image-gathering format for narrative shorts and features (even standard definition DV) is rapidly gaining in popularity. Add to this the increasingly powerful and inexpensive digital editing software programs currently available, which often include HD editing, and you have a complete, powerful, and accessible moviemaking system. Obviously, there are aesthetic considerations that trump efficacy and even frugality, but digital video has reached a point where the question "Why shoot or finish on film?" is one that should be very carefully deliberated.

Shoot: Film / Edit: Digital / Finish: DV Tape / Release: DVD

The Picture Path

Whenever we choose to shoot on film (usually for aesthetic reasons), the workflow is not as self-contained. We are always required to use a laboratory, not only for processing, but also to transfer that footage to a digital format that we can use to both view and download our footage into the NLE system. This service, of course, costs money, and like all format conversions there are some technical considerations that must be carefully observed in order to make the entire process run smoothly. Of primary concern is the transfer between a format with one frame rate (film's 24 fps) to a format with a different frame rate (standard DV's 29.97 fps). Tangled up in this format conversion is synchronous audio, which, if it is to remain in sync, must also undergo its own conversion. Even though this transfer process is very common, it is easy to be confused by all of the associated details, minutiae, and extenuating factors.

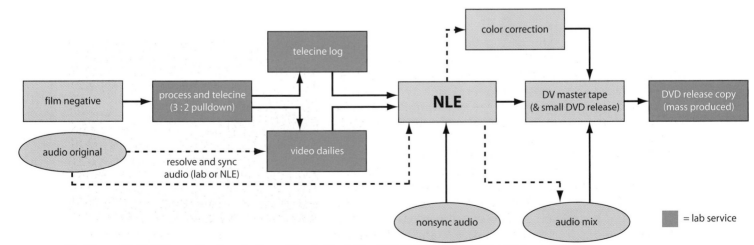

■ **Figure 19-11** Picture and audio paths for workflow 2: Shoot: Film / Edit: Digital / Finish: DV tape / Release: DVD.

The Film-to-Tape Transfer

It's not difficult to find very cheap, down-and-dirty, film-to-tape transfers, often called **film chain** transfers. Basically, a film chain is a projector that pushes light through your negative onto a CCD chip mounted where the projector lens usually sits. While film chain transfers are cheap, they give you thoroughly wretched results. Contrast is extreme, color is dull, and a stroboscopic throb is evident, caused by the crude method for reconciling the different frame rates. In essence, using a cheap film-to-tape transfer method is totally counterproductive because it eliminates all of the reasons to shoot film in the first place (primarily, rich image quality and detailed response to light).

In order to maintain all of the hard work you put into your lighting and exposures (not to mention your story, performances, sound, etc.) you should go the final yard and get a professional **telecine** transfer. The telecine is the standard machine used for film-to-tape transfers, which are sometime also called "rank" transfers, after the commonly used Rank/Cintel flying spot scanner, telecine machine. The **flying spot scanner** is a CRT telecine system that works like a reverse CRT.

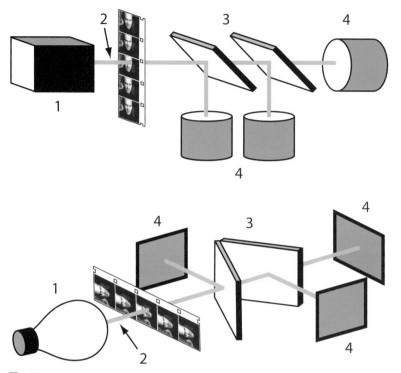

■ Figure 19-12 A flying spot scanner (top) uses a photon light beam (1) to scan the negative (2); the resulting beam is separated by dichroic mirrors (3) into primary colors, and their output is received by photodiodes (4). A CCD scanner (bottom) uses a xenon bulb (1) to scan the negative film frame (2). Dichroic mirrors (3) separate the resulting beam into primary colors that are registered by CCD chips (4).

A photon light beam scans the negative film frame, passing right through and registering the color and brightness information, pixel-by-pixel, onto red, green, and blue photodiodes (Figure 19-12 and 19-13). However, many labs also use the Philips **CCD telecine** system, which uses light from a xenon bulb; the light passes through the negative and into a prism block, which in turn separates the image into red, green, and blue components to be registered by respective R, G, and B CCD chips, similar to the CCD camcorder (Figure 19-12).

The film-to-tape transfer process essentially accomplishes four things: (1) It converts the film image into digital data to be recorded as DV tape formats, (2) it reconciles the difference between film and DV frame rates, (3) it inverts the colors from negative film into a positive image on your tape, and (4) it allows for color and exposure correction. Let's look at each procedure.

1. *Converting the film image into digital data.*
   As your camera original negative film runs through the telecine machine, it scans your negative, separating the color components (RGB and luminance information), and converts these values into binary code (or digital data), ready to be recorded on whichever DV format you need for your NLE system (MiniDV, DVCPRO, DVCAM, etc.). It is essential that you tell the lab to which DV format you wish to transfer.

2. *Reconciling the difference between film and DV frame rates.*
   It is the telecine scanning process that allows us to reconcile the difference in frame rates between film and video, through a process called 3:2 pulldown. There are two components to this process, the "3:2" part and the "pulldown" part. We know that the frame rate of film is 24 frames per second and the frame rate for standard video is essentially 30 frames per second. We also

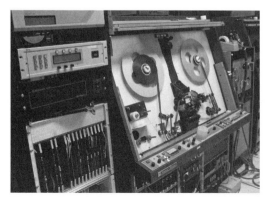

■ Figure 19-13 A Rank/Cintel flying spot scanner telecine machine.

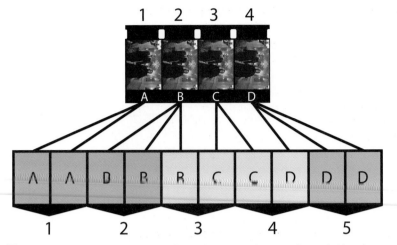

■ **Figure 19-14** To reconcile the different frame rates between film and video, the 3:2 pulldown transfer process creates 5 video frames from 4 film frames by duplicating every other film frame across 3 video fields.

know that each video frame is made up of two fields (30 frames per second = 60 fields per second). The "3:2" process involves duplicating *every other* film frame as three fields, instead of two fields. If we look at how the 3:2 process affects four frames of film we see that frames A and C are each scanned onto two fields (1 video frame each), while frames B and D are each scanned onto *three* fields (1.5 frames each). So, after four frames of film we will have ten fields, or five frames of video (Figure 19-14). Following this pattern, after 24 frames of film, we will have created an extra six video frames, to arrive at 30 frames of video (60 fields).

But wait a minute! By now we all know that video *really* runs at the slightly slower rate of 29.97 frames per second (see p. 172), so what are we going to do about that? This is where the "pulldown" part of the process comes in. The 29.97 video frame rate is precisely 0.1% slower than 30 fps, so, to compensate, the telecine machine actually slows down the speed of your film as it passes through the transfer machine, to 23.976 fps, which is exactly 0.1% slower than 24 fps. Both of the adjustments in the 3:2 pulldown, film-to-tape transfer process (adding extra fields and slowing the film transport speed) are amazingly imperceptible to the human eye.

Incidentally, this elaborate process of converting frame rates with 3:2 pulldown is not a global problem. For example, if you're a filmmaker in a country that uses PAL or SECAM, like France, for example, the standard frame rate for video and film are the same, 25 fps, so the transfer from film-to-tape is a simple frame-for-frame conversion.

This whole 3:2 pulldown process can be avoided if you shoot your film at a frame rate of 29.97 fps, instead of 24 fps because then the transfer would be a one-to-one (frame-for-frame) conversion. In fact, many film cameras have variable-speed motors in which 29.97 fps is a preset option (see Figure 8-15 in Chapter 8). However, keep in mind that you would also be using up much more film per take at the faster frame rate, which means buying and processing more film. In addition, 29.97 fps is a "transfer-to-video-ONLY" frame rate; you can never go back to film, even if a big-time film festival tells you that they love your movie but you have to send a film print to participate in the festival. Since there are no film projectors that run at 29.97 fps, you can *only* show on DV.

3. *Inverting the colors from negative film into a positive image.*

   Once the frame rate issue is resolved and the image information of each frame has been scanned and turned into binary code, the telecine outputs that data to a highly sophisticated console called a color corrector. The primary job of the color corrector at this point is to invert the color values of the negative film so that you get a positive image on the DV tape. However, the color corrector console can do much more than simply invert a negative image to a positive image.

4. *Correcting color and exposure.*

   Names like "DaVinci" (film-to-tape color correction) and "Rembrandt" (tape-to-tape/film color correction) might give you a sense for what these consoles aspire to in their abilities to adjust the colors and exposures in your scene. Well, maybe these machines aren't quite as astonishing as DaVinci himself, but in the hands of an experienced **colorist** (the person who operates the color corrector), you can have enormous control over the tonalities and exposures of each scene. The colorist is able to adjust the red, green, blue, and luminance values of each scene independently and with a remarkable degree of flexibility (Figure 19-15). Adjusting the original negative image is called **color correction** or **color timing.** Subtle and common adjustments include fixing inconsistencies and minor problems with color temperatures and exposure, while extreme color timing can include shifting an entire color tonality of a scene or altering the contrast for an entire film. Yes, all of this can be yours! For a price!

Film labs offer several different levels of color correction that you can use, depending on the stage of your project. **Supervised color correction** sessions involve the filmmaker sitting with the colorist at the color correction console as adjustments are made to each scene. This is a service that is charged by the hour, so it is not in your best interest to supervise the transfer of all your raw footage. Usually, supervised transfers are reserved for after the editing process, when you can color correct only those shots that actually made it into the final cut. At this stage, when transferring raw footage to video in preparation for editing, what is returned from the lab is called **video dailies** (Figure 19-16). For this process we generally use one of two **unsupervised color correction** processes. The quickest and cheapest is called the **one-light transfer**: the colorist establishes the transfer settings based on the skin tones and luminance contrast range of your first shot, or better, based on the color chart at the head of each film roll—if you remembered to shoot it. Once set, the entire roll is run through the telecine and transferred. So, what you shot is what you get. If you've underexposed a few scenes, it'll show. The other option is called a **best-light transfer**. This costs more, but the colorist resets the chrominance and luminance settings for each change in location or lighting situation (for which there should be a new color chart). With this transfer, minor color temperature and exposure problems will be fixed and often your video dailies will be of high enough quality to take you all the way to your finished movie—with a little additional color correction toward the end of the process, either with your own software (e.g., color correction in Final Cut Pro) or in a supervised session at the lab.

Once the lab has processed and transferred your film to DV tape, you are ready to capture the footage into your NLE systems and start editing.

The Audio Path

As we mentioned before, film shooting is a double-system sound process, so all synchronized audio must be brought into sync with the picture before editing. A filmmaker has two options for this. You can send your field audio to the lab with your film (and your sound logs) and request that they sync your audio for you, take-for-take. This service, as with all lab services, costs money and is charged by the hour. If your slating and logging procedures on the set were inconsistent and sloppy, then you can expect it to take them many more hours to figure out exactly where sync is on each take. The final cost can be sig-

■ **Figure 19-15** A colorist using a DaVinci color correction station to fine tune color and exposures during a film-to-tape transfer.

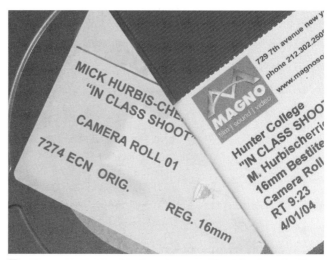

■ **Figure 19-16** My original negative and video dailies from the lab. Notice on the DV tape label that I had requested a best light transfer for this in class shooting exercise.

Shooting a Color Chart at the Head of Every Film Roll

A **color chart** (also called **chip chart**) is a piece of cardboard with a series of standardized colored squares. The chip chart is shot at the head of every roll of film to help the colorist achieve accurate and consistent colors when transferring your film to DV tape. It is standard procedure to shoot a color chart at the head of every roll of film, but some film crews will also shoot a chip chart on the first shot whenever the lighting situation changes

dramatically (e.g., moving from outside to inside in the middle of a roll). Here are a few tips to follow concerning this procedure:

1. Shoot just a few feet of film. You don't need to waste too much film on the chip chart; the colorist will freeze one frame to set up the telecine transfer colors.

2. Shoot under representative light. Always shoot the chip chart under the representative light for the scene (e.g., tungsten or daylight) but without using any special color effects (gels or filters) you wish to add into the scene. If, for example, you are shooting indoors with tungsten lights and you want to create a red edge to the image by adding red gels to some of the lights, this effect could easily be "corrected" right out of your image if you've shot the chip chart under the red glow. In this case, shoot the chip chart under tungsten lights first, THEN add the red gels. This will signal to the colorist that the red glow in the image is actually intentional.

3. Include skin for fine-tuning. Many colorists ultimately will rely on skin tones to fine-tune the color balance. For this reason, many labs prefer that you include the face of the crew member holding up the color chart.

■ **Figure 19-17** It's important to shoot a few feet of a color chart (with skin tone) at the head of each camera roll to help the colorist make color adjustments during the film-to-tape transfer

nificantly reduced if your slates are readable in the frame, your audible markers are clearly articulated on each take (e.g., "scene 2b, take 3"), and your logs are accurate and readable. Using a timecode slate that is receiving T.C. from the audio recorder also makes the job go much faster, because syncing is simply a matter of reading timecode off the image and typing the corresponding number into the audio transfer deck to find the sync point. When you ask the lab for this service, what you get back from the lab are video dailies, with the audio already synced, ready to be captured and edited. Or, to save on your budget you can sync your transferred footage with the audio yourself in your NLE system, by capturing audio and video separately and then lining up the sync points yourself. This process is discussed in detail on p. 386.

Sync drift and audio resolving: There is one additional step that must be accomplished before film, transferred to DV, and field audio can be synced-up: **resolving the audio**. As we just discussed, when film is transferred to tape, the 3:2 pulldown process effectively slows the film down by one-tenth of one percent (0.1%). This slowdown of the picture essentially throws the audio, which was recorded in sync with a film rolling at a rate of 24 fps, out of sync. With the image running slightly slow, our synchronous audio is now slightly faster than the picture; image and sound are out of sync. While a 0.1% difference doesn't seem like much, over long takes the difference becomes more and more pronounced; this is called **sync drift**. The pulldown speed's discrepancy amounts to an offset of 1.8 frames every minute; that's 18 frames every 10 minutes. Loss of sync becomes noticeable after only 20 or 30 seconds. To compensate and resolve our audio, we need to perform the pulldown process on the audio as well, i.e., slow *it* down 0.1%, to match the slower rate of the transferred footage. Film labs, of course, resolve audio as a matter of course when you ask them to sync your audio. Most NLE systems, like Final Cut Pro, offer some type of "modify speed" command that will quickly and easily resolve your audio, essentially by playing it a 99.9% speed (Figure 19-18). You will then be able to easily sync up picture and audio by lining up the slate (see p. 386).

Some digital recorders offer the ability to slightly alter their sampling rate to accomplish a pulldown frame rate setting (23.976 or 29.97). Recording at pulldown sample rates, your field audio will be "pre-resolved" to the (3:2 pulldown) video dailies you get back from the lab. However, altering your field recording rate can be tricky, as it can be confusing, or impossible, to "pull-up" to resolve to 24 fps, should you wish to go back to a genuine film at some point in the future. Most people opt for the very simple, and somewhat more flexible, option of resolving their audio in postproduction. In either case, it is important to remember to indicate precisely (by writing it directly on the label and announcing it at the head of each audio roll) exactly what sample rate and T.C. setting you used for your recording. This allows you or the lab to properly set up the transfer system accordingly.

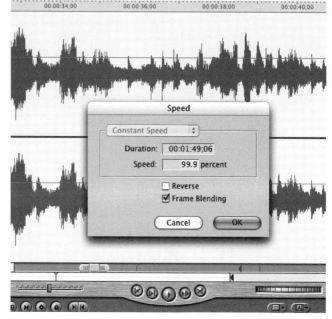

Figure 19-18 The "modify speed" command in Final Cut Pro allows you to easily resolve your audio to your pulled-down footage when syncing dailies yourself.

---

in practice

3:2 Pulldown: It's Not Just a Film Issue!

3:2 pulldown, as you know, is the process that allows us to convert from 24 fps to 29.97 fps, to display our footage in a standard NTSC system. However, this process is necessary not only for film, but also for 24P video (both SD and HD) as well. In fact, 24P video doesn't exactly capture at 24 fps; it captures at 23.976 fps for the same reason we slow film's 24 fps frame rate down by 0.1%—for a compatible transfer to 29.97. The important thing to remember is that while 24P cameras *capture* at 23.976, they in fact *record* at 29.97. The 3:2 pulldown is accomplished in your cam-

corder's digital signal processor (DSP), which then sends the 29.97 DV (with extra fields, interlacing, and all) to be written onto your tape. In fact, all video outputs in 24P mode are actually 29.97 video. So, when you view your 24P DV footage on a monitor or even on the camera LCD screen, you're seeing the standard frame rate, NTSC version.

With software like Cinema Tools, most NLE systems are able to easily remove the extra frames when you capture, so that you may edit in 24 fps mode with the **original frames**. Whether you plan to go back to film or finish on DVD for distribution, staying in the 24 fps mode is advantageous. In the first case, the transfer to film is much simpler, and in the second case, the amount of data you need to pack onto your DVD is greatly reduced.

Figure 19-19 The Panasonic DVX100b is just one of many cameras that has the option to shoot 24p video.

Shoot: Film / Edit: Digital / Finish: Film / Release: Film and DVD

So, you want to shoot on film, edit on an NLE system, and finish the project back to film? This is where it can get complicated—not impossible, but complicated. Shooting and finishing on film requires *two* format conversions. The first format transfer is the same film-to-tape process as already discussed, so that you can get your footage into a digital format for editing. All issues of pulldown, sync drift, etc. apply to this workflow as well. However, when the editing is over and you need to then the transfer *back* from your digitally edited version, into a film print, you will require extensive services from a film lab, a negative cutter, and quite possibly a head-shrinker.

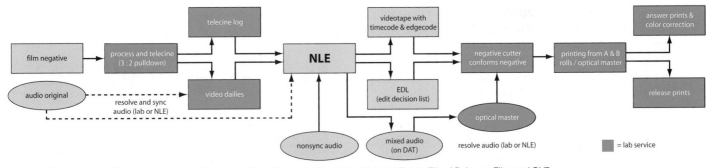

■ Figure 19-20 Picture and audio paths for workflow 3: Shoot: Film / Edit: Digital / Finish: Film / Release: Film and DVD.

The Picture Path

The first part of this workflow is similar to workflow 2: shoot film, edit digital, however, the image portion of the second conversion isn't done directly from digital to film; rather, all of the creative decisions you made during the digital edit are then manually duplicated, cut for cut, with your original camera negative. Once this is accomplished, we can then strike film prints, from that original negative, for exhibition. This duplication of the creative decisions you made is accomplished in two steps, the **matchback** step and the **conforming** step.

Matchback: Matchback is the process by which the edgecode numbers on the original camera negative are coordinated with the timecode numbers on the DV transfer, so that the creative edit decisions we made in the NLE system can be replicated on our camera original film, cut-for-cut and frame-for-frame. The first step to the matchback, during the telecine transfer process, is to have the lab begin creating an edgecode/timecode database called a **telecine log** (also called **a Flex File**) (Figure 19-21). The telecine log database compares the original footage edgecode numbers (either latent image numbers or the proprietary film barcode system) and the newly generated timecode numbers on the transfer in order to keep track of each and every "phantom" frame and field created in the 3:2 pulldown process. The lab will give you the telecine log as a text file on disk. Then, once you've captured your footage and transferred the telecine log database into your project file, you are free to fully engage your creative brain and edit the movie. When you have no more cutting to do, and the editing is done, the matchback begins. Each edited shot begins and ends on a specific timecode number. All professional editing software, like Avid or Final Cut Pro, can easily print out an **edit decision list** (**EDL**), which is a list detailing the beginning and ending timecode numbers of each and every shot in your movie. However, a timecode EDL includes all of those phantom fields inserted during the 3:2 pulldown process. So, all editing software designed to accommodate film shooting has a matchback tool (e.g., Avid's *Film Scribe* and Final Cut Pro's *Cinema Tools*), which uses the information in the telecine log to compare the timecode EDL with the negative film's edgecode numbers and interpolates the data to create a corresponding, frame-accurate, film edgecode EDL. This EDL now corresponds (or has been matched back) to the edgecode numbers from your camera original negative and tells us exactly which frames of *film* begin and end every shot in the movie. This list also includes the information for the visual transitions between shots (straight cut, dissolve, fade to black, etc.). This list is

```
#Film Title      ANDREW LUND/"LOST & FOUND"
#Episode         All
#Trsfr Facility  CINE TRANSFER 1-ATLANTA-USA
#Aaton ATN       Version 2.2, Keylink S/N 134 V. 6.91
#Telecine Speed  NTSC @ 23.98
#Film Format     16mm @ 24fps
#AudioTC fps     29.97nd
#AudioTC Origin  Keylink Generated: Kc breaks
#Transfer Date   06-05-16 12:45 mod:06-05-16 13:29 CINE TRANSFER 1-ATLANTA
#Video Reel      006
#Lab Reel        000011
#
#   Video TC    Audio TC    Aux TC    Keycode         Acmade
# ----------  ----------  --------  ----------     -----------
001 11:00:08:00 12:45:41:00           KI652425 7580&00
    11:11:13:20 12:56:46:20           KI652425 8378&16
    Dr.11:05:20 06 05 16    Camera A  Dt +00:00:00:00.00  r  g  b
    CamRol 26   S:    /     Tg 21AEA2CD i     e     v      -  -  -
    Scen 1      Take

002 11:11:13:20 12:56:46:20           KI652425 8388&00
    11:21:45:20 13:07:18:20           KI65242  9146&08
    Dr.10:32:00 06 05 16    Camera A  Dt +00      00.00  r  g  b
    CamRol 27   S:    /     Tg 21AEA2CD i
    Scen 2      Take

003 11:21:45:20 13:07:18:20           KI7
    11:31:39:25 13:17:12:25           KI
    Dr.09:54:05 06 05 16    Camera A  D
    CamRol 28   S:    /     Tg 21AEA2CD i
    Scen 3      Take
```

■ Fig. 19-21 The lab's telecine log is created during the transfer process to keep track of original negative edge code and video dailies time code information. Labs often deliver this text file on disk or via email.

called the **matchback cut-list** because it essentially becomes the roadmap for the literal cutting of the negative during the next step, **conforming** (Figure 19-22).

Conforming: Conforming (also called **negative matching**) is the process by which we cut and splice the camera original negative film to match, frame-for-frame, the cuts made during the editing process, so that we can make high-quality film prints directly from the original footage. Because there is only one original negative, which is vulnerable to damage, this process is done by trained professionals, called **negative cutters** (Figure 19-23), in special, filtered-air **clean rooms** to ensure that your precious negative remains free of dust and scratches. Should your negative get scratched, that mark will appear on each and every film print or DV transfer made from the original. Negative cutters match your creative decisions to the original footage by using the telecine log and matchback cut-list data and literally cut and glue the film together from the negative, performing the edits with cement splicing glue for a strong and permanent bond. This is the reason that this step is done at the very end, after all creative editing decisions are settled once and for all. You cannot go back after the film has been conformed and say, "Uh . . . can you just add three more frames at the end of that shot?" Can't be done.

Usually, negatives are cut by alternating consecutive shots onto two strands, called **A&B rolls** (Figure 19-24); odd-numbered shots are on the A roll and even numbered shots are on the B roll. The "missing" shot on each roll is replaced by black leader. When the lab makes a print from the A&B rolls onto a single strand of film, the A roll is threaded up first and printed by pushing light through the negative onto the print stock in a **contact printer** (Figure 19-25). The odd shots are now rendered as positive images, but the areas of black leader protect the print stock from exposure. The print film is then rewound to the beginning and the B roll is threaded up and printed, filling in those unexposed spaces with the even shots. However, where you have two shots that must overlap, as with dissolves and superimpositions, the print film is indeed printed over twice (Figure 19-26). In the case of dissolves, the printer light fades out at the

```
Avid Cut Lists
Project: AX Matchback
List Title: 35mm Matchback

35mm Matchback                10 events      handles = -1
Picture 1                      0 dupes       total footage:    74+04
Assemble List                  0 opticals    total time: 00:00:49:13
-----------------------------------------------------------------------------
       Footage   Duration    First/Last Key     Address TC   Cam Roll  Sc/Tk    Clip Name

  1.    0+00      10+04    KW 42 9137-4866+15   06:22:47:24    A85     A10G/2   A10G/2
       10+03               KW 42 9137-4877+02   06:22:54:18

  2.   10+04       8+04    KW 35 3532-5791+11   06:18:07:29    A83     A10B/1   A10B/1
       18+07               KW 35 3532-5799+14   06:18:13:13

  3.   18+08      11+08    KW 42 9137-4884+05   06:22:59:11    A85     A10G/2   A10G/2
       29+15               KW 42 9137-4895+12   06:23:06:29
       Matchback lengthened the tail of the clip by 1 frame.

  4.   30+00      12+04    KW 35 3532-5812+01   06:18:21:16    A83     A10B/1   A10B/1
       42+03               KW 35 3532-5824+04   06:18:29:20

  5.   42+04       5+06    KW 42 9137-4904+14   06:23:13:03    A85     A10G/2   A10G/2
       47+09               KW 42 9137-4910+03   06:23:16:20
       Matchback shortened the tail of the clip by 1 frame.

  6.   47+10       4+00    KW 46 7331-2663+04   06:25:54:15    A87     A10K/1   A10K/1
       51+09               KW 46 7331-2667+03   06:25:57:04

  7.   51+10       2+09    KW 42 9137-4914+01   06:23:19:06    A85     A10G/2   A10G/2
       54+02               KW 42 9137-4916+09   06:23:20:26

  8.   54+03      10+11    KW 35 3532-5907+07   06:19:25:04    A83     A10C/1   A10C/1
       64+13               KW 35 3532-5918+01   06:19:32:07

  9.   64+14       4+12    KW 42 9137-4926+01   06:23:27:06    A85     A10G/2   A10G/2
       69+09               KW 42 9137-4930+12   06:23:30:10

 10.   69+10       4+10    KW 35 3532-5923+00   06:19:35:15    A83     A10C/1   A10C/1
       74+03               KW 35 3532-5927+09   06:19:38:16

(end of Assemble List)
```

■ **Figure 19-22** The matchback cut-list helps the conformer cut precisely the right frames of original negative film to match the edits made in the NLE system.

■ **Fig. 19-23** A negative matcher literally cuts film and then uses cement glue and a hot splicer to connect the shots. Delicate handling and a clean environment is required around camera original negative.

A

B

■ **Figure 19-24** By printing the alternating shots on the A&B rolls onto a new strand of print film, we get a print with no physical splices.

Figure 19-25 A contact printer like this one is used to print A&B rolls onto a new strand of film. The print film is commonly run through from beginning to end three times: once to print the A roll shots, a second time for the B roll shots and a third time to print the optical sound track along the edge.

end of the outgoing shot and fades in at the head of the incoming shot on the next roll.

A&B rolling, also called **checkerboarding**, allows the lab to print transition and visual effects, like dissolves, superimpositions, titles over images, and fades. It also ensures that there are physically no image-to-image edits that require overlapping a tiny portion of the frame when cement-splicing and can lead to noticeable splices. Checkerboarding ensures "invisible splices." The printing process also allows for extensive color and exposure correction by controlling the color and intensity of the printer light.

Most negative cutters like to have a video copy of the film to double check each cut when in doubt. Some prefer a video copy that displays the timecode and corresponding edgecode numbers right on the screen. Depending on your lab, it is possible to get DV copies of your footage, called **window dubs**, with the actual T.C. numbers and edgecode numbers **burned in** the image (Figure 19-27). Editing with window dubs can help you manage the process of going back to a film print, but you cannot get rid of the numbers, so this footage is useless for mastering on DV.

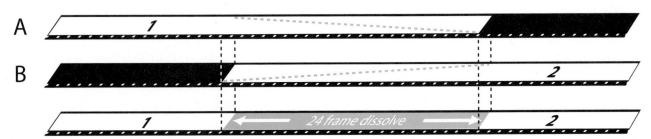

Figure 19-26 Dissolves are achieved by overlapping shots on the A&B rolls and adjusting the contact printer light during the print process: fading out the outgoing shot (1) and fading in the incoming shot (2).

The newest development in the film-to-digital-to-film matchback/EDL process is the recording of exact barcode edge number information (e.g., Kodak's *Keycode* or Fuji's *Mr. Code*) written as meta-data directly into the data tracks of the DV transfer. With this you theoretically can capture your footage into your computer using a "reverse telecine" process, which captures only the original 24 fps frames. All of your editing can then be done in the computer at 24 fps and a direct edgecode cut-list can be quickly and accurately generated for the conformer—theoretically. I have yet to find someone for whom this process actually worked as smoothly as it sounds, but I have no doubt that the wrinkles will soon be ironed out.

The Audio Path

Just as the image requires *two* conversions to go back to film, so, too, does the audio. Like the picture, the first step in the process, getting your field audio synced and into your NLE system, is the same as for the film/digital/DV workflow, with all of the same issues of pulldown and sync drift. However, when the editing is over and you need to then move the audio into the realm of film printing, there is another conversion process necessary to reestablish sync between your audio (now including many edits and tracks of sound) and the film print, which will now be running again at 24 fps.

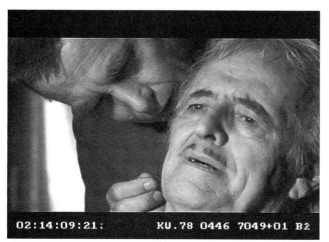

Figure 19-27 A window dub has "burned in" timecode (lower left) and edgecode numbers (right), providing an easy way for a negative cutter to check edits. (Frame from Lund's *Snapshot*.)

Figure 19-28 François Truffaut's *Day for Night* (1973) starts with a typical New Wave self-referential nod to filmmaking: it shows the optical track of the sound of an orchestra rehearsing the music that will be used later in the film.

After all picture and sound editing has been completed (called **picture lock**; see p. 389) and your sound mixing has been completed (see Chapter 23), you will send the final audio mix track to the lab (usually on a DAT tape, but, again, check with your lab) and they will perform a reverse resolving process called **pull-up**. It makes sense that if audio *pulldown* slows the rate of audio 0.1%, to match the slowed rate (23.976 fps) of the transferred image, then when the image goes back to film (24 fps) the audio needs to be pulled-up again (sped up) to 100% speed, to sync with the film. Your film lab will do the pull-up conversion while they transfer your audio from the DAT tape (the digital world) to an **optical master** (film world).

Motion picture film projection predominantly uses an **optical sound track**, which is an analog audio system in which the film's sound track is represented by a clear stripe of varying widths, which is photographically printed right into the black edge of the film (Figure 19-28). An exciter lamp pushes light through this clear stripe and onto a photodiode. Changes in the width of the stripe create varying pulses of light hitting the photodiode, which in turn transforms the fluctuating voltages into analog audio. The concept is not unlike the jagged grooves of an LP record, only created and read with light instead of with a needle, and this would be a pretty good metaphor if LP records still existed!

in practice

Attention—Hidden Cost Alert!!

If you plan to shoot film, edit digital, and finish on film, you should always consult with the film lab and the negative cutter way ahead of time to determine what they need from you to perform a smooth matchback, and what they charge. There are two things to keep in mind when employing this workflow. The first is that effects, like dissolves, wipes, superimpositions, color effects, motion effects, etc., are so easily created on an NLE system that we hardly even think about it while we edit. But if you plan to go back to film, every one of these transitions and effects is a billable lab process. When creating a film print, most labs charge you a per-foot fee and an additional fee for each transition or special effect. Creating a 48-frame dissolve was just a minor mouse movement in digital editing, but in film printing it can cost you $20 for each dissolve! Second, talk with your negative cutter to find out what they need from you to do the matchback and conforming, and how they bill. Often a negative cutter will charge an hourly rate and a *per-edit* fee. The more edits you have and the more the conformer has to fish around for the right matchback numbers, the more expensive it will be to conform your movie.

These are the kinds of "hidden costs" that can be anticipated and budgeted for if you consult with your lab and negative cutter in pre-production, while you prepare your budget.

The optical master is printed on a strip of film all on its own and then, after both the A roll and B roll have been run through the contact printer and printed onto the print stock, the film is once again rewound and the optical track is threaded up and printed on the same strip of film. In the end, the print film has been exposed three times, once for the A roll, again for the B roll, and a third time for the optical track. Finally, the image and sound are photographically and permanently joined onto a single, projectable strip of film called a **married print**. There are several versions of married prints. The first time you print the A&B and optical tracks onto the film, you get what is called an **answer print**. This print is used for evaluation. The director is now able to see the finished film, projected, on the big screen for analysis. If there are any corrections that need to be made to the color or exposure, these are noted and executed during the second printing (again from the original A&B and optical rolls). Once again, the director checks this print out on the big screen. If there is still more work to be done, then this print is your **second answer print**, and the lab will go back to the original rolls with your notes again and print another one. If all is well, then you are the proud owner of a **release print**—ready for distribution and exhibition.

Finishing on tape and finishing on film are not mutually exclusive. It is entirely possible to finish your project on DV for mass distribution and then, when the need arises (e.g., a producer needs a film print to put your movie into theatrical distribution), you can always go back to your negative to create a film print. In other words, always finish on tape—it's inexpensive, it greatly expands your exhibition possibilities, and it's the easiest format to send out to festivals, production companies, producers, or your mom.

Shoot: DV (SD or HD) / Edit: Digital / Finish: DV Tape / Release: Film and DVD

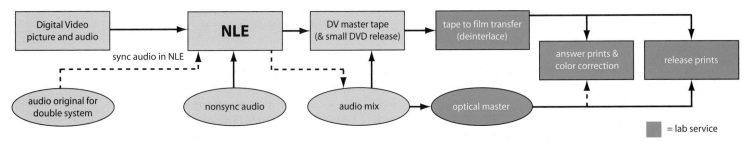

Figure 19-29 Picture and audio paths for workflow 4: Shoot: DV (SD or HD) / Edit: Digital / Finish: DV Tape / Release: Film and DVD.

As we mentioned earlier in the chapter, this workflow process is becoming increasingly prevalent. Successful films like *Dancer in the Dark* (2000), *Bamboozled* (2000), and *Ten* (2002) have shown emerging filmmakers how to capitalize both on the unique storytelling qualities of the DV aesthetic and on the physical advantages of the lightweight production gear, to energize their camerawork and their ideas. However, the substantial costs of striking a film print worthy of projection from a DV original (especially standard definition DV) are somewhat contradictory to DV's capacity for ultra low-budget production. Since staying within the DV workflow is so simple, and because of the hefty additional cost of the of the tape-to-film transfer, people tend not to go this route unles s there is a real demand to put the film into theatrical distribution, where a commercial distributor will foot the bill. The D.P. Ellen Kuras (Figure 19-30) commented on this issue concerning Spike Lee's *Bamboozled,* the first film she shot on MiniDV:

Digital definitely does have its advantages and is appropriate in certain applications. With my strong desire to give the film a look and the need for a full color correction, we ended up spending quite a bit on the back end in post. Unless aesthetics or theory dictate choosing video—whether Hi-def or mini-DV—I caution everyone to consider all costs involved, not just the dollars you'd save during a production shoot.

**(From *The Digital Cinematographer*, by Kevin H. Martin,
The International Cinematographers Guild)**

Again, it is best for you to consult with the DV-to-film transfer facility to get all of the details. If you have a sense that you will, or might, strike a film print from your DV-mastered film (from the DV/digital/DV workflow scheme), then this consultation should happen in preproduction. Each transfer facility prefers specific camera settings during the production process for compatibility with their system. In doing the research for this book, for example, many facilities told me that PAL footage transfers "much better" than NTSC does, because of the more compatible frame rate (25 fps) and the increased resolution (20% better) and color stability. However, I was told by other facilities that they've maximized their system so that NTSC transfers look nearly equal to PAL and that it's not worth the other inconveniences, like not being able to finish on NTSC DV for video screening, to use the PAL system. Most facilities also prefer you to shoot and edit your footage in interlace mode (i.e., NTSC 60i), preferring to do the de-interlacing in-house with their own proprietary software, rather than in-camera. Some facilities will even tell you which DV cameras transfer best on their system! So, as with any other lab service, go directly to the transfer facility if your workflow ultimately involves a tape-to-film transfer.

■ **Figure 19-30** Cinematographer Ellen Kuras is one of the most versatile and sought-after DPs working today. She has produced brilliant images on 35mm and super 16 film as well as high definition and standard definition DV.

Once you have mastered your film from the digital edit (and mixed your audio), the transfer facility pretty much takes over both the video and audio processes. The facility captures your master tape into their computer system, which de-interlaces and resamples the footage at 24 fps. These new image frames are then recorded onto 35mm or 16mm negative film with a **cathode ray tube** (CRT) **recorder** (less expensive) or a **laser scanner** like the Kodak Cineon (more expensive).

The audio goes through a process similar to the film/digital/film workflow path. The audio from your master tape is transferred to timecode DAT by the facility (or you may be asked to provide a DAT audio master), after which it is then resolved to the 24 fps film rate and transferred to a negative optical sound master. Once the facility has created both a picture and optical sound negative master, they are printed to the same positive film strip to create a married print ready for projection in a theater.

In Conclusion

In the old days, not really so long ago, when I was in school myself, the choices for a filmmaker were much simpler. Anything destined for a theater was shot, edited, and finished on film. Projection could only be done adequately on film. Video was only for projects destined for the television broadcast or gallery installations. A few people were editing commercials on video (because they were destined for TV broadcast) and were predicting that video and video editing would make film obsolete in ten years—but a funny thing happened; that's about how long it took for analog video and videotape editing to become obsolete. While film as a production medium was resilient, film as an editing process went the way of video. The cause of all this upheaval? The digital revolution. The 21st-century filmmaker has accessible to them an extraordinary array of powerful tools and aesthetic capabilities, but the digital revolution has also opened up so many more workflow avenues that, quite frankly, it boggles the mind.

These workflow overviews are designed to help you understand the basics of the technical stages and the format interfaces involved in the most common production routes. Just as a road map cannot show you every sight or building or pathway, it would be impossible for me to explain every detail in every workflow scenario. These are details you need to discover for yourself by talking to the lab, talking to filmmakers who have been through the same process, and hitting the Web for the most up-to-date information. By now, you know that this book concentrates on ideas, aesthetics, and creativity as the most important tools for a filmmaker. But film is a technical art form, and just as all technical knowledge is worthless without imagination and a story to tell, so, too, all of the creativity in the world remains unnoticed if you can't get your movie to an audience. Thankfully, technology is not like talent; there really is no mystery to it—it can be taught and you can learn it. And you can harness it for your creative goals to get your story onto a screen. A little bit of forethought, planning, and legwork is all it takes. It will always pay off.

Principles and Process of Digital Editing

■ DIGITAL EDITING FUNDAMENTALS

Virtually all film projects, whether they're destined for television, DVD, or theatrical release, regardless of being shot on film, standard DV, or HD, are edited on a **digital**, **nonlinear editing system** (or **NLE** for short). Editing in the digital domain means that all visual and aural components of the project, no matter what their original form, must be turned into digital data called **media files** and brought into a computer running specialized editing software. In Final Cut Pro, the video media files are saved in the **QuickTime** format, and in the Avid system, they are saved as **Open Media Framework** (.omf) files. In both systems, audio files are saved in the **Audio Interchange File Format** (AIFF). In data form, any piece of visual footage or any piece of sound can be instantly accessed through a computer's **random access** capability and easily labeled, organized, duplicated, cut, arranged, rearranged, trimmed, mixed, and manipulated with a mere drag and click of a mouse. This simple fact is why, even in the technologically conservative arena of narrative filmmaking, digital editing completely revolutionized the postproduction process in only a few years.

Nonlinear Editing

So why *do* they call it **nonlinear editing**? The label "nonlinear" basically means that we are not limited by the linear characteristic of videotape. For example, if you want to preview a shot in a digital editing system, just a click will open it up on the screen in a flash, and another click will instantly position you on any frame within that shot. A nonlinear system allows us to move around in the footage in any direction, instantaneously. On videotape, if the shot we wanted to preview happened to be at the end of the tape, we would have to wait while the tape fast forwarded to the cue point; and if the next shot we wanted to preview happened to be at the head of the tape, we'd have to rewind all the way to the beginning again. Even more significantly, however, is the fact that, with digital editing, we can delete (or insert) a shot anywhere along our edited sequence and all succeeding shots will move up to close the gap or push down to accommodate the new shot. In short, inserting or deleting shots has no effect on the other shots in the sequence. At this point, I can imagine a young film student, weaned exclusively on hard drives and data, blinking hard and saying "Yeah? So?" The fact is, there are those of us who, in the dark ages, struggled with tape-to-tape video editing, which is essentially a process of rerecording material from a source tape directly onto a record tape. We remember a time when you would string together, say, twenty-five edits, only to realize that you wanted to insert a new shot after edit #4. Videotape's "linearity problem" meant that if you inserted (literally recorded) a new shot #5, you covered over the old shot #5 and so had to rerecord it as shot #6, which covered over the next shot, which you had to then re-lay, and so on. Every time you inserted or deleted a shot in an existing sequence you had to re-lay every shot that came after that point. I'd rather not contemplate the hours of my life I lost doing exactly this in videotape editing rooms. Digital editing, on the other hand, never actually lays any media down onto tape until you are completely done editing. Instead, it uses the computer's **RAM (random access memory)** to perpetually "preview" all of the edits in your program. You can insert shots, delete shots, rearrange sequences, and build several versions and still make it home in time to get eight hours of sleep. So the term "nonlinear editing" was introduced to announce that, while digital editing was done electronically, it didn't have video's "linearity problem," and hearing this, we all traded in our play decks, record deck, and RM440 edit controllers for a mouse and a hard drive, in record time!

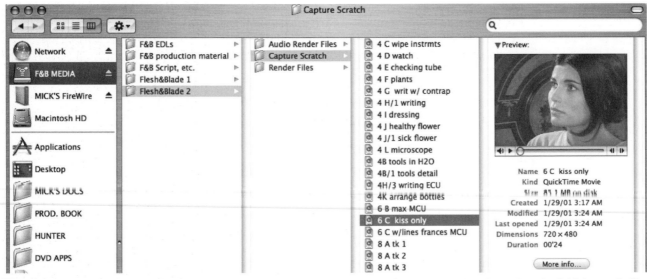

■ **Figure 20-1** Media files are saved on an external firewire drive and are not actually altered during editing. Pictured are the Quicktime media files for a project on Final Cut Pro located in the capture scratch folder.

Nondestructive Editing

To be fair, editing on film was also a form of nonlinear editing. Yes, you still had to rewind and fast forward through rolls of film to find specific shots, but if you had a twenty-five-edit sequence cut together and decided to insert (or delete) a shot early in the sequence, you would simply unsplice two shots and insert the new shot (or remove a shot) and redo the splice. The rest of the shots in the sequence would slide up or down. This is why video-tape editing, despite all predictions, did not win over many film editors, especially in the feature film world. However, "cutting" on film literally meant cutting a strip of cellulose acetate to define the shot you wanted to edit into the film. If you changed your mind often and recut many times, you had little pieces of film scattered across the flatbed like spilled cornflakes, and every one of these frames had to be saved and labeled just in case you changed your mind again. Additionally, film editing is done on a workprint (a low-resolution print struck from the original negative), and because a workprint costs money to make, there was usually only one copy—especially for students. After cutting together a sequence, it was painstaking to pull it apart and try another version of the sequence. If the new version didn't work, you'd have to redo the old sequence. So, while film editing was nonlinear, it was unfortunately also "destructive editing," which means that the physical material you were editing with was permanently changed (damaged) with each cut. Digital NLE is **nondestructive editing**, which means that any cutting, arranging, trimming, corrections, or effects you might perform occur only virtually, in a preview mode. The original media files that you captured are not altered in any way (**Figure 20-1**).

All editing is done via **media file indicators**, which only "point" to the original data without ever altering the media file. For example, let's say you have a camera take that is ten seconds long and you want to use two seconds from the middle of that media file for an edit. In film you would have to literally cut that portion out of the longer take. But digitally, you simply indicate the timecode numbers where you want the shot to begin (the **in-point**) and end (the **out-point**). Then you edit that portion of the shot into program sequence. However, you are in fact not cutting any actual media into the sequence, rather, only the numbers (or pointers) that tell the computer what piece of that QuickTime media file to load into RAM and play back at that point. This is why it's easy to make changes to that shot, to trim it a few frames longer or shorter, to try numerous versions of the same sequence using the same shots: because you're simply altering the data indicators, the numbers, not the media file itself. Nothing is actually recorded until the very last stage, when all of the editing has been completed and you send your final project out to be recorded onto DV tape (or DVD) for mastering.

One great advantage to this system has been the ability to do long-distance collaborative editing. Remember, all of the editing decisions you make—length of shots, order of shots, layering of audio, etc.—that constitute your **edit decision list** (**EDL**) are simply pointer numbers referencing the media files. Without any actual media, an EDL is a very small file. Because of this, it is common to have two sets of hard drives with the same raw media files on them—say, one with the movie's director in New York and another with the editor in Chicago, who then can email the EDL file back and forth. This way the director is able to see and respond to the work of the editor, several times a day, if necessary, without ever leaving New York.

Nonlinear and nondestructive editing solved two of the most pernicious drawbacks of previous editing methods, film and video, which is why NLE systems pushed both film and video editing into obsolescence in fairly short order. Add to this the fact that the cost for all of this power is considerably cheaper than for the old processes, since so many procedures and capabilities have been taken out of the hands of labs, rental facilities, and technical specialists (and their assistants) and placed in our hands, making the process of filmmaking easier, faster, more accessible, and cheaper, and that's great. But the digital revolution is not without its own drawbacks.

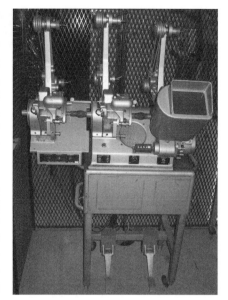

■ **Figure 20-2** The upright Moviola. Even though countless wonderful movies have been edited on this machine, it is thankfully a relic of a bygone era.

Too Much of a Good Thing?

These days I can edit a short film, with titles, effects, sound mix, and color correction by myself, in no time flat and in the comfort of my own home or on my laptop. So what's to complain about? In the past, I've done a lot of editing on both film and video. My first three student films were edited on a cantankerous machine called an upright Moviola (Figure 20-2). Our professor kept telling us not to complain when the "green monster," as we called it, ate our film. He'd remind us of "all the great movies that were made on machines just like this one, including *Citizen Kane!*" At the mention of *Citizen Kane,* we were all obliged to stop our whining. We'd looked at the green monster and conclude that Orson Wells might well be considered a genius, if only for his ability to actually finish a movie with this beast! I, for one, will tell you that if I never have to get on my hands and knees to hunt for three missing film frames that dropped behind the flatbed, or spend an hour re-laying twenty edits just so I could add one new shot in a videotape sequence, it will be too soon (Figure 20-3).

However, as I started writing these postproduction chapters, I bought the latest version of one of those very popular, relatively inexpensive NLE programs that are on the market. The software for all that power and technical capacity came on just a few slim little disks—but the box it came in was *huge!* Why was the box so big? Because the user's manual came in five (!) volumes of around 300 pages each. The manual for this "easy to use" editing software takes up more than twice the space on my bookshelf as the complete works of William Shakespeare. Think about that. I looked at these NLE tomes, after nearly dislocating my shoulder putting them on the shelf, and wondered—Is this *really* going to simplify my life? Or even more to the point is the question—Will all this technology really make me a better filmmaker? Is *all* of it really necessary? Does one need to read all 1,500+ pages before one can call themselves an editor? Sometimes, when I sit in front of my hyper-turbo-charged editing software, I acutely feel the burden of an excess of riches. I think about the sort of editing resources truly great filmmakers like Robert Bresson, Yasujiro Ozu, Roberto Rossellini, and Satyajit Ray had when they were making the films that profoundly resonated around the world and established cinema as an artistic force. Take a

■ **Figure 20-3** The convenience of today's editing software. Two students do some last minute cutting in the hallway before their film production class begins.

Figure 20-4 Ozu's masterpiece *Tokyo Story* (1953) is told using only straight cuts, two fades, and no "spinning 3D cubes."

look at any one film from each director (*A Man Escaped, Tokyo Story, Rome: Open City,* and *The World of Apu*) and you'll see mostly simple cuts and occasionally you'll see a fade-out or fade-in, maybe a few dissolves, and only very rarely a slow motion shot. But you'll *never* see a "shattering-glass" transition effect, or a "chroma key composite" layering two images, one with a "radial blur filter" and the other with a "ripple effect" and both spinning through space inside a "cube-spin 3D motion effect". I can do that! I can do what these legendary filmmakers never imagined, in a matter of minutes. But how important is this ability, truly (Figure 20-4)?

What you *will* see in these films, is eloquent and thoughtful visual storytelling using simple, precise, and fundamental editing techniques that have become the essential vocabulary for anyone wishing to make movies. With all this technology, *how* we make a dissolve is super easy, but *why* we use a dissolve is still the most important question, the complexity of which cannot be changed by technology. If we are not careful with all of this technological power we are gaining, we run the risk of losing much (Figure 20-5).

How to Approach Surplus Technology

The boon and the burden of the digital revolution is the remarkable ease with which we can manipulate sound and image. We are offered so many bells and whistles in our editing software, not because we *asked* for six different kinds of image blur filters, but simply because engineers could easily include it. The best way to approach your software is to learn the basic functions first, the essential tools. Learn how to choose the shots you want, how to perform cuts and make a sequence. Learn how to arrange those shots and how to trim them longer or shorter as you need. Learn how to layer a few tracks of audio and adjust sound levels and keep your footage in sync. Maybe try a dissolve or two. That's all you really need at first. Now go make a movie. If your shots don't work together with a cut, then a "page-peel" transition isn't going to help. If your images aren't carefully composed, spinning them across the screen won't make them more eloquent. If your actors aren't convincing, not one of the numerous image-effect filters will make their performance ring more true. Strengthen your fundamental storytelling techniques and use only what you need to tell your story. Don't worry: those 1,500-page user manuals are waiting for you. As soon as you discover that you truly need to use a wipe transition, then look it up and learn how to do it. When you find that

Figure 20-5 The NLE surplus. Does anyone truly need the "checkerboard wipe" (left) or the "jaws wipe" (right) to tell a good story?

your film will be improved by adding an image filter to reduce contrast; it's there, it's not hard, go learn it. There may come a day when you want to try a green screen key effect; no problem, it'll be there when you need it. As you make your movies, you will be adding one useful technique at a time—but on your schedule and as your movies require. The tail should not wag the dog. Make the technology work for your ideas and resist the temptation to let snazzy technology lead the way.

in practice

The film director Michel Gondry developed his filmmaking skills in the world of music videos before he tackled feature-length narrative films. He created memorable videos for such pop musicians as Björk, The Chemical Brothers, Cibo Matto, and others. Although he has a reputation for fairly low-tech special effects, his music video works are nonetheless highly stylized and technically flamboyant. However, when it came to feature film storytelling, the music video director surprisingly used no extreme digital technology or even fancy transitions in his 2004 film *Eternal Sunshine of the Spotless Mind*. In telling a very complex story—which traces the labyrinth of a man's mind as he slowly loses his memories of a woman through a scientific process designed to erase her from his brain—Gondry opted for a highly stripped down style including a handheld camera and natural lighting. His editing approach is equally simple. In the entire film, Gondry uses exclusively straight cuts with only four exceptions: one fade-in, two fades to black, and one fade to white. It is the structure of the film itself that conveys the layered storyline, and not the flashy effects.

The Dardenne brothers' film *La Promesse* (1997) (Figure 20-7) presents a fictional drama in a cinema vérité documentary style. The film derives its realism and credibility from the immediacy of the raw, unembellished documentary approach. In this case, the use of digital effects, dissolves, or other fancy transitions in video or audio would be completely inappropriate for the realist content and corresponding style and would weaken the film's impact.

However, I certainly wouldn't want to close off any of a filmmaker's potential creative avenues. If your story will benefit from all of the bells and whistles, if the fancy transitions, key effects, and digital processing are appropriate and can actually enhance your story, then by all means use them. In *The Matrix* trilogy (1999–2004) (Figure 20-8), the Wachowski brothers certainly exploited technology for all it was worth in creating the matrix, an entire world and consciousness, a complete construction of technology. In this case the filmmakers are practically obligated by the subject matter and themes of the film to push high technology to its limits.

Figure 20-6 Michel Gondry needed little more than straight cuts to intricately explore the mind and memories of Joel (Jim Carrey) in *Eternal Sunshine of the Spotless Mind* (2004).

Figure 20-7 In *La Promesse* (1996), the Dardenne brothers tell the story of Igor's (Jérémie Renier) moral awakening in a documentary style, devoid of any flashy techniques that would detract from the gritty realism of the film.

Figure 20-8 The Wachowski brothers had to push the limits of filmmaking technology to render the dystopian future world of *The Matrix* (1999).

■ THE BASIC SYSTEM: INTERFACE AND WORKFLOW

Nonlinear editing systems are a lot like camcorders. There are the bare-bones consumer programs, like iMovie, which are usually free and ultra-easy, but are not flexible enough (especially in their limited sound-editing abilities) for anyone who seriously wishes to make narrative films. Then there are the mid-range programs, like Final Cut Pro HD, Avid Xpress Pro, and Adobe Premiere Pro, which are extremely reasonable in price for their capabilities and quality—especially with the educational discount. And finally there are the ultra high-end systems, like Avid's Symphony Nitris system, which can claim the mantle of highest image finishing quality and most visual effects. The truth is, however, that the mid-range systems add new features and higher quality by the bucket-full every year, so it is no wonder that Walter Murch edited Anthony Minghella's feature film *Cold Mountain* (2003) (Figure 20-9) on a Final Cut Pro system. These days, there are many filmmakers, especially on the introductory and intermediate levels, who find no practical advantage to moving beyond these mid-range, highly accessible editing systems.

While there are a number of different nonlinear editing systems around, they all work on the same basic principles and interface. True, there are enough differences in terminology, lay-out, and small details to keep most people from switching around once they're comfortable with one particular system, but learning one system certainly prepares you for working with any other system. It's like learning to drive in one car and then getting behind the wheel of a different car. Sure, you need to figure out where the headlight switch is, and the windshield wipers, and if the gas cap is on the driver's or passenger's side, but other than that, you can drive.

The Hardware Setup

The hardware for a typical, low-end, nonlinear editing station consists of a computer and monitor(s) (Mac or PC) running NLE software, an external firewire hard drive, a DV deck, speakers, and a comfortable chair (Figure 20-10).

Editing sound and picture, especially if you plan to incorporate any effects at all, requires a fairly powerful personal **computer**. Also, as we saw earlier, a computer's random access

■ **Figure 20-9** Walter Murch edited Minghella's *Cold Mountain* (2003) and Mendes' *Jarhead* (2005) using off-the-shelf Final Cut Pro software. Still from Apple's *The Cutting Edge* (2004).

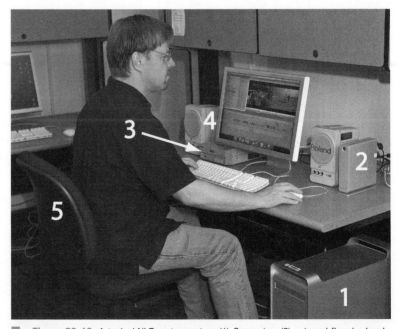

■ **Figure 20-10** A typical NLE system setup. (1) Computer; (2) external firewire hard drive; (3) DV deck; (4) speakers and monitor; (5) comfortable chair.

memory is critical to the functioning of editing software, so maximum RAM is always recommended. Always check the system specifications against the software requirements. It is important that your computer **monitor** be of high resolution so that you can have some sense for the picture quality of your footage and any image effects you may employ. Many editing setups will also include a high-end NTSC monitor to get a truer sense for the video quality. Also, while you can edit just fine with a single monitor, many system setups will use two, simply for ease and to keep the desktop from being too cluttered.

An **external firewire hard drive** stores your media files. Most NLE software recommends not putting media files onto the internal drive of your computer where your software resides. This is a speed issue and also a convenience issue. Media saved on a portable, firewire hard drive can be used on any editing station running the same software. Keep in mind that media files take up a lot of space. For sync sound DV, 5 minutes of video will take up a little more than 1 gigabyte of drive space. In addition to holding your original media files, your NLE system will also create new media each time you add a transition effect (like a dissolve), special effect, or text and graphics, which all require additional space. So, for example, if you have 60 minutes of raw footage to download, you'll need at least 13 GB of drive space, but with the potential of new media being created in the edit you'd be wise to allow for 18 GB of drive space for the project.

The **DV deck** is used to download your footage into the NLE system and ultimately to record your finished program to tape. This can be accomplished with your DV camcorder or with a dedicated DV deck interfacing with the computer via a firewire cable, but a dedicated DV deck is preferable because it reduces wear and tear on the camcorder. In the case of footage recorded on hard drives or P2 cards, the interface is made via a firewire or USB cable (or through the DVD player in the case of optical disk recording) and the data can be read directly off the record media. If you need to reuse the record media, then the data transfer to another hard drive is much faster than the real time necessary for DV tape downloads.

A good set of powered **speakers** is important to get a true sense for your audio. Often, in editing facilities where there are multiple systems in a single room, you'll be forced to edit with headphones, so that no one disturbs the other editors in the room. Headphones are fine while you're constructing the first few rough cuts of your movie, but the final sound track mix should always be done with high-quality speakers to get an accurate sense for how the balance and presence of the audio will sound to an audience who will themselves be listening to speakers.

A **comfy chair** is a must. The familiar film industry saying, "Never trust an editor with a tan," reminds us that editing requires that you remain inside an editing room, sitting on your behind, in front of an NLE system for hours and days on end. For this reason, a comfy, adjustable, ergonomically correct chair is important. A comfortable editor is a happy, creative, and productive editor; an uncomfortable editor takes frequent breaks to go to the beach.

The data transfer rate for standard DV is 3.8 MB/sec:

30 sec = 108 MB
1 min = 216 MB
5 min = 1.08 GB
10 min = 2.16 GB
30 min = 6.5 GB
60 min = 13 GB

The Software Interface

In standard editing mode, all NLE systems divide the **edit environment** (or **desktop**) into four main windows (Figure 20-11): (1) the browser [Final Cut Pro (FCP)] or project window (Avid), (2) the viewer (FCP) or source monitor (Avid), (3) the timeline window (FCP and Avid), and (4) the canvas (FCP) or composer monitor (Avid).

■ **Figure 20-11** The four main editing windows in the Avid Xpress Pro HD (top) and Final Cut Pro HD (bottom).

The Browser (FCP) or Project Window (Avid)

The **browser window/project window** is the main window for storing, organizing, and accessing all of the visual and audio elements for your project. These elements, which you use to edit your film, are organized in folders called **bins**. In traditional film editing, the **film bin** was where editors would store and organize the **selects**, which are all the individual shots to be used in the film. In NLE systems, **bins** serve the same function. **A bin** is where you store and organize your separate editing elements, including **video clips**, which are individual shots, and **audio clips**, which can be pieces of music, sound effects, or voice-over. The clips in the bins are saved on the internal hard drive and are not actual media; they are simply the pointers that reference the original media files that are stored on the external hard drive (Figure 20-12).

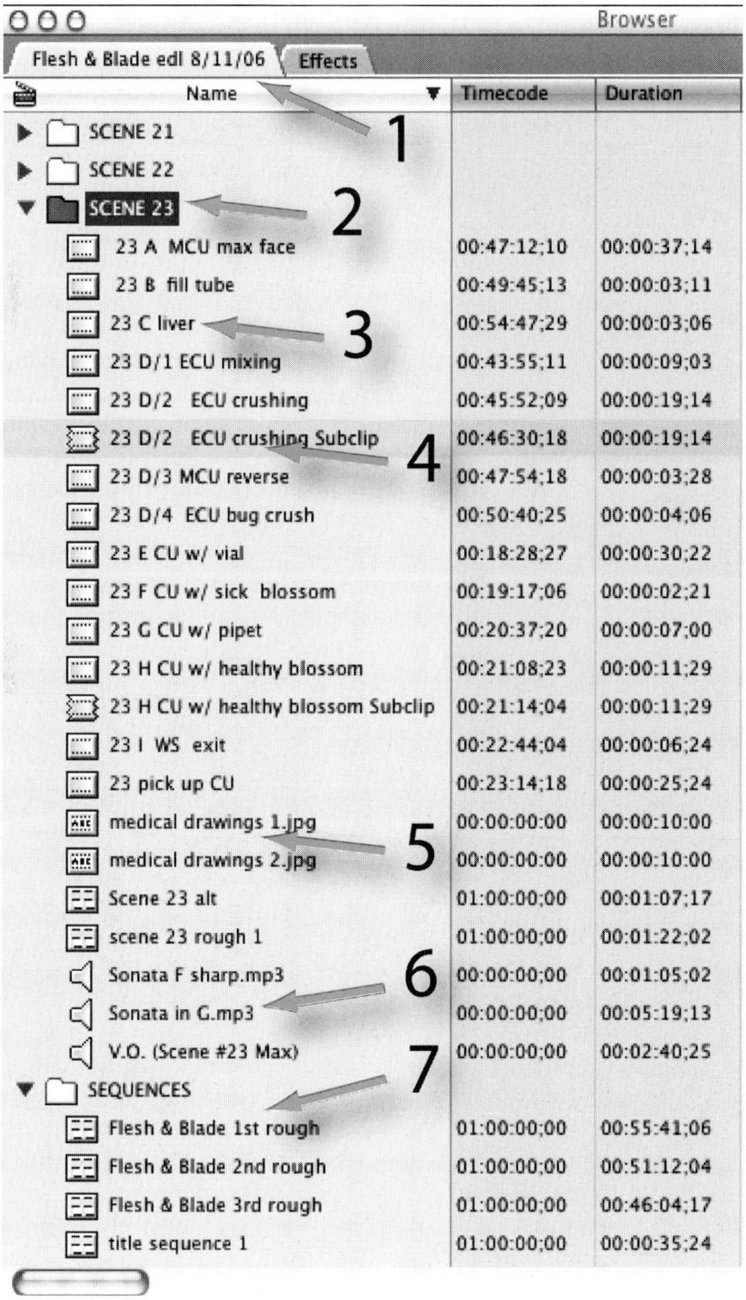

Figure 20-12 The organization of project files in Final Cut Pro: The project folder (1) contains all project files including the bin folders (2) that themselves hold all necessary files for each scene including: master clips (3); sub-clips (4); graphic files (5) and sound files (6). Sequences (7) are also found in the project folder.

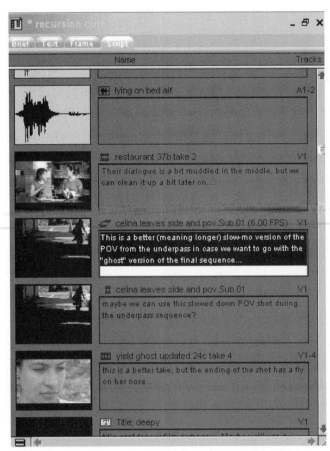

Figure 20-13 Most NLE systems, like AVID Xpress Pro HD (pictured), allow you to keep fairly extensive notes about each take with the clip itself, to help you remember editing ideas and shot details.

You can create multiple bins within the larger project window (or browser). Organizing your bins so that you can easily find the material you need is essential for efficiency—but *how* you organize the bins is a very personal matter. Often, editors will create one bin for each scene, including all of the elements (camera takes and audio) needed to edit the scene. Most NLE systems provide great flexibility for customizing, organizing, and identifying clips. Clip information can include the *in* and *out* timecode numbers, shot duration, scene, take, and camera roll numbers. You can also include notes on any clip. For example, you might write a note on a specific clip with the indication, "sound is no good, but good expressions toward end for reaction shots" (Figure 20-13).

The Viewer (FCP) or Source Monitor (Avid)

If you want to view, evaluate, and work with any particular video clip, you simply click on it and the shot will open up in the FCP **viewer** (or **source window** on the AVID). In the viewer you can view the entire shot and then set **in-points** and **out-points** to delineate the exact piece of footage from the longer shot that you want to edit into your film. If you're working with a sound clip in the viewer, like a piece of music, you will see the audio waveform in the viewer, which can be enormously helpful in finding beats or sound peaks and determining where you want to cut into and out of the sound track (Figure 20-14).

The Timeline Window (FCP and Avid)

Once you've decided on the specific parameters of the shot you'd like to insert into your film, you place it into the **timeline**. The timeline is where all the action is—this is where you truly edit your movie by inserting, deleting, arranging, rearranging, and fine-tuning your clips as you build your movie, both sound and image, one cut at a time.

The timeline is divided into discrete **video** and **audio tracks** for maximum creative flexibility. You have the option to cut, rearrange, or apply effects to only the picture, or only the sound, or any combination of picture and sound tracks, or all tracks simultaneously. A typical timeline will automatically provide one video track and four audio tracks when you start a project, but you can add as many audio tracks as you need—Final Cut Pro allows up to 99 audio tracks. Additional video tracks can also be added when you want to create superimpositions, text over image, and other image layering effects (Figure 20-15).

As you lay down a string of shots and audio tracks in the timeline, you are creating a **sequence**, which is a graphical representation of your edited movie. Sequences should be clearly named and saved frequently. Sequences are also saved in the browser, along with the clips. One of the great flexible advantages of digital editing is that you can create multiple sequences, copy sequences, create versions of sequences, and treat a sequence like a clip and insert them into other sequences.

In both Avid and Final Cut Pro, the number of tools and possibilities for working in the timeline are staggering. Some capabilities, like the ability to **trim** shots shorter or longer with frame precision, are essential tools for editing. Other timeline functions you will use only occasionally, while others you may never need at all (Figure 20-16).

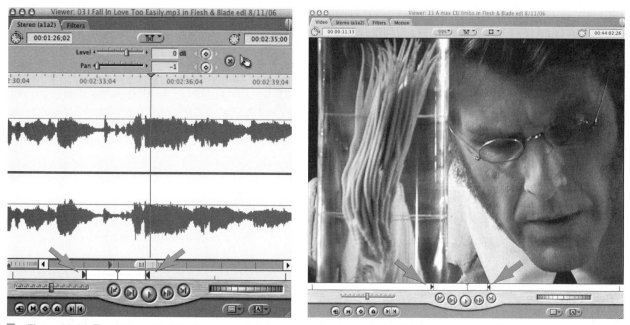

■ **Figure 20-14** The viewer in Final Cut Pro can toggle between soundtrack view (left) and picture view (right). The in point and out point on the clip timeline (arrows) show exactly what portion of the entire clip you have chosen to use.

It is not possible to cover timeline functions in detail in this book, so I refer you to the software instruction manuals. Both Avid and Final Cut Pro have a "Getting Started" manual, which is the best place to begin. Also, there are many third-party books on the market that are written in a much more intuitive and useful way than the full software manuals are. I have mentioned a few of the more popular publications in the Recommended Reading list in the back of the book.

Inside the timeline is a **playhead**, which is a horizontally scrolling vertical line running through all edited tracks. The playhead tells you where you are in the timeline and is used to move around your sequence quickly. We also use the playhead to determine where edit points are placed and where shots are inserted. With the mouse, you can drag the playhead across the sequence to locate a specific shot quickly, or, if you hit play, the playhead moves across the sequence in real time.

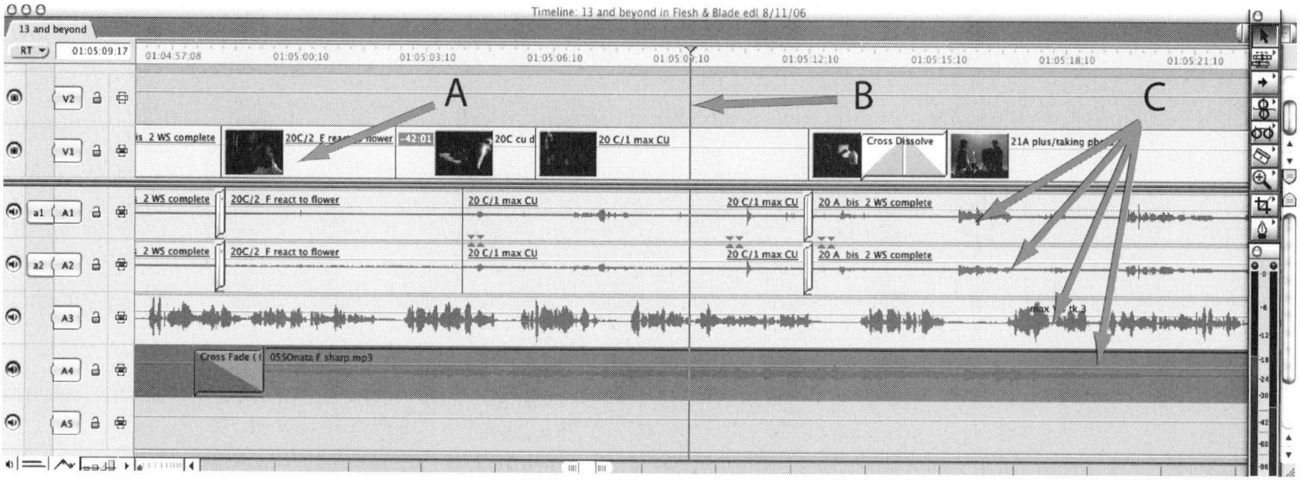

■ **Figure 20-15** The timeline consists of the picture track(s) (A); sound tracks (C) and the playhead (B).

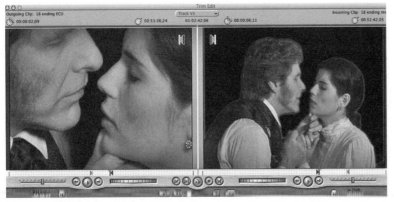

Figure 20-16 Most of your editing tasks can be accomplished right from the timeline, including trimming, which is a tool that allows for precise, one frame adjustments to the end of the outgoing shot (left) and the beginning of the incoming shot (right).

The Canvas (FCP) or Composer Monitor (Avid)

Wherever the timeline playhead rests, that frame of video is viewable in the FCP **canvas** (or composer monitor on an AVID). The canvas is where you watch your sequence to see how your shots are holding together. You can move through the sequence in real time by using the **transport control buttons** at the bottom of the window, or scroll through in slow motion (forward and backward) with the **shuttle control**, or frame-by-frame with the **jog control wheel**. Or you can drag the playhead with the mouse to move around the sequence extremely quickly. The playhead in the canvas window is a duplicate of the playhead in the timeline window (**Figure 20-17**). Notice that the viewer window (**Figure 20-14**) has all of the same playback controls for viewing clips.

In addition to the four main windows, there are other auxiliary windows that you can include on your desktop if you need them for convenience' sake. The two most common are the **sound levels window**, to monitor your sound as you lay down audio, and the timeline **toolbar window**, which allows you to access timeline tools and various edit modes with the click of your mouse (**Figure 20-18**).

Figure 20-17 The Final Cut Pro canvas includes transport control buttons (A); a shuttle control slider (B) and a jog control wheel (C) allowing you to view your footage at practically any speed you desire.

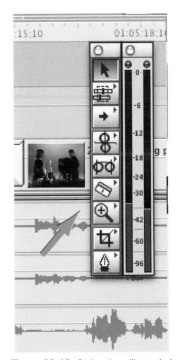

Figure 20-18 Optional auxiliary windows include the sound levels window and the timeline toolbar window (arrow).

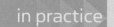

Summary: The Four Basic NLE Windows

1. Browser/bin: This is where you store and organize your editing elements; video clips, audio clips, and graphics files and sequences.
2. Viewer window: This is where you preview clips and determine edit parameters for your shots.
3. Timeline: This is where you edit and arrange your shots and sound tracks to create a sequence.
4. Canvas: This is where you view and move through the sequence.

■ **Figure 20-19** Many functions can be accomplished in multiple ways. For example, you can set in- and out-points on the keyboard (left) through a menu (middle) or by clicking icons.

Menu, Icon, or Keyboard: Take Your Pick

One thing you'll discover on all NLE systems is that there are usually *three* ways of doing exactly the same thing. You can find any given command inside pulldown menus or you can trigger the same command by clicking an icon on the desktop, or you can use a keyboard shortcut for the same action. For example, setting in- and out-points in the viewer can be accomplished three ways: by hitting the "i" or "o" button on the keyboard, by clicking on the *mark in/mark out* icons on the viewer window, or by scrolling down the "mark" menu to the "mark in" or "mark out" command (Figure 20-19). You don't need to memorize all three ways of doing every task. If you don't like to take your fingers off the keyboard, then learn the keyboard shortcuts; if you're a mouse person who loves to click on icons, learn what the icon symbols stand for; if your brain organizes the world through lists and menus, then use the pulldown menus; or, if you're like me, and like to mix it up, then go that way. I use the keyboard for some functions (setting in- and out-points) and icons for others (taking an edit). In short, customize your process, find the easiest and fastest route (for you) for each function and ignore the alternatives!

That said, there are two special keyboard functions that are extremely handy to know:

1. The J, K, and L buttons are universal, transport control buttons. J is play/reverse, K is pause, and L is play/forward. Pressing J and L multiple times (up to four) increases or decreases the play speed from normal speed (one press) to 2× to 4× to 8× (four presses) (Figure 20-20).
2. The **command** + **Z** keystroke combination instantly undoes your last action. Inevitably, as you edit, you will click a wrong icon or drag and drop something where it doesn't belong, or accidentally delete an entire sequence. Well, if you've made a

■ **Figure 20-20** Some keyboard shortcuts, like the J, K, and L buttons for playing footage, can be extremely helpful.

mistake, simply hit command-Z, and voilà!—all is forgiven and put back where it was before your little blunder. I've often wished for a command-Z function in the less technological areas of life, but alas most things are not so easily undone.

Making a Simple Edit

The more you edit, the more tools, edit modes, and shortcuts you will incorporate into your routine. As I mentioned earlier, the best way to learn software is one function at a time, as the need arises. It only takes cutting a few short films before you have a thorough knowledge of a program's capabilities. However, the place to start, where you'll do the majority of your editing, is using the four basic windows to do simple cuts. Let's go through the process of using the basic windows to make two simple edits.

The moment is from George Racz' *The Miracle* and involves Kate walking to the window of the toy store, seeing a homeless woman digging through the garbage, before Kate is led away from the window by her parents (see line script on p. 89). This scene moves from interior to exterior and includes a POV sequence. For this example, we have already laid down the interior shot of Kate walking to the window (#1a). The next shot is of Kate, from outside, watching the homeless woman (#2a).

1. *View and evaluate the shot.* In your bin (within the browser window), locate the shot you wish to cut into the film (Kate looking outside, scene #2a) and click on it. The entire clip will be loaded into the viewer. If the clip includes sync sound, then both sound and image will be loaded. Play through the clip a few times to determine what portion of the longer shot (the camera take) you will edit into the film at this moment. When you have a sense for where you want the shot to start and end, set an in-point by using the mark in-point button (or by hitting the "i" key on the keyboard) and an out-point by using the mark out-point button (or by hitting the "o" key on the keyboard).

2. *Make the edit.* Once the parameters of the shot have been established, you can simply drag the shot from the viewer window into the timeline and place it where you'd like it (**Figure 20-21**). Again, if the shot includes sync sound, you will simultaneously be dragging and adding two tracks, the picture track and the sync audio track. This drag-and-drop editing approach is used primarily for simply putting one shot after another. In this case, we simply drop the shot after the previous (interior) shot of Kate walking to the window. But, again, you can "take" this edit in other ways (keyboard or menu), as you'll see in the next cut.

3. *Evaluate the edit.* Play through your timeline and watch your edit in the canvas window. How does the shot work with the other shots in the sequence? Is it right? Does it belong there? How is the rhythm? Perhaps the shot is great, but the precise edit point, where the two shots meet, is a little off and needs adjusting. Adjusting

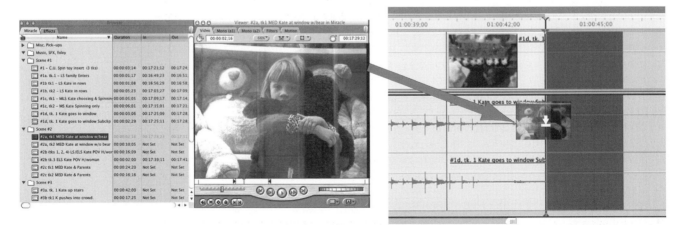

■ **Figure 20-21** Simple edits can be accomplished by choosing your clip from the bin (left) setting your in- and out-points in the canvas (middle) and drag-and-dropping the clip image into your timeline (right).

Figure 20-22 When you place your playhead on an edit point and enter trim mode (1), you will get two windows that show the very last frame of the outgoing shot and the very first frame of the incoming shot (2) allowing you to adjust the precise frames of the cut.

the out- and in-points of adjacent shots from within the timeline is called **trimming** (Figure 20-22).

4. *Fine-tune the edit.* Enter **trim mode**, and trim the edit points of either or both shots. In trim mode you can add or subtract one, five, or ten frames at a time. At first, trim mode can be tricky, but with a little practice, this tool becomes the editor's primary implement for fine-tuning edits. Trim mode is one of the most powerful features introduced by digital nonlinear editing.

The Three-Point Edit

Now, the next shot we want to cut in is Kate's POV shot for the sequence: Kate's looking shot (#2a) → POV of homeless person (#2b) → Kate's reaction (#2a). Although the edited sequence consists of three shots, Kate's looking and reaction shots are originally only one shot, with the POV inserted and splitting it in two (see marked script p. 89). For this sort of edit, dragging and dropping isn't accurate enough. We need to perform a very common cut called the **three-point edit**, in which three in- and out-points (two on the source material and one in the timeline, or vice versa) determine the cut.

As usual, we find the POV shot in the bin and click on it to bring it up in the viewer. After deciding on the in- and out-points, we turn to the timeline and position (or **park**) the playhead on the precise point where we want to insert the POV shot, which will be in the middle of the looking shot, and we mark an in-point on the timeline (Figure 20-23). When we click on the "insert edit" icon, the shot will be inserted at that exact frame in the timeline, pushing everything after the in-point down the timeline. We now have Kate's looking shot, next to the POV shot, followed by her reaction. Again, you can go into trim mode to finesse where each of the three shots begins and ends in relation to the shots immediately adjacent.

These two sample edits pretty much describe the predominant cutting routine for editing any movie. As I mentioned before, there are many other tools, functions, and capabilities in your software with which you will no doubt become familiar as you use it.

■ **Figure 20-23** Inserting a shot with a typical three point edit. Mark the in- and out-points of the shot you wish to cut in (1); mark the in-point on the timeline where you wish to place that shot (2) and click on "insert edit" to make the edit (3). Notice how the long take (along with its sync audio) has been split by the newly inserted POV shot. (right).

■ THE EDITING STAGES

You know you've achieved perfection in design,
Not when you have nothing more to add,
But when you have nothing more to take away.

Antoine de Saint-Exupéry

The editing process is one that has become somewhat standardized over time, yet remains extremely flexible to fit the scale of the specific project and the working preferences of the editor. A large-budget Hollywood film has no trouble shooting 500,000 feet of 35mm film, and features shot on DV, where scene coverage is extreme and the attitude "it's only tape," can easily generate well over 100 hours of footage to wade through, consider, evaluate, and edit. Because of the volume of material and the cost of production, most commercial feature film editors begin cutting during the shooting of the film. As the dailies come back from the lab, the editor immediately starts reviewing footage and cutting scenes. This way, if there are serious holes in the coverage of scenes, the director can re-shoot while the cast, crew, and equipment are still assembled. In this sense, to call editing a "postproduction" process is a bit of a misnomer. Yes, it deals with material that emerges from the production process, but it also often commences along with production.

Short narrative films, on the other hand, have much less footage, especially when shot on film. And since low budgets tend to reduce the number of shooting days, the amount of footage generated is manageable and there is no time to edit along the way. Add to this that short films, especially student films, are often directed and edited by the same person. So, editing on shorts tends to truly be a postproduction process, starting once the shooting is over.

In either case, whether you're dealing with 100 hours of raw footage and a team of editors cutting scenes while the film is in production, or just 10 minutes of footage being cut by the director, after the shooting stops, the process is somewhat similar.

Viewing Dailies

The total footage that is the result of your production process, whether you're shooting on DV or film, is your **raw footage**. Raw footage is also known as **dailies**, especially when

in practice

When shooting *Bamboozled* (2000), Director Spike Lee and his D.P. Ellen Kuras usually had three MiniDV cameras, shooting from different angles, running at the same time. The MiniDV format was used for the "real world" sections of the film, which constitute nearly 90% of the movie, while the television broadcast segments were photographed on Super 16mm film. In one scene, in which the Mantan TV show is filmed along with the live studio audience reactions, Lee and Kuras had fifteen cameras running simultaneously: three Super 16mm film cameras and twelve DV camcorders. The scene coverage on *Bamboozled* was staggering; there were over 100 hours of footage to consider. This is where editor Sam Pollard's experience editing documentary films, which routinely generate much more footage than narrative films, came in handy. Also, Pollard started editing the day after the first day of shooting, meaning he sifted through and logged the raw footage, selected and narrowed down the potential shots he would use, and edited quick rough cuts of scenes, in an effort to remain on top of the avalanche of footage.

■ **Figure 20-24** For *Bamboozled* (2000) Director Spike Lee always had multiple camas running, generating an enormous amount of footage for editor Sam Pollard to work with.

lab processing is involved. The term "dailies" comes from the early vernacular of Hollywood studio productions, where film was shot on one day, processed overnight, and viewed the next day, so that any reshoots could be undertaken before the set was taken down. It still works that way in commercial film, only now, with digital editing, it's not only raw footage being viewed, but rough cuts of scenes as well. If you're shooting on film, what comes back from the film lab after processing are **video dailies**, which are the processed footage transferred to DV.

Viewing dailies means watching your footage for the first time and evaluating each and every camera take for exposures, composition, scene coverage, and performance. This should be done on the highest quality monitor (or projection) you can find so that your image is as clear and true as possible. As you view your dailies, take detailed notes on which shots are great, called **selects**, which shots simply don't work, called **outtakes**, and which shots have some portion that can be used. Selects, which have an abundance of great material for editing, are naturally marked for downloading by noting the roll and timecode information for the shot. Outtakes, usually early takes of a shot, do not need to be downloaded into the computer. This saves hard drive space and helps with organization and efficiency because you only have what you can use. Still, you should always know where to find your outtakes, just in case you need a piece of one later. It is not unusual to be cutting a scene and remember just a look or a gesture from an outtake that would fit perfectly into the edit. Some shots are neither selects nor outtakes. They are great in one part, but lacking in another. These shots are marked for downloading, too, but notes should be made about what you liked about them and what wasn't working.

Viewing dailies can be an emotional experience. All of the effort, struggles, victories, and tears from the production process are in that footage, yet a filmmaker needs to detach themselves from what went on during the shoot and watch the footage as objectively as possible. You need to keep reminding yourself that no one in the audience will know what went into making these shots; no one knows what's just out of the frame or how you struggled or how much money you spent or how ingenious you were to get that shot. Only the image on the screen counts and that is exactly what you need to evaluate when you watch dailies. Often, when I mention to a student that a particular shot simply isn't working, I hear the response "But it took me all day to get that damned shot so it's got to be in the film!"

In addition to this, it's easy to succumb to the "daily blues," which is a sort of letdown feeling you can have viewing your raw footage. You've put so much time, effort, and

Figure 20-25 The log and capture window allows you to see the clip you are capturing (1) and log each one with pertinent information, like the scene and take numbers, (2) as you go.

money into production, that you'd like to sit down and just watch your movie! But it's not a movie yet. It's still in pieces and there's a lot of work yet to be done. The "daily blues" happens to me every time. The footage never looks quite as good as I thought it would, and everything seems lifeless and flat. But then, once I start editing, and the individual shots start connecting and talking to other images, and the sound track adds its alchemical dimension, the story and emotions start to emerge from the edited sequences, and my original excitement returns as the film starts to become what I thought it might be at the very beginning.

Capturing and Logging

Once you've settled on all of your useable footage, you need to get it into the computer environment to edit. In fact, all other film elements you plan to use in the film—music, sound effects, graphics, etc.—need to be put into the computer for editing. This process is called **capturing**. Capturing turns your raw elements from whatever format into media files that the NLE software can work with. Capturing your footage is usually done with a DV deck via a firewire cable. All nonlinear editing software has a **capture mode** that will control the external deck (**external device control**) from the computer interface. Before you capture, it's important to set a single destination for your media files (called a **capture scratch file** in Final Cut Pro) or you run the risk of spraying footage throughout your system and ultimately losing some.

As you capture, you will also be **logging** your footage, which involves labeling your clips, adding descriptive information, and organizing clips into bins (Figure 20-25). Taking some time at this stage to put your materials in order will save a lot of searching for clips during the editing stage. Generally, bins are organized such that you have one bin per scene that contains all the video and audio clips necessary for editing that particular scene. The bins themselves are then organized in the scene order as they appear in the movie.

There are three ways you can capture footage: **clip capture**, **capture now**, or **batch capture**:

1. *Clip capture.* As you view your DV tape, you can pause to set in- and out-points to determine where you'd like the capture to begin and end, and then execute the clip capture. This will give you one media file in your hard drive and one **master clip** (that references the media file) to label and place in your bin. You can capture one take at a time (and label them by their scene and take number) or you can capture multiple takes (or even an entire tape) and split them up later into sub-clips (see Figure 20-12). **Sub-clips** are smaller clips that reference master clips, which in turn reference media files. Be careful, however: if you lose your master clip, then you lose your associated sub-clips.
2. *Capture now.* As you play your footage from the DV tape, you can simply hit the "capture now" button and download your footage "on the fly," and then hit the space bar to end the capture. This method is fast, but can be inaccurate and often leads to disorganized bins. However, you can use this function if your input deck is not controllable by the software preventing you from entering in- and out-points (if you want to capture footage from a standard VHS deck, for example). Capture now can also be used to download "live" video, streaming into the computer.
3. *Batch capture.* With this method, you can create bins and log all of your select clips first, naming shots and entering the in and out timecode numbers for each clip from the DV tape. Then with the "batch capture" command, the editing software takes over and

automates the entire capture process. It shuttles to the cue points, captures, and moves on to the next shot on the tape. If there are multiple tapes, the computer will prompt you to insert the next tape when the previous one is finished. This method saves time on the editing system but requires that you compile the timecode numbers for your selects as you view dailies. Batch capture is especially useful if, for some reason, you lose or need to delete your original media files from the hard drive after you've already captured your shots. In this case, your clip information (pointers to media, remember?) still contains the tape number and timecode information for every shot. So, you simply choose the clips and batch capture the media back onto the hard drive (Figure 20-26).

	Name		Timecode	Duration	In
▼	roll 1				
	7 A CU "blight"		00:08:06;16	00:00:04:02	00:09:12;29
	10 (?) pick up CU		00:26:13;20	00:00:00;01	Not Set
	10 A WS w/ plant etc.		00:24:52;01	00:00:03;25	00:25:12;09
	10 B CU hands		00:25:40;23	00:00:16;25	Not Set
	10 B CU hands1		00:26:00;25	00:00:13;05	Not Set
	7 J coat off-leave		00:16:06;19	00:00:18;15	00:16:18;11
	7 B "blight"		00:04:20;15	00:00:39;00	Not Set
	7 B bis "blight"		00:06:49;01	00:00:06;11	00:07:12;06
	7 C bis m w/ apparat WS		00:00:07;06	00:00:11;12	00:00:14;10
	7 C m w/ apparatus WS		00:17:14;03	00:00:07;11	00:17:51;01
	7 C/ 1 dropper CU		00:01:20;17	00:00:12;20	00:02:24;17

■ **Figure 20-26** In Final Cut Pro, clips that have had the original media files deleted appear in your bin with a red slash. It's an easy procedure to chose all clips that have lost their media and batch capture new media without re-logging the clips.

One additional note about capturing: always remember to capture more footage at the beginning and end of every clip than you think you'll need for the actual edited shots. This will give you room for trimming and transitions like dissolves. These extra seconds are called **handles**. If you capture entire camera takes—from "Action!" to Cut!"—then you'll have all the handles you need.

If the footage you're capturing is single-system DV footage, or if you shot film and had the lab sync your dailies for you, then both sound and picture are captured in sync at this stage. However, if you shot film or double-system DV and planned to sync the footage yourself in the NLE system, then you must capture the image (from DV tapes) and sound (from original recording media) individually, creating separate clips and media files. You will then need to perform one extra step before you can start editing: syncing dailies manually.

First Assembly Edit

The **assemble edit** means placing end-to-end all the shots of a scene, or a sequence of scenes, or even an entire short film, without selecting too precisely the parameters of each shot. The shots are slapped in "very fat" without any finessing. The assemble edit is your first opportunity to see the broad strokes of the general order of the shots, to get a sense of the relationships between scenes and to get a feel for the overall flow of the story. Because it's like a preliminary sketch, rearranging shots and scenes is quick and simple and allows you to see various versions without too much effort. During the assemble edit stage you will ask yourself the larger questions of sequencing: How is the story unfolding scene by scene and shot by shot? Do these scenes belong next to each other? How many shots and which shots should I include to cover this scene? It is more efficient to make structural adjustments in this very broad form, than to waste time carefully finding precise edit points and frame-accurate transitions for five consecutive shots, only to discover that they really don't belong in that order at all.

The first assembly is a first draft. When you first put an assembly together, you put in everything the director shot. You don't try to give it too much shape yet. Then, you attack it in the second cut. So, it's like a first draft of someone's writing.

Thelma Schoonmaker (editor, *Raging Bull, Goodfellas, The Aviator*) (From *MovieMaker*, Vol. 5, Issue #2)

Syncing Dailies in a Digital Edit System

The procedure for syncing dailies is very simple and uses the basic edit interface windows we explained earlier. Syncing dailies takes a little time at first, but once you get the hang of it, it's quick and easy. For each sync take you will be working with the two related clips, the sound clip and the image clip, and the all-important slate, so you must be sure to capture the slating in all of your sync clips (Figure 20-27).

1. Open the image clip in the viewer and, using the jog control wheel, find the exact frame where the clapper arm on the slate closes. Place a marker on that frame with the **marker button**. A marker is not an in-/out-point: it just tags a specific frame, the way a bookmark marks a page. Finally, drag the video clip into an empty timeline sequence.

2. Open the corresponding sound clip. You will see a sound wave representing the audio on that clip. If you have shot on film, at 24 fps, then you'll need to compensate for the speed slowdown of the telecine 3:2 pulldown process (see p. 355). With the "modify speed" command, simply enter 99.9% and the clip will be slowed down the required 0.01% to match the image (see Figure 10-10). Now, find the exact point on the timeline with the "clap" sound of the clapper arm meeting the slate. You will also be able to see a drastic peak in the sound wave at this point. **Audio scrub**, which allows you to hear frame-by-frame audio as you drag the viewer playhead, is a helpful tool here. Again, place a marker at the "clap" point and drag the clip into the timeline audio track just below the image.

3. Slide the video clip until the two markers are lined up. Make sure the **snap** function is on, which will line the markers up with a snap when they are brought close to each other. When the markers are perfectly aligned, the clips are in sync, but can still easily be moved out of sync.

4. The next step is to choose the two tracks and, using the **link** command, to merge them together. Link simply associates the two tracks as one **merged clip**. You can now drag the new synced and linked clip back into the browser window. You should create a separate bin for your synced clips to distinguish them from the unsynced sound and video clips as you proceed.

5. Once you have created new, synced clips (that point to the original media files) you can delete the unsynced clips, to avoid confusion.

6. Voilà! Now you're ready to edit!

■ **Figure 20-27** The marker button (1) is extremely helpful for lining up the slate closing frame with the slate closing sound (bottom arrows) when syncing dailies.

Rough Cuts

Once you've laid down the general structure off the film, it's time to dive into the individual scenes to rearrange, add, eliminate, split, or trim footage to make each scene work on its own. A **rough cut** is a version of the film in which all scenes have been edited fairly tightly, but usually with the blunter tools available in the edit system, like straight cuts instead of other transitions effects. Rough cuts are edited with picture track and the essential audio

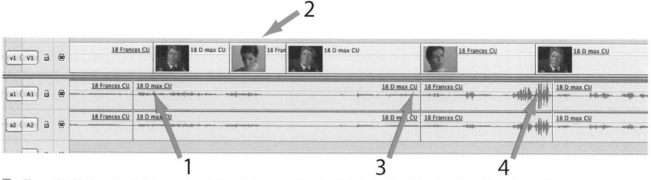

■ **Figure 20-28** A variety of dialogue edits within a single scene. Sound cuts in before the picture in a J-cut (1), an insert edit simply places an image over the ongoing sound of a shot (2), sound and picture cut at the same time in a straight cut (3), and picture cuts in before sound in an L-cut (4).

tracks only. For example, if your scenes involve extensive sync sound dialogue, then you should be editing picture and dialogue; if your film has no dialogue, but instead a music sound track throughout, then you'll cut picture to the music; if voice-over is a major component of a sequence, then you'll need to lay that down on the audio track and cut to it. Usually, you will cut several rough edits of your movie, tightening and improving the film with each version. Remember, the idea here is not to spend too much time on the ultrafine points until you know absolutely that all of the cuts are just right.

Cutting Dialogue

If your film involves extensive dialogue, then you will probably start to cut audio during this stage as well. Remember, all of our film elements, audio and video, are on separate tracks and can be edited and manipulated independently. Therefore, sync audio does not necessarily need to remain with the corresponding images. When editing picture and dialogue there are three basic cutting techniques: the straight cut, the split edit, and the insert cut (**Figure 20-28**).

As the name suggests, the **straight cut** cuts the picture and sound on the same frame. When the picture cuts to another image, the sound cuts as well. When using straight cuts for dialogue, we go from one person speaking to the other speaking, then back to the first person speaking, etc., as in the example in **Figure 20-29**. This sort of back-and-forth dialogue cutting has a certain rhythm that can be effective at times, but in most instances the predictable edits, always coming between lines of dialogue, are too monotonous to use for an entire scene.

Ruth, there's one more thing I need to say: I love you.	No, no you don't really love me.	But I do, with all my heart and soul!	You're just in love with the idea of being in love.

■ **Figure 20-29** A scene with all straight cuts on dialogue has a very predictable pattern and rhythm.

Split edits (also called **L-cuts** and **J-cuts**) are edits in which the transition from one image to the other happens at a different time than the transition in the audio track. In an **L-cut**, the picture cuts to the next shot first, and the audio cuts occur later. The **J-cut** is the opposite: the audio cuts out first, while the picture plays a bit longer before cutting to the next shot. The timing of these edits—how many frames or seconds to displace the cut in image versus the cut in audio—depends on a number of factors, some creative and some practical. Split edits are used frequently in dialogue scenes to produce smooth edits that are practically invisible.

Beyond invisibility, however, split edits are an essential technique for dialogue editing and play an important role in establishing the internal rhythm of an encounter, in the dramatic timing of reactions, and in the construction of character point of view, which are all key storytelling considerations. Holding the camera on a character's face, a few seconds longer as someone else speaks, can communicate a strong sense of point of view in the scene; likewise, cutting to someone on just the right word is a juxtaposition that can make powerful, subtextual, and emotional associations.

An **insert cut** involves completely disconnecting either the sync audio or video from its original linked clip and inserting it over a shot that is continuous. This is commonly done with reaction shots where you wish to continue one person's dialogue during the reaction of the other person and then return to the image of the first person talking. All that's needed in this case is the image of person #2 laid over the dialogue. Conversely, you can insert someone else's dialogue only, without ever cutting to their image.

Most films liberally combine J-cuts, L-cuts, and insert cuts even within the same scene. Figure 20-30 is an example of three additional versions of the melodramatic scene, with exactly the same dialogue, but cut using various dialogue editing options in order to alter the tone and POV of the dramatic moment. Bob and Ruth are coworkers out for lunch and Bob takes the opportunity to announce that he's in love with Ruth. As you can see with these simple illustrations, dialogue editing can have a substantial impact on the shaping of performances and the interpretation of a scene. The first version (Figure 20-29), using only straight cuts when each person speaks, presents the moment in a rather neutral way. The second version (Figure 20-30 A) allows two moments where Ruth reacts while Bob delivers his most ardent lines. The L-cut in particular brings Ruth in at a crucial moment ("I love you"), giving her a great moment for a reaction. This dialogue edit announces that Ruth's reaction is more important than Bob's proclamation and therefore draws the audience into a closer identification with Ruth, who clearly does not share Bob's feelings. The third version (Figure 20-30 B) draws us closer to Bob's POV, who now gets to respond to what Ruth is saying. The last insert, in particular, leaves us with Bob's forlorn reaction at the end of the scene. The final version (Figure 20-30 C) is all Ruth's POV: not only does she get that strong L-cut reaction on "I love you," but Ruth also gets the rest of the scene, in a close-up, and we get to watch her struggle with Bob's declaration of love.

■ **Figure 20-30** Dialogue editing. These three versions of the same scene illustrate how simple J-cuts, L-cuts, and inserts provide an editor with a great deal of control over the POV and emotional impact of a scene.

On a more practical note, for split edits to work in a continuity style scene, you need to make sure your actors don't step on each other's lines during the shooting. Also, split edits are frequently used to fine-tune continuity edits, especially when cutting to match action, or to hide continuity errors altogether. While the dialogue may cut perfectly on a particular point, the gesture in the video track might not exactly match, so simply trimming only the video a few frames earlier or later than the audio cut might just give you either the perfect action match or the ability to avoid the problematic movement all together.

Rough cuts are where you spend the majority of your time and creative thinking. There is a lot of cutting and recutting during this stage as you discover the final style, shape, order, and rhythm of your movie. And as you edit, you become intimately familiar with every frame of your footage. Because of this, new ideas will emerge as you notice details, rhythms, and connections between shots. Experimenting with different juxtapositions will reveal the full potential of your footage over the course of the editing process.

However, be careful: familiarity can also be a liability when you start seeing things in the footage or assuming information in a sequence that a first-time viewer would never be aware of. For example, it happens with some frequency that a student will screen a film that, let's say, includes a conversation between two people, with the scene consisting entirely of close-ups. The audience will become disoriented, wondering where this scene is taking place. The response of the director/editor is usually something like "They were in her father's house. Didn't you see the yellow walls behind her head? That was the same house as in the first scene!" The fact is no, we didn't notice the yellow walls. While the director/editor, who knows the script and has seen the footage a million times, can immediately match the wall color between two disparate scenes, we, drawn in by the close-ups, looked at faces, not walls. The editing did not establish the location because it all seemed clear enough to the editor. By the same token I have seen students struggle for hours to fix a teeny-tiny continuity problems, which no one watching the film would ever notice.

One remarkable skill that all great editors share is the ability to step back and look at the footage and sequences with fresh eyes—the way an audience will experience it in a theater. It's also important to show rough cuts to selected people for a fresh perspective and to get some constructive criticism while you are editing and can do something about it. It's better to have a few people raise red flags during the rough-cut stage than to have a theater full of confusion at your premiere.

The Fine Cut and Picture Lock

Once you're happy with the basic editing of your film, and all of the sequences are working the way you need them to work, and you've determined that there will be no more big changes to the film, now you can start to fine-tune the rough cut. **The fine cut** involves finessing all of the edits one-by-one; it's the time to make those small edit adjustments to, for instance, get that cut on action just right, or add the dissolve between two scenes, or trim a few frames off a POV shot to get the timing of the reaction just perfect. The fine cut is also where we make final decisions concerning effects and transitions. Although you can preview many effects while you edit, like fades and dissolves, most need to be rendered before you can output them to your master. **Rendering** is the process of combining the video and audio with the applied effect to create a new media file. For example, a dissolve involves a slow fade-in of the incoming shot simultaneously with the slow fade-out of the outgoing shot. We can see two images super-

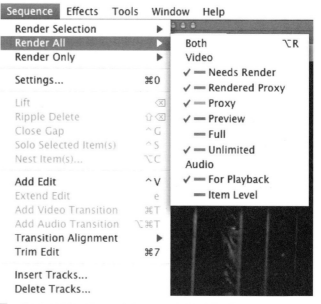

Figure 20-31 The rendering menu in Final Cut Pro.

imposed for the duration of the dissolve. But there is no actual media like this, so, by rendering, the edit system creates this media. It's most efficient to render during the fine-cutting stage after you've decided on the type and duration of your effects, and when you can simply render all of the effects on any single track at the same time (Figure 20-31).

This stage is also where you begin to add additional sound tracks (like sound effects, music, etc.) and get the film into it's final form. Once the film is perfect, and all of the creative editing decisions are done, and you've decide you will not trim a single frame more, you have arrived at **picture lock**.

Finishing

Picture lock does not mean all of the creative the work is over, however. The film still needs finishing, which means that you turn your attention to two areas, the sound design and color correction. Once all of the images are locked in place and the film has been edited to the essential sound track(s), you can then start to do the serious work of building the broader sound design, which includes adding music, sound effects, and ambience tracks, which will ultimately lead to the mixing down of all of the audio tracks into one mixed track. The sound design for a film is a major creative endeavor and I have devoted an entire chapter to the art and craft of postproduction sound (see Chapter 22).

Color correction is another area of the finishing process. **Color correction** is the process of tweaking the tonalities and exposures in each scene for balance and consistency and to polish the final visual impression of the film. Digital editing systems like Final Cut Pro and Avid are becoming increasingly sophisticated in their color correction capabilities. For most short and low-budget films finishing on tape, there is more than enough power to make your final adjustments within your editing system. If you are finishing on film, however, the color correction is done by the film lab. Color correction for film prints and video masters will be covered in more detail in Chapter 24.

Mastering

The final step in the editing process is to master the film. This means outputting the final film to a sturdy, archivally sound digital form from which distribution copies can be made. While most NLE systems offer a wide range of output options, you will, no doubt, want to master to a format that does not involve any video data compression. The robust DV tape formats, like DVCPRO and DVCAM, are recommended over standard MiniDV, but MiniDV is certainly sufficient for most introductory film projects. If your computer has a DVD burner, you can master to DVD, but DVDs have limited data space (typically 4 GB), and if your project exceeds that space, you will be forced to compress the image. This means image compromises, which is never a good option for a project master. Also, the jury is still out concerning the robustness and longevity of recordable DVDs.

Think!

Everything we've discussed so far has revolved around the process and even the technology of editing, but I have saved discussing the most essential part of the editing process for last—creative thinking, imagining how the film will hold together, thinking about how one shot will work next to another shot. This is not something you do with your fingers on a keyboard or something that is saved for one specific moment in the process. Imagining the way the story will reveal itself and the way the film will play out on the screen is something that is done, as one of my students said, with the "technology of the mind."

In his book "In The Blink of an Eye," editor Walter Murch devotes a chapter to figuring out how much time he (and his editing associates) actually spent *physically* cutting Coppola's *Apocalypse Now*. His calculations included the number of days the editors worked divided by the number of cuts in the finished film. The rate of cuts, per editor for each 12-hour day, came out to 1.47. He then goes on to figure that for each cut in the film, there were probably five "shadow splices" that were cuts that were undone. His conclusion?

Since it takes under ten seconds to make one-and-a-half splices, the admittedly special case of Apocalypse Now serves to throw into exaggerated relief that fact that editing—even on a "normal" film—is not so much a putting together as it is a discovery of a path, and that the overwhelming majority of an editor's time is not spent actually splicing film.

[T]he remaining eleven hours and fifty-eight minutes of each working day were spent in activities that, in their various ways, served to clear and illuminate the path ahead of us: screenings, discussions, rewinding, re-screenings, meetings, scheduling, filing trims, note-taking, bookkeeping and lot of plain deliberative thought.

Walter Murch (From *In The Blink of an Eye*)

What Murch is telling us is that, like all other aspects of filmmaking, the creative work of the editor is not about the technology, it's about the ideas and the imagination, which are then expressed through the technology. Interestingly, he reminds us that all of those seemingly mundane, organizational tasks, like logging and bookkeeping, have their role in allowing us to think, consider, and reflect.

Murch also makes the point that making an actual cut on film takes no time at all, and this is doubly true in the digital age. It's so easy to perform many editing procedures these days that we run the risk of confusing the creative task of the editor, which takes time, with the practical task of making a cut, which takes no time at all. Sam Pollard expressed it this way in an interview with Jennifer M. Wood (*MovieMaker,* Vol. 3, Issue #4):

What's happened now with the digital medium, because everything can be done so fast, is that people don't have the tendency to understand that editing is really about what you think—not about what you do physically. It's really how you think in terms of conceptualizing the way a sequence should unfold, particularly when you're cutting documentary footage. How the sequence should build structurally—it's a real thinking process. To me that's the one downside to digital technology. People are so impatient now and things are on TV so quickly, there's no opportunity to think.

An editor should never lose sight of the fact that "why" we make an edit is much more important than "how" we make an edit. This is as important and powerful a question as "why put the camera here, instead of there," or "why use this lens, instead of that lens," or "why cast this person in the role instead of that person." In the next chapter we'll look at the "why" of it, the creative and storytelling dimension of the art of editing.

Editing Stages Summary

1. *Viewing dailies:* All of the footage must be reviewed, evaluated, and logged. This is done on a high-quality playback system.
2. *Capturing:* All useable footage (and other project elements) are downloaded into the computer for editing.
3. *First assembly:* Scenes and sequences are loosely arranged to determine general scene sequencing and story structure.
4. *Rough cuts:* Scenes are cut and recut, progressively tightening the film.
5. *Fine cut:* Transitions, small edit adjustments, and additional sound tracks are added to finesse the movie into its final form.
6. *Picture lock:* The film is ready for finishing, after all creative editing decisions are done and not another frame will be added or subtracted.
7. *Finishing:* The various tracks in the sound design are mixed down into one track and the picture is corrected for color and exposure consistency (see Chapter 23 for mixing, Chapter 24 for color correction).
8. *Mastering:* The final film is outputted to tape or DVD for mastering (see Chapter 24 for mastering).

The NLE Project Structure
Media Elements

- ***Original Media***—Your media elements *before* they are brought into the NLE environment for editing. This includes your original DV tapes (e.g., DV footage or telecine transfer footage), music or sound-effects CDs, and graphic files from third-party software (e.g., Photoshop or Illustrator files).
- ***Media Files***—The media that is created when you capture video or audio from the original source, including video and audio. In FCP the video format is QuickTime, and in the Avid system video is saved as .omf files. The standard audio format for both is AIFF (.aif). Media files can also be text, photos, or graphics imported from other software applications. Media files are saved on an external HD.
- ***Render Files***—Media files that are created by the NLE system from rendering special effects (like dissolves, superimpositions, motion effects, etc.).

Editing Elements (in project window/ browser)

- ***Master Clips***—A master clip references the media file. Clips are trimmed, altered, and manipulated during the edit session, but since they are only "pointers" to the media file, all edit decisions occur only virtually, leaving the media unaltered.

- ***Sub-clips***—Smaller clips made from, and referencing, the master clip. Sub-clips do not reference the media file; if you delete the master clip you will lose the sub-clip information and it will not play.
- ***Sequences***—The edited sequence of video, audio, and graphic clips arranged in the order you need to tell your story. Clips used in the sequence are essentially "edited copies" of the information from the master clip, known as "associated clips," and therefore directly reference the media files. If you delete a master clip, the associated clip within the sequence will play nonetheless. Your movie can comprise only one long sequence or you can create multiple sequences and bring them together later. Multiple sequences can also be used to edit various versions.

Organizational Elements

- ***Project***—A top-level folder (located in the project/browser window) that includes all of the elements of the movie, including sequences, bins, clips, and graphics.
- ***Bins***—Second-level folders that are used to organize all audio and video clips and graphic files. You can create as many bins as you need to organize your footage.

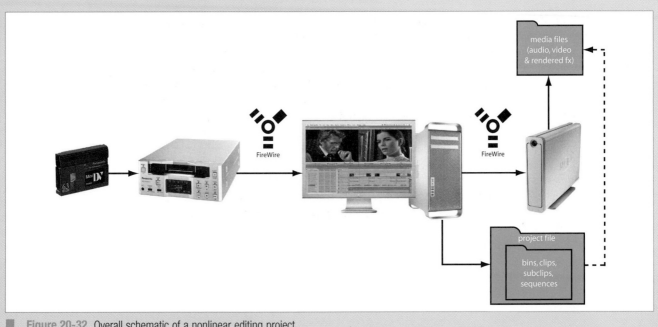

media files
(audio, video
& rendered fx)

FireWire   FireWire

project file

bins, clips,
subclips,
sequences

■ Figure 20-32 Overall schematic of a nonlinear editing project.

The Art and Technique of Editing

For my style, for my vision of cinema, editing is not simply one aspect; it is the aspect.
Orson Wells (From *Cahiers du Cinéma*, n°84, 1958)

As an editor, you decide the meaning the spectator is going to get from the combination of pictures and sounds you give. Film [is not] a film until it is edited and that's so important you almost don't see it.
Mathilde Bonnefoy (editor, *Run, Lola, Run*) [From *Edgecodes.com: The Art of Motion Picture Editing* (2004; directed by A. Shuper)]

I love editing. I think I like it more than any other phase of filmmaking. If I wanted to be frivolous, I might say that everything that precedes editing is merely a way of producing film to edit. Editing is the only unique aspect of filmmaking which does not resemble any other art form—a point so important it cannot be overstressed. (I know I've already stressed it!) It can make or break a film.
Stanley Kubrick (From *Stanley Kubrick Directs,* by Alexander Walker)

■ WHY WE EDIT I: NARRATIVE ORDER AND EMPHASIS

When I was a student, I remember taking an introductory editing class in which the teacher gave seven students exactly the same batch of found footage (which, in fact, consisted of outtakes from several films). Using the outtakes, each student created a film. It was a surprise to the students that the same footage yielded seven very different films; one was even a comedy, while another was edited as a mystery. Now, as a professor, having seen this phenomenon repeated many times, the range of films that can emerge from the very same footage comes as no surprise at all. The differences between all of those student films, made from the same raw materials, were the result of the conceptual plasticity and creative flexibility of the editing process.

The art of telling of a story, even a verbal or written story, involves carefully ordering the events of that tale, controlling the unfolding information, and elevating certain dramatic details over other, more utilitarian, details. We, as filmmakers, don't just objectively show actions, we narrate, which means interpreting the story through the voice of a storyteller. And much of the filmmaker's voice is located in the domain of the editing process. The primary reason we edit is to tell a particular story in our unique way: to guide the audience to see what we want them to see, to understand what we want them to understand, and at the moment when we want them to see and understand it. And, of course, all of this story manipulation is to get them to feel what we want them to feel.

Although one could write volumes trying to define the art of editing in narrative filmmaking, for the sake of concise definitions we could say that **editing** is the process of selecting, arranging, and assembling the essential visual and sound elements to tell a unique version of the story of the film.

Editing for Story Order

Here is a simple three-shot sequence:

A. Sandra drives up to her house and gets out of her car.
B. Sandra walks to the front door, opens it, and discovers . . .
C. A burglar is in her house stealing her TV!

A   B   C

■ Figure 21-1

These three shots (Figure 21-1), put in this order, tell us the story of Sandra, who comes home one day and discovers a burglar in her house. The film is told strictly from Sandra's point of view, and because of that, we discover the burglary at the same moment she discovers it. It's a shock to all of us, character and audience, when that front door opens.

One of the broader and essential creative considerations in the editing process is **story order**: the shot-by-shot and scene-by-scene connections to the events of the story. The same material can yield very different approaches to the same story, when placed in a different order. Let's reedit the preceding sequence by simply rearranging the order of shots (Figure 21-2).

A. A burglar is in Sandra's house stealing her TV!
B. Sandra drives up to her house and gets out of her car.
C. Sandra walks to the front door, opens it, and discovers the burglar . . .

A   B   C

■ Figure 21-2

This sequence no longer develops strictly from Sandra's point of view. Showing the burglary in progress to the audience, before Sandra herself discovers it, gives the audience more information than Sandra has. And what will the audience do with this information? Well, they will certainly anticipate Sandra stumbling upon the burglary in progress, and we hope that they start to fear for her, to worry about what will happen when she opens that door. This is the essence of suspense: give the audience a little bit more information than the character has so that they anticipate the conflict. Not only has the audience's perspective on the events been completely altered simply by rearranging the same shots, but the emotional effect changes also. In the first sequence the emotional effect is surprise, and in the second it is suspense. Both are powerful, so now the director and editor need to choose which one works best for the story.

Editing for Dramatic Emphasis

Imagine the inside of an empty apartment (Figure 21-3):

LONG SHOT; A man enters the apartment and crosses to a desk. Looking for something, he moves stuff around the desktop, knocks a picture frame over, and then opens a drawer and pulls out a letter. He stuffs it into his pocket and leaves.

Surely we can present this scene in real time—long shot, from one angle, in one single take, with no edits—much the way we would see it in live theater. Some might say that this would be the most democratic way to present the scene, allowing the audience to pick and choose what they wanted to look at and when. Here's one interpretation of the preceding scene (Figure 21-4).

■ Figure 21-3

A. LONG SHOT; A man enters the apartment and crosses to a desk. Looking for something, he moves stuff around the desktop and knocks a picture frame over.

B. CUT TO a MEDIUM CLOSE-UP on the drawer as he opens it, revealing a letter.

C. CUT TO a CLOSE-UP of his face looking at the letter; we can see sweat forming on his anxious brow.

D. We CUT back to the drawer (CU) as his trembling hand enters the frame and slowly takes the letter out.

E. CUT back to our LONG SHOT; the man stuffs the letter into his pocket and leaves.

Cutting into the scene with close-ups at just the right moments creates dramatic emphasis, a moment of discovery, and turns that letter into a LETTER! In addition, the back-to-back close-ups of the man's anxious face and the letter imply a complicated relationship; it may not be explicit, but clearly that letter is of great importance to him and we've already started a mystery. The audience is led to wonder, "What is it with that letter?"

A B C

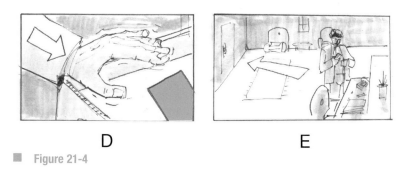

D E

■ Figure 21-4

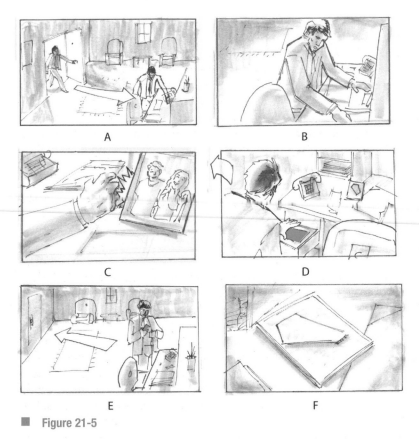

■ Figure 21-5

Now, let's try another interpretation through cutting (Figure 21-5).

A. LONG SHOT; A man enters the apartment and crosses to a desk.

B. CUT to a MEDIUM shot as he moves stuff around the desktop, looking for something.

C. CUT TO a CLOSE-UP of a photograph of him and a beautiful woman; he carelessly knocks over the photo.

D. CUT back to the MEDIUM shot; clearly he hasn't noticed the photo, as he opens the drawer, pulls out a letter, and stuffs it in his pocket.

E. As he leaves the room we CUT back to the CLOSE-UP of the picture frame, tipped over on its face.

Now the scene is no longer about the letter, it's about that photo. We're no longer asking why the man is so anxious about getting that letter; we're asking what it means that he knocked over the photo. We suspect that it will become a clue—someone will know he was here when they notice the photograph knocked out of place. We might even be wondering who that woman is in the photograph.

Beyond the editing, these interpretations obviously also involve slightly different scene coverage, and this is where shooting and editing are absolutely linked. When shooting a scene we must anticipate what the editor will need to create the particular emphasis we are after. This is why the director and D.P. need to "think like editors" on the set—and editing your own films in the beginning will help you understand, in a practical way, what editors need.

> *In telling a story, the task of a director is to emphasize what is significant by under-emphasizing what is less so. The actor's performances, the camera's coverage of the performances and the film editor's re-construction of these during post-production: all are designed to make certain things more significant than others to an audience.*
>
> **Alexander Mackendrick (From *On Filmmaking,* 2004)**

Although Mackendrick is talking about the larger task of the director as storyteller, there is a significant lesson in this quote for the editing stage. Films rely extensively on editing to create those dramatically elevated moments and details. However, you can't have dramatic peaks without a few valleys. Most films have moments that must be elevated through expressive or stylized editing to reveal their true dramatic importance, with, say, a well-timed cut to a close-up, or a series of graphically stunning juxtapositions, or energetically disjunctive jump cuts, or whatever visual acrobatics the scene needs. But all narrative films also have many fairly utilitarian passages that should be cut, simply just to get us from narrative point A to narrative point B efficiently. And then there are those scenes of enormous dramatic importance that acquire their power *without* the intervention of editing. In these cases, the primary dramatic weight is not necessarily carried by the editing, but perhaps instead by the dialogue or the mise-en-scène. These scenes, too, are either cut very simply or, in some cases, not edited at all. Keep in mind that NOT cutting is an editorial decision, too, and it can be a powerful one.

Martin Scorsese's *Raging Bull* (1980) brilliantly illustrates the use of stylized editing, functional editing, and expressive nonediting approaches, all within the same film. Editor Thelma Schoonmaker, a longtime collaborator with Scorsese, won an Academy Award in 1980 for her work on *Raging Bull*, which itself constitutes a complete textbook on editing and sound design.

Stylized editing: "Sugar Ray Robinson, Round 13"

Among the great achievements in cinema for editing (and sound design) is the "Sugar Ray Robinson Round 13" fight scene (Figure 21-6). It stands as a tour de force of rhythm, energy, and raw impact accomplished through editing and sound. This scene is central in the movie, because it is more than a boxing match: it is the moment when LaMotta allows Robinson to savagely beat him as an act of sacrifice and contrition for the violence he has visited on the people he loves, namely his wife Vickie and his brother Joey. In planning the scene, Scorsese looked to the famous "shower" murder sequence in Hitchcock's *Psycho* for inspiration. What he admired about that scene was that "every shot had it's

own energy." Scorsese meticulously storyboarded each and every shot in the fight sequence himself—shot size, movement, and angle. Continuity was not a huge concern for this sequence, as Scorsese said during a filmmaking master class with students: "I wanted every shot to have enough raw energy that we could edit them in any configuration and it would work."

Thelma Schoonmaker worked with that visual energy and employed everything from perfectly matched action edits to intentional jump cuts to convey to the audience what it must feel like to be in a ring with a prizefighter who is trying to knock you out. In her hands, time becomes completely elastic; moments are extended by packing in multiple shots between a raised fist and its crushing blow, yet later a flurry of ferocious punches are cut so quickly that they all seem to land on LaMotta's face within a fraction of a second. Relatively long shots are juxtaposed with images just a few frames long; Schoonmaker duplicates actions and creates jarring edits between radically different angles and different frame rates. Scorsese and Schoonmaker vividly create an altered state in which time

■ Figure 21-6 The speed, power, ferocity and pain as Jake LaMotta (Robert DeNiro) is pummeled by Sugar Ray Robinson (Johnny Barnes) is vividly conveyed through the stylized editing of Thelma Schoonmaker.

itself alternately slows down and abruptly lurches forward. There's pain, numbness, power, brutality, and beauty. The walls spin, punches come out of nowhere; what you thought was up is down. This is precisely the feeling they wanted to convey. Strict adherence to rules of continuity and the 180° line, which organize time and space in a standardized and coherent way, would be antithetical to the chaotic, visceral experience of being in the boxing ring getting your head beaten in.

Simple editing, shot/reverse shot: "Pelham Parkway, 1950"
Earlier in the film, after Jake wins the boxing title from Cerdan, his personal life completely falls apart and he succumbs to jealous paranoia about his wife being unfaithful. One scene (Figure 21-7), which begins innocuously with Jake and his brother trying to get a TV to work, carefully traces the workings of his deluded mind as he falls so deeply into suspicion that he asks his own brother if he's had sex with his wife. This scene is the beginning of a slow burn sequence that culminates, several scenes later, in a violent rage against those who love Jake the most. Here we recognize the point of the scene through the dialogue, which reveals the tangled logic of a dangerously warped mind. The scene is shot and edited in a simple shot/reverse shot structure—starting wide and moving in tighter as the conversation becomes more intense. It adheres to the principles of continuity, maintaining proper looking direction and angles and never once crossing the line of action. Understanding that the dialogue is doing the heavy lifting in the scene, Thelma Schoonmaker knows that the editing doesn't need to be acrobatic, de-

spite the tension and simmering violence, and should simply support the rhythms of this disturbing interrogation.

Unbroken shots: "Dade County Stockade"
Toward the very end of the film, Jake LaMotta's fall from glory is nearly total. He's an overweight has-been, running a tacky nightclub in Florida. He has no friends and has long alienated anyone who once loved him, most importantly Vickie and Joey. He is picked up by the police for allowing a 14-year old girl into his nightclub and is thrown into the Dade County stockade. Totally alone, stuck in a cage, Jake hits rock bottom. The realization of what he is and what he's done overwhelms him and he releases his anger onto himself. Screaming "Why, why, why? . . ." and calling himself "stupid," he ferociously beats his head and fists against the concrete walls of the jail cell (Figure 21-8), inflicting the same physical punishment on himself that he's inflicted on everyone else throughout the film, whether a boxing opponent or family member. When his anger is spent, he collapses onto the jail cell bed and cries, "I'm not an animal." In this devastating scene, a man is realizing that he is an animal, like a raging bull, and Robert De Niro's performance is shattering. The scene lasts for over two minutes and there is only one discrete cut. Knowing that editing would diffuse the power of the scene, Scorsese and Schoonmaker allow the moment to play out, in real time—essentially unbroken. Because the scene is unbroken, the audience becomes not so much viewers, but witnesses to this man's most private and pathetic pain. It's so uncomfortable for the audience that we want to look away; we're begging for a cut to show us

■ Figure 21-7 The unobtrusive editing in the "Pelham Parkway, 1950" scene supports the tension that is simmering in the dialogue.

something else, and we secretly want a little bit of "editing style" as an emotional buffer, reminding us that it's only a movie. We need anything that could take us away from Jake's naked misery. But Scorsese and Schoonmaker don't cut away and they don't flinch; they keep us right in there, in that cell with Jake as he reaches the nadir of his life. We thought it was tough being in the boxing ring with Jake, with all of those punches coming out of nowhere, but the Dade County stockade proves to be much rougher.

■ **Figure 21-8** A good editor also understands when it is more powerful *not* to cut into a scene, as in the "Dade County Stockade" scene (left). Editor Thelma Schoonmaker with Martin Scorsese in the editing room (right).

We have already discussed many of the fundamental shooting and editing patterns in Chapters 3 and 4. It might be helpful to review them again in the context of this editing chapter.

- Shots, sequences, and scenes (p. 35)
- Juxtaposition and cumulative meaning (p. 36)
- Continuity shooting and editing (Chapter 4)
- 180° principle and the 20mm/30° rule (pp. 59–61)
- Match action cuts (p. 62)
- Shot/reverse shot technique (pp. 63–65)
- POV sequences (p. 68)
- Moving people through space and elliptical editing (p. 70–72)
- Meeting and chase/follow sequences (pp. 73–75)
- Parallel action sequences (including temporal, graphic, and action matches) (pp. 75–80)
- Jump cuts and long takes (pp. 81–83)

Fundamental Image-to-Image Transitions

To be sure, there are many ways to get from one shot to another, but in the world of narrative filmmaking, there are really only three bread-and-butter transitions—that constitute the vast majority of visual transitions in films throughout history—the cut, the dissolve, and the fade. Sure, there are others transitions, but they're specialty effects that are concocted when the need arises from a special circumstance. But these three—cuts, dissolves, and fades—are the core.

The Cut

For the most part in this chapter, and in the previous chapters, we're exploring the function, power, and versatility of the cut, which is the joining of two shots such that the last frame of the first shot is directly spliced to the first frame of the next shot. The visual shift in a cut from one shot to the next is sequential, instantaneous, and complete. First we're looking at a man running out of an apartment . . . CUT; now we're looking at a picture frame on a desk. A direct cut is by far the most commonly used shot-to-shot transition in film and we have already explored some of the vast spatial, temporal, and narrative associations created by adjoining two images and some of the numerous techniques for making a cut work. This chapter will shed some light on a few additional creative considerations, beyond the formally conventional, for making cuts work expressively in your films.

in practice

One of the most famous cuts in motion picture history is the elliptical edit from Kubrick's *2001: A Space Odyssey* (1968), in which the image leaps hundreds of thousands of years, from man's first major evolutionary step, i.e., the discovery of "tools," a bone notably first used as a weapon, to our next evolutionary step, a moment in the space-age in which the dominance of man and technology over nature is superseded by an alien intelligence, perhaps a deity, which is unfathomable. This single instantaneous edit seems to imply, by skipping over our entire history, that everything in between these two evolutionary points was comparatively insignificant, amounting simply to the development of more tools with which to conquer nature on Earth, in space, and even man's own nature.

This is an **intellectual edit**; yes, it moves the story forward, fast forward as it were, but it also invites us to think thematically about why these two particular moments are juxtaposed. Encouraging this deeper connection is the fact that this is a **formal edit**; it is both a **match on action cut** (see p. 62) and a **graphic match** (see p. 411). The physical similarities between the shape of the bone and the orbiting nuclear-powered satellite make the point that the primitive tool and the sophisticated satellite are fundamentally more similar than they are different. Kubrick does not want us to be awash in emotions in this film; he wants us to put the pieces together, and, in encouraging us to think about the relationship between shots and events of the story, we are also inevitably led to ponder our own place in the universe.

■ Figure 21-9 Elliptical edit, from Kubrick's *2001: A Space Odyssey* (1968) (Editor, Ray Lovejoy). This single cut takes us from the "dawn of man" to the end of mankind as we've known it.

The Dissolve

The **dissolve** is a transition in which the first shot gradually disappears (fades out) as the second shot gradually appears (fades in). With a dissolve we see, for a moment, the merging of both images on the screen simultaneously. A dissolve can have any duration the filmmaker needs, from a few frames that overlap to dissolves that occur over many seconds, becoming a prolonged **superimposition** (two images layered over one another) before giving way to the second shot entirely. Because the dissolve holds both images, and is a shot-to-shot transition that occurs over time, the audience is invited to think about the deeper relationship between the two shots. Dissolves are often used to imply a temporal shift, or a change in location on a more thematic level. They're also used as a transitional device that implies a character-based psychological motivation for the transition, like moving into a memory, dream, or fantasy. A dissolve is a transition that promises something to the audience. It says, "look at these two images merging, think about it"; the complex associative relationship between these images is developing.

The Dissolve

Anthony Minghella's *The English Patient* (1996) (edited by Walter Murch) is set during the final days of World War II and revolves around the memories of Hungarian Count Almásy, a cartographer, who has been severely burned in a plane crash. Almásy recounts to his attending nurse the story of his complex and tragic involvement with Katherine Clifton. Dissolves are often used to bring us into and out of the flashback sequences, which take place much earlier in North Africa.

In one flashback scene Almásy and Katherine are stranded in a truck during a fierce sandstorm. As Almásy talks to her, Katherine reaches up and touches the window of the truck, behind which the sandstorm is raging. This image dissolves slowly into the horribly burned face of the "present day" Almásy, bringing us out of the memory. The merging of her hand and his face looks for a moment as if she, a woman who in present tense is dead, is caressing his face. The dissolve not only brings us back in time, but it intimately and viscerally connects Almásy to his now dead lover. It is as if he, by conjuring her memory, can still feel Katherine's caress, her hand on his face.

Michael Ondaatje, the author of the novel on which the film was based, said this of that specific dissolve: "It's a remarkable scene and it suggests so many things, of compassion and forgiveness; all of these things that are there, again, is that emotional result of that technical device that makes it work" [from *Edgecodes.com: The Art of Motion Picture Editing* (2004; directed by A. Shuper)]. Once again we hear expressed the interconnection between technology and artistic expression.

■ Figure 21-10 In Minghella's *The English Patient* (1996), a dissolve merges the images of a dying man (Ralph Fiennes) and his dead lover (Kristin Scott Thomas) so that, for a moment, it appears that past and present are merging in this flashback.

The dissolve can be a very powerful transition, but it is frequently abused, especially in the era of digital editing where a simple movement of a mouse can create a dissolve. Any film professor can tell you stories of students whose footage isn't cutting together well and who simply plop a dissolve between every shot, hoping to "smooth out" the rough edges. The effect of using dissolves willy-nilly is to strip them of their expressive potential, which they can retain only through careful and restrained use.

The Fade

The **fade-out** is a slow disappearing of an image into a color, and a **fade-in** is the slow appearing of the image from a color. Most commonly, one sees a fade to (or from) black, and a little less frequently, a fade to (or from) white. Very often a fade-out and fade-in are used back to back as a transition from one image to another. In other words, from the first image we fade to black and then we fade up from black to bring in the second image. Again, the duration of the fades and the black between the images can be short or long, depending on the effect you want. The **fade-out/fade-in** technique is frequently used as a time ellipse or to punctuate a major shift in the dramatic direction of the movie. There is a strong sense of closure after a fade-out, and if followed by a fade-in, the audience feels a sense of a new beginning.

The Fade

Orson Welles' seminal film *Citizen Kane* (1941) tells the fictional life story of the powerful and imposing Charles Foster Kane through the device of a reporter, Mr. Thompson, who is trying to solve the mystery of the last word Kane uttered on his deathbed, "Rosebud." Thompson follows up on numerous leads, hoping to discover the essence of Kane's life, primarily by interviewing anyone who knew Kane personally. In the end, the film compiles an intricate and multifaceted portrait of a man through multiple perspectives. Each source of information is handled as a separate chapter and Wells often uses fades to delineate these various accounts. For example, early in the film Thompson tries to interview Susan Alexander Kane, "the second Mrs. Kane." But Miss Alexander is drunk and in no mood to talk. When it's clear that the "Alexander chapter" has yielded everything it can concerning "Rosebud," which is essentially nothing, Wells fades out to black and then fades up on a statue of Walter Parks Thatcher at the Thatcher memorial Library, where Thompson is given access to Mr. Thatcher's journals. We then begin a new account of Charles Foster Kane from the perspective of Thatcher's diary, pages 83–142 to be precise. The use of this fade-out/fade-in is Wells' way of turning the page, closing off one chapter and opening on the next.

■ **Figure 21-11** This fade-out/fade-in from *Citizen Kane* (1941) effectively closes off one investigative lead and introduces another "chapter" (Editor, Robert Wise).

■ WHY WE EDIT II: EXTRA-NARRATIVE CONSIDERATIONS

Although we've looked at some of the more systematic approaches to cutting shots and sequences in previous chapters, let's now fill in some of the gaps and add a few more creative considerations that inform editing decisions. Editing for dramatic structure or continuity is only part of the editor's expressive vocabulary. When you listen to professional editors talk they just as often use words like "rhythm," "feeling," "pace," and "energy." Great editors and great musicians are a lot alike: great musicians, while thoroughly understanding the formal aspects of their craft (i.e., how to play their instrument, musical scales, harmonic modulation), also play from their gut to "get it right." As Jazz great Duke Ellington reminds us, *"It don't mean a thing if it ain't got that swing."* Well, it's the same with filmmaking, and the editing process is where a movie finds its "swing."

Given that editing is a craft that involves sequencing, action, and movement played out over time, there are limits to what can be illustrated with words and still frames. I have used a lot of examples from films in this section and encourage the reader (the serious student of film) to rent the films and watch these examples play out in time and in the context of the larger story, to really fill out these lessons.

Condensing and Expanding Time

Time is an endlessly elastic entity in the hands of a screenwriter, director, and editor. Some films tell a story whose events take place over two hours, in two hours; these are **real-time** films. Other films will take two hours to tell stories which occur over two days, or two years, or two-hundred years. Look at the example from *2001: A Space Odyssey* (Figure 21-9). One edit covers 200,000 years! Some people call this **reel time** (alluding to a film reel).

There are quite a few notable examples in the history of cinema of entire features which play out in real time—Hitchcock's *Rope* (1948), Chantal Akerman's *Jeanne Dielman, 23 Quai du Commerce, 1080 Bruxelles* (1976), and Agnès Varda's *Cleo from 5 to 7* (1961) (Figure 21-13), to name just a few. But for the most part, these films are exceptions,

in practice

Real Time and Short Films

Real time can work quite well in short films, which often revolve, as closely as possible, around a single, pivotal moment in the life of a character, as opposed to depicting the slow transformation of a character found in feature-length narratives. Rodrigo García's DV film *Nine Lives* (2005), is composed of nine real-time, one-shot vignettes that depict a particularly critical moment in the personal lives of nine women. Each episode is essentially a self-contained short film on its own, lasting only ten to twelve minutes. The only edits in the film are those which take us from one woman's story to the next.

The power of each short vignette is located in the tight POV that the audience shares with each woman. The unbroken shots and the uninterrupted passage of time allow the audience to experience the moment-by-moment development of each highly emotional and often tragic event along with the central character. It is as if we are following each woman, inhabiting their space and time with them. Maintaining temporal integrity also foregrounds small details, and the audience is reminded how anyone's life can be turned upside down in only ten minutes.

■ Figure 21-12 Nine stories, nine shots. García's *Nine Lives* (2005) skillfully uses single, unbroken shots and a fluidly moving camera on a stabilizing arm to tell each of its nine stories.

even within the broader oeuvres of these particular filmmakers. The primary task of film editing, from larger structural choices to cutting within scenes, is to compress time for efficiency's sake, and we've already explored the temporal and spatial economy of elliptical editing (see p. 70). However, beyond simple storytelling efficiency (i.e., taking out the unnecessary bits), the elliptical edit can also be used as a strategy to create highly expressive moments.

A great example of how the compression of time and actions can be used expressively comes in a scene from Stephen Gaghan's *Syriana* (2005) (edited by Tim Squyres). The scene (Figure 21-14) begins with CIA operative Bob Barnes returning to his hotel room, hav-

■ Figure 21-13 Varda's *Cleo from 5 to 7* (1961) is one of a handful of films that play out in real time.

ing just been told by another CIA agent that the Prince Nasir Al-Subaai will be kidnapped and killed. While standing at his window, watching for evidence of the pending kidnapping, Barnes is suddenly grabbed from behind by four men, who throw him to the ground, tie him up, drag him out of his room, and toss him into the back of a waiting SUV.

Barnes was set up. It was he who was the kidnapping target after all. But by whom? Why? The kidnapping sequence, which in real time would likely take several minutes at least, takes 35 seconds and is accomplished in eighteen quick shots. The quickness of the actions and rapid edits reinforces the fact that this was totally unexpected and takes Barnes (and us) completely by surprise. The action is over "in a flash," certainly before he (or we) can figure out what's going on. Just like Barnes, we're left in a state of breathless confusion about what just happened. The highly elliptical, noncontinuity, rapid cutting also in-

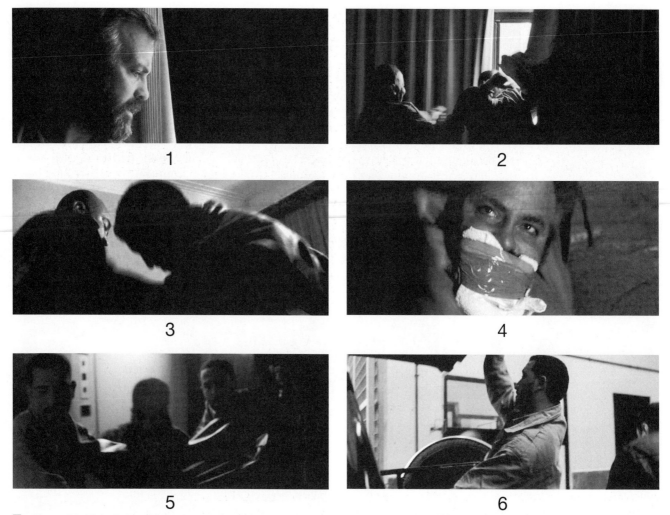

■ **Figure 21-14** In *Syriana* (2005), the six shots of Bob Barnes' (George Clooney) kidnapping are edited with rapid jump cuts to connect the audience to the confusion that Barnes must be experiencing, as well as to the professional efficiency of this brutal act.

fuses the scene with the "feeling" of the brutal efficiency and the instantaneous change of fortunes on this level of espionage.

In a central scene in Soderbergh's *Traffic* (2000) (edited by Stephen Mirrione), the drug czar's daughter, Caroline Wakefield, and her friends are having a drug party in her living room. This scene uses two different edit transitions to imply the passing of time (Figure 21-15). Frequent jump cuts lurch us forward in little, discontinuous bits of time, while slow dissolves give us the feeling that hours and hours are passing while these kids do nothing but drink, snort coke, and engage in mindless banter. The cumulative effect of these two elliptical devices is remarkable because, while the editing does in fact greatly condense time (the scene lasts only three minutes and ten seconds), it "feels" like they, and we, have been in that living room all night long. In addition, the jump cuts reinforce the partiers' disorientation due to their drug-induced state.

While the vast majority of temporal editing is done to condense time, editing also has the ability to **expand** or even **suspend time** as well. There are more or less obvious ways to use this technique, depending on how apparent you want the device to be. Rob Reiner's *Misery* (1990) (edited by Robert Leighton) employs a very subtle, but effective, time expansion device that is commonly used to heighten suspense. The famous novelist Paul Sheldon is wheelchair bound and literally imprisoned by the violently unpredictable Annie, his

■ Figure 21-15 Dissolves (top) and jump cuts (bottom) are used in this party scene from Soderbergh's *Traffic* (2000) to both condense time and convey a sense of drug-induced disorientation.

most ardent fan, after she rescues him from a terrible car accident. In one scene, while Annie is away, Paul picks the lock on the door of his room and ventures into the rest of the house to find a way out. He is some distance from his room when he hears Annie's car coming up the driveway.

Paul must not be discovered out of his room or he'll face Annie's wrath, so he races down the hallway to his room, and that action is intercut with Annie walking to the house and up the front stairs (Figure 21-16). But each time we cut back to Paul, furiously rolling his wheelchair down the hall, he seems to be getting nowhere; it's taking him forever to get down that short little hallway! Editorially speaking, each time we cut to Paul he is a bit farther back than we left him in the previous shot, so he is in fact traveling over some of the same territory. So, not only time but also distance seems to be elongating for Paul, while Annie makes quick progress to the front door of the house. The longer it takes Paul to get down the hallway, the more anxiety the audience feels for him. The editor expands Paul's trip down the hallway, not so much that it's visibly obvious, but just enough that we "feel" the suspense more intensely, causing us to scream to ourselves, "Go faster, Paul. Go!" Horror, action, and mystery genres thrive on this sort of emotional manipulation, this delicious, suspenseful anxiety.

Overlap editing is one of the more stylistically overt devices for suspending time, and is often used to punctuate a heightened moment. **Overlap editing** is the obvious repetition of the same moment, action, or gesture, several times—sometimes from different camera angles. In Mike Nichols' *The Graduate* (1967), the recently graduated Benjamin finds himself alone with Mrs. Robinson, an old friend of his parents, in her house. She proceeds to seduce the highly confused Benjamin. When he refuses her advances, she slyly manages to get him into her daughter's bedroom, where she pounces.

The moment Mrs. Robinson enters the bedroom, totally naked, and locks the door behind her, Benjamin's head turns in total surprise—not once, not twice, but three complete times (Figure 21-17). Benjamin's stupefaction at that moment—his shock, confusion, and panic—is brilliantly punctuated by duplicating the gesture and extending the moment of discovery with an overtly stylistic flourish (not to mention that it's funny, too). The continuation of the scene is also wonderfully edited. Benjamin doesn't want to, but he can't help looking at Mrs. Robinson's body, and his attracted-but-reluctant POV is reflected in little rapid close-up insert shots of various parts of her naked body, inter-cut with his furtive glances (Figure 21-18)—which brings us to our next editing consideration: timing, rhythm, and pace.

■ **Figure 21-16** The edits in this sequence from Reiner's *Misery* (1990) add tension and drama by making it seem that it takes forever for Paul (James Caan) to traverse a few feet of hallway, in his effort to avoid Annie (Kathy Bates).

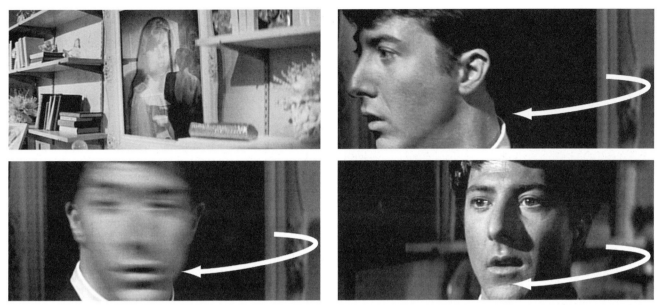

■ **Figure 21-17** In Nichol's *The Graduate* (1967), the moment when Benjamin (Dustin Hoffman) sees Mrs. Robinson (Anne Bancroft) naked is punctuated by three quick shots of him turning his head edited together.

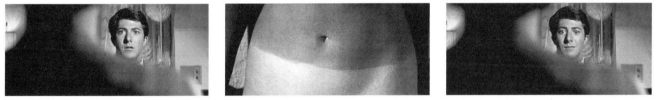

■ **Figure 21-18** The rapid intercutting between Mrs. Robinson's naked body parts and Benjamin's stare in *The Graduate* mimic his inability to keep his eyes off her even though he doesn't want to look.

Timing, Rhythm, and Pace

Timing

Timing refers to the specific placement of a shot within the sequence, meaning the precise moment one cuts to a new shot for maximum impact. Good editors have a sixth sense for timing: it seems to be in their bones; the rest of us experiment—we try an edit here or there and then trim it until it's right. One good example of a sharp, perfectly timed edit is the first moment of death for Charlie Company in Terrence Malick's World War II film *The Thin Red Line* (1998) (edited by Saar Klein), which is edited with absolutely precise timing.

At 45 minutes into *The Thin Red Line,* Charlie Company has already landed on Guadalcanal and the men have made their way to the front lines, where the Japanese are firmly dug in. Up to this point the company has seen only the aftermath of war during encounters with American soldiers returning from battle, but have suffered no casualties themselves. At the edge of the Japanese fortifications, a Second Lieutenant, on orders from the First Lieutenant, sends the first two soldiers out to press forward and scout. Slowly, carefully they move toward the heavily armed Japanese bunkers while everyone watches (Figure 21-19). While the audience can feel the apprehension, visually the journey doesn't seem so dangerous—the soldiers travel across a stunningly beautiful hill covered with long, brilliantly green grasses, gently swaying in a soft breeze. Suddenly, seemingly out of the blue—Bap! Bap!—two quick gunshots from the top of the hill, and both men drop. Before they even hit the ground, Malick cuts to the stunned Second Lieutenant, and then quickly to the stunned First Lieutenant. They blink hard, staring in disbelief, trying to comprehend what just happened, in a flash—Bap! Bap!—just like that, two men dead. Is that possible? That swiftly, that easily, life is gone? We, too, like the First and Second Lieutenants, are stunned and disbelieving. Malick's strategy, not to linger on the deaths but to rapidly show

■ **Figure 21-19** The rapid cutting, from the falling soldiers to their stunned commanding officers, reflects the fragility of life in a war situation in Malick's *The Thin Red Line* (1998).

the witnesses who are just as shocked as we are, compels us to ask the same questions they must be asking. The environment seemed so beautiful and quiet—how can death be so close? The precision of the editing, just a few quick cuts, constructs a huge existential moment from very little and dramatically understated material.

Verbal and visual timing are, of course, essential for comedy, too. A genuinely funny joke will elicit only a polite chuckle if the punch line isn't delivered with just the right timing—trust me on this one: I know! On the other hand, something decidedly silly can have people rolling on the floor in hysterical laughter. If the delivery is sharp—John Cleese knows all about this. It's the same with editing a film that hopes to provoke laughter, and in comedy everything is secondary to making people laugh, including the story. The comic timing in Bobby and Peter Farrelly's 1998 comedy, *There's Something About Mary* (edited by Christopher Greenbury), is flawless. One special editing tactic the Farrelly brothers frequently use is to allude to something off screen, but not reveal it until the moment is just right.

Early in the film, when teenage Ted is getting ready to take his dream girl to the prom, he goes to the bathroom to relieve himself. As he does so, he glances out the window at a pair of cooing doves—the perfect image for how he feels, but when the doves fly away they reveal a half-naked Mary, seen through her bedroom window as she is getting dressed, with her mother. They naturally assume Ted is a peeping tom, and in his haste to get out and explain himself, he zips up a bit too quickly and, well, gets his "frank and beans" mangled in his zipper. A few scenes later, the bathroom is filled with Mary's parents, a police officer, and a fireman, all staring at his zipper predicament. The cop decides to resolve the situation and approaches to unzip his fly to free him from the zipper's teeth. He tells Ted that it'll be just like taking off a Band-Aid. Below the frame line (Figure 21-20), the cop takes hold of the zipper and counts "A-one, and a-two and a-. . . ." Just then, the they cut to a close-up of a person we've never seen before—now outside. Huh? And the person screams, "We've got a bleeder!" The next quick cut is a wide shot. Poor Ted is on a stretcher, a towel covering his wound, and the entire neighborhood is watching as he's rushed into a waiting ambulance by the EMTs. All of the audience's anxiety, built up while anticipating the pain of the cop's brutal action, is funneled through those two quick edits into the punch line of the joke. We feel the pain, and understand the bloody aftermath, and laugh, all at the same time. At the conclusion of Ted's tragic and traumatic prom night, as the ambulance takes him to the hospital, he starts to cry and the Farrellys cut to . . . years later, a scene in which adult Ted is on a therapist's couch. Again, a sharp edit efficiently and comically tells us that he's still suffering the psychic wounds of that fateful night at Mary's house.

■ **Figure 21-20** The careful timing of the edits in this scene from the Farrelly brothers' *There's Something About Mary* (1998) creates a terrific punch line to an already funny situation.

Rhythm

Rhythm within a sequence refers to the duration of the shots relative to each other within a sequence, and the patterns of emphasis, or pulses, these durations create. If you consider an edited shot as a pulse or a beat, like a musical beat, then you will be able to manipulate the duration of these image "beats" to create regular, irregular, or syncopated visual rhythms. For example, if you were to edit a sequence such that every shot was exactly 24 frames, then the sequence would have a very constant rhythmic beat, as if it were cut to a metronome, and each image would have equal weight in the sequence. Cutting a sequence of shots that are all 48 frames long would obviously be slower and longer, but would nonetheless also have a very even rhythm. If, however, you were to cut your film in a repetitive pattern in which three shots had 12 frames and the fourth shot had 48 frames, and repeated this twice, you would get a visual rhythm in which there was a strong accent on the fourth and eighth shots, not unlike the opening of Beethoven's Fifth Symphony (da, da, da, duummm / da, da, da, duummmm).

Obviously, finding a cutting rhythm is much more organic than arbitrarily imposing frame counts to edited shots. The visual cutting strategy of a sequence can find the drive for its rhythm in a number of places, especially action within the frame, camera movement, dialogue rhythms, or beats in the music sound track. The opening sequence in Fernando Meirelles and Kátia Lund's film *City of God* (2002) (edited by Daniel Rezende) intercuts between two scenes with contrasting visual rhythms. The very first scene plunges the audience into the sounds, colors, people, food, music, and dangers of the favelas of Rio de Janeiro.

A street party is in progress with food being prepared and music playing. The sequence is put together with familiar editing patterns. For example, there is a POV sequence involving a tied up chicken; the chicken looks (looking shot) and sees a knife cutting the throat of another chicken (POV shot), and when we cut back to the chicken (reaction shot) we see panic in his eyes (thank you Mr. Kuleshov) (Figure 21-21). The chicken then tries to pull free of his bindings (cause and effect). Once the chicken is free, a chase sequence ensues, with gun-wielding kids trying to kill the frantic chicken in the alleys of the favela (Figure 21-22).

However, while the basic patterns are familiar, the editing (and camerawork) does not strictly adhere to the rules of continuity. Through rapid cutting, combined with dynamic visual discontinuity and percussive jump cuts, the editor creates a visual equivalent for the driving and syncopated Brazilian Batucada rhythms that play on the sound track. By varying the length of shots, which creates surprising accents throughout the scene, the cutting assiduously avoids a constant rhythm. Instead, the cuts create a complex syncopated visual rhythm that instantly holds the audience through its momentum and visual audacity. The propulsive energy of the scene would be destroyed by smooth, continuity style cuts, perfect matches on action, strict adherence to the 180° rule, and editing that was too metrically regular. When you watch this sequence, you can turn off the sound track and still dance to it!

■ **Figure 21-21** A clever POV sequence serves as a metaphor for the violence found in the favelas of Meirelles and Lund's *City of God* (2002).

■ **Figure 21-22** The jarring editing style and lapses in continuity augment the energetic introduction of the street gangs in *City of God.*

During the dynamically rhythmic chicken chase scene, the film cuts to Buscapé, the level-headed protagonist of the film, who is casually walking and talking with a friend (Figure 21-23). Buscapé has a calm, thoughtful, and sensible demeanor (and no gun). The editing abruptly stops and yields to a long, steady shot that reveals this shift in character energy. Within the first minutes of the movie, we "feel," through the shift in editing rhythm, the contrast between Buscapé and the activity of the streets around him—which is one essential dimension of the conflict driving the film.

Pace

Pace (also called **tempo**) is, of course, related to rhythm, in that it is determined by the duration of shots next to other shots, but pace refers specifically to the rate of speed that a scene, or sequence of scenes, plays out. A **fast-paced** editing approach can suggest intensity, excitement, energy, or even confusion or chaos; depending on the narrative context. **Slowly paced** editing can lend a feeling of casualness, fluidity, calm, contemplation, or even torpor or stasis to a movie; again depending on the story.

The story line of a film often suggests an overall pace, or tempo, and is an important consideration that can be incorporated right up in the scripting stage by carefully controlling the length of scenes on the page. Overall tempo is then carried through in the production phase by controlling the length of shots, number of shots, and camera movements, and then is finally realized in the editing room. However, very few films strictly maintain a single pace from beginning to end. Contrasting the pace of scenes is a very important tool for creating narrative emphasis and a general sense for overall story shape.

Thomas McCarthy's film *The Station Agent* (2003) (edited by Tom McArdle) is about Finbar McBride, a dwarf who inherits a pathetic little plot of land in New Jersey and simply wants to live his life in calm solitude doing what he loves the most, trainwatching (Figure 21-24). The pace of this film is broad, calm, and contemplative; Finbar is in no hurry, so neither is the editing pace.

■ **Figure 21-23** Buscapé's (Alexandre Rodrigues) introduction in *City of God* is marked by a shift in editing and cinematographic styles, immediately establishing him as a level-headed, decent character.

■ **Figure 21-24** The leisurely pace of McCarthy's *The Station Agent* (2003) is exemplified by this 30-second shot of the main characters watching a train roll along.

■ **Figure 21-25** A change in the pace of the cutting effectively fore-shadows Finbar's (Peter Dinklage) outburst in this scene from McCarthy's *The Station Agent* (2003).

However, as Finbar becomes reluctantly involved in the dramatic personal lives of his neighbors, he is eventually forced to confront that which he sought to escape, his own loneliness. In one extraordinary scene (Figure 21-25), Finbar becomes drunk in a bar, and the suppressed anger and frustration he's been holding suddenly erupts and this normally quiet and reserved man becomes publicly confrontational. To emphasize this profoundly disquieting moment, the editing pace accelerates and the length of each cut decreases.

Associative Editing

Associative edits are cuts that are designed to build additional meaning by juxtaposing two shots together with a stylized technique that encourages the audience to think about the connection. Broadly speaking, associative editing works by comparing or contrasting the content of the shots to create an association that is not contained in the individual shots. The connective content can be either the **formal/graphic** compositional elements of the frame (e.g., color, shape, and movement) or the **thematic/metaphoric** (based on actions and other visual detail), and these properties provide a link between shots that don't otherwise have an immediate, direct, or obvious narrative connection.

We have already explored this phenomenon of creating an association between two juxtaposed images in its most basic form, with the examples from Kuleshov and Lucas (see p. 37). But there can be more overt and complex connections created through associative editing; these encourage the audience to *think* instead of merely respond emotionally, which is why this technique is also referred to as **intellectual editing**. Again, we saw a classic example of this technique in our discussion of *2001: A Space Odyssey*. In the cut in Figure 21-9, Kubrick used a strong **formal/graphic edit** (on shape and movement) to forge a metaphoric connection between a bone and an orbiting satellite.

Intellectual editing is a product of early Soviet filmmakers and their rigorous writings on, and uses of, an editing theory that has been labeled "Soviet montage." Soviet montage eschewed the smooth, invisible Hollywood style of continuity editing, which historically had been primarily about facilitating the dramatic goals of the story, for a more intellectually engaging, overtly visible and political style. Associative editing, like many Soviet montage techniques, is meant to call attention to itself as a device. Consequently, the audience is encouraged to thoughtfully participate in the construction of the film's meaning. The early Soviet filmmakers, like Vertov, Eisenstein, and Pudovkin, who each developed their own theories of montage, had a profound influence on the art of editing in general and on specific filmmakers, including Wells, Hitchcock, Godard, Kubrick, Scorsese, and Coppola, to name only a few. At this point in cinema history, the editing theories and practices of Soviet montage, Hollywood editing, French New Wave styles, Hong Kong cinema, and the rest of the cumulative history of national and individual editing approaches have merged into one big, global aesthetic, cinema toolbox, available and accessible to any filmmaker, for any project, anywhere on the planet.

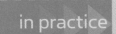

In his book "Making Movies," Director Sidney Lumet says about editing, "To me there are two main elements to editing: juxtapositioning images and creating tempo." He then goes on to talk about how his careful control over editing tempo was used for narrative emphasis and characterization in his classic film *Long Day's Journey into Night* (1962):

On Long Day's Journey into Night, *I found that I could use editing tempos to reinforce character. I always shot Kather-ine Hepburn in long, sustained takes, so that in editing, the legato feel of her scenes would help us drift into her narcotized world. We would move with her, into her past and into her own journey into night. Jason Robard's character was edited in exactly the opposite way. As the picture went on, I tried to cut his scenes in a staccato rhythm. I wanted him to feel erratic, disjointed, uncoordinated.*

(From *Making Movies,* **by Sidney Lumet, Vintage Books, 1995)**

■ Figure 21-26 In Lumet's *Long Day's Journey into Night* (1962) the characterization of Mary (Katherine Hepburn) and Jamie (Jason Robards) was reinforced through editing tempo.

Emotion

We started this chapter by talking about cutting to tell a story, but a story without emotion is lifeless. Notice how in many of the examples we have discussed that the word "feel" is used. Many editors believe that the first consideration of an editing strategy, and indeed the motivation for individual edits, is emotion—how you want the audience to feel at any given moment. Do you want them to laugh? Worry? Jump in their seat? Do you want them to feel an impending doom, or a sense of relief? Do you want them to feel what your protagonist is feeling? Emotion is aroused in the audience when they become participants in the drama. The editing principle for the Robinson fight sequence from *Raging Bull* (see Figure 21-6) was not to be stylistic for its own sake, but to make the audience feel what it's like to be in a boxing ring, to feel the surreal malleability of time as your adrenaline surges, to feel the powerful blows from a prizefighter. The Farrelly brothers also want us to feel pain, in *There's Something About Mary* (see Figure 21-20), the pain of catching your "frank and beans" in a zipper, but they also want to make us howl with laughter as we simultaneously grimace in pain; Rob Reiner, in *Misery* (see Figure 21-16), wants us to feel anxiety that our hero will not make it to the room in time—and so on.

in practice

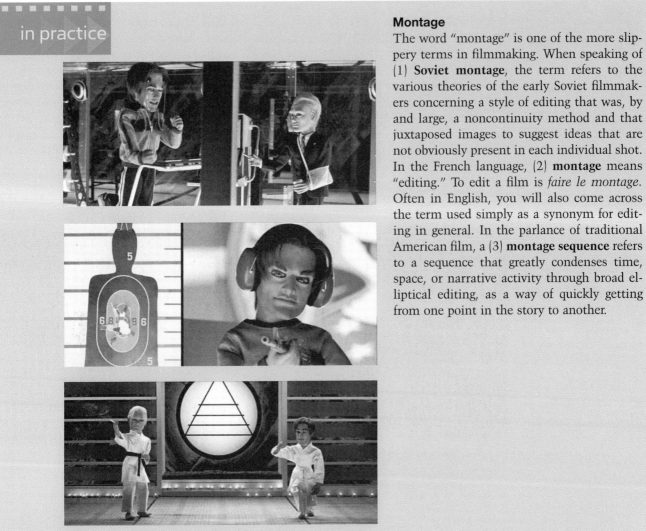

Figure 21-27 Trey Parker and Matt Stone playfully parody a common cinematic device, the montage sequence, in their "Montage Song" sequence in *Team America: World Police* (2004).

Montage

The word "montage" is one of the more slippery terms in filmmaking. When speaking of (1) **Soviet montage**, the term refers to the various theories of the early Soviet filmmakers concerning a style of editing that was, by and large, a noncontinuity method and that juxtaposed images to suggest ideas that are not obviously present in each individual shot. In the French language, (2) **montage** means "editing." To edit a film is *faire le montage*. Often in English, you will also come across the term used simply as a synonym for editing in general. In the parlance of traditional American film, a (3) **montage sequence** refers to a sequence that greatly condenses time, space, or narrative activity through broad elliptical editing, as a way of quickly getting from one point in the story to another.

Never forget that we are telling a story to move people emotionally in very particular ways. So, the next time you're watching a movie and have an emotional reaction, pull yourself out of the filmmaker's spell and try to figure out how they did that. Try to recall, cut for cut, how the filmmaker drew that emotion out of you. If you can do that, then you'll *really* be learning how to make movies.

So of course there are basic rules. But even today, people are struggling with new ways of telling stories through film, and they're still using the same old tools—establishing shots, medium shots, close-ups—but not necessarily with the same intent. And it's the juxtaposition of these shots in the editing process that is creating new emotions or, more precisely, a new way to communicate certain feelings to the audience.
Martin Scorsese (From *Moviemakers' Master Class*, by Laurent Tirard)

Associative Editing
Metaphoric Visual Links—Natural Born Killers (1994)

In *Natural Born Killers*, Oliver Stone and editors Brian Berdan and Hank Corwin use extremely fast, disjunctive, highly associative editing and wildly stylized camerawork to depict the vicious anarchy of Mickey and Mallory's killing sprees. In several episodes, Stone cuts in (or projects right onto the scene) images of horses, snakes, spiders, and rabbits that do not come from the world of the film at all but that are inserted, to force us to consider the murderous brutality of Mickey and Mallory in the context of the often cruel laws of nature. Where does the ability to kill come from? Is it natural or is it a by-product of our particularly violent culture? These questions are posed relentlessly through associative editing. Are Mickey and Mallory natural born killers, as the title suggests? Or have they been shaped by a violent upbringing and a sick society? Stylized devices like this never allow the audience to become entirely taken in by the fictive world; we are consistently reminded that we are watching a movie, a construction, an artifice from which we are deriving a perverse, prurient pleasure through a narrative of mass murder and mayhem. Hey, that's entertainment, no? This self-reflectivity is nowhere more apparent than at the end of the film, when Stone creates a didactic juxtaposition by cutting from the movie's final fictional events to true news events, such as the O.J. Simpson trial (Figure 21-29).

■ **Figure 21-28** The violent journey of Mickey (Woody Harrelson) and Mallory (Juliette Lewis) in Stone's *Natural Born Killers* (1994) is punctuated with documentary images from the natural world.

■ **Figure 21-29** Oliver Stone juxtaposes the fictional world of Mickey and Mallory with real news events to illustrate his central theme concerning the American public's insatiable appetite for violence as entertainment.

The Sound Design in Film

We gestate in Sound, and are born into Sight
Cinema gestated in Sight, and was born into Sound
Walter Murch (From the foreword to *Audio-Vision*, by Michel Chion)[1]

Roughly, the first thirty-three years of film's early history—between the introduction of Edison's kinetoscope in 1894 and the commercial success of Warner Brothers' *The Jazz Singer* in 1927—established the "motion picture" as a fundamentally visual art form, with images telling the entire narrative. In those early decades, before the introduction of "talking pictures," the movies themselves were silent and sound was incorporated almost exclusively in the form of live musical accompaniment played during the screenings, long after the production of the motion picture. Even though it's been roughly eighty years since *The Jazz Singer* transformed film production into an art form with multiple layers of synchronized audio, filmmaking is all too often still considered (and taught) as a primarily visual art form—with sound as a sort of addendum. However, as Walter Murch, Michel Chion, Randy Thom, and others have so eloquently expressed, the filmmaker's art has evolved to the point where the aural dimension of a movie is at least as important as, and sometimes even more dominant than, the picture for creating tone, mood, and meaning. For too many filmmakers, the audio component remains at one of two poles; for some it plays a purely supporting role as an auxiliary to the image, an accompaniment (often redundant) to the story being told through the visual action, and others shackle it to the hard labor of expository dialogue that explains the film story in the absence of truly expressive imagery. Because of its powerful dramatic potential, you should consider sound as a costar of your movie, capable of much more than expository drudgery—capable, in fact, of profound narrative eloquence. The filmmaker who learns to harness the power of a film's aural realm and fully develops sound as an essential storytelling component that enhances, but does not duplicate, the visual dimension of a movie will have vastly more opportunity and territory for creative expression. This requires imagining and incorporating aural story elements from the very earliest scriptwriting stages straight through to postproduction. It's unfortunate that all too often, filmmakers think about sound only after the shooting is done.

■ SOUND DESIGN OVERVIEW

The final form of a movie's total aural impression is called the film's **sound design**. A film's sound design consists of layering multiple tracks of sound, anywhere from two to a dozen. The creative manipulation, placement, layering, enhancing, composing, juxtaposing, and mixing of these audio tracks is done in the postproduction stage. It is important to understand that in film production visual and aural components remain separate for as long as possible in order to allow for maximum creative manipulation, right up to the very end of the filmmaking process, when the movie (picture) and all sound tracks are locked together and prepared for distribution. For this reason, we gather and lay down the elements of the sound design, each separate and distinct from the others. For example, as we construct our movie in postproduction we may have three separate audio tracks for our sync sound dialogue, a fourth track for the music, and a fifth track for sound effects, and maybe a sixth track for ambient sound. Taken as a whole, all of these audio tracks and the way they are mixed together comprise the sound design.

[1]*Audio-Vision*, by Michel Chion, Columbia University Press, New York, 1994.

Whether you are cutting to only one music track or layering fifteen tracks of audio, there is virtually no end to the contributions a well-crafted sound design can bring to a film. Sound can establish a tone or mood with unmatchable nuance and it can vividly establish the legitimacy and emotional impression of a location. Sound is able to bring dramatic emphasis to actions or details inside or outside of the frame; in fact, sound can create an entire world off screen (how many times have we seen characters reacting to the sound of a terrible car crash just outside the frame's edge?). Sound can contribute to establishing a character's point of view even to the point of reflecting their particular psychology. In short, sound is an essential cinematic storytelling component that deserves considerable attention throughout all phases of the film production process.

Before we go any further, I need to express one caveat at this point. It is already quite a challenge to discuss the visual aspects of cinema (a time- and movement-based art form) through written language, aided only by still frame illustrations. However, the insufficiencies of this approach expand exponentially when exploring the sound world of films. So again, I greatly encourage readers of this book to rent the films I mention and listen closely to the sound design examples in this chapter.

■ SOUND DESIGN I: SOUND, SYNC, AND SOURCE

In closely exploring or devising the sound design of a motion picture we need to consider three closely related aspects of the movie's sonic world: (1) What kinds of sounds make up the sound design? (2) Is the sound synchronous (in sync) with the picture or not? (3) Where are those sounds emanating from or, where is the source?

■ **Figure 22-1** A scene from Polanski's renowned short film *Two Men and a Wardrobe* (1958) which includes no dialogue.

Sounds: Speech, Sound Effects, and Music

The sound components of a film, the aural elements of the sound design, can pretty much be organized into three broad categories: **speech**, **sound effects**, and **music**. These sounds comprise the way a film can aurally communicate to an audience, but not every scene within a film will have all three types of sound. For example, many scenes are edited to music without any dialogue or sound effects at all, while other scenes may have dialogue and no music. Short films very often tell their stories without the use of the human voice at all, either as dialogue or voice-over. One of the most famous examples is Roman Polanski's celebrated short, *Two Men and a Wardrobe* (1958), which is a very complex social satire about two men who are ostracized from "civilized" society because they carry a huge wardrobe around with them (**Figure 22-1**).

This 14-minute short film, which garnered prizes all over the world, has no dialogue or voice-over whatsoever. The sound design consists only of a music track and a few sound effects. Also, it is not uncommon to find narrative films, even feature films, which do not have music. Some filmmakers, especially those working in a more realist mode, assiduously avoid the overt infusion of emotion that music supplies. Abbas Kiarostami (*Ten, Taste of Cherry*) (**Figure 22-2**) is one filmmaker who rarely uses music in his movies, while other filmmakers, like Tsai Ming-Liang (*Goodbye, Dragon Inn*), use very little or no speech (either dialogue or narration). The general categories of speech, sound effects, and music

■ **Figure 22-2** Abbas Kiarostami's films rarely have music in them, diegetic or otherwise, as exemplified in his film *Taste of Cherry* (1997).

can obviously be broken down into more detailed categories, which we will do, but first let's look at the question of sync and source that also inform the more specific elements of a sound design.

Synchronous, Nonsynchronous, and Postsynchronous Audio

The second consideration for sound is whether the audio as it is realized in the sound design is **in sync** with the picture or not, in which case it is called **nonsync audio** (or **asynchronous sound**). Sync audio has a frame-accurate, direct correspondence with the image and appears to be generated from what we are watching, like a character speaking lines of dialogue or the sound that accompanies the image of a car starting up and driving off. Sync sound that is recorded on location and in sync with the image (for example, the car image and the sound of the car) is called **direct sound**. As we explored in Chapter 15, if we're not happy with the quality of the sync sound (perhaps the camera framing didn't allow us to position our mikes for optimum sound) we can always get another, better recording in the field, of a car starting and pulling away without the camera rolling, as **wild sound**. In the postproduction world, sound effects recorded on location are called **pfx**, for **production sound effects**. This sound is recorded nonsync, but will be aligned to appear in sync later in postproduction. But perhaps in building our sound design we don't like *either* car sound from the field recordings. Well, we can easily replace it with a "car starting and drive away" sound from a **prerecorded sound effects** library; such libraries are found on CDs or through online sound effect resources. In this case, the sound will also be aligned with the image in postproduction (i.e., just as the key is turned in the ignition). Both the pfx and prerecorded effects are called **postsynchronous** sound effects because their synchronous relationship to the picture is accomplished in post-production rather than in the shooting.

Nonsync audio (either speech, sound effects, or music) is sound that has no corresponding image and so has no visible source. For example, just as the car drives off screen, we hear the sound of a car crash. Nonsync audio always carries with it the question: Where is this sound coming from? Because there is no visible source, nonsync sound is often used to create a sense for the area outside of the camera's field of view (as in the car crash example) or to layer an additional emotional tone over the image. An example would be the hoot of an owl and the howl of a coyote, as two frightened Boy Scouts desperately try to light a campfire in the dark woods at night.

Source

The question of the location of the source of a sound has a profound interrelationship with the other categories of sound. The film theorist Michel Chion makes the astute observation, in his book "Audio-Vision," that in film, all images are contained within the frame. But sound, the aural universe of the film, has no such "container," no such strictly delineated limits. Not only are we free to layer as many sounds as we want on top of other sounds, but we can also have various rationales for where those sounds are ostensibly coming from. As we just mentioned, sounds can emanate from **on screen** (a source within the frame) or from **off screen** (a source outside the frame). In addition, sounds can have different relationships to the fictive world that the film has created. In film theory terms, the world of the film—consisting of the characters, actions, objects, locations, time, and story—is called the film's **diegesis**. A sound track can have sounds that seem to come from the world of the movie, called **diegetic sound**, and it can have **nondiegetic sounds**, which don't come from anything in the world of the film. These are supplementary sounds, like music, included by the filmmaker to add further emotional or narrative dimensions.

Examples of diegetic sound would be the dialogue spoken by a character, music playing on a radio that is visible in the scene, or the sound of a car crash that our characters respond to, whether it is on screen or not. All of these sounds come from the world of the movie and can be heard by the characters in the film. Nondiegetic sound, on the other hand would include the voice of a narrator commenting on the scene we are watching, music that has no source in the world of the film, like the romantic orchestral music that

Mel Brooks, Jokin' Around with Diegesis

Off screen, on screen, diegetic, nondiegetic; these terms may sound theoretical, but their application is simple and evident in practically every film you see. Mel Brooks even found a way to play to the audience's expectations concerning diegetic and nondiegetic sounds for laughs. In his 1977 comedy *High Anxiety*, which is a hilarious spoof of Alfred Hitchcock thrillers, Dr. Richard H. Thorndyke is the new chief administrator for the prestigious "Psychoneurotic Institute for the Very, Very Nervous." But Dr. Thorndyke quickly discovers that there are some VERY sinister goings-on at the hospital. On his first day, as he is being driven from the airport to the institute, his chauffer Brophy announces that the sudden demise of the previous chief administrator was "highly suspicious!" True to the genre conventions, ominous orchestral music (nondiegetic music) punctuates this portentous revelation.

As soon as the music kicks in, Dr. Thorndyke and Brophy start looking around. The audience wonders: What are they looking for? And at that moment a bus carrying the entire Los Angeles Philharmonic passes their car, playing the very ominous orchestral music that we (and they) are hearing. In one moment, the music that we assumed was simply the musical score becomes diegetic music coming from just outside their car.

■ **Figure 22-3** Mel Brooks pokes fun at cinematic conventions by exposing the "true source" of the ominous music that underscores this scene from *High Anxiety* (1977).

surges when two characters finally kiss, or the sound of a car crash just as an infatuated boy says something stupid to the girl he's trying to win. There is no literal car crash in the world of the film, neither the boy nor the girl hears this sound, but the filmmaker is making a sound metaphor for the boy's crash-and-burn attempt to get the girl.

■ SOUND DESIGN II: THE SOUND ELEMENTS IN DETAIL

Now let's look in more detail at those basic audio categories (speech, sound effects, and music), with the added aspects of sync and source. When we consider these other factors, we are able to break down the general categories even further and define all of the kinds of sounds we can employ in a sound design. Remember, not every sound design contains every kind of sound.

Speech

Sync Dialogue and Off-Screen Dialogue

Sync dialogue is dialogue that is recorded in sync with the picture during the production phase. The picture and sound from the shot are both used and sync is maintained during editing. Off-screen dialogue is dialogue that comes from a person who is assumed to be in the time and space of the film (diegetic sound), but simply is not in the view of the camera. For example, we are with a character inside a hotel room when someone knocks on the door and screams, "Let me in or I'll break the door down!" Because there is no visual reference in the frame this is a nonsync sound element, although many times we use sound that was recorded as sync sound, but in the edit we decide not to use the corresponding image.

Voice-over Narration

Voice-over narration is also nonsync sound and has no direct visual sync reference in the frame; however, it differs from off-screen sound in that it is understood by the audience that the voice cannot be heard by the people in the scene. This means that the voice-over is either not in the time and space of the film world (nondiegetic sound), as in the case of narrator who is commenting on the events or narrating the story of the film, or it can be the unspoken thoughts of a character in the scene.

ADR

ADR is the acronym for **automatic dialogue replacement**, which is the rerecording, of sync dialogue, in a studio, in cases where the production sound is not usable. ADR is also referred to as **looping** because the

■ **Figure 22-4** In this scene from Haneke's *Code Unknown* (2000), he replicates a typical ADR session, where actors are brought back to re-record their lines as they watch themselves on screen.

method of rerecording and syncing up the dialogue involves the actor standing in a studio in front of a microphone watching a loop of the scene whose dialogue needs replacing over and over again (**Figure 22-4**). The actor watching the scene also listens to the field recordings of their performance on headphones while trying to duplicate the words, timing, and emotional intensity. ADR can be used to replace poorly recorded audio, improve articulation or performance, or even "re-voice" a character (meaning to replace an actor's voice with another's).

ADR can be an expensive and elaborate process, especially if you have to pay Tom Cruise to come back into a rented ADR studio to redo the dialogue for entire scenes. But on shorts and independent films, where field recordings are mostly used, ADR can simply mean replacing an unintelligible line or two here and there, while the talent watches the scene on a laptop computer in a soundproof room.

---

in practice ▶

Speech in Films
Dialogue

With very few exceptions, narrative films after the silent era have used some degree of sync dialogue. In some film genres, dialogue is *the* dominant storytelling element. The screwball comedy genre is known for its reliance on wall-to-wall, fast-paced, witty verbal repartee, and nowhere is this more clearly illustrated than in the following conversation between two recently divorced newspaper re-

porters, from *His Girl Friday* (1940), by Howard Hawks (**Figure 22-5**).

Hildy: Walter!

Walter: What?

Hildy: The mayor's first wife, what was her name?

Walter: You mean the one with the wart on her . . .?

Hildy: Right.

Walter: Fanny!

■ **Figure 22-5** Fast and witty repartee is central to the screwball comedy genre as epitomized in Hawks's *His Girl Friday* (1940), with Cary Grant and Rosalind Russell.

Stanley Kubrick, on the other hand, used quite a different approach in *2001: A Space Odyssey*, where his use of dialogue was extremely spare. In his article "*2001: A Space Odyssey* Re-viewed" (from the book, "The Making of *2001: A Space Odyssey*"), Alexander Walker claims that, "there are barely forty minutes of dialogue in a 141 minute film." By far, the most verbal character in this film is the com-

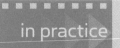
in practice

puter HAL 9000, whose dialogue expresses much more emotion than do any of the human beings in the movie (Figure 22-6). In fact, while crewmember Poole dies a quick and

■ **Figure 22-6** Much of the sparse dialogue in Kubrick's *2001: A Space Odyssey* (1968) is given to HAL 9000 (voiced by Douglas Rain), allowing the audience to identify with it more than with the human protagonists.

silent death in space, Kubrick gives HAL 9000 a very talky and stirringly melodramatic dying scene. As crewmember Bowman is shutting HAL 9000 down by removing one artificial intelligence bank at a time, HAL at first protests, but then, weakened, it (he?) comes to terms with its (his?) impending death:

HAL: I'm afraid. I'm afraid, Dave. Dave, my mind is going. I can feel it. I can feel it. My mind is going. There is no question about it. I can feel it. I can feel it. I can feel it. I'm afraid. Good afternoon, gentlemen. I am a HAL 9000 computer. I became operational at the H.A.L. plant in Urbana, Illinois on the 12th of January 1992. My instructor was Mr. Langley, and he taught me to sing a song. If you'd like to hear it I can sing it for you.

Dave Bowman: Yes, I'd like to hear it, HAL. Sing it for me.

■ **Figure 22-7** Hitchcock's use of off-screen dialogue expertly manipulates audience expectations in this scene from *Psycho* (1960).

HAL: It's called "Daisy."

[HAL progressively slows down as he sings]

Daisy, Daisy, give me your answer do. I'm half crazy all for the love of you. It won't be a stylish marriage, I can't afford a carriage . . .

[slows down further]

But you'll look sweet . . . upon the seat of a bicycle . . . built . . . for two. . . .

Off-Screen Voice

Alfred Hitchcock uses the physical absence of a character as an essential element of mystery and suspense in his film *Psycho* (1960) (Figure 22-7). After the brutal stabbing of Marion, we hear the off-screen voice of Norman Bates shouting, "Mother! Oh God, mother! Blood! Blood!" By keeping Norman off screen we assume he's addressing his mother, and that she may have been the one to kill Marion, but we can't be entirely sure. Randy Thom, in his article "Designing a Movie for Sound" (1999, http://www.filmsound.org), says "starving the eye will inevitably bring the ear, and therefore the imagination, into play." This is exactly Hitchcock's strategy: by suggesting the presence of Norman's mother strictly through off-screen dialogue he piques the audience's curiosity (Where is she? What does she look like?) and a mystery forms in their minds.

Voice-over

François Truffaut's classic short film *Les Mistons* (1957) (Figure 22-8) uses a sound track with two primary elements: voice-over and music. There are also a few sound effects and postsynchronously dubbed dialogue, but it is the voice-over that dominates and recounts the story of a group of preadolescent boys who spy on, tease, and torment Bernadette and Gérard, a young couple in love. When Gérard leaves to go on a mountain-climbing expedition, the boys play a trick on Bernadette, sending her a postcard that suggests that Gérard is not being faithful while he is away, but after they mail it to her they learn from the newspapers that Gérard was killed in a mountaineering accident.

in practice

Figure 22-8 Truffaut's use of voice-over in *Les Mistons* (1957) adds emotional complexity and poignancy to this story of five mischievous boys.

Voice-over as a storytelling element is frequently poorly used. It seems so easy to tell a story simply by slapping on a voice-over, but one must be sure that this technique contributes additional layers of meaning to the image rather than simply duplicating what we are seeing, or, worse, doing all of the storytelling while the images accomplish nothing. Les Mistons is a great example of well-used voice-over. The story is told from the point of view of one of the boys (we never know which), who is now a man. The young boys could not possibly understand at the time that they are experiencing a profound, tragic, and indelible life lesson as they struggle with their newly emerging and confusing desires—their first romantic crush on a woman. But it is the now grown man, reflecting on his childhood experiences in the voice-over, who reveals the emotional complexity of what would otherwise be seen simply as the irritating antics of a group of childish brats.

Sound Effects

Hard Effects

Hard effects are sound effects that are essentially gathered as a nonsync sound and then inserted into the sound design either as post-synchronous sound (synced up to a corresponding image in the editing) or as an asynchronous sound effect. Hard effects are sounds like shattering glass, dog barks, gunshots, explosions, creaking stairs, doorbells, telephones, exotic birdcalls, and a Huey helicopter fly-by. A hard sound effect can come from the production wild sound track (pfx) (e.g., a clean, nonsync recording of the actual car starting), or can be found as a prerecorded sound effects from commercial sound effects libraries (on CDs or the Internet), or can be constructed from a collection of sounds, like mixing a car starting sound with a lion's roar to reflect a character's anger as he starts the car and pulls away (Figure 22-9).

25.	Small group gasp - astonished.	:01
26.	Party - social gathering - medium	1:04
27.	Shopping in supermarket	1:00
28.	Pool hall - general atmosphere	1:00
29.	Patchinco - continuous play	:30
30.	Karate workout atmosphere	1:00
31.	Boxing match - small arena	1:00
32.	Hot air balloon rising	:18
33.	Hot air - 1 long blast	:09
34.	Sailing with surf	1:00
35.	Golf Swing - driving club whoosh	01
36.	Factory with automated machines	1:00
37.	Sleigh Bells - jingling	1:00
38.	Door Bell - Avon type - 1 ring	:04
39.	Clock - church - strikes 1/2 hour	:13
48.	High performance car - engine turning over - won't start	:19
49.	High performance car - fast departure (burn out)	:05
50.	High performance car - driving - interior perspective	:30
51.	Motorcycle passing	:10
52.	Light traffic	1:00
53.	Medium traffic	1:00
54.	Outboard boat - approach	:16
55.	Tractor - start idle & stop	1:00
56.	Tractor - driving by	:30
57.	Harp - diminished glisses down and up	:10
58.	Harp - C chord - cracked	:05
59.	Harp - C chord - cracked slower	:07
60.	Slide whistle - gliss up slow	:04
61.	Slide whistle - gliss down slow	:03
62.	Vibra - slap - accent	:03
63.	Boat whistle - orchestral - 2 blasts	:06

Figure 22-9 An enormous repository of prerecorded hard effects and ambient sounds can be found through commercial sound effect libraries on CDs or on the Internet.

It's extremely important to record, create, or find the sound effect that will have the particular impact you need, and this is a task that requires great attention to detail. One doesn't just say, "Hey, I need a dog barking." That's way too general. To get just the right one, each sound effect needs to be considered from a number of different angles. You need to have a specific sense for the size and kind of dog (the "yap" of a Yorkie or the lazy "woof-woof" of a hound dog), the kind of bark (playful, serious, or rabid barking), and the dramatic context for the bark (Is the film a drama or comedy? Is the barking realistic or expressionistic?), and so on.

Foley Effects

Foley effects, named after Universal Picture sound department head Jack Foley, differ from hard effects in that they are recorded in synchronization with the edited film. A foley session involves watching a scene in a soundproof room, with whatever objects or sur-

■ **Figure 22-10** Professional foley rooms are sound studios designed to record post-synchronous sound effects while the foley artist watches the scene projected. As you can see here, they are outfitted with a wide array of objects that can make a variety of noises.

faces you need to create the right noise, and creating and recording the sounds as you watch the film. The recording is done onto a digital sound recorder and input into the NLE system to be aligned with the scene. The intention of a foley effect is always to create a sound in sync with the picture. Just like ADR, a foley session can be an extremely elaborate and expensive event, requiring professional **foley artists** and a special **foley room** equipped with, among other things, different floor surfaces (gravel, concrete, wood, carpet, etc.), in order to create the right "walking sounds" (**Figure 22-10**). But for shorts and independent films, a foley session can simply mean watching your footage on a laptop computer in a soundproof room and re-creating a sound effect or two onto a digital recorder, then putting it back into the NLE and making the necessary frame adjustments to get the sequence in sync.

Ambient Sound and Walla-walla

Ambient sound is the overall aural environment in which a scene takes place—the background noises and other acoustic properties. Ambient sound can come from the field recordings at the actual locations or can be pulled off commercial sound effects libraries, which can offer hundreds of different ambient environments ("stormy night," "horse stable," "rainforest with birds," "city streets/rush hour," "sheet metal factory," and so on). While shooting an early film of mine, I was lucky to record the sounds of some beautiful birds chirping in the trees. I used this ambient sound in two other short films of mine before I retired the track. It is not uncommon to use multiple ambient tracks in a single scene.

It's important to note that "silence" in film, as well as in real life, does not mean "utterly no sound." During "silent" passages, we should be able to hear the ambient sound of the environment, the naturally occurring background noises. What this means is that there is never a time when a sound track has no audio track. At the very least, it will contain very quiet ambient sound that only feels like silence.

Walla-walla is the term used for ambient sound that involves the general, unintelligible chatter of a group of people. You can have, for example, the walla-walla of a theater audience before the curtain goes up, or of a cocktail party or an art gallery opening. Walla-walla is a great resource for a low-budget filmmaker, because it is often used under a scene to give the impression that there are many more people in the location (off screen) than there actually were in production. For example, a medium close-up of two people sitting in a restaurant may have been shot in an empty restaurant during off hours, but by putting "crowded restaurant ambience and walla-walla" under the scene, it will feel like the place is full. Like ambient sound, you can record this yourself as wild sound or you can get it from a sound effects library.

As with everything else in film, ambient sound has a practical use and a creative application. Practically speaking, the ambient track is used to smooth out any ambient shifts that would be apparent when cutting from one shot to another in the same scene. For

Using Sound Effects in Film
Hard (Hitting) Effects

Anyone who has seen a fight in real life knows that a real punch doesn't sound like much—it sounds quite a bit like a slap, only a little more solid. It certainly doesn't sound as bad as it *feels*. A real punch sound is decidedly undramatic, which is why many "punch" sound effects are constructed out of layers of other sounds (not to mention that you can't go around hitting people just to get the pfx of a punch). But when constructing a sound effect, like a punch, you need to consider the visual and dramatic context for the effect. The sound of a bare-fisted punch would be different than one with a boxing glove; a punch to the jaw should sound different than a punch in the gut. Also, the sound of a punch seen in a long shot would have less vivid presence than would a punch in a close-up shot. Additionally, a punch in a comedy film will sound very different than the same punch in a hard-hitting drama. A student of mine, in an editing class exercise, created a punch sound effect for his "found footage" that included one quick shot of a knockout punch from a boxing match. He blended the sound of a baseball bat hitting the soft cushion of a sofa, for the low "thud," and the sound of crushing a small head of lettuce, for the high "crunch" of damaged nose cartilage, and his own fist hitting his wet palm, for the "slap" of leather on flesh. The effect was pretty darn good, if a little bit too visceral for his exercise. The "knockout punch" effect stole the show (Figure 22-11).

In the world of sound design, it's universally recognized that supervising sound effects editor Frank Warner created some of the greatest "punch" sounds in the history of movies for Scorsese's *Raging Bull.* Warner created punches that acutely reflected the subjective *feel* of receiving blows from a prizefighter. Not only do the boxers get punched, but everyone in the audience *feels* each uppercut right on their own jaw. How did Warner construct these sound effects? So far, he hasn't shared with anyone this particular sound effect recipe and he has since destroyed the original multitrack tapes. Although there are rumors that melons and tomatoes were involved, no one really knows exactly how he created those punches. It has remained a secret even from Martin Scorsese himself, who admits that he indeed asked, but wasn't told.

Less Is More

Sometimes with sound effects, less is more (Figure 22-12). A former student of mine in an intermediate production class made a simple, high-energy comedy chase scene, in which a high school kid on a skateboard is being chased by his mother, who turns out to be the superior athlete. She ultimately catches the kid and forces him to finish his breakfast. The end. At one point, as the mother chases her son, the boy bumps into an old lady carrying groceries, knocking her onto her fanny (the mother later hurdles right over the woman as she picks up her oranges). The old lady was played by a sophomore dance major (wearing loads of makeup) and she was miked with an ultra-cardioid to get good sync sound. The stuntwoman did a great job of getting knocked backward, sprawling, onto the sidewalk. But when the student showed his synced dailies in class, rather than laugh, the students groaned with sympathetic pain. The sounds were too good, too real, too close. We could hear flesh and bone hitting the hard concrete and we felt this

Figure 22-11 Among the most famous and mythologized sound effects in film history are Frank Warner's "punch" sounds in Scorsese's *Raging Bull* (1980).

Figure 22-12 To keep us laughing, the slapping, poking, punching, and falling sounds in the *Three Stooges* are given a comedic rather than a visceral tone. Mo is no Jake LaMotta. From *Nutty but Nice* Dir. Jules White (1940).

poor old woman's pain and it was anything but funny. Clearly, the student filmmaker needed a different "fall" sound effect. He removed the sync sound and found a funny "yelp and fall" sound effect on a sound effects CD that had a huge selection of "cartoon" sound effects. The new "fall" sound included a soft "splat" and comical "boioing," clearly not realism. When he showed the edited film, the old lady's fall was now a truly comic pratfall.

Simple Foley

I once edited a scene that had no dialogue and involved a man standing in a bathtub, up to his ankles in water, bathing (Figure 22-13). After his bath he steps out of the tub and leaves the bathroom. The scene was shot MOS (without sound) so I needed to create all

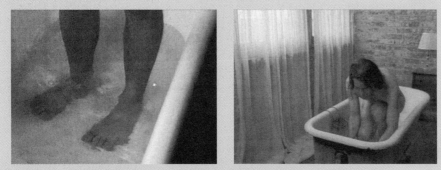

■ **Figure 22-13** Simple Foley effects were used to create all the bath water sounds in K. Hurbis-Cherrier's short film *Ode to a Bar of Soap* (1998).

of the sounds in foley. After the scene was cut, I simply brought the footage on my laptop into a music practice room (a soundproof space) along with a large plastic tub of water and a microphone hooked up to a DAT recorder. I positioned the mike above the water and plunged my hands in. When the man moved in the tub, I swirled my hands around, making the sound his legs might make. When he stepped out of the tub, I quickly removed both arms from the water, to make the right "splash" sound, and when his feet hit the tiled floor, I patted my wet hands on the linoleum floor of the practice room to make the "pit-pat" sound of wet flesh on tile. After downloading the sound into my NLE, it took only a little tweaking and the entire scene had

perfectly convincing sound to accompany the image. All that was left was to add ambience to the location.

Ambience and Walla-walla

Andrew Lund's *Snapshot* (2006) is a low-budget short film that revolves around the kidnapping of the wildly popular photographer Marcello, who has enjoyed a lucrative career taking candid photos of people on the street (Figure 22-14). His kidnapper is Nathan, the disgruntled subject of one of his photos who believes that Marcello ruined his life when he published the fateful photograph showing Nathan at a highly compromised moment. In order to establish the popularity of the photographer, the film opens with an elaborate and well-attended museum retrospective of the photographer's work. But Lund did not have the time or money to wrangle a large, well-heeled crowd of extras to populate the museum opening. So he and his editor/sound designer, Dave Monahan, created the crowd through sound. In the museum scene Lund kept his framing fairly tight and carefully selected several ambience and walla-walla tracks to sonically create the excited buzz and murmurs of a large crowd—but just off screen! Once in a while Lund would have an extra pass in front of the lens, implying that people are milling about, but we never see more than a few people. The effect is totally convincing; the audience gets a clear sense of a huge turnout for Marcello's big museum retrospective.

■ **Figure 22-14** Clever use of ambience and walla-walla, along with tight framing, in his short film *Snapshot* (2006) allowed Lund to convincingly conjure a crowded museum retrospective without having a real crowd.

example, in a scene in which we cut between two people sitting at a sidewalk cafe, one facing the traffic and another facing away, there might be a noticeable discrepancy between the traffic noise we hear in their respective sound recordings. Often, this ambience shift (the amount of traffic picked up by the mike) can be too abrupt for continuity's sake when cutting from one shot to the other. While we can't get rid of the traffic noise from one character's audio, we could add a little traffic ambience on another track, under the character who has less, in order to even them out.

The creative dimension of ambient sound is not to be underestimated. Finding just the right ambient sound for a scene can, with any degree of subtlety, establish an environment that makes the scene truly come alive or adds additional narrative information or an emotional tone. Ambience is also often used to create a subjective sound space, meaning that the sound environment the audience hears is a reflection of what a specific character hears. We will further explore the expressive uses of ambience and other sound effects.

Music

Source Music

Source music is the name for any music that has a visible source in the scene—for example, a song playing from a jukebox in the corner of a bar, or the guitar that a character is playing, or the orchestral music of the Los Angeles Philharmonic in a bus driving down the highway (see Figure 22-3). Source music is always diegetic music, but it is not always direct sound (recorded in sync). Many times source music is postsynchronous sound, either gathered from prerecorded music (the jukebox playing in the bar) or recorded in postproduction (the orchestral music on the bus) and synced up in the editing. The guitar music, however, could very easily be recorded on location as sync sound or handled as post-synchronous sound (Figure 22-15).

■ Figure 22-15 The music emanating from Radio Raheem's (Bill Nunn) boom box in Lee's *Do the Right Thing* (1989) is a prime example of source music, even though it was dubbed in later.

The Score

The **musical score** (or **background music**) is nonsync and nondiegetic music that generally accompanies action or dialogue to underscore the events of a scene with a tone, a mood, or musical commentary. Score music is usually barely noticed, but deeply felt. Score music is often composed specifically for the film. In this case, the edited film is given to a composer who, in close consultation with the director, will compose music timed to the actions, rhythms, and durations of specific scenes. Sometimes, the performance and recording of scored music are done while watching the scenes on a monitor (or projected) to ensure perfect timing, not unlike ADR or foley sound effects (Figure 22-16). Other times, the composer will record a number of **musical motifs**, smaller musical phrases, which can be easily combined, elongated, and rearranged in the editing process to fit the temporal dimensions of the sequences.

Motifs can have a close association with an emotion, a psychological state, or an event such that the repetition of that musical phrase will evoke that feeling or event. For *Gone With the Wind*, Max Steiner created one of the most famous motifs in film history, called "Tara's Theme," a grand sweeping melody that conjured the glory of the plantation and Scarlett's love for the land. Motifs can also be associated with a character and repeated whenever that character appears in the film or when you wish to evoke them. A character motif always contains something of the spirit of the character—for

■ Figure 22-16 On major motion pictures an entire orchestra plays and records score music while the conductor watches the scene on a monitor for timing. Pictured is a scoring session for the *Lord of the Rings* Trilogy.

■ Figure 22-17 Shigeru Umebayashi's bittersweet theme for Wong's *In the Mood for Love* (2000) perfectly encapsulates the film's slower pace and sad story, and is frequently repeated, particularly during slow motion sequences.

example, accompanying the shark in *Jaws* (1975) is the frighteningly efficient "dum-duum, dum-duum," that gathers momentum and malevolence the closer the shark gets. In either case, the music is aligned with the scenes in editing. You can also use prerecorded music from CDs for your background music, like a jazz tune or a baroque suite from a CD. Using prerecorded music, however, means that you'll be cutting your picture to a musical track that is fixed. This is a major difference between these two types of background music. With one, the editing rhythm and tempi of the picture determine the music, and with the other, the music determines the rhythms and pace of the editing. Also, the length of prerecorded music is fixed, and getting into or out of a piece can be tricky—especially if you want the score to be somewhat understated.

Film music has been around for the entire history of cinema and is in itself a complex art form. It's beyond the scope of this book to elaborate in complete detail the uses of music in films, but a few concepts might be helpful. Obviously, the **tempo** and **rhythm** of music can infuse a scene with fast and explosive energy, as in the opening of *City of God* (see p. 409), or with slow sensual fluidity, as in the case of Wong Kar-Wai's *In The Mood for Love* (Figure 22-17).

■ Figure 22-18 John Williams' majestic score for the *Star Wars* films is designed to augment the emotional tone of the action, as seen in the triumphant final destruction of the second Death Star in Lucas' *Star Wars: Episode VI – Return of the Jedi* (1983).

We are also all familiar with music that provides an **emotional tone** or **mood** in a scene. No one can resist feeling the exhilaration of victory in *Star Wars: Episode VI—Return of the Jedi* (1987) when the Rebel Alliance destroys the Death Star (Figure 22-18) and restores justice and order to the galaxy—especially when the heroism is underscored with John Williams' exuberant and energetic orchestral score. Incidentally, throughout the *Star Wars* series, Williams also created individual musical motifs for Darth Vader, Princess Leia, Luke Skywalker, and other major characters.

Even though the audience may not be aware of it at the time, most people understand how scary music can underscore frightening scenes, how lush and sweeping violins can infuse passion in a romantic moment, and how a jaunty score can encourage laughs for a funny scene. But music, like sound effects, can do much more than simply reinforce the existing mood, tone, or rhythm of a scene. In one scene in Quentin Tarantino's 1992 film *Reservoir Dogs,* an up-beat pop song ("Stuck in the Middle with You," by Stealers Wheel) plays on the radio as the cold-blooded killer, Mr. Blonde, tortures a captured police officer by slicing off his ear (Figure 22-19). The peppiness of the song completely plays against the mood, actions, and horror we're witnessing on the screen, and this ironic juxtaposition only accentuates the cruelty of the moment.

Prerecorded Music and Copyright Clearance

Using a prerecorded music track from a commercial CD, whether it's a rap song from last year, a classical symphony from the 18th century, or a folk song recorded in the 1950s, will usually require **copyright clearance**. Copyright clearance means that you have been given, or you have purchased, the rights to use specific music

■ Figure 22-19 The pop music that plays on the radio (source music) as Mr. Blonde (Michael Madsen) cruelly taunts a captured police officer creates a highly disturbing tonal dissonance in this scene from Tarantino's *Reservoir Dogs* (1992).

in your film. Getting copyright clearance requires a number of steps. Sometimes the process is painless, especially for students who do not expect to make any money from the exhibition of their project, but other times it can be prohibitively difficult and expensive.

1. First you must ascertain and contact the person (or entity) who holds the rights to the song. This can be anywhere from simple to impossible. As a student, I once tried to get the rights to use a Rolling Stones song in a film of mine. After contacting four of the numerous entities who held a piece of that song, I simply gave up. Each person passed the buck and I eventually realized that no one wanted to say yes to a proposition that held absolutely no financial gain for them. I was also discouraged because I knew that for me to legally use the song in my film I would need not just one rights holder to grant permission, but *all* of them. Obviously, the more popular the performer and composer, the more difficult it becomes because you enter into the corporate world of big money. In general, the musical composition (music and lyrics) are owned by the music publisher and recordings are owned by the record company.

2. Once you have contacted the rights holder, you need to tell them specifically (a) what you want, (b) how much of it you want, (c) in what context it will be used, and (d) how the music will be credited. As you can understand, people who create or control artistic works are very careful about how the works are used. A composer who wrote a lovely ballad may not want his song used in and associated with a slasher film bloodbath. Complicating matters is that there is often not just one "right" you need to acquire, but a bundle of rights, including clearance for lyrics, clearance for music composition, clearance for performance, etc. Also, obtaining the right to cover a song is a totally different proposition than trying to get rights to prerecorded material from a CD. In other words, you really need to know what you're asking for. But let's move on . . .

3. If the rights holders are okay with your use of the music, then you negotiate the price of getting the rights. What's important to the rights holder here is how much money the filmmaker stands to make from the film for which the music is helping to sell tickets. So you need to be honest about what sort of distribution your film is expected to get. If your movie is a short movie made for a class, and you hope to show the movie only at a few film festivals, then what you're asking for is called "festival rights." The cost of festival rights is often manageable. Occasionally, my students are given permission to use commercial music in their films for nothing.

If you have any intention of getting your film into festivals (which is a public screening), then you should take the time to acquire the necessary clearance. You never know. It's not uncommon for low-budget, independent films to become surprise festival hits, ones that attract commercial distributors. One of the first questions an interested distributor will ask is, "Do you have the rights to all of the music?" If you don't, then they'll probably back away. Why? A music rights holder is more likely to give a filmmaker a cheap price for rights *before* it has a distribution company attached, because they think the film is small, but if you attempt to buy music rights post-festival success (i.e., it has commercial value), then the earning potential of the movie skyrockets, as does the price for the music. The price for clearance can easily become more than a distributor wants to pay and so they pass, even though they love the movie. This is such a sad story and so common, but so crushing for the filmmaker that I dare not name examples, though I could.

I certainly cannot cover this topic in nearly enough detail, but it is necessary for you to be alerted to the fact that you cannot simply grab music from your CD collection to use in a film you plan to distribute to festivals or broadcast on TV. In the Recommended Readings and the Web Resources at the back of the book you will find some resources that can help you negotiate this complex terrain. Obtaining clearance, in any case, is usually a time-consuming process that requires patience, research, and persistence. Filmmakers on tight schedules, like students, are usually better off finding musicians to write original music for their films. There are many benefits to this: namely, you can acquire perfectly matched, custom-made music *and* collaborate with more creative people along the way.

Common Music Pitfalls

Music, when used correctly, can be a profoundly expressive option in the filmmaker's toolbox of storytelling elements. The use of music to enhance a motion picture's impact can seem so easy, and yet there are a number of pitfalls to be wary of. A poorly employed musical score can bury what would otherwise be a fine film. Most problems with poorly used music come from "too much." Music is like a strong cooking spice—just because a little bit is good does not mean that more is better.

1. Use music only where it is necessary. **Wall-to-wall music** is the phenomenon of the excessive and indiscriminate use of music from the beginning to the end of a film. Music that relentlessly "cues emotions" from the audience can be exhausting and counterproductive because it ultimately impedes authentic audience involvement.

2. Don't try to evoke an emotion that is not in the film. It doesn't help to throw music under a scene simply because the scene isn't working. If a suspenseful scene does not create suspense in the actions, adding suspenseful music will not necessarily help. It will simply become an unsuspenseful scene with mismatched music.

3. Too loud! Often in student films the music is mixed in so loudly that it dominates anything else in the scene. In especially bad cases, loud music makes dialogue unintelligible. This is a sound mixing issue.

4. Watch out for mismatched tempo. Rhythm and tempo come from many places: the cutting pace, the actions in the frame, the camerawork, and the dialogue. Be careful that your music fits well with the tempo you've established in the picture editing. This doesn't necessarily mean to duplicate the rhythms beat-for-beat, because music can often serve as a rhythmic counterpoint.

5. Lyrics can be difficult to manage, especially in dialogue scenes. Lyrics tend to fight with dialogue for attention, even if you're using low-level source music, like a radio softly playing in the background. The more compelling the lyrics, the more they'll scream "listen to me!"

6. A related problem is inappropriate lyrics. I've seen many films where students will use a piece of music because they love the beats or the melody, but they're so familiar with the song that they've stopped really listening to the words. Remember: the words are expressing something. They will invariably add a layer of meaning to your film. Make sure it's something you want to include.

7. Emotional associations are not fixed. While music is especially useful for conjuring emotions, the relationship between the particular music and the individual listener can be highly subjective. This is especially a problem when using popular music. You may decide to use a song in a love scene because it was on the radio two summers ago when you fell in madly love, so that piece of music resonates, for you, with all of those feelings. But this may not be a universal feeling about that song; in fact, there are no universal feelings about any song. When you use a very popular song, people bring their feelings about that song (and that band or that musical genre) with them into your movie instead of gleaning the emotional context from within the world of your movie.

---

in practice

Simple Score Music

Keep in mind that you certainly do not need the Los Angeles Philharmonic and a professional recording studio to score a film. One of my own short films, *Ode to Things* (1997) (7 minutes), was scored by Byron Estep, a very talented musician playing only a guitar, and the music was recorded in a small soundproof recording room Byron built in his apartment. *Ode to Things* is an adaptation of a poem by Pablo Neruda; it follows a day in the life of a married couple, detailing the myriad "things" they use over the course of that day: keys, pencils, napkins, shoelaces, spoons, sunglasses, etc. Byron and I sat in his apartment and watched the film a few times, discussing the overall feeling I wanted to evoke in the film, which was affection. The film, I told him, was an affectionate and appreciative look at those simple objects that help us live our daily lives, but that we scarcely even notice. It was a paean to common objects. I also pointed out to him the place where the film/poem shifts from a literal discussion of "things" into a more metaphysical mode. I indicated to him that there needed to be a marked shift in the tone of the music right at that point, telling him where the music needed to dig a little deeper. As we watched and talked he played me a few riffs on the guitar and together we found the musical mood and themes we were looking for. Then Byron moved to his soundproof room, opened a mike, and, as he watched the film one more time, expertly improvised on those themes, modulating into a minor key and slowing the tempo just a hair when the film shifted into its metaphysical mode; then he resolved back to the bright major key just as the final images faded to black. He nailed it in one go! I took that track, which was recorded on DAT, and downloaded it into the Avid, laid it into my sound track, and adjusted a few frames, and voilà, my scored sound track was done. All in all it took one great musician and about four hours.

■ **Figure 22-20** The lovely original score music for Hurbis-Cherrier's short *Ode to Things* (1998) was conceived, written, performed and recorded by Byron Estep—in his apartment!

■ SOUND DESIGN STRATEGIES

> *Sound may be the most powerful tool in the filmmaker's arsenal in terms of its ability to seduce. That's because "sound," as the great sound editor Alan Splet once said, "is a heart thing." We, the audience, interpret sound with our emotions, not our intellect.*
>
> **Randy Thom (sound designer, *Wild at Heart, Forrest Gump, The Incredibles*)**
> **(From "Designing a Movie for Sound," 1999, http://www.filmsound.org)**

In film production we have a great degree of control over the actual sounds used in the sound design and we are able to create a sound environment that can be anything from highly objective, using a direct sound, documentary approach, to highly subjective, reflecting the emotional or psychological state of a character. A sound design can provide a tone of irony or hyperbole, or even create fantastic or intellectual associations between sound and image. Moreover, one can combine any number of approaches in a single film. The possibilities are endless. The question to ask yourself is: What are you trying to say with this film and how can sound help you accomplish that?

From Realism to Stylized Approaches

The continuum from **realism** in sound to a **stylized** sound design, as with cinematography, cannot be broken down into strict categories. The differences between approaches can be subtle and practices can overlap. Films that overall employ a realistic sound design often use stylization to elevate certain dramatic moments.

Realism obviously can be achieved through **direct sound**, which is the use of sounds recorded at the actual location (usually in sync). This "realism" is a documentary type of realism, but depending on microphone placement can be more or less convincing. Realism is also achievable through the careful and judicious addition of other nondirect sounds, which are motivated by the scale of a shot (close-ups requiring "closer" sounds and long shots requiring remote sounds), by the dramatic magnitude of the actions, or by character psychology. For

Figure 22-21 The barking of this dog in Kurosawa's *Dreams* (1990) is manipulated to sound much more aggressive than in real life. Michel Chion calls this type of sound manipulation "added value sound."

example, the sound of a gun firing in an extreme long shot is expected to sound lower and further away than is a gun going off in a close-up. However, the direct sound of a man firing a gun in a long shot might be "realistic," but will also, in all likelihood, be thinner than what most movie audiences expect from a gunshot in a fictional narrative film. If the narrative context calls for a big and violent sound, then adding a closer, darker gunshot sound effect will be necessary and not necessarily unrealistic. Using a sound that enriches the image and adds an expressive or emotional feel to the action from which it emanates is referred to (originally by the sound theorist Michel Chion) as **added value sound**. This "hyper-real" sound effect doesn't in and of itself create a stylized sound approach. Although it is an artifice, it in fact gives a stronger impression of realism by reinforcing the emotional energy of the dramatic moment. Remember, sound is "a heart thing."

However, if we should add a sound effect of a lion's roar inside the gunshot, to augment the menace and power of the gun, we would then be pulling away from realism into stylization. A simple example of this can be seen in Akira Kurosawa's *Dreams* (1990) (Figure 22-21).

In "The Tunnel" segment an officer walks along a small mountain road, returning home from a battle in which his entire platoon has been annihilated. As he enters a tunnel, he is confronted by rabid dog, which bares its teeth, growls, and barks at him. Through a layered sound design, each bark and growl of the dog includes real vicious dog barks with what sounds like gunshots and cannon fire. The sound effect not only increases the ferociousness of the dog, but through it we understand that this is decidedly not a "real" dog . . . it is a hound from hell, a dog from the hell of war. In keeping with the otherworldliness of this particular "dream" (or nightmare, in this case), Kurosawa employs an otherworldly, stylized sound approach.

in practice

Story and Realistic Design

The Dardenne brothers' 1996 film *La Promesse* is an excellent example of a realist film that uses a direct sound approach almost exclusively to express its tragic story in an utterly honest and immediate way. The Dardenne brothers' aesthetic approach to this film, as with all of their other films, is a fairly strict vérité documentary style: handheld camera, real locations, natural light, and almost exclusively direct audio recorded by the microphone in the field. An example of the effectiveness of the Dardennes' uncompromising approach occurs early in the film, when the main character, Igor, a 15-year-old boy, is running through a building under construction, warning all of the illegal immigrant workers to flee because inspectors are on their way. As he climbs a staircase, Igor hears Amidou, an illegal immigrant from Africa, fall several floors from the scaffolding. Igor races down the stairs; when he reaches Amidou, Igor sees that he is badly hurt. Just before the man dies, he asks the boy to take care of his wife and the boy promises that he will. It's a central and highly dramatic moment in the film—but the audio remains absolutely realistic and without any embellishment. What the boy hears in the stairwell is the very faint and simple clank of a scaffolding pipe breaking loose. It's easy to miss and we certainly don't know what has happened until the boy reaches Amidou outside. During the dialogue between them, not one additional sound is used to pull pathos from the moment. There is no sad music, no added value sound effects, no special ambience to enrobe these characters at this moment in which everything is suddenly and dramatically changed. The track consists of whatever was picked up on the boom mike in the field. The strict use of nothing but direct sound leads the audience to feel that this is not a constructed fictional film, that this did indeed truly happen. In this unembellished moment we feel that we are kneeling next to Amidou and Igor (Figure 22-22).

Story and a Stylized Design

Jonathan Demme's *The Silence of the Lambs* (1991), on the other hand, is a classic example of a film, shot in a highly precise and dramatic style, which uses added value sounds (ambience and sound effects) in a more or less "realistic" way throughout most of the film, and then selectively elevates other, highly dramatic moments by incorporating overtly stylistic flourishes to the sound design. For example, early in the film, just as the lead character, Clarice Starling, is about to meet the serial killer, Hannibal Lecter, for the first time, the Chief Administrator of the institution, Dr. Chilton, shows Clarice a photograph of one of Hannibal's victims. We do not see the photograph she is looking at, only her reaction, but the sound track leaves no doubt as to the gruesomeness of the image and the savagery of Lecter's actions. On the dialogue track Chilton talks about the attack on a nurse, "When she leaned over him he did *this* to her . . . they managed to save an eye, reset her jaw more or less . . ." and his voice is recorded oppressively close, too close for comfort, like he's right at our ear. The ambience track suddenly becomes thick with a portentous low bass rumble and a sound effects track additionally layers the diabolical groans and malevolent breathing of a madman. Although Clarice is trying to remain professional and confident, the sound track infuses the scene with fear (for her and the audience) and the feeling that when she sees Hannibal, she will in fact see the face of evil. A few moment later, as Clarice enters the secure cell block where Hannibal is imprisoned, the automatic prison bars close behind her with a decisive, resounding, and exaggerated *clang*, giving her and us the feeling that she is well and good locked in with a madman who eats people's faces. Then, the moment she begins her tentative progress toward Hannibal's cell, the music track slips in. A slow, low-pitched dirge, a frightening musical scale, descends lower and lower the closer she gets to "Hannibal the Cannibal," who, once he sees her, greets her with a surprisingly courteous "Good Morning." All of these sounds (ambience, sound effects, and music) are not merely hyper-real, but they are downright expressionistic. The sound design not only amplifies the terror that the young FBI agent is feeling at meeting her first serial killer face-to-face, but it communicates her emotional point of view so directly that we feel what she is feeling as well.

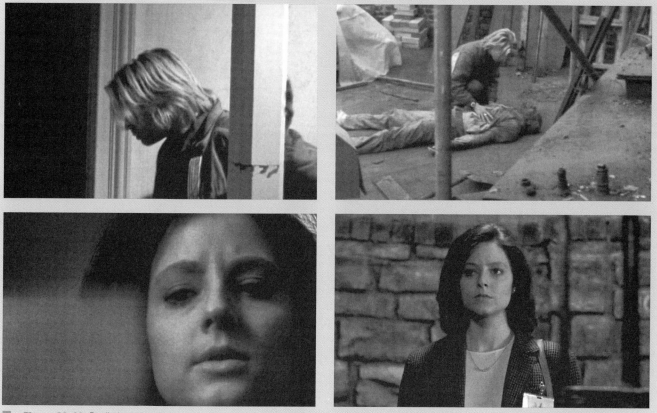

■ **Figure 22-22** Realistic and stylized sound design. In *La Promesse* (1996) the Dardenne brothers maintain audio that matches the documentary style of their cinematography (top). In Demme's *The Silence of the Lambs* (1991) sound is manipulated to heighten the dramatic tension (bottom).

Cutting Sound and Working with Multiple Tracks

One of the things that I try to hold on to is some sort of creative constraint. For example, one of those creative constraints might be: "I'm going to only give myself eight channels to edit" . . . and if I can't make something interesting in that eight channels, I am going to get rid of something and replace it with something else until I get something that is, in fact, interesting. And the reason why that's an important way to work is that it helps you focus on what the music and the sound is truly about. Because if you can't figure out the essence of "what it's about" within a creative constraint of a minimum amount of channels then you're probably doing something wrong.

Ren Klyce (sound designer, *Panic Room, Fight Club, Seven*)
(From DVD extras, *Panic Room*, 2002)

■ WORKING WITH MULTIPLE TRACKS

In the previous chapter we defined a film's sound design as the complete aural impression of a movie created through the layering of multiple tracks of sound, and we concentrated on defining the various sound elements, discussing their creative application. In this chapter we will look closely at the more practical aspects of building the sound design, specifically how to work with multiple tracks within a nonlinear editing timeline. The most basic principle of multiple tracks is that it allows us to layer sounds that occur simultaneously in the film—for example, music playing under dialogue while we also hear waves crashing on the shore, which would involve three layered tracks running simultaneously (Figure 23-1).

There are three fundamental tasks in audio postproduction: **finding**, **positioning**, and **enhancing**. The first task we have already covered in detail (choosing the best lines of dialogue, the perfect sound effects, and the most appropriate music). The second task is to locate the precise placement for each sound element in your sound design, meaning the right dramatic moment (horizontally along the timeline) and the best track for individual equalizing and creative sound manipulation (vertically along the layered tracks). The third task involves the enhancement of each sound element to craft a multilayered sound design that works toward the same goal as the writing, directing, cinematography, and editing—telling your story in the style you choose.

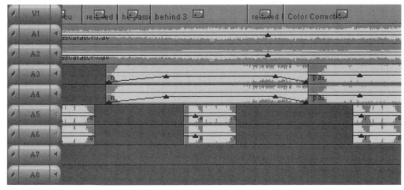

■ **Figure 23-1** The timeline for this project has 8 tracks of audio—4 stereo pairs. NLE systems can layer upwards of 99 tracks of audio.

Building Your Audio Tracks

Even though popular NLE systems allow us to create 99 tracks, clearly most films use only a small fraction of this capacity. The sound design for *Apocalypse Now* included more than 75 audio tracks, but short films and low-budget productions can easily be made with anywhere from 3 to 12 tracks of audio.

The construction of your sound design follows various stages, from the most important sounds (those that are essential to understanding the story) to the supplementary sounds (those that add tone, mood, or other sonic dimensions to the film). We begin to build our tracks from the moment we start to put shots together in the first assembly and first rough cut. If your film is driven primarily by a music track, then start with that. If you're cutting a narrative that is dialogue based, then picture and dialogue editing will happen simultaneously. As you edit your early rough cuts you will find it necessary to start adding other sound track layers that also play a vital role in the progress of the story and are therefore necessary for picture editing. Again, the basic rule for rough editing applies: don't fine-tune something that may have to be undone later. Start with the cake, and then later add the icing. The typical progression for the gradual buildup of audio tracks for a narrative film with sync sound dialogue goes something like this:

- Audio tracks from rough cut to fine cut:

1. *Dialogue:* The first assembly and first rough cut include rough picture and production dialogue editing involving only a few tracks of audio (see Chapter 20).
2. *Essential sound effects:* Subsequent rough cuts add a sound effect track for important hard sound effects, especially those that are central to the story and to which characters in a scene respond.
3. *Music–I:* If necessary, an additional track is then added for sequences that are intended to be edited to music (for example, chases or montage sequences cut to prerecorded music).

- Audio tracks after picture lock:
  Once you have arrived at picture lock, with the image and essential audio tracks in their fixed places, you then turn your attention to the supplementary sounds—those sounds

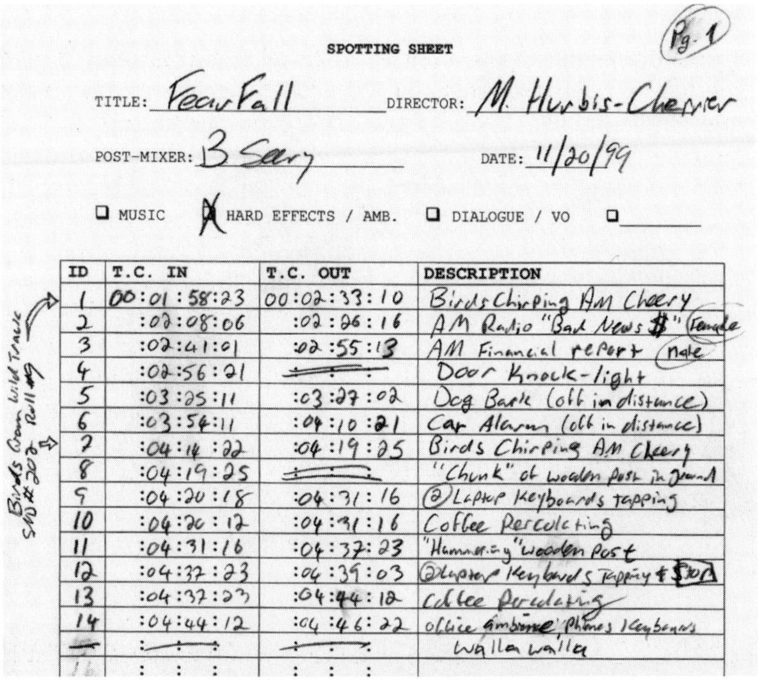

SPOTTING SHEET

Pg. 1

TITLE: FearFall DIRECTOR: M. Hurbis-Cherrier

POST-MIXER: B Seary DATE: 11/20/99

☐ MUSIC ☒ HARD EFFECTS / AMB. ☐ DIALOGUE / VO ☐

ID	T.C. IN	T.C. OUT	DESCRIPTION
1	00:01:58:23	00:02:33:10	Birds Chirping AM Cheery
2	:02:08:06	:02:26:16	AM Radio "Bad News $" Female
3	:02:41:01	:02:55:13	AM Financial report Male
4	:02:56:21	—	Door Knock-light
5	:03:25:11	:03:27:02	Dog Bark (off in distance)
6	:03:54:11	:04:10:21	Car Alarm (off in distance)
7	:04:14:22	:04:19:25	Birds Chirping AM Cheery
8	:04:19:25	—	"Chunk" of wooden post in ground
9	:04:20:18	:04:31:16	(2) Laptop Keyboards tapping
10	:04:26:12	:04:31:16	Coffee Percolating
11	:04:31:16	:04:37:23	"Hammering" wooden post
12	:04:37:23	:04:39:03	(2) Laptop Keyboards Tapping +
13	:04:37:23	:04:44:12	Coffee Percolating
14	:04:44:12	:04:46:22	Office Ambience Phones Keyboards Walla walla
—	: : :	: : :	
	: : :	: : :	

Birds from Wild Track SND # 203 Roll

■ **Figure 23-2** The first page of the sound effects spotting sheet for *FearFall* (2000). After picture lock, all missing sound effects are listed in the order they occur in the program with their approximate timecode in- and out-points.

that provide extra layers of mood, tone, and information. This is where much of the creative sound design work begins. The first step in this process is called **spotting for sound** (or just **spotting**). Spotting is the process of sitting down and closely watching the picture-locked movie to identify, scene-by-scene, the placement and character of any additional sound effects, ambience tracks, or music that are needed. Notes are taken on a "**spotting sheet**" detailing the location (scene, shot, and time code reference) of each sound effect and music track (sync and nonsync), along with your thoughts on the tone, mood, or other contribution that each sound is supposed to provide in the film (Figure 23-2). Do you want to add an off-screen siren under a tense confrontation? What sort of siren? How far off? On what line exactly does it come in and how long can we hear it before it fades away? If someone else is composing the music or creating the sound design, then this process is done in collaboration between them and the director.

Continuing with the track progression, the next steps involve:

4. *Adding final hard sound effects:* Once the film has been thoroughly spotted, all of the sound effects must be composed (or found) and placed in the appropriate audio track. This usually involves adding a few more tracks if several effects overlap. This step is where you replace all scratch sound effects as well.

5. *Room tone tracks:* An additional track is added for production room tone when it is needed to smooth over dialogue edits and fill in dialogue gaps. Remember: with extremely rare exceptions, there should be no place in your sound design where there is utterly no sound. Silence almost always means adding quiet room tone. A complete absence of sound signals to viewers a technical problem with the audio.

6. *Ambient tracks:* Further tracks can be added if you need additional ambient sounds to add a mood or sense of location for a certain scene (like adding the ambient sound of off-screen waves on the beach to indicate that a scene takes place in the kitchen of a beachfront home).

7. *Score music and background source music:* Finally, after the composer has created the score (specifically to the locked picture edit) and/or you've located any background source music used in the film, you'll need to add still more tracks to accommodate these elements.

By now you should be getting a good idea how a film like *Apocalypse Now* ended up with close to 75 tracks of audio! However, again, remember that many films do not necessarily use all of these sound tracks; in fact, many short films might need only four or fewer tracks.

What Are Scratch Tracks?
Scratch tracks (also called **temp tracks**) are audio cuts (either music, voice-over, or special effects) that are slugged in temporarily during the editing process when the actual sounds still need to be composed, recorded, or located. Rather than hold up the picture cutting, we insert scratch tracks that have a similar character (rhythm, feel, duration) to the sound we will ultimately use. Scratch tracks are often used in editing the rough cuts to establish basic placement and timing and are replaced when the actual sound is ready.

■ BASIC SOUND DESIGN: ANALYSIS OF AN AVERAGE SCENE

Figures 23-3 and 23-4 shows an example of the audio track layout for a relatively ordinary scene that has a few stylistic flourishes. This scene, from the final moments of a film I made in 2000 called *FearFall,* takes place in an average, middle class, sub-

■ **Figure 23-3** The scene from *FearFall* (2000) in which detailed attention to sound design was considered early in the script-writing stage.

```
                                                                    46

          INT. WILSON BEDROOM - NIGHT

          Ray is standing at the window, eyes fixed on the Jones
          house.  Ellen sits up in the bed, telephone next to her,
          re-reading Sophie's note.

          Ray sees a light go on and for the first time he sees a
          figure next door: against the closed curtains a man's
          silhouette crosses from the front of the house to the
          back.  The light goes off.  Then Ray faintly hears the
          Jones' BACKDOOR open and close.  The dog BARKS, then
          stops.  A METALLIC SCRAPE, the lock on his gate?  Some
          RUSTLING outside...

          A beat of silence, suddenly Ray cocks his head to listen.

                              RAY
                         (whispering)
                    Did you lock the back door?

                                   ELLEN (O.S.)
                         Ray, I'm not...

                              RAY
                         (sharp but still a whisper)
                    Ssshhh!  Did you lock the door?

          Ellen is getting scared.

                              ELLEN
                         (whispering)
                    I think so...I don't know.

          Suddenly, a dull THUD downstairs, definitely IN their
          house!  They freeze.

                              RAY
                         (very softly)
                    They're in here.

          INT. WILSON KITCHEN

          Sophie has just opened the refrigerator which has caused
          bottles to rattle.  She pokes around for munchies and
          beer.
```

urban neighborhood. Ray Wilson has become completely paranoid about the people who recently moved in next door, although he's never met or even seen them. His mania has caused his 15-year-old daughter to "run away" from home, which means she's just hanging out at a friend's house (which she explains in a note to her parents). Ray, however, is sure that she's been lured next door by the neighbors, whom he is convinced are very dangerous.

In this scene sound was central to the progress of the story and psychology of the character. Ray hears a collection of ambiguous noises that, in his paranoid state, signify that the neighbors have broken into his house. To him, the sounds are clear evidence of someone moving from the Jones' house, to the backyard, and into his house. On screen, Ray's head pivots as his eyes follow exactly this path. In fact, the sounds are a circumstantial

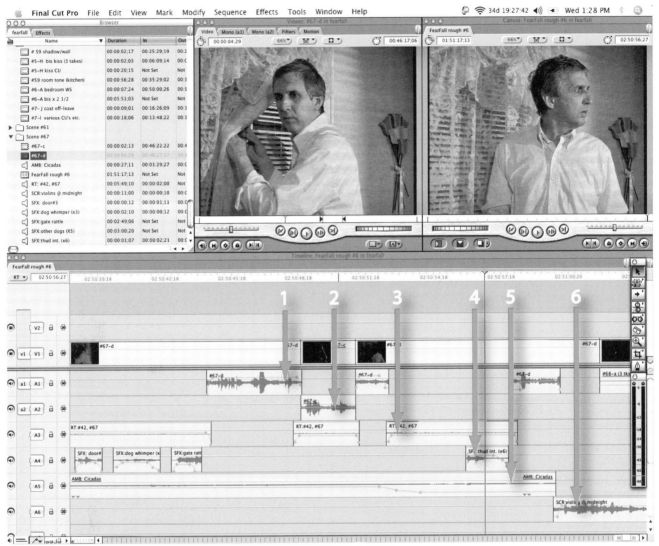

■ Figure 23-4 A careful selection of sounds serves to deepen Ray's (James Rutledge) paranoia in this scene from *FearFall*. Audio tracks: Track #1, Ray's dialogue; Track #2, Ellen's dialogue; Track #3, production room tone; Track #4, sound effects; Track #5, ambience; Track #6, music.

combination of noises from the neighbor's house and from his own daughter, who has snuck back home to nab some food for her friends. While these sounds have real (off screen) sources, the scenario Ray spins with them emerges from his paranoid imagination (Figure 23-4).

Dialogue Tracks

We have already discussed the craft of dialogue editing and the role of L-cuts, J-cuts, and insert edits for creating dialogue rhythms, point of view, and emphasis (see Chapter 20). Now let's look at a few technical aspects of handling dialogue on the timeline.

The dialogue for the *FearFall* scene discussed in the preceding section was edited as **split tracks**, meaning each character's dialogue is placed on its own audio track. The idea behind splitting tracks that occur in the same location and same time is that you have greater ability to equalize (or EQ, for short) each track separately. **Equalizing** basically means adjusting the various frequencies and characteristics of a sound to achieve a specific quality (see later, The Sound Mix). In the case of dialogue, a shift in microphone proximity, recoding quality, or ambient sound can make the edits between lines of dialogue too apparent for continuity's sake. Splitting the dialogue allows you to easily EQ

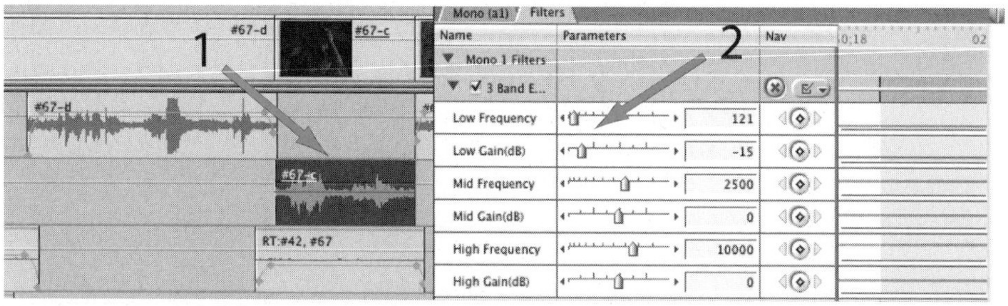

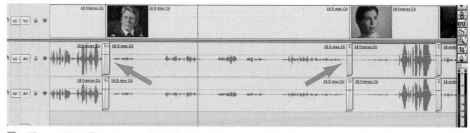

Figure 23-5 By applying the 3-band equalizer filter to a specific clip (1) you can select and attenuate very specific frequencies in the sound spectrum (2).

one or both tracks so that they match better. In the case of *FearFall,* Ellen's shots were taken later, after it had gotten very hot at the location. There was a fan going in the next room, which no one on the set noticed, but that gave her sync audio a very slight low-frequency hum. By splitting her dialogue off it was easy to select her clips and remove some low frequencies until the ambient sound of Ellen's dialogue matched Ray's perfectly (Figure 23-5). The EQing of tracks is not done in the editing stage, but is accomplished during final sound mixing (see later).

If the sound quality of your dialogue matches perfectly, then there is no reason to split tracks, and any slight smoothing out of cuts can be accomplished with quick cross-fades (four frames or so) between dialogue edits to smooth out the cut point (Figure 23-6). Splitting Ray's and Ellen's tracks also allowed me to create a slight overlap when Ray interrupts her. Scenes in which people step on each other's lines can be created by overlapping split dialogue.

Figure 23-6 The arrows point to the four frame cross-fades that are commonly used to smooth over sound edits when cutting dialogue on a single track.

Room Tone

The room tone you gathered during the production of the film is downloaded into the computer and saved as a sound clip with the other editing elements for the each scene. Room tone is used primarily to fill in "silent" gaps between lines. Remember that silence in film, as in real life, does not mean the total absence of sound. Background noises in the environment are always present and audible (with the exception of outer space, where there is no sound) (see p. 293). So, in the moment when Ray remains quiet, listening, the ambient sound of the room must fill in that space (Figure 23-7).

You may ask: Why I didn't simply use the sync take as Ray looks around and hears noises? A sync take would have had the same room tone, so why did I have to slug in new room tone? New room tone was necessary here because to get the performance I needed, i.e., the very sharp reaction to a series of noises, I "verbally cued" each noise at precisely the moment Ray was supposed to hear them. During the take I would say "the dog barks . . . stops . . . The gate, they're opening the gate! What's that rustling?" etc. All of this, of course, was picked up by the sound recordist, so the original sync take was cut out and

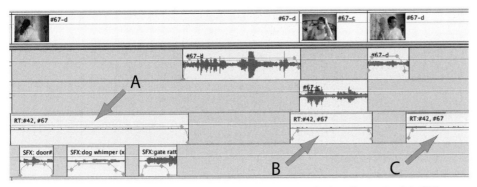

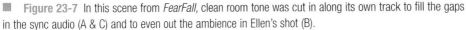

■ Figure 23-7 In this scene from *FearFall*, clean room tone was cut in along its own track to fill the gaps in the sync audio (A & C) and to even out the ambience in Ellen's shot (B).

replaced with nice, clean room tone. This illustrates another use of room tone: replacing any parts of the existing ambience that contains noises the recordist picked up, but that you'd rather not have in the sound design. If your dialogue ambience matches perfectly and you wanted to cut the dialogue on a single track, then ambience would be used between the lines to fill in the "silent" gaps (Figure 23-8).

There may be times when you look in your bin for some desperately needed room tone, only to discover that you forgot to record it on the set. This can happen, especially when the shooting schedule is particularly tight. In these cases you need to hunt through the various sound takes from that location and "steal room tone" from any spot in the recoding that has no dialogue, and duplicate that presence until you have enough to fill in the gaps.

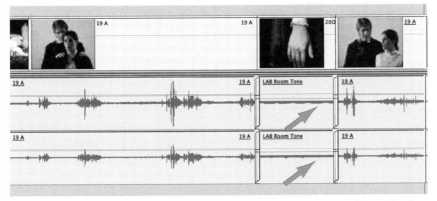

■ Figure 23-8 When cutting single strand dialogue, matching room tone can be seamlessly added under MOS shots using quick (4-frame) cross fades at the edit points (arrows).

Hard Effects Track

Hard effects are either downloaded from a digital recording or from the Internet, or imported from an audio CD as sound clips; they are then logged and named and, like room tone, saved along with the sync takes and other editing elements for each scene for quick access.

Even though all of the hard effects in the Ray/Ellen scene are nonsync, they nonetheless required very careful alignment with Ray's head and eye movements, which precisely indicated where his attention was focused and when he heard a noise. So I created the effects track right in the very first rough cut with the dialogue (Figure 23-9). Two of these effects were recorded on production. We got a great recording of the "screen door" opening and closing (with tinny spring and latch sounds) right in the house where we were

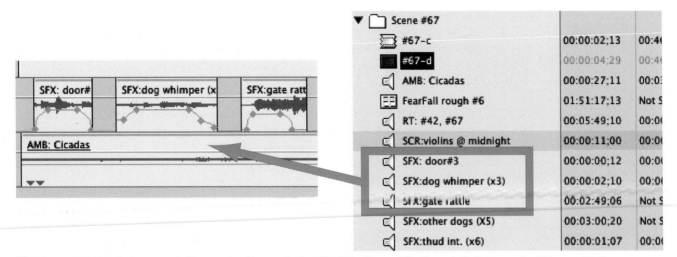

▼ ☐ Scene #67		
▦ #67-c	00:00:02;13	00:4(
▉ #67-d	00:00:04;29	00:4(
◁ AMB: Cicadas	00:00:27;11	00:0;
▦ FearFall rough #6	01:51:17;13	Not S
◁ RT: #42, #67	00:05:49;10	00:0(
◁ SCR:violins @ midnight	00:00:11;00	00:0(
◁ SFX: door#3	00:00:00;12	00:0(
◁ SFX:dog whimper (x3)	00:00:02;10	00:0(
◁ SFX:gate rattle	00:02:49;06	Not S
◁ SFX:other dogs (X5)	00:03:00;20	Not S
◁ SFX:thud int. (x6)	00:00:01;07	00:0(

■ **Figure 23-9** Detail of the sound effects and ambient tracks from FearFall. All sound files for a particular scene should be saved in the same folder as the scene clips.

shooting. And the "rustle" effect was stolen from another scene entirely (one in which Ray is in the bushes, hiding from his neighbors), but was tweaked a bit; it worked beautifully in the scene. These effects I cut in right away. Initially, I had to use a scratch "dog bark" and "metal gate" sound because it took me some time (and two CD sound effects libraries) to find just the right dog and I had to create the metal gate from scratch a few weeks later (in another location with a wrench and a chain link fence).

It's important that your sound effects be as pure as possible, without too much ambience behind the noise you want. Also, cut the effect as tightly as possible, without clipping off any of the sound. When adding additional tracks you want to avoid piling ambience on ambience each time to cut in a different sound effect. This is why good CD and Internet sound effects libraries are useful: the sounds are generally quite pure. If you record your own hard effects try to find as quiet a location as possible and close-mike the recording. You can always create sound perspective later in the mix (see later).

Ambience
Ambience is related to room tone, which is a kind of ambience also. However, in sound cutting terms, ambience is a background effects track that creates a unique sense of space and location. Many films work quite well with just the production ambience recorded in the field, but ambience can, as we saw in the previous chapter, add another layer of narrative meaning or emotional tone.

For *FearFall,* I added a nighttime ambient track with cicadas. Initially I was interested in cricket sounds, but after trying few tracks, I found it didn't add anything to Ray's highly agitated psychological state. The cicadas, with their extra annoying buzzing, were a better emotional fit, because their sound seemed to push Ray's anxiety further. In general, this track level remained quite low and worked on a more subliminal level. But you may notice (Figure 23-11) that I dipped the level of the ambient sound just a little bit when Ray is listening hard and imagining what's going on. I wanted at that moment to create a subjective sound space for Ray, who is focusing hard on the sounds next door, mentally filtering out extraneous noises. I was hoping that this would bring the audience slightly further inside his head.

Adding separate ambience allows us to shoot our scenes in as quiet a location as possible, and concentrate on getting the best possible recording of the dialogue, knowing that we can create the specific sonic background context for the location and the scene in the sound editing. We can also control volume levels and equalize all of these tracks totally independently.

Sound Effects Libraries

Sound effects collections come either on CDs (Figure 23-10) or can be found through numerous sites on the Internet, where you pay per sound effect download. A good sound effects library can provide you with sounds you could only dream of recording on your own: dozens of factory noises, hundreds of airplane and helicopter fly-bys, and more dog barks than you can imagine. If you need the sound of a 1965 Mustang starting up and pulling away, you'll find it. If you want the wheels to screech, they've got that too.

But beware, not all commercial effects libraries are created equal and some are mostly garbage. Wading through the bad stuff to find the sounds you can actually use can take a lot of research time. Also be aware that sound effects libraries come from different countries and can, for many effects, sound different.

The difference in police sirens is an obvious instance, but interestingly, even though you cannot make out any words, walla-walla most definitely contains national characteristics. When I was an undergraduate (before there was such a thing as Internet sound effects libraries) my department had only one sound effects library on cassette tape, which was produced by the BBC. In one of my first sync sound films I had a scene in a restaurant and tried to use the "restaurant walla-walla" from the BBC collection. The effect was not exactly what I was after. While my actors were clearly from the American mid-west, the walla-walla restaurant patrons in the background were right out of Notting Hill. And forget about getting a "car starting up" sound: our choices were a Mini-Cooper, a Jaguar, an Austin-Healey, a Land Rover, and a Rolls Royce Silver Shadow. Sure, they've got motors, but they also had a British accent.

Apocalypse Now "This Is War" (The American Zoetrope SFX Collection)

Set Code	Disc Number	Track Number	Duration	Description
AZ	AZ-01	01	0:21	Radio spot: 'Psychedelic Music Show'. Mono.
AZ	AZ-01	02	0:38	A-6 Intruder: power-up and takeoff. Stereo.
AZ	AZ-01	03	0:30	F-4 Phantom: takeoff medium-distant, 2 versions. Stereo
AZ	AZ-01	04	1:42	F-4 Phantom: taxi, idle and takeoff. Stereo.
AZ	AZ-01	05	0:41	F-4 Phantom: idle, power-up adn takeoff. Stereo.
AZ	AZ-01	06	0:43	F-4 Phantom: in, by and afterburner distant. Stereo
AZ	AZ-01	07	0:06	Fighter jet: hot fly-by, close-up. Stereo
AZ	AZ-01	07	0:08	Fighter jet: fly-by. Medium close-up. Stereo
AZ	AZ-01	07	0:12	Fighter jet: fly-by distant overhead. Stereo
AZ	AZ-01	07	0:08	Fighter jet: fly-by medium-distant. Stereo
AZ	AZ-01	08	1:10	C-130 Hercules: taxi by, medium close-up. Stereo
AZ	AZ-01	09	1:11	AH-1 Cobra: hover overhead, medium-distant. Mono
AZ	AZ-01	10	0:39	AH-1 Cobra: fly-by while firing 2.75' rockets. Mono
AZ	AZ-01	11	0:46	Ch-46 Chinook: idle on ground, medium close-up. Stereo
AZ	AZ-01	12	1:01	CH-46 Chinook: takeoff and hover. Stereo
AZ	AZ-01	13	1:15	Jet Ranger: cockpit interior start-up. Stereo
AZ	AZ-01	14	0:32	Jet Ranger: idle. Interior perspective. Mono.

Figure 23-10 This excerpt from the extensive list of sound effects used in Coppola's *Apocalypse Now* (1979) illustrates how precise sound effects must be in order to be convincing, including specific model, action and distance perspective. The sound designer was Walter Murch.

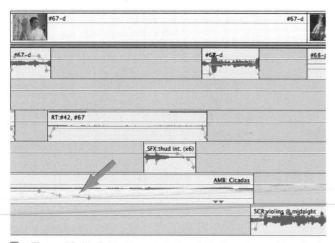

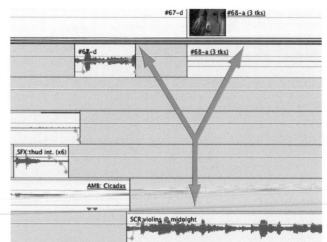

■ **Figure 23-11** Subjective sound. The dip in the volume of the cicada ambience track (arrow) reflects Ray's selective aural perception and brings us closer into his POV.

■ **Figure 23-12** A music sound bridge in *FearFall.* The violins on the music track begin slightly before the end of scene #67 and continue into scene #68 creating a strong connection between the two scenes.

Music

The music in *FearFall* was composed by Randy Wolff. For some scenes he scored music to the picture lock edit and for other scenes, like the one shown in **Figure 23-12**, he provided me with short motifs that I could easily adapt to the picture editing. The music here is simply a strident, dissonant, and insistent violin chord that starts the minute the narrative takes a new turn; Ray, now convinced "they" are inside his house, must do something. The music was cut in at this moment to punctuate this dangerously flawed realization and to infuse the moment with tension and foreboding, but it continues into the next scene, in which Sophie is innocently getting food out of the refrigerator. This is called a **sound bridge** and it is designed to carry the emotional tension from one scene to the next.

The Sound Bridge

Sound bridges are a very common sound editing technique involving any sound that overlaps from one scene into another. Sound bridges can involve a sound from one scene continuing into the following scene (as in the *FearFall* example, Figure 23-12) or, vice versa, the sound from the second scene beginning early, at the tail end of the preceding scene. Sound bridges create a very strong and smooth connection between scenes by carrying over the emotional content of one scene into the other. Musical sound bridges are the most common, but sound effects and dialogue can also be used as sound bridges. Like any other technique that creates strong associations, sound bridges can be extremely powerful and adaptable in their specific application.

Music Sound Bridge

The story of Bernard Rose's *Immortal Beloved* (1994) (Figure 23-13) revolves around the mystery of Ludwig van Beethoven's famous love letter to his unnamed "immortal

■ **Figure 23-13** Rose's *Immortal Beloved* (1994) uses the music from the premiere of Beethoven's Ninth Symphony to bridge several scenes in one of the last sequences of the film.

beloved." The ending sequence of the film includes a sound bridge constructed around Beethoven's most famous and influential composition, the mighty Ninth Symphony. The sequence begins with an investigator talking to one of Beethoven's presumed mistresses, while the last movement of the Ninth Symphony underscores the scene (as non-diegetic music). The music continues as we cut to a concert hall, which shows an orchestra playing the symphony (the music is now diegetic). When Beethoven comes onto the stage the sound is drastically muted and muffled to reflect his near total deafness (now it is subjective sound). The full dimension of the music returns as the film cuts to a flashback of Beethoven as a child, tormented by his father. The Ninth Symphony in this sequence serves as a sound bridge for three scenes that take place in three different eras and locations. In addition, the music transforms into three different sounds modes: non-diegetic score music, diegetic source music, and subjective sound.

Dialogue Sound Bridge

Fritz Lang's *M* (1931) contains perhaps one of cinema's earliest sound bridges and it remains one of the most eloquent and moving films. After we see the little girl Elsie lured away by a man who has bought her a balloon, Lang cuts to her mother, who anxiously waits for her child to come home. The mother goes to her window, opens it wide, and calls for her little girl, "Elsie!" "Elsie!" (Figure 23-14). The sound of her voice bridges the next few edits, which take us out of the apartment, to the staircase, and to an attic, places where the little girl should be and that are still in earshot of the mother's continuing cries of "Elsie!" Elsie!" But suddenly the calling stops and Lang presents us with three stunning shots in silence. Elsie's empty place at the family table, the little girl's toy ball rolling out of a thicket of brush, and the balloon, tangled in the wires of an electrical pole. The meaning couldn't be clearer: Elsie is another victim of the child killer.

■ **Figure 23-14** Although made only a few years after the introduction of sync sound in film, Lang's *M* (1931) experimented with sophisticated techniques, such as using a dialogue sound bridge.

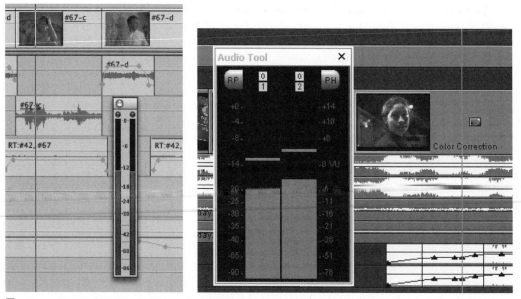

■ **Figure 23-15** Audio level adjustments are done right on the timeline and can be monitored on the sound tool's level meter window. Final Cut Pro (left); AVID (right).

Sound Levels and Effects during the Edit

During the editing stage you will need to manipulate the audio levels of all your tracks somewhat to give yourself an idea for the perspective and balance of the various tracks in relation to the others. This is especially important if you plan to screen rough cuts to get feedback along the way. All NLE systems offer some sort of easily accessible level control right in the timeline (Figure 23-15). You can adjust tracks globally, by selecting the entire track, or adjust individual clips. Adjusting clip levels in the timeline does not alter the master clip or the original media in any way. You can also add simple transitions like sound fades and cross-fades into your sequence very simply as well (Figure 23-16).

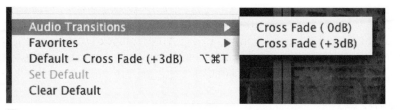

■ **Figure 23-16** The audio transition menu in Final Cut Pro. Simple audio effects, such as preset cross fades, can be applied as you edit, but save the more detailed sound work for the mixing stage.

But be careful. It's very easy to waste hours tweaking the volume or dissolve parameters for this shot, that shot, and the other. Don't take too much time fine-tuning details that will only be undone and redone later in the sound mixing phase. The editing stage is not the place to get the sound absolutely perfect. Finessing the track levels, creating transition effects, and enhancing the sound through equalization and audio filters are done in the next and final stage of the sound design process—sound mixing.

■ THE SOUND MIX

For most student and independent films that are edited and finished on an NLE system, it's hard to strictly delineate the editing and sound cutting phase from the sound mixing stage.

To be sure, as you work with your rough cuts and build your sound design, you will be doing some rough sound mixing along the way, especially if you screen your rough cuts. But at some point, after picture lock and after you've more or less gathered all of the actual sounds you will use for your sound design and placed them more or less where they need to be, you need to turn your attention exclusively to perfecting the way your movie sounds. The **sound mix** is the process of polishing and finalizing the various audio tracks in your sound design, and creating a single **mixtrack**, which is the mono or stereo sound track track that is then married to your images and accompanies your film into distribution and exhibition. The ultimate goal of a sound mix is to create a harmonious sonic environment for your film, harmonious meaning that the completed sound design is both believable and appropriate for the conceptual and aesthetic aims of your motion picture. In this respect, the sound mix should not be viewed as merely a polishing process; rather there are substantial creative decisions to me made here. The sound mix process involves five steps, generally in this order: (1) final sound selection and placement, (2) audio sweetening, (3) creating audio transitions, (4) audio level balancing, and (5) the mix down.

Before we look at each step in detail, let me just mention that sound mixing should be done in an environment that most accurately represents a high-quality exhibition space. In a professional mixing facility, the **rerecording mixer** handles the hardware and the mixing tasks while the director and editor watch the film projected on a fairly large screen and listen to the sound mix on high-quality reference speakers. The whole mixing suite is also sound baffled to minimize reverberation. Most students in introductory or intermediate production courses, however, mix right on their NLE system—which is certainly fine—but it is recommended to mix in a space that is quiet and to use good speakers. Be aware of what the mixing environment itself sounds like; traffic noise, reverberant surfaces, and the cooling fan of a CPU all blend with what's coming out of your speakers. Mixing with headphones is also a viable alternative, but again, make sure the headphones are of very high quality and are isolation-type headphones, meaning that they have foam that surrounds your ears to keep external noises from leaking in. Poor quality headphones, especially those that do not press firmly against your ear, can give you a less than accurate impression of your sound track.

The Sound Mixing Steps

Final Sound Selection and Placement

As we discussed previously, the editing process involves the somewhat expeditious use of sound in order to get the film to a picture locked phase. This means using some sounds that will end up in the final film (like dialogue, pfx, or prerecorded music) and inserting scratch tracks as place holders until you find or record the perfect sound (like sound effects or score music). But the final sound mix is the moment of truth: you must select (or record) all final sounds that make up your sound design and precisely place these sounds into your timeline, replacing all scratch tracks.

Audio Sweetening

Audio sweetening simply means making your audio sound better. This is accomplished by evaluating, and adjusting when necessary, every individual audio clip, across each audio track (i.e., dialogue, sound effects, ambience), one track at a time. Sweetening includes a variety of audio signal processing tools that can be employed to accomplish three goals: to generally enhance the quality of the audio, to repair poor audio, and to create audio effects. Remember: like every other effect in nonlinear editing, changes you make to an audio clip or track are nondestructive, meaning the original media are not affected in any way, so feel free to experiment; you can always undo anything you try.

Audio Filters

At the heart of audio sweetening is the application of **audio filters**. Audio filters are audio signal processors that digitally alter the audio data, and therefore the characteristics of your sound, in some way. Each audio filter manipulates the spectrum in a unique way to produce a specific effect. It is certainly not possible to explore in this chapter the capabilities of every processing tool found in most NLE systems, but a few basics should get

Figure 23-17 The three-band equalizer in Final Cut Pro. A common audio filter used in sound mixing.

you started. The effect and function of a specific audio filter generally falls into one of three categories: (1) equalization, (2) reverb/echo, and (3) compression/expansion.

Filters for frequency equalization and noise reduction.
Equalization, or **EQ**, means the manual manipulation of the various frequencies in your signal. Generally, we divide the frequency spectrum of an audio signal into three **frequency bands**: low frequencies, which are the deep, bass quality (around 25 Hz – 250 Hz); mid-range frequencies, which are the most perceptible range for the human ear, which includes the human voice (250 Hz – 4 kHz); and high frequencies, which include the bright, treble quality of the sound (4 kHz – 20 kHz). Most NLE systems offer a filter called a **three-band equalizer**, which allows you to manipulate these three broad areas of the sound spectrum more or less independently (Figure 23-17).

So when might we use an EQ filter? Let's say you have a romantic scene (shot in fairly tight close-ups) of a couple talking and clearly falling in love. In this situation, you may want to boost the low end of your audio just a drop, to "warm up" the audio, make it sound close, resonant, and intimate. Or let's say you shot a scene with a microphone that accentuated the high, treble end of the audio and, to your ear, it sounds too "crispy." You can use the EQ filter to bring down the high frequencies. Completely removing high frequencies and low frequencies, leaving only the mid-range, will make voices sound like they're coming through the telephone or over a PA system.

Primarily, however, EQ is used to fix audio that includes some sort of unwanted noise. Also, in the *FearFall* sound design analysis (see pp. 437–438), I mentioned that Ellen's dialogue was recorded while an unnoticed fan hummed in the next room. The microphone picked up this vibration as a low-frequency hum. So, I split Ellen's dialogue onto its own track, selected all of her clips from that scene, and equalized the low frequencies until that low hum was all but eliminated. High frequencies can also be equalized out. One of my students shot a scene that took place around a computer, and when he listened carefully to the recoding he discovered an extremely high-pitched whine coming from the computer monitor. This sound was fairly easy to eliminate through EQing. In both his film and in mine, the frequency of the offending noise was either higher or lower than any other sounds, especially the voices in the scene, so there was no discernible change to the quality of the voices. However, if you need to EQ out a frequency that is found in other areas of the recorded sound spectrum, then the EQing will remove that frequency throughout the recording and will alter sounds you want to alter, as well as those you don't want changed. Also keep in mind, as a general rule, you can fairly successfully remove (or accentuate) frequencies that are in the recording, but you cannot add frequencies that are not in the audio in the first place. The removal of high- and low-frequency noise is so common in sound mixing that you'll find numerous **filter presets** for high-end and low-end roll-off filters designed exactly for these problems. In fact, in Final Cut Pro you'll even find a preset **vocal de-esser** setting to remove excessive sibilance from the dialogue of an actor who has particularly piercing S-es.

Filters for reverb and echo.
Echo and **reverb** are very similar in that they both involve the reflection and return of sound after a slight delay. The return delay for reverb is fast (think small rooms, like tiled bathrooms and concrete stairwells). The return delay for an echo is much longer (think Gothic cathedrals or the Grand Canyon). Reverb and echo effects change the audio signal to make it sound as if it were recorded in an acoustically live space, where sound reverberates off hard surfaces.

There are several preset filters (small hall, large hall, tunnel, etc.) (Figure 23-18) or you can control the loudness and delay of the return manually. Reverb and echo can sound great, but be careful not to use too much or to use it without narrative and visual justification. Inappropriate reverb can sound cheesy and too much will make otherwise clear sound, especially dialogue, murky and unintelligible. Also remember that reverb filters do not remove reverberation—they can only add it! So, when do we use these filters? Let's say you have a scene in which a man is being chased up a concrete stairwell by an unseen dog. You want that dog to be barking and growling (off screen) as the man makes a desperate dash up the stairwell to the rooftop doors. If you found your barking sound effects from a sound effects library, it's likely that the "mean dog barking" will have been recorded as closely and as flat as possible. All you need to do to make it sound as if that dog is only one landing below him in the stairwell is to choose the "barking" clips and add the appropriate amount of reverb.

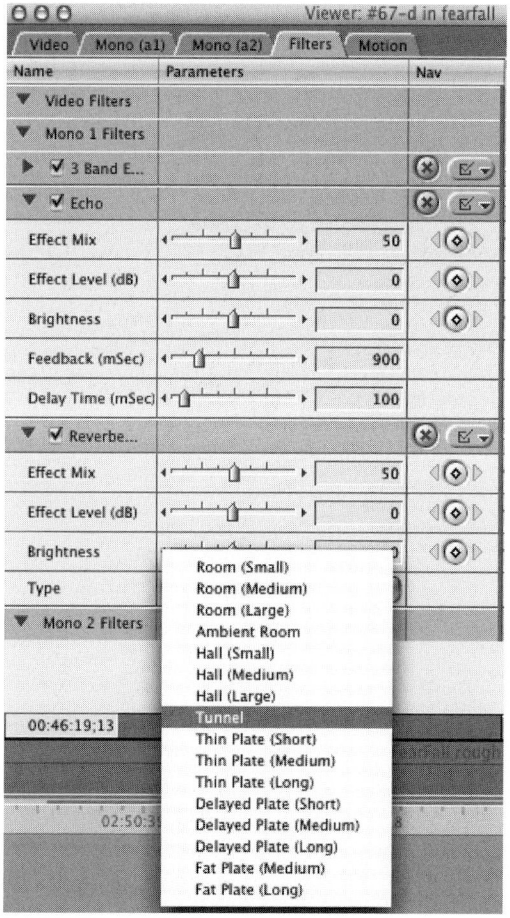

Filters for amplitude compression or expansion.
Compression and **expansion filters** work on the amplitude of a sound signal, or, more accurately, on the dynamic range (see p. 296) of a given recording. As I mentioned previously (p. 319), the result of audio that peaks above 0 dB on a peak meter is distortion,

Figure 23-18 Do you want your audio to sound like it's reverberating in a tunnel? A large hall? In Final Cut Pro you can choose from a range of acoustic effects when you apply the reverb filter.

and in digital audio this means the loss of data and very noticeable crackling in the sound. A compression filter detects when a sound will peak above 0 dB and it will suppress it to keep it within range without affecting the average audio levels of the track.

This is very different than simply lowering the overall (or average) audio level to keep loud sounds from peaking above 0 dB. This approach would lower everything on that track. Here's an example: Let's say you've shot a scene in which a married couple is talking while the husband washes the dishes. The sound recordist did their job well and kept the sound from peaking above 0 dB in the field recordings, but now that you're mixing your sound, you want to be able to hear the dialogue very clearly, and so you've set the audio levels for the dialogue track fairly high. But now you discover that every time the husband bumps a plate in the sink or in the dish drainer, the audio spikes above 0 dB and crackles. If you simply lower the average track level overall so that this doesn't happen, you'll be lowering the dialogue as well. The solution here is a compression filter, which will suppress only the audio that threatens to peak above 0 dB, leaving the rest at the level established in the timeline.

While compression filters lower loud, peaking sounds, **expansion filters** lower the amplitude of extremely low-level sounds, in order to drop them below the level of audibility. Let's say you finally go into your sound mix, with super high-quality speakers, and suddenly notice that during the shooting of a tight, close-up monologue, the microphone picked up the ticking of the boom operator's watch. It's very, very faint but, by revealing the presence of a crew person, the fictive world you're trying to create is shattered. An expansion filter will drop this very

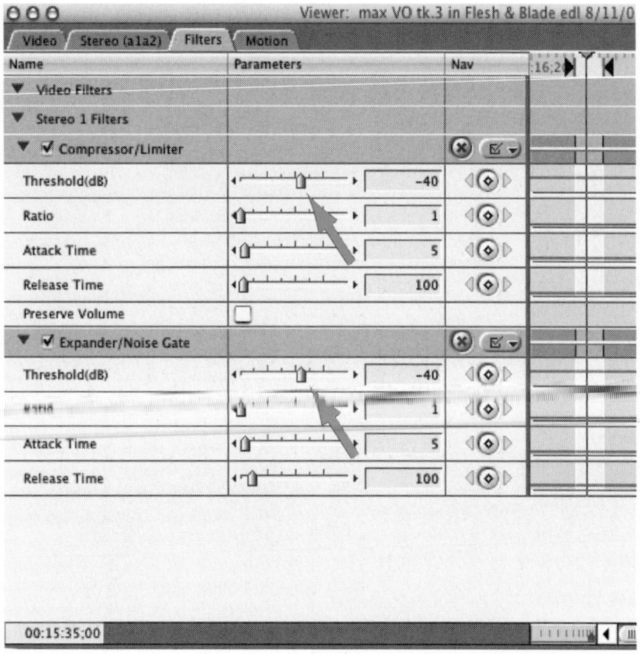

Figure 23-19 The manual threshold level adjustments for the compressor audio filter (top arrow) and the expander audio filter (bottom arrow) in Final Cut pro.

quiet noise even lower, hopefully out of the range of hearing, without affecting the rest of the audio on track. Expansion filters can also be used to minimize the room tone in a dialogue recording, allowing you to more successfully replace it with another ambient track without worrying about compounding ambience over a noticeably different presence.

With both compression and expansion, you can manually set the **threshold level** (Figure 23-19), which is the amplitude level above which (compression) or below which (expansion) the sound must be in order to be attected by the filter.

Audio Filter Toggle for Reference

The human ear is a very adaptable and intricate mechanism that subconsciously equalizes, attenuates, filters, and selectively perceives the sounds in the world around us in order to reduce what we perceive to the essentials. For example, sitting around a table talking with our friends, it's automatic that we no longer perceive the hum of the air conditioner, or the sound of traffic outside the window, or even the refrigerator kicking on. Just as our olfactory sense can adapt to and "normalize" smells such that we don't smell them anymore, so, too, our hearing can adapt and normalize a wide variety of audio qualities. For this reason, all filter effects have the ability to toggle instantly on and off (Figure 23-20). In order to really hear what effect an audio filter is having on your sound, you need to compare it regularly to the reference of the original track. Without toggling back to your reference, your ear can get lost as you apply effect after effect, straying further from the parameters of acceptable audio manipulation.

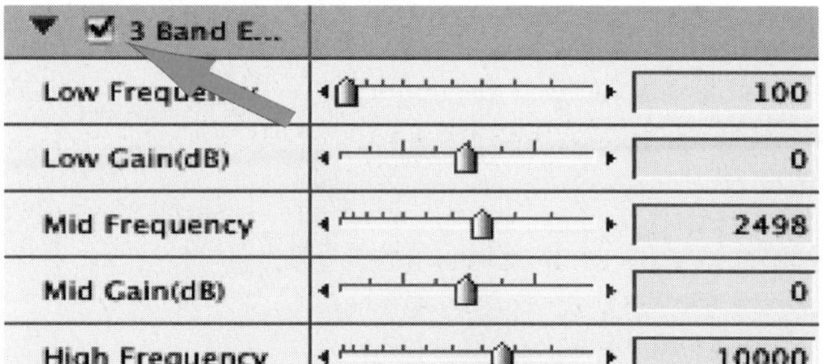

Figure 23-20 The audio filter toggle icon (arrows) enables you to easily switch a filter effect on and off, allowing you to compare the effect to your original audio for reference.

Creating Audio Transitions

Most of the creative audio editing choices, like split edits for dialogue, sound bridges, and ambient track layering, are accomplished during the rough cut and fine cut stage. During the sound mixing phase, what concerns us most is the smooth transition from sound to sound across an entire track. This includes the use of room tone to fill in gaps of "silence" on the sound track and to even out the ambience quality of two pieces of audio that are supposed to sound continuous. However, most audio edits that are straight cuts, especially in dialogue editing, also require a little extra attention. A straight cut between two audio clips not only magnifies small ambient shifts, but the inconsistent waveforms of the two directly abutted audio clips will also result in a audible "pop" or "click" right at the edit point. To correct this, sound editors routinely add a very quick, four- to six-frame **cross-fade** right at the edit point between two connected sound clips, and two- to four-frame **fades** (in and out) at the beginning and end of sound clips that are not directly joined to another audio clip (Figure 23-21).

A **cross-fade** is the audio equivalent of a dissolve in the image. As the level of the first audio clip fades out, the

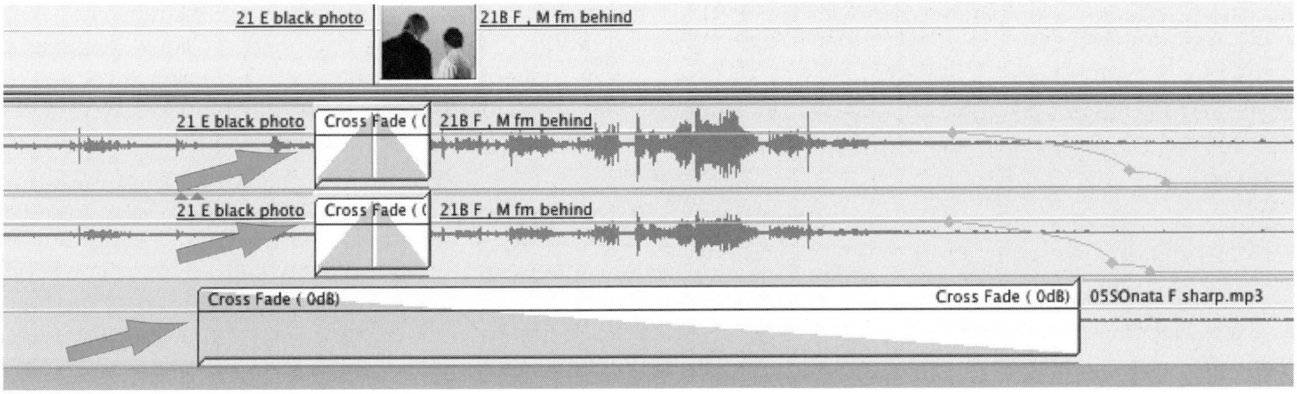

■ **Figure 23-21** You can manually determine the length of audio cross-fades to suit the requirements of the effect. Pictured are a 6 frame cross-fade (top arrows) used to create an invisible dialogue edit and a 60 frame fade-in from silence to gradually introduce music on the sound track.

level of the incoming clip fades up. Obviously, like an image dissolve, you can create long cross-fades of many seconds to, for example, slowly introduce some background music as sync sound fades away. But quick cross-fades are extremely helpful in smoothing a cut from one audio clip to another. Very often, cross-fades of twelve to twenty-four frames is enough to smooth an edit between two dialogue clips with more noticeable room tone differences.

When you cross-fade between two clips, the audio of the first clip is extended beyond the cut point by half the duration of the cross-fade in order to accommodate the full fade-out, and the incoming shot is extended at the head by half the cross-fade duration to accommodate the fade-in. This is called a **center on cross-fade** (Figure 23-22).

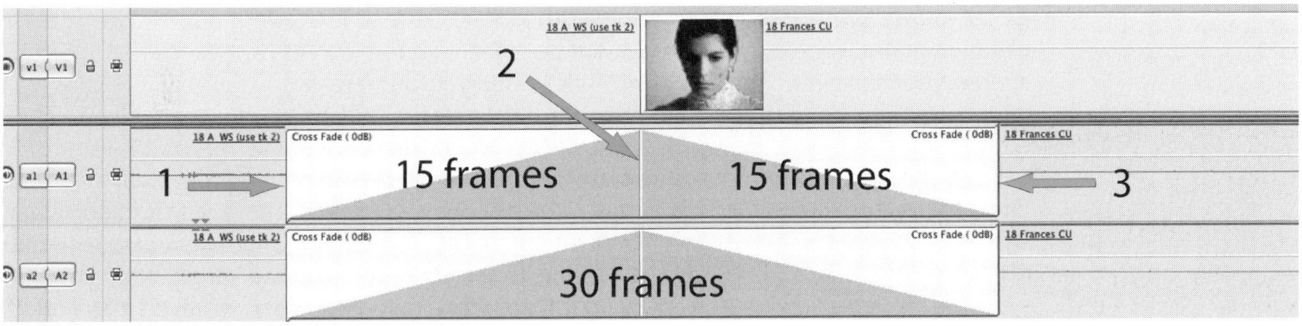

■ **Figure 23-22** Handles. To accommodate a 30 frame cross-fade, the incoming audio clip requires 15 additional clean frames (1) before the cut point (2) and the outgoing audio clip needs an additional 15 frames beyond the cut point (3).

For example, if you decide that a cut point needs a twelve-frame cross-fade to smooth out a slight ambience discrepancy, then the first shot will end twelve frames after the cut point before it completely fades out and the second clip will begin twelve frames before the edit point to accommodate the fade-in. These extra frames are called **handles**, and you must be sure that there are no unwanted sounds, like the tail end of some dialogue that you wanted to cut out, within those extra frames.

Audio Level Balancing

Once all of the tracks sound good on their own, and all of the edit points are clean and smooth, it's time to think about adjusting the overall volume balance between the clips in each track and between the various tracks in relation to the others. This stage is critical not only for the intelligibility of your sound (for example, important dialogue shouldn't be drowned out by music that is too loud), but it also is critical for the general

audio headroom
-20 to -6

■ **Figure 23-23** The Final Cut Pro mixing tool allows you to adjust and meter the levels for each track independently. You should first establish your headroom by adjusting your dominant audio track and then adjust the others to that reference.

believability of the world of your film. An ambience track that is too loud can make a scene ring false; dialogue levels that are all over the map can make the editing painfully obvious; music that is too low will cause the audience to turn around and scream "louder!" at the poor projectionist. If all tracks have equal volume levels, then all you'll get is a sonic stew. The dynamics of track levels helps you to create emphasis and direct the ear and the eye to what is most important at a particular moment. Keep in mind that when you screen your film for an audience you cannot ride the levels; the final sound track has to work all on its own from start to finish. Once, when I was judging a student film festival, we had an entry that came with a little note marked "URGENT!" The note said something like, "Please be advised, sound dips at TC 00:08:12:13 (after scene under tree) but it goes back up at TC 00:09:18:23." Even though this is totally unacceptable, we, the three judges, decided to watch it anyway, but we were certainly not disposed to like it.

When establishing audio levels we start with the most important tracks first and then adjust all other tracks relative to this central reference. For example, if a film is primarily music driven, with an occasional special effect tossed in here and there, then you'll set levels for the music track first. For dialogue-driven projects, start with dialogue tracks and then later adjust the effects, music, and ambience tracks relative to the dialogue. In either case, the first, and most important, track we mix is called our **reference track**.

Establishing Average Level Range

Just as with field recording, we use a peak meter as our primary reference tool as we adjust levels. Yes, we monitor with the headphones as well (see later), but the peak meter helps us maintain consistency **across time**, meaning from clip to clip, from start to finish, across your timeline. The first track that we adjust, our reference track, establishes our **average audio level range** (also called **headroom**) (Figure 23-23).

Let's say we're adjusting dialogue first. Just as with field recording (see p. 319), the level for normally spoken dialogue is around –20 dB, and the loudest peaks in your sound mix should not exceeded –6 dB (to give you a comfortable margin before the ultimate limit of 0 dB). The area, between –20 and –6 dB, becomes our average audio range. Now you can adjust the levels of each and every clip, across the dialogue tracks, relative to this reference. A whisper should obviously dip below –20 dB, loud voices will register around –16 dB, and a scream will clearly be even louder, but should not peak above –6 dB. If pre-recorded music is your most important track (say you're making a music video), then you'd simply find the loudest peak in the track and adjust the levels so that it falls on –6 dB. The rest will fall into place below that top headroom point.

As you adjust your clip levels for the reference track across time, you should use the peak meter to maintain consistency from clip to clip to clip. For example, if character A's average voice in the first scene held around –20 dB, then in the last scene it should also be at the same level. By comparing the levels of the two clips, you can easily see if your mix levels have drifted over time.

Compositional and Dramatic Sound Perspective

Keep in mind that composition and dramatic content can have an important effect on audio levels. The sound of a man talking in a close-up should obviously be somewhat louder than the same dialogue shot in a long shot or extreme long shot. For this reason it's important not only to *listen* to your sound mix, but also to *watch* and consider the images you're trying to match the sound to. Dramatic content also has a profound effect on levels, especially when working with **subjective sound**, in which you are trying to represent the POV and selective perception of a character. Just as we can either "tune out" or hone in on someone who is talking to us from across the table, you can use your audio level mixing to duplicate this effect.

Bob Fosse's *All That Jazz* (1979) (Figure 23-24) tells the story of hard-living and hard-working Joe Gideon, a musical theater director on Broadway who is putting up a show while his life and health fall apart. During the first reading of the play, with the entire cast and principal crew of the production gathered around him, Gideon has a mild heart attack. At this moment, Fosse completely mutes all sounds, except for those that Gideon himself makes, which are amplified. Although we see everything going on around him, we cannot hear the obvious sounds, like lines being read or the uproarious laughter of the people gathered in the room. Instead we hear his fingernails scratching on a metal pipe, the rustle as he removes yet another cigarette from its box, his pencil snapping, and his spent cigarette landing on the floor. The effect is one of extreme character subjectivity in which we are enclosed completely and deeply in Gideon's perspective and consciousness.

Adjusting the Other Tracks

Once you have established the levels of your reference track, you can then adjust the other tracks (sound effects, ambience, music) relative to this one. Keep in mind that the reference track does not mean that this is always the loudest track in the movie. There are many times, for example, when music levels will be set well under dialogue levels and then later fade up to become the most prominent track in the sound design. Also, some sound effects, like explosions, should clearly be mixed louder than average dialogue; other sounds can be mixed hotter than dialogue to intentionally drown out the speakers for dramatic value.

■ **Figure 23-24** In Fosse's *All That Jazz* (1979), sound design is manipulated to reflect Joe Gideon's (Roy Scheider) subjective experience as he has a mild heart attack.

■ **Figure 23-25** The famous Albert Hall sequence from Hitchcock's *The Man Who Knew Too Much* (1956). The diegetic orchestral sound track drowns out all other sounds in the scene and playfully recalls the silent era films of Hitchcock's early career.

A good example of a music track taking over in prominence and volume level can be seen in the famous "Albert Hall sequence" in Alfred Hitchcock's *The Man Who Knew Too Much* (1956) (**Figure 23-25**). In this film an average American couple finds themselves unwittingly tangled in a plot to assassinate a Prime Minister; to keep them quiet, the plotters kidnap their son. Looking for their son, the couple finally converges on one of the kidnappers as he is about to carry out the assassination during an orchestral concert at the Royal Albert Hall. The killer's plan is to shoot the diplomat when the music reaches its climax, with a crash of cymbals, to cover the sound of the shot. The sequence dramatically inter-cuts the police and parents searching for the killer, while the killer takes aim at the diplomat and the audience simply enjoys the orchestral music. Although the rest of the film is primarily dialogue driven, in this sequence the music itself becomes the driving force of the narrative as we get closer and closer, measure by measure, to the assassination. Additionally, the music completely drowns out all dialogue exchanges, essentially creating a sequence that harkens back to the silent era.

NLE Systems and Audio Levels

As with most other functions in NLE systems, there are a number of ways to adjust the audio levels of clips and tracks. The most controlled and accurate method for adjusting audio levels is a combination of using the timeline and the viewer. Most NLE systems make it extremely easy to adjust audio levels right in the timeline. To do this, you must select the timeline setting that shows the clip **audio level overlay** within each track (**Figure 23-26**). The line that you see drawn through each clip is the system's default level. Using your mouse, you can simply grab the audio overlay and manually raise or lower it to raise or lower the entire clip level.

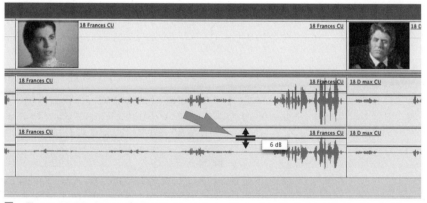

■ **Figure 23-26** In most NLE systems, audio levels can be adjusted right in the timeline by clicking/dragging clip overlays. Notice the box showing the changing dB levels on this Final Cut Pro timeline.

If you have a clip that has multiple dynamic level adjustments (for example, music in which the volume dips and then rises again), you can use the **pen tool** to create key frames. Audio levels between key frames can be adjusted independently. You can create as many key frames as you need, allowing for enormous flexibility for dynamic level adjustment (**Figure 23-27**).

If you require a much more detailed view of the audio track than you see in the timeline, you can simply bring your clip into the viewer and you will see both a waveform represen-

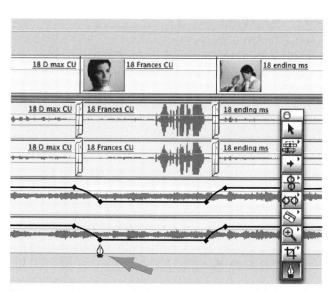

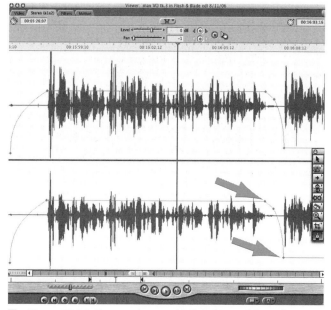

■ **Figure 23-27** The pen tool allows you to create multiple level adjustments within a single clip.

■ **Figure 23-28** For a much more detailed picture of the audio waveform, level adjustment can be made in the viewer. In this Final Cut Pro viewer you can clearly see the end of one musical phrase and the beginning of the next. The arrows show where a pen tool was used to drop the audio out during this pause.

tation of the sound and the audio level overlay. You can also magnify or reduce the audio clip. The viewer also allows you to work with key frames and dynamic adjustments, but with a much more detailed and precise picture of the sound (Figure 23-28).

Obviously this discussion only scratches the surface of the capabilities and procedures for adjusting levels in an NLE system. You should look over the manual for your particular system carefully to fully understand how to achieve the audio balance you are after.

The Mix Down

Finally, with all of the tracks sounding their best and mixed to the perfect balance relative to the other tracks, you are ready to mix down and output your multiple tracks to create a master **mix track**. Your NLE program's mix tool is used for this purpose (Figure 23-29).

When you open the mix tool, you will see one audio gain slider for every audio track in the program, and as you play through your sound design, the gain sliders will move,

Audio Monitor Reference

When setting audio levels during the sound mix it is essential that you keep the output level to your speakers, or headphones, absolutely consistent. Audio levels are relative, so if your headphone level is low one day, you might raise the levels of your clips higher than you need, and if the headphone levels are higher another day, then you may be tempted to set clip levels lower than on the previous day. So set the output volume to a comfortable level and leave it alone for the duration of the sound mix. This includes the computer audio output volume settings and the monitor out on an external mixer, if you're using one.

Clean dialogue edits and consistent levels are essential for the maintenance of continuity in dialogue-driven films. Here is a summary of techniques we use to keep an edited sequence feeling like it's unfolding seamlessly and continuously:

1. Stay in sync.
2. Use split audio edits.
3. Maintain consistent room tone.
4. Cross-fades for hard cuts.
5. Never let audio peak above 0 dB.
6. Maintain consistent and appropriate audio levels from clip to clip and scene to scene across time.

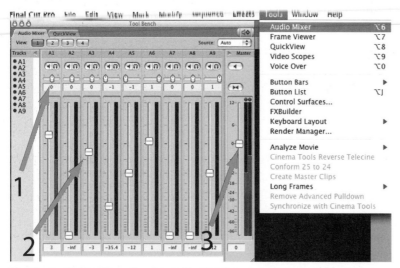

Figure 23-29 The audio mixer in Final Cut Pro mixes all your audio tracks down to two master output stereo channels (3). With the panning slider (1) you can send each track to either one or both stereo channels. Each track also has its own fader (2) for independent level adjustment. Both the panning slider and faders automatically respond to all the choices you made in the timeline.

corresponding to the level adjustments you made in each clip. At the top of each level slider is a **pan slider**. Generally, whether you are finishing on film or on DV tape, you will be outputting your audio as a two-channel stereo master. The pan sliders allow you to select which channel each audio track should be recorded to and later play from. If you want both channels of audio to be the same, then all of the pan sliders remain in their central position. This is especially important if you plan to finish on a 16mm film print, because 16mm optical sound is a mono format.

In any case, if you are mastering to DV tape, you will output your audio mix down along with your program to the master tape, creating a master that has both video and stereo sound. If your workflow involves finishing on film, then you will need to output the audio only to a DAT tape (or whatever format the lab requires) and take that master mix track to the laboratory, where they will use it to strike an optical sound track master (see p. 363).

■ ADVANCED SOUND MIXING PROGRAMS

The audio sweetening and sound mixing capabilities found in most NLE systems are truly remarkable, but to a professional sound mixer they offer only basic functions. As your films get more complex and your sound track needs become more demanding, you may find yourself needing to use more advanced, stand-alone, sound mixing programs. Remember, Avid and Final Cut Pro are picture editing programs, and a professional sound mixer would never use these to mix sound; instead, they use a **digital audio workstation** (or **DAW**, for short). There are numerous DAWs on the market, but many are exclusively for mixing music. **Soundtrack Pro**, (from the Final Cut Pro Studio software bundle) and **Pro Tools** (the current industry standard DAW) (Figure 23-30) are designed to mix both music and film sound tracks, and contain many more features and capabilities compared to NLE picture editing programs. Both mixing programs offer dozens more (and much more powerful) audio filters for special effects and "audio fixing," many more transition effects, and much more precise (subframe) editing and effects capabilities.

These programs are also designed to import both your edited video (for visual reference) as well as all of the sound tracks and adjustments you've made along the way. Sound track Pro is designed to let you move seamlessly from Final Cut Pro and back again with-

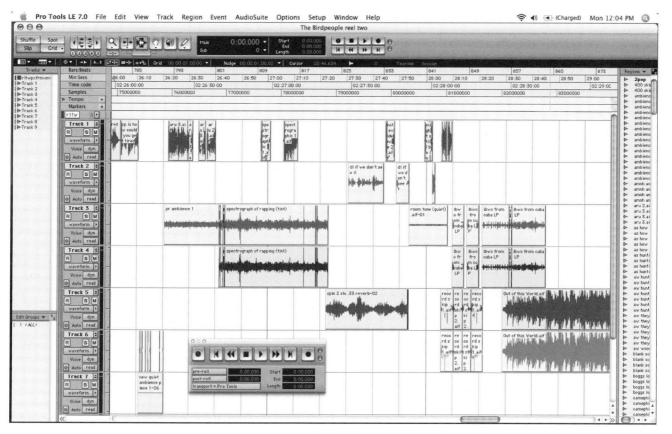

| File | Edit | View | Mark | Modify | Sequence | Effects | Tools | W |

New ▶
New Project ⇧⌘N
Open... ⌘O
Open Recent ▶
Close Window ⌘W
Close Tab ^W
Close Project

Save Project ⌘S
Save Project As... ⇧⌘S
Save All ⌥⌘S
Revert Project
Restore Project...

Import ▶
Export ▶
Send To ▶
Batch Export

Batch Capture... ^C
Log and Capture... ⌘8
Media Manager...
Reconnect Media...
Set Logging Bin

Print to Video... ^M
Edit to Tape...

QuickTime Movie...

Using Compressor...
Using QuickTime Conversion...

For Soundtrack
For LiveType

Audio to AIFF(s)...
Audio to OMF...
Batch List...
Cinema Tools Audio EDL...
Cinema Tools Change List...
Cinema Tools Film Lists...
EDL...
XML...

■ **Figure 23-31** The "export audio" menu allows you to convert audio from a Final Cut Pro timeline into OMF files for importing into a Pro Tools sound mix session. Be aware that FCP audio levels settings are not retained in the OMF export.

out any format conversions. Pro Tools, on the other hand requires that all sound files be converted into the **OMF** (**open media framework**) file format. Realizing that most sound mixing professionals use Pro Tools, Apple has made it relatively easy to migrate and has an option for exporting all audio clips and timeline information in the OMF format (Figure 23-31). You can even set the conversion to export each clip with handles, extra frames on either end of the edit points to accommodate cross-fades, or trims to the individual audio clip during the mix.

Why Go Pro?

Venturing into the territory of highly advanced software applications for sound mixing means acquiring the not insubstantial expertise to use them. This itself begs the question: Why not go to a professional sound mixer?

Certainly, as you are starting out, the benefits of mixing your own sound tracks on your first, fairly simple films are enormous. Mixing your own sound gives you an intimate and nuanced understanding of the power of layered audio tracks. Creating an intricate sound design, placing a sound effect with perfect timing, adjusting the audio balance to create dramatic emphasis, changing the mood by inserting a different ambient track, and literally seeing the way a music track can weave its way throughout a film and therefore in and out of a viewer's consciousness are all invaluable lessons that will inevitably have an impact on the way you look at movies and how sound is used in your future projects. To actually lay your hands on the stuff and make it happen, quite simply, will make you a better filmmaker; it may even convince you that you'd like to be a sound designer like Walter Murch, Ben Burtt, or Ren Klyce.

But, at some point, you may find that your ideas and sound requirements have become more complex than your abilities. It's then time to turn to those people who absolutely adore postproduction sound, those who have dedicated their careers to it and have a talent for it, those people who know exactly what every one of those audio filters and third-party plug-ins in a Pro Tools system does—those people called professional **post-production sound mixers**.

I remember the first film for which I had a professional digital mix on a Pro Tools system (before that, my mixes were done on 16mm magnetic stock, which is a different experience entirely). Anyway, I dutifully brought in my video and all of my audio and sound track data in OMF format to the postproduction mixer, Bill, having carefully arranged and "fixed" my tracks. I had a very small budget and needed the mix session to proceed as quickly as possible, so, to save time, I had done meticulous level balancing, inserted quick cross-fade dissolves for every cut, and applied a few simple filters. I thought that by doing that, all Bill would have to do is tweak things here or there, replace a few special effects, and I could go home. When Bill loaded my sound design into his Pro Tools system he indeed told me to go home and we would start the next day. When I returned I found that overnight he had undone everything I had done, with the exception of the basic sound cutting and placement. All of the lovely audio smoothing and finessing I had labored over for over a week was gone. Bill had removed all audio filters and transitions, undone all level settings and split all tracks. I went from six tracks to about twenty-five in less than ten hours! Then Bill got down to work.

Yes, he had a high-end mixing program with audio processors, scopes, and equalizers I had never even heard of, but more importantly he had experience and a sensibility for the world of sound that I simply couldn't match. He not only made everything sound much better with his more accurate and powerful mixing tools, and his vast selection of sound effects and ambient tracks, but he heard problems in the tracks that I couldn't hear until after he fixed them. Most importantly, he made creative suggestions, especially for sound bridges between scenes, which quite frankly improved the movie. And that's why we go to a professional, in any area of filmmaking; experience, talent, and technical experience will enhance the expressive impact of your movie.

When you decide to start using a professional sound mixer, it is important to consult with them before you start editing your film. They will tell you the details of the mixing system they use and how it interfaces with your particular editing system. They will tell you what resources they have, what they need, and in what format they prefer the audio data and video delivered. It is especially important to consult with them ahead of time if you have problematic sound that will need significant fixing in the mix. Some things can be fixed; others, like too much reverb in a recording, are nearly impossible to correct.

Keep in mind that the options are not limited to DIY or going with a professional sound mixer charging $200 an hour. Just as with acting, cinematography, directing, writing, and any other filmmaking task, there are people who have a talent for sound design and mixing, who are good, but not yet professionals. This person might be your classmate or it might be you! These people need to establish themselves in the field and gain experience, and the only way to do that is to work and practice and show what they've got—so they are looking to mix your movie, and you are looking for a postproduction mixer . . . sounds like a perfect match.

Finishing, Mastering, and Distribution

Once you have a picture-locked film and a mixed sound track the big creative choices are over, but there is still some finishing work to be done and perhaps a few smaller creative considerations to think about before you transfer your film from your NLE system and onto a format that will allow you to send it out into the world.

■ FINISHING

Digital Color Correction

The **color correction tool** found in many NLE systems is a powerful image correction device; it takes some time and patience to learn, but once mastered can put a truly professional and individualized polish on the look of your motion picture. Color correction is used primarily to accomplish four things:

1. **Match** color and brightness values across all clips in a single scene.
2. **Correct** color temperature or exposure problems.
3. **Enhance** colors to create subtle tonalities for an individualized "look" or mood.
4. **Create** color effects, like stripping an image of all but one specific color.

The main color filter used for correcting your image is called the **three-way color corrector** (Figure 24-1). The three-way color corrector allows you to alter the **luminance values**, which are the brightness of gray tones from black to white, and the **chrominance values**, which are **hue** (the color) and **saturation** (the intensity of color) within three separate areas of your image, more or less independently of one another. Altering the chrominance values in an image is called **color balancing**. The three areas within which we make adjustments are the **blacks**, **mids**, and **whites**, and each area has its own **color wheel** and **luminance slider** for executing the modifications (Figure 24-2).

Brightness or color adjustments made with the blacks control will affect the darkest parts of the image, like dark objects and shadows. Using the whites control will affect the very brightest parts of the image, like practical lights, windows, and white objects. The mids control has the broadest range and generally includes everything in between blacks and whites. Keep in mind that these areas are not strictly distinct; they do overlap somewhat, as will the adjustments you make.

Making changes to the brightness of the image is done simply by clicking and dragging the luminance slider. Adjustments are made to the color balance by clicking and dragging the **balance indicator**, which starts at the middle of each color wheel by default. Dragging the indicator toward any area of the color spectrum infuses the image with that particular color; the further you move away from the center, the more intense the

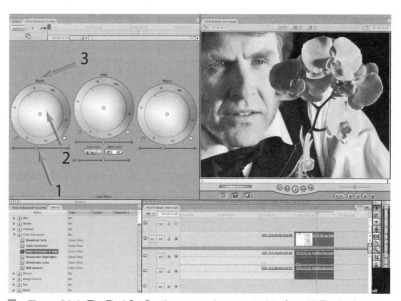

■ **Figure 24-1** The Final Cut Pro three way color corrector interface. (1) The luminance slider; (2) the color balance controls (with the balance indicator at center); (3) the color correction control range (blacks, mids or whites). Notice that the shot selected in the timeline is brought up in the viewer for color correction. See the color insert in Chapter 13.

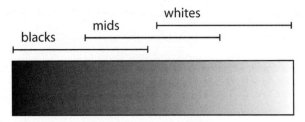

■ **Fig. 24-2** The color correction controls for blacks, mids, and whites actually overlap somewhat, which means that changes to a specific area of the image will have some effect on other areas as well.

A

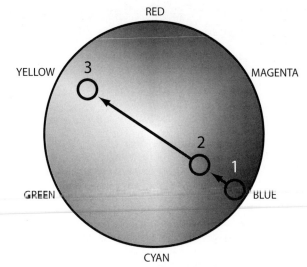

■ **Figure 24-3** Dragging the balance indicator into a specific areas of the color wheel balances the image toward that particular color. The closer to the edge you go, the more intense the color becomes. (1) Intense blue; (2) lighter blue; (3) intense yellow. See the color insert in Chapter 13.

color becomes (Figure 24-3). **Complementary colors,** like blue and yellow, are opposite each other on the color wheel because, by adding more of one color, you are reducing its complement. Beyond correcting wayward white balancing or removing color to make your film black and white, there is an enormous number of visual possibilities with this tool. You can, for example, use the luminance slider in the blacks to brighten up the shadows a tad so that we can see some detail in the shadows, or if in one scene the light outside a window is a little too bright, you can use the luminance slider in the whites areas to bring it down a bit. Perhaps you want to push a little blue into the shadows to create a certain mood. Just click and drag the blacks color balance indicator slightly further into the blue range of the color wheel (Figure 24-4).

If you're using the three-way color correction filter for the first time, you'll quickly realize that simply pushing sliders and dragging your mouse around the color wheel can create a visual mess: skin tones suddenly take on a Martian quality, or an image that had fine exposures suddenly looks terribly dull or terribly crispy, or while you're adjusting the color of the grass, the sky takes on a sickly tone. The color correction tool is something that should be researched thoroughly before you go grabbing sliders and whanging them around. Also, color correction is not just about the buttons you need to push: there is considerable technique involved that goes beyond the scope of this book, so I have listed some resources in the Recommended Readings section at the back of the book to help familiarize you with this step of the finishing process, should you find it necessary.

C

■ **Figure 24-4** A typical use of color correction. The original image (A) appears somewhat flat and pale. By adjusting luminance values we can create sharper contrast and more depth to the image (B). Adjusting the color further refines the image. In this case adding a slight amber hue provides a sense of the heat of the summer sun (C). See the color insert in Chapter 13.

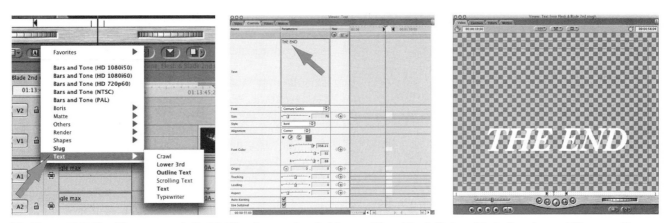

■ **Figure 24-5** The titling generator in Final Cut Pro allows you to select from a wide variety of effects and fonts. Superimposed titles are written over a checkerboard background that is later replaced by the image.

One more word of caution. Color correction, like any other visual effect, should be used with intelligence and some restraint. Creating red highlights in the shadows might look cool, but you need to consider what its purpose is in your film. Once again, technology is there to serve our ideas, so we need to be clear about what our ideas are in the first place, in order to use these tools only when they are really called for. To be sure, few films need extensive color correction, and some need none at all. If it ain't broke, don't fix it, but if you can improve your movie's look with this tool, then by all means, use it. That's what it's there for.

A Word about Color Correction and Finishing on Film

We have already discussed the color correction process for projects that finish as a film print (see p. 356). But it's worth noting that, during the digital editing stage, you should not apply any colorization effects (or any other visual effects, for that matter) that cannot be duplicated on your film print—or which you cannot afford to have done to your film print. Colorizing and special effects are so simple to achieve in your NLE system that it's easy to forget that a lab will need to duplicate those effects when you print from your A&B rolls to your answer print, and you will have to pay for those effects as well. Adjusting color temperature balance is fine, but achieving other effects, like stripping all but one color, might require that you go through a costly digital intermediate step. So think twice about applying visual effects if you're going back to film and, of course, consult with your lab.

Titles and Credits

The final step, before we can send our film out of the computer and onto a format we can show to our eager public, is to put titles and credits on the film. Again, most NLE systems contain a titling generator with more typographical options than you could ever use in a lifetime (Figure 24-5). You can choose from dozens of fonts, sizes, and colors; you can adjust the opacity of the text, create drop shadows or fuzzy edges, make the text scroll up and down, or crawl sideways, or fly in from the four corners of the screen; you can have your credits fade-in, wipe-in, or all of the above at the same time. You can, of course, create titles against simple color backgrounds, like any color text on black, or any color on white. Or by adding an additional video track to your timeline, you can superimpose your opening credits over scenes from your film (Figure 24-6).

Titling generators are fairly straightforward to learn and use, but you should always remember, when creating your titles and credits, to use the **title safe overlay**, on the screen. The title safe overlay is like the title safe viewfinder marking in a camera. It indicates the area of the frame, 20% smaller than the full video frame, which will not be covered up by the masking used on any television set to hide the very edges of the video image where signal information is located. Depending on the manufacturer of the television, those masks can be of varying widths and can create a significantly smaller viewable frame. In any case, the title safe overlay allows you to keep your credits within the area where they

■ **Figure 24-6** Superimposed titles are placed on a second video track and the final result can be seen in the viewer. Notice the title safe overlays that help your text remain within the "safe area" of all television monitors.

can be read on any screening system out there. The title safe overlay is only viewable in the preview pane and is not recorded as part of your video.

Despite the myriad titling options included in all popular NLE systems, some filmmakers who have a very specific graphic look for their title designs might go to an even more powerful, third-party graphics or typography software, like Adobe Illustrator, to create customized titles and import these files back into the NLE system to cut into the program like any other clip.

One important word of advice: take your time creating your credits. The people who worked on your movie deserve proper credit. Especially for people initiating their careers in film, credits can be as important as pay—it is not unusual for talented people to work only for the credit, especially if they believe the film will be good. If you slap your credits together at the last minute, you run the risk of forgetting people, or giving them improper credit, or misspelling their names. All of these are serious faux pas and can alienate the people you've worked with, who are among your most important resources as a filmmaker. In Chapter 18 I talked about treating everyone on the film with respect. Giving proper credit is at the core of this respect. Also, do not forget to acknowledge those people who helped make your film a reality, though they may not have directly worked on it, by putting them on a "thanks to . . ." or "special thanks to . . ." list.

■ MASTERING YOUR PROJECT

Picture locked, sound mixed, color corrected, and titles on, you are ready to take your film out of the computer and into the real world. The first step is to create full-resolution **program masters**. **Mastering** simply means getting your film onto a high-quality format, both for archiving and so that you can make distribution copies for exhibition. Even if your workflow ends with a film print, it is recommended that you master the project on DV anyway. First, most people can afford only a limited number of film prints, which limits the number of places you can send your film; additionally, many festivals require a tape or DVD submission for the first round of judging.

Output Formats

NLE systems offer a huge range of output options depending on your intended distribution avenues. Each output option uses a different **codec** (compression/decompression) mathematical algorithm that reduces the amount of video information (compression) to match your exhibition needs (Figure 24-7) (see p. 191 for a discussion of compression). Different codecs are compatible with different uses. For example, the MPEG 2 codec is used for making DVDs and MPEG 4 is commonly used for distribution over the Web. The Sorenson codec is used for CD-ROMs, and DV-NTSC codec is the same one used in DV video systems and for capturing DV footage. You can also export a QuickTime movie of your project at different levels of compression depending on your distribution outlet. Outputting NTSC DV (or any of the HD formats) is done via firewire to a DV tape, but many of these other output options, like QuickTime movies or MPEG 2, simply create media files on your hard drive; these files can be exported into third-party programs for multimedia playback, for further compression, or for authoring DVDs. It's best to consult with your software manual for a complete rundown of the various output options, their workflow, and their uses.

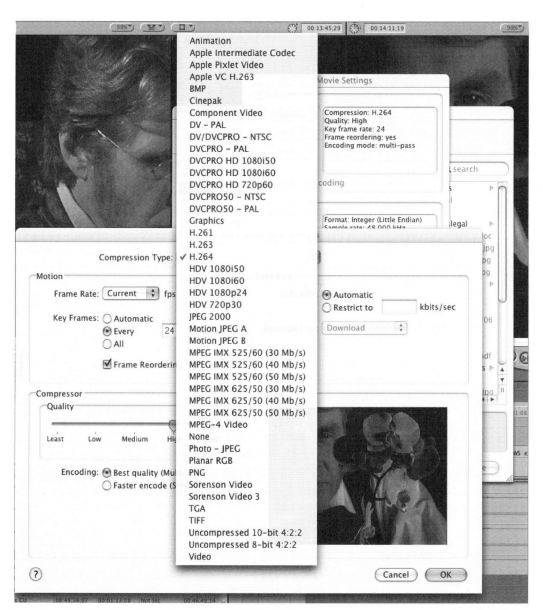

■ Figure 24-7 All NLE systems offer a wide range of output options, as you can see from this extensive menu in Final Cut Pro.

Mastering Formats

When we make **program masters** of our film, however, we want the highest quality possible. Masters are used for archiving our final film and as the source for subsequent duplication in order to create distribution copies. *The recommended method for mastering your film is to simply output your project to a DV tape deck, via firewire, with the same codec and to the same format in which you shot and captured* (Figure 24-8). For example, if you shot standard NTSC DV, then this should be your output option. If your acquisition and capture format was either HDV or DVCPRO HD, then you will likewise output using the same codec to create your master. Mastering to the same format ensures that you will lose no image quality at all from acquisition to output and it also ensures that all of your elements, raw footage and program master, are all in the same compatible format.

Whether you are editing on Final Cut Pro or Avid, outputting to tape is simply a matter of hooking up a record deck, or your camcorder, to the computer via a firewire cable. You should always use a fresh tape for each master. As usual, NLE software offers various methods for outputting, but for creating a master tape you should use the method that

■ **Figure 24-8** When mastering to DV tape simply output your project, via firewire, with the same codec and to the same format in which you shot and captured.

allows you to add a **program leader** to the head of your tape before your film begins; leaders include **color bars** and **tone**, a **slate**, and **countdown** (Figures 24-9 and 24-10). In Final Cut Pro, this output method is called **print to video**.

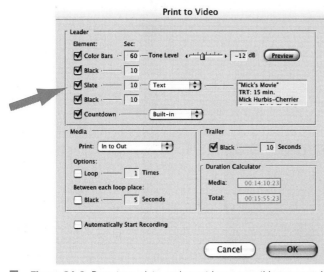

■ **Figure 24-9** Bars, tone, slate, and countdown; everything you need for a professional program leader can be found in the "Print to Video" dialogue box in Final Cut Pro.

You can, of course, output your final film more than once. You should always make several master tapes, called **safety masters**, and then, if necessary, you can output your film as a QuickTime movie (or MPEG 4) in preparation for distribution over the Web, and/or as an MPEG 2 file that you can later bring into a DVD authoring program (like iDVD or DVD Studio Pro) in order to create DVDs. None of these other options need, or should have, the added program leader mentioned above.

■ DISTRIBUTION COPIES

In the not so distant future, distribution will mean simply a video-on-demand, full-resolution transfer of data via the Web or satellite download. But at this point, the common coin of exchange for mass distribution is the DVD, and for high-quality exhibition, digital videotape. Once you have created your program and safety masters, you need to think about distribution copies. In the era of digital reproduction, it's so easy to make multiple copies that it seems silly to have to put this in print, but *do not send or give to anyone your one and only program master!* While this may seem painfully self-evident, novices, who are pushing deadlines right up to the last minute, will whip off one copy, and send it away. I'll tell you a quick story. Recently a student from my school, a very fine filmmaker, was selected with four other students to represent our school in a prestigious production award competition, which was by invitation only. Sample work had to be submitted on DVD. About a week later the judges called the school back asking for another copy of this student's work, because the submitted DVD wasn't playing. When we called the student he said, "I don't have another one, I only made one copy and didn't have time to duplicate it." When we asked if he could simply output another copy from his NLE system, he said that he had used a friend's laptop to edit and the friend was out of town, traveling with his computer! The lesson here is clear, you should output several safety masters and then use them only as a source to create distribution copies.

DVDs for Distribution

DVDs are by far the most prevalent distribution format. It's staggering to think that they first entered the commercial market place in only 1997. Most festivals, television programmers, museum curators, online festivals, and online sales and distribution outlets all take DVD submissions for screening and consideration. Also, if you want to send a sample of your work to a production company, ad agency, or producer, you will most likely send a DVD. These DVDs are called **screening copies** (or **screeners**). The more polished and professional your DVD package, meaning a DVD with extras, printed covers, and a plastic case,

in practice

Elements of the Program Leader

The program leader is inserted at the very beginning of your master tape and has a standardized order and duration for each element.

- *Bars and tone* (60 seconds):
  If you plan to broadcast your movie over television or cable, or submit it to film festivals, it's important to give the recipient of your film some way to accurately calibrate their equipment so that your images (color and brightness) and your audio levels are accurately played back. The standard calibration tools, which we lay down at the head of our tape, are **color bars** and **tone**. We have already mentioned color bars with respect to calibrating field monitors in Chapter ••. The leader elements discussed here are the same Society of Motion Picture and Television Engineers (SMPTE) standard color bars, which allow the projectionist or broadcast engineer to accurately calibrate the chrominance and luminance of their playback equipment. The 1 kHz reference tone, which is recorded on the sound track under the color bars, allows them to calibrate the audio so that your program is played back neither too soft nor too loud.

- *The program slate* (10 seconds):
  In addition, standard professional tape leader includes a **program slate**, which is a simple list of all of the information that would be important to a broadcaster or programmer, including (a) the film title, (b) producer, (c) total running time (TRT), (d) starting timecode (standard start timecode is 1:00:00:00), (e) audio configuration (i.e., mixed or stereo unmixed), and (f) production date.

- *SMPTE countdown* (10 seconds):
  SMPTE countdown is a numeric countdown in seconds, from 10 to 2, which cuts to black for the last 2 seconds of the countdown. Your project then begins precisely after the end of the 2 seconds of black. Countdown allows the broadcast engineer or projectionist to easily cue your tape for screening. By simply pausing in the black, after the #2 frame, they can be sure to begin your program with a little buffer of black before the first images appear on screen (Figure 24-10).

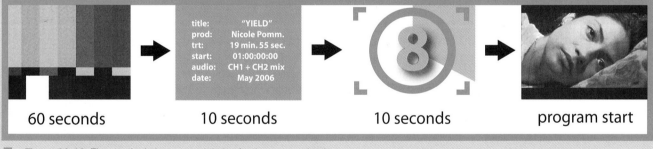

title:	"YIELD"
prod:	Nicole Pomm.
trt:	19 min. 55 sec.
start:	01:00:00:00
audio:	CH1 + CH2 mix
date:	May 2006

60 seconds   10 seconds   10 seconds   program start

Figure 24-10 The standard elements and timing for the program leader.

the better your film will be represented. DVDs are also standard for selling your film and for giving your movie to family, friends, and the people who participated in the production.

A **DVD** (for **digital versatile disc**) stores the binary data for your sound and images as microscopic bumps and indentations, called **pits**, in the surface of the disc. These pits are written as one long, ultra fine spiral called the **data track**. Your DVD player reads these pits with a laser beam as the disc spins in the DVD drive bay at speeds between 200 and 500 rpm (depending on the position of the laser tracking system on the disc). All DVDs encode the image and sound data using the MPEG 2 compression codec. Your software encodes your film as MPEG 2 when you create the disc and your DVD player contains the MPEG 2 decoder to uncompress the data as you watch it. What is also essential to know, for projects shot on film or 24P DV and captured into the NLE system with reverse telecine for editing at 23.976 fps (see p. 359), is that you can output, encode, and author your DVD at 23.976 fps as well. When a DVD player decompresses the data, it also has the ability to perform as a mini-telecine machine and convert your 23.976 fps movie to 29.97 NTSC for screening on conventional TV sets. Keeping your frame rate at 23.976 fps allows you to put more footage, less compressed, onto the DVD, because you have fewer frames and less data per minute. This is the encoding method used for most commercial films on DVD.

Pressed DVDs are manufactured as either single sided or double sided. In addition, they can have either one or two layers of data storage. These variables determine the storage capacity of the DVD.

DVD-5: Single sided, single layer. Stores 4.7 GB of data, around 2 hours of video and audio.

DVD-9: Single sided, dual layer. Stores 8.5 GB of data, around 4 hours of video and audio.

DVD-10: Double sided, single layer. Stores 9.4 GB of data, around 4.5 hours of video and audio.

DVD-18: Double sided, dual layer. Stores 17 GB of data, around 8 hours of video and audio.

Pressed or Burned?

Not all DVDs are created equal: there are two basic types, pressed and burned. **Pressed DVDs** (also called **replicated discs**) physically mold the pits of the data track into the surface of the DVD polycarbonate plastic, which is then coated in aluminum. This is the kind of DVD you find when you buy or rent a commercial movie. **Burned DVDs** are created using a laser to burn a color dye layer in the media surface, which turns various colors and densities; this mimics the depth and shadows of the physical pits in a pressed DVD.

Pressed DVDs are 100% compatible with all DVD players but must be created by a professional disc mastering service. The cost for having discs professionally mastered is quite low, but this kind of DVD manufacturing is only available for bulk quantities, which means 300 or more discs! That's a lot of distribution. If you plan to go this route, most disc mastering services prefer that you deliver your film uncompressed in the form of a program master on DV tape or an uncompressed QuickTime file on a portable hard drive or digital linear tape (DLT). You should check with the facility to see how they prefer delivery of your project. Ordinarily, DVD mastering services do not want you to compress your own files to MPEG 2, as their encoding tools are substantially more sophisticated.

But what if you don't need 500 DVD copies? What if you only need twelve or so? Then you're likely to burn your own using **recordable DVDs** (also called **burned DVDs**). Recordable DVDs come in four flavors: DVD+R and DVD−R are record-once-only formats, and DVD+RW and DVD−RW can have their data erased and rewritten, so are not a good choice for distribution. All four types are single-sided, single-layer media and so hold no more than 4.7 GB of data. Currently, there are some serious format wars going on, primarily between HD-DVD and Blu-Ray technology, over the next generation of high-capacity, high-definition recordable DVDs, but for the time being, the standard for burning your own DVDs remains DVD+R or DVD−R. So what's the difference between +R and −R? Not much. This is the format war that wasn't. Two rivals looking for exclusivity wound up both being compatible on nearly every new DVD player manufactured. Either one works fine, for the most part. Occasionally you will find an older model DVD player that will not play one or the other or either. As someone who gives lectures at various colleges and conferences, I always keep duplicate copies (one +R and one −R) just in case of compatibility problems, and, if possible, I have someone check the system for compatibility ahead of time.

When we create a DVD+R or −R copy it's called "burning" a disc, instead of "pressing" a disc, because of the laser technique used to create recordable disks. The faux "pits" (color dye layers) fool the DVD player's laser into thinking that it's scanning and reading into the dimensions of a pressed pit. DVD+R (−R) media claim 90%–95% compatibility with existing DVD players. But all new DVD player's are now manufactured to be compatible with both +R and −R DVD media, so that number will likely edge closer and closer to 100%. Unfortunately, my mother's old DVD player happens to be one from the 5% minority!

In any case, encoding, authoring, and burning your own DVDs requires a computer with a DVD burner and a DVD authoring program like DVD Studio Pro or iDVD (for simple projects) on the Apple platform, or Adobe Encore or Pinnacle Studio for the PC (Figure 24-11). It is usually recommended that you import your projects as an uncompressed file into these programs (i.e., uncompressed QuickTime movie) and do the necessary encoding from within the program. Make sure you thoroughly research the capabilities and options these programs offer before you encode, author, and burn your DVDs.

■ **Figure 24-11** The interface for Adobe Encore DVD, a powerful DVD authoring program.

Screening Dubs for Film Festivals and Broadcast

Cable companies and film festivals are two of the most visible and important outlets for your film, so screening your movie at its best quality is essential. While most festivals and broadcast stations accept DVDs for application submissions or as a preview copy, once you are accepted for screening, you must find out what their preferred exhibition format is and use one of your safety masters to make a screening dub. Two common DV formats used for projection at film festivals and broadcasting are DigiBeta and DVCPRO.

■ WEB DISTRIBUTION AND THE FUTURE

The Web is a fact of life for the student and independent filmmaker. More and more films, especially shorts, are being streamed on one of the many film outlets proliferating on the Web. Some of these sites are **video hosting sites**, which provide a wide variety of services, from video-on-demand to online marketing, distribution, and DVD sales. Some of these sites hold online film festivals while others simply lay out a smorgasbord of media and keep a running tally of the most popular works (those that get the most hits) on the site. Divining who the major players are in the Web video hosting world can be difficult, in that Web culture is notoriously unstable and subject to constant change, so it would be folly to commit to a list of the most popular sites in print here. I have listed a few sites in the Web Resources section that hopefully will still be around when you try to visit them. Among the most stable video streaming sources are conventional film festival websites; Sundance, The Tribeca Film Festival, and Slamdance, to name just a few, all stream some of their short film winners from their websites. Other Web platforms, like individual **filmmaker websites**, **video podcasts**, and **vlogs**, are also becoming a significant new outlet for the self-distribution and self-promotion of films.

Without much trouble, a filmmaker can create a series of video podcasts of their work, list the video podcast on Apple's music store, and subscribers will receive new video episodes downloaded to their video iPods automatically. The most recent trend in media for the small screen is cell phone distribution. Cell phone companies are currently in a mad scramble to find "byte-sized" video content for downloading into their cell phones. This

Filmmakers Susan Buice and Arin Crumly created both a website and an ongoing series of video podcasts around their first feature film, *Four Eyed Monsters,* which was shot on DV and screened at numerous film festivals, including Slamdance. The strategy of the filmmaking duo was to generate interest in the film by "creating an audience" through regular, 5-minute podcasts. These podcasts are not episodes from the film; rather, they are an ongoing, behind-the-scenes look at the filmmaking process and the couple's developing romantic and creative relationship during the period of making and distributing the movie.

The video podcasts are the movie about the movie, delivered in 5-minute episodes.

"In about nine months, we went to 16 film festivals and 3,000 people saw the film. Yet in the first 36 hours [our podcasts] were viewed 3,000 times online" (from *The Independent,* May/June 2006). Buice and Crumly self-distribute their film, which has opened to sold-out audiences around the country. Most of those in attendance are primed and eager to see the film because they've been closely following the story of the film and the couple via the podcasts.

In podcast episode 7.6, in which the couple screen their film in New York City, Susan and Arin interview audience members standing in line to attend their film. Many spoke of the connection they felt with the filmmakers, even though they had yet to see the film itself: "I guess since I've been seeing the podcasts for a little while, I feel like I have a connection." . . . "I'm really invested in Susan and Arin as people even though I don't know them; it's creepy." . . . "I like you guys and I want things to work out."

Looking at their website, especially through the "Friends" links, it's clear that the feature film is only one part of what Buice and Crumly have accomplished; the podcasts have a life of their own and have essentially created a broader film community through innovative online outreach.

■ **Figure 24-12** Filmmakers Susan Buice and Arin Crumly successfully promote and self-distribute their film *Four Eyed Monsters* (2005) through the use of a website and regular podcasts.

means a whole new outlet for very short, low-resolution films. By and large, cell phones also use MPEG 2 encoding.

At this moment, all Web-based outlets require super low-resolution distribution compression. MPEG 4 and QuickTime (.mov) and Windows movies (.wmv) are the current standard encoding formats. Most Web-based video hosting sites that stream (or download) video require that you keep files very small, meaning a total file size no more than 100 MB (a few sites go as high as 200 MB) and the average required screen size is 320 × 240 pixels (Figure 24-13)!

At the required compression and size, a six-minute movie will take up 80 MB. That's pushing the limit. Personal websites, of course, can hold and stream longer films in larger sizes and better resolution, but all of these factors increase the download time for the viewer. In any case, what the Web is able to handle, in general, at this point are very short movies, with poor visual quality. But this assessment can only serve as a snapshot of this rapidly changing arena. The current level of technology and quality isn't causing serious filmmakers to abandon the large screen yet, but they are monitoring the Web's progress very carefully. Currently the World Wide Web is a space that is more appropriate for advertising your film, than actually distributing it with any quality; it is, as yet, an emerging distribution outlet—not a fully developed one. But Web and satellite distribution will sure enough arrive at some point in the near future. The technology and capacity advance monthly and it is consistently improving, step by step, achieving better and better visual resolution. A published book like this one can never remain current with a developing organism like the Web; it is up to you, the emerging filmmakers, to stay current with the technological state of the art. You must also carefully consider all of the creative, aesthetic, and formal implications that the Web, cell phones, vlogs, video podcasts, and all other screening formats that await, right around the next evolutionary bend, will have on your art form—filmmaking. In the 2006 Tribeca Film Festival Catalogue, Martin Scorsese summed up the heart of the debate between seeking distribution of your film in a theatre vs. online:

■ **Figure 24-13** High compression, low resolution and brief running times are typical of films downloaded from online sources like You Tube. Still from the 1 minute and 45 second "Le Machine" (2006) by Michael Griffin and Luke Rimmelzwaan.

When I read that the newest generation of Apple's iPod allows for movie as well as music downloads, I was taken aback. An iPod screen is, I believe, an inch and a half by an inch and a half. Now, the iPod is a tremendous product. But can this really be called an innovation?

In other words, if you're watching a movie on a screen that small, are you actually watching a movie? What, in fact, are you looking at?

Scorsese poses a central and vital question for all of us to consider (**Figure 24-14**). What are we looking at? Is this a new mode of media? One that requires its own approaches, its own aesthetic, its own forms? Or is this simply another outlet, a further extension of filmmaking as we've always known it? That's not just for you to decide, it's for you to define!

■ **Figure 24-14** An audience enjoys the action on the big screen (left), from Keaton's *Sherlock Jr.* (1924). The convenience and portability of your own pocket sized movie screen (right) with Apple's iPod.

Production Format Workflow Table

Likely production format for anticipated output and distribution:

PRODUCTION	EDIT	FINISH, OUTPUT, AND DISTRIBUTION
Film	NLE (23.976 or 29.97 fps)	Film
Film	NLE (29.97 fps)	SD or HD DV DVD Internet
60i DV	NLE (29.97 fps)	DVD SD DV Internet
24p SD DV	NLE (29.97 fps)	DVD SD DV
24p SD DV	NLE (23.976 or 29.97 fps)	Film
720p or 1080i HD	NLE (HD compressed)	HD (uncompressed)
24p HD	NLE (HD compressed)	HD (uncompressed)
24p HD	NLE (HD compressed)	Film (from uncompressed HD)

Common Filters for Black-
and-White Cinematography

COLOR	KODAK WRATTEN #	EFFECT	LIGHT LOSS (IN STOPS)
Light Yellow	#3	Absorbs some blue. Will slightly darken blue areas, like skies, blue jeans, blue water.	2/3 stop
Yellow	#8	Absorbs blue. Darkens blue areas. Very natural contrast.	1 stop
Deep Yellow	#15	Absorbs much blue. Will darken blue areas more than #8.	1 2/3 stop
Orange	#21	More extreme effects on blue. Quite dark. Also will lighten skin tones.	1 2/3 stop
Reds (#29 more extreme effect)	#25 & #29	Absorbs most blue. Blue skies and water appear nearly black. Not recommended with skin. Used in day-for-night effects, often with #56 below to improve flesh tones.	3 1/3 stops & 4 2/3 stops
Greens (#58 more extreme effect)	#56 & #58	Lightens green foliage and darkens blues areas, like the sky.	2 stops & 2 2/3 stops
Blue	#47	Lightens blue areas, darkens red areas, and accentuates haze.	2 1/3 stops

How to Calibrate a Field Monitor to NTSC Color Bars

| gray | yellow | cyan | green | magenta | red | blue |

| I | White (100 units) | +Q | Black | | | Black |

3.5/7.5/11.5
(pluge bars)

Standard NTSC color bars. Please refer to color insert Figure 12-19 for a color illustration of the NTSC bars.

Color bars are a standardized electronic signal that allow you to calibrate your reference monitor with accuracy and consistency so that you can be sure the colors and exposures you see on the monitor are what you are actually recording. It is important that you carefully calibrate your monitor each and every time you set up your equipment. While it seems like a lot of steps, calibrating a monitor to color bars becomes quick and easy after you do it a few times.

Locate the adjustment controls for brightness, contrast (a.k.a. picture), chroma (a.k.a. color) and hue (a.k.a. tint).

■ STEP 1: ADJUST BRIGHTNESS

a) Be sure that no ambient light (sunlight, movie lights, etc.) is hitting the face of the monitor. Monitor hoods are designed to block light from falling onto the monitor.

b) Send a color bar feed to the monitor. Some cameras generate color bars, or you may use a portable color bar generator. In a pinch, you can play back a tape of pre-recorded color bars.

c) Set the contrast adjustment to the middle point. There will usually be a notched indicator.

d) Turn the chroma all the way down so that the monitor renders a black-and-white image of the bars.

e) Adjust the brightness control of the monitor while watching the effect on the three pluge bar strips (Picture Lineup Generating Equipment). Adjust the brightness to the precise point at which center pluge bar (7.5) disappears and becomes indistinguishable from the left pluge bar (3.5). These two bars should become like one black bar, but you should still be able to distinguish the right pluge bar (11.5) as a slightly brighter shade of gray. If you do not see the right pluge bar, turn your brightness up a bit until it becomes visible.

Your brightness level is now set.

■ STEP 2: ADJUST CONTRAST

a) To adjust contrast, turn your attention to the white square at the bottom left. Turn the contrast all the way up. You'll notice the white square get hot and flare out a bit.

b) Turn the contrast down until the white square starts to show a change and gets sharper around its edges.

Your contrast level is now set.

■ STEP 3: ADJUST CHROMA SATURATION

Next adjust the intensity of the color in the signal.

a) Turn up the chroma to the point that the colors appear to be very saturated. You will notice especially that the magenta and red bar bleed into the surrounding bars. Turn the chroma down until all of the color bars, but especially the red bar, show clean, distinct edges and borders with the neighboring bars.

Your chroma level is now set.

■ STEP 4: ADJUST CHROMA HUE

The final step involves adjusting the hue, or the "tint," of the color in the signal. This step requires a little experience and judgment. Most video professionals judge their hue adjustments by the yellow and the magenta/red bars.

a) Adjust the hue until the yellow is "canary yellow," meaning that it has no orange or green mixed into the color. Also look at the magenta and red bars. They should be clearly distinct colors. You know that your hue is off when the magenta looks too much like the red bar or starts to look purple.

Once you're happy with the hue, your monitor is fully calibrated.

Scheduling, Budgeting, and Production Forms

There are several commercial software packages available to filmmakers that include all of the necessary scheduling and production forms to make a movie. *Gorilla* (Jungle Software) and *Movie Magic* (Entertainment Partners) are two of the most commonly used packages for film scheduling, budgeting, and production management. However, these software packages are usually created for the feature filmmaker and often include far too much detail for filmmakers working on short films or exercises. In other words, they are often overkill for small films. Appendices 4-1–4-8 contain forms designed for filmmakers who are working on short and exercises.

SHORT FILM BUDGET
Summary Page

Title:	Length:

Format:	Shoot:	Edit:	Distribute:

PERSONNEL:	PHONE #:
Director:	
Producer:	
Prod. Manager:	
Dir. of Photog.:	
Art Director:	
Sound:	
Editor:	

BUDGET SUMMARY:
1) Preproduction Total   _____
2) Production Total   _____
3) Postproduction Total   _____
4) Contingency (10%)   _____
   GRAND TOTAL   [_____]

PROJECT TIMETABLE:

	Begin:	Complete:
1) Preproduction		
2) Production		
3) Postproduction		

PROJECT DESCRIPTION:

Short Film Budget Breakdown

Title:	Dir:

Format:	*Shoot:*	*Edit:*	*Distribute:*

Length:	Shooting Ratio:	Shooting Days:

1) Preproduction Breakdown:

Item/Service/Personnel	Unit Price/Rate	Cost:
Advertising (casting)		
Transportation (scouting)		
Photocopying		
Audition facility/equip.		
Hospitality		
Legal		
Research		
Production asst.		
Miscellaneous I		
Miscellaneous II		
1) PREPRODUCTION TOTAL		

2) Production Breakdown:

Item/Service/Personnel	Unit Price/Rate	Cost:
SUPPLIES:		
Film stock		
Raw DV tape stock		
Audio tape stock		
Batteries		
Gels & diffusion		
Miscellaneous		
EQUIPMENT RENTAL:		
Camera/lenses		
Camera support		
Misc. (meters/bag/slate)		
Sound recorder		
Microphones		
Misc. audio (boom/cable)		
Lighting		
Grip		
Misc. lighting & grip		

Production Breakdown (cont'd)

ART DEPARTMENT:		
Set construction/material		
Set dressing (rental)		
Set dressing (purchase)		
Prop (rental)		
Prop (purchase)		
Wardrobe (rental)		
Wardrobe (purchase)		
Wardrobe (cleaning)		
Hair & makeup		
Special Effects		
Miscellaneous		
LOCATION EXPENSES:		
Location rental -1		
Location rental -2		
Studio rental		
Strike & restitution		
Truck/van rental		
Car rental		
Parking		
Fuel		
Public transport		
Meals		
Phone		
Insurance		
Location stills		
Miscellaneous		
PRODUCTION PERSONNEL:		
Director		
Production manager		
Director of photography		
Asst. camera		
Gaffer		
Grips		
Prod. designer/art dir.		
Sound recordist		
Asst. sound (boom op.)		
Makeup/stylist		
Talent #1		
Talent #2		
Talent #3		
Extras		
Production asst.		
2) PRODUCTION TOTAL		

Item/Service/Personnel	Unit Price/Rate	Cost:
LAB WORK		
Process & video dailies		
Syncing dailies		
Color timing		
Misc. lab work		
FILM EDIT SUPPLIES & FACILITY:		
Digital edit suite #1		
Digital edit suite #2		
Misc. (DV tape, etc.)		
SOUND:		
Sound transfers		
Music license fees		
Sound effects		
Studio (foley/ADR/etc.)		
Sound mix		
LAB PRINTING (for finishing on film):		
Negative matching		
Optical effects		
Titles		
Optical audio master		
1st answer print (A/B)		
Corrected answer print		
Master positive (A/B)		
Release print		
DISTRIBUTION:		
Mastering		
DVD copies		
Packaging		
Promotion & fest. fees		
Miscellaneous		
POST PERSONNEL:		
Editor		
Sound designer/mixer		
Foley/sound engineer		
Musicians		
3) POSTPRODUCTION TOTAL		

Script Breakdown Sheet

TITLE _____ Shoot Date _____ Page # _____

Producer _____ Director _____

❏ INT. / ❏ EXT. Location _____ ❏ DAY. / ❏ NIGHT.

Scene #.	Script pp.	Description

Cast	Wardrobe	Props

Extras & Bit Players:

Set Dress	Vehicles	Atmosphere

Hair & Makeup	Special Effects	Miscellaneous

STORYBOARDS
(Format: 16:9)

Title:	Page #
Director:	Producer:

Scene/Shot #:

Scene/Shot #:

Scene/Shot #:

Scene/Shot #:

Scene/Shot #:

Scene/Shot #:

STORYBOARDS
(Format: 16:9)

Title:		Page #
Director:	Producer:	

Scene/Shot #:

Scene/Shot #:

Scene/Shot #:

Production Call Sheet

Title:				Shooting Date:	
Producer:				PM:	
Director:				AD:	

SET	SCENES	PAGES	LOCATION

CAST CALL TIMES

CAST MEMBER	PART OF	MAKEUP	SET CALL

EXTRAS & STAND INS	MISC. INSTRUCTIONS

CREW CALL TIMES

CREW MEMBER	SET CALL
Director	
A.D.	
Art Dept.	
Makeup & Wardrobe	
Camera Dept.	
Sound Dept.	
Grips	
Other #1	
Other #2	

SOUND REPORT

Project Title _____ Date_____

Dir._____ Recordist_____ Boom Op._____

Sound Roll # _____ Location _____ Recorder # _____

Rate _____ Sample Freq. _____ Head Tone_____

Notes:

SND #	SCENE	TAKE	TIMECODE	COMMENTS
			: : :	
			: : :	
			: : :	
			: : :	
			: : :	
			: : :	
			: : :	
			: : :	
			: : :	
			: : :	
			: : :	
			: : :	
			: : :	
			: : :	
			: : :	
			: : :	
			: : :	
			: : :	
			: : :	
			: : :	
			: : :	
			: : :	
			: : :	
			: : :	
			: : :	
			: : :	

Page#_____ of _____

CAMERA REPORT

Project Title _____ Date_____

Director_____ D.P. _____ A.C. _____

Camera #_____ DV Format_____ Film Stock _____ Emulsion #_____

PROCESSING INSTRUCTIONS:

ROLL	SCENE	TK	SND #	Footage or T.C.	REMARKS
				: : :	
				: : :	
				: : :	
				: : :	
				: : :	
				: : :	
				: : :	
				: : :	
				: : :	
				: : :	
				: : :	
				: : :	
				: : :	
				: : :	
				: : :	
				: : :	
				: : :	
				: : :	
				: : :	
				: : :	
				: : :	
				: : :	
				: : :	
				: : :	
				: : :	

Notes:

TALENT RELEASE FORM

PRODUCTION TITLE: _____

PRODUCTION DATES: _____

PRODUCER: _____ DATE: _____

For good and valuable consideration of _____receipt of which is hereby acknowledged, I (the undersigned) hereby grant to the Producer the right to photograph me and to record my voice, performances, actions and appearances, and use my picture, photograph, silhouette, and other reproductions of my physical likeness in connection with the motion picture tentatively entitled _____ _____ (the "Picture").

I hereby grant to the Producer, his successors, assigns, and licensees the perpetual right to use, as you may desire, all still and motion pictures and sound track recordings and records that you may make of me or of my voice, and the right to use my name or likeness in or in connection with the exhibition, advertising, exploiting, and/or publicizing of the picture.

I agree that I will not assert or maintain against the Producer, your successors, assigns, and licensees, any claim, action, suit or demand of any kind or nature whatsoever, including but not limited to those grounded upon invasion of privacy, rights of publicity or other civil rights, or for any reason in connection with your authorized use of my physical likeness and sound in the Picture as herein provided.

By my signature here I understand that I will, to the best of my ability, adhere to the schedule agreed to prior to the beginning of my engagement. Additionally, I agree, to the best of my ability, to make myself available should it be necessary, to rerecord my voice and/or record voice-overs and otherwise perform any necessary sound work required after the end of filming. Should I not be able to perform such sound work, I understand that the Producer may enter into agreement with another person to rerecord my dialogue and/or record voice-overs and use this sound work over my picture or however they deem appropriate.

I hereby certify and represent that I am over 18 years of age and have read the foregoing and fully understand the meaning and effect thereof.

Talent Name: _____

Address:_____

_____ Telephone:_____

Talent Signature: _____

Producer Signature: _____

This form is for informational purposes only and should not be construed as legal advice. The facts of your situation may make it inappropriate for you, and you should consult your school or an attorney before using it. The author expressly undertakes no responsibility for the reliance on, or consequences of, using this sample form.

LOCATION CONTRACT

PRODUCTION TITLE: _____

PRODUCER: _____ DATE: _____

Permission is hereby granted to _____ (hereinafter referred to as "Producer"), to use the property and adjacent area, located at:

_____

for the purpose of photographing and recording scenes (interior and/or exterior) for motion pictures with the right to exhibit and license others to exhibit all or any part of said scenes in motion pictures throughout the world; said permission shall include the right to bring personnel and equipment (including props and temporary sets) onto said property, and to remove the same therefrom after completion of work.

The above permission is granted for the following days/period:

_____

at the agreed upon rental price of _____.

Producer hereby agrees to use reasonable care to prevent damage to said property and will hold the undersigned harmless of and from any and all liability and loss that the undersigned may suffer, or incur by reason of any accidents or other damages to the said premises, caused by any of their employees or equipment, on or about the above-mentioned premises, ordinary wear and tear of the premises in accordance with this agreement excepted.

The undersigned does hereby warrant and represent that the undersigned has full right and authority to enter into this agreement concerning the above-described premises, and that the consent or permission of no other person, firm, or corporation is necessary in order to enable Producer to enjoy full rights to the use of said premises, herein above mentioned, and that the undersigned does hereby indemnify and agree to hold Producer free and harmless from and against any and all loss, costs, liability, damages or claims of any nature, including but not limited to attorney's fees, arising from, growing out of, or concerning breach of the above warrant.

Name (print): _____ Company: _____

Signature: _____ Title: _____

Producer Signature: _____

16mm Film Camera Depth of Field Tables

These depth of field tables are for 16mm film shooting and were derived from the website www.dofmaster.com. They can be photocopied so that you have them handy on the set. They cover some of the most common lenses used in 16mm film photography. If you do not find your specific lens among these examples, you can easily create your own charts at www.dofmaster.com or at www.panavision.com/tools.php. DOF master also offers depth of field software for the Palm OS® platform, which can be used for both film and video shooting. To calculate depth of field, it's essential to remember that the circle of confusion (CoC) for 16mm film is 0.0006 inch (.015 millimeters).

16mm Camera DOF
Lens Focal Length: 10mm

CoC = 0.015 mm (0.0006")

FOCUS DISTANCE (FEET)	F/1.4 NEAR	F/1.4 FAR	F/2 NEAR	F/2 FAR	F/2.8 NEAR	F/2.8 FAR	F/4 NEAR	F/4 FAR	F/5.6 NEAR	F/5.6 FAR	F/8 NEAR	F/8 FAR	F/11 NEAR	F/11 FAR	F/16 NEAR	F/16 FAR	F/22 NEAR	F/22 FAR
2	1.77	2.29	1.70	2.44	1.59	2.68	1.47	3.12	1.33	4.07	1.16	7.13	0.99	∞	0.82	∞	0.66	∞
3	2.52	3.71	2.36	4.12	2.17	4.87	1.94	6.56	1.70	12.9	1.44	∞	1.18	∞	0.95	∞	0.74	∞
4	3.18	5.38	2.94	6.28	2.64	8.21	2.32	14.6	1.97	∞	1.63	∞	1.31	∞	1.03	∞	0.78	∞
5	3.78	7.37	3.44	9.16	3.04	14.0	2.62	55	2.19	∞	1.78	∞	1.40	∞	1.08	∞	0.81	∞
6	4.33	9.77	3.88	13.2	3.39	26.3	2.87	∞	2.36	∞	1.89	∞	1.47	∞	1.12	∞	0.84	∞
7	4.83	12.7	4.28	19.3	3.68	71	3.08	∞	2.50	∞	1.97	∞	1.52	∞	1.15	∞	0.85	∞
8	5.28	16.5	4.63	29.5	3.94	∞	3.26	∞	2.61	∞	2.04	∞	1.56	∞	1.17	∞	0.87	∞
9	5.70	21.4	4.95	50.0	4.17	∞	3.41	∞	2.71	∞	2.10	∞	1.60	∞	1.19	∞	0.88	∞
10	6.08	28.1	5.23	113	4.37	∞	3.54	∞	2.79	∞	2.15	∞	1.62	∞	1.21	∞	0.88	∞
12	6.77	53	5.73	∞	4.71	∞	3.76	∞	2.93	∞	2.23	∞	1.67	∞	1.23	∞	0.90	∞
14	7.36	144	6.15	∞	4.99	∞	3.94	∞	3.04	∞	2.29	∞	1.70	∞	1.25	∞	0.91	∞
16	7.87	∞	6.50	∞	5.22	∞	4.08	∞	3.12	∞	2.34	∞	1.73	∞	1.26	∞	0.91	∞
18	8.33	∞	6.81	∞	5.42	∞	4.20	∞	3.19	∞	2.38	∞	1.75	∞	1.27	∞	0.92	∞
20	8.73	∞	7.08	∞	5.58	∞	4.30	∞	3.24	∞	2.41	∞	1.77	∞	1.28	∞	0.92	∞
30	10.2	∞	8.02	∞	6.15	∞	4.63	∞	3.43	∞	2.51	∞	1.82	∞	1.31	∞	0.94	∞
∞	15.5	∞	11.0	∞	7.77	∞	5.50	∞	3.90	∞	2.77	∞	1.97	∞	1.40	∞	1.00	∞

All measurements are in feet.

16mm Camera DOF
Lens Focal Length: 16mm

CoC = 0.015 mm (0.0006")

FOCUS DISTANCE (FEET)	F/1.4 NEAR	F/1.4 FAR	F/2 NEAR	F/2 FAR	F/2.8 NEAR	F/2.8 FAR	F/4 NEAR	F/4 FAR	F/5.6 NEAR	F/5.6 FAR	F/8 NEAR	F/8 FAR	F/11 NEAR	F/11 FAR	F/16 NEAR	F/16 FAR	F/22 NEAR	F/22 FAR
2	1.91	2.10	1.87	2.15	1.82	2.22	1.76	2.32	1.67	2.49	1.56	2.77	1.44	3.30	1.28	4.51	1.12	9.39
3	2.79	3.24	2.71	3.35	2.61	3.52	2.48	3.80	2.31	4.27	2.11	5.18	1.88	7.42	1.63	19.0	1.37	∞
4	3.64	4.44	3.51	4.66	3.33	5.00	3.12	5.57	2.86	6.65	2.56	9.17	2.23	19.8	1.88	∞	1.54	∞
5	4.44	5.71	4.25	6.07	4.00	6.67	3.69	7.73	3.33	10.0	2.93	17.1	2.50	∞	2.07	∞	1.67	∞
6	5.22	7.06	4.95	7.62	4.61	8.58	4.21	10.4	3.75	15.0	3.24	39.9	2.73	∞	2.22	∞	1.76	∞
7	5.96	8.49	5.61	9.31	5.18	10.8	4.68	13.9	4.11	23.5	3.51	949	2.91	∞	2.34	∞	1.84	∞
8	6.66	10.0	6.23	11.2	5.71	13.4	5.10	18.5	4.44	40.6	3.75	∞	3.07	∞	2.45	∞	1.90	∞
9	7.34	11.6	6.82	13.2	6.20	16.4	5.49	24.9	4.73	94	3.95	∞	3.21	∞	2.53	∞	1.95	∞
10	7.99	13.4	7.38	15.5	6.66	20.1	5.85	34.6	4.99	∞	4.13	∞	3.32	∞	2.60	∞	1.99	∞
12	9.22	17.2	8.41	20.9	7.48	30.3	6.47	82	5.44	∞	4.43	∞	3.51	∞	2.72	∞	2.06	∞
14	10.4	21.6	9.34	27.9	8.21	47.4	7.01	3862	5.81	∞	4.68	∞	3.67	∞	2.81	∞	2.11	∞
16	11.4	26.8	10.2	37.2	8.86	82	7.48	∞	6.13	∞	4.88	∞	3.79	∞	2.88	∞	2.15	∞
18	12.4	32.9	11.0	50	9.44	193	7.89	∞	6.40	∞	5.05	∞	3.89	∞	2.94	∞	2.18	∞
20	13.3	40.3	11.7	70	9.96	∞	8.25	∞	6.63	∞	5.19	∞	3.98	∞	2.99	∞	2.21	∞
30	17.1	123	14.5	∞	11.9	∞	9.56	∞	7.45	∞	5.68	∞	4.25	∞	3.14	∞	2.29	∞
40	19.9	∞	16.5	∞	13.3	∞	10.4	∞	7.94	∞	5.96	∞	4.41	∞	3.22	∞	2.33	∞
50	22.1	∞	18.0	∞	14.2	∞	10.9	∞	8.27	∞	6.15	∞	4.51	∞	3.27	∞	2.36	∞
∞	39.6	∞	28.0	∞	19.8	∞	14.1	∞	9.95	∞	7.05	∞	5.00	∞	3.55	∞	2.53	∞

All measurements are in feet.

16mm Camera DOF
Lens Focal Length: 25mm

CoC = 0.015 mm (0.0006")

FOCUS DISTANCE (FEET)	F/1.4 NEAR	F/1.4 FAR	F/2 NEAR	F/2 FAR	F/2.8 NEAR	F/2.8 FAR	F/4 NEAR	F/4 FAR	F/5.6 NEAR	F/5.6 FAR	F/8 NEAR	F/8 FAR	F/11 NEAR	F/11 FAR	F/16 NEAR	F/16 FAR	F/22 NEAR	F/22 FAR
2	1.96	2.04	1.95	2.06	1.92	2.08	1.89	2.12	1.85	2.17	1.80	2.25	1.73	2.38	1.63	2.58	1.52	2.93
3	2.91	3.09	2.88	3.13	2.83	3.19	2.76	3.28	2.68	3.41	2.56	3.62	2.42	3.96	2.24	4.56	2.02	5.80
4	3.84	4.17	3.78	4.24	3.70	4.35	3.59	4.52	3.44	4.77	3.25	5.19	3.02	5.92	2.74	7.39	2.43	11.4
5	4.76	5.27	4.66	5.39	4.54	5.57	4.37	5.84	4.15	6.28	3.88	7.02	3.55	8.43	3.17	11.8	2.76	26.9
6	5.65	6.39	5.52	6.57	5.35	6.84	5.11	7.26	4.82	7.95	4.46	9.18	4.03	11.8	3.54	19.5	3.03	294
7	6.53	7.54	6.36	7.79	6.12	8.17	5.82	8.78	5.44	9.81	4.98	11.8	4.45	16.4	3.87	36.8	3.26	∞
8	7.39	8.71	7.17	9.05	6.87	9.57	6.50	10.4	6.03	11.9	5.47	14.9	4.83	23.2	4.15	109	3.46	∞
9	8.24	9.91	7.96	10.4	7.60	11.0	7.14	12.2	6.57	14.3	5.91	18.8	5.18	34.4	4.40	∞	3.63	∞
10	9.07	11.1	8.73	11.7	8.30	12.6	7.75	14.1	7.09	17.0	6.33	23.8	5.49	56	4.63	∞	3.79	∞
12	10.7	13.7	10.2	14.5	9.63	15.9	8.90	18.4	8.04	23.7	7.07	39.7	6.04	880	5.01	∞	4.04	∞
14	12.2	16.4	11.6	17.6	10.9	19.7	9.95	23.6	8.88	33.0	7.72	75	6.51	∞	5.33	∞	4.24	∞
16	13.7	19.2	13.0	20.9	12.0	23.9	10.9	29.9	9.65	46.9	8.28	234	6.90	∞	5.59	∞	4.40	∞
18	15.2	22.1	14.3	24.4	13.1	28.6	11.8	37.8	10.3	70	8.79	∞	7.25	∞	5.81	∞	4.54	∞
20	16.6	25.2	15.5	28.2	14.2	34.0	12.6	47.9	11.0	114	9.24	∞	7.55	∞	6.00	∞	4.65	∞
30	22.9	43.4	20.9	53	18.5	79	16.0	241	13.4	∞	10.9	∞	8.63	∞	6.66	∞	5.04	∞
40	28.3	68	25.3	96	21.9	230	18.4	∞	15.1	∞	12.0	∞	9.29	∞	7.05	∞	5.26	∞
50	33.0	103	28.9	185	24.6	∞	20.3	∞	16.3	∞	12.8	∞	9.74	∞	7.31	∞	5.40	∞
∞	97	∞	68	∞	48.4	∞	34.3	∞	24.2	∞	17.2	∞	12.2	∞	8.63	∞	6.12	∞

All measurements are in feet.

16mm Camera DOF
Lens Focal Length: 50mm

CoC = 0.015 mm (0.0006")

FOCUS DISTANCE (FEET)	F/1.4 NEAR	F/1.4 FAR	F/2 NEAR	F/2 FAR	F/2.8 NEAR	F/2.8 FAR	F/4 NEAR	F/4 FAR	F/5.6 NEAR	F/5.6 FAR	F/8 NEAR	F/8 FAR	F/11 NEAR	F/11 FAR	F/16 NEAR	F/16 FAR	F/22 NEAR	F/22 FAR
3	2.98	3.02	2.97	3.03	2.96	3.04	2.94	3.06	2.91	3.09	2.88	3.13	2.83	3.19	2.77	3.27	2.68	3.40
4	3.96	4.04	3.94	4.06	3.92	4.08	3.89	4.12	3.85	4.17	3.79	4.24	3.71	4.34	3.60	4.51	3.45	4.75
5	4.94	5.06	4.91	5.09	4.88	5.13	4.83	5.18	4.76	5.26	4.67	5.38	4.55	5.56	4.38	5.82	4.17	6.25
6	5.91	6.09	5.87	6.13	5.82	6.19	5.75	6.27	5.66	6.39	5.53	6.56	5.35	6.82	5.12	7.24	4.83	7.91
7	6.88	7.13	6.83	7.18	6.76	7.26	6.67	7.37	6.54	7.53	6.36	7.78	6.13	8.15	5.83	8.75	5.46	9.76
8	.84	8.17	7.78	8.24	7.69	8.34	7.57	8.49	7.40	8.71	7.18	9.04	6.88	9.55	6.51	10.4	6.04	11.8
9	8.80	9.21	8.72	9.30	8.61	9.43	8.45	9.62	8.25	9.91	7.97	10.3	7.61	11.0	7.15	12.1	6.59	14.2
10	9.75	10.3	9.65	10.4	9.52	10.5	9.33	10.8	9.08	11.1	8.74	11.7	8.31	12.6	7.77	14.0	7.11	16.9
12	11.6	12.4	11.5	12.5	11.3	12.8	11.0	13.1	10.7	13.7	10.2	14.5	9.64	15.9	8.91	18.4	8.05	23.5
14	13.5	14.5	13.3	14.7	13.1	15.1	12.7	15.6	12.2	16.3	11.6	17.6	10.9	19.6	9.97	23.5	8.90	32.8
16	15.4	16.7	15.1	17.0	14.8	17.4	14.3	18.1	13.7	19.1	13.0	20.8	12.1	23.8	10.9	29.8	9.67	46.4
18	17.2	18.9	16.9	19.3	16.5	19.8	15.9	20.7	15.2	22.1	14.3	24.4	13.1	28.5	11.8	37.6	10.4	69
20	19.0	21.1	18.6	21.6	18.1	22.3	17.5	23.4	16.6	25.2	15.5	28.2	14.2	33.9	12.7	47.7	11.0	112
30	27.9	32.5	27.0	33.7	26.0	35.5	24.6	38.4	22.9	43.4	20.9	53	18.5	78	16.0	236	13.4	∞
40	36.3	44.6	34.9	46.8	33.2	50	31.0	56	28.3	68	25.3	96	21.9	228	18.5	∞	15.1	∞
50	44.3	57	42.3	61	39.8	67	36.6	79	33.0	103	28.9	185	24.6	∞	20.3	∞	16.3	∞
∞	387	∞	274	∞	193	∞	137	∞	97	∞	69	∞	48.5	∞	34.3	∞	24.3	∞

All measurements are in feet.

16mm Camera DOF
Lens Focal Length: 75mm

CoC = 0.015 mm (0.0006")

FOCUS DISTANCE (FEET)	F/1.4 NEAR	F/1.4 FAR	F/2 NEAR	F/2 FAR	F/2.8 NEAR	F/2.8 FAR	F/4 NEAR	F/4 FAR	F/5.6 NEAR	F/5.6 FAR	F/8 NEAR	F/8 FAR	F/11 NEAR	F/11 FAR	F/16 NEAR	F/16 FAR	F/22 NEAR	F/22 FAR
3	2.99	3.01	2.99	3.01	2.98	3.02	2.97	3.03	2.96	3.04	2.95	3.05	2.93	3.08	2.90	3.11	2.86	3.16
4	3.98	4.02	3.98	4.02	3.97	4.03	3.95	4.05	3.93	4.07	3.90	4.10	3.87	4.14	3.81	4.21	3.74	4.30
5	4.97	5.03	4.96	5.04	4.95	5.06	4.92	5.08	4.89	5.11	4.85	5.16	4.79	5.23	4.71	5.33	4.60	5.48
6	5.96	6.04	5.94	6.06	5.92	6.08	5.89	6.11	5.85	6.16	5.78	6.23	5.70	6.34	5.58	6.49	5.43	6.71
7	6.95	7.05	6.92	7.08	6.89	7.11	6.85	7.16	6.79	7.22	6.71	7.32	6.59	7.46	6.43	7.67	6.23	7.99
8	7.93	8.07	7.90	8.10	7.86	8.15	7.80	8.21	7.72	8.30	7.62	8.42	7.47	8.61	7.27	8.90	7.00	9.33
9	8.91	9.09	8.87	9.13	8.82	9.18	8.75	9.26	8.65	9.38	8.52	9.54	8.33	9.79	8.08	10.2	7.75	10.7
10	9.89	10.1	9.84	10.2	9.78	10.2	9.69	10.3	9.57	10.5	9.40	10.7	9.18	11.0	8.87	11.5	8.48	12.2
12	11.8	12.2	11.8	12.2	11.7	12.3	11.6	12.5	11.4	12.7	11.1	13.0	10.8	13.5	10.4	14.2	9.87	15.3
14	13.8	14.2	13.7	14.3	13.6	14.5	13.4	14.7	13.2	14.9	12.9	15.4	12.4	16.0	11.9	17.0	11.2	18.7
16	15.7	16.3	15.6	16.4	15.4	16.6	15.2	16.9	14.9	17.2	14.5	17.8	14.0	18.7	13.3	20.1	12.4	22.5
18	17.6	18.4	17.5	18.5	17.3	18.8	17.0	19.1	16.6	19.6	16.1	20.3	15.5	21.5	14.6	23.4	13.6	26.7
20	19.6	20.5	19.4	20.7	19.1	21.0	18.8	21.4	18.3	22.0	17.7	22.9	16.9	24.4	15.9	26.9	14.7	31.4
30	29.0	31.1	28.6	31.5	28.1	32.2	27.4	33.2	26.4	34.8	25.1	37.2	23.6	41.3	21.6	48.9	19.4	66
40	38.3	41.9	37.6	42.8	36.7	44.0	35.4	45.9	33.8	48.9	31.8	54	29.3	63	26.4	83	23.1	149
50	47.3	53	46.3	54	44.9	56	43.0	60	40.7	65	37.8	74	34.3	92	30.4	142	26.1	589
75	69	82	67	85	64	91	60	99	56	114	50	146	44.4	240	38.0	2694	31.6	∞
100	90	113	86	119	81	130	76	148	69	185	61	285	52	1209	43.5	∞	35.3	∞
∞	870	∞	615	∞	435	∞	308	∞	218	∞	154	∞	109	∞	77	∞	55	∞

All measurements are in feet.

16mm Camera DOF
Lens Focal Length: 100mm

CoC = 0.015 mm (0.0006")

FOCUS DISTANCE (FEET)	F/1.4 NEAR	F/1.4 FAR	F/2 NEAR	F/2 FAR	F/2.8 NEAR	F/2.8 FAR	F/4 NEAR	F/4 FAR	F/5.6 NEAR	F/5.6 FAR	F/8 NEAR	F/8 FAR	F/11 NEAR	F/11 FAR	F/16 NEAR	F/16 FAR	F/22 NEAR	F/22 FAR
5	4.98	5.02	4.98	5.02	4.97	5.03	4.96	5.04	4.94	5.06	4.92	5.09	4.88	5.12	4.83	5.18	4.77	5.25
6	5.98	6.02	5.97	6.03	5.96	6.04	5.94	6.06	5.91	6.09	5.88	6.13	5.83	6.18	5.76	6.26	5.67	6.37
7	6.97	7.03	6.96	7.04	6.94	7.06	6.92	7.09	6.88	7.12	6.83	7.18	6.77	7.25	6.67	7.36	6.55	7.52
8	7.96	8.04	7.94	8.06	7.92	8.08	7.89	8.11	7.84	8.16	7.78	8.23	7.69	8.33	7.57	8.48	7.41	8.69
9	8.95	9.05	8.93	9.07	8.90	9.10	8.86	9.15	8.80	9.21	8.72	9.29	8.61	9.42	8.46	9.61	8.26	9.89
10	9.94	10.1	9.91	10.1	9.88	10.1	9.83	10.2	9.76	10.3	9.66	10.4	9.52	10.5	9.34	10.8	9.09	11.1
12	11.9	12.1	11.9	12.1	11.8	12.2	11.7	12.3	11.6	12.4	11.5	12.5	11.3	12.8	11.1	13.1	10.7	13.6
14	13.9	14.1	13.8	14.2	13.8	14.3	13.7	14.4	13.5	14.5	13.3	14.7	13.1	15.1	12.7	15.6	12.3	16.3
16	15.8	16.2	15.8	16.2	15.7	16.3	15.6	16.5	15.4	16.7	15.1	17.0	14.8	17.4	14.4	18.1	13.8	19.1
18	17.8	18.2	17.7	18.3	17.6	18.4	17.4	18.6	17.2	18.9	16.9	19.2	16.5	19.8	15.9	20.7	15.2	22.0
20	19.7	20.3	19.6	20.4	19.5	20.5	19.3	20.7	19.0	21.1	18.7	21.6	18.2	22.3	17.5	23.4	16.6	25.1
30	29.4	30.6	29.2	30.8	28.9	31.2	28.5	31.7	27.9	32.5	27.1	33.7	26.0	35.4	24.6	38.3	23.0	43.3
40	39.0	41.1	38.6	41.5	38.0	42.2	37.3	43.1	36.3	44.6	34.9	46.8	33.2	50	31.0	56	28.4	68
50	48.4	52	47.8	52	47.0	53	45.8	55	44.3	57	42.3	61	39.8	67	36.7	79	33.0	103
75	72	79	70	80	68	83	66	87	63	93	59	103	54	122	48.5	165	42.3	330
100	94	107	92	110	89	115	85	122	80	135	73	157	66	206	58	369	49.2	∞
∞	1547	∞	1094	∞	774	∞	547	∞	387	∞	274	∞	194	∞	137	∞	97	∞

All measurements are in feet.

16mm Camera DOF
Lens Focal Length: 120mm

CoC = 0.015 mm (0.0006")

FOCUS DISTANCE (FEET)	F/1.4 NEAR	F/1.4 FAR	F/2 NEAR	F/2 FAR	F/2.8 NEAR	F/2.8 FAR	F/4 NEAR	F/4 FAR	F/5.6 NEAR	F/5.6 FAR	F/8 NEAR	F/8 FAR	F/11 NEAR	F/11 FAR	F/16 NEAR	F/16 FAR	F/22 NEAR	F/22 FAR
4	3.99	4.01	3.99	4.01	3.99	4.01	3.98	4.02	3.97	4.03	3.96	4.04	3.95	4.05	3.93	4.07	3.90	4.11
5	4.99	5.01	4.99	5.01	4.98	5.02	4.97	5.03	4.96	5.04	4.94	5.06	4.92	5.08	4.89	5.12	4.84	5.17
6	5.98	6.02	5.98	6.02	5.97	6.03	5.96	6.04	5.94	6.06	5.92	6.09	5.88	6.12	5.83	6.18	5.77	6.25
7	6.98	7.02	6.97	7.03	6.96	7.04	6.94	7.06	6.92	7.08	6.88	7.12	6.84	7.17	6.77	7.24	6.68	7.35
8	7.97	8.03	7.96	8.04	7.95	8.06	7.92	8.08	7.89	8.11	7.85	8.16	7.79	8.22	7.70	8.32	7.59	8.46
9	8.97	9.03	8.95	9.05	8.93	9.07	8.90	9.10	8.86	9.14	8.81	9.20	8.73	9.29	8.62	9.41	8.48	9.59
10	9.96	10.0	9.94	10.1	9.91	10.1	9.88	10.1	9.83	10.2	9.76	10.3	9.67	10.4	9.53	10.5	9.35	10.7
12	11.9	12.1	11.9	12.1	11.9	12.1	11.8	12.2	11.8	12.3	11.7	12.4	11.5	12.5	11.3	12.8	11.1	13.1
14	13.9	14.1	13.9	14.1	13.8	14.2	13.8	14.2	13.7	14.4	13.5	14.5	13.3	14.7	13.1	15.0	12.8	15.5
16	15.9	16.1	15.8	16.2	15.8	16.2	15.7	16.3	15.6	16.5	15.4	16.7	15.2	17.0	14.8	17.4	14.4	18.0
18	17.9	18.1	17.8	18.2	17.7	18.3	17.6	18.4	17.4	18.6	17.2	18.8	16.9	19.2	16.5	19.8	16.0	20.6
20	19.8	20.2	19.8	20.3	19.7	20.4	19.5	20.5	19.3	20.7	19.1	21.0	18.7	21.5	18.2	22.2	17.5	23.3
30	29.6	30.4	29.4	30.6	29.2	30.8	28.9	31.2	28.5	31.7	27.9	32.4	27.1	33.6	26.1	35.3	24.7	38.1
40	39.3	40.7	39.0	41.0	38.6	41.5	38.1	42.1	37.3	43.1	36.3	44.5	35.0	46.6	33.3	50	31.1	56
50	48.9	51	48.5	52	47.9	52	47.0	53	45.9	55	44.4	57	42.4	61	39.9	67	36.9	78
75	73	78	72	79	70	80	69	83	66	87	63	93	59	102	54	121	48.8	162
100	96	105	94	107	92	110	89	114	85	122	80	134	74	156	66	202	58	352
∞	2228	∞	1575	∞	1114	∞	788	∞	557	∞	394	∞	279	∞	197	∞	140	∞

All measurements are in feet.

16mm Camera DOF
Lens Focal Length: 2000mm

CoC = 0.015 mm (0.0006")

FOCUS DISTANCE (FEET)	F/1.4		F/2		F/2.8		F/4		F/5.6		F/8		F/11		F/16		F/22	
	NEAR	FAR	NEAR	FAR	NEAR	FAR	NEAR	FAR	NEAR	FAR	NEAR	FAR	NEAR	FAR	NEAR	FAR	NEAR	FAR
6	5.99	6.01	5.99	6.01	5.99	6.01	5.99	6.01	5.98	6.02	5.97	6.03	5.96	6.04	5.94	6.06	5.92	6.08
8	7.99	8.01	7.99	8.01	7.98	8.02	7.97	8.03	7.96	8.04	7.95	8.05	7.92	8.08	7.89	8.11	7.85	8.15
10	9.98	10.0	9.98	10.0	9.97	10.0	9.96	10.0	9.94	10.1	9.92	10.1	9.88	10.1	9.83	10.2	9.76	10.2
12	12.0	12.0	12.0	12.0	12.0	12.0	11.9	12.1	11.9	12.1	11.9	12.1	11.8	12.2	11.8	12.3	11.7	12.4
16	16.0	16.0	15.9	16.1	15.9	16.1	15.9	16.1	15.8	16.2	15.8	16.2	15.7	16.3	15.6	16.5	15.4	16.7
18	17.9	18.1	17.9	18.1	17.9	18.1	17.9	18.1	17.8	18.2	17.7	18.3	17.6	18.4	17.4	18.6	17.2	18.8
20	19.9	20.1	19.9	20.1	19.9	20.1	19.8	20.2	19.8	20.3	19.7	20.4	19.5	20.5	19.3	20.7	19.0	21.1
30	29.9	30.1	29.8	30.2	29.7	30.3	29.6	30.4	29.4	30.6	29.2	30.8	28.9	31.2	28.5	31.7	27.9	32.5
40	39.7	40.3	39.6	40.4	39.5	40.5	39.3	40.7	39.0	41.0	38.6	41.5	38.1	42.1	37.3	43.1	36.3	44.5
50	49.6	50	49.4	51	49.2	51	48.9	51	48.5	52	47.8	52	47.0	53	45.9	55	44.3	57
75	74	76	74	76	73	77	73	78	72	79	70	80	68	83	66	87	63	93
100	98	102	98	102	97	103	96	105	94	107	92	110	89	115	85	122	80	135
∞	6187	∞	4375	∞	3094	∞	2188	∞	1547	∞	1094	∞	774	∞	547	∞	387	∞

All measurements are in feet.

Recommended Readings

GENERAL FILM STUDY

Looking at Movies: An Introduction to Film
Richard M. Barsam; W.W. Norton and Co.

The Film Experience
by Timothy Corrigan and Patricia White; Palgrave Macmillan.

The Cinema Book
by Pam Cooke and Mieke Bernink; British Film Institute.

Film Style and Technology: History and Analysis
by Barry Salt; Starword.

SCREENWRITING AND SCREENPLAYS

The Shooting Script (Newmarket Shooting Script Series)
(esp. *Pieces of April,* by Peter Hedges; *The Squid and the Whale,* by Noah Baumbach; and
Sideways, by Alexander Payne and Jim Taylor); New Market Press.

Rushmore
by Wes Anderson and Owen Wilson; Faber and Faber.

Developing Story Ideas
by Michael Rabiger; Focal Press.

Crafting Short Screenplays that Connect
by Claudia Hunter Johnson; Focal Press.

Alternative Scriptwriting
by Ken Dancyger and Jeff Rush; Focal Press.

The Screenwriter's Manual: A Complete Reference of Format & Style
by Stephen E. Bowles, Ronald Mangravite, Peter A. Zorn; Allyn & Bacon

PRE-VISUALIZATION

Film Directing Shot by Shot: Visualizing from Concept to Screen
by Steven D. Katz; Michael Wiese Productions.

PRODUCING

Producing and Directing the Short Film and Video
by Peter W. Rea and David K. Irving; Focal Press.

Contracts for the Film & Television Industry
by Mark Litwak; Silman-James Press.

IFP/Los Angeles Independent Filmmaker's Manual
by Eden H. Wurmfeld and Nicole Laloggia; Focal Press.

Film Budgeting: Or, How Much It Will Cost to Shoot Your Movie?
by Ralph S. Singleton; VNU Inc.

Clearance and Copyright: Everything the Independent Filmmaker Needs to Know
by Michael C. Donaldson; Silman-James Press.

■ DIRECTING

On Filmmaking: An Introduction to the Craft of the Director
by Alexander Mackendrick; Faber and Faber.

Film Directing Fundamentals: See Your Film Before Shooting
by Nicholas Proferes; Focal Press.

Directing Actors: Creating Memorable Performances for Film & Television
by Judith Weston; Michael Wiese Productions.

The Film Director's Intuition: Script Analysis & Rehearsal Techniques
by Judith Weston; Michael Wiese Productions.

Directing Feature Films: The Creative Collaboration Between Director, Writers, and Actors
by Mark W. Travis; Michael Wiese Productions.

■ ART DIRECTION

Production Design and Art Direction (Screencraft Series)
by Peter Ettedgui; Focal Press.

The Art Direction Handbook for Film
by Michael Rizzo; Focal Press.

■ CINEMATOGRAPHY

Lighting for Film and Digital Cinematography
by Dave Viera and Maria Viera; Wadsworth Publishing.

Motion Picture and Video Lighting
by Blain Brown; Focal Press.

Contemporary Cinematographers on Their Art
by Pauline B. Rogers; Focal Press.

New Cinematographers
by Alex Ballinger; Collins Design.

Cinematography (Screencraft Series)
by Peter Ettedgui; Focal Press.

Masters of Light: Conversations with Contemporary Cinematographers
by Dennis Salvato and Larry Salvato; University of California Press.

■ SOUND

Audio-Vision
by Michael Chion; Columbia University Press.

Practical Art of Motion Picture Sound
by David Yewdall; Focal Press.

Sound for Film and Television
by Tomlinson Holman; Focal Press.

■ PRODUCTION TECHNICAL REFERENCE

American Cinematographer Manual
by Stephen Burum; American Society of Cinematographers.

Selected Tables, Charts and Formulas for the Student Cinematographer from the American Cinematographer Manual
by ASC, Stephen Burum (Ed.); American Society of Cinematographers.

ASC Video Manual
by Michael Grotticelli (Ed.); ASC Holding Corp.

Camera Assistant's Manual
by David E. Elkins; Focal Press.

The Professional Cameraman's Handbook
by Sylvia E. Carlson and Verne Carlson; Focal Press.

Working with HDV: Shoot, Edit, and Deliver Your High Definition Video
by Chuck Gloman and Mark J. Pescatore; Focal Press.

Digital Cinematography
by Paul Wheeler; Focal Press.

■ POSTPRODUCTION

In the Blink of an Eye
by Walter Murch; Silman-James Press.

Technique of Film and Video Editing: History, Theory, and Practice
by Ken Dancyger; Focal Press.

On Film Editing
by Edward Dmytryk; Focal Press.

Avid Editing: A Guide for Beginning and Intermediate Users
by Sam Kauffmann; Focal Press.

Apple Pro Training Series: Final Cut Pro
by Diana Weynand; Peachpit Press.

Visual Quickpro Guide: Avid Express Pro
by James Monohan; Peachpit Press.

Advanced Color Correction and Effects in Final Cut Pro 5 (Apple Pro Training Series)
By Alexis Van Hurkman; Peachpit Press.

■ **ON FILMMAKERS AND METHODS**

Notes on the Cinematographer
by Robert Bresson; Green Integer.

Hitchcock
by Helen G. Scott and François Truffaut; Simon & Schuster.

On Directing Film
by David Mamet; Penguin.

Making Movies
by Sidney Lumet; Vintage.

Who the Devil Made It: Conversations with Legendary Film Directors
by Peter Bogdanovich; Ballantine Books.

Moviemakers' Master Class: Private Lessons from the World's Foremost Directors
by Laurent Tirard; Faber and Faber.

Web Resources

The World Wide Web offers an enormously wide range of resources for the filmmaker. The usefulness of individual websites ranges from absolutely indispensable to completely disposable fluff. Below I have listed some of the more useful websites for a working filmmaker. Also, as anyone who visits the web regularly knows, it is a rather unstable organism—websites come and websites go. I have tried my best to list the most stable resources out there, but I cannot guarantee that all of these links will still be up and running when you try to visit. Best of luck.

GENERAL FILM INFORMATION

http://www.imdb.com

http://www.filmmaker.com

http://www.moviemaker.com

http://www.filmthreat.com

http://www.sensesofcinema.com

http://www.indiewire.com

http://www.studentfilmmakers.com

SCRIPTS

http://www.scriptcity.net

CASTING AND LEGAL

http://www.backstage.com

http://www.breakdownservices.com

https://www.nowcasting.com

http://www.marklitwak.com

GUILDS, UNIONS, AND ORGANIZATIONS

http://www.wga.org

http://www.theasc.com

http://www.editorsguild.com

http://www.dga.org

http://www.mpaa.org

http://www.aivf.org

http://www.ufva.org

http://www.pbs.org/independentlens

http://www.ifp.org

http://www.sagindie.org

http://www.filmarts.org

http://www.wif.org

http://www.creative-capital.org

■ CINEMATOGRAPHY

http://www.theasc.com

http://www.cinematography.com

http://www.cinematography.net

■ SOUND AND MUSIC

http://www.filmsound.org

http://www.ascap.com

http://www.bmi.com

■ PRODUCTION TECHNICAL REFERENCE

http://www.smpte.org

http://www.atsc.org

http://www.kodak.com/US/en/motion

http://www.fujifilmusa.com/JSP/fuji/epartners/MPHomePage.jsp

http://www.panavision.com/tools.php

http://www.dofmaster.com

http://web.mac.com/angelodp1/iWeb/USC/Welcome.html

http://www.adamwilt.com

http://www.davideubank.com

http://digitalcontentproducer.com

http://www.colorlab.com

■ FESTIVALS AND DISTRIBUTION

http://www.filmfestivals.com

http://www.withoutabox.com

http://www.atomfilms.com

http://www.ifilm.com

http://www.shorts.org

http://filmfestivalworld.com

http://www.slamdance.com

http://www.current.tv

http://medialab.ifc.com

http://www.indieflix.com

http://www.indiepix.net

http://www.res.com

Filmography

■ CHAPTER 1

Pieces of April. Dir. Peter Hedges. IFC Productions, 2003.
(DVD distribution: MGM Home Entertainment) (Figure 1-3)

Nan va Koutcheh (*Bread and Alley*). Dir. Abbas Kiarostami, 1970 (Figure 1-4)

The Miracle. Dir. George Racz, 2006. (Figure 1-5)

Raiders of the Lost Ark. Dir. Steven Spielberg. Lucasfilm Ltd., 1981.
(DVD distribution: Paramount Home Video)

La Jetée. Dir. Chris Marker. Argos Films, 1962.
(DVD distribution: BijouFlix Releasing) (Figure 1-6 R)

Dwaj ludzie z szafa (*Two Men and a Wardrobe*). Dir. Roman Polanski. Panstwowa Wyzsza
Szkola Filmowa, 1958.
(DVD distribution: Available on *Knife in the Water.* The Criterion Collection, 2003)

Meshes of the Afternoon. Dir. Maya Deren, 1943.
Available on *Maya Deren: Experimental Films.* Mystic Fire Video, 2002. (Figure 1-6 L)

El Mariachi. Dir. Roberto Rodriguez. Columbia Pictures, 1992.
(DVD distribution: Columbia Tristar). (Figure 1-7)

Old Joy. Dir. Kelly Reichardt. Washington Square Films, 2006.
(DVD distribution: Kino International Corp.) (Figure 1-8)

■ CHAPTER 2

The Miracle. Dir. George Racz, 2006.

Ocean's Eleven. Dir. Steven Soderbergh. Village Roadshow Pictures, 2001.
(DVD distribution: Warner Home Video) (Figures 2-4, 2-7, 2-8, 2-9)

The Thin Red Line. Dir. Terrence Malick. Fox 2000 Pictures, 1998.
(DVD distribution: 20th Century Fox Home Entertainment) (Figure 2-5)

The Silence of the Lambs. Dir. Jonathan Demme. Orion Pictures Corporation, 1991.
(DVD distribution: The Criterion Collection) (Figure 2-10)

Sideways. Dir. Alexander Payne. Fox Searchlight Pictures, 2004.
(DVD distribution: Twentieth Century–Fox Film Corporation) (Figures 2-11, 2-12)

■ CHAPTER 3

Psycho. Dir. Alfred Hitchcock. Shamley Productions, 1960.
(DVD distribution: Universal Home Entertainment)

Russian Ark. Dir. Aleksandr Sokurov. Egoli Tossell Film AG, 2002.
(Distribution: Wellspring Media)

The Fisher King. Dir. Terry Gilliam. Columbia Pictures Corp., 1991.
(DVD distribution: Columbia Tristar Home Video) (Figure 3-1)

The Thin Red Line. Dir. Terrence Malick. Fox 2000 Pictures, 1998.
(DVD distribution: 20th Century Fox Home Entertainment) (Figure 3-2)

Star Wars: Episode VI - Return of the Jedi. Dir. Richard Marquand. Lucasfilm Ltd., 1983.
(DVD distribution: 20th Century Fox Home Entertainment) (Figure 3-3)

Young and Innocent. Dir. Alfred Hitchcock. Gaumont British Picture Corporation, 1937.
(DVD distribution: Delta Expedition, 2000) (Figure 3-4)

Down by Law. Dir. Jim Jarmusch. Island Pictures, 1986.
(DVD distribution: The Criterion Collection) (Figure 3-5)

Yield. Dir. Gustavo Mercado. Gustavo Mercado, 2006. (Figures 3-6, 3-7, 3-14)

Stranger than Paradise. Dir. Jim Jarmusch. Cinesthesia Productions, 1984.
(DVD distribution: MGM Home Entertainment) (Figure 3-8 T)

Le Samouraï. Dir. Jean-Pierre Melville. TC Productions, 1967.
(DVD distribution: The Criterion Collection) (Figure 3-8 B)

Letyat zhuravli (The Cranes Are Flying). Dir. Mikheil Kalatozishvili. Ministerstvo Kinemato-grafii, 1957. (DVD distribution: The Criterion Collection) (Figure 3-9 T)

Smala Sussie (Slim Susie). Dir. Ulf Malmros. Götafilm, 2003.
(DVD distribution: Home Vision Entertainment (HVE)) (Figure 3-9 M)

Masculin/Féminin: 15 faits précis. Dir. Jean-Luc Godard. Argos Films, 1966.
(DVD distribution: The Criterion Collection, 2005) (Figure 3-9 B)

The Usual Suspects. Dir. Bryan Singer. Polygram Filmed Entertainment, 1995.
(DVD distribution: Polygram Home Video) (Figure 3-10)

Vozvrashcheniye (The Return). Dir. Andrei Zvyagintsev. Ren Film, 2003.
(DVD distribution: Kino International) (Figure 3-11 T)

Naked. Dir. Mike Leigh. Thin Man Films, 1993.
(DVD distribution: The Criterion Collection, 2005) (Figure 3-11 B)

Sin City. Dir. Frank Miller. Dimension Films, 2005.
(Distribution: Miramax Films) (Figure 3-12 T)

La vie rêvée des anges (The Dreamlife of Angels). Dir. Erick Zonca. Canal+, 1998.
(DVD distribution: Columbia TriStar Home Video) (Figure 3-12 B)

A Zed & Two Noughts. Dir. Peter Greenaway. Channel Four Films, 1985.
(Distribution: Skoures Pictures) (Figure 3-13 T)

L'eclisse. Dir. Michelangelo Antonioni. Interopa Film, 1962.
(DVD distribution: The Criterion Collection, 2005) (Figure 3-13 B)

The Constant Gardener. Dir. Fernando Meirelles. Potboiler Productions, 2005
(DVD distribution: Focus Features) (Figure 3-15)

Raging Bull. Dir. Martin Scorsese. Chartoff-Winkler Productions, 1980.
(DVD distribution: MGM Home Entertainment) (Figures 3-7 B, 3-16 through 3-23)

Der himmel über Berlin (*Wings of Desire*). Dir. Wim Wenders. Argos Films, 1987.
(DVD distribution: MGM/UA Home Entertainment) (Figure 3-24)

Annie Hall. Dir. Woody Allen. Rollins-Joffe Productions, 1977.
(DVD distribution: MGM/UA Home Entertainment) (Figure 3-25)

Le fils (*The Son*). Dirs. Jean-Pierre Dardenne and Luc Dardenne. Archipel 35, 2002.
(DVD distribution: New Yorker Video) (Figure 3-27)

The Crying Game. Dir. Neil Jordan. Channel Four Films, 1992.
(DVD distribution: Live Home Video) (Figure 3-28)

Bakushû (*Early Summer*). Dir. Yasujiro Ozu. Shochiku Films Ltd., 1951.
(DVD distribution: The Criterion Collection, 2004) (Figure 3-29 L)

Angst essen Seele auf (*Ali: Fear Eats the Soul*). Dir. Rainer Werner Fassbinder. Tango Film, 1974.
(DVD distribution: The Criterion Collection) (Figure 3-29 R)

La belle et la bête (*Beauty and the Beast*). Dir. Jean Cocteau. DisCina, 1946.
(DVD distribution: The Criterion Collection) (Figure 3-31)

Elephant. Dir. Gus Van Sant. HBO Films, 2003.
(DVD distribution: HBO Films) (Figure 3-32)

The Silence of the Lambs. Dir. Jonathan Demme. Orion Pictures Corporation, 1991.
(DVD distribution: The Criterion Collection) (Figure 3-33)

Raising Arizona. Dir. Joel Cohen. Circle Films, 1987
(DVD distribution: 20th Century Fox Home Entertainment) (Figure 3-34)

■ CHAPTER 4

Bamboozled. Dir. Spike Lee. 40 Acres & A Mule Filmworks, 2000.
(DVD distribution: New Line Home Video)

Riget (*The Kingdom*). Dirs. Morten Arnfred and Lars von Trier. Zentropa Entertainments, 1994.
(DVD distribution: Warner Home Video)

My Own Private Idaho. Dir. Gus Van Sant. New Line Cinema, 1991
(DVD distribution: The Criterion Collection) (Figure 4-2)

New Jack City. Dir. Mario Van Peebles. Warner Bros. Pictures, 1991.
(DVD distribution: Warner Home Video)

River of Things: "Ode to Things." Dir. Mick Hurbis-Cherrier, 1998. (Figure 4-7)

Sideways. Dir. Alexander Payne. Fox Searchlight Pictures/Michael London Prod., 2004.
(DVD distribution: 20th Century Fox) (Figures 4-10, 4-11, 4-12)

Down by Law. Dir. Jim Jarmusch. Island Pictures, 1986.
(DVD distribution: The Criterion Collection)

The Squid and the Whale. Dir. Noah Baumbach. American Empirical Pictures, 2005.
(DVD distribution: Sony Pictures) (Figure 4-13)

Angst isst Seele auf (Fear Eats the Soul). Dir. Shahbaz Noshir. Yilmaz Arslan Filmproduktion GmbH, 2003.
(DVD distribution: The Criterion Collection with *Angst essen Seele auf* Dir. R.W. Fassbinder) (Figure 4-14)

Yield. Dir. Gustavo Mercado. Gustavo Mercado, 2006. (Figure 4-15)

L'Avventura. Dir. Michelangelo Antonioni. Cino del Duca, 1960.
(DVD distribution: The Criterion Collection) (Figure 4-11)

Raising Arizona. Dir. Joel Cohen. Circle Films, 1987
(DVD distribution: 20th Century Fox Home Entertainment) (Figure 4-18)

Strangers on a Train. Dir. Alfred Hitchcock. Warner Bros. Pictures, 1951.
(DVD distribution: Warner Home Video) (Figure 4-22)

Diva. Dir. Jean-Jacques Beineix. Les Films Galaxie, 1981
(DVD distribution: Anchor Bay Entertainment) (Figure 4-23)

Romuald et Juliette (Mama, There's a Man in Your Bed). Dir. Coline Serreau. Union Générale Cinématographique, 1989. (Figure 4-24)

The Godfather. Dir. Francis Ford Coppola. Paramount Pictures, 1972.
(DVD distribution: Paramount Home Video) (Figure 4-25)

The Constant Gardener. Dir. Fernando Meirelles. Potboiler Productions, 2005
(DVD distribution: Focus Features) (Figure 4-26)

Breathless (À Bout de Souffle). Dir. Jean-Luc Godard. Impéria, 1960.
(DVD distribution: Fox Lorber)

The Limey. Dir. Steven Soderbergh. Artisan Entertainment, 1999.
(DVD distribution: Artisan Entertainment)

Dancer in the Dark. Dir. Lars von Trier. Zentropa Entertainment, 2000.
(DVD distribution: New Line Home Video) (Figure 4-27)

Happy Together (Cheun gwong tsa sit). Dir. Wong Kar-Wai. Jet Tone Prod. Co., 1997.
(DVD distribution: Kino Video) (Figure 4-28)

Aiqing wansui (Vive L'Amour). Dir. Tsai Ming-Liang. Central Motion Pictures Corporation, 1994. (DVD distribution: Strand Releasing) (Figure 4-29)

Elephant. Dir. Gus Van Sant. HBO Films, 2003.
(DVD distribution: HBO Films)

■ CHAPTER 5

The Miracle. Dir. George Racz, 2006. (Figure 5-3)

The Birds. Dir. Alfred Hitchcock. Universal Pictures, 1963.
(DVD distribution: Universal Home Entertainment)

Sideways. Dir. Alexander Payne. Fox Searchlight Pictures/Michael London Prod., 2004.
(DVD distribution: 20th Century Fox)

Sabotage. Dir. Alfred Hitchcock. Gaumont British Picture Corporation, 1936.
(DVD distribution: Laserlight Entertainment) (Figure 5-7)

Finders Keepers. Dir. Andrew Lund, 2006. (Figure 5-10 L)

Snapshot. Dir. Andrew Lund, 2005. (Figure 5-10 R)

■ CHAPTER 6

Pieces of April. Dir. Peter Hedges. IFC Productions, 2003.
(DVD distribution: MGM Home Entertainment) (Figure 6-1)

Something Wild. Dir. Jonathan Demme. Religiosa Primitiva, 1986.
(DVD distribution: MGM/UA Home Entertainment) (Figure 6-2)

Paul & Steve. Dir. Alessandra Kast. 2005 (Figure 6-3)

Looking for Richard. Dir. Al Pacino. 20th Century Fox, 1996.
(Distribution: Fox Searchlight Pictures) (Figure 6-4)

Aria "Rigoletto" Segment. Dir. Julien Temple. Lightyear Entertainment, 1987
(DVD distribution: Image Entertainment) (Figure 6-5)

■ CHAPTER 7

Man Push Cart. Dir. Ramin Bahrani. Noruz Films, 2005.
(DVD distribution: Koch/Lorber) (Figure 7-1)

The Miracle. Dir. George Racz, 2006. (Figure 7-3)

The Last Temptation of Christ. Dir. Martin Scorsese. Universal Pictures, 1988.
(DVD Distribution: The Criterion Collection) (Figure 7-4)

River of Things: "Ode to Things." Dir. Mick Hurbis-Cherrier, 1998.

Vive le premier mai. Dir. Didier Rouget, 1999. (Figure 7-13)

■ CHAPTER 8

2001: A Space Odyssey. Dir. Stanley Kubrick. Metro-Goldwyn-Mayer, 1968.
(DVD distribution: MGM/UA Home Video) (Figure 8-4 T)

A Clockwork Orange. Dir. Stanley Kubrick. Warner Bros. Pictures, 1971.
(DVD distribution: Warner Home Video) (Figure 8-4 B)

Adaptation. Dir. Spike Jonze. Propaganda Films, 2002.
(DVD distribution: Columbia TriStar Home Video) (Figure 8-5)

What's Up, Tiger Lily? Dirs. Woody Allen & Senkichi Taniguchi. Benedict Pictures, 1966.
(DVD distribution: Vestron Video) (Figure 8-11)

Fa yeun nin wa (In the Mood for Love). Dir. Wong Kar-Wai. Paradis Films, 2000.
(DVD distribution: The Criterion Collection) (Figure 8-16 T)

Requiem for a Dream. Dir. Darren Aronofsky. Artisan Entertainment, 2000.
(DVD distribution: Lions Gate Films) (Figure 8-16 B)

Manhattan. Dirs. Woody Allen. Jack Rollins and Charles H. Joffe Productions, 1979.
(DVD distribution: MGM/UA Home Entertainment) (Figure 8-35 B)

Good Night, and Good Luck. Dir. George Clooney. Warner Independent Pictures, 2005.
(DVD distribution: Warner Bros. Pictures) (Figure 8-35 T)

Hero (Ying xiong). Dir. Zhang Yimou. Beijing New Picture Film Co., 2002.
(DVD distribution: Miramax Films) (Figure 8-38)

Pi. Dir. Darren Aronovsky. Harvest Filmworks, 1998
(DVD distribution: Lion's Gate Films) (Figure 8-43)

The Miracle. Dir. George Racz, 2006. (Figure 8-44)

Cidade de Deus (City of God). Dirs. Fernando Meirelles and Kátia Lund. O2 Filmes, 2002.
(Distribution: Miramax Films) (Figure 8-48 L)

Leaving Las Vegas. Dir. Mike Figgis. Initial Productions, 1995
(DVD distribution: MGM/UA Home Entertainment) (Figure 8-48 R)

◼ CHAPTER 9

Timecode. Dir. Mike Figgis. Red Mullet Productions, 2000.
(DVD distribution: Columbia Tristar Home Video) (Figure 9-8)

Star Wars: Episode II - Attack of the Clones. Dir. George Lucas. Lucasfilm Ltd., 2002.
(DVD distribution: 20th Century Fox Home Entertainment) (Figure 9-11 L)

Sex and Lucía (Lucía y el sexo). Dir. Julio Medem. Alicia Produce/Canal+ España, 2001.
(DVD distribution: Trimark Video) (Figure 9-11 R)

November. Dir. Greg Harrison. IFC Productions, 2004
(DVD distribution: IFC Films) (Figure 9-13, 9-34)

Taste of Cherry (Ta'm e guilass). Dir. Abbas Kiarostami. Abbas Kiarostami Productions/
CiBy 2000, 1997.
(DVD distribution: Criterion Film Corp.) (Figure 9-15 L)

Ten. Dir. Abbas Kiarostami. Abbas Kiarostami/Key Lime/MK2 Productions, 2002.
(DVD distribution: Zeitgeist Films) (Figure 9-15 R)

The Rocking Horse Winner. Dir. Michael Almereyda. 1997 (Figure 9-34 L)

◼ CHAPTER 10

Goodfellas. Dir. Martin Scorsese. Warner Brothers Pictures 1990
(DVD distribution: Warner Home Video) (Figure 10-5)

The Fisher King. Dir. Terry Gilliam. Columbia Pictures Corp., 1991. (Figure 10-6 T)
(DVD distribution: Columbia Tristar Home Video)

Searching for Bobby Fischer. Dir. Steven Zaillian. Mirage Entertainment, 1993.
(Distribution: Paramount Pictures) (Figure 10-6 M)

Man Push Cart. Dir. Ramin Bahrani. Noruz Films, 2005.
(DVD distribution: Koch/Lorber) (Figure 10-6 B)

Ed Wood. Dir. Tim Burton. Touchstone Pictures, 1994.
(DVD distribution: Buena Vista Home Video) (Figure 10-12)

Sideways. Dir. Alexander Payne. Fox Searchlight Pictures/Michael London Prod., 2004.
(DVD distribution: 20th Century Fox) (Figure 10-16)

▪ CHAPTER 11

Café Lumière (Kôhî jikô). Dir. Hou Hsiao-Hsien. Shochiku Co., 2003,
(DVD distribution: Fox Lorber) (Figure 11-1 T)

Elephant. Dir. Gus Van Sant. HBO Films, 2003.
(DVD distribution: HBO Films) (Figure 11-1 M)

24 Hour Party People. Dir. Michael Winterbottom. Revolution Films, 2002.
(DVD distribution: MGM/UA Home Entertainment) (Figure 11-1 B)

Eternal Sunshine of the Spotless Mind. Dir. Michel Gondry. Focus Features, 2004.
(DVD distribution: Universal Studios Home Video)

La Promesse. Dirs. Jean-Pierre and Luc Dardenne. Eurimages, 1996.
(DVD distribution: New Yorker Films)

Dancer in the Dark. Dir. Lars von Trier. Zentropa Entertainments, 2000.
(DVD distribution: New Line Home Video)

Chelovek s Kino-Apparatom (Man With Movie Camera). Dir. Dziga Vertov. VUFKU, 1929.
(DVD distribution: Kino Video) (Figures 11-3 and 11-6)

Tokyo-Ga. Dir. Wim Wenders. Chris Sievernich Filmproduktion, 1985.
(DVD distribution: Gray City/Pacific Arts) (Figure 11-8)

Rocky. Dir. John G. Avildsen. Chartoff-Winkler Productions, 1976.
(DVD distribution: MGM Home Entertainment)

Marathon Man. Dir. John Schlesinger. Paramount Pictures, 1976.
(DVD distribution: Paramount Home Video)

The Shining. Dir. Stanley Kubrick. Warner Bros. Pictures, 1980.
(DVD distribution: Warner Home Video)

The Evil Dead. Dir. Sam Raimi. Renaissance Pictures, 1981.
(DVD distribution: Anchor Bay Entertainment) (Figure 11-15)

Blood Simple. Dir. Joel Coen. Foxton Entertainment, 1984.
(DVD distribution: Columbia TriStar Home Video)

The Celebration (Festen). Dir. Thomas Vinterberg. Nimbus Film, 1998.
(DVD distribution: Universal Studios)

Breathless (À Bout de Souffle). Dir. Jean-Luc Godard. Impéria, 1960.
(DVD distribution: Wellspring Media)

Barry Lyndon. Dir. Stanley Kubrick. Hawk Films Ltd., 1975.
(DVD distribution: Warner Home Video) (Figure 11-17)

Nine Lives. Dir. Rodrigo García. Mockingbird Pictures, 2005.
(DVD distribution: Sony Pictures Home Entertainment) (Figure 11-18)

The Constant Gardener. Dir. Fernando Meirelles. Potboiler Productions, 2005
(DVD distribution: Focus Features) (Figure 11-19)

■ CHAPTER 12

Wings of Desire. Dir. Wim Wenders. Argos Films, 1987.
(DVD distribution: MGM/UA Home Entertainment) (Figure 12-1)

Masculin/Féminin. Dir. Jean-Luc Godard. Argos Films, 1966.
(DVD distribution: The Criterion Collection) (Figure 12-4 T)

The Graduate. Dir. Mike Nichols. Embassy Pictures Corporation, 1967.
(DVD distribution: MGM DVD) (Figure 12-4 B)

Naked Doom. Ed Rankus, 1983 (Figure 12-13)

Personal Velocity: Three Portraits. Dir. Rebecca Miller. IFC Productions, 2002.
(DVD distribution: MGM Distributing Corp.) (Figure 12-18 T)

The Celebration (Festen). Dir. Thomas Vinterberg. Nimbus Film, 1998.
(DVD distribution: Universal Studios) (Figure 12-18 B)

■ CHAPTER 13

Masculin/Féminin. Dir. Jean-Luc Godard. Argos Films, 1966.
(DVD distribution: The Criterion Collection) (Figure 13-1 TL)

Personal Velocity: Three Portraits. Dir. Rebecca Miller. IFC Productions, 2002.
(DVD distribution: MGM Distributing Corp.) (Figure 13-1 TM)

Chungking Express (Chung hing sam lam). Dir. Wong Kar-Wai. Jet Tone Production Co.,
1994. (DVD distribution: Miramax Home Entertainment) (Figure 13-1 TR)

Ali: Fear Eats the Soul (Angst essen Seele auf). Dir. R. W. Fassbinder. Tango Film, 1974.
(DVD distribution: The Criterion Collection) (Figure 13-1 BL)

Reconstruction. Dir. Christoffer Boe. Nordisk Film, 2003.
(DVD distribution: Palm Pictures) (Figure 13-1 BR and 13-9 R)

The Blair Witch Project. Dirs. Daniel Myrick and Eduardo Sánchez. Haxan Films, 1999.
(DVD distribution: Lions Gate Films) (Figure 13-2 B)

River of Things: "Ode to a Bar of Soap." Dir. Katherine Hurbis-Cherrier, 1998. (Figure 13-3)

Persona. Dir. Ingmar Bergman. Svensk Filmindustri AB, 1966.
(DVD distribution: MGM Home Entertainment) (Figure 13-4)

Lost In Translation. Dir. Sophie Coppola. American Zoetrope, 2003.
(DVD distribution: Universal Home Entertainment) (Figure 13-9 L)

Der himmel über Berlin (*Wings of Desire*). Dir. Wim Wenders. Argos Films, 1987.
(DVD distribution: MGM/UA Home Entertainment) (Figure 13-15 and 13-18)

Veronika Voss. Dir. R. W. Fassbinder. Tango Film, 1982.
(DVD distribution: The Criterion Collection) (Figure 13-20)

The Godfather. Dir. Francis Ford Coppola. Paramount Pictures, 1972.
(DVD distribution: Paramount Home Video) (Figure 13-26 L)

Mr. Arkadin. Dir. Orson Wells. Mercury Productions, 1955
(DVD distribution: The Criterion Collection) (Figure 13-26 R)

Beauty and the Beast (*La belle et la bête*). Dir. Jean Cocteau. DisCina, 1946.
(DVD distribution: The Criterion Collection) (Figure 13-29 TL)

Sweet Smell of Success. Dir. Alexander Mackendrick. Hill-Hecht-Lancaster Prods., 1957.
(DVD distribution: MGM/UA Home Entertainment) (Figure 13-29 TR)

The Last Laugh (*Der Letzte Mann*). Dir. F.W. Murnau. Universum Film A.G., 1924.
(DVD distribution: Kino Video) (Figure 13-29 BL)

Citizen Kane. Dir. Orson Welles. Mercury Productions/RKO Radio Pictures. 1941.
(DVD distribution: Warner Home Video) (Figure 13-26 BR)

Night of the Hunter Dir. Charles Laughton. Paul Gregory Prod., 1955
(DVD distribution: MGM/UA Home Entertainment) (Figure 13-30)

Ed Wood. Dir. Tim Burton. Touchstone Pictures, 1994.
(DVD distribution: Buena Vista Home Video) (Figure 13-32)

Pretty See, Pretty Do. Dir. Kelly Lewis. 2006 (Figure 13-33)

Bringing up Baby. Dir. Howard Hawks. RKO Radio Pictures, 1938
(DVD distribution: Warner Home Video) (Figure 13-34)

To Kill a Mockingbird. Dir. Robert Mulligan. Universal International Pictures, 1962.
(DVD distribution: Universal Pictures) (Figure 13-35)

Stardust Memories. Dir. Woody Allen. Rollins-Joffee Productions, 1980
(DVD distribution: MGM Home Entertainment) (Figure 13-36)

Ferris Bueller's Day Off. Dir. John Hughes. Paramount Pictures, 1986.
(DVD distribution: Paramount Home Video) (Figure 13-37 TL)

Tony Takitani. Dir. Jun Ichikawa. Wilco Co. Ltd., 2004.
(DVD distribution: Strand Home Video) (Figure 13-37 TR)

Crash. Dir. Paul Haggis. Bull's Eye Entertainment, 2004.
(DVD distribution: Lions Gate Films Home Entertainment) (Figure 13-37 BL)

Raiders of the Lost Ark. Dir. Steven Spielberg. Lucasfilm Ltd., 1981.
(DVD distribution: Paramount Home Video) (Figure 13-37 BR)

Becoming. Dir. Gustavo Mercado (2007) (Figure 13-38)

Days of Heaven. Dir. Terrence Malick. Paramount Pictures, 1978.
(DVD distribution: Paramount Home Entertainment) (Figure 13-41 L)

Cycle Unknown. Dir. Jessica Daniels, 2006 (Figure 13-41 M)

Yield. Dir. Gustavo Mercado, 2005. (Figure 13-41 R)

■ CHAPTER 14

Masculin/Féminin. Dir. Jean-Luc Godard. Argos Films, 1966.
(DVD distribution: The Criterion Collection) (Figure 14-1)

Felicia's Journey. Dir. Atom Egoyan. Alliance Atlantis Communications, 1999.
(DVD distribution: Artisan Entertainment) (Figure 14-6)

The Son (Le Fils). Dirs. Jean-Pierre and Luc Dardenne. Les Films du Fleuve, 2002.
(DVD distribution: New Yorker Films) (Figure 14-21)

The Dreamlife of Angels. Dir. Eric Zonca. Diaphana Films, 1999.
(DVD distribution: MGM Columbia Tristar Home Video) (Figure 14-22)

New York Stories, "Life Lessons." Dir. Martin Scorsese. Touchstone Pictures, 1989.
(DVD distribution: Touchstone Home Video) (Figure 14-23)

Mildred Pierce. Dir. Michael Curtiz. Warner Bros. Pictures, 1945
(DVD distribution: Warner Home Video) (Figure 14-24)

Black Narcissus. Dirs. Michael Powell & Emeric Pressburger. Independent Prods, 1947.
(DVD distribution: The Criterion Collection) (Figure 14-25)

Do The Right Thing. Dir. Spike Lee. 40 Acres & A Mule Filmworks, 1989
(DVD distribution: The Criterion Collection) (Figure 14-26 T)

Election. Dir. Alexander Payne. Paramount Pictures, 1999.
(Distribution: Paramount Pictures) (Figure 14-26 B)

Repulsion. Dir. Roman Polanski. Tekli British Productions, 1965.

(Laserdisc distribution: The Criterion Collection) (Figure 14-27)

Mo' Better Blues. Dir. Spike Lee. 40 Acres & A Mule Filmworks, 1990.
(DVD distribution: Universal Pictures) (Figure 14-28)

The Last Laugh (Der Letzte Mann). Dir. F.W. Murnau. Universum Film A.G., 1924.
(DVD distribution: Kino Video) (Figure 14-29 L)

Delicatessen. Dirs. Jean-Pierre Jeunet and Marc Caro. Miramax Films, 1991.
(DVD distribution: Miramax) (Figure 14-29 R)

Flesh & Blade. Dir. Katherine Hurbis-Cherrier. Two Bugs Prod., 2007.(Figures 14-30 L and R)

Personal Velocity: Three Portraits. Dir. Rebecca Miller. IFC Productions, 2002.
(DVD distribution: MGM Distributing Corp.) (Figure 14-31)

■ CHAPTER 15

Alien. Dir. Ridley Scott. 20th Century Fox, 1979.
(DVD distribution: 20th Century Fox Home Entertainment)

2001: A Space Odyssey. Dir. Stanley Kubrick. Metro-Goldwyn-Mayer (MGM), 1968.
(DVD distribution: Warner Home Video) (Figure 15-2)

Brokeback Mountain. Dir. Ang Lee. Focus Features, 2005
(DVD distribution: Universal Home Entertainment) (Figure 15-7)

Don't Look Back. Dir. D.A. Pennebaker. Leacock-Pennebaker, 1967.
(DVD distribution: New Video) (Figure 15-12)

Monterey Pop. Dir. D.A. Pennebaker. The Foundation, 1968.
(DVD distribution: The Criterion Collection)

■ CHAPTER 16

Urban/Suburban. Dir. Didier Rouget, 2006.

■ CHAPTER 17

Snapshot. Dir. Andrew Lund, 2006. (Figure 17-17)

Nashville. Dir. Robert Altman. American Broadcasting Company (ABC), Paramount Pictures, 1975.
(DVD distribution: Paramount Home Video) (Figure 17-18)

■ CHAPTER 18

Old Joy. Dir. Kelly Reichardt. Washington Square Films, 2006.
(Distribution: Kino International Corp.)

Baloon Girl. Dir. Sharone Vendriger, 2007. (Figure 18-2)

Shift. Dir. Kelly Anderson. Anderson Gold Films, 1999. (Figure 18-19)

■ CHAPTER 19

Bamboozled. Dir. Spike Lee. 40 Acres & A Mule Filmworks, 2000.
(DVD distribution: New Line Home Video)

Fallen Angels. Dir. Wong Kar-Wai. Jet Tone Production Co., 1995.
(DVD distribution: Kino International Corp.) (Figure 19-2)

Close Up. Dir. Abbas Kiarostami. The Institute for the Intellectual Development of Children & Young Adults, 1990.
(DVD distribution: Facets Multimedia Distribution) (Figure 19-3)

Meatpacking District. Dir. Jonathon Gibson (2006) (Figure 19-4)

Dance Mania Fantastic. Dir. Sasie Sealy. -45 cm Productions, 2005. (Figure 19-5)

Hoop Dreams. Dir. Steve James. Kartemquin Films ,1994.
(DVD Distribution: The Criterion Collection) (Figure 19-16)

The Blair Witch Project. Dirs. Eduardo Sánchez and Daniel Myrick. Haxan Films, 1999.
(DVD distribution: Artisan Entertainment) (Figure 19-7 L)

The Celebration. Dir. Thomas Vinterberg. Nimbus Film ApS, 1998.
(DVD distribution: Universal Studios) (Figure 19-7 R)

Pieces of April. Dir. Peter Hedges. IFC Productions, 2003.
(DVD distribution: MGM Home Entertainment) (Figure 19-8 L)

You Me and Everyone We Know. Dir. Miranda July. IFC Films, 2005
(DVD distribution: IFC Films) (Figure 19-8 R)

La Nuit Américain (*Day for Night*). Dir. François Truffaut. La Films du Carrosse, 1973
(DVD distribution: Warner Home Video) (Figure 19-28)

■ CHAPTER 20

Un condamné a mort s'est échappé ou Le vent souffle où il vout (*A Man Escaped*). Dir. Robert Bresson. Nouvelles Éditions de Films, 1956.
(DVD distribution: NewYorker Video)

Tokyo monogatari (*Tokyo Story*). Dir. Yasujiro Ozu. Shochiku Films, Ltd., 1953.
(DVD distribution: The Criterion Collection, 2003) (Figure 20-4)

Roma, città aperta (*Rome, Open City*). Dir. Roberto Rossellini. Excelsa Film, 1945.
(DVD distribution: Image Entertainment Inc.)

Apur Sansar (*The World of Apu*). Dir. Satyajit Ray. Satyajit Ray Productions, 1959.
(DVD distribution: Columbia TriStar Home Entertainment, 2003)

Eternal Sunshine of the Spotless Mind. Dir. Michel Gondry. Focus Features, 2004.
(DVD distribution: Universal Studios Home Video) (Figure 20-6)

La Promesse. Dirs. Jean-Pierre Dardenne and Luc Dardenne. Touza Productions, 1996.
(DVD distribution: New Yorker Films) (Figure 20-7)

The Matrix. Dirs. Andy Wachowski and Larry Wachowski. Warner Bros. Pictures, 1999.
(DVD Distribution: Warner Bros. Pictures) (Figure 20-8)

The Cutting Edge: The Magic of Movie Editing. Dir. Wendy Apple. A.C.E. Prod., 2004. (DVD Distribution: Warner Home Videos) (Figure 20-9)

The Miracle. Dir. George Racz, 2006. (Figures 20-21, 20-22, 20-23, and 20-25)

Bamboozled. Dir. Spike Lee. 40 Acres & a Mule Filmworks, 2000.
(DVD distribution: New Line Home Video) (Figure 20-24)

Apocalypse Now. Dir. Francis Ford Coppola. Zoetrope Studios, 1979.
(DVD Distribution: Paramount Home Video)

■ CHAPTER 21

Edge Codes.com: The Art of Motion Picture Editing. Dir. Alex Shuper. Travesty Productions Inc., 2004.

Raging Bull. Dir. Martin Scorsese. Chartoff-Winkler Productions, 1980.
(DVD distribution: MGM Home Entertainment) (Figures 21-6, 21-7, and 21-8 L)

2001: A Space Odyssey. Dir. Stanley Kubrick. Metro-Goldwyn-Mayer, 1968.
(DVD distribution: MGM/UA Home Video) (Figure 21-9)

The English Patient. Dir. Anthony Minghella. Tiger Moth Prod./Miramax Films, 1996.
(DVD Distribution: Miramax films) (Figure 21-10)

Citizen Kane. Dir. Orson Welles. RKO Radio Pictures, 1941.
(DVD distribution: Warner Home Video) (Figure 21-11)

Rope. Dir. Alfred Hitchcock. Warner Bros. Pictures, 1948.
(DVD distribution: Universal Home Entertainment)

Jeanne Dielman, 23 Quai du Commerce, 1080 Bruxelles. Dir. Chantal Akerman. Paradise Films, 1976.

Nine Lives. Dir. Rodrigo García. Mockingbird Pictures, 2005.
(DVD distribution: Sony Pictures Home Entertainment) (Figure 21-12)

Cléo de 5 à 7 (*Cleo from 5 to 7*). Dir. Agnès Varda. Rome Paris Films, 1961.
(DVD distribution: The Criterion Collection) (Figure 21-13)

Syriana. Dir. Stephen Gaghan. Warner Bros. Pictures, 2005.
(DVD distribution: Warner Bros. Entertainment) (Figure 21-14)

Traffic. Dir. Steven Soderbergh. USA Films, 2000.
(DVD distribution: Focus Entertainment) (Figure 21-15)

Misery. Dir. Rob Reiner. Castle Rock Entertainment, 1990.
(DVD distribution: MGM DVD) (Figure 21-16)

The Graduate. Dir. Mike Nichols. Embassy Pictures Corporation, 1967.
(DVD distribution: MGM DVD) (Figures 21-17 and 21-18)

The Thin Red Line. Dir. Terrence Malick. Fox 2000 Pictures, 1998.
(DVD distribution: 20th Century Fox Home Entertainment)

There's Something About Mary. Dirs. Bobby & Peter Farrelly. 20th Century Fox, 1998.
(DVD distribution: 20th Century Fox Film Corporation) (Figure 21-20)

Cidade de Deus (*City of God*). Dirs. Fernando Meirelles & Kátia Lund. O2 Filmes, 2002.
(Distribution: Miramax Films) (Figures 21-21, 21-22, and21-23)

The Station Agent. Dir. Thomas McCarthy. SenArt Films, 2003.
(DVD distribution: Miramax Films) (Figure 21-24)

Long Day's Journey Into Night. Dir. Sidney Lumet. Embassy Pictures Corporation, 1962.
(DVD distribution: Embassy Pictures Corp.) (Figure 21-26)

Team America: World Police. Dir. Trey Parker. Paramount Pictures, 2004
(DVD distribution: Paramount Home Entertainment) (Figure 21-27)

Natural Born Killers. Dir. Oliver Stone. New Regency Pictures, 1994.
(DVD Distribution: Warner Home Video) (Figures 21-28 and 21-29)

■ CHAPTER 22

The Jazz Singer. Dir. Alan Crosland. Warner Bros. Pictures (as The Vitaphone Corporation), 1927. (DVD Distribution: Warner Home Video)

Dwaj ludzie z szafa (*Two Men and a Wardrobe*). Dir. Roman Polanski. Panstwowa Wyzsza Szkola Filmowa, 1958.
(DVD distribution: Available on *Knife in the Water* (*Nóz w wodzie*). Dir. Roman Polanski. The Criterion Collection) (Figure 22-1)

Ta'm e guilass (*Taste of Cherries*). Dir. Abbas Kiarostami. Abbas Kiarostami Productions, 1997. (DVD distribution: The Criterion Collection) (Figure 22-2)

High Anxiety. Dir. Mel Brooks. Crossbow Productions, 1977.
(DVD distribution: 20th Century Fox Film Corporation) (Figure 22-3)

Code inconnu: Récit incomplet de divers voyages. Dir. Michael Haneke. Canal+, 2000.
(DVD distribution: Kino International Corp.) (Figure 22-4)

His Girl Friday. Dir. Howard Hawks. Columbia Pictures Corporation, 1940.
(DVD distribution: Columbia Classics Home Video) (Figure 22-5)

2001: A Space Odyssey. Dir. Stanley Kubrick. Metro-Goldwyn-Mayer, 1968.
(DVD distribution: MGM/UA Home Video) (Figure 22-6)

Psycho. Dir. Alfred Hitchcock. Shamley Productions, 1960.
(DVD distribution: Universal Home Entertainment) (Figure 22-7)

Les Mistons. Dir. François Truffaut. Les Films du Carrosse, 1957.
(DVD distribution: The Criterion Collection, 2003) (Figure 22-8)

Raging Bull. Dir. Martin Scorsese. Chartoff-Winkler Productions, 1980.
(DVD distribution: MGM Home Entertainment) (Figure 22-11)

Nutty but Nice. Dir. Jules White. Columbia Pictures Corporation, 1940. (Figure 22-12)

River of Things: "Ode to a Bar of Soap." Dir. Katherine Hurbis-Cherrier, 1998. (Figure 22-13)

Snapshot. Dir. Andrew Lund, 2006. (Figure 22-14)

Do The Right Thing. Dir. Spike Lee. 40 Acres & A Mule Filmworks, 1989
(DVD distribution: The Criterion Collection) (Figure 22-15)

Gone With The Wind. Dir. Victor Fleming. Selznick International Pictures, 1939
(DVD Distribution: Warner Home Video)

Jaws. Dir. Steven Spielberg. Universal Pictures, 1975.
(DVD distribution: Universal Studios Home Video)

Fa yeun nin wa (*In the Mood for Love*). Dir. Wong Kar-Wai. Paradis Films, 2000.
(DVD distribution: The Criterion Collection) (Figure 22-17)

Star Wars: Episode VI - Return of the Jedi. Dir. Richard Marquand. Lucasfilm Ltd., 1983.
(DVD distribution: 20th Century Fox Home Entertainment) (Figure 22-18)

Reservoir Dogs. Dir. Quentin Tarantino. Dog Eat Dog Prods., 1992
(DVD distribution: Artisan Entertainment) (Figure 22-19)

River of Things: "Ode to Things." Dir. Mick Hurbis-Cherrier, 1998. (Figure 22-20

Yume (*Dreams*). Dir. Akira Kurosawa. Akira Kurosawa USA, 1990
(DVD Distribution: Warner Home Video)

La Promesse. Dirs. Jean-Pierre Dardenne and Luc Dardenne. Eurimages, 1996.
(DVD distribution: New Yorker Films) (Figure 22-22 T)

Silence of the Lambs. Dir. Jonathan Demme. Orion Pictures Corporation, 1991.
(DVD Distribution: The Criterion Collection) (Figure 22-22 B)

▧ CHAPTER 23

Apocalypse Now. Dir. Francis Ford Coppola. Zoetrope Studios, 1979.
(DVD Distribution: Paramount Home Video)

FearFall. Dir. Mick Hurbis-Cherrier, 2000.

Immortal Beloved. Dir. Bernard Rose. Majestic Films International, 1994.
(DVD Distribution: Columbia Home Video) (Figure 23-13)

M. Dir. Fritz Lang. Nero-Film AG, 1934.
(DVD Distribution: The Criterion Collection) (Figure 23-14)

All That Jazz. Dir. Bob Fosse. Columbia Pictures Corporation, 1979.
(DVD Distribution: 20th Century Fox Films) (Figure 23-24)

The Man Who Knew Too Much. Dir. Alfred Hitchcock. Paramount Pictures, 1956.
(DVD Distribution: Universal Home Video Inc.) (Figure 23-25)

▧ CHAPTER 24

Four Eyed Monsters. Dirs. Susan Buice & Arin Crumley. Less Life Lived LLC, 2005.
(Figure 24-12)

La Machine. Dirs. Michael Griffin & Luke Rimmelzwaan (2006) (Figure 24-13)

Shirlock Jr. Dir. Buster Keaton. Buster Keaton Productions,1924
(DVD Distribution: Kino Video) (Figure 24-14 L)

Bibliography

■ INTRODUCTION

Broughton, James. "Making Light of It," City Lights Books, San Francisco, CA, 1992

Mackendrick, Alexander. "On Filmmaking," Faber & Faber, New York, NY, 2004.

Tirard, Laurent. "Moviemakers' Master Class," Faber & Faber, New York, NY, 2002.

■ CHAPTER 1

Hedges, Peter. "Pieces of April: The Shooting Script," Newmarket Press, New York, NY, 2003.

Locarno International Film Festival, 1996. Excerpt from an interview with Houshang Golmakani, "48th Locarno International Film Festival." Available July 27, 2006 at http://www.pardo.ch/1995/95ret1.htm.

Mamet, David. "On Directing Film," Penguin Books USA, Inc., New York, NY, 1991.

Pfeiffer, Mark. "A Conversation with 'Pieces of April' director Peter Hedges," *The Film Journal,* November 2003. Available July 27, 2006 at http://www.thefilmjournal.com/issue7/hedges.html.

Tirard, Laurent. "Moviemakers' Master Class," Faber & Faber, New York, NY, 2002.

■ CHAPTER 3

Mackendrick, Alexander. "On Filmmaking," Faber & Faber, New York, NY, 2004.

Tirard, Laurent. "Moviemakers' Master Class," Faber & Faber, New York, NY, 2002.

■ CHAPTER 5

Bourke, Philippa. "Taking the Digital Medium Into Their Own Hands: Storytelling by Women Filmmakers Evolves with DV." Available at http://www.moviesbywomen.com/articles (posted August 9, 2002).

Kohn, Bill. "Hitchcock at Work," Phaidon Press, London, New York, 2003.

Truffaut, François, and Helen G. Scott. "Hitchcock," Simon & Schuster, France, 1985.

■ CHAPTER 7

Cronin, Paul. "Four Golden Rules," *The Guardian,* June 17, 2005. Available September 4, 2006 at http://film.guardian.co.uk/interview/interviewpages/0,6737,1508057,00.html.

■ CHAPTER 8

Anderson, Joseph, and Barbara Anderson. "The Myth of Persistence of Vision Revisited," *Journal of Film and Video,* Vol. 45, No. 1 (Spring 1993): 3–12.

Eastman Kodak Corp. "Kodak: Film Tools." Available September 4, 2006 at http://www.kodak.com/US/en/motion/16mm/resources/.

Gregpak. "Film Tools: Footage Calculator & Charts." Available September 4, 2006 at http://www.gregpak.com/filmhelp/tools/footagechart.html#calculator.

■ CHAPTER 9

Fahs, Chad. "HDV Filmmaking (Aspiring Filmmaker's Library)," Thomson Course Technology PTR, Boston, MA, 2006.

■ CHAPTER 10

Burum, Stephen H. "American Cinematographer Manual," 9th edn. ASC Press, Hollywood, CA, 2004.

DOFMaster. "Hyperfocal Distance and Depth of Field Calculator." Available September 4, 2006 at http://www.dofmaster.com.

Panavision. "Technical Information: Tools." Available September 4, 2006 at http://www.panavision.com/tools.php.

■ CHAPTER 12

McDonough, Tom. "Light Years: Confessions of a Cinematographer," Grove Press, New York, NY, 1987.

■ CHAPTER 14

Ballinger, Alexander. "New Cinemtographers," Laurence King/Harper Design, London, New York, NY, 2004.

Bourke, Philippa. "Taking the Digital Medium Into Their Own Hands: Storytelling by Women Filmmakers Evolves with DV." Available at http://www.moviesbywomen.com/articles (posted August 9, 2002).

Calhoun, John. "Photographing Angels," *Live Design Online,* April 1, 1999. Available September 4, 2006 at http://livedesignonline.com/mag/lighting_photographing_angels/index.html.

Herrell, Al. "Variations on the Mo' Better Blues," *American Cinematographer,* September 1990.

Rogers, Pauline. "Emmanuel Lubezki, ASC puts a twisted look on the macabre myth of *Sleepy Hollow,"* The International Cinematographers Guild. Available at http://www.cameraguild.com/index.html?magazine/stoo1199.htm~top.main_hp.

Salt, Barry. "Film Style and Technology: History and Analysis," 2nd edn. Starword, London, 2003.

Schaefer, Dennis, and Larry Salvato. "Masters of Light," University of California Press, Berkeley, CA, 1984.

Torneo, Erin. "Interview: Cinematography as Poetry: Ellen Kuras Talks About the DV Challenges of "Personal Velocity," *indieWIRE,* November 25, 2002. Available at http://www.indiewire.com/people/int_Kuras_Ellen_021125.html.

Wood, Jennifer M. "Where the Girls Are: DP Ellen Kuras talks about shooting Rebecca Miller's Personal Velocity," *MovieMaker Magazine: Hands On Pages,* Issue #17. Available at http://www.moviemaker.com/hop/ (go to "cinematography" and then vol. #17)

■ CHAPTER 19

Lumet, Sidney. "Making Movies," Vintage Books, New York, NY, 1995.

Martin, Kevin H. "The Digital Cinematographer: Ellen Kuras, ASC, discusses *Bamboozled* and the travails of digital filmmaking," The International Cinematographers Guild. Available at http://www.cameraguild.com/technology/bamboozled.htm.

Rodriguez-Ortega, Vicente. "Zen Palette: An Interview with Christopher Doyle," *reverse shot online,* summer 2004. Available at http://www.reverseshot.com/legacy/summer04/doyle.html.

Wood, Jennifer M. "Life with Spike: Moviemaker Sam Pollard discusses his most frequent collaborator," *MovieMaker Magazine: Hands On Pages,* Issue #22. Available August 2, 2006 at http://moviemaker.com/hop/ (go to "editing" and issue #22).

■ CHAPTER 20

Doughton, KJ. "A Cut Above: Editor Thelma Schoonmaker celebrates in Seattle," *Movie-Maker Magazine: Hands On Pages,* Issue #35. Available August 2, 2006 at http://www.moviemaker.com/hop/ (go to "editing" and Issue #35).

Murch, Walter. "In the Blink of an Eye," Silman-James Press, New York, NY, 2001.

Wood, Jennifer M. "Life with Spike: Moviemaker Sam Pollard discusses his most frequent collaborator," *MovieMaker Magazine: Hands On Pages,* Issue #22. Available 2 August 2006 at http://moviemaker.com/hop/ (go to "editing" and issue #22).

■ CHAPTER 21

Bazin, André, et al. "Entretiens avec Orson Welles," *Cahiers du Cinéma* (June 1958), no. 84: 1–13.

Lumet, Sidney. "Making Movies," Vintage Books, New York, NY, 1995.

Mackendrick, Alexander. "On Film-Making: An Introduction to the Craft of the Director," Faber & Faber, New York, NY, 2004.

Tirard, Laurent. "Moviemakers' Master Class: Private Lessons from the World's Foremost Directors," Faber & Faber, New York, NY, 2002.

Walker, Alexander. "Stanley Kubrick Directs," Harcourt Brace Co., New York, NY, 1972.

■ CHAPTER 22

Chion, Michel. "Audio-Vision," Columbia University Press, New York, NY, 1994.

Schwam, Stephanie (Ed.). "The Making of 2001: A Space Odyssey," Modern Library, New York, NY, 2000.

Thom, Randy. "Designing A Movie For Sound," *FilmSound.org,* 1999. Available August 2, 2006 at http://www.filmsound.org/articles/designing_for_sound.htm.

Index